Building
Amerika

Jean-Louis Cohen

Building a new New World
Amerikanizm in Russian Architecture

Canadian Centre for Architecture
Yale University Press

This is a story about the circulation of ideas across countries and cultures, and about how the world is shaped by this flow. For Jean-Louis Cohen, who has spent most of his life probing the role of cultural transfers in the construction of the modernist project, this is not a fully new story, but an extension of and a deeper dive into his previous exhibition and book projects at the CCA. Ultimately, it is an invitation to once again reconsider the locations and origins of modernism from a different vantage.

The first of Cohen's projects at the CCA, *Scenes of the World to Come* (1995), traced and documented the impact that the idealization of American skyscrapers, industrial plants, and urban form had on the development of European cities from the end of the nineteenth century through the 1960s. The project was based on a hypothesis Cohen had put forward in the 1980s with Hubert Damisch that the cultural and economic hegemony of the U.S.A. from the 1893 World's Columbian Exposition on fuelled global modernization.

The second project, less directly connected at first glance but equally relevant, is *Architecture in Uniform: Designing and Building for the Second World War* (2011), which saw in the traumatic geopolitical conflicts of the mid-twentieth century an ideal breeding ground for that process of modernization and, in particular, for the consolidation and dissemination of modern architecture as a global language. Stemming from research also initiated in the 1980s on Germany and France that asked why the war era was absent from established histories of modern architecture, *Architecture in Uniform* revealed the extent to which international warfare drove technological innovation and industrialization across the world.

Building a new New World, assembled with materials from institutions across Russia and North America, including the Shchusev State Museum of Architecture, Avery Library at Columbia University, and the CCA's rich holdings on the Soviet avant-garde, once again aims to dismantle dominant readings of the long twentieth century by exploring the contributions of architecture to the modernization process. Tracing the many journeys of Russian writers, politicians, and planners through the American territory, foregrounding the constant streams of cultural and technological transfer from the U.S.A. to Russia, and revealing the parallel fascination among Russian and American intellectuals with the ongoing pursuit of land occupation and development within their respective borders, the following story weaves together a long thread of bonds and interdependencies between the two superpowers that calls into question the myth of a Cold War marked by antagonistic worldviews. Looking back on that era today, the book also offers a challenge to the lingering contemporary political view that internationalization is fundamentally opposed to national culture.

In each of these three projects, Cohen assembles stories to deploy, test, and validate research. The act of reading, interpreting, and describing the world is inevitably framed by narratives, including those passed on by others and those that themselves travel the world. We hope you enjoy this one.

Albert Ferré
Associate Director, Publications
CCA

Table of contents

Note on the Russian transliteration

The norm used throughout the book for the transliteration of the Russian terms is a simplified version of the ALA-LC romanization table, easier to grasp for most readers. The soft and hard signs have been ignored, and the short i character is rendered by a simple i. The usual form of persons' names–such as Lissitzky, Gorky or Eisenstein–has been kept, as well as their first names–Leon Tolstoy. In the notes, the spelling of the authors' names follows the one used in the original publication cited and might thus differ from the rigorous transliteration. JLC. Unless otherwise indicated, all translations are by Luba Markovskaia.

Introduction

Roman Cieslewicz. *The Two Superman*, montage published on the cover of *Opus International* (December 1967).
Offset print on paper. Private collection.

"There are now two great nations in the world which, starting from different points, seem to be advancing toward the same goal: the Russians and the Anglo-Americans. Both have grown in obscurity, and while the world's attention was occupied elsewhere, they have suddenly taken their place among the leading nations, making the world take note of their birth and of their greatness almost at the same instant. [...] One has freedom as the principal means of action; the other has servitude. [...] Their point of departure is different and their paths diverse; nevertheless, each seems called by some secret desire of Providence one day to hold in its hands the destinies of half the world."

Alexis de Tocqueville, *Democracy in America*, 1835[1]

1   Alexis de Tocqueville, *De la démocratie en Amérique* [1835] (Paris: Pagnerre, 1848), 413-414; in English: *Democracy in America,* ed. Jacob P. Mayer, trans. George Lawrence (Garden City, NY: Doubleday, 1969), vol. 1, 412–13.

Alexis de Tocqueville's memorable prophecy described a rivalry that persisted until the end of the 20th century, sealing the fate of both nations in the political, economic, and cultural spheres. Architecture stood at the heart of this often contentious relationship, both as a symptom and as its monumental expression. In the context of industrialization and modernization, the transformations undergone by this discipline were determined by an American ideal that could be too reductively described by its most apparent manifestation: a skyscraper fetish. This ideal has shaped German, British, French, and Japanese architectural cultures, but nowhere has it been as powerful and wide-ranging as in Russia over the past two centuries.

Despite China's recovery of its formerly long-held power, the American-Russian enmity has survived the collapse of the Soviet Union, as evidenced by Vladimir Putin's alleged attempts to undermine the American political system in 2016 through his secret services. In the second half of the 19th century, the conflictual relationship between the two ideologies had already shaped the divide that would come to characterize the global balance. As in other fields, the developing relationship between Russia and the United States played out in the realm of architecture, understood as widely as possible and with respect to its connections to urban planning, landscaping, and design. In the 1960s, this "parallel history" of two nations inspired the French writers Louis Aragon and André Maurois to write a homonymous monumental work about the confrontation set during the post-war era[2].

But the opponents in this geopolitical duel, depicted in the evocative 1968 collage "The Two Superman" by the Paris-based Polish graphic artist Roman Cieslewicz, were of unequal strength, contrary to what is shown in this illustration[3]. The USSR, defeated in the Cold War, was heavily dependent symbolically on America. Both socialist and capitalist Russia's fascination with the United States was multifaceted, enduring, and complex, and extended far beyond the architectural sphere discussed within these pages. Consistent with the overall workings of Americanism, this fascination offers a somewhat distorted view, comparable to anamorphosis, deforming certain traits of a phenomenon that can only be understood by examining the network of relations between Russia and the West at large, as well as America's ties to the rest of the world.

Modernity and Americanism

A brief history of what I will refer to as Americanism is in order. The term was coined in 1781 by the Scottish minister John Witherspoon, the sixth president of Princeton University, to describe certain aspects of the English spoken in the United States[4]. Thomas Jefferson expanded its meaning to characterize the new nation's political principles[5]. Some decades later, the word came to denote reception, when Pierre Larousse defined it in his *Dictionnaire universel* as the "pronounced and exclusive admiration for the government, laws, and usages of the Americans, chiefly the inhabitants of the United States," which he distinguished from "Américanomanie," the "affected, ridiculous admiration for everything associated with America."[6] As for Baudelaire, he was mostly referencing the prosaic aspect of the notion when he wrote of Edgar Allan Poe that "the day that he wrote 'All certainty is dreams,' he thrust back his own Americanism into the region of inferior things."[7] In Russia, one of the earliest allusions to Amerikanizm can be found in 1873 in Fedor Dostoevsky's *Diary of a Writer*[8]. Without necessarily endorsing this critical stance, numerous

19th-century thinkers amalgamated America in their worldview. Goethe, in his 1827 poem "America," praised the benefits of a nation free from the weight of the past:

"America, a better fate
Of thee than of Europe's expected.
No ruined castles of ancient date
Nor basalts in thee are detected
The past disturbs thee not; nor rages
In this, thy surging modern life
Vain memory of by-gone ages,
Nor futile antiquated strife."[9]

By contrast, Hegel, in his 1830 *Lectures on the History of Philosophy*, considered that: "What has taken place in the New World up to the present time is only an echo of the Old World—the expression of a foreign Life; and as a Land of the Future, it has no interest for us here, for, as regards *History*, our concern must be with that which has been and that which is."[10] Karl Marx similarly disagreed with Goethe's point of view, which made America a "new world" cut off from the old one. His friend Friedrich Engels, after briefly travelling across the Atlantic in 1888, was most cautious: "We usually think of America as a new world, new not merely because of when it was discovered, but new in all its institutions—a world far ahead of us old-fashioned sleepy Europeans, with its disdain for everything traditional, handed down from the past, a world entirely built anew on virgin soil by modern people and founded on modern, practical, rational principles."[11] On the contrary, he observed the old-fashioned aspect of American cities and material culture. Like Marx, he supported the Union during the Civil War. As for Friedrich Nietzsche, in *The Gay Science*, he compared the Americans to fifth-century Athenians, describing "the American conviction of the present day, which wants also more and more to become a European conviction: whereby the individual is convinced that he can do almost anything, that he can play almost any role, whereby everyone makes experiments with himself, improvises, tries anew, tries with delight, whereby all nature ceases and becomes art."[12]

2   Louis Aragon and André Maurois, *Les deux géants: histoire des États-Unis et de l'URSS, de 1917 à nos jours* (Paris: Éditions du Pont-Royal, 1964).
3   Roman Cieslewicz, "The Two Superman," cover of *Opus International*, vol. 3, no. 4 (1967).
4   John Witherspoon, *The Works of the Rev. John Witherspoon* (Philadelphia: William W. Woodward, 1801), vol. 4, 182.
5   He discusses the principles of "pure americanism" in a letter to Edward Rutledge, 24 June 1797, in *The Works of Thomas Jefferson*, ed. Paul Leicester Ford (New York: G.P. Putnam's Sons, 1904), vol. 8, 316.
6   Pierre Larousse, *Grand dictionnaire universel du XIXe siècle* (Paris: Administration du Grand dictionnaire universel, 1866), vol. 1, 262.
7   Charles Baudelaire, "Notes nouvelles sur Edgar Poe," in Edgar Allan Poe, *Nouvelles histoires extraordinaires* [1857] (Paris: Michel Lévy, 1875), x; in English: *Baudelaire as a Literary Critic, Selected Essays*, intro. and trans. Lois Boe Hyslop and Francis E. Hyslop, Jr. (University Park, PA: Pennsylvania State University Press, 1964), 121-122.
8   Fedor Dostoevsky, "Malenkie kartiny," [1873] in *Dnevnik Pisatelia* (Berlin: Izd-vo Dadyzhnikova, 1922), 374-75; in English: *The Diary of a Writer*, trans. Boris Brasol (New York: George Braziller, 1954), 121.
9   J.W. von Goethe, "Den Vereinigten Staaten" [1827], in *Goethes Werke* (Hamburg: Wegner, 1952), vol. 1, 333; in English: Paul Carus, *Goethe: With Special Consideration of His Philosophy* (Chicago: The Open court Pub. Co, 1915), 61.
10   G. W. F. Hegel, *Lectures on the Philosophy of History* [1830], trans. J. Sibree (London: Henry G. Bonn, 1861), 87.
11   Friedrich Engels, "American Travel Notes," in Friedrich Engels, Karl Marx, *Letters to Americans, 1848-95: A Selection* (New York: International Publishers, 1963), 291-92.
12   Friedrich Nietzsche, *The Gay Science* [1882], trans. Walter Kaufman (London: Penguin, 1974), §356. p. 194.

When the Russians' understanding of the United States grew more substantial, through writings, reports, and exhibitions visited by the masses, the "American scene"—as Henry James called it, while cautiously keeping it at a distance[13]—began to foreshadow what the future had in store for Europe. This was especially true as World War I had allowed the United States to gain a firm foothold in a battered European economy. According to its leader George Creel, the Committee on Public Information, created in 1917 by President Woodrow Wilson to support the war effort, preached "the Gospel of Americanism."[14] In 1928, the Spenglerian book *This American World* by the foreign correspondent Edgar Ansel Mowrer, then stationed between Rome and Berlin, was translated in German under the eloquent title *Amerika, Vorbild und Warnung* [America, Example and Warning][15]. In his foreword to the original edition, T. S. Eliot noted that "the literature of Americanism […] ha[d] been steadily accumulating."[16] In the years after the war, examples of this propagation could be found even in the most revolutionary texts. One of the subtlest critics of Americanism was then the Italian communist leader Antonio Gramsci, who was familiar with Ford's industrial policy, as it had been replicated by Fiat. In a 1934 entry from his prison notebooks on "Americanism and Fordism," he examined the principles behind the American industrial doctrines and their effects, based on Trotsky's writings, among others[17]. Indeed, the latter had declared to an American senator, in 1923, that "[t]he words 'Americanism' and 'Americanization' are used in our newspapers and technical journals in an altogether sympathetic way and by no means in the sense of reproach."[18]

Russia's Singular Case

This sympathy was not solely the result of the 1917 revolution, as a form of Russian Amerikanizm was already becoming apparent by the end of the nineteenth century. According to the historian Hans Rogger, "Americanism was both a perception of the United States as an industrial civilization from which more could and should be learned or borrowed than mere isolated techniques or pieces of equipment, and the acceptance of the inevitability of doing so and of Russia's becoming more like America in the process."[19] The semantic field around the notion was particularly broad. As opposed to Americanism, which mainly concerned ideas and representations, Americanization—*Amerikanisierung* in Germany and *amerikanizatsia* in Russia—, often confused with the former, became commonly used as of 1918[20]. It denoted the direct presence of capital and American operatives in material or cultural production, two manifestations whose timeframes often collided, but not necessarily so. These two objective aspects went hand in hand with their morbid and grotesque expressions, identified early on in the Soviet Union, as though to prove Larousse right several years later: an "*amerikanshchina*" [Americanitis], a childhood illness of Soviet cinema, was diagnosed as early as 1922 by the filmmaker Lev Kuleshov[21].

The film industry played a major part in the phenomenon, not only because Hollywood was central in global film production, but also because its spectacular nature was intrinsic to Americanism. In one of the most popular works of interwar fiction, the French novelist Georges Duhamel, a critic of American mass entertainment, described "scenes from the life of the future"[22] as he perceived them in American society. More than theatre or cinema, phantasmagoria seems to be the medium through which the New World appeared to the eyes of the old one. Characters, products, and buildings emerged as apparitions, much like in Walter Benjamin's analysis of the nineteenth-century Parisian spectacle of commodity. Like the great industrial age displays, these spectres—appearing in print, in photographs, on screens, or in three dimensions, in the case of exhibits—conveyed an ideology of progress associated with America and carrying the promise of happiness. These representations, as much as the reality of production and construction, sang the praises of Americanism. Construction site mystique, as imagined in the late 1920s Soviet Union, was embodied by a ghostly ballet of workers and engineers set against a backdrop of cranes, drawbridges, and machines. Later, Broadway's nocturnal spectacle rolled out the screen onto which Moscow's Stalin-era "seven sisters" were projected.

The particular pervasiveness of the Americanist phantasmagoria in Russia was derived from the identification between the "two great nations" proposed by Tocqueville and revisited by Walt Whitman as he called for a Russian publication of his *Leaves of Grass*: "You Russians and we Americans;—our countries so distant, so unlike at first glance—such a difference in social and political conditions, and our respective methods of moral and practical development the last hundred years;—and yet in certain features, and vastest ones, so resembling each other. The variety of stock-elements and tongues to be resolutely fused in a common Identity and Union at all hazards— the idea, perennial through the ages, that they both have their historic and divine mission—the fervent element of manly friendship throughout the whole people, surpassed by no other races—the grand expanse of territorial limits and boundaries—the unformed and nebulous state of many things, not yet permanently settled, but agreed on all hands to be the preparations of an infinitely greater future—the fact that both peoples have their independent and leading positions to hold, keep, and if necessary fight for, against the rest of the world—the deathless aspirations at the inmost centre of each great community, so vehement, so mysterious, so abysmic—are certainly features you Russians and we Americans possess in common."[23]

Nevertheless, the parallel drawn by Tocqueville and Whitman did not describe symmetrical attitudes. Though many authors saw Russia as a "new America"—and though the Bolsheviks intended, according to the Russian lyrics

13   Henry James, *The American Scene* (London: Chapman and Hall, 1907).

14   Emily S. Rosenberg, *Spreading the American Dream: American Economic and Cultural Expansion, 1890-1945* (New York: Hill and Wang, 1982), 108.

15   Edgar A. Mowrer, *Amerika, Vorbild und Warnung*, trans. Annemarie Horschitz (Berlin, Rohwolt, 1928); originally *This American World* (London: Faber and Gwyer, 1928).

16   T. S. Eliot, preface to Mowrer, *This American World*, ix.

17   Antonio Gramsci, "Americanism and Fordism" [1934], in *Prison Notebooks*, trans. Quintin Hoare and Geoffrey Nowell Smith (New York: International Publishers, 1971), 277–318.

18   Leon Trotsky, *Pravda*, 30 September 1923, quoted by Jeffrey Brooks, *Thank You, Comrade Stalin! Soviet Public Culture from Revolution to Cold War* (Princeton: Princeton University Press, 2000), 37.

19   Hans Rogger, "Americanism and the Economic Development of Russia," *Journal of the Society for Comparative Study of Society and History* 23, no. 3 (July 1981): 407.

20   See for example Pierre Musso, "Américanisme et américanisation: du fordisme à l'hollywoodisme," *Quaderni*, no. 50–51 (2003): 231–47.

21   Lev Kuleshov, "Americanitis," in *Kuleshov on Film*, texts assembled by Ronald Levaco (Berkeley: University of California Press, 1974), 127-130.

22   Georges Duhamel, *Scènes de la vie future* (Paris: Mercure de France, 1930); in English: *America the Menace*, trans. Charles Miner Thompson (Boston: Houghton Mifflin, 1931).

23   Walt Whitman, letter to John Fitzgerald Lee, 20 December 1881, in Walt Whitman, *The Correspondence, vol. III, 1876-1885* (New York: New York University Press, 1969), 259, quoted in Alan M. Ball, *Imagining America: Influence and Images in Twentieth-Century Russia* (London: Rowman & Littlefield, 2003), 15.

to the *International*, to build a "New World," which would actually be a *new* "new world," more perfect than the first one—, even the strongest American supporters of the Soviet Union never imagined creating a "new Russia" between the Atlantic and Pacific oceans. And while there was no symmetry between the two positions, the Russian stance was far from monolithic. Americanism and anti-Americanism incessantly combined and conflicted as of the mid-19th century among writers, ideologists, and politicians. Critical accounts of racial segregation in the South and of the supremacy of capital in the North contrasted with the general exaltation of civil liberties. Maxim Gorky's damning indictment after his 1906 trip is a perfect example of this critical discourse. A terrifying phantasmagoria alternated with the naïvely optimistic one depicting the wonders of America.

The opposition between a static European civilization and a dynamic American industrial culture was a cliché in writings about America by intellectuals who either visited the country themselves or drew on second-hand accounts. This dichotomy was largely accepted in the 1920s, as one of the most popular works in Soviet publishing was Oswald Spengler's *Decline of the West*. The book was discussed in Russia as of 1921—by the philosopher Nikolai Berdyaev, among others—and translated in 1922[24]. Writing in a tone meant to bring solace, Spengler noted, much to his readers' outrage, that Russia would avoid the decline because it was not part of Europe[25]. A more liberated outlook on America thus became possible for this nation on the brink of an unprecedented rise.

24   Oswald Spengler, *Der Untergang des Abendlandes*; vol. 1, "Umrisse einer Morphologie der Weltgeschichte: Gestalt und Wirklichkeit" (Munich, Vienna: Braumüller, 1921); and vol. 2, "Welthistorische Perspektiven" (Munich: C.H. Beck, 1922). On Spengler's reception in Soviet Russia, see Carol Avins, *Border Crossings: The West and Russian Identity in Soviet Literature 1917–1934* (Berkeley: University of California Press, 1983), 36–37.
25   Maria Gough aptly pointed it out in *The Artist as Producer: Russian Constructivism in Revolution* (Berkeley: University of California Press, 2014), 132–36.
26   For analyses of national scenes, see among others Hans Ibelings, *Americanism: Dutch Architecture and the Transatlantic Model* (Rotterdam: NAI Publishers, 1997); Murray Fraser, with Joe Kerr, *Architecture and the "Special Relationship": The American Influence on Post-War British Architecture* (London: Routledge, 2007); Paolo Scrivano, *Building Transatlantic Italy: Architectural Dialogues with Postwar America* (London: Routledge, 2017). On Brazil, see Fernando Atique, *Arquitetando a "Boa Vizinança": Arquitetura, Cidade e Cultura nas relações Brasil-Estados Unidos 1876–1945* (Campinas: Pontes Editores, 2010).
27   Jean-Louis Cohen and Hubert Damisch, eds., *Américanisme et modernité: l'idéal américain dans l'architecture* (Paris: Flammarion/École des hautes études en sciences sociales, 1993); Jean-Louis Cohen, *Scenes of the World to Come: European Architecture and the American Challenge, 1893–1960* (Paris: Flammarion; Montreal: Canadian Centre for Architecture, 1995).
28   Frederick Charles Barghoorn, *The Soviet Image of the United States: A Study in Distortion* (New York: Harcourt Brace, 1950). For a view in *longue durée*, see William Appleman Williams, *American Russian Relations 1781–1947* (New York: Rinehart & Co, 1952).
29   Rogger, "Amerikanizm and the Economic Development of Russia." See also his diachronic analysis "How the Soviets See Us," in *Shared Destiny: Fifty Years of Soviet-American Relations*, Mark Garrison and Abbott Gleason, eds (Boston: Beacon Press, 1985), 107–45.
30   Dieter Boden, *Das Amerikabild im russischen Schrifttum bis zum Ende des 19. Jahrhunderts* (Hamburg: Cram, de Gruyter & Co., 1968); Robert V. Allen, *Russia Looks at America: The View to 1917* (Washington, DC: Library of Congress, 1988).
31   Robert Linhart, *Lénine, les paysans, Taylor* (Paris: Seuil, 1976); Kurt Johansson, *Aleksej Gastev: Proletarian Bard of the Machine Age* (Stockholm: Almqvist & Wiksell International, 1983); Kendall E. Bailes, "Alexei Gastev and the Soviet Controversy over Taylorism, 1918–1924", *Soviet Studies* 29, no. 3 (July 1977), 372–94.
32   Antony Sutton, *Western Technology and Soviet Economic Development* (Stanford: Hoover Institution Press, 1971–1973); Lewis H. Siegelbaum, *Cars for Comrades: The Life of the Soviet Automobile* (Ithaca: Cornell University Press, 2011).

As of the last third of the 19th century, the field of European architecture, in its broadest geographical sense, was particularly prone to American phantasmagoria, as shown by various works on France, Germany, the Netherlands, and Italy published over the past three decades[26]. Along with Hubert Damisch, I had provided an initial overview of the phenomenon in 1993, after a conference held in Paris several years earlier as part of a seminar at the École des hautes études en sciences sociales. In 1995, I had presented the many topical registers of Americanism in an exhibit organized by the Canadian Centre for Architecture[27]. The premise of this work, which was that America had established the model for future European buildings and cities, remains unrefuted to this day.

But to comprehend the many dimensions of architectural Americanism in Russia, a mechanical extension of previous readings focusing on the only architectural manifestations specific to this national stage, would be insufficient. An analysis confined to the limits of architectural history would spawn an impoverished narrative, reduced to mundane stylistic considerations. Americanism, characterizing a rapidly changing discipline, also fell within the interaction between politics, economics, technology, and literary and artistic culture. Its study must therefore consider the sizable body of research conducted since the 1980s, which is in stark contrast with previous scholarship, produced mostly by American researchers as part of a collective attempt to understand the Soviet "adversary" and their vision of the United States. At the start of the Cold War, the "biased" Soviet literature, considered as pure propaganda, was a focal point for Western researchers[28]. Some time later, considerations on Amerikanizm and *Amerikanizatziia*, appearing in numerous academic works and several dozen major volumes, have continued to proliferate, with the work of historians, economists, and political science researchers interested in the history of political, diplomatic, and trade relations between the two countries. I have made a point of mentioning these studies stemming from various sectors of the academic community, whose intersections with my own research have shaped the backbone of this book.

I will not turn this long introduction into a bibliographical essay, a most thankless genre, but I will mention the main lessons that can be derived from this abundant and scattered research, analyzing them in their respective fields. First, the various aspects of nineteenth-century Russia's relation to America have been from an economic standpoint—as the country slowly found its place in the global economy, though without surpassing the European nations—as well as in the literary sphere. Hans Rogger has demonstrated the significance of American ideas for early Russian capitalism[29]. Studies of this period have shown that interest in America predated Lenin's fascination with the country[30]. In the realm of industrial policy, the early adoption of Frederick Winslow Taylor's doctrine, which the Bolsheviks initially condemned, and later espoused with great determination, has been analyzed as of the 1970s, along with its transposition by the poet Aleksei Gastev into his Central Institute of Labour[31].

The contribution of American industrial firms to the rise of Soviet industry has been mapped from a general perspective, for instance by the condescending Antony Sutton, and for specific sectors of activity, like the automotive industry, by Lewis Siegelbaum[32]. As for science, where American programmes were crucial after World War II, nuclear research has been thoroughly examined, as well as computer science and communication net-works[33]. Studies on the social transformation of Russia, as well as of its political elites and technologies, also shed light on the country's relationship with America[34]. In the literary realm, anthologies of Russian writings on America were published along with poetical analyses[35]. More recently, Aleksandr Etkind applied contemporary literary theory concepts to these texts[36]. Very few critics have addressed the connections between architecture and literature, explored in Rem Koolhaas's *Delirious New York*, which brought back to light Maxim Gorky's contribution to the rise of metropolitan culture[37].

33   David Holloway, *Stalin and the Bomb: The Soviet Union and Atomic Energy 1939–1956* (New Haven: Yale University Press, 1994); Seymour E. Goodman, "Soviet Computing and Technology Transfer: An Overview," *World Politics* 31, no. 4 (July 1979): 539–70; Steven T. Usdin, *Engineering Communism: How Two Americans Spied for Stalin and Founded the Soviet Silicon Valley* (New Haven: Yale University Press, 2005); Benjamin Peters, *How Not to Network a Nation: The Uneasy History of the Soviet Internet* (Cambridge, MA: MIT Press, 2017).

34   Moshe Lewin, *The Making of the Soviet System: Essays in the Social History of Interwar Russia* (New York: Pantheon Books, 1987); Kendall E. Bailes, "The American Connection: Ideology and the Transfer of American Technology to the Soviet Union," *Comparative Studies in Society and History* 23, no. 3 (July 1981): 421–48; Sheila Fitzpatrick, *The Cultural Front: Power and Culture in Revolutionary Russia* (Ithaca, London: Cornell University Press, 1992); Sheila Fitzpatrick, *Everyday Stalinism: Ordinary Life in Extraordinary Times. Soviet Russia in the 1930s* (New York and Oxford: Oxford University Press, 1999).

35   Olga Peters Hasty and Susanne Fusso, *America through Russian Eyes: 1874–1926* (New Haven: Yale University Press, 1988); Charles Rougle, *Three Russians Consider America: America in the Works of Maksim Gor'kij, Aleksandr Blok and Vladimir Maiakovskij* (Stockholm: Almqvist & Wiksell International, 1976).

36   Aleksandr Etkind, *Tolkovanie puteshestviei: Rossia i Amerika v travelogakh i intertekstakh* (Moscow: Novoe literaturnoe obozrenie, 2003).

37   Rem Koolhaas, *Delirious New York: A Retroactive Manifesto for Manhattan* (New York: Oxford University Press, 1978), 67–68.

38   Alan M. Ball, *Imagining America*.

39   William Nelson, *Out of the Crocodile's Mouth: Russian Cartoons about the United States from Krokodil, Moscow's Humor Magazine* (Washington, DC: Public Affairs Press, 1949).

40   Erika Wolf, *Aleksandr Zhitomirsky: Photomontage as a Weapon of World War II and the Cold War* (New Haven: Yale University Press, 2016).

41   Jeffrey Brooks, "The Press and Its Message: Images of America in the 1920's and 1930's," in Sheila Fitzpatrick, Alexander Rabinowitch, and Richard Stites, ed., *Russia in the Era of NEP: Explorations in Soviet Society and Culture* (Bloomington: Indiana University Press, 1991), 231–52; Owen Hatherley, *The Chaplin Machine: Slapstick, Fordism and the International Communist Avant-garde* (London: Pluto Press, 2016).

42   S. Frederick Starr, *Red & Hot: The Fate of Jazz in the Soviet Union 1917–1980* (London, New York: Oxford University Press, 1983); expanded edition (New York: Limelight Editions, 1994).

43   David Caute, *The Dancer Defects: The Struggle for Cultural Supremacy During the Cold War* (Oxford: Oxford University Press, 2003); Greg Castillo, *Cold War on the Home Front: The Soft Power of Midcentury Design* (Minneapolis: University of Minnesota Press, 2010). Susan E. Reid has published insightful analyses, such as "Cold War in the Kitchen: Gender and the De-Stalinization of Consumer Taste in the Soviet Union under Khrushchev," *Slavic Review* 61, no. 2 (Summer 2002): 211–52; and "The Khrushchev Kitchen: Domesticating the Scientific-Technological Revolution," *Journal of Contemporary History* 4, no. 2 (2005): 289–316.

44   Richard Stites, *Revolutionary Dreams: Utopian Vision and Experimental Life in the Russian Revolution* (Oxford, New York: Oxford University Press, 1989).

45   Susan Buck-Morss, *Dreamworld and Catastrophe: The Passing of Mass Utopia in East and West* (Cambridge, MA: MIT Press, 2000).

46   Julia Vaingurt, *Wonderlands of the Avant-Garde: Technology and the Arts in Russia of the 1920s* (Evanston, IL: Northwestern University Press, 2013).

47   Anatole Kopp, "Foreign Architects in the Soviet Union During the First Two Five-Year Plans," in *Reshaping Russian Architecture: Western Technology, Utopian Dreams*, William Craft Brumfield, ed. (Cambridge: Cambridge University Press; New York: Woodrow Wilson International Center for Scholars, 1990), 176–214.

48   Sonia Melnikova-Raich, "The Soviet Problem with Two 'Unknowns': How an American Architect and a Soviet Negotiator Jump-Started the Industrialization of Russia, Part I: Albert Kahn" and "Part II: Saul Bron," *Journal of the Society for Industrial Archeology* 36, no. 2 (2010): 57–80, and 37, no. 1–2 (2011): 5–28; Christina Crawford, "The Socialist Settlement Experiment: Soviet Urban Praxis, 1917–1932," PhD dissertation (Cambridge, MA: Harvard University, 2016).

49   William Craft Brumfield, "Russian Perceptions of American Architecture 1870–1917," in William Craft Brumfield, *Reshaping Russian Architecture*, 43–66.

50   Katherine E. Zubovich, "Moscow Monumental: Soviet Skyscrapers and Urban Life under High Stalinism", PhD dissertation (Berkeley: University of California, 2016); published as *Moscow Monumental: Soviet Skyscrapers and Urban Life in Stalin's Capital* (Princeton: Princeton University Press, 2021).

51   Maria Gough, "Lissitzky on Broadway," in *Object: Photo; Modern Photographs: The Thomas Walther Collection 1909–1949*, Mitra Abbaspour, Lee Ann Daffner and Maria Morris Hambourg, eds. (New York: Museum of Modern Art, 2014).

52   For an attempt at an overview of the mirroring relationship between the two countries, see Fabien Bellat, *Amériques–URSS: Architectures du défi* (Paris: Éditions Nicolas Chaudun, 2014).

Investigations on visual culture such as the work of Alan Ball have also been rather sparse, despite the importance of images in the idealized and critical portrayals of the United States[38]. Anti-American caricatures published in the satirical weekly *Krokodil* have been reprinted in the late 1940s, with their round-bellied Wall Street capitalists, their emaciated proletarians, and all the imaginable takes on the Statue of Liberty and skyscrapers[39]. Vladimir Zhitomirskii's photomontages, developed over several decades in John Heartfield's shadow, were not taken seriously as aesthetic objects until the 21st century[40]. The press of the early Soviet Union has been revisited by Jeffrey Brooks, while Owen Hatherley studied its mass culture and new media, such as film, in a dynamic interpretation of the role cultural industries played in shaping the Americanist discourse[41]. As for jazz, imported as well as locally produced—and temporarily obscured during the most xenophobic phase of Stalinism—, S. Frederick Starr explored it in a masterful 1983 publication[42]. More recently, the Cold War has become a research theme in itself, as Russian archives became available, allowing for more thorough investigations of official documents and letters[43].

Alongside the fragmented considerations on explicit Americanism, its phantasmagoric aspect has been unearthed in three books describing its dreamlike elements. In his sweeping fresco *Revolutionary Dreams*, Richard Stites unveils various motifs of the Russian imagination since the middle of the 19th century[44]. In *Dreamworld and Catastrophe*, Susan Buck-Morss revisits the revolutionary project and reveals its unremitting debt to capitalist streamlining[45]. Finally, several of the issues raised between these pages have been tackled by Julia Vaingurt in *Wonderlands of the Avant-Garde*, where she has uncovered popular literature, the scientific organization of labour, theatre, and urban utopias, tracing a trajectory that my discourse will at times overlap[46].

Architecture at Play

In Russia, as well as in the West, there has been no shortage of research on architecture and urban planning since the 1980s. In keeping with his role as a pioneer, Anatole Kopp, who had been among the first to revisit the Russian avant-gardes, endeavoured to study Albert Kahn's contribution to the industrialization of the USSR, at a time when Moscow's archives were still out of reach[47]. Based on field work as well as on uncharted archives, Sonia Melnikova-Raich's excellent work on the Detroit architect and his Russian patrons, as well as Christina Crawford's path-breaking study of the new cities of the first five-year plan, attest to the road travelled since[48]. Among earlier works, William Craft Brumfield explored pre-revolutionary journals, uncovering several articles on construction and urban planning in the United States[49]. The spectacular episode of Moscow's post-1945 high-rise building construction did not go unnoticed among researchers, who have highlighted its poorly concealed debt to American structures, a debt now thoroughly identified owing to Katherine Zubovich's remarkable research[50].

Between the intense professional and artistic life of capitalist Russia and its post-war endeavours, the two decades during which the rise and fall of the avant-gardes have been deeply impacted by Americanism have not yet been studied from the standpoint of architecture. Maria Gough has briefly mentioned El Lissitzky's engagement in a perceptive analysis of a collage made from a Broadway photograph[51]. But the mutual attraction between Soviet architects and Frank Lloyd Wright has unfortunately been examined only unilaterally. Thus, more studies need to be conducted to circumscribe and comprehend many aspects of Americanism[52]. This quick overview would be incomplete without mentioning my own work, which began four decades ago, when I became interested in the topic. Russian Americanism became part of my own personal phantasmagoria, shaped by visions of Russia instigated by my 1960s encounter with the works of Kopp, as well as with the scholar himself, and my discussions with Damisch as of the late 1970s. My familiarity with the United States, which developed later, fostered this growing interest. Frequently travelling to Moscow and delving ever deeper into the archives, I have disseminated my research in works addressed to a larger audience, such as my 1984 essay on the "American ideal" and my 1995 book *Scenes of the World to Come*, where I studied Russian innovations alongside those of the rest of Europe[53]. I have focused on periods such as the 1920s and the early 1930s, the golden era of the first radical Americanism[54]. Individual architects have also retained my attention, such as the visionary creator Iakov Chernikhov, or travellers like Erich Mendelsohn and Frank Lloyd Wright[55]. I have also ventured beyond the preserve of architecture to study a few industrial artifacts that had migrated eastward and to peruse some of the most recent Russian literary works on the United States[56]. These fragments, however, do not suffice to paint an intelligible picture and will be either discarded or largely remodeled into the following ambitious chronicle.

The Figures of Amerikanizm

The multiple discourses and practices, only partly reflected in the aforementioned analyses, resist a comprehensive mapping by a single author. I will thus deliberately focus on architecture, as I believe that spatial and formal manifestations can shed light on other dimensions of Americanism. I will also put strong emphasis on material production, since the social construction of Russian technological systems owes a great debt to the American model[57]. Exploring the sedimented layers of the phenomenon will involve constant shifts between representations and practices, as well as continuous fluctuations in scale. Indeed, in Russia more than in any other nation, Amerikanizm has served as a general metaphor for urbanization, modernity, and modernization.

Architecture is an integral part of Amerikanizm for two reasons. First, it is one of the manifestations of the urban American identity that the various observers—be they economists, politicians, sociologists, or writers—were most eager to describe. But it was also a prism, a mirror, and a telltale sign of Amerikanizm at large, as embodied in the successive theoretical projects, city plans, and buildings designed and created in Russia, such as skyscrapers or standalone houses. It also allows us to decipher the major eras of Americanization. Architecture will thus serve as a unifying thread for this analysis conducted in the realm of visibility, as well as in the field of concrete and symbolic production.

Ever since I undertook my initial analyses, the study of relations between national cultures has become a major component of historical research. The transnational circulation of ideas seems to have become a discipline onto itself, as the outdated concept of "influence" has been replaced by those of "cultural transfer" and "interference."[58] Furthermore, reception studies allow us to measure the distant effects of one political, technical, or cultural group on another, as long as the relationship is envisioned within a dynamic model, such as the one proposed by Reinhart Koselleck. His concept of "horizon of expectation," borrowed from Hans Robert Jauss, is particularly useful to understand how a future-oriented nation such as industrialization-era Russia strove towards Americanism, as well as to comprehend its initial goals of emancipation and social change. As for the idea of "space of experience," it allows for an understanding of the often-contradictory execution of these aspirations[59].

Rather than revealing a single horizon, it would be more appropriate to shed light on the many distinct perspectives of the various agents of Amerikanizm—politicians, writers, engineers, architects, and artists—appearing in travel narratives, documentary works, novels, poetry, and projects of all scales. The proliferation of these productions cannot be measured comprehensively, and they will be brought up in a fragmentary fashion. The geographical scope of Amerikanizm in Russia is significant. It could be mapped in a bilateral way, with, on the American side, recurring regions, such as the South and California, and cities that were the object of such focus that they often seemed to serve as a synecdoche for America as a whole. In turn, Chicago, New York, Detroit, or Los Angeles condensed the wonders to be replicated and the woes to avoid. As such, a true inter-urbanity was shaped, with each Russian city containing fragments of one or several American metropolises. On the Russian side, Amerikanizm could be depicted in various areas of focus, as revealed by informal place names. Novosibirsk thus became the Chicago of a Siberia imagined as a new Midwest or a reversed Far West. In popular culture, while a particularly productive worker of a Soviet collective was nicknamed "the American" in the 1920s, the places and buildings embodying the USSR's initial impulse were nicknamed "little Americas."[60]

The West-to-East movement of representations, models, and techniques was not always straightforward, especially during the halt in diplomatic relations between the two countries between 1919 and 1933. At that time, before reaching Russia, images of the United States were refracted in the prism of the Weimar Republic, with which the early Soviet Union had strong ties, forming a triangular relationship. Later, transfers became more direct, in a form of "translation," in the geometrical sense of the term. This was the case of products or production systems borrowed without a license, such as the first tractor of the Putilov factory, copied from Ford, and the Tupolev Tu-4 aircraft plagiarized from Boeing. Other such borrowings were based on explicit agreements, such as for Kahn's factories, which migrated from Dearborn, Michigan to cities such as Cheliabinsk, in the Urals. "Translation" was also the rule for standards, procedures, and technical specifications regarding the hundreds of factories created during the first five-year plan, as well as for those specific to architecture.

53   Jean-Louis Cohen, "America, a Soviet Ideal," *AA Files*, no. 5 (January 1984): 33–40; *Scenes of the World to Come*, 1995. The earliest of my articles is "Il collettivo all'assalto del cielo: i paesi socialisti in cerca del grattacielo," *Hinterland* 1, no. 2 (March–April 1978): 42–48.

54   Jean-Louis Cohen, "L'Oncle Sam au pays des Soviets: le temps des avant-gardes," in id. and Hubert Damisch, ed., *Américanisme et modernité*, 403–435.

55   Jean-Louis Cohen, "Le ballet mécanique de Tchernikhov, ou l'Amerikanizm fantastique," in *Iakov Tchernikhov,* Carlo Olmo and Alessandro de Magistris, eds. (Paris: Somogy; Turin: Allemandi, 1995), 61–78; Id., "Postface", in Erich Mendelsohn, *Amerika, livre d'images d'un architecte* (Paris: Éditions du Demi-Cercle, 1992), 225–41; Id., "Useful Hostage: Constructing Wright in Soviet Russia and France," in *Frank Lloyd Wright: Europe and Beyond,* Anthony Alofsin, ed. (Berkeley: University of California Press, 1999), 100–20.

56   Jean-Louis Cohen, "[American] Objects of [Soviet] Desire," in *Forty Ways to Think About Architecture: Architectural History and Theory Today,* Iain Borden, Murray Fraser, and Barbara Penner, eds. (Chichester: Wiley, 2014), 127–33; Id., "Retour d'Amérique: pages d'écriture russes," *Europe* 95, no. 1055 (March 2017): 43–54.

57   Wiebe E. Bijker, Thomas P. Hughes, and Trevor J. Pinch, *The Social Construction of Technological Systems* (Cambridge, MA: MIT Press, 1987).

58   Pierre–Yves Saunier, *Transnational History* (Basingstoke, NY: Palgrave Macmillan, 2013); Sanjay Subrahmanyam, *Aux origines de l'histoire globale* (Paris: Collège de France, Fayard, 2014).

59   Reinhart Koselleck "Representation, Event, and Structure," in *Futures Past: On the Semantics of Historical Time* [1979] (Cambridge, MA: MIT Press, 1985), 105–114.

60   Brooks, "The Press and Its Message," 241–42.

Other figures of displacement can easily be identified. The quotation is the most obvious one, as evidenced by the use of tectonic or decorative elements borrowed from New York skyscrapers in early 1950s Soviet high-rise build-ings. Similarity, or transformation, multiplies all distances by the same positive real number, called a constant. Following this principle, the circular shape of the Pan Am terminal at Idlewild was condensed at the Moscow-Sheremetyevo Airport. Homothety, a particular type of similarity, occurs when the vertical American city is miniaturized while maintaining the relation between sky-scraper and islet. More complex transformations materialize, such as anamor-phosis, in which an agglomeration of buildings like Kharkov's Gosprom, in certain angles, takes the shape of a great metropolis. Isomorphism—or struc-tural correspondence—between Russian and American configurations can also be found, for example in the relation between factories and the towns housing their workforce, or in the layout of collective farms, as well as scien-tific or military grounds. The most obvious case of isomorphism can be found in the industrial sector, for instance in the manufacturing of machines, auto-mobiles, or airplanes, as well as in the food industry.

The most determinant and all-encompassing figure of displacement remains the metaphor, which portrays the United States as the *speculum*, the mirror, reflecting the future of Russia. But this figure is far from stable, and it is reconfigured along with the changes in horizons of expectation specific to each historical period. Lastly, I must mention the figures of *maskirovka* (cam-ouflage) of borrowings and their outright denial. Anti-Amerikanizm is the *doppelgänger* of Amerikanizm, and as of the 19th century, the two tendencies constantly combined and resisted one another in the words of writers, ideo-logues, and politicians. Nowadays, they persist in Putin's Russia.

Cycles and Fluctuations

An intellectual attitude as well as a symbolic dependence spanning all discur-sive fields, Amerikanizm was not borne out of the Bolshevik revolution, though it was adopted as a quasi-doctrine in the early years of the Soviet Union. Neither did it magically disappear along with the USSR in 1991. A two-century period must thus be examined to understand its mechanisms and attachment points and to paint a picture informed by studies from these past decades. Rather than applying a topical principle, roughly outlined above, which would involve identifying the manifestations of Amerikanizm in various fields of the social practice, a comprehensive discourse can be shaped only by shedding light on the context of these oft-delayed manifestations. The most obvious historical markers are political ones: 1861, when the abolition of serfdom made way for the modernization of Russia, after the Crimean War; and 1991, with the collapse of the Soviet Union. But this time frame should not obscure the events that occurred after the 1776 American Revolution, as they were significant for the development of future attitudes.

In this time frame covering around 130 years, two events determined both the Russians' horizon of expectation towards America and their space of experience. The first was a visit paid by a group of Russian scientists and technicians to the 1876 Philadelphia World's Fair, commemorating the 100th anniversary of the Declaration of Independence. The second was the 1959 American National Exhibition held in Moscow shortly before Nikita Khrushchev's departure for an epic journey in the United States. The first event was experi-enced by the elite, while the second was open to the masses. Between these two dates, numerous successive trips were undertaken by politicians, technicians, writers, architects, artists, and filmmakers, whose travels were dictated by political circumstances. The great expositions held in Chicago (1893 and 1933), in New York (1939), and in Moscow (1959) were privileged areas of interaction. However, wars and revolutions had the most powerful effects, namely because they caused migrations and exiles towards the West, with the exception of the fifteen years where American technicians and activists participated in the Soviet industrialization. The time frame of Amerikanizm is thus non-isotopic, spanning distinct horizons and experiences.

The ties formed after 1861 remained unsevered by the October Revolution, especially as thousands of exiles returned to Russia following the uprising. But as Russia's industrial development coincided with the rise of revolutionary movements, the resulting advances must be examined for themselves, in the complex layering of discourses, and not only as a prelude to what would follow. Though the focus on industry and daily life characteristic of late-czarist Americanism persisted during the Soviet period, the interest in democratic life waned, leaving only recurring mentions of racial segregation. Conventional breakdowns also have their limitations during the Bolshevik period: in a centralized system traversed by conflicts and contradictions, the rhythms of politics, economics, and visual culture do not perfectly overlap.

Between the October Revolution and the 1930s era of repression, the regime initially endorsed Taylorism and Fordism, while the avant-gardes borrowed a portion of their paradigms from American models. The subsequent undivided power of Stalin's coterie failed to suspend borrowings from America. They remained considerable in the second half of the 1930s—as a large part of those involved with the United States perished in the purges—and regained their intensity during the Second World War. In the post-war period, a disguised Americanism endured throughout the early years of the Cold War despite the prevalence of hysterical propaganda. Between 1953 and the late 1960s, the relationship became more porous, namely when Nikita Khrushchev advocated for a peaceful coexistence between the two blocs, all the while presiding over the restoration of modernity. During the Brezhnev stagnation, Soviet attempts to create an economy centred on consumption and foreign markets were also the result of American contributions. The arms race, however, ended up devastating an economy that was impossible to reform.

In each of these cycles, the imagined and concrete ties with America were the product of generations involved in implicit or deliberate collective movements: the focus of many Russian intellectuals on American democracy in the 19th century, the industrial enthusiasm expressed by leaders and engineers in the 1920s, or the discovery of daily life in the West by reporters in the 1970s. As for architecture, it was comprehended both through its own codes and procedures, as swayed by Amerikanizm, and as a symptom of more general symbolic and material displacements, though without an all-encompassing understanding of these interactions. This book will follow these shifts between the macroscopic and microscopic scales: the only way to measure the interrelations between the fates of societies and those of individuals[61].

61   Jean-Louis Cohen, *Architecture, modernité, modernisation*, inaugural lecture at the Collège de France (Paris: Collège de France/Fayard, 2017), 86.

To capture what permeates from the phantasmagoria into reality, perhaps we should revisit Walter Benjamin and his identification with the figure of the rag-picker, patiently collecting items and fragments, which served as a model for his *Arcades Project*[62]. The final step would involve combining them in a mosaic, or field-based approach, such as the one applied by Marshall McLuhan in *The Gutenberg Galaxy*[63]. With its recognizable shapes, where the shards can be assembled, along with its gaps and omissions, this is the sort of mosaic I wish to present to the reader.

62   Irving Wohlfarth, "Et Cetera? The Historian as Chiffonnier," *New German Critique*, no. 39 (Autumn 1986), 142–168.
63   Marshall McLuhan, *The Gutenberg Galaxy: The Making of Typographic Man* (Toronto: University of Toronto Press, 1962).

Czarist Russia and its Americas

1

George Washington Whistler (1800-1849). American railway engineer, active in Russia.

Aleksandr S. Pushkin (1799-1837). Russian poet and playwright, curious about developments in America.

Fedor M. Dostoevsky (1821-1881). Russian writer, always ironic in the mention he made of America.

Aleksandr I. Herzen (1812-1870). First Russian revolutionary, attracted by the American *republic*.

Dmitri I. Mendeleev (1834-1907). Russian chemist, discovered the United States in 1876.

Vladimir G. Shukhov (1853-1939). Russian civil engineer, discovered the United States in 1876.

Mikhail I. Khilkov (1834-1909). Railroad minister, built upon his American experience.

Maxim Gorky (1868-1936). Russian writer, returned in horror from his 1906 trip to New York.

Aleksandr A. Blok (1880-1921). Russian poet celebrated industrial Russia as a *New America*.

"It is such an amazing fantasy of stone, glass, and iron, a fantasy constructed by crazy giants, monsters longing after beauty, stormy souls full of wild energy. All these Berlins, Parises, and other 'big' cities are trifles in comparison with New York. Socialism should first be realized here—that is the first thing you think of when you see the amazing houses, machines, etc."

Maxim Gorky, letter to Leonid Krasin, 1906[1].

1   Maxim Gorky, letter to Leonid Krasin, 1906, in Maxim Gorky, *Letters of Gorky and Andreev 1899–1912*, ed. Peter Yershov (New York: Columbia University Press), 85.

Long before Tocqueville foretold parallel fates for Russia and the United States, the two countries had already forged a strong relationship. Russia was an American power before its California trading posts and Alaska were relinquished to the Union in 1867. But the Russians' perception of American politics, society, and culture was not in line with their trade objectives in Alaska, a land they believed to be contiguous to Siberia until Vitus Bering's explorations, commissioned by Peter the Great in 1728, revealed the existence of a water mass between the two continents.

At the start of the eighteenth century, as demonstrated by Dieter Boden, Russians were discovering America through numerous literary translations and works imbued with exoticism, such as the 1788 comic opera *The Americans* by the fabulist Ivan Krylov. One of the more widely circulated books at the time was Raynal's *A History of the Two Indies*, written in part by Diderot, which described American society with a critical perspective[2]. Russian and American scholars came into contact against the backdrop of the triple hegemony exerted by France, Germany, and Great Britain. This is evidenced by the 1784 publication, in Saint Petersburg, both in Russian and in French, of Benjamin Franklin's *Poor Richard's Almanack*, which he had begun writing in 1732. The Almanack was one of Catherine the Great's favourite bedside books. On the political front, the empress refused to support the British forces during the American Revolutionary War. This refusal, however, was dictated not so much by genuine sympathy for a republican form of government as by Russian interests in weakening the British Empire[3]. In 1780, Congress dispatched attorney Francis Dana to Saint Petersburg with the aim to establish diplomatic relations with the Russian Empire. For two full years, he danced attendance on the empress, alas, in vain, before President James Madison finally sent John Quincy Adams as Ambassador in 1809[4].

A distant horizon, America was nevertheless present in Russian politics and literature at the start of the nineteenth century, if only in reverence to Benjamin Franklin and George Washington. A hastily repressed reformist, Aleksandr Radishchev extolled the virtues of the "Transatlantic Republic's" civil freedoms in his 1790 *Ode to Liberty*, which appears in his *Journey from Saint Petersburg to Moscow*[5]. Aleksandr I, having exchanged letters with Thomas Jefferson, momentarily devised reforms inspired by the American model, which also played a significant role in shaping the political ideas of the Decembrists, who instigated the failed uprising of 1825.

Early Literary and Technological Transfers

One of the first Russians to visit the United States was Pavel Svinin, a diplomat, artist, and controversial figure of 1820s literary society. From September 1811 to September 1813, he travelled across the American northeast, all the while disseminating his writings about Russia and his sketches of landscapes from his homeland[6]. He expressed admiration for the greatness of the United States in his 1815 *Picturesque Journey through North America*, illustrated by some fifty engravings based on his watercolours, which depicted skylines, landscapes, and daily life in America[7] [ill. p. 38]. Celebrating the "perfection" of American factories and machines, he broke away from the conventional narrative about "noble savages" and natural wonders such as Niagara Falls, painting instead a picture of an inventive and energetic civilization. For this reason, his compatriots often considered his travel accounts to be tall tales[8]. He also described the brand new bridge across the Schuylkill River in Philadelphia, known as the Colossus of Fairmount. Built in 1812 by Louis Wernwag and spanning 103 metres, it was then the country's longest wooden bridge, reinforced with steel rods. Svinin was particularly interested in Robert Fulton's steamboat, the *Paragon*, so much so that he sought to become its exclusive distributor in Russia, where Fulton was planning to establish a route between Saint Petersburg and Kronstadt[9]. But the inventor's demise brought these attempts to a halt. In his correspondence, Svinin marvelled at the spectacle of New York, predicting that it would surpass all other cities thanks to its harbour and foreseeing its brilliant future[10].

This early response to American technical innovation laid the foundation for an enduring disposition. The nearly instant popularity of inventors such as Franklin and Fulton foretold the significant notoriety of Alexander Graham Bell, Thomas Edison, and Henry Ford. The earliest display of any consequential interest towards American engineering on the Russian Empire's part occurred during the construction of the railway between Saint Petersburg and Moscow. Military engineer Pavel Melnikov, author of the first book in Russian on the theme of railroads, was sent to America to prepare the creation of the line[11]. In 1839, he recruited his colleague George Washington Whistler, who introduced truss bridges to Russia, where he settled, immediately after their invention in the United States[12]. Most significantly, he issued a recommendation to then minister of transportation, Count Petr Kleinmichel, to widen the rails by five feet, or 1.524 metres. This gauge was larger than other European railways but typical of those of the American South until 1886[13]. Steam-powered excavators were commissioned to William Otis[14], while the locomotives and rolling stock, based on a design brief created by Whistler, were manufactured by Harrison, Winans & Eastwick, an American company that had opened a factory in Saint Petersburg for this purpose. This was also a trailblazing event[15]. The American engineer died in the Russian capital in 1849, where his son James, who would later surpass his father's fame, studied fine arts.

2	Abbot Guillaume Thomas Raynal, *Histoire philosophique et politique des établissements et du commerce des Européens dans les deux Indes* (Amsterdam: [s.n.], 1770). See Dieter Boden, *Das Amerikabild im russischen Schrifttum bis zum Ende des 19. Jahrhunderts* (Hamburg: Cram, de Gruyter & Co., 1968), 16–26.
3	On Catherine the Great's pro-American views, see Max M. Laserson, *The American Impact on Russia; Diplomatic and Ideological, 1794–1917* (New York: MacMillan, 1950), 31–39.
4	Nikolai N. Bolkhovitinov, *Stanovlenie russko-amerikanskikh otnoshenii 1775-1815* (Moscow: Nauka, 1966); in English: *Russia and the American Revolution* (Tallahassee: The Diplomatic Press, 1976).
5	Aleksandr N. Radishchev, *Puteshestvie iz Peterburga v Moskvu* (Saint Petersburg: Tip. Radishcheva, 1790); in English: *A Journey from Saint Petersburg to Moscow* (Cambridge, MA: Harvard University Press, 1958). For the meaning of the ode, see Bolkhovitinov, *Russia and the American Revolution*, 152–63.
6	Pavel P. Svinin, *Sketches of Moscow and Saint Petersburg* (Philadelphia: Thomas Dobson, 1813).
7	Pavel P. Svinin, *Opyt zhivopisnogo puteshestvia po Severnoi Amerike* (Saint Petersburg: Tip. F. Drekhslera, 1815), 64–65; see reproductions of the original drawings in *Traveling across North America 1812–18: Watercolors by the Russian Diplomat Pavel Svinin* (New York: Harry N. Abrams, 1992); and his published notebooks and correspondence in Pavel P. Svinin, *Amerikanskie dnevniki i pisma* (Moscow: Parad, 2006).
8	Boden, *Das Amerikabild*, p. 55–56.
9	Correspondence published in Alice Clary Sutcliffe, "Fulton's Invention of the Steamboat," *The Century Magazine* 78, no. 6 (October 1909), 833.
10	Pavel P. Svinin, second letter to Nikolai Ia. Kozlov, n.d., in *Amerikanskie dnevniki i pisma*, 181.
11	Richard Mowbray Haywood, *Russia Enters the Railway Age, 1842–1855* (Boulder: East European Monographs, 1998), 20–21.
12	D. A. Gasparini, K. Nizamiev, and C. Tardini, "G. W. Whistler and the Howe Bridges on the Nikolaev Railway, 1842–1851," *American Society of Civil Engineers, Journal of Performance of Constructed Facilities* 30, no. 3 (2015): https://dx.doi.org/10.1061/(ASCE)CF.1943-5509.0000791 [accessed 2 September 2019].
13	George Washington Whistler, "Report to His Excellency the Count Kleinmichel on the Gauge of the Russian Railways, Saint Petersburg, 9 September 1842," James McNeill Whistler Papers, 1830–1894, New York Public Library. A rail gauge of 1.524 metres has remained standard in Russia.
14	Samuel Stueland, "The Otis Steam Excavator," *Technology and Culture* 35, no. 3 (1994): 571–74.
15	Haywood, *Russia Enters the Railway Age*, 256ff; Robert V. Allen, *Russia Looks at America: The View to 1917* (Washington, DC: Library of Congress, 1988), 26–27.

Pavel P. Svinin. *New York City and its Harbor Seen from Weehawken*, ca. 1811.
Watercolour and gouache on off-white wove paper, 15.2 × 25.4 cm. Metropolitan Museum of Art, 42.95.5.

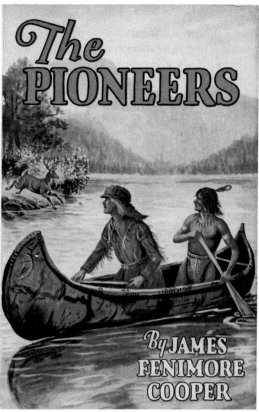

Left: James Fenimore Cooper, *The Pioneers* [1823], New York: Grosset & Dunlap, 1930, cover. CCA.
Right: Vladimir Arsenev and the trapper Derzu Uzala, between 1902 and 1907, illustration in *La Taïga de l'Oussouri.*
Mes expéditions avec le chasseur gold Dersou. Paris: Payot. 1939.

As for writers and political reformers, America was ever-present in their considerations regarding the future of Russia. They viewed the New World as an alternative means of political development, different from that of European powers. Aleksandr Pushkin was rather pessimistic, underlining in 1836, the flaws of a society he nevertheless admired. He lamented the extermination of the "Indians" and the replacement of grasslands with cultivated fields: "the respect felt for this new nation and its code, the fruit of the most advanced enlightenment, has been greatly shaken. People saw with astonishment democracy in its disgusting cynicism, with all its cruel prejudices, in its unbearable tyranny. Everything noble and disinterested, everything that elevates man's spirit, crushed by implacable egoism and a passion for comfort; the majority, and insolently persecuting society; Negro slavery in the midst of freedom and education; class persecution among a people who have no nobility, and envy on the part of the electorate."[16] The tempting connection between the slavery practised in Southern states and Russian serfdom would soon establish widespread recognition for Harriet Beecher Stowe's *Uncle Tom's Cabin*, translated in 1858, six years after its original publication[17].

The most critical writer towards America was Fedor Dostoevsky, who never missed an opportunity to portray America as another, albeit more materialistic, Siberia, where wretched Russian emigrants were destined to go astray, like the characters in his 1872 *Demons*. One of the novel's protagonists admits to having admired "everything: spiritualism, lynching, sixshooters, hoboes", sadly noting that Russians are "pygmies compared to the soaring ideas of the North American States."[18] In *Crime and Punishment*, published six years earlier, Dostoevsky alluded to a distant haven that Raskolnikov aspired to reach, exclaiming: "Better escape altogether…far away…to America."[19] In 1873, in *A Writer's Diary*, he commented ironically on the characteristics of the new Saint Petersburg buildings, such as Ludwig Fontana's Europe Hotel, then in construction on Nevsky Prospekt: "finally, here we have the architecture of a modern, enormous hotel: this is a businesslike trend – Amerikanizm, hundreds of rooms, a formidable industrial enterprise. One sees at once that we, too, have built railroads, and that all of a sudden we have become businessmen."[20]

Dostoevsky's sarcastic tone is typical of a subset of Russian fictional and journalistic writings on America. The parallel with Siberia remained a trope in Russian literature as well as in politics. An equally central recurring theme was that of the frontier, employed by Tolstoy in his novella *The Cossacks*, who borrowed it from *Le lac Ontario*, the French translation of James Fenimore Cooper's *Pathfinder*[21]. The popularity of the author of the *Leatherstocking Tales*

16   Aleksandr Pushkin, "Dzhon Tenner," *Sovremennik* (1836), 205–207, quoted in Glynn R. V. Barratt, "Pushkin's America: A Survey of the Sources," *Canadian Slavonic Papers* 15, no. 3 (1973): 274–96.

17   For this comparison, see Michael Confino, "Servage russe, esclavage américain," *Annales; Économies; Sociétés; Civilisations* 45, no. 5 (1990): 1119–41.

18   Fedor Dostoevsky, *Besy* (1872); in English: *Demons*, trans. Richard Pevear and Larissa Volokhonsky (New York: Alfred A. Knopf, 1994), 140. See Hans Rogger's comments in "America in the Russian Mind – or Russian Discoveries of America," *Pacific Historical Studies* 47 (February 1978): 27–28.

19   Fedor Dostoevsky, *Crime and Punishment*, in *Polnoe sobranie sochinenii v tridsati tomakh*, vol. 6 (Leningrad, Nauka, 1973), 100; in English: *Crime and Punishment*, trans. Constance Garnett (New York: P. F. Collier & Son, 1917), 129.

20   Fedor Dostoevsky, "Malenkie kartiny," [1873] in *Dnevnik Pisatelia* (Berlin: Izd-vo Dadyzhnikova, 1922), 374-75; in English: *The Diary of a Writer*, trans. Boris Brasol (New York: George Braziller, 1954), 121.

21   James Fenimore Cooper, *Œuvres*, t. XVII, *Le lac Ontario*, trans. A.-J.-B. Defauconpret, (Paris: C. Gosselin, 1840).

in Russia would prove enduring[22]. His tales of indigenous peoples inspired Vladimir Arsenev, a twentieth-century writer and explorer, whose novel *Dersu the Trapper*, written in 1907 and published in 1921 in Vladivostok, centered on the Nanai trapper Dersu Uzala, a distant cousin of the last of the Mohicans. Arsenev devoted another volume to this character in 1923[23] [ill. p. 38]. In 1929, Sergei Tretiakov described the tale as a work of *factography*, a non-fictional form of storytelling that claims Cooper as a forerunner, based on the book's numerous allusions to North American material culture and ritual practices[24].

America in the Eyes of the Revolutionaries

The divide between members of the Russian intelligentsia was mirrored in their respective perceptions of America, fuelled by ever simpler and more frequent travels. According to a recurrent dichotomy in nineteenth-century Russia, two main visions prevailed: Slavophile cautiousness and Occidentalist optimism, although the latter group perceived Western Europe to be a closer frame of reference than the United States. The leader of the Slavophiles, poet and theologist Aleksei Khomiakov, viewed America as a place where European corruption was multiplied, and saw no virtue in democracy[25]. As for liberal Ivan Golovin, he ruthlessly critiqued American daily life and democracy in *Stars and Stripes*, and was pessimistic concerning the future of the Union[26].

One of the first Russian revolutionaries, Aleksandr Herzen, although a great admirer of Alexis de Tocqueville, disagreed with his prophecy. Herzen read the first volume of *Democracy in America* in 1837, a year after Pushkin, and rejected the idea of a perfect parallel between the fates of Russia and America[27].

22   Boden, *Das Amerikabild*, 96–103; Willard Thorp, "Cooper Beyond America," *New York History 35*, no. 4 (1954): 522–39.
23   Vladimir K. Arsenev, *Po ussuriiskomu kraiu [Along the Ussuri Land]* (Vladivostok: Tip. Ekho, 1921). Id., *Dersu Uzala* (Vladivostok: Svobodnaia Rossiia, 1923); in English: *Dersu the Trapper*, trans. Malcolm Burr (New York: E.P. Dutton & Co, 1941). Akira Kurosawa released his film of the same title in 1975.
24   Sergei Tretiakov, "Zhivoi 'zhivoi' chelovek (o knige V. K. Arseeva 'V debriakh ussuriiskogo kraia', izd. Knizhnoe delo, Vladivostok, 1926)," in *Literatura fakta: pervyi sbornik materialov rabotnikov LEF-a*, N.F. Chuzhak and O.M. Brik, eds. (Moscow: Federatsia, 1929), 243–45.
25   Boden, *Das Amerikabild*, 127–31; Hans Rogger, "Russia and the Civil War," in *Heard Round the World; the Impact Abroad of the Civil War*, Harold M. Hyman, ed. (New York: Knopf, 1969), 183–184.
26   Ivan Golovin, *Stars and Stripes, or American Impressions* (London: W. Freeman, 1856).
27   Alexander Kucherov, "Alexander Herzen's Parallel Between the United States and Russia," in *Essays in Russian and Soviet History in Honor of G. T. Robinson*, John S. Curtiss, ed. (Leiden: Brill, 1969), 34–47.
28   Michel Mervaud, "L'Amérique dans l'œuvre d'Alexandre Herzen," *Cahiers du monde russe et soviétique 13*, no. 4 (octobre-décembre 1972): 524–554; id., "La découverte de l'Amérique par le jeune Herzen: du romantisme au réalisme," *Revue des études slaves 49* (1973): 301–14.
29   Aleksandr Herzen, quoted in David Hecht, *Russian Radicals Look to America 1825-1894* (Cambridge, MA: Harvard University Press, 1947), 24.
30   Aleksandr Herzen, "Amerika i Sibir," *Kolokol*, 1 December 1858, 233, quoted in Mervaud, "L'Amérique dans l'œuvre d'Alexandre Herzen," 548.
31   Mikhail Bakounine, *Œuvres de Michel Bakounine*, ed. James Guillaume (Paris: Stock, 1907), vol.1, 28, quoted in Hecht, *Russian Radicals*, 58. See also *Correspondance de Michel Bakounine: lettres à Herzen et Ogaroff, 1860-1874*, published by Mikhail Dragomanov (Paris: Perrin, 1896), 123, quoted in Hecht, *Russian Radicals*, 62
32   See the nuanced and stimulating analysis of Hans Rogger, "Russia and the Civil War," *loc. cit.*, 179–256. See also Mark M. Malkin, *Grazhdanskaia voina v SShA i tsarskaia Rossiia*, (Leningrad: Sotsekgiz, 1939).
33   Nikolai G. Chernyshevskii, "Politika," a report from *Sovremennik* (Feb 1861), in *Polnoe sobranie sochinenii* (Saint Petersburg: Yip. Ts. Kraiza, 1906), VIII, 390, quoted in David Hecht, *Russian Radicals*, 100-101.
34   Nikolai G. Chernyshevskii, *Chto delat?* (Vevey: P. Benda, 1867 [first edition in one volume]); in English: *A Vital Question, or What Is to Be Done?*, trans. Nathan H. Dole and S.S. Skidelsky (New York: Thomas Y. Crowell, 1886).
35   Hecht, *Russian Radicals*, 137-141.
36   The archives for Frey/Geins are kept at the New York Public Library; for more on him see Avrahm Yarmolinsky, *A Russian's American Dream; A Memoir on William Frey* (Lawrence: University of Kansas Press, 1965).
37   Grigorii Machtet, *Polnoe sobranie sochinenii*, vol. 1, *Putevye kartiny amerikanskoi zhizni* (Saint Petersburg: Knigoizd-vo t-va Prosveshchenie, 1911), 200–5.

In 1839, although his knowledge of the New World was entirely based on his readings, Herzen wrote a Tocqueville-inspired drama entitled *William Penn*, in which the most positive characters were Quakers[28]. Drawing from observations made by Giuseppe Garibaldi, whose knowledge of the United States stemmed from a two-year stay in New York City, he surmised that the country was "more practical than intelligent," "cold and calculating," albeit capable of transcending bourgeois narrowness, and celebrated its federalism and local democracy[29]. In his articles for *Kolokol* (The Bell), Herzen imagined a future where both countries would cooperate on the grounds of a geographical resemblance, as "both stretch out into boundless plains, searching for their borders and, from opposite sides, marking their path with countless mountains, villages, and colonies, reach the Pacific Ocean, this '*mare nostrum* of the future'", a passage that was quickly circulated in the American press[30]. He thus replaced Tocqueville's parallelism with geopolitical symmetry.

While he garnered some of Herzen's ideas, having met him in Russia and in France, the anarchist Mikhail Bakunin was undoubtedly the first revolutionary who had not only read Fenimore Cooper, but also experienced America first-hand, as he spent several months in San Francisco, New York, and Boston on his way to Europe after escaping Siberian exile in 1861. In his nuanced commentary on the New World's social divide, he contrasted the relative well-being of American workers to the misery of their European counterparts, noting that "in less than a century, America has been able to catch up to Europe and even to surpass it." However, he lamented the "banality of material comfort" and the "heartlessness" he encountered there[31]. He nevertheless approved of the federal system, to such a degree that the project he presented in Prague in 1848 for the creation of a Slavic federation bore striking resemblance to the American model.

During the American Civil War, all levels of Russian society were overwhelmingly in favour of the Union. Russian emigrants joined the Union Army to fight against Southern slavery[32]. As the battles continued and in light of the 1863 Polish Insurrection, Russian conservatives opposed a democratic and federalist form of government in Russia. In the *Sovremennik* (The Contemporary), a journal founded by Pushkin, the revolutionary writer Nikolai Chernyshevskii spoke highly of Abraham Lincoln, equating the abolition of slavery—to him, a form of "social despotism"—with the beginning of a broader fight for social justice that involved Russia[33]. Chernyshevskii was an avid reader of Tocqueville and Cooper and generally well informed, but he had no contact with the United States other than through his diversified readings. However, he portrayed an idealized America in his 1863 novel *What Is to Be Done?*[34], with an American character named Charles Beaumont. To better serve his thesis, the author exaggerated the realities of US democracy, the emigrants' ability to assimilate—namely that of the Irish—, and the significance of utopian communities in the New World[35]. Some alternative insular communities were created in the United States by Russian populists inspired by Auguste Comte's "Religion of Humanity." For instance, Nikolai Chaikovskii and Vladimir Geins (also known under his pen name, William Frey) established a commune in Cedar Vale, Kansas in 1871[36]. The writer Grigori Machtet, who stayed there in 1873, disparaged the wretched living conditions of this self-described "communist" initiative—and Frey disbanded the community four years later[37].

Russian revolutionaries were concerned with their portrayal in the eyes of the American public. To demonstrate good will, members of the anarchist organization *Narodnaia Volia* (The People's Will) sent Leo Hartmann, who created the Russian-American National League in 1887, as a permanent representative to the United States. After 1865, the heroic depiction of an America at war gave way to a more critical perception of civilian life during the Reconstruction, characterized by injustice, brutality, and unlawful enrichment. This disappointment regarding social and political evolution in America is palpable in Bakunin's later writings as well as in those of Petr Lavrov, a sociologist and populist who described a "republic of humbug" and a "kingdom of the dollar" based on his extensive readings, but without ever crossing the Atlantic. In the journal *Vpered* (Forward), published between 1873 and 1876 and slightly tinged with Marxist discourse, Lavrov highlighted the values of the American constitution, but also shed light onto the violence specific to class relations. According to him, "the social question smashed, destroyed, and buried the political creations of the revolutionary period."[38] His one-time associate in the 1880s, Georgii Plekhanov, one of the first authentic Russian Marxists and founder of the Social Democratic Party, claimed in 1886, in an appeal to the immigrant Russian workers in the United States, that American democracy does not invalidate the working-class revolution and that even in "the freest of all countries, the yoke of capital continues to press down upon the working class."[39]

As the American social and political system was being thoroughly debated, the writings of economist Henry George on land reform, which had a worldwide reception, were widely circulated in Russia[40]. His strongest advocate was Leo Tolstoy, who read his 1879 treatise *Progress and Poverty* in 1885.[41] Though initially skeptical, and despite his hostility towards property fuelled by the writings of Pierre-Joseph Proudhon, he sustained indirect relations with George. The economist's central argument was that private land

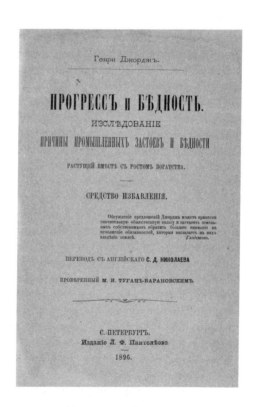

Henry George, *Progress and Poverty* [1879], Saint Petersburg: L.F. Panteleev, 1896. Title page. CCA, BIB 249319.

ownership is fundamentally unfair and that its detrimental impacts can be compensated by taxing land value. After his book was translated into Russian in 1896, George's thesis was supported by the populists, but rejected by Marxists such as Mikhail Tugan-Baranovskii.[42] In 1894, Tolstoy declared that "the possession of land as such is illegitimate, like the possession of serfs," berating himself for having understood it only twenty years after the 1861 abolition, while George "for thirty years has clearly and simply explained everything."[43] From that moment on, he ceaselessly invoked the teachings of the Pennsylvania prophet, and even tried to meet him shortly before the economist's passing in 1897[44]. Tolstoy became a proponent for George's ideas a decade later, advocating them to Piotr Stolypin, Minister of the Interior who was charged with modernizing agriculture across the Russian Empire. The Bolsheviks' decree nationalizing all land in 1917 was clearly derived from George's principles. They were also well received by European social democrats, had an impact on the garden city movement, and were substantially reclaimed by reformist architects such as Frank Lloyd Wright, who mentioned them as the basis for his Broadacre City in 1935[45].

The World Fairs: Philadelphia and Chicago

In the middle of the nineteenth century, Russians' understanding of America and its inhabitants remained fragmentary, until they were nourished by books written by travellers who had gathered information during relatively long stays. The account written by the historian Aleksandr Lakier and published in 1859, two years after his travels to America, was especially informative. In his book, he reflected upon the rise of the American power and its potential impact on the Old Continent: "will the Americans remain confined in America alone or are they destined to return to Europe, bringing to it the institutions which, having been implanted in virgin soil, were regenerated and cleansed of the excrescences acquired in their long European past? A young, an energetic, a practical people that has been fortunate in its undertakings can see no reason to give a negative answer to such a question and is certain to exert its influence over Europe. But it will do so not by force of arms, not by fire and sword, not by death and destruction, but by the power of invention, by commerce and industry, whose influence will be more lasting than any conquests."[46] A subversive

38   Petr Lavrov, *Izbrannye sochinenia na sotsialno-politicheskie temy* (Moscow: Izd-vo Vses. Ob-va politkatorzhan i ssylno-poselentsev, 1934), vol. II, 132, quoted in Hecht, *Russian Radicals*, 155.

39   Georgii Plekhanov, *Perepiska G.V. Plekhanova i P.B. Akselroda* (Moscow: Izd. P.M. Plekhanovoi, 1925), vol. 1, 219, quoted in David Hecht, "Plekhanov and American Socialism," *Russian Review*, no. 2 (1950): 115.

40   "Henry George in Russia," in Laserson, *The American Impact on Russia*, 269-292.

41   Henry George, *Progress i bednost: isledovanie prichiny promyshlennykh zastoev i bednosti, rastushchei vmeste s rostom bogatsva. Sredstvo izbavlenia* (Saint Petersburg: M.M. Lederpe, 1896); originally: *Progress and Poverty: An Inquiry Into the Cause of Industrial Depressions and the Increase of Want with Increase of Wealth; The Remedy* (New York: United States Books Co., 1879).

42   Mikhail Tugan-Baranovskii, "Genri Dzhordzh i natsionalizatsii zemli," *Novoe Slovo* 6, no. 9 (June 1897): 108–9.

43   Leo Tolstoy, statement reported in the journal of V.F. Lazurskii, 24 June 1894, quoted in Kenneth C. Wenzer, "The Influence of Henry George's Philosophy on Lev Nikolaevich Tolstoy: The Period of Developing Economic Thought (1881–1897)," *Pennsylvania History* 63, no. 2 (Spring 1996): 244.

44   Rob Knowles, "Tolstoy's Henry George," in *Henry George's Legacy in Economic Thought*, John Laurent, ed. (Northampton, MA: Edward Elgar Pub., 2005): 51–70.

45   Frank Lloyd Wright, *The Disappearing City* [1932], in *Collected Writings, vol. 3, 1931–1939*, ed. Bruce Brooks Pfeiffer (New York: Rizzoli, 1993), 87.

46   Aleksandr B. Lakier, *Ocherki po Severo-Amerikanskikh soedinnennym Shtatam, Kanade i Kube* (Saint Petersburg: Tip. Leonida Demisa, 1859), vol. 2, 399, quoted in Hans Rogger, "Amerikanizm and the Economic Development of Russia," *Comparative Studies in Society and History* 23, no. 3 (July 1981): 395.

Architects & Engineers of the U.S. Commission. Bird's-eye view of the International Exhibition in Philadelphia in 1876, in *Album of the International Exhibition in Philadelphia to Commemorate the Centennial of the United States of America*, New York: J. Bien, ca. 1875. 53 × 71 cm. CCA, ID:87-B2387.

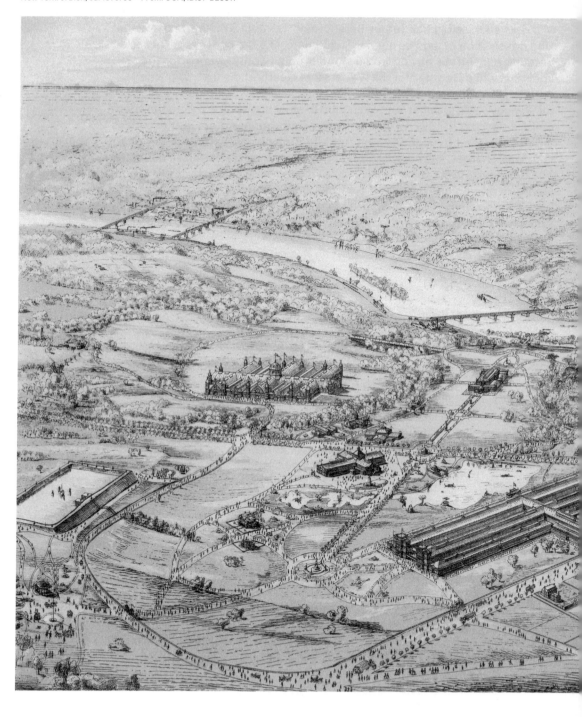

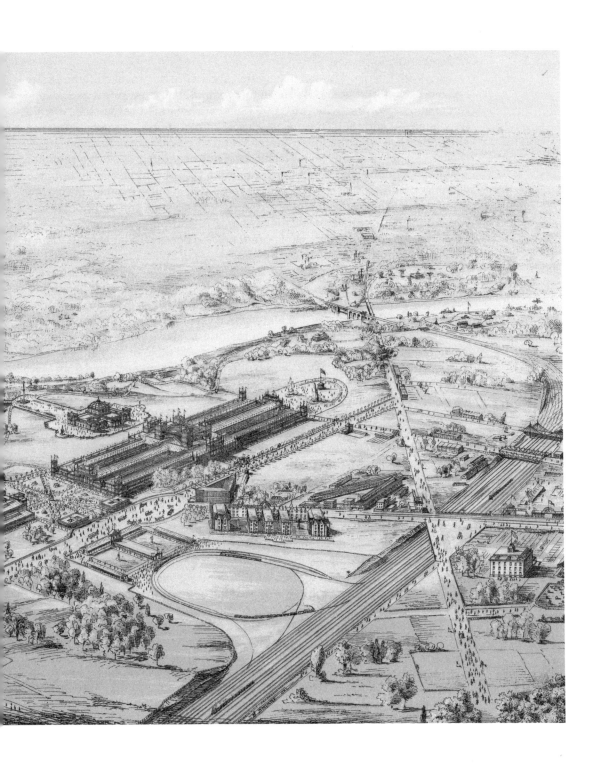

ex-officer, Pavel Ogorodnikov likewise waxed lyrical about the virtues of mass education, comfort, and mechanization he had observed during his trip from New York to San Francisco, while mitigating his fellow countrymen's criticism of democratic excesses[47].

With the rise of steam navigation and railroads, travel became easier and more comfortable, and was no longer restricted to a few privileged adventurers and explorers[48]. Some 40,000 Russians relocated across the Atlantic between 1871 and 1880, in a major wave of immigration[49]. Ten years after the end of the Civil War, the United States World's Fairs attracted Russian industrialists, engineers, and technicians, who not only discovered the realm of American industry and agriculture within the walls of these events but also witnessed a new urban environment beyond. Two of these expositions played a decisive role in the dissemination of American science and technology to a wider public: those held in Philadelphia in 1876 and Chicago in 1893.

In 1876, the French ship *Labrador* sailed across the Atlantic, carrying the arm and torch of Auguste Bartholdi's Statue of Liberty to Philadelphia, as well as the sculptor himself, on his way to gather funds for the monument's construction. On board was also a group of distinguished Russian scholars and engineers, including the mining engineer Konstantin Skalkovsky, the aerodynamicist Nikolai Petrov, and the metallurgist Nikolai Iossa. The Russian delegation, comprised of over a hundred members, also included the chemist Dmitri Mendeleev, who had completed his periodic table of elements in 1869 and was to present his newly invented differential barometer[50]. Held from May to September to celebrate the centenary of the Declaration of Independence, the Philadelphia Exhibition took place in a glass and iron building even larger than the Crystal Palace built in London in 1851 [ill. p. 44-45]. The environment was rather chaotic, as witnessed by Louis Simonin, who had accompanied the Russians on their journey: "One cannot commend the American curators for their classification system. Do you like chaos? It is everywhere."[51] In this pandemonium, alongside the latest steam engines, visitors discovered the newest inventions by American engineers, including the Westinghouse air brake, Bell's telephone, and the Singer sewing machine.

Mendeleev did not fail to take interest in a project based on the classification of human activity and devoted to the extraction and transformation of raw materials[52]. He described his nuanced impressions of the rampant mechanization of American society in an account entitled "Visit to America": "I got the general impression at the exposition and in the refineries that Americans have a special attachment for mechanical processes, using them everywhere, sometimes even where there would be an advantage without them."[53] Mendeleev was somewhat reticent towards American society at large, and more specifically regarding New York's urban spectacle. Although he was impressed with the elevated railway, he was "surprised by the plainness of the streets of the famous city. They were narrow, paved with cobbles, and especially bad, worse than the streets of Saint Petersburg or Moscow. The stores and shops reminded me not of Saint Petersburg, but of a provincial town of Russia."[54] While celebrating American vigour and individualism and recognizing the country's scientific and technical contributions, he had strong reservations about its society: "Why do they constantly quarrel, why do they hate Negroes, Indians, even Germans, why do they not have science and poetry commensurate with themselves?" He noted that "in the United States there was a development not of the best, but of the middle and worst sides of European civilization. [...] A new dawn is not to be seen on this side of the ocean."[55]

Dmitri I. Mendeleev, *The Oil Industry in the North American State of Pennsylvania and in the Caucasus,* Saint Petersburg: Tipografia Tovarishchestva Obshchestvennaia Polza, 1877. Title page. CCA.

НЕФТЯНАЯ ПРОМЫШЛЕННОСТЬ

въ

СѢВЕРО – АМЕРИКАНСКОМЪ ШТАТѢ

ПЕНСИЛЬВАНІИ

и

НА КАВКАЗѢ.

Д. МЕНДЕЛѢЕВА.

САНКТПЕТЕРБУРГЪ.
ТИПОГРАФІЯ ТОВАРИЩЕСТВА «ОБЩЕСТВЕННАЯ ПОЛЬЗА».
БОЛЬШАЯ ПОДЬЯЧ., д. № 39.
1877.

Upon his return, Mendeleev published a book on the American oil industry and the lessons to be learned from it for the Caucasus region, where he contributed to the development of the oil fields of Baku before working on metal extraction in the Ural Mountains at the end of the century[56]. Over several decades, he continued to observe the progress of industry and technical training in the United States, setting aside his initial reserve and urging his fellow countrymen to "catch up to America," in 1899[57]. Mendeleev thus coined the phrase that would later be reprised as a recurrent Bolshevik slogan.

47   Pavel I. Ogorodnikov, *Ot Niu-Iorka do San Frantsisko i obratno v Rossiiu* (Saint Petersburg: Izd-vo F. Koleshova i F. Mikhina, 1872).
48   Gennadii P. Kuropiatnik, "Russkie v Amerike: obshchestvennye, kulturnye, nauchnye kontakty v 1870-kh godakh," *Novaia i Noveishaia Istoria,* no. 4 (1981): 143–56 and no. 5 (1981): 136–49.
49   *Historical Statistics of the United States, Colonial Times to 1970* (Washington, DC: Bureau of the Census, 1975), 106.
50   Efrosinia M. Dvoichenko-Markova, "Uchenye Rossii na mezhdunarodnoi vystavke v Filadelfii v 1876 g.," *Novaia i noveishaia Istoria* 18, no. 4 (1975): 153. Gennadi P. Kuropiatnik, *Rossiia i SShA: ekonomicheskie, kulturnye i diplomaticheskie sviazi 1867–1881* (Moscow: Nauka, 1981), 174–79.
51   Louis Simonin, "Le Centenaire américain et l'exposition de Philadelphie," *Revue des Deux Mondes* 17 (16 October 1876): 798.
52   Robert W. Rydell, *All the World's a Fair: Visions of Empire at American International Exhibitions, 1876–1916* (Chicago, University of Chicago Press, 1999), 9–37.
53   Dmitrii Mendeleev, "Poezdka v Ameriku," in *Neftianaia promyshlennost v Severo-amerikanskom shtate Pensilvani i na Kavkaze* (Saint Petersburg: Tip. Tov. Obshchestvennaia Polza, 1877), 99. For the chemist's impressions, see H.M. Leicester, "Mendeleev's Visit to America," *Journal of Chemical Education* 34, no. 7 (July 1957): 332. Kuropiatnik, "Russkie v Amerike," no. 5 (1981): 139–44; and *Rossia i SShA,* 179–91.
54   Mendeleev, "Poezdka v Ameriku," 77.
55   Ibid., p. 146 and 150.
56   Mendeleev, *Neftianaia promyshlennost,* 1877.
57   Dmitrii Mendeleev, "Raboty po selskomu khoziaistvu i lesovodstvu," in *Sochineniia* (Moscow, Leningrad: Izd-vo Akademii Nauk, 1952), vol. 20, 501, quoted in Rogger, "Amerikanizm," 406.

Vladimir G. Shukhov. Adzhigol lighthouse, Kherson, 1911, general view.
Gelatin silver print mounted on cardboard. Archives of the Russian Academy of Sciences.

Vladimir G. Shukhov (from left to right and top to bottom): water reservoirs in Nizhnii Novgorod, 1896; Ivanovo-Voznesensk, 1924; Baku, 1925; and Orekhovo-Zuevo, 1924. Heliographic prints on paper. Russian State Archive of Scientific and Technical Documentation.

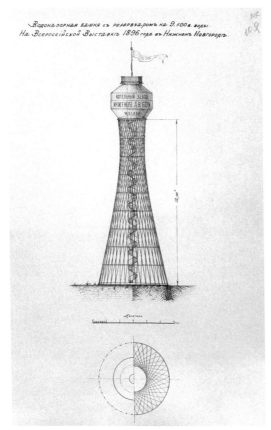

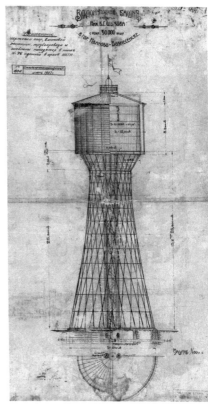

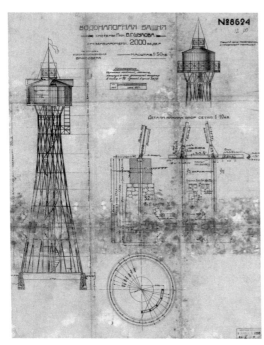

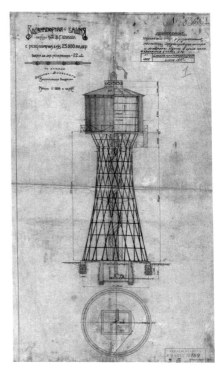

The South Carolina dreadnought of the United States Navy, with masts designed by Vladimir G. Shukhov, ca. 1910. Postcard, 9 × 14 cm.

U. S. S. South Carolina.

REBUILT CHICAGO.—PALMER'S GRAND HOTEL, STATE AND MONROE STREETS.

The Palmer Hotel in Chicago, general view, in *Two Years After the Fire: Chicago illustrated*,
Chicago: J.M. Wing, 1873. CCA, ID87B7787.

While some Russian scientists and technicians shared their impressions of America[58], others, like the young civil engineer Vladimir Shukhov, remained more discreet. Having studied at the Moscow Superior Technical School (MVTU) between 1870 and 1876, Shukhov visited the Philadelphia Exhibit as part of a student expedition to present the establishment's pedagogical approach[59]. There, he met Mendeleev and, more importantly, Aleksandr Bary, whose drafting firm had created one of the pavilions for the fair. Born in Saint Petersburg to an American family and a graduate of the Zurich Polytechnic, Bary was recruited by Robert Nobel to work on the development of the Baku oil fields. He invited Shukhov to accompany him, and later, to join the office he established in Moscow in the beginning of the 1880s. The scope of Shukhov's inventions is extraordinary, ranging from the creation of the first Russian pipelines, spanning hundreds of kilometres, to the development of a pumping system and a cracking process for the oil industry. He also created metal barges and innovative water tanks that sat atop hyperboloids of revolution [ill. p. 48-49]. His structures were highly acclaimed at the Nizhnii Novgorod exhibition in 1896, and, in a rare occurrence of technological transfer from the East to the West, the US Navy purchased his patents to build masts for its cruisers. After the 1917 Revolution, Shukhov remained in Russia, at the helm of Stalmost, Bary's nationalized design office[60].

A decisive event in Shukhov's career, the Philadelphia Exhibition was described in the professional journal *Zodchii* (The Architect), which issued a regular column about construction in the United States from 1872, often borrowing from the pages of the *American Architect and Building News*. According to William C. Brumfield, the three articles written by Sergei Kuleshov upon his return from Philadelphia constitute the first Russian publication describing the architecture and layout of American cities[61]. Kuleshov, the author of several articles on farm buildings, recounted his observations on dwellings, churches, and urban systems from New York to Philadelphia. He gave detailed and sometimes illustrated information on hydraulic elevators and vault lights paving the Manhattan sidewalks, and was fascinated with a new miraculous substance: asbestos. Observing the street spectacle as Mendeleev had done before him, he offered a general interpretation of America's social and material characteristics, donning the sociologist's hat[62].

Four years earlier, in the same publication, an unnamed author had marvelled at the remarkable reconstruction after the Great Chicago Fire of 1871, attributing its speed to the "use of large amounts of iron, including entire façades made up of a row of columns attached with iron rods," to the presence of night lighting on construction sites, and the use of cranes to hoist up prefabricated housing components. The article mentioned an illustrated book—likely *Two Years After the Fire. Chicago Illustrated*[63]—, declaring Chicago to be "the Paris of the

58   Konstantin Skalkovskii, *V strane iga i svobody* (Saint Petersburg: 1878); Nikolai Iossa, "O metallurgicheskom otdele na filadelfiiskoi vystavke," *Zapiski Imperatorskogo Tekhnicheskogo Obshchestva*, no. 1 (1877).
59   It was very well received, as indicated in a letter from MIT president John D. Runkle: Grigorii M. Kovelman, *Tvorchestvo potchetnogo akademika inzhenera Vladimira Grigorevicha Shukhova* (Moscow: Gos. Izd-vo po stroitelstve, arkhitekture i stroitelnykh materialov, 1961), 16–17.
60   Rainer Graefe, Murat Gappoev, and Ottmar Pertschi, eds., *Vladimir Suchov 1853–1939; die Kunst der sparsamen Konstruktion* (Stuttgart: Deutsche Verlags-Anstalt, 1990); Mark Akopian and Elena Vlassova, eds, *Shukhov, Formula of Architecture* (Moscow: Kuchkogo Pole, 2019).
61   William Craft Brumfield, "Russian Perceptions of American Architecture 1870–1917," in id., *Reshaping Russian Architecture: Western Technology, Utopian Dreams* (Cambridge: Cambridge University Press; Washington, DC: Woodrow Wilson International Center for Scholars, 1990), 47–51.
62   Sergei Kuleshov, "Eskizy amerikanskoi arkhitektury i tekhniki," *Zodchii*, no. 4 (1877) 32; no. 5 (1877): 48–56; and no. 11–12, 100–105.
63   *Two Years After the Fire: Chicago Illustrated* (Chicago, J.M. Wing, 1873).

Daniel H. Burnham, project for the World's Columbian Exposition, Chicago, 1893. Aerial view.
Lithographic print on paper, 23 × 29 cm. CCA, ID 0010036 EXP T500; ID:97-F61.

American West, the centre of its commerce, the prime location of its industry and its literature, its true heart, whose beat propels a vital force into the country's veins." The author noted that "the hotel buildings are the tallest, with the highest one, the Palmer Hotel, containing two five-story façades, with thirty windows each. It is believed to be the most beautiful and luxurious hotel in the world. Its impressive porch decorated with columns and statues would be the envy of Italian Renaissance palaces."[64] [ill. p. 50] The article spares no hyperboles to characterize "an unprecedented moral and material activity in the history of human cultural development."[65]

Some fifteen years later, an even larger Russian contingent visited the 1893 Chicago Columbian Exposition. No fewer than 59 official representatives were sent, a delegation surpassed in number only by the English one, to conduct an exhaustive study of the thematic sections.[66] Upon their return, the visitors highlighted the freedom with which they were able to lead their investigation, in contrast with the secrecy maintained by the Europeans: "here there was no policy of jealously guarding special installations from the eyes of those interested in them, as there was in general little in the way of trade secrets. In particular, our Russian delegates could make free use in this respect of the openness of the Americans since between the two distant countries there can be no question of mutual competition through jealousy."[67]

Visiting the exhibition was made simpler by various guidebooks issued in a great number of languages, proof that the affluence was deemed sufficient to gather profits from the initiative. Of note among these guides is the most detailed one, Nikolai Pliskii's document focusing on the skyscrapers of "the Queen of the West"[68]. The visit was considered significant enough to throw a dinner in celebration of the Russian expedition. The event was held in Saint Petersburg, in 1894, and attended by Sergei Witte, Minister of Finance. Several publications described the Chicago Fair and American advances in all sectors of the industry, highlighting the critical need for systematic observation on the Russians' part. Among these, the book issued by Sergey Kareisha in 1896, after a nearly 12,000-kilometre journey on the railroads of the American continent, was among the most detailed studies of infrastructure and rolling stock, such as locomotives. Kareisha also referred to the economy at large, namely by examining the connection between railways and grain silo construction, an association that allowed the United States to surpass Russia in the grain trade[69].

64   "Vnov ostroennyi gorod Chicago," Zodchii, no. 7 (1873): 107.
65   Ibid., 108.
66   Allen, Russia Looks at America, 18
67   Ochet generalnogo komissara russkago otdela Vsemirnoi Kolumbovoi Vystavki v Chicago,
        (Saint Petersburg: Tip. V. Kirshbauma, 1895), quoted in Allen, Russia Looks at America, 190.
68   Nikolai Pliskii, Podrobnyi putevoditel na Vsemirnuiu Kolumbovu Vystavku v Chicago 1893 goda
        (Saint Petersburg: Tipo-lit. "Stefanov i Kachka," 1893).
69   Sergei D. Kareisha, Severo-amerikanskie zheleznye dorogi (Saint Petersburg: Tip. P. P. Soikina, 1896).
70   Aleksandr Shuprov, letter to Ivan Ianzhul, in Ivan Ianzhul, Vospominania, vol. 2 (Saint Petersburg:
        Elekro-tip. N. Ia. Stoikovoi, 1911), 126, quoted in Hans Rogger, "Americanism," 407.
71   Ivan I. Ianzhul, Promyslovye sindikati ili predprinimatelskie soyuzi dlia regulirovania proizvodstva
        preimushchestvennogo v SShA (Saint Petersburg. Tip. M.M. Stasiulevicha, 1895).
72   Nikolai Melnikov, Chudesa vystavki v Chicago (s 70 risunkami) (Odessa: Tip. Odesskikh Novostei, 1893).
        Melnikov was a prolific writer and an engineer who was particularly knowledgeable about chemistry;
        he visited the Exposition Universelle in Paris in 1889. See Tekhnicheskie pisma s parizhskoi vystavki 1889 g.,
        (Odessa: Slavianskaia Tip. N. Khristogelos, 1890).
73   Vladimir G. Korolenko, Bez iazyka, published in four parts in Russkoe Bogatsvo in 1895;
        in Sobranie sochinenii (Moscow: Izd. Pravda, 1971), vol. 4, 5–146; in English: In a Strange Land, trans.
        Gregory Zilboorg (New York, Bernard G. Richards Co., 1925).
74   Vladimir G. Korolenko, "Fabrika smerti, eskiz", originally published in Samarskaia Gazeta, no. 11–12, 1896;
        in Sobranie sochinenii (Moscow: Izd. Pravda, 1971), vol. 4, 147–157.

The founder of the Society for the Dissemination of Technical Knowledge, the economist Aleksandr Chuprov, wrote to his colleague Ivan Ianzhul: "America, and the Chicago Fair in particular, is so important to us as a model in various sectors of the economy that the government should spare no funds to send our specialists there."[70] Incidentally, upon reaching Chicago, Ianzhul wrote several books about work and education in the United States, his main publication focusing on industry unions[71]. The Odessan technologist Nikolai Melnikov was one such specialist searching for practical processes applicable to Russia. In a popular collection of his writings, he insisted on the importance of the Fair for the development of the nation's industrial field. He also drew on his experience to reflect upon the projected exposition in Nizhnii Novgorod in 1896, in line with the European events, which he regularly frequented[72].

The 1893 event was held in two different locations in Chicago: the Midway Plaisance, a long rectangular stretch of land perpendicular to Lake Michigan, where the world's ethnic and cultural diversity was on display, and Daniel Burnham's "White City," along the lakeshore [ill. p. 52-53]. But behind the curtains of the Fair, there was a city made black by a booming industry. The populist writer Vladimir Korolenko was particularly interested in this backdrop. Upon his return from Chicago, he published the novel *Bez iazyka* (Without a Tongue)[73] and dedicated several pages of his journal to his travels, unsparingly describing what he witnessed behind the scenes at the Exposition. In a 1896 essay entitled "Factory of Death, a Sketch," published in Samara, he used the Chicago slaughterhouses as a metaphor to portray the workings of American capitalism[74]. To Korolenko, "the stockyards are untidy, somber, and rather cynical.

It is dirty and ugly, it smells bad, and at times visitors to Chicago, who have gathered here from the world over to see the Fair, are forced to hold their noses. What can you do? The city is forced to tolerate these unpleasant traits in the stockyards' character: after all, the city has made a dazzling name for itself and can receive dazzling society, thanks, for the most part, to its ugly grandfather: the stockyards"[75]. The impact of Korolenko's description, published in a regional paper, was comparable to that of Paul Bourget's *Outremer, impressions d'Amérique*, published around the same time, and to Upton Sinclair's *The Jungle*, which raised a public scandal in 1906[76]. Highly critical of America, Korolenko would later declare in his writings that he preferred his land of exile, Yakutia, to a country overrun by exploitation, corruption, and commercial cynicism[77].

Petr Tverskoi, a publicist who emigrated in 1881 and died in California in 1919, focused on the Exposition and the city of Chicago in his 1895 *Essays* describing the exponential growth and variety of populations. He observed the sprawl of a city still riddled with vacant spaces, noting that "aside from a few new corporate buildings downtown, Chicago is scarcely different from most cities in the Western United States in that the land that has been recently adjoined to it seems more deserted and less developed than large cities usually are."[78] He also wondered about the inevitable contradictions that would arise between the density of the development and the capacity of the streets: "In the future, buildings will have more and more stories in correlation with the rising prices of the lots on which they are built. The only way to face these increasing prices is to make sure that the houses grow taller. Some buildings house over 4,000 tenants, and their elevators carry up to 20,000 people a day. Soon, street conditions will restrain human circulation, and

Petr A. Tverskoi, *Essays on the North American United States*, Saint-Petersburg: Tip. Skorokhodova, 1895. Private collection.

American communities will need to both address the complicated issue of what to do with them and try to reconcile the upward growth of houses with the motionlessness of street space"[79].

The inventions displayed at the exhibition were also discovered by distinguished guests such as the Grand Duke Aleksandr Mikhailovich, grandson of Nicholas I, who arrived in the United States aboard the frigate *Dmitrii Donskoi*, visiting America to mark the 400th anniversary of Columbus' landing. He would later strive for the technological modernization of Russia, looking to America as an example, as he wrote in his memoirs after the Revolution: "[Russia] was even richer than this new country, confronting the same problems, such as an immense population incorporating in its midst several scores of nationalities and religions, tremendous distances between the industrial centres and agricultural hinterland, crying necessity for extensive railroad building, etc. American liabilities were not smaller than ours, while our assets were bigger, if anything. [...] What was the matter with us? Why did we not follow the American way of doing things? We had no business bothering with Europe and imitating the methods befitting nations forced by their poverty to live off their wits."[80] Upon returning to the United States twenty years after the Fair, he expressed his disenchantment to the *New York Times*: "Of course, one might comment upon your tall buildings, but then they are only somewhat taller than the buildings I saw when I was here before. You have grown, and your buildings have grown up in the air, as trees would. [...] I like America and New York very much. There is one thing in America, however, which I cannot say I wholly enjoy. That is the rush, the hurry that is characteristic of everything and everywhere."[81]

As for architects, along with journalists and critics such as Korolenko, they were interested not only in the exposition pavilions, but in the city itself. In 1892, *Nedelia Stroitelia* (Builders' Weekly) described the ongoing projects, marvelling at the number of buildings being erected and noting that in spite of the insurance companies' resistance to cover structures dozens of stories tall, such endeavors were proliferating: "These buildings, intended as offices, use a specific type of structure, first designed in Chicago six years ago, which has surpassed the others in practicality. At first, a steel skeleton or carcass is formed out of posts, linking, and diagonals, whose exterior is then covered with ceramic blocks, bricks, or cut stone." The journal recounted the common use of iron and steel and the rise of a corporation of assemblers capable of raising an entire level in less than four days[82].

The following year, an article in *Nedelia Stroitelia* depicted the landscape of The White City, relishing in the enumeration of the countless styles: the Moorish fisheries pavilion, the ionic arts building, the Italian Renaissance

75   Vladimir G. Korolenko, "Factory of Death: a Sketch", in Olga Peters Hasty, Susanne Fusso,
        America through Russian Eyes: 1874–1926 (New Haven: Yale University Press, 1988), 87.
76   Paul Bourget, *Outre-mer: Impressions of America* (New York: Scribner's Sons, 1895).
        Upton Sinclair, *The Jungle* (New York: Doubleday, Jabber & Company, 1906); in Russian: *Debri*,
        trans. K. Zh (Moscow: Tip. T-va I. D. Sytina, 1907).
77   Vladimir G. Korolenko, Letter to Evelina L. Ulanovskaia, n.d., in *Puteshestvie v Ameriku*
        (Moscow: Zadruga, 1923), 7.
78   Petr A. Tverskoi [pseud. of Petr A. Dementev], *Ocherki Severo-Amerikanskikh Soedinennykh Shtatov*
        (Saint Petersburg: Tip. Skorokhodova, 1895), 410.
79   Ibid., 410-411.
80   Alexander, Grand Duke of Russia, *Once a Grand Duke* (New York: Cosmopolitan Book Corp.;
        Farrar & Rinehart, 1932), 123.
81   "Grand Duke Alexander Does Not Like the Rush," *New York Times*, 6 September 1913.
82   "Stroitelnaia deatelnost v Chicago," *Nedelia Stroitelia* 20, no. 46 (1892): 313.

electricity pavilion; the Spanish pavilion of mechanics, and the French building of administration[83]. Lamenting that "all these architectural wonders were
destined for demolition," the journal applauded Daniel H. Burnham's artistic
direction and "the exposition's general striking appearance," adding that "it
is impossible not to marvel at the spectacle of this city filled with lush palaces,
appearing as if by magic. The Chicago Exhibition will, without a doubt, outshine, with its luxury and lustre, all past universal expositions."[84]

Capitalism and Amerikanizm

As Russians gained a more concrete understanding of American cities and
as it became possible for them to follow current events overseas with shorter
delays, the future embodied by the New World seemed to be within reach for
the country's industrial development. As Alexander Gershenkron wrote in his
analysis of Russia's economic growth, "increasingly the eyes of engineers
and factory managers turned toward the United States."[85] The impressions
left by the Chicago Fair seemed to prove Tverskoi right in his depiction of
America as Russia's future, a vision he presented in such a stark and simplistic
way that Maxim Gorky would later characterize his claims as "idiotic."[86] But
this idea of a country offering "so much to learn" and "rapidly barrelling forward" is also present in the 1903 publications of Ivan Ozerov, a professor of
financial law and member of the State Council. He had not witnessed the
Chicago Exposition himself, but nevertheless refused to see America as a
"threat" and called for "a healthy dose of Americanism" in Russian economy
and education, necessary in his view to awaken the country from its slumber
and humdrum[87]. For instance, he saw American methods in civil engineering
and management as means to promote and develop Siberia, a critical issue
at the time.

   Following the 1856 Russian defeat in the Crimean War, which led the
Empire to open its economy to Europe, the Emancipation Manifesto of 1861 abolishing serfdom instated a new era for Russian society. The population was eager

83   "Opisanie zdanii vystavki v Chicago," Nedelia Stroitelia 21, no. 1 (3 January 1893): 3.
84   Ibid., vol. 21, no. 3 (17 January 1893), 11.
85   Alexander Gerschenkron, "Russia: Patterns of Economic Development 1861-1958," in Economic
        Backwardness in Historical Perspective (Cambridge, MA: Belknap Press, 1962), 128.
86   Maxim Gorky, Letter to Ivan P. Ladyzhnikov, mid-August 1906, in Sobranie sochinenii v 30-ikh tomakh
        (Moscow: Gos. Izd-vo khudozhestvennoi literaturii, 1948-1955), vol. 28, 429.
87   Ivan Ozerov, Chemu uchit nas Amerika (Moscow: Knigoizd-vo Polza, 1903), 74; quoted in Hans Rogger,
        "America Enters the Twentieth Century: The View from Russia," in Felder und Vorfelder russischer
        Geschichte, Studien zu Ehren von Peter Scheibert, Ingrid Auerbach, Andreas Hillgruber, and Gottfried
        Schramm, eds. (Freiburg: Verlag Rombach, 1985), 168; Ozerov also published Otchego Amerika idiot tak
        bystro vpered? (Moscow: Tipo-litogr. T-va I. N. Kushneneva i Ko, 1903).
88   Sergei U. Witte, The Memoirs of Count Witte [1921], trans. and ed. by Abraham Yarmolinsky
        (New York: Howard Fertig, 1967), 75.
89   Henry Reichman, Railwaymen and Revolution: Russia, 1905 (Berkeley, University of California Press, 1987).
90   Witte, The Memoirs of Count Witte, 171.
91   Jonathan Coopersmith, The Flectrification of Russia, 1880-1926
        (Ithaca, NY: Cornell University Press, 1992), 21-24.
92   Valerian F. Agafonov, "Peredacha sily na rastoianie i belyi ugol," Russkaia mysl, no. 6 (1913): 41-55.
93   Gleb M. Krzhizhanovskii, "Oblastnye elektricheskie stantsi na torfe i ikh znachenie dlia tsentralnogo
        promyshlennogo raiona," in Izbrannoe (Moscow: Gospolitizdat, 1957), 16. Quoted in Coopersmith,
        Electrification of Russia, 116-17.
94   "American Contracts in Russia," Scientific American 78, no. 26 (25 June 1898): 406.
95   Frederick V. Carstensen, American Enterprise in Foreign Markets; Studies of Singer and International
        Harvester in Imperial Russia (Chapel Hill: University of North Carolina Press, 1984), 133-35; Frederick V.
        Carstensen and Richard H. Werking, "International Harvester in Russia: The Washington-St. Petersburg
        Connection?," The Business History Review 57, no. 3 (1983): 347-66.

for new travel narratives and analyses, such as those, encouraged by major public servants who wished to demonstrate the necessity for the observation, and even imitation, of America in sectors such as industrial planning and infrastructure. The authoritarian Count Sergei Witte, minister of finance from 1892 to 1903, was skilled at establishing decisive agreements with Germany and France, but wished to offset European influence nonetheless. Viewing rail transportation as the critical basis for Russia's industrialization, he spearheaded the launch of the Trans-Siberian Railway, based on the American example of transcontinental lines, a project he convinced the young Nicholas II to complete[88].

Engaged in 1891, the line reached Vladivostok in 1916. Its construction was given considerable impetus under the authority of Prince Mikhail Khilkov, who was minister of railway Communications from 1895 to 1905. A temporary emigrant who had donated his land to his former serfs, he spent a few months in the United States in 1860, followed by several years starting in 1862, working as a labourer, and later as an executive in a railway company. Khilkov was famous for entertaining guests in English with an impeccable Yankee accent. Owing to this background, his running of European projects in Asia was informed by a direct experience of the industry. Less successful was his blundering attempt to respond to railway workers' demands during the 1905 Revolution[89]. At the time, Sergei Witte himself spent long months in the United States, where he negotiated the peace treaty with Japan, marvelled at the New York skyscrapers, and visited Harvard and Columbia universities with avid curiosity. After a discussion with a professor from Columbia, he was pleased to find out that Henry George's doctrine was only taught there to "expose its fallaciousness," remarking that "many of our home-spun economists and also our great writer but naïve thinker, Leo Tolstoy, would do well to go to school to that American teacher."[90]

Scholarly and technical societies played a major part in the process of studying foreign experiments and developing a self-sufficient technological community. The networks of engineers created at the end of the nineteenth century, namely in the field of electricity, became crucial in the Empire's industrialization and in that of the Soviet Union, where they persisted. The Russian military launched the first electrification measures, inspired by the use of projectors during the American Civil War. Initiated in 1886 and funded by foreign investments, the development of electric supply networks favoured major cities and its public transportation infrastructures. In 1914, as Jonathan Coopersmith noted, only 41 Russian cities had electric tramways, eight times fewer than in the United States twenty years earlier[91]. The use of hydroelectric power also remained negligible, despite its dominant position in the press[92], while peat was so widespread that in 1915, one of the main electrical engineers, Gleb Krzhizhanovskii, recommended supplying in energy the entire central economic region with eight peat-burning power plants, based on American standards[93].

At the turn of the 19th and 20th centuries, American companies, with their advanced and proven technologies, were prevalent in certain specific sectors. Westinghouse sold electrical and rail equipment, providing the Manchuria railroad with air brakes, while its locomotives were supplied by Baldwin[94]. Cyrus McCormick's motorized farming equipment appeared in the fields as early as in the 1880s, outshining the rudimentary harvesters (*lobogreiki*) that were used until then. When the International Harvester Company was founded in 1902, bringing together McCormick and four of his competitors, it controlled two thirds of the Russian market, which was its second global outlet after Canada[95]. In 1910, the firm purchased the factory built by

the New York Air Brake Company in Liubertsy, on the outskirts of Moscow, and began manufacturing its machines there, along with brakes and gasoline engines. Meanwhile, it also established a close-knit network of distributors disseminating its equipment as far as Siberia. Incidentally, the correlation between the agricultural expansion of the United States and that of the Russian steppes is not happenstance[96].

The multinational Singer was an early adopter of direct commercialization. Its sewing machines were produced industrially since the 1860s, and the firm started exporting them to the promising Russian market a decade later[97]. Created in 1897, the Kompania Zinger decided, as a way of evading customs barriers, to establish a factory some thirty kilometres away from Moscow, in Podolsk, hiring 5,000 workers as of 1901. Its European representative, Neidlinger, recruited Walter F. Dixon, an American engineer who had just founded a locomotive factory for Baldwin in Sormovo, near Nizhnii Novgorod[98]. To an unnamed observer, the plant seemed "so essentially American throughout that one almost feels upon entering it that he is back in the United States."[99] The initiative was met with such resounding success that most of Singer's global growth before 1914 was due to the Russian market. The company became the largest commercial organization worldwide thanks to a particularly decentralized crediting system allowing it to sell five million machines over the course of the decade preceding the First World War. Singer was praised as an example by American diplomats, who were in favour of a stronger American presence in the Russian markets[100]. The development of advertising, which Singer was pioneering, lent what some viewed as an American appearance to the urban landscape[101].

All commentators agreed that one of Russia's main impairments was the archaic state of its educational system, and many cited America as an example. Pavel Mizhuev, who had visited the Chicago Fair with education experts and who wrote the first important Russian study on African-Americans, also contributed to one of the official reports on American schooling[102]. He offered a thorough policy analysis from kindergarten to university, highlighting the considerable portion of private resources differentiating the American model from the European one. In his 1902 book *Shkola i obshchestvo v Amerike* (School and Society in the United States), Mizhuev emphasized the unique nature of the American school system and its society's commitment to education[103]. Ten years later, he published a comparative analysis of the various levels of instruction in Europe and the United States[104]—from kindergarten to

96   David Moon, *The Plough that Broke the Steppes; Agriculture and Environment on Russia's Grasslands, 1700–1914* (Oxford: Oxford University Press, 2013).

97   Ruth Brandon, *Singer and the Sewing Machine: a Capitalist Romance* (New York, Tokyo, London: Kodansha International, 1977), 100–110.

98   Carstensen, *American Enterprise*, 43–48. See also Robert Bruce Davies, *Peacefully Working to Conquer the World: Singer Sewing Machines in Foreign Markets, 1854–1920* (New York: Arno Press, 1976), 243–305; Irina V. Potkina, "The Singer Company in Russia, 1897–1917," in Hubert Bonin et al., *American Firms in Europe (1890–1980)* (Geneva: Droz, 2008), 283–98.

99   Carstensen, *American Enterprise*, 73.

100   Davies, *Peacefully Working to Conquer the World*, 275-280.

101   Sally West, "The Material Promised Land: Advertising's Modern Agenda in Late Imperial Russia," *The Russian Review* 57, no. 3 (1998): 345–63.

102   Evgraf P. Kovalevskii, *Narodnoe obrazovanie v Soedinnenykh Shtatakh Ameriki* (Saint Petersburg: Tip. V.S. Balasheva i Ko, 1895), 187–230, in Allen, *Russia Looks at America*, 202.

103   Pavel G. Mizhuev, *Shkola i obshchestvo v Amerike* (Saint Petersburg: Tip. I. I. Skorokhodova, 1902), 160.

104   Pavel G. Mizhuev, *Sovremennaia shkola v Evrope i Amerike* (Moscow: Polza, 1912). For more on this author, see Irina R. Chikalova, "Professor Pavel Grigorevich Mizhuev: rossiiskii angloved i liberal," *Dialog so vremenem*, no. 34 (2011): 5–30.

university—and continued writing on the theme after the Revolution. As for advanced technical training, *Zodchii* (The Architect) published an investigative piece on this issue in 1894[105].

Despite all these developments, the rise of Russian capitalism remained largely dependent on trade with Europe, and particularly with Germany, which was responsible for nearly half of Russian imports before 1914[106]. This inclination is evidenced by the fact that in 1913, 55% of Saint Petersburg Polytechnic University graduates spoke German, while only 28% spoke English. Russians therefore became acquainted with America chiefly through translations of major German writings about the country, such as *Die Amerikaner* by Hugo Münsterberg, a psychology professor at Harvard University. Its two thick volumes were translated by his colleague Aleksandr Grombakh, just twenty-four months after their original publication. This expert on education—namely sexual—and psychology, who had also translated William James, wrote a foreword underlining its novelty in breaking away from widespread Russian stereotypes about American ways of thinking and living. "America is often portrayed as a nation of machines, a nation of profit, a nation of innovation and political experiments, and many readers of this book will be frankly surprised at its firm contentions, claiming that Americans are a sentimental, massively conservative people, and that the 'race for the dollar' has deep moral grounds."[107]

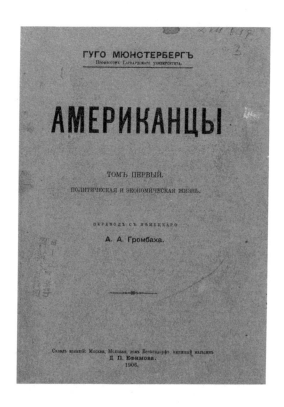

Hugo Münsterberg, *The Americans* [1904], Moscow: D.P. Efimov, 1906. CCA, BIB 247261.

Looking at the American City

The rise of capitalism in Russia went hand in hand with urbanization. On the eve of the 1917 Revolution, when Russian cities were home to 17% of the total population, Russian observers became interested in urban and architectural transformations. For some, this interest was sparked because they saw them as the expression of an inevitable and desirable modernization, whereas others were attempting to detect characteristics of the "Americanness" advocated in 1853 by sculptor Horatio Greenough, who claimed that "the mind of this country has never been seriously applied to architecture."[108]

Russian urban development was compared to the rise of American cities, whose struggles did not go unnoticed. Tales of American slums echo those of Moscow's and Saint Petersburg's *trushchoby* (hovels)[109]. The expansion of Moscow after 1861 was also viewed as "American" by contemporaries. After the 1905 Revolution, as more powers were given to local autonomous communities, the first studies on regulation and modernization of Russian cities transformed by industrialization described American urban experiments. One such publication was the report on the capital's transformations drafted in 1912 by Fedor Enakiev, a civil engineer involved in the development of the Donbass. He described the policies established in Cleveland and St. Louis and advocated for a general plan for the city. He also recommended the creation of a metropolitan railway, based on previous studies led by Andrei Gorchakov, his colleague from the Ministry of Railway Communications[110].

Published that same year, *Blagoustroistvo gorodov* (City Planning), the first Russian urban planning manual, was written by Vladimir Semenov, an architect who had worked in London with Raymond Unwin, a pioneer of garden-city designs. A passionate Anglophile who was also interested in the Parisian model, Semenov wrote that "the scope of American projects is dazzling. They cost hundreds of millions of dollars, are efficiently built and swiftly completed. Their cities, sprawling through farmlands, adapted to harsh climates, are a prototype for Russians."[111] His book brought a strong focus on reform strategies for American cities and introduced figures such as Frederick Law Olmsted, the father of the Park Movement, highlighting his Emerald Necklace, a chain of gardens linked by parkways created in Boston in the 1890s.

Semenov also analyzed projects stemming from the City Beautiful Movement, such as the McMillan Commission plan for the National Mall in Washington, which he viewed as a model administrative centre[112]. He touched upon methods for the study of plans, such as those employed by Daniel

105   "Vysshee tekhnicheskoe obrazovanie i universitety v Soedinnennykh Shtatakh," *Zodchii*, 22, no. 36 (4 September 1894): 181–82; no. 37 (11 September 1894): 187–88.
106   Kendall E. Bailes, "The American Connection: Ideology and the Transfer of American Technology to the Soviet Union," *Comparative Studies in Society and History* 23, no. 3 (July 1981): 421–48.
107   Aleksandr A. Grombakh, preface to Hugo Münsterberg, *Amerikantsy*, trans. Aleksandr A. Grombakh (Moscow: D.P. Efimov, 1906), 7; in German: *Die Amerikaner* (Berlin, Mittler, 1904). I would like to thank Alla Vronskaya for this information on Grombakh.
108   Horatio Greenough, "American Architecture," in *Form and Function: Remarks on Art by Horatio Greenough*, Harold A. Small, ed. (Berkeley: University of California Press, 1947), 55.
109   E.N. Matrosov, "Amerikanskie trushchoby (sotsiologichesko-opisatelnyi ocherk)," *Istoricheskii vestnik*, vol. 95 (January–March 1904): 1072–93; see also Daniel R. Brower, *The Russian City Between Tradition and Modernity, 1850–1900* (Berkeley: University of California Press, 1990), 143.
110   Fedor E. Enakiev, *Zadachi preobrazovania S. Peterburga* (Saint Petersburg: T-vo R. Golike i A. Vilborg, 1912); see also S. Frederick Starr, "The Revival and Schism of Urban Planning in Twentieth-Century Russia," in *The City in Late Imperial Russia*, Michael F. Hamm, ed. (Bloomington: Indiana University Press, 1986), 228.
111   Vladimir Semenov, *Blagoustroistvo gorodov* (Moscow: Tip. I.I. Riabushinskago, 1912), 1.
112   Ibid., 129–32 [park systems], 38–40 [Washington].

Если ту же площадь, которая занята бульварами, распределить по лондонской системѣ, т.-е. въ видѣ отдѣльныхъ скверовъ, то вышеприведенные недостатки исчезнутъ, а всѣ достоинства и удобства распредѣленія могутъ быть сохранены. Такой скверъ Черт. 103. представляетъ компактную массу зелени, способную устоять противъ изсушающаго дѣйствія городской пыли. Онъ долженъ быть густо засаженъ по границамъ, имѣя солнечныя площадки внутри. Растительность идетъ бы въ немъ гораздо лучше, чѣмъ на бульварѣ. Скверъ можетъ дѣйствительно содѣйствовать освѣженію воздуха и, во вся-

105. Планъ парковой системы Бостона. Разработанъ городскими управленіемъ.

комъ случаѣ, даетъ больше удобствъ жителямъ. При расположеніи скверами, внутри ихъ всегда возможно найти мѣста для дѣтскихъ площадокъ, лаунъ-тенниса и пр., вообще использовать площадь зелени болѣе цѣлесообразнымъ способомъ, чѣмъ дѣлать изъ него проходное, хотя бы и широкое мѣсто.

Расположеніе входовъ и выходовъ въ скверахъ обыкновенно дѣлается такъ, чтобы не привлекать сквознаго движенія пѣшеходовъ. Если же скверъ достаточно великъ, то особая аллея сбоку отводится для уличнаго движенія. То же относится до экипажнаго и коннаго движенія. Не лучшія центральныя аллеи, какъ это

9

Однимъ изъ типичныхъ англійскихъ примѣровъ является пригородъ Лондона — Hampstead. Онъ совмѣщаетъ и особенности и достоинства англійской планировки. Улицы его, гдѣ возможно, Черт. 24. правильны, но для правильности ихъ архитекторъ-планировщикъ не принесъ ни одной жертвы и, въ особенности, не испортилъ природной красоты мѣста. Поселокъ имѣетъ явно обозначенные два центра—первый, распредѣляющій движеніе, — площадь, съ которой лучами расходятся улицы; второй—назначенъ для общественныхъ нуждъ. Сообразно своему значенію онъ занимаетъ и болѣе центральное и болѣе высокое мѣсто. Вокругъ него расположены церкви,

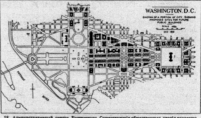

18. Административный центръ Вашингтона. Существующія общественныя зданія показаны чернымъ цвѣтомъ, проектируемыя заштрихованы. Планъ со всѣми измѣненіями разработанъ комиссіей «объ улучшеніи системы парковъ». 1. Капитолій. 2. Бѣлый домъ—дворецъ президента. 3. Монументъ Вашингтону.

концертный залъ, музей — это центръ муниципальный. Торговыя помѣщенія обрамляютъ первую-лучевую площадь — тамъ они доступнѣе всему населенію и сами находятся вблизи главныхъ артерій, соединяющихъ поселокъ съ Лондономъ. Остальная часть поселка назначена только для жилыхъ домовъ-коттеджей.

Застроенная площадь составляетъ приблизительно ¼ часть всего поселка, и увеличеніе ея уже не допускается. Предѣлъ застроенія въ Англіи обыкновенно опредѣляется количествомъ домовъ, расположенныхъ на одномъ акрѣ. Принятое въ Hampstead число домовъ—8 на акръ, т.-е. приблизительно 20 на десятину. Самый пригородъ окруженъ полосой парковъ, тщательно охраняемыхъ

Burnham and Edward Bennett in Chicago (1908–1909), and demonstrated, through various examples, the necessity of conducting collective initiatives to establish a general city layout: "this issue has been resolved in an especially practical way in America. There, virtually every city either already has an expansion plan or is currently developing one. In each city, a committee comprised of representatives from the city and independent entities from the local government oversees the general guidelines for urban planning."[113] Semenov's interest in Chicago might be explained by the parallel he possibly perceived with Saint Petersburg: the converging pathways towards the centre of Burman's plan were reminiscent of the three main avenues culminating at the Admiralty Building in Saint Petersburg, while Lake Michigan echoed the Gulf of Finland, and the eye was drawn to the Eastern American continent rather than towards Europe[114].

Along with publications focusing on methodology and carefully pondered projects such as Enakiev's, proposals for more targeted initiatives were also put forth, such as the 1912 plan for a "high-speed railway line," or elevated metro, for the Moscow city centre, projected to cross over the Red Square on a metal viaduct. The engineer behind this proposal was Evgenii K. Knorre, a graduate from the Zurich Polytechnic, who had built several structures for the Trans-Siberian Railway[115]. The face of Moscow "in 200 years" was drafted in 1914 in a set of eight postcards issued by the Einem candy factory—renamed *Krasnyi Oktiabr* (Red October) after 1917—, which had its own printing press. The intentions behind this publication, whose illustrator remains unknown, were clearly stated: "Leaving to the wise historians the task of describing and studying the past, we have imagined in this little album, to the best of our abilities and through colourful fantasy, the relatively distant future of the Mother Moscow we all know and love."[116] [ill. p. 66-67] Lofty edifices were shown: a cavernous central station for "aerial or ground-based means of communication;" massive office buildings; suspension bridges thrown across the Moskva River, where large steamboats were afloat; monorails erupted from houses, while the sky was obscured by clouds of aircraft, and the streets were filled with sledges and streamlined buses. The sleepy commercial town seemed to rise in a dizzying vertical expansion and was agitated by a three-dimensional frenzy of constant motion[117].

This futuristic representation is reminiscent of similar European endeavours, such as the images of Albert Robida, a Parisian illustrator whose work was certainly well known in Russia[118], a parallel made even clearer by the fact that the details on some buildings were typical of the Art Nouveau aesthetic. But the most obvious roots for this portrayal are found in America, where prophetic views of cities were commonly published, such as the 1910 montage of San Francisco, where monorails, blimps, and other flying vehicles can be seen hovering above Market Street[119]. These images were issued as postcards and used to preface albums with more realistic illustrations. Among the boldest were Harry McEwen Pettit's 1908 depictions of a vertically expanding New York City overrun by flying machines in *King's Views of New York*. Three years later, Richard W. Rummel pushed them further in *Future New York*, replacing the blimps with triplanes and inserting existing constructions such as Ernest Flagg's Singer Building within the structures of taller skyscrapers[120] [ill. p. 68].

Beyond the community of architects and pioneering urban planners, Russians' perception of America was increasingly urban. Descriptions of Chicago, Philadelphia, Boston, or Baltimore were progressively overshadowed by New York City. As for Los Angeles, its first literary mentions surfaced in the final decade of the nineteenth century, namely in the writings of Tverskoi, the author of dozens of articles in *Vestnik Evropy* (The European Herald) between the turn of the century and the Revolution. Promoting a positive view of the American system, as previously noted, Tverskoi's articles touched upon all aspects of daily life in major cities[121]. After 1905, the Marxist economist Izaak Rubinov was commissioned by the Moscow City Duma, an assembly created after the Revolution, to study the effects of the new domestic reports on lodging and various types of public policy in the fields of social housing and communal facilities[122].

In this historical period when city management became an important political issue, professional journals such as *Zodchii* broadened their coverage of America. Although *Zodchii* remained focused on disasters, including

113   Semenov, *Blagoustroistvo gorodov*, 24.
114   On this parallel between Chicago and Saint Petersburg, see Ross Miller, *American Apocalypse: The Great Fire and the Myth of Chicago* (Chicago, University of Chicago Press, 1990), 245–46.
115   *Osnovy proekta inzheniera E. K. Knorre po ustroistvu dorogi bolsho skorosti v cherte goroda Moskvy* (Moscow: Levenson, 1912).
116   *Moskva cherez 200 let* (Moscow: Izd. Tov. Einem, 1914).
117   On the city during this period, see Joseph Bradley, *Muzhik and Muscovite: Urbanization in Late Imperial Russia* (Berkeley: University of California Press, 1985); Robert W. Thurston, Liberal City, *Conservative State: Moscow and Russia's Urban Crisis, 1906–1914* (Oxford: Oxford University Press, 1987).
118   Albert Robida, *Le vingtième siècle* (Paris: La Librairie illustrée, 1893).
119   "Market Street, San Francisco, Cal. in Fifty Years," photomontage, postcard, San Francisco, circa 1910.
120   *King's Views of New York* (New York: Moses King, 1908); *Future New York* (New York: Moses King, 1911).
121   Tverskoi, *Ocherki*.
122   Izaak M. Rubinov, "Evoliutsia domashnei zhizni v Soedinennykh Shtatakh," *Russkaia Mysl* (1905), 194–207; Rubinov, "Ocherki munitsipalnoi zhizni v Amerike," *Izvestiia Mosk. Gor. Dumy* (1907), 113–34 and 159–74; Rubinov, "Igornye ploshchadki v amerikanskikh gorodakh," *Izvestiia Mosk. Gor. Dumy* (1909), 91–107.

Moscow of the Future, advertising cards published by the Einem candy factory in Moscow, 1912, 9 × 14 cm. CCA, BIB 249349.

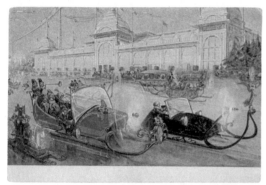

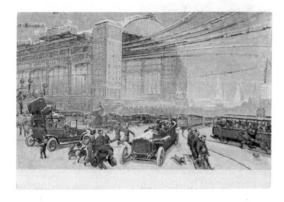

Moses King, *King's Views of New York: Four Hundred Illustrations*, New York: Moses King, ca. 1912.
Drawing by Richard W. Rummell, 37 × 25 cm. CCA, ID:86-B1493.

the Great Baltimore Fire of 1904, followed by the 1906 San Francisco Fire, and on the safety measures they inspired, the journal also provided regular and detailed documentation on the construction of metal bridges and public buildings, developments in housing, and the introduction of electricity in homes and throughout the city. These articles were often reprised from German publications such as the *Deutsche Bauzeitung* or the *Zentralblatt der Bauverwaltung*. F. Rudolf Vogel's 1910 book on the "American house," intended as a counterpart to *Das englische Haus*, the three influential volumes by Hermann Muthesius, was quickly cited by the journal, highlighting the Americans' "absence of traditions" and the fact that their homes were more "lively" in considering practical considerations than European constructions[123].

Among first-hand accounts, the one published by Saint Petersburg architect Aleksandr Dmitriev upon his return from a 1904 trip stands out for several reasons, including the fact that it was illustrated with the author's sketches[124]. In 1904, Dmitriev, the capital's chief architect from 1908 to 1912, having created several public buildings and the first affordable housing projects in Saint Petersburg, undertook an extensive journey across the United States as part of his visit to the St. Louis World's Fair. There, Russian participation was limited to an exhibition of paintings, which were never returned to their homeland[125]. Dmitriev was unimpressed with American urban centres and criticized their density and uniformity. However, he was won over by the suburban landscapes and construction technologies, which inspired him to conclude his seven-article series with the following declaration: "In terms of civil engineering, America is the most interesting country in the world."[126] In his analyses, collected in a single volume and undoubtedly representing the first serious Russian study on American architecture, Dmitriev discussed and illustrated grain silos several years before Walter Gropius's celebrated article, and described the embellishments projected by the City of New York[127] [ill. p. 70-71].

Russian Buildings Shatter the Ceiling

American buildings themselves were also a theme of interest. A professor at the Saint Petersburg University of Civil Engineering, Victor Evald, also a cellist and a composer, and one of the editors of *Zodchii*, was interested in the artificial stone cladding used in American construction, devoting a book to the matter[128]. As of 1891, *Nedelia Stroitelia* highlighted the "colossal" nature of New York City's urban landscape, from its bridges to its office buildings, including that of Joseph Pulitzer's daily newspaper, the *New York World*[129].

123   Rudolf Berngard, "Das amerikanische Haus von F. Rud. Vogel," *Zodchii* 40, no. 46 (13 November 1911): 487.
124   Aleksandr I. Dmitriev, "Iz poezdki v Severnuiu Ameriku," *Zodchii*, vol. 34, 1905, no. 27, 313–314; no. 28, 321–324; no. 29, 329–332; no. 30, 337–339; no. 31, 345–346; no. 35, 381–385; no. 36, 395–398. On Dmitriev, see Boris Kirikov, *Aleksandr Ivanovich Dmitriev, arkhitektor pervoi poloviny XX veka* (Saint Petersburg: Kolo, 2009).
125   Robert C. Williams, "America's Lost Russian Paintings and the 1904 St. Louis Exposition," in *Russia Imagined: Art, Culture and National Identity, 1840–1995* (New York: P. Lang, 1997), 187–213.
126   Dmitriev, "Iz poezdki v Severnuiu Amerikou," *Zodchii* 34, no. 36 (1905): 98.
127   Aleksandr I. Dmitriev, *Nekotorye osobennosti sovremennoi zheleznoi arkhitektury v Severo-amerikanskikh Soedinnennykh Shtatakh* (Saint Petersburg: Tip. zhurnala Stroitel, 1905). It was in 1913 that Walter Gropius discussed this theme in "Die Entwicklung moderner Industriebaukunst," in *Die Kunst in Industrie und Handel, Jahrbuch des Deutschen Werkbundes 1913* (Jena: Eugen Diederichs, 1913): 17–22.
128   Viktor V. Evald, *Konstruktivnye osobennosti amerikanskikh zdanii i estestvennye kamni, primeniaemye v sooruzheniakh v Soedinennykh Shtatakh* (Saint Petersburg: Tip. A. S. Khomskago i Ko.), 1895.
129   *Nedelia Stroitelia* 19, no. 3-4 (1891): 20.

впрочемъ, не особенно много, то для ихъ постройки, при соединеніи нѣсколькихъ обществъ, оказывается возможнымъ затратить несравненно большія суммы, нежели при постройкахъ отдѣльнымъ обществомъ.

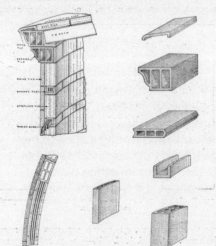

115. Общій видъ огнеупорныхъ зернохранилищъ на озерѣ Эри въ Канадѣ.

Хотя Нью-Іоркъ, наибольшій изъ американскихъ городовъ (второй по размѣрамъ въ свѣтѣ), и обладаетъ около 20 отдѣльныхъ желѣзнодорожныхъ линій, но въ центрѣ собственно Нью-Іорка (островъ Mannhatan) имѣется,

116. Детали огнеупорныхъ конструкцій зернохранилищъ на озерѣ Эри въ Канадѣ.

покамѣстъ, лишь одинъ центральный вокзалъ. Наиболѣе-же богатая изъ жел.-дорожныхъ линій Pennsylvania R. R. кончается въ правобережномъ предмѣстьи Нью-Іорка—New-Jersey City. Вокзалъ этой дороги (черт. 119),

по наружному виду, весьма типичному для желѣзнодорожной конечной станціи въ большомъ городѣ, очень похожъ на большой машинный сарай. Внутри, впрочемъ, распредѣленіе помѣщенія столь-же просто, какъ и въ большихъ центральныхъ вокзалахъ, о нѣкоторыхъ изъ которыхъ ниже будетъ сказано подробнѣй. Единственнымъ «украшеніемъ» этого зданія, въ чисто американско-рекламномъ духѣ, служитъ огромная надпись изъ электрическихъ лампочекъ надъ главной дугой стропильной фермы—«Pennsylvania R. R». Надпись эта по вечерамъ ярко свѣтитъ черезъ Hudson River (вродѣ того, какъ у насъ на циркѣ Чинизелли въ Петербургѣ) и должна заманивать жителей Нью-Іорка пользоваться именно этой, а не другой желѣзной дорогой.

Что касается общаго расположенія зданій вокзаловъ, то по даннымъ *Mr. Elmer L. Corthell* (гражд. инженера по занятію), строителя зданія пассажирской станціи въ гор. Буфалло (N. I.) въ Сѣв. Амер. С. Шт., ихъ можно распредѣлить слѣдующимъ образомъ:

1) *Конечныя станціи, главныя операціи въ коихъ происходятъ почти на уровнѣ земли.* Къ такому виду относятся: главная центральная станція въ Нью-Іоркѣ (на островѣ Mannhatan), и въ С. Луи штатъ Минезота (о ней

117. Огнеупорный элеваторъ въ южной части Чикаго на берегу озера Мичигана.

будетъ сказано подробнѣй ниже), южная конечная станція въ Бостонѣ (Mass), The Dearbor Station Chicago Ill. (The Liverpool Street, Euston, Great Central, Victoria etc въ Лондонѣ и Франкфуртскій вокзалъ въ Германіи).

2) *Конечныя станціи, лежащія полностью или только частью выше улицы.* Напримѣръ—New-Jersey City Station Pennsylvania Railroad, того-же желѣзно-дорожнаго обще-

ства—Broad Street Station въ Филадельфіи Ра. Въ той-же Филадельфіи—The Reading Terminal (въ Европѣ—вокзалъ

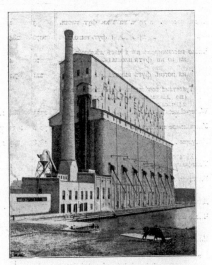

118. Общій видъ зернохранилища въ сѣверной части Чикаго, извѣстнаго подъ названіемъ „Rialto Elevator".

St.-Lazare въ Парижѣ, Центральная станція въ Антверпенѣ и почти всѣ зданія вокзаловъ въ Берлинѣ).

частью подъ землею. Соотвѣтственно этому подраздѣ-ленію, (a)—вокзалъ въ Буффало шт. N. I., (b)—Кельнскій и Дрезденскій вокзалы въ Германіи, (c)—проектируемое зданіе вокзала Pennsylvania R. R. въ центрѣ Нью-Іорка, (въ Лондонѣ, Европа—Waverley Station) (d)—новая ко-нечная станція въ Вашингтонѣ.

Наконецъ, зданія вокзаловъ и ихъ архитектура, какъ мы ранѣе упоминали, въ высокой степени зависятъ отъ того,—заняты-ли они однимъ обществомъ или нѣсколь-кими. Соединяться нѣсколько обществъ вмѣстѣ для по-стройки вокзаловъ побуждаютъ исключительно денежныя соображенія, съ одной стороны—вслѣдствіе высокой стоимости земли въ центрѣ городовъ, а съ другой—въ виду удешевленія пассажирамъ проѣзднаго билета, при отъѣздѣ съ вокзаловъ, лежащихъ въ центрѣ города. Такъ, напр., въ Нью-Іоркѣ, тѣ компаніи, которыя владѣютъ центральнымъ вокзаломъ—единственнымъ сре-ди острова Mannhatan'a, взимаютъ столь значительную доплату съ каждаго прицѣпленнаго вагона чужого об-щества, что съ пассажира за пріятность выйти не въ New Jersey City Pennsylvania R. R., а въ главномъ вокзалѣ взимается *доплата 4 рубля.*

Обращаясь теперь къ разсмотрѣнію отдѣльныхъ по-строекъ вокзальнаго типа, приведемъ нѣкоторыя стати-стическія данныя по разсматриваемому вопросу.

Изъ наблюденій надъ операціями слѣдующихъ исклю-чительно американскихъ зданій желѣзнодорожныхъ вок-заловъ:

Reading Terminal Philadelphia, Pa;
Broad Street Station, Pennsylvania Railroad Philadelphia, Pa;

119. Общій видъ переходныхъ пристаней на р. Гудзонѣ и вокзала Пенсильванской жел. дор. (Pennsylvania R. R.) въ право-бережной части Нью-Іорка—Хабокенѣ.

3) *Вокзалы со сквозными проѣздами поѣздовъ, распо-ложенные на уровнѣ земли* («Thougth» station). Въ С. Амер. С. Шт.—Indianopolis Union Station, а также въ городахъ: Omaha, штат. Nebraska, St. Paul, Min. (въ Германіи—вокзалъ въ Гановерѣ).

4) *Соединенія изъ конечной и сквозной станціи.* Послѣд-нія, въ свою очередь, могутъ быть: a) на уровнѣ земли, b) надъ землей, c) подъ землей, d) частью на землѣ и

South Terminal Station, Boston, Mass;
Lake Shore and Rock Island, Chicago, Ill;
Union Terminal Station, St Louis, Mo;
Grand Central Station, New Iork City;

выведена нижеслѣдующая таблица № I, являющаяся ре-зультатомъ наблюденій за протекшую зиму 1903—904 года.

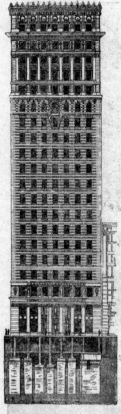

Рис. 9.

представляющемъ основаніе зданія Зингера въ Нью-Іоркѣ. На рисункѣ видны кессоны, кирпичные столбы на нихъ, гранитные штучные камни, чугунные башмаки подъ балки и колонны, ростверки изъ двутавровыхъ балокъ и, наконецъ, кантиливерная большая клепаная балка.

Общій видъ узкаго и высокаго зданія, выходящаго на уголъ двухъ улицъ, показанъ на рис. 9.

Это — зданіе American Surety Building въ Нью-Іоркѣ, выходящее на улицы Broadway и Pine; глубина кессоновъ 24 метра. На рисункѣ видны кессоны, кирпичные столбы, ростверки изъ двутавровыхъ балокъ и анкера.

III. Каменныя постройки съ желѣзнымъ остовомъ.

а) Скелетныя и каркасныя конструкціи.

Указанныя выше условія: дороговизна земли, стремленіе строить промышленныя и торговыя зданія въ одномъ небольшомъ районѣ города, маломѣрность земельныхъ участковъ, спѣшность постройки—все это привело къ типу зданій узкихъ и очень высокихъ, съ минимальной толщиной стѣнъ.

Высота кирпичныхъ зданій обычнаго типа въ Америкѣ долго ограничивалась 9 — 10 этажами; толщина стѣнъ такихъ зданій въ нижнихъ этажахъ достигала 2 м. При участкахъ иногда не болѣе 7 метровъ шириной такія толстыя стѣны были слишкомъ неэкономичны; было необходимо найти конструкцію съ меньшей толщиной стѣнъ и при значительно большемъ числѣ этажей.

Въ 1883 г. въ Чикаго было построено первое зданіе въ 10 этажей, но уже съ тонкими стѣнками, которыя не несли совершенно никакой нагрузки, кромѣ своего собственнаго вѣса, нагрузка же всѣхъ перекрытій воспринималась колоннами, поставленными какъ внутри зданія, такъ и по контуру наружныхъ стѣнъ.

Конструкція эта, названная *скелетной*, получила дальнѣйшее развитіе, и число этажей было доведено до 20 въ Чикаго въ 1890 году (Masonic Temple) и до 30 въ Нью-Іоркѣ въ 1893 году (Manhattan Life Building).

Въ скелетной конструкціи (skeleton construction)

металлическій жесткій остовъ принимаетъ нагрузку отъ внутреннихъ легкихъ стѣнъ и отъ всѣхъ перекрытій; наружныя же свободныя стѣны, для устойчивости связанныя съ остовомъ анкерами, несутъ только свой собственный вѣсъ, а потому наружныя стѣны въ скелетныхъ конструкціяхъ могутъ быть сдѣланы болѣе тонкими, чѣмъ при обычныхъ конструкціяхъ.

Дальнѣйшее развитіе высокія зданія получили, когда на желѣзный остовъ стали передавать также и вѣсъ стѣнъ, а не только нагрузку отъ перекрытій.

Конструкціи эти названы *каркасными* (cage construction); онѣ состоятъ изъ желѣзнаго жесткаго остова, несущаго не только вѣсъ внутреннихъ стѣнъ и перекрытій, но и вѣсъ наружныхъ стѣнъ, а потому толщина наружныхъ стѣнъ каркасныхъ зданій можетъ быть сдѣлана еще меньшею, чѣмъ при скелетной конструкціи.

Въ каркасной конструкціи весь остовъ состоитъ изъ вертикальныхъ жесткихъ желѣзныхъ стоекъ, идущихъ во всю высоту зданія, отъ фундамента до кровли, и расположенныхъ какъ по периметру зданія, такъ и внутри его; стойки эти поддерживаютъ горизонтальныя желѣзныя балки, охватывающія по этажамъ по наружному его периметру и проходящія внутри его; балки поддерживаютъ какъ перекрытія, такъ и стѣны.

Пространство между стойками и балками, а также между самыми балками, задѣлывается камнемъ, кирпичемъ, бетономъ; каркасъ обдѣлывается тѣми же матеріалами. Такимъ образомъ наружныя стѣны какъ бы ,висятъ на каркасѣ и могутъ быть сдѣланы во всю высоту зданія снизу до верху не толще 300 мм. (С. Франциско).

Новѣйшія высокія зданія всѣ каркаснаго типа (рис. 10). При этой конструкціи должно, однако, имѣть въ виду

Рис. 10.

надежное укрѣпленіе стоекъ къ фундаменту и солидное устройство вѣтровыхъ связей, о которыхъ будетъ сказано ниже.

Половые и охватывающія зданія по этажамъ по его периметру балки укрѣпляются по мѣрѣ наращиванія стоекъ въ высоту; построенный, но еще не заполненный, каркасъ чрезвычайно напоминаетъ гигантскую клѣтку, что вполнѣ оправдываетъ англійское названіе этой конструкціи.

б) Работы по заполненію каркаса.

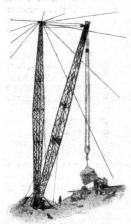

Рис. 11.

При крайней тѣснотѣ улицъ Нью-Іорка и другихъ городовъ, необходимо производить сборку каркаса и заполнять его такъ, чтобы можно было обходиться безъ подмостей и лѣсовъ, которые, кромѣ того, при высокихъ зданіяхъ столь же нецѣлесообразны и трудно исполнимы, какъ и при кладкѣ кирпичныхъ фабричныхъ трубъ.

Весь матеріалъ подвозится къ постройкѣ и немедленно поднимается многочисленными кранами (рис. 11), рѣшетчатыя мачты которыхъ укрѣплены канатами.

Выгода каркасныхъ построекъ заключается еще въ томъ, что заполненіе между балками и стойками можетъ быть начато одновременно въ нѣсколькихъ этажахъ, и его можно продолжать въ верхнихъ этажахъ, когда матеріалъ для заполненія нижнихъ этажей не доставленъ еще на работы (рис. 12).

Заполненіе между стойками для образованія стѣнъ производится обычно изъ пустотѣлыхъ красныхъ кирпичей, устанавливаемыхъ пустотами вертикально; укрѣпленіе этихъ кирпичей, въ случаѣ надобности, производится горизонтальными желѣзными полосами, укладываемыми между рядами кирпичей и закрѣпляемыми въ концахъ къ стойкамъ. Кирпичи эти бываютъ съ однимъ или съ двумя рядами пустотъ, но двѣ или по три пустоты въ каждомъ рядѣ; пустоты расположены вдоль большаго измѣренія кирпичей, равнаго 300 мм.; прочіе размѣры кирпичей различны — отъ 80 × 150 до 200 × 300 мм.; боковыя поверхности кирпичей обычно имѣютъ бороздки для лучшаго сцѣпленія съ растворомъ.

Полы подвальнаго и 1-го этажей выполняются зачастую изъ желѣзобетона, а полы слѣдующихъ этажей дѣлаются изъ пустотѣлыхъ фасонныхъ красныхъ кирпичей; при этомъ желѣзобетонные полы играютъ роль діафрагмы для закрѣпленій всѣхъ стоекъ въ уровнѣ земли.

Все желѣзо предохраняется отъ огня цементнымъ растворомъ въ 25 мм. и терракотой въ 75 мм.

Высоту комнатъ обычно дѣлаютъ отъ 3,8 до 6 метровъ.

Рис. 12.

в) Висячія подмости.

Вслѣдствіе отмѣченной выше нецѣлесообразности и неудобоисполнимости обычныхъ лѣсовъ, при постройкѣ

Рис. 13.

Pavel Iu. Siuzor. Singer Building, Nevskii Prospekt, Saint-Petersburg, 1904, section.
Plate from the *Ezhegodnik Obshchestva Arkhitektorov Khudozhnikov*, Saint-Petersburg, 1906. CCA, W.E933.

Ernst-Richard Nirnzee, High-rise buiding, Bolshoi Gnezdikovskii pereulok, Moscow, 1912, view c. 1935, Moskva kotoroi net.

Shortly after, the journal informed its readers that the "gigantic houses"—increasingly common 18- or 19-story structures—were called "sky scrapers" [neboskreby] and that their abundance in Chicago was "astounding." The journal also applauded the powerful and swift construction of Dankmar Adler and Louis Sullivan's Auditorium Building, erected between 1887 and 1889, but failed to mention its architects[130]. Upon his return from a mission to America in 1913, the engineer Nikolai Lakhtin described the latest trends in skyscraper construction in Zodchii, claiming that such buildings would soon become crucial for Russia[131] [ill. p. 72-73].

A parallel can be drawn between certain Russian structures whose height had until then remained unknown and their American predecessors. In 1904, Singer inaugurated a building intended for shops and offices in Saint Petersburg, located on the angle lined by the Nevskii Prospekt and the Ekaterinskii Canal[132]. George Neidlinger had wished to implement his offices in the capital rather than in Moscow, where they would have been closer to the Podolsk factory. Following this initiative, the first project was drawn by Ernest Flagg, who would later design the company's New York skyscraper, the world's tallest building for a time. There was nothing similar in the Russian capital, where no structure was allowed to surpass the Winter Palace cornice, which was 11 sazhens (23.5 metres) high. In 1902, The Architectural Record presented a project that was "ready to be launched" and was meant to be built in stone "on the city's main square" and intended for a "showroom" and offices[133] [ill. p. 75].

A more spectacular alternative was designed and completed by the renowned Saint Petersburg architect Pavel Siuzor, recruited by the leaders of Singer's Russian division, who exchanged fiery letters on this matter with the American branch[134]. Siuzor shattered the regulatory limits by placing a glass dome on the corner roof of the building and by topping it off with a luminous sphere, making it the tallest structure in the city [ill. p. 74]. Widely discussed in the architectural press, his construction was the first in Russia to use a steel skeleton revealed by the façades, with many more openings than those sketched by Flagg. It had three electric Otis elevators, also a first in Russia, as well as fireproof floors. The two lower stories were meant for the sale and exhibition of machines and textile goods, while the five upper floors were arranged into "Anglo-American-style private offices," the last of which was sheltered by a vaulted ceiling covered by the attic[135]. Not only did the Singer building tower impressively over the capital's main artery, it also proved to be much more American than the New York City skyscraper designed by Flagg, then viewed as the most Parisian architect working in Manhattan.

In Moscow, no regulatory limit was set to protect symbolic manifestations of power. In 1912, an eight-story tenement house was built on the Bolshoi Gnezdnikovskii pereulok by Ernst-Richard Nirnzee, a prolific residential architect, for A. V. Lobozev [ill. p. 75]. Occupying a block on the corner of Tverskaia Street and rising above the landscape of the Garden Ring, it was described as the city's first "cloud cutter." In addition to inaugurating Moscow's upward growth, the building served as an American-style apartment hotel, complete with residential services. Its terrace hosted a café, and its floors were frequented by members of the capital's intelligentsia for several decades to come[136]. Also in Moscow, a considerably more ingenious and creative architect, Fedor Shekhel, designed constructions that were much more radical in their utilitarian aesthetic, if not as tall. Details evocative of Berlin-style architecture were mixed in with American themes. Horizontally stretched windows, inspired from Chicago office buildings, lighten the understated brick façade of the bank created by the Riabushinskii brothers in

1903–1904 and located in Kitai-Gorod. The corner edifice of the Moscow Merchant Society is similarly unadorned, its façade so vastly covered in glass that its pillars seem rather spindly[137].

Amerikanizm of the Poets: Balmont, Gorky, and Blok

At the start of the twentieth century, Russian emigration to America was increasing. The movement included numerous Jews fleeing pogroms, as well as idealists seeking a more welcoming world. Among the 2.3 million Russians who emigrated to the United States between 1899 and 1913 in search of a utopian American land replete with communitarian experiences, many were inspired by Edward Bellamy's socialist-leaning anticipation novel *Looking Backward*, released to instant acclaim in *Nedelia* (The Week) in 1889, a year after its original publication in Boston[138] [ill. p. 79]. The developments of American socialism were later surveyed by such authors as Izaak Rubinov, who contributed to the newspaper *Russkaia mysl* (The Russian Thought) and the journal *Russkoe Bogatsvo* (The Russian Wealth)[139]. In 1902, in his novel *Za Okeanom* (Across the Ocean) issued under the pen name N. A. Tan, the ethnologist and linguist Vladimir Bogoraz described the social climb and political success of Russian workers established in the United States[140]. In 1932, despite repeated attacks on behalf of the Soviet government, he still managed to publish a book on "the people and customs" of America[141].

Tolstoy, who initially approved of America, became increasingly vocal in his condemnation of its "materialism" at the start of the century, while conservative commentators feared "the new messianism of the nation of dollars."[142] The most in-depth investigations came from the field of political science, such as those of Maksim Kovalevskii, and especially Moisei Ostrogorskii, whose critical analysis of democracy and political parties in *La démocratie et les partis politiques* was printed in Paris in 1903, and remained untranslated until the 1920s. Upon its Russian publication, it was read as a "ruthless exposé" of bourgeois democracy[143]. Only two writers crossed the Atlantic in the first decade of the century, both bringing back accounts with detailed notations

130   "Kolossalnye postroiki v Amerike," *Nedelia Stroitelia* 21, no. 14 (4 April 1893): 64.
131   Nikolai Lakhtin, "Iz komandirovki v Ameriku," *Zodchii* 52, no. 18 (5 May 1913): 203–11.
132   Carstensen, *American Enterprise*, 48–50.
133   "The Works of Ernest Flagg," *The Architectural Record* 11, no. 3 (April 1902): 35.
134   Mardges Bacon, *Ernest Flagg: Beaux-Arts Architect and Urban Reformer* (Cambridge, MA: MIT Press, 1986), 213, 215 and 375. See in particular William Craft Brumfield, *The Origins of Modernism in Russian Architecture* (Berkeley: University of California Press, 1991), 216–19.
135   *Zodchii* 35, no. 39 (24 September 1906): 390, 41–43; *Ezhegodnik Obshchestva Arkhitektorov-Khudozhnikov*, 1906, 114–15.
136   Vladimir Besonov and Rachit Iangirov, *Dom Nirnzee, Bolshoi Gnezdikovskii pereulok 10* (Moscow: Intellekt-Tsentr, 2012).
137   Liudmila Saigina, *Arkhitektor Fedor Shekhtel; paviliony, banki, doma, khramy epokhi eklektiki i moderna* (Moscow: Muzei Arkhitektury im. Shchuseva, 2017), 206–11.
138   Edward Bellamy, *Looking Backward, 2000–1887* (Boston: Benjamin, 1888); in Russian: *Cherez sto let – sotsiologicheskii roman* (Saint Petersburg: Novosti, 1891).
139   In addition to the articles mentioned, Rubinov published "Detskii trud v Amerike," *Russkaia mysl*, no. 3 (1903): 18–57; "Zhenskii professionalnyi trud v Amerike," *Russkaia mysl*, no. 9 (1906): 52–73; "Rabochii vopros v amerikanskom zakonodateltsve," *Russkoe bogatsvo*, no. 9 (1909): 103–31. See also Rogger, "America Enters the Twentieth Century," 163–64.
140   N.A. Tan, *Za okeanom* (Moscow: 1902), published as a serial in *Mir bozhii*, 1904; republished in vol. 6 of *Sobranie sochninenii* (Saint Petersburg: Prosveshchenie, 1911).
141   Vladimir G. Bogoraz-Tan, *USA: liudi i nravy Ameriki* (Moscow: Federatsia, 1932).
142   Evgeni Pravdin, "Novorozhdennyi messianizm strany dollarov i Stary Svet," *Istoricheskii vestnik* 74 (November 1898): 704–21, quoted in Laserson, *The American Impact on Russia*, 343.
143   Moisei Ostrogorski, *La démocratie et les partis politiques* (Paris: Calmann-Lévy, 1903). The translations of both volumes of this work, the second of which focuses on the United States, were published in Moscow in 1927 and 1930, with a preface by Evgenii Pashukanis.

on landscapes and cities, but to radically different effect. Symbolist poet Konstantin Balmont penned a few pages summarizing his impressions from his quick crossing of the continent, whereas realist writer Maxim Gorky published, in Germany, a fierce condemnation of American society.

Balmont's "A Few Words on America, Travel Notes" was printed in Russian and in French in the first issue of the symbolist journal *Zolotoe Runo* (The Golden Fleece), created as a successor to *Mir Iskusstva* (The Art World). After crossing the Mexican border in El Paso, on his way to San Francisco, the poet felt as if he had "dived into the vivifying waters of the Narzan Baths," referencing the spa city of Kislovodsk in the North Caucasus: "lively and cheerful faces everywhere, a sense of freedom, music, train whistles, the tremor of life—nothing is amiss here, not even the grotesque Salvation Army parade."[144] Balmont was amused by the fact that the Art Institute of Chicago displayed only casts, and lamented finding only two meager bookstores in San Francisco. But New York City reconciled him with America. He deemed its "main park" to be "charming," comparing it to San Francisco's Golden Gate Park: "It is more withdrawn, more intimate, it doesn't have the pomp and circumstance of a hymn, rather the brightness of lyrical poetry, the softness of an elegy."[145] Travelling across the city on the subway, he "experienced a sense of freedom, of space" and "his heart joyfully expanded," as he expressed in verse:

I race along the aerial railroad
In mighty New York. The ocean is close by.
Hovels whizz past; palaces whizz past
I race along the aerial railroad—
And the heart rejoices in the iron lie.
Machines, machines. A victory over height.
A twining of metal. Patterns of networks[146].

Although he viewed Americans as "deeply unlikable," Balmont expressed his "faith in the great destiny" of the country. He added: "when natural talents are supported by great passion, failure is impossible. For the time being, Americans are insufferable and extravagant, like adolescents mistaking themselves for adults. Their heads shine with hair wax, but their hands are still dirty." He believed Americans to be destined to a bright future, because "a wilderness such as the one thriving between the immensities of the Pacific and the Atlantic oceans will compel its inhabitants to grow tall and beautiful, as has often been the case in the past."[147]

Whereas for Balmont, the metal twining surrounding New York was an "iron lie," for Gorky, who used the same metaphor, the iron was the expression of a threat: "Everywhere—overhead, underfoot, alongside, iron clangs, exulting in its victory. Awakened to life and animated by the power of gold, it casts its web about man, strangles him, sucks his blood and brain, devours his muscles and nerves, and grows and grows, resting upon voiceless stone, and spreading the links of its chain ever more widely."[148]

144   Konstantin Balmont, "Dva slova ob Amerike, is pisem s dorogi: Deux mots sur l'Amérique, notes de voyage," in Russian and French in *Zolotoe runo* 1, no. 1 (1906): 72.

145   Ibid., 74.

146   Ibid., 75.

147   Ibid., 75-76.

148   Maxim Gorky, *V Amerike, ocherki* (Stuttgart: J.H.W. Dietz, 1906), 13–14; in English: *In America* (Moscow: Foreign Languages Publishing House, 1949), 10.

Maxim Gorky (front row second to left) and Mark Twain (to his left) at the latter's Writer's Club in New York, 1906, Photographer unknown.

Published in 1906, Gorky's essays are the result of a stay in New York and in a few other east coast cities from April to October that same year. Invited by the socialist millionaire Gaylord Wilshire, who had settled in the East after leaving his mark on Los Angeles' urban landscape[149], the writer had travelled to America to collect funds for political activists incarcerated after the 1905 Revolution. His first impressions were enthusiastic. He wrote to Leonid Krasin, who had initiated the mission: "It is such an amazing fantasy of stone, glass, and iron, a fantasy constructed by crazy giants, monsters longing after beauty, stormy souls full of wild energy. All these Berlins, Parises, and other 'big' cities are trifles in comparison with New York. Socialism should first be realized here—that is the first thing you think of when you see the amazing houses, machines, etc."[150]

Gorky's later reactions, radically opposite, were dictated by his personal mishaps. After a warm welcome from colleagues such as Jack London, Upton Sinclair, and Mark Twain, agents of the Czarist police conspired to have the writer evicted from the hotel where he was staying with his partner, actress Mariia Andreeva, to whom he was not married. A vicious press campaign ensued, and several of his new friends turned away from him. The fundraising turned out to be most disappointing[151].

Gorky insisted in his writing on the difference between the widespread idealized perception of America and the mundane reality, aligning his view with Tolstoy on this matter. He challenged the conception, common in Russian narratives, that New World capitalism was fundamentally different from that of Europe. He denounced the tyranny of gold, the "Yellow Devil," in the ravenous metropolis, his anti-urban critique reaching beyond New York City, attacking the monstrosity and bestiality of all great agglomerations. This vision was inspired by Émile Verhaeren's poems, which he had published in the journal *Znanie* (Knowledge) and whose poem "The Tentacular Cities" was translated into Russian under the title "The Octopus-City."[152] As for Gorky's obsession with gold, it is reminiscent of Nietzsche, another widely read author in Russia, who wrote, in *The Gay Science*: "There is an Indian savagery, a savagery peculiar to the Indian blood, in the manner in which the Americans strive after gold: and the breathless hurry of their work—the characteristic vice of the New World—already begins to infect old Europe, and makes it savage also, spreading over it a strange lack of intellectuality."[153]

For Gorky, the "surprising fantasy" of New York City turned into a terrifying and predatory environment: "This is a city. This is New York. Twenty-storied houses, dark soundless skyscrapers, stand on the shore. Square, lacking in any desire to be beautiful, the stiff ponderous buildings tower gloomily and drearily. A haughty pride in its height, its ugliness is felt in each house. [...] From this distance the city seems like a vast jaw, with uneven black teeth. I breathe clouds of black smoke into the sky and snuffles like a glutton suffering from his obesity. Entering the city is like getting into a stomach of stone and iron, a stomach that has swallowed several million people and is consuming and digesting them."[154] [ill. p. 82-83]

In another essay entitled "The Mob," Gorky derided the enslaved masses populating the city streets, describing their commercialized leisure on display in Coney Island's Luna Park, where he discovered "the kingdom of boredom." [ill. p. 84] He delighted in picturing a redeeming fire that would burn the amusement park's huts down to the ground, unwittingly foreboding its misfortune: "The air is filled with the even hissing of the arc lights, ragged fragments of music, the pious whining of wooden organ pipes and the thin, incessant whistle of the peanut stands. All this merges in an irritating hum as some invisible string, thick and taut, and when a human voice invades this incessant sound it seems like a frightened whisper. Everything glitters insolently, baring its dismal ugliness. [...] The soul is gripped by a burning desire for a live, red, flowering flame that would deliver people from the bondage of this mottled boredom that deafens and blinds. One would wish to set fire to all this prettiness, and to dance in wild merriment, to shout and sing in the tempestuous play of the colourful tongues of a living flame, to revel in a voluptuous feast of destruction of lifeless magnificence of spiritual poverty."[155] As he became one of the most celebrated writers in Stalinist Russia—although the dictator likely had him assassinated in 1936 while continuing to publicly glorify him—, Gorky's horrified impressions were repeatedly reissued as an antidote against the rampant Amerikanizm of Soviet culture.

The gold-plated iron Gorky so vehemently rejected was exalted by the symbolist writer Aleksandr Blok in a 1913 Christmas poem. Although he had not crossed the Atlantic, he had read the Russian translations of Walt Whitman's *Leaves of Grass*, which were then being thoroughly discussed[156]. In "New America," Blok envisions the United States as the light of destiny, waking Russia from its secular slumber and guiding it towards a New World. The poet claims he has seen the glow of American industrial culture in the Donbass coal mines, illuminated by what turns out to be the Christmas star, coinciding with the December 25 publication date. This premise allows him to criticize the stagnant state of Russian civilization.

The black coal – subterranean Messiah,
The black coal – tsar and bridegroom out there,
But the voice of your stone songs, O Russia,
O bride, tells of nothing to fear!

The coal groans and the salt becomes whiter,
And unceasingly screams the iron ore…
Yes, above the bleak steppe-lands, the rising
New America shines like a star![157]

Blok's intention is all the more obvious when you consider that all of the poem's rejected variants referred explicitly to America. He embraced the widespread Russian perception of America as a restorative force, a vision scorned by Gorky, whose resistance to urbanization he did not share. His attentive reading of Mendeleev's last work, focused on the virtues of great American cities, is a

149   Lou Rosen, *Henry Gaylord Wilshire: The Millionaire Socialist* (Pacific Palisades: School Justice Institute, 2011).

150   Gorki, Letter to Krasin.

151   Filia Holtzman, "A Mission that Failed: Gorky in America," *Slavic and East European Journal* 6, no. 3 (1962): 227–35; Tovah Yedlin, *Maxim Gorky, a Political Biography* (New York: Praeger, 66–78).

152   Charles Rougle, *Three Russians Consider America: America in the Works of Maksim Gor'kij, Aleksandr Blok and Vladimir Majakovskij* (Stockholm: Almqvist & Wiksell International, 1976), 46–50.

153   Friedrich Nietzsche, *The Gay Science* [1882], trans. Walter Kaufman (London: Penguin, 1974), §329.

154   Maxim Gorky, "Gorod zheltogo diavola," in *V Amerike*, 12–13; in English: *In America*, 9–10. This text was published before he even left the United States, "The City of the Yellow Devil: My Impressions of America," *Appleton's Magazine*, no. 8 (August 1906): 177–82.

155   Maxim Gorky, "Tsarstvo skuki," in *V Amerike*, 44–45; in English: *In America*, p. 34. This passage drew the attention of Rem Koolhaas in *Delirious New York* (New York: Oxford University Press, 1978), 67-68.

156   Rougle, *Three Russians Consider America*, 64.

157   Aleksandr Blok, "Novaia Amerika," *Russkoe Slovo* (25 December 1913); in English: "The New America," in Alexander Blok, *Selected Poems* (Moscow: Progress Publishers, 1971), 244. See also Anna A. Arustamova, "'Novaia Amerika' A. Bloka i A. Ladinskogo," *Artikult* 27, no. 3 (2017): 99–105.

George P. Hall & Son. Panorama of the Lower West Side of Manhattan, New York, ca. 1899.
Gelatin silver print, 31.3 × 105.7 cm. CCA, PH1982:0285.

testament to this conception[158]. To him, Amerikanizm, which he also mentioned in his diaries, "this manner of resolving life's practical issues on a vast scope and an extensive scale," was the core strength of the "culture" that would resurrect a country fatally asleep in its archaic and Asian "civilization"[159].

Poets belonging to other new literary movements were also interested in the New World. The Acmeists set off to search, if not for America, then at least for its female inhabitants. In his 1913 poem "Amerikanka," echoing

158   Dmitrii Mendeleev, *K poznaniu Rossii* (Saint Petersburg: Izd-vo. A. V. Suvorina, 1907) 60–61, quoted in Rougle, *Three Russians Consider America*, 72.

159   Aleksandr Blok, in Boris Solovev, *Poet i ego podvig, tvorcheskii pout Aleksandra Bloka* (Moscow: Sovetskii Pisatel, 1973), 439; quoted in Rougle, *Three Russians Consider America*, 86.

160   Tatiana L. Pavlova and Elena V. Merkel, "K konfliktu kultur v akmeisme: obraz amerikanskoi turistki v poezi N. Gumileva i O. Mandelshtama," *Kultura i tsivilizatsiia* 7, no. 4 (2017): 304–12; Aleksandra Miliakina, "K interpretatsii stikhotvorenia 'Amerikanka' O. Mandelshtama," *Russkaia filologia* 25 (2014): 169–74.

161   Aleksandr Benois, "Poslednaia futuristicheskaia vystavka," *Rech* (9 January 1916).

162   Jeffrey Brooks, "The Press and Its Message: Images of America in the 1920's and 1930's," in Sheila Fitzpatrick, Alexander Rabinowitch, Richard Stites, eds., *Russia in the Era of NEP: Explorations in Soviet Society and Culture* (Bloomington: Indiana University Press, 1991), 236.

163   Lev G. Zhdanov, Dva miliona v god (nishchi millioner): fantasticheskii roman (Saint Petersburg: Prometei, 1914).

164   Bernhard Kellerman, *Der Tunnel* (Berlin: S. Fischer Verlag, 1913). In Russian: *V tunnele* (Saint Petersburg: Izd. M. M. Gutsatza, 1913).

165   Jeffrey Brooks, *When Russia Learned to Read: Literacy and Popular Literature, 1861–1917* (Princeton, Princeton University Press, 1985), 142.

166   Boris Dralyuk, *Western Crime Fiction Goes East: The Russian Pinkerton Craze 1907–1934* (Leiden; Boston, Brill, 2012), 10–20.

167   S. Frederick Starr, *Red & Hot: The Fate of Jazz in the Soviet Union 1917–1980* [1983] (New York: Limelight Editions, 1994), 20–36.

168   Jacqueline D. St. John, "John F. Stevens, American Assistance to Russian and Siberian Railroads, 1917–1922," PhD dissertation, Norman: University of Oklahoma, 1970.

169   Nikolai Borodin, *Amerikantsi i amerikanskaia kultura* (Petrograd: Tip. Tov. Obshchestvennaia polza, 1915); *Severo-amerikanskie Soedinnennye Shtaty i Rossiia* (Petrograd: Ogni, 1915). A professor at Harvard, Borodin died in Cambridge, Massachusetts, in 1937.

Nikolai Gumilev, Osip Mandelstam brings to life an ignorant tourist from the New World[160]. In "Amerikan Bar," he mocks the proliferation of such establishments in Russia. Representatives of Suprematism and Futurism staged their irreverent performances in Saint Petersburg's Luna Park, an amusement park created in 1912 based on the London version of the Coney Island original. In 1913, the park hosted Kazimir Malevich and Mikhail Matiushin's opera *Victory over the Sun*, as well as the play *Vladimir Mayakovsky, a Tragedy*. Another sign of the permeation of American culture in avant-garde circles can be found in Aleksandr Benois's 1916 article in the newspaper *Rech* (Speech). The artist and historian lamented the manifest "amerikanizm" in *The Last Futurist Exhibition of Paintings 0,10*, where the rivalry between Malevich's Suprematism and Vladimir Tatlin's protoconstructivism became apparent[161].

From Pulp Fiction to Political Fiction

Beyond the avant-garde's experimentations, American narratives proliferated in the popular press at the start of the twentieth century. The *Gazeta kopeika* (The One-Kopek Paper) and the *Russkoe slovo* (The Russian Word) described its unlimited resources, all the while criticizing its sweeping focus on business[162]. Lev Zhdanov's best-selling novel *Dva milliona v god* (Two Million a Year) cast capitalism in a more appealing light[163]. Speculative fiction was particularly popular, namely Bernhard Kellerman's 1913 book *Der Tunnel*, a telling of the lengthy construction of an underwater connection between the United States and Europe, translated on the first year of its original publication and reissued several times before and after the Revolution[164]. The tale propagated the notion that heroic enterprises were essential to modernization, paving the way for the discourse that would accompany industrialization during the first five-year plan, in which the construction site became a symbol of the manufacturing revolution.

Russian kiosks were flooded with regular serialized novels, such as *Nick Carter, the American Sherlock Holmes* and *Nat Pinkerton, the King of Detectives*, set in urban America. This escapist literature spawned a wave of *Pinkertonovshchina*, or "Pinkertonite." In 1908 alone, nearly 10 million booklets with stories about Carter, Pinkerton, and Holmes, mostly translated from German editions of American dime novels, were sold[165]. Schoolchildren, blue-collar labourers, and office workers alike devoured them, diving into the reassuring realm of big-city storylines where the wicked were always punished. Their illustrated covers, echoing the aesthetic of *luboks*, popular Russian prints, were particularly appealing and caught the attention of such readers as a young Sergei Eisenstein. Poets from Sergei Esenin to Aleksandr Blok were fascinated by them, with the latter going as far as to spoof their dialogues[166]. Another popular culture crossover was jazz, with multiple orchestras appearing in Saint Petersburg; cake-walk and ragtime provided the musical backdrop for the last months of Czarist society[167].

During the First World War, Russian-American trade exchange dramatically increased, with the United States replacing Germany as the major provider of industrial equipment. American companies like General Electric and Standard Oil entered several markets, such as electrical and railway equipment[168]. The pre-war bilateral relations were strengthened with the 1915 creation of the Society for Promoting Mutual Friendly Relations between Russia and America. One of its founders was Nikolai Borodin, an ichthyologist and journalist, who wrote several books about the United States[169]. After his 1891 and 1913 travels to America, he praised the "help yourself" mentality he observed there, drawing on writings such as *The American As He Is* by Nicholas Murray Butler, president of Columbia University, and popular accounts by French reporters Firmin Roz and Jules Huret[170]. Pavel Miliukov, the founder of the Constitutional Democratic Party, gave talks at the University of Chicago in 1903 and presented his political theories in New York, at the 1908 Civic Forum[171].

The February 1917 Revolution, which allowed for the return of exiled Russian activists, put Miliukov in a position of power as minister of foreign affairs. At war with Germany as of April, the United States made use of its networks to ensure that Russia kept fighting alongside the Allies[172]. European pre-war operatives hoped to quickly resume their business and expected Russia to rise to America's economic level, as a brochure distributed by the Parisian publication Comptoir franco-anglo-russe boldly stated: "Since the beginning of America's industrial development, the whole world has largely benefited from the progress made in the industrial and scientific realm, and these modern methods will serve Russia's growth. One can thus safely claim that Russia will not only follow America's rapid rise but will also surpass the great Western Republic."[173]

On November 11, 1917, only a few days after the Bolsheviks took over in Petrograd, *Niva* (The Field), a widely circulated weekly paper, devoted an issue to the theme of America, prefaced by an enthusiastic foreword about the star-spangled banner by Aleksandr Kuprin[174]. One page was dedicated to Ambassador David R. Francis—who had likely funded the issue—, and several pages carried a short story by N. A. Tan. One of the posters replicated in an insert showed "Ivan and Uncle Sam," two "democrat comrades," one wearing a cap and the other, a top hat, exchanging a firm handshake against the backdrop of the New York City skyline and the Statue of Liberty[175]. Aleksandr Blok wrote to his mother in March 1917 that to him, "the future Russia can be envisioned as a great democracy, but not necessarily a new America."[176] The Bolsheviks, who took control of the country in October, had no respect whatsoever for the American political system, if they were on the other hand close to the industrialist movement that had risen before 1900 and shared its fascination for large factories and streamlined production. As many of them had experienced America first-hand, once settled at the helm of the economy, they had no trouble complementing their existing post-war and post-revolutionary relationship with Germany with an intense focus on the United States, specifically on its companies and its industrial doctrines.

170   Nicholas Murray Butler, *The American as He Is* (New York: Macmillan, 1908); Firmin Roz, *L'énergie américaine (évolution des États-Unis)* (Paris: Flammarion, 1910); Jules Huret, *L'Amérique moderne* (Paris: Pierre Lafitte, 1911); see also Allen, *Russia Looks at America*, 226.

171   Paul Miliukov, *Constitutional Government for Russia: An Address Delivered Before the Civic Forum in Carnegie Hall*, New York City, January 14, 1908 (New York: The Civic Forum, 1908).

172   George F. Kennan, *Russia Leaves the War: The Americans in Petrograd and the Bolshevik Revolution* (Princeton: Princeton University Press, 1956).

173   *La Russie: ses possibilités économiques* (Paris: Comptoir franco-anglo-russe, 1917), 13–14.

174   Aleksandr I. Kuprin, "Zvezdnyi flag," *Niva*, no. 45 (11 November 1917), 675–78.

175   "Tovarishchi demokraty – Ivan i Diadia Sem," illustration in ibid., 683.

176   Aleksandr Blok, Letter to his mother, 19–20 March 1917, *Sobranie sochinenii v vosmi tomakh*, vol. 8 (Moscow: Gospolitizdat, 1963), 479.

Left: *Nat Pinkerton, the King of Detectives: The Nest of Criminals Under the Clouds*, Saint Petersburg: Razvlechenie, 1908. CCA.
Right: "Democratic Comrades: Ivan and Uncle Sam," poster reproduced in *Niva*, 11 november 1917. Private Collection.

Taylorism and Fordism for the Soviet Industrial Development

2

Aleksandra M. Kollontai (1872-1952). Bolshevik activist, stayed in New York in 1917.

Leon D. Trotsky (1879-1940). Bolshevik leader, stayed in New York in 1917.

Nikolai I. Bukharin (1888-1938). Bolshevik leader, stayed in New York in 1917.

Frederick W. Taylor (1856-1915). American engineer, developed scientific management.

Lillian M. (1878-1972) and Frank B. (1868-1924) Gilbreth. American engineers who engaged in motion studies, using apparatuses of their own invention.

Vladimir I. Lenin (1870-1924). Main bolshevik leader, with a passion for Taylorism.

Albert Kahn (1869-1942). American architect, his team built more than 500 factories in the Soviet Union.

Armand Hammer (1898-1990). American businessman, used his connections with Lenin to create a pencil factory in Moscow.

Walter N. Polakov (1879-1948). Russian engineer, emigrated to the United States and advised the USSR.

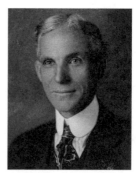

Henry Ford (1863-1947). American entrepreneur, supported the trade with the USSR.

Saul G. Bron (1887-1938). Soviet economist, coordinated the technological imports from the United States.

"Incredible as it may seem, more people in Russia have heard of him [Ford] than of Stalin, the Commander-in-Chief of the one-million-odd Communists who are governing the destiny of the vast Slavic empire. I visited villages far from railroads, where I talked to illiterate peasants who didn't know of Stalin, or Rykov, or Bukharin, but who had heard of the man who made 'iron horses.'"

Maurice Hindus, "Henry Ford Conquers Russia," 1927[1].

The Bolsheviks' coup on 25 October 1917, had significant consequences, not only on Russia's political system and its war with Germany—which ended in March 1918 with the Treaty of Brest-Litovsk—, but also on its economy and culture, marking the dawn of a new era in the country's attitude towards America. Defence measures against the white armies and foreign contingents as well as Vladimir I. Lenin's reforms aiming to revive production, and the ensuing electrification and industrialization programmes, made use of various elements of a paradoxically flourishing Amerikanizm.

Trotsky, Bukharin, and Kollontai in New York City

Several Russian revolutionaries travelled to the United States for prolonged stays at the end of the war, and this first-hand experience of America informed these leaders' ideals. Following Anatolii Lunacharsky, ultimately appointed People's Commissar for Education, Aleksandra Kollontai, who had a long string of responsibilities after 1917, toured the United States between September 1915 and the beginning of 1917 with a series of 123 lectures. She visited San Francisco and Los Angeles, gazing at the passing deserts from train windows, and later admitting to having "fallen in love" with those views[2]. She served as Lenin's special envoy at the time, as he grew impatient, harbouring grand illusions of an imminent socialist revolution in the United States[3]. She stayed there a second time between September 1916 and February 1917. Kollontai's general attitude towards America was critical, though her remarks about New York City were positive, similar to Maxim Gorky's first impressions. She recognized the city's "majestic beauty," describing its outlines, "the huge, twisting, relentlessly upward-thrusting lines of the New York skyscrapers,"[4] but lamented the fate of the poor statue of Liberty: "so tiny, lost in the noise of the harbour and framed against the soaring skyscrapers of the Wall Street banks. Was this powerless, tiny figure shrinking before the all-powerful gigantic skyscrapers, those guardians of financial deals, the Statue of Liberty we had pictured to ourselves?"[5]

Kollontai recounted her travels in an article published by the German daily *New-Yorker Volkszeitung*, "above all, to answer the question of what we, socialists, can learn from America—the country of trust kings and of the most advanced form of capitalist economy."[6] America served as a backdrop to her 1922 novel *Vasilisa Malygina*, in which Vladimir, the main character's love interest, has held multiple jobs in the United States. Nicknamed "the American," Vladimir, whose anarchist beliefs cause him some trouble, paints a rather positive portrait of businessmen, while remaining critical towards bourgeois women, specifically the customers of the department store where he had been employed. He celebrates the daily life of workers, enviable in the eyes of Russian readers, "with their pianos, their Ford motor-cars and motor-cycles."[7]

In New York, Kollontai crossed paths with Leon Trotsky, who would go on to establish the Red Army. He stayed in the city from January to March 1917, taking part in the publication of *Novy Mir* [The New World], a paper for socialist emigrés[8]. As evidenced by his memoirs, Trotsky did not experience the same nauseating feeling at the sight of Manhattan as Gorky had: "Here I was in New York, city of prose and fantasy, of capitalist automatism, its streets a triumph of Cubism; its moral philosophy that of the dollar. New York impressed me tremendously because, more than any other city in the world, it is the fullest expression of our modern age.[9]" Later, he even seemed to regret the shortness of his stay, abruptly interrupted by his sudden return to Petrograd in the aftermath of the February 1917 Revolution: "The Russian Revolution came so soon that I only managed to catch the general life rhythm of the monster known as New York." He lamented having only caught a "peep" of "the foundry in which the fate of man is to be forged."[10] Interestingly, the American press basked in the illusion that, thanks to Trotsky, "Russia [would] be a republic built on the lines of the great American republic."[11]

Nikolai Bukharin, the "darling child" of the party, as Lenin called him, reached the banks of the Hudson River in November 1916, preceding both of his compatriots and later working with Trotsky at *Novy Mir*. In daily contact with local activists, the two revolutionaries engaged in a major controversy on the future of the American socialist movement. According to his biographer Stephen Cohen, Bukharin did not hide his "abiding respect for American technological and scientific achievements."[12] His 1922 political programme thus combined the "reform of human psychology" and the "merging of Marxist theory with American practicality and business know-how."[13] Bukharin often referred to American culture in his musings on politics and, as he begged Stalin to spare him while awaiting the verdict of his 1937 trial, he asked to be sent to New York to spread propaganda[14]. Along with these three leaders, thousands of Russians living in exile in New York City returned to their homeland in 1917. Many of them would come to occupy important positions in the new government structure, as the *New York World* was prompt to point out in August of that year[15].

Taylorism Before and After the Revolution

Business administration was one of the areas where the new Russian state was most overtly inclined to forge constructive ties with the American industrial sector, thus remaining relatively consistent with the discourse prevailing in the years leading up to the war. The rise of Russian capitalism had then been characterized by a great openness towards novel methods of production and

2   Aleksandra Kollontai, "Iz amerikanskogo dnevnika 1915-1916 gg. ," in *Iz moei zhizni i raboty: vospominania i dnevniki*, Moscou, Izd-vo Sovetskaia Rossiia, 1974, 210-211. Cathy Porter, *Alexandra Kollontai. The Lonely Struggle of the Woman Who Defied Lenin*, (New York: The Dial Press, 1980), 227–34.
3   Beatrice Farnsworth, *Aleksandra Kollontai: Socialism, Feminism and the Bolshevik Revolution* (Stanford, Stanford University Press, 1980), 59.
4   Aleksandra Kollontai, "Iz amerikanskogo dnevnika 1915–1916 gg.," 225.
5   Alexandra Kollontai, "Statuia Svobody," *Inostrannaia literatura*, no. 2 (1970): 244; in English: "The Statue of Liberty," in *Selected Articles and Speeches* (New York: International Publishers, 1984), 113.
6   Aleksandra Kollontai, "Moia agitatsionnaia poezdka po Soedinnennym Shtatam," March 1916, in *Iz moei zhizni i raboty*, 230.
7   Aleksandra Kollontai, *Vasilisa Malygina* [1922] (Moscow: Gos. Izd-vo, 1927); in English: *Love of Worker Bees*, trans. Cathy Porter (Chicago: Cassandra Editions, 1978), 31, 34–35, 44–45, 74.
8   Ian D. Thatcher, "Leon Trotsky in New York City," *Historical Research* 69, no. 169 (June 1996): 166–80; Kenneth D. Ackerman, *Trotsky in New York, 1917: Portrait of a Radical on the Eve of Revolution* (Berkeley, CA: Counterpoint, 2017).
9   Leon Trotsky, *My Life; The Rise and Fall of a Dictator* (London: Thornton Butterworth, 1930), 268.
10   Ibid., 278.
11   *New York American*, 9 November 1917, quoted in Ackerman, *Trotsky in New York*, 287.
12   Stephen F. Cohen, *Bukharin and the Bolshevik Revolution: a Political Biography, 1888–1938* (New York: Oxford University Press, 1971), 43.
13   Nikolai Bukharin, *Pravda*, 11 October 1922, quoted in Kendall E. Bailes, "Alexei Gastev and the Soviet Controversy over Taylorism, 1818–1924," *Soviet Studies*, no. 3 (July 1977), 387.
14   Nikolai Bukharin, Letter to Joseph Stalin, 12 October 1937, in Edvard Radzinsky, *Stalin: The First In-Depth Biography Based on Explosive New Documents from Russia's Secret Archives* (New York: Doubleday, 1997), 380.
15   Arno Dosch-Fleurot, "Russians from US Leading Lenin Radicals," *New York World*, 25 August 1917, quoted in Ackerman, *Trotsky in New York*, 288.

governance developed in Western Europe and in the United States. The most
successful approach was scientific management, devised in Pennsylvania in the
1890s by the steel industry engineer Frederick Winslow Taylor, and promptly
embraced in Western Europe[16].

Russia welcomed Taylor's ideas a few years before they spread to
Germany and France, implementing them in eight factories by 1914[17]. Taylor's
1906 treatise on metal cutting, a method that allowed to streamline the Beth-
lehem Steel workshops, cemented his reputation, and consolidated his fortune, was published in Saint Petersburg in 1909[18]. The proponents of Taylorism
in Russia were Aleksandr Pankin, a professor at the Artillery Academy of Saint
Petersburg and an expert on metal cutting involved in the Polytechnic Institute, and L. A. Levenshtern, a mining engineer and a publisher. In 1909, they
printed a translation of Taylor's "A Piece Rate System, Being a Step Toward
Partial Solution of the Labor Problem" (1896),[19] followed in 1912 by the article
"Shop Management" (1903).[20] As for Taylor's main work, *Principles of Scientific Management*, the Russian edition was issued in 1912, a year after its initial
publication. The near immediacy of these translations demonstrates the great
level of interest for this bestselling author, whose writings were also propagated by reglonal publishers[21].

The basic principles of Taylorism applied to both a specific reality and
a very broad one. The method, which Taylor presented as universal, involved a
double division of labour that dissected the working process into fragmented
and juxtaposed tasks, and separating conception from execution. Each position was defined according to the decomposition of successive operations into
simple segments, whose sequence, once measured with a chronometer, was

rigorously enforced. Applied to brick or concrete construction as well as to office work, Taylorism was also used to manage social relationships beyond the workplace[22].

Taylor's propositions stemmed from the systematic management already practised in the United States to streamline staff functions, but went beyond this purpose, as they prompted a complete overhaul of companies' structures by instilling in them a new frame of mind[23]. His ideas were combined with past administrative techniques and doctrines, adapted and reprised during his lifetime, namely in the research led by Frank and Lillian Gilbreth in the realm of ergonomy. Taylor devised his own public relations strategies to popularize his discoveries and made a deliberate effort to extend them to various markets, through press, publishing, and ad hoc professional organizations such as the Taylor Society, created in 1911. This strategy explains his method's extraordinary outreach in all of Europe, including Russia, in the years leading up to the First World War.

In Russia, original American publications were disseminated along with a great deal of commentary and tales of personal experience. Among the many areas where Taylorism could be enforced, Russians were particularly focused on workspace organization[24]. Their interest went beyond Taylor's contributions, extending to several other engineers and technologists applying his methods. All were members of the Taylor Society, like Henry Gantt, who had met the father of the doctrine in the Pennsylvania steel mills. Starting in the 1890s, he had worked to arrange the workflow and scheduling into clear graphic tables. His writings were made available in Russian in 1913[25]. As of 1910, one of Gantt's associates was the engineer Walter Polakov, who had emigrated from Russia in 1908. An active member of the American Locomotive Company, he attempted to reconcile his socialist beliefs with the teachings of Taylorism. He created his

16   On the consolidation and spread of Russian Taylorism, see Angelika Ebbinghaus, "Taylor in Russland," Autonomie. Materialen gegen die Fabrikgesellschaft 1 (1975): 3–15; Melanie Tatur, "Wissenschaftliche Arbeitsorganisation, zur Rezeption des Taylorismus in der Sowjetunion," Jahrbücher für Geschichte Osteuropas, no. 25 (1977): 34–51; Judith A. Merkle, Management and Ideology, the Legacy of the International Scientific Management Movement (Berkeley: University of California Press, 1980), 103–35; Richard Stites, Revolutionary Dreams: Utopian Vision and Experimental Life in the Russian Revolution (New York: Oxford University Press, 1989), 145–64.

17   Aleksei K. Gastev, "2–ia konferentsia po NOT i TsIT v Moskve," Organizatsia truda, no. 3–4 (1924): 33, quoted in Ulf Brunnbauer, "The League of Time (Liga Vremia): Problems of Making a Soviet Working Class in the 1920s," Russian History 27, no. 4 (2000): 475. On Taylor's initial receptions, see Anton L. Dmitriev, Andrei A. Semenov, "Pervye shagi amerikanskoi sistemy nauchnogo manadzhmenta v dorevoliutsionnoi Rossi," Vestnik Sankt-Peterburgskovo Universiteta, series 8 (Saint Petersburg, 2012).

18   Frederick W. Taylor, Iskusstvo rezat metally (Saint Petersburg: L.A. Levenshtern, 1909); originally "On the Art of Cutting Metals," Transactions of the American Society of Mechanical Engineers 28 (1906): 31–350.

19   Frederick W. Taylor, Usovershenstvovannaia sistema sdelnoi platy (Saint Petersburg: L.A. Levenshtern, 1914); originally "A Piece Rate System: Being a Step Toward Partial Solution of the Labor Problem," Economic Studies 1, no. 2 (June 1896): 88–129.

20   Frederick W. Taylor, Administratvno-tekhnicheskaia organizatsia promyshlennykh predpriatii (Saint Petersburg: L.A. Levenshtern, 1912), trans. and ed. by A.V. Pankin and L.A. Levenshtern, republished in 1916 and 1918; originally, "Shop Management," Transactions of the American Society of Mechanical Engineers 24 (1903): 1337–480.

21   Frederick W. Taylor, Nauchnye osnovy organizatsii promyshlennykh predpriatii (Saint Petersburg: L.A. Levenshtern, 1912); originally Principles of Scientific Management (New York: Harper, 1911); Pochemu zavodchiki ne liubiat tolko chto okonchivshikh inzhenerov? (Kharkov: Tip. i lit. M. Zilberberga i s-via, 1910).

22   Maurice de Montmollin and Olivier Pastré, Le Taylorisme (Paris: La Découverte, 1984).

23   David A. Hounshell, From the American System to Mass Production: The Development of Manufacturing Technology in the United States (Baltimore: Johns Hopkins University Press, 1984).

24   V. P. Salamatin, Nauchnoe rukovodstvo rabotami; ocherk sistemy F. Teilora (Moscow: Kruzhok tekhnologov Moskovsk. r-na, 1912).

25   Henry L. Gantt, Sovremennye sistemy zarabotnoi platy i podbor rabochikh v sviazi s dokhodnostiu predpriatii (Saint Petersburg: L.A. Levenshtern, 1913), trans. and ed. by A.V. Pankin and L.A. Levenshtern; originally The Compensation of Workmen: A Lecture Delivered Before the Harvard Graduate School of Business Administration, December 15, 1910 (Cambridge, MA: Harvard University, 1910).

own consulting firm and, as discussed further, was hired for the first five-year plan as part of Stalin's industrial policy[26].

The most popular experiments inspired by Taylor's doctrine were those conducted by Frank Bunker Gilbreth and his wife Lillian Moller Gilbreth, who were less concerned with the time spent completing a task and more with the executed movements, studied with ingenious equipment. The main tool they used was the chronocyclegraph, which Gilbreth proudly introduced to Taylor[27]. By means of an electric lightbulb attached to the hand of the worker, the device filmed the trajectory of each of his or her gestures in the darkness, with the aim of analyzing it and enhancing its efficiency [ill. p. 106]. The first investigation describing the mechanism, *Motion Study: A Method for Increasing the Efficiency of the Workman*, published in 1911, was translated into Russian two years later by A.V. Pankin and L.A. Levenshtern[28] [ill. p. 107]. But this transition from *time study* to *motion study* displeased the founder of the doctrine, casting a shadow on Gilbreth and Taylor's relationship, which remained strained until the latter's death.

The rise of Taylorism did not go unnoticed among the social democrats. Aleksandr Bogdanov was a member of the populist group *Vpered* (Forward) along with Maxim Gorky and Anatolii Lunacharsky. In 1909, he was expelled from the Bolshevik Party, which he had cofounded. He described the impact of the American doctrine in 1913: "Taylor, an American engineer, a scientist, and a talented inventor, has created a new machine, although using an old, but original, method. This machine is the worker, but reconfigured according to Taylor's 'scientific' system." Bogdanov's analysis was nuanced: "Taylor's system is a complex thing. It combines various elements, some good and some bad, meaning some useful and others detrimental to the development of society. We must identify them and distinguish clearly between the latter and the former."[29] A medical doctor turned philosopher, with an enduring interest for physiology, Bogdanov noted that the perpetual replication of identical tasks could lead to the deterioration of the worker's senses. He was also

26   Daniel Wren, "Scientific Management in the U.S.S.R., with Particular Reference to the Contribution of Walter N. Polakov," *The Academy of Management Review* 5, no. 1 (1980): 1–11; Diana J. Kelly, *The Red Taylorist: The Life and Times of Walter Nicholas Polakov* (Bingley (UK): Emerald Press, 2020).

27   Frank B. Gilbreth, Letters to Frederick W. Taylor, 6 February 1908 and 3 April 1913 (Taylor Collection, Stevens Institute of Technology, Hoboken, NJ), quoted in Hugo J. Kijne, "Time and Motion Study: Beyond the Taylor–Gilbreth controversy," in J.-C. Spender and Hugo J. Kijne, eds, *Scientific Management: Frederick Winslow Taylor's Gift to the World?* (Boston, Dordrecht: Kluwer Academic Publishing, 1996), 68.

28   Frank B. Gilbreth, *Izuchenie dvizhenii kak sposob povychit proizvoditelnost pri vsiakoi rabote* (Saint Petersburg: L.A. Levenshtern, 1913), translated and published by A.V. Pankin and L.A. Levenshtern; originally, *Motion Study: A Method for Increasing the Efficiency of the Workman* (New York: D. Van Nostrand, 1911).

29   Aleksandr A. Bogdanov, *Mezhdu chelovekom i mashinoi; o sisteme Teilora* (Moscow: Izd. Volna, 1918[1916]), 6 and 9.

30   Zenovia A. Sochor, *Revolution and Culture: the Bogdanov-Lenin Controversy* (Ithaca: Cornell University Press, 1988).

31   On Taylorism in the USSR, see the early analyses of Robert Linhart, *Lénine, les paysans, Taylor* (Paris: Seuil, 1976); Jean Querzola, "Le chef d'orchestre à la main de fer: Léninisme et Taylorisme," in *Le Soldat du Travail* (Paris: Recherche, 1976), 57–94.

32   Vladimir I. Lenin, "A 'Scientific' System of Sweating", *Pravda*, 13 March 1913; in *Collected Works* (Moscow, Foreign Languages Publishing House, 1958), vol. 18, 594-595.

33   M. M. [Vladimir I. Lenin], "The Taylor System—Man's Enslavement by the Machine;" *Put Pravdy*, no. 35 (March 13, 1914); in *Collected Works* (Moscow, Foreign Language Publishing House, 1964), vol. 20, 154.

34   Lenin, "The Taylor System," 154.

35   Vladimir I. Lenin, in *Leninskii sbornik* (Moscow: Partiinoe Izd-vo, 1933), vol. 2, 226, quoted in Merkle, *Management and Ideology*, 103.

36   Vladimir I. Lenin, Notebook ß, in *Polnoe sobranie sochinenii* (Moscow: Gospolitizdat, 1962), vol. 28, 126–32; in English: *Collected Works*, vol. 39, 152-9.

37   Izrail M. Besprozvannyi, *Rasplanirovochnoe biuro v nebolshom zavodskom predpriatii organizovannom po sisteme Teilora* (Nizhnii Novgorod: Tipo-lit. t-va I. M. Masistova, 1915); id., *Sovremennaia organizatsiia amerikanskikh zavodov (sistema Teilora)* (Moscow: Tipo-lit. t-va petchatnogo i izd. dela v. M., 1919).

concerned with the threat of a divide among the working class, between those promoted by the system and those left behind. He was especially worried about the potential inordinate growth of the engineering and executive workforce, which would lead to a drop in overall productivity.

While he opposed Bogdanov's philosophical theses in *Materialism and Empirio-Criticism*,[30] Lenin was even more critical of Taylorism and engaged in the first of a long series of considerations on labour organization[31]. In a 1913 *Pravda* article, Lenin denounced what he called "a 'scientific' system to pressure the worker." He drew on a presentation made at the Saint Petersburg Institute of Railway Engineers to describe a method aiming to "squeeze out of the worker three times more labour during a working day of the same length as before. The sturdiest and most skilful worker is put to work; a special clock registers—in seconds and fractions of a second—the amount of time spent on each operation and each motion; the most economical and most efficient working methods are developed; the work of the best worker is recorded on cinematographic film, etc." The result is that "within the same nine or ten working hours as before," capitalists "squeeze out of the worker three times more labour, mercilessly drain him of all his strength, and are three times faster in sucking out every drop of the wage slave's nervous and physical energy." He concluded that this was the equivalent of "sweating in strict accordance with all the precepts of science."[32]

Barely a year later, in "The Taylor system—Man's Enslavement by the Machine," a more thorough analysis published in *The Path of Truth*, his perspective had changed. Lenin was now interested in the Gilbreth chronocyclegraph, describing it in the following way: "an electric lamp was attached to a worker's arm, the worker's movements were photographed, and the movements of the lamp studied. Certain movements were found to be 'superfluous' and the worker was made to avoid them, i.e., to work more intensively, without losing a second for rest. The layout of new factory buildings is planned in such a way that not a moment will be lost in delivering materials to the factory, in conveying them from one shop to another, and in dispatching the finished products. The cinema is systematically employed for studying the work of the best operatives and increasing its intensity, i.e., 'speeding up' the workers."[33] Lenin began distinguishing what pertained to labour enhancement as opposed to capitalist exploitation, and identified methods that a working-class power could assimilate: "The Taylor system—without its initiators knowing or wishing it—is preparing the time when the proletariat will take over all social production and appoint its own workers' committees for the purpose of properly distributing and rationalizing all social labour. Large-scale production, machinery, railways, telephone—all provide thousands of opportunities to cut by three fourths the working time of the organized workers and make them four times better off than they are today."[34] During the war, Lenin carefully read Gilbreth's *Motion Study*, leaving a margin note in his copy in 1915: "An excellent example of technical progress under capitalism towards socialism."[35] He compiled long quotations from Taylor in his notebooks the following year, interested in all the measures that could help speed production and increase staffing in charge of establishing working norms[36].

After 1914, as was the case in all warring countries, the dissemination of Taylor's ideas and its concrete implementation accelerated in Russia, providing Lenin with the opportunity to apply the theories[37]. Even before the end of the Russian Civil War, he was strongly committed to forming direct relations with American industrialists and importing their equipment and technologies,

preferring them to those of any other nation[38]. His expectations were laid out in a patently clear equation: "Soviet power + the structure of Prussian railways + the techniques and organization of American trusts + American public education, etc., etc. = Socialism."[39] The "organization" Lenin alluded to was essentially the implementation of the scientific management doctrine. A few weeks following the October 1917 Revolution, speaking of the "immediate tasks of the Soviet government," Lenin stressed the urgent need to rely on Taylorism, no matter the price to pay, mentioning its capitalist origins only in passing: "The Taylor system [...] is a combination of the refined brutality of bourgeois exploitation and a number of the greatest scientific achievements in the field of analysing mechanical motions during work, the elimination of superfluous and awkward motions, the elaboration of correct methods of work, the introduction of the best system of accounting and control, etc. The Soviet Republic must at

38   John Lewis Gaddis, *Russia, the Soviet Union and the United States: An Interpretive History* (New York: McGraw-Hill, 1978), 57–85.

39   Vladimir I. Lenin, "Plany stati 'Ocherednye zadachi sovetskoi vlasti'," *Polnoe sobranie sochinenii* (Moscow: Gospolitizdat, 1962), vol. 36, 550.

40   Lenin, "Ocherednye zadachi sovetskoi vlasti," in *Polnoe sobranie sochinenii* (Moscow: Gospolitizdat, 1962), vol. 36, 189-90; in English: "The Immediate Tasks of the Soviet Government," in *Collected Works* (Moscow: Foreign Languages Publishing House, 1965), vol. 27, 259.

41   Lenin, "Vystuplenie na zasedanii prezidiuma VSNKh 1 aprelia 1918 g." in *Polnoe sobranie sochinenii*, vol. 36, 213; in English: "Speech at a meeting of the Presidium of the S.E.C., 1st April 1918," in *Collected Works* (1969), vol. 42, 213.

42   Vladimir I. Lenin, Letter to Joseph Stalin, 24 May 1922, in Vladimir I. Lenin, *Lenin on the United States: Selected Writings* (New York: International Publishers, 1970), 586.

all costs adopt all that is valuable in the achievements of science and technology in this field. The possibility of building socialism depends exactly upon our success in combining the Soviet power and the Soviet organization of administration with the up-to-date achievements of capitalism. We must organise in Russia the study and teaching of the Taylor system and systematically try it out and adapt it to our own ends."[40]

In the precarious political and economic context of April 1918, in preparation for the decree on workers' control, Lenin issued absolutely unambiguous guidelines: "The decree should definitely provide for the introduction of the Taylor system, in other words, every use should be made of the scientific methods of work suggested by this system." Furthermore, he added that "in the application of this system, American engineers are to be enlisted"[41]. As he wrote to Stalin in 1922, Lenin sought in all matters, after the end of the civil war, at least a "small path leading to the American business world," which to him was embodied by Armand Hammer and a handful of his fellow countrymen[42]. He scrupulously followed the progress of the American political and social situation by perusing all the publications available to him. But as he told the painter Iurii Annenkov while posing for an official portrait, his perspective was more cynical than friendly: "the slogan 'catch up with and surpass America' must not be understood literally: any optimism should stay within reasonable limits. Catching up with America and surpassing it mostly means that we must corrupt, dismantle, and destroy its political and economic balance as quickly as possible, undermine it until its strength and drive for resistance crumble to

Frank B. Gilbreth, *Motion Study: A Method for Increasing the Efficiency of the Workman* [1911],
Saint Petersburg: L. A. Levenshtern, 1913. Purdue University Libraries, Frank and Lillian Gilbreth Papers.

pieces. It is only then that we might hope to 'catch up to and surpass' the United States and their civilization."[43]

Lenin was not the only Bolshevik leader to insist on the importance of Taylorism for the post-revolutionary economy. All high-ranking party members were unanimous on this issue. Trotsky focused on introducing its methods in railway workshops to achieve a form of militarization of production. In 1920, he drew his discourse on the theme from Lenin's rhetoric: "All of the characteristics of militarism line up with what we call Taylorism. What is Taylorism? On one hand, it is the most sophisticated form of exploitation of the workforce, as well as the most brutal, in that each gesture, each breath is compiled and observed by capitalist tormentors, with the aim of converting them into profits. But on the other hand, it is a system allowing a discerning expense of the human force participating in production. [...] Socialist leaders must espouse this side of Taylorism, and by examining militarism, they will find that it has always been very close to Taylorism."[44] Trotsky broadened his position in 1924, stating: "We lack the technique of the Americans and their labour proficiency. [...] To have Bolshevism shod in the American way, there is our task!"[45] The founder of the Red Army hoped to see the rise of a Bolshevik "superman." He quipped in a striking slogan that "Americanized Bolshevism will crush and conquer imperialist Americanism," but showed only disdain for American politicians, such as Woodrow Wilson[46].

In the right wing of the party, Bukharin, Trotsky's former companion in New York exile, prophesied, in a 1923 speech delivered in Petrograd that "Soviet Russia, once on its feet, will become a new America, not in the bourgeois sense, but in the proletarian sense."[47] According to him, a framework was needed, with leaders possessing "psychological traits similar to that of the old Russian intelligentsia, knowledgeable about Marxism, far-sighted, and able to analyze facts from a theoretical standpoint, but combined with the practical steadfastness of Americans." He stated, yet more clearly, criticizing the Bolshevik's inability to grasp material issues: "What we need is Marxism as well as Americanism."[48]

Vladimir Lenin died in January 1924, and Joseph Stalin, who was then the General Secretary of the Party, wasted no time before writing, in *The Foundations of Leninism*, that "American efficiency is that indomitable force

43   Iurii Annenkov, *Dnevnik moikh vstrech, tsikl tragedii* (Moscow: Khudozhestvennaia literature, 1991), vol. 2, 270.
44   Leon Trotsky, "Osnovnye zadachi i trudnosti khoziaistvennogo stroitelstva," 6 January 1920,
      in *Sochinenia* (Moscow: Gos. Iz-vo, 1927), vol. 15, p. 92. See also Leon Trotsky, "Nauchno–tekhnitcheskaia
      mysl i sotsialisticheskoe khoziaistvo," *Izvestiia* (2 June 1925).
45   Leon Trotsky, « K voprosu o perspektivakh mirovogo razvitiia », *Pravda*, 5 August 1924, 3-4;
      in English: "Perspectives of World Development," in *Europe & America*, transl. by John G. Wright
      (Colombo, Lanka Sama Samaja, 1951), 35; reprinted from *Fourth International* 6, no. 8 (August 1945).
46   Ibid.
47   Nikolai Bukharin, *Proletarskaia Revoliutsia i kultura*, (Petrograd: Priboi, 1923), 16.
48   Ibid., 48 and 49.
49   Joseph Stalin, "Ob osnovakh leninizma" [1924], in *Sochineniia* (Moscow: OGIZ, 1947), 188; in English:
      The Foundations of Leninism (New York: International Publishers, 1939), 126.
50   René Fülöp-Miller, *Geist und Gesicht des Bolchewismus, Darstellung und Kritik des kulturellen Lebens in
      Sowjet-Rußland* (Zurich: Amalthea-Verlag, 1926), 30; in English: *The Mind and Face of Bolshevism:
      An Examination of Cultural Life in Soviet Russia* (New York: G. P. Putnam's Sons, 1927), 22.
51   Carol Willcox Melton, *Between War and Peace: Woodrow Wilson and the American Expeditionary Force in
      Siberia, 1918-1920* (Durham, NC: Duke University Press, 1991).
52   *Making Things Work: Russian-American Economic Relations, 1900-1930* (Stanford: Hoover Institution
      Press, 1992), 67-76; Jacqueline D. St. John, "John F. Stevens: American Assistance to Russian and Siberian
      Railroads, 1917-1922," PhD dissertation (Norman: University of Oklahoma, 1969). Georges H. Emerson's
      archives include photographs of train stations and bridges damaged in the fighting, as well as correspon-
      dence with Stevens (Hoover Institution Library & Archives, 58003-9.17, box 1).
53   Charles H. Smith, "Four Years of Mistakes in Siberia," *Asia* 22 (1922): 481.
54   Herbert G. Wells, *Russia in the Shadows* (New York: George H. Doran, 1921), 178.

which neither knows nor recognizes obstacles; which with its businesslike perseverance brushes aside all obstacles; which continues at a task once started until it is finished, even if it is a minor task; and without which serious constructive work is inconceivable." To him, therefore, "the combination of Russian revolutionary sweep with American efficiency is the essence of Leninism in Party and State work."[49]

From that point forward, it seemed that the Russian revolutionary intelligentsia had looked away from Germany and France to try to build the new America Aleksandr Blok had foreseen. The Austrian journalist René Fülöp-Miller took note of this passion in his best-selling 1926 essay *The Mind and Face of Bolshevism*: "[I]ndustrialized America became the Promised Land. At an earlier period, the 'intelligentsia' still looked for their models in Europe, but, immediately after the Revolution, a wild enthusiasm for America started; the magnificent industrial works of Germany and the highly perfected plants of France and England, all at once appeared paltry to Soviet Russia, they began to dream of Chicago and to direct their efforts towards making Russia a new and more splendid America."[50]

Humanitarian Aid and Concessions: Towards the Electrification of the USSR

These musings were complemented by an authentic American presence. Since the February 1917 Revolution, President Wilson had become interested in Russian finances and infrastructure, sending the ex-Secretary of State Elihu Root to Petrograd to discuss the former, and creating a Commission of Railway Experts to Russia to manage the latter[51]. Led by John F. Stevens, who had recently overseen the construction of the Panama Canal, the Commission re-established efficient circulation on the Trans-Siberian Railway, the only connection for the delivery of American products from East to West. As of December, the three hundred engineers of the Russian Railway Service Corps, under the helm of Colonel George H. Emerson, repaired the line and its ancillary facilities[52]. Charles H. Smith, initially commissioned by the Allies to manage the Trans-Siberian Railway, continued his work under the new government, fighting both the Japanese and the White armies of Admiral Alexander Kolchak. He became an outspoken advocate for the preservation of economic relations between the United States and Russia in order to enable the development of Siberia. In 1922, he wrote that after "four years of mistakes," the state of the region was deplorable because "we had mushroom governments and military governments in Siberia, and not harvesting machines, binder twine, locomotives, rakes and hoes."[53]

During the Russian Civil War, which was waged from April 1918 to November 1920, many American specialists worked in Russia. Some were motivated by humanitarian concerns, others by political sympathies, some simply by a keen flair for business. Even though diplomatic relations were severed on 15 December 1917, and despite America's siding with the White armies during the civil war, a continuity soon became apparent, as American finances paradoxically helped the Bolsheviks. Upon his return from Moscow in 1920, the novelist H. G. Wells wrote that "the only power capable of playing this role of eleventh-hour helper to Russia single-handed is the United States of America."[54] As for humanitarian efforts, the American Red Cross passed on its operations to the American Relief Administration (ARA), thanks to the personal intercession of Herbert C. Hoover, the former director of the US Food Administration during the war, who responded to Maxim Gorky's call for help[55]. The ARA, led in Russia by Colonel William N. Haskell, was active as of 1921 in the struggle against the famine that raged in the aftermath of the civil war. By deploying its officials, the ARA succeeded in feeding 10 million Russians daily, in addition to disseminating American scholarly writings[56]. Significant assistance programmes were also put in place by philanthropic organizations related to the Rockefellers, who devoted substantial resources to the cause between 1922 and 1927. As Susan Gross-Solomon and Nikolai Krementsov have shown by examining the Rockefeller Foundation's archives, these organizations were at first responding to cries for help on behalf of several groups of emigrants, but later decided to intervene directly in Russia, despite the termination of diplomatic relations between the two countries.

While Germany remained their primary Western partner in the research sector, the Russians resumed issuing missions abroad in 1923, following the initiative of the People's Commissariats for Health and Education and by the Academy of Sciences. Although the International Health Division refused to support the creation of a social pathology clinic or any other programme, the Rockefeller Foundation started sending scientific literature to Moscow in 1922. As for the International Education Board, it offered scholarships to Russian researchers, emigrants, and those who had remained in the USSR, until 1927. The Laura Spelman Rockefeller Memorial established food aid programmes for Soviet educators and students, while the Medical Education Division sent over scientific publications in English. In 1927, Alan Gregg, an agent for the International Health Division who travelled to Moscow and Leningrad to study the state of medicine, promoted increased support for Soviet laboratories, while Rockefeller representatives, on location, negotiated their technical assistance to oil extraction in Baku. This policy remained in force until Stalin cut off incoming international aid in 1933. One of the strongest proponents of using "bourgeois money" was Olga Kameneva, president of VOKS, the society for cultural relations with foreign countries, who was also Trotsky's sister[57].

In the industrial sector, the Bolshevik policy concerning foreign concessions, devised as of December 1917 but interrupted by the civil war, was effectively established in 1920, with arrangements ranging from limited agreements to the creation of joint societies[58]. Certain concessions were strategic, such as the one Lenin planned to offer directly to Washington B. Vanderlip, Jr., a financier and cousin of the banker Frank A. Vanderlip, to counter Japanese claims on the Kuril and Sakhalin islands and to warrant exploitation of their minerals and oil. Significant misunderstandings between Vanderlip and the Soviet government rendered the tactic unsuccessful[59]. The relationship between the Soviets and the industrialist Armand Hammer turned out quite differently.

55   Leo J. Bacino, Reconstructing Russia: U.S. Policy in Revolutionary Russia, 1917–1922 (Ashland, OH: Kent State University Press, 2013); Antony Sutton, Wall Street and the Bolshevik Revolution: the Remarkable True Story of the American Capitalists Who Financed the Russian Communists (Forest Row: Clairview, 2011).
56   Harold H. Fisher, The Famine in Soviet Russia 1919–1923: The Operations of the American Relief Administration (New York: Macmillan, 1927); J.D. Parks, Culture, Conflict and Coexistence: American–Soviet Cultural Relations, 1917–1958 (Jefferson, NC; London: McFarland, 1983), 16–17.
57   Susan Gross Solomon and Nikolai Krementsov, "Giving and Taking Across Borders: the Rockefeller Foundation and Russia, 1919–1928," Minerva 39, no. 3 (2001): 265–98.
58   Floyd James Fithian, Soviet–American Economic Relations, 1918–1933: American Business in Russia during the Period of Non–Recognition (Lincoln, NE: University of Nebraska, 1964).
59   Albert Parry, "Washington B. Vanderlip, the 'Khan of Kamchatka'," Pacific Historical Review 17, no. 3 (1948): 311–30.

During his brief stay in New York City before the Revolution, Trotsky lived in the Bronx next door to Julius Hammer, Armand's father and one of the founders of the American Communist Party. In 1921, Armand organized wheat shipments to Russia, before helping revive asbestos production in the Ural site of Alapaevsk, with his Amalgamated Drug and Chemical Corporation, the first concession granted by the new government to a Western operator[60].

In 1926, cunningly making use of his father's relationship with Lenin, Hammer junior opened a pencil factory in Moscow, employing 800 workers and giving his name to the products. Although the concession was revoked in 1930, generations of Russian schoolchildren would continue to use the term *Gammer*—with the Russian G instead of the Latin H—to refer to their pencils[61] [ill. p. 111]. Most significantly, Hammer created a network of relations that was destined to last for decades and was particularly effective in exporting works of art from Czarist collections[62]. William Averell Harriman, son of the railway mogul Edward Henry Harriman, obtained a concession to extract manganese, though he was unlikely to have shown any sympathy for the Bolsheviks. He returned to Moscow as an ambassador in 1943[63]. In total, some 150 companies were thus created in 1927 throughout the country, from major industrial projects to modest mills, from the most mercenary undertakings to the most idealist ventures[64].

Along with the industrialists, whether they harboured communist sympathies or not, thousands of American workers played a part in rebuilding and industrializing the nation. These were often "reimmigrants," among the 3 million Russians settled in the United States. Wells observed within these masses "flowing back from America and the West to rejoin their comrades a considerable number of keen and enthusiastic young and youngish men, who had in that more bracing Western world lost something of the habitual impracticability of the Russian and acquired a certain habit of getting things done." He noted that many among them were Jews who, according to him, were to become the "living force of Bolshevism."[65] The new government wished to recruit 100,000 overseas workers, but the actual turnout was more modest. In total, roughly 22,000 Americans and Canadians came to work in Russia before 1925, while almost half a million immigration requests were filed, mainly by Americans[66].

60   Philip S. Gillette, "Armand Hammer, Lenin, and the First American Concession in Soviet Russia," *Slavic Review* 40, no. 3 (Fall 1981): 355–65.

61   For more on the company, see for example *Economic Review of the Soviet Union*, 1 January 1928, 7; a statement published by Hammer in the *Economic Review of the Soviet Union*, 1 December 1928, 373–74; and "The Hammer Pencil and Stationary Company," *Economic Review of the Soviet Union*, 1 July 1929, 243.

62   Armand Hammer, *Quest of the Romanoff Treasure* (New York: William Farquhar Payson, 1932); Armand Hammer with Neil Lyndon, *Hammer* (New York: Putnam, 1988), 89–140.

63   William Appleman Williams, *American Russian Relations 1781-1947*, New York, Rinehart & Co, 1952, 212.

64   For more on this, see Antony Sutton, *Western Technology and Soviet Economic Development, 1917 to 1930* (Stanford: Hoover Institution Press, 1968), 4–11. For a Soviet perspective on the issue, see Vassili I. Kasianenko, *How Soviet Economy Won Technical Independence* (Moscow: Progress Publishers, 1966), 147–53.

65   Wells, *Russia in the Shadows*, 87–88.

66   Galina Ia. Tarle, *Druzia strany Sovetov* (Moscow: Nauka, 1968). See the biographies collected in Paula Garb, *They Came to Stay: North Americans in the USSR* (Moscow: Progress Publishers, 1987), 27. On idealization of the ongoing transformations in the USSR, see David C. Engerman, *Modernization from the Other Shore: American Intellectuals and the Romance of Russian Development* (Cambridge, MA: Harvard University Press, 2003).

67   Lewis H. Siegelbaum, *Cars for Comrades: The Life of the Soviet Automobile* (Ithaca, NY: Cornell University Press, 2011), 13–14.

68   Seth Bernstein and Robert Cherny, "Searching for the Soviet Dream: Prosperity and Disillusionment on the Soviet Seattle Agricultural Commune, 1922–1927." *Agricultural History* 88, no. 1 (2014): 22–44. Benjamin W. Sawyer, "Shedding the White and Blue: American Migration and Soviet Dreams in the Era of the New Economic Policy" *Ab Imperio*, no. 1, 2013, 65–84.

69   Joseph P. Morray, *Project Kuzbas: American Workers in Siberia (1921-1926)* (New York: International Publishers, 1983), 68–69.

70   Ibid., 19.

In Moscow and in Petrograd, the Amalgamated Workers of America union strived to establish a garment industry. The US-Canadian Society for Technical Assistance to the Soviet Union organized travel for some hundred mechanics who claimed to have worked in Detroit, as well as the shipment of equipment to relaunch automobile manufacturing at the Moscow AMO plant. They were led by Arthur A. Adams, who had returned from political exile and was a proponent of "American methods." He went back to the United States decades later as an agent of scientific espionage[67]. In 1922, brigades of American tractor drivers were deployed in the Don region by the Department of Industrial Immigration of the People's Commissariat of Commerce and Industry. These units had names such as "California," "Seattle," or "San Francisco," and brought together born-and-bred Americans as well as re-immigrants, who were quickly disappointed by the disarray of the 33 communes operating in 1925[68].

The most remarkable venture to employ American workers and engineers was pursued in the small Siberian town of Kemerovo, south of Tomsk. Two American revolutionary labourers, William (Big Bill) Haywood and Herbert S. Calvert, and the Dutch communist engineer Sebald Justinus Rutgers, a concrete specialist, established the Autonomous Industrial Colony Kuzbass (AIK), a near-symmetrical experiment to those of the Russians who had built utopian communes in the United States. After initiating preparation for their project in 1918, the three partners signed a contract in October 1921[69]. Lenin trusted Haywood, whom he had met in Copenhagen before the war[70].

Workers of the World, Unite!

KUZBAS

A Bulletin devoted to the Affairs of the Industrial Colony Kuzbas

| Vol. 1. No. 9 | January 20, 1923 ☞ New York, N. Y. | 5 Cents |

Out Among the Corn, Kemerovo. 54° North.

REPORT AND FINANCIAL BUDGET OF THE KUZBAS INDUSTRIES

Endorsed by the Council of Labor and Defense, December, 1922

The detailed information and general plans, as far as the coal mines and the Kemerovo chemical plant are concerned, will be found in the reports of Eng. Alfred Pearson (in No. 10) and Dr. Eng. W. H. Mahler in our next issue.

The most urgent need in Kemerovo to be considered is the completion of the housing program to such an extent that the present overcrowding will be relieved and so that the machine farm will be able to provide the more important food products for the American and Russian workers connected with the industries. (See Pearson's report on the farm.) Simul-taneously immediate action must be taken to finish the chemical plant in order to bring the first battery of fifty coke ovens and the corresponding productive apparatus for by-products into operation in the spring of 1923. For the next few years the chemical plant offers the best possibility for immediate financial returns and no time should be lost in placing this modern plant into operation. The money required is estimated at 150,000 gold roubles (the gold rouble is equivalent to 51½ cents), 40,000 of which are to be expended in America. For an estimate of the production after the completion of the first battery of ovens and the

Kuzbas, bulletin of the Kuzbas Autonomous Industrial Colony 1, No. 9, January 1923.
Library of the University of California, Davis.

113

In the United States, the AIK received support from Walter Polakov, an expert on the organization of labour sympathetic to the Soviet Regime [ill. p. 113].

Hundreds of Americans financed their own equipment and journey to Kemerovo, where they relaunched coal production in Kuzbas and created farms and factories to tackle "the task of Americanizing the industry" with the energy of New World pioneers. This led to outlandish incidents, as "the period of excitement, romance and adventure" wore out and was followed by "drudgery of reconstruction." Remembering this disheartening process, which delighted the American press, Ruth Epperson Kennell, the colony's librarian, wrote in *The Nation* that the goal was not to build "a new Atlantis, but rather a new Pennsylvania," as "Russia need[ed] American machinery with human machines to operate it."[71] In 1926, the leadership of the AIK, having failed to gather the 6,000 projected members, finally became productive after several setbacks. When it was claimed by the Soviets, the most engaged Americans, who had remained on-site, left the country[72].

The other sponsor of this colony was Ludwig Martens, a Bolshevik engineer and a friend of Lenin from the 1890s. As of 1912, he had worked for the New York-based engineering firm Weinberg & Posner, and took part in the publication of *Novyi Mir*, before returning to Russia at the same time as Trotsky, in March 1917. After crossing the Atlantic, this time from east to west, in 1919, Martens created the Russian Soviet Government Bureau, which was used for diplomatic purposes in lieu of an official embassy. Established at the heart of the business centre, in downtown Manhattan, instead of Washington D.C., the Bureau signed financial agreements and contracts with hundreds of American companies. Martens was expelled from the U.S. in 1921, after the anti-communist Lusk Committee, created by the State of New York in the midst of the "Red Scare," had searched the premises on 12 June 1919[73]. That same year, the Bureau launched the bi-monthly publication *Soviet Russia*, the first propaganda medium of Red Russia in the United States. The periodical survived the shutdown of the organization in 1921 and was taken over by the Friends of Soviet Russia. Upon his return to Moscow, Martens headed the Department of Industrial Immigration and was a strong supporter of the AIK.

71   Ruth Epperson Kennell, "Kuzbas: A New Pennsylvania," *The Nation* 116, no. 3017, 2 May 1923, 512.
72   See the perspectives collected in Vadim S. Golubtsov, "The Americans at Kuzbass, 1922–24: A Story of Internationalism," *New World Review* 39 (Fall 1971): 68–103. In the USSR, the story of the colony was recounted in "Rabota zarubezhnykh trudiashchikhsia v sovetskoi promyshlennosti (Avtonomnaia industrialnaia kolonia 'Kuzbass')," in Tarle, *Druzia strany Sovetov*, 287–347.
73   Todd J. Pfannestiel, *Rethinking the Red Scare: The Lusk Committee and New York's Crusade Against Radicalism, 1919–1923* (London: Routledge, 2003).
74   Sutton, *Western Technology*, vol. 1, 16–44.
75   Grigory M. Kovelman, *Tvorchestvo pochetnogo akademika inzhenera Vladimira Grigorevicha Shukhova* (Moscow: Gos. Izd-vo po stroitelstvu, arkhitekture i stroitelnykh materialov, 1961), 56–69.
76   Fithian, *Soviet–American Economic Relations, 1918–1933*, 1–39.
77   Alex K. Cummins, *The Road to NEP, The State Commission for the Electrification of Russia (GOELRO): A Study in Technology, Mobilization, and Economic Planning* (Ann Arbor, MI: UMI, 1994); Anne D. Rassweiler, *The Generation of Power: The History of Dneprostroi* (Oxford: Oxford University Press, 1988), 12–29.
78   Wells, *Russia in the Shadows*, 158–159.
79   "Ot redaktsii," *Elektrichestvo*, no. 7–8 (1917): 111, quoted in Jonathan Coopersmith, *The Electrification of Russia, 1880–1926* (Ithaca, NY: Cornell University Press, 1992), 124.
80   "Deiatelnost Soiuza elektrotekhnikov," *Elektrichestvo*, no. 3–4 (1918): 40–45, quoted in Coopersmith, *The Electrification of Russia*, 124.
81   The principal trade journal for electricians published Pankin's articles: Aleksandr Pankin, "Nauchnaia organizatsiia truda," *Elektrichestvo*, no. 10 et 11 (1910): 297–305 and 327–35.
82   Electrification pioneer Gleb Krzhizhanovskii worked on power plants based on American models: Coopersmith, *The Electrification of Russia*, 116–117.
83   Peter Rutland, *The Myth of the Plan: Lessons of Soviet Planning Experience* (London: Hutchinson, 1985); Eugène Zaleski, *Planning for Economic Growth in the Soviet Union, 1918-1932* [1962] (Chapel Hill, University of North Carolina Press, 1971).
84   Coopersmith, *The Electrification of Russia*, 162 and 170.
85   Ibid., 174–185.

Beyond utopian endeavours such as the Kuzbas colony, oil well production in Baku, which was essential for Russian economy and foreign trade, resumed in 1921 thanks to an agreement with the International Barnsdall Corporation. Using American technologies, drilling systems were modernized, pipelines were laid in the direction of the Black Sea, and refineries were built according to the cracking method developed by Vladimir Shukhov whose patent, issued in 1891, had remained unexploited before 1914[74]. After the Revolution, to sidestep the Burton patent practised by the Standard Oil Company, the Sinclair Oil Company sent a mission to Moscow to purchase Shukhov's patent, but he refused to sell it[75]. Coal and steel production were revamped with the help of the Chicago Freyn Engineering Company, whose engineers introduced wide-strip rolling mills, used by the firm in Gary, Indiana, to the USSR. As for transportation equipment, the Soviets delayed the nationalization of companies such as Westinghouse until they could replicate the technology by their own means[76].

Nationwide, the new economic policy launched by Lenin in 1921 revived the private sector and reinstated a market economy in agriculture. This was part of an initiative aiming to establish a socialized industry, whose linchpin was the State Plan for the Electrification of Russia. Also known as the GOELRO plan, it stemmed from the efforts of Bolshevik engineers working under Lenin. His old acquaintance from his years in exile, Gleb Krzhizhanovskii, was the most influential and committed among them[77]. Ever since his first writings on the rise of capitalism in Russia, Lenin focused on electrification as one of the essential components of the country's development. His passion for this issue was so deep that H. G. Wells wrote, after his legendary 1920 visit, that the "dreamer in the Kremlin [...] who like an orthodox Marxist denounces all 'Utopians,' has succumbed at last to a Utopia, the Utopia of the electricians."[78]

As reported by Jonathan Coopersmith, in the spring of 1917, these engineers had established the Union of Electrotechnicians to participate in the "great tasks of national economic reconstruction and growth" and to contribute to "raising the productivity of national labour."[79] Inspired by the German Verband Deutscher Elektrotechniker and by the American Institute of Electrical Engineers, the new organization, presided over by the engineer Petr Osadchii, strived to impose its vision and to influence all aspects of the energy policy[80]. Instrumental in the development of post-revolutionary planning, this association was also interested in innovative methods such as the scientific organization of work[81]. During the war, ambitions arose for a unified network for the production and distribution of electricity, generated either with hydropower or by peat-burning plants, citing the American example[82]. These initial considerations on electrification gave way to the idea of general planning under the Bolshevik regime[83].

The GOELRO plan, established as a result of these engineers' activism, aimed to electrify a country divided into disconnected territories, but also to determine concrete indicators for production and planning. The companies used American methods to calculate energy consumption and localization and, in a territorial projection of Taylorism, focused on streamlining and the concentration of resources[84]. The plan was approved during the 8th Congress of Soviets, in reference to the United States, although similar projects such as the Pennsylvania Giant Power and Superpower in the northeast were not launched there before the 1920s[85]. One of the first accomplishments was the hydroelectric plant located on the Volkhov River, which supplied Leningrad. In 1924, Petr Voevodin introduced it as a product of the New World: "Here you see the current America—noise, thunder—all, all America. In a word, there is not a Russian approach but an American tempo."[86] This statement was informed by personal experience, as Voevodin had lived in the United States in 1912 and 1913. In 1927, the plant was used as a backdrop for Semen Timoshenko's film *Pobediteli nochi* [The Conquerers of the Night], an "industrial drama" based on Fedor Gladkov's novel *Cement*.

86   Petr I. Voevodin, "Na Volkhovstroe," *Elektrifikatsia*, no. 2 (1924): 24, quoted in Coopersmith, *The Electrification of Russia*, 246–47.

87   *Trudy I-oi vserossiiskoi initsiativnoi konferentsii po nauchnoi organizatsii truda i proizvodstva*, Osip A. Ermanskii, ed. (Leningrad: Org. troika konf. po nauch. org. truda i pr–va, 1921).

88   Ivan I. Ianzhul and E.G. Liberman, *Chto tchitat po nauchnoi organizatsii truda* (Kharkov, Proletarii, 1925).

89   Frederick Winslow Taylor, *Nauchnaia organizatsia truda*, trans. A.I. Zak and B. Ia. M., foreword by Platon M. Kerzhentsev (Moscow: NKPS Transpechat, 1924), reissued in 1925; Frederick Winslow Taylor, *Teilor o Teilorizme* (Leningrad; Moscow: Tekhnika upravleniia, 1931).

90   Clarence B. Thompson, *Nauchnaia organizatsia proizvodstva; sistema Teilora* (Moscow: Izd–vo NKRKI, 1925); id., *Nauchnaia organizatsia proizvodstva, opyt Ameriki* (Petrograd: Petrogr. otd. Red.-izd–vo kollegii Narkomfina, 1920); translation of *Scientific Management: A Collection of the More Significant Articles Describing the Taylor System of Management* (Cambridge, MA: Harvard University Press, 1914).

91   Iosif L. Kan and Zakharii A. Papernov, *Amerikanskie ratsionalizatory; ocherki i etiudy*, (Moscow: Tekhnika upravlenia, 1928).

92   Franziska Baumgarten, *Arbeitswissenschaft und Psychotechnik in Rußland* (Munich; Berlin: R. Oldenbourg, 1924); and "Russland, Arbeiterwissenschaft," in Fritz Giese, ed., *Handbuch der Arbeitswissenschaft*, Halle a. S., Marhold, 1930, Sp. 3794.

93   Frank B. Gilbreth, *Azbuka nauchnoi organizatsii truda i predpriatii*, ed. R.S. Maizels, trans. E. G. Shteinberg (Moscow: Vsia Rossia, 1923); Frank B. Gilbreth, *Azbuka nauchnoi organizatsii truda*, trans. and preface by L. Shcheglo (Moscow: L.D. Frenkel, 1925). On the dissemination of Gilbreth's methods in Europe, see Ivan Rupnik, "Exporting Space-Time: American Industrial Engineering and European Modernism," in Eva Franch y Gilabert, Amanda Reeser Lawrence, Ana Miljački and Ashley Schafer, eds., *Office US Agenda* (Zurich: Lars Müller, 2014), 114–16.

94   Frank B. Gilbreth, *Sistema kladki kirpicha*, trans. B.V. Babin-Koren (Leningrad; Moscow: Tekhnika upravlenia, 1930); originally *Bricklaying System* (New York; Chicago: The M.C. Clark Pub. Co. 1909); *Izuchenie dvizheniia*, trans. I.F. Popov, 2nd edition (Leningrad; Moscow: Tekhnika Upravlenia, 1931); previously *Izuchenie dvizhenii* (Moscow: Knigoizd-vo tsentralnogo Instituta Truda, 1924); originally *Motion Study: A Method for Increasing the Efficiency of the Workman* (New York: D. Van Nostrand Co., 1921); Frank B. Gilbreth with Lillian Moller Gilbreth, *Prikladnoe izuchenie dvizhenii*, trans. and adapted by Arkadi A. Ialovoi (Moscow: Izd–vo VSPS); originally *Applied Motion Study* (New York: Macmillan, 1919); Lilian M. Gilbreth, *Psikhologiia upravleniia predpriatiami; znachenie psikhologii dlia vyrabotki metodov naimenshikh poter, dlia obucheniia im i dlia provedeniia ikh v zhizn*, trans. and preface by Ia. G. Abramson (Petrograd: Seatel, 1924).

95   Irene Witte, *Taylor, Gilbreth, Ford*, trans. L. V. Shcheglo (Leningrad: Vremia, 1925); originally: *Taylor. Gilbreth. Ford. Gegenwartsfragen der amerikanischen und europäischen Arbeitswissenschaft* (Munich; Berlin, R. Oldenbourg, 1925). On Witte, see Rita Pokorny, "Die Rationalisierungexpertin Irene Witte (1894-1976), Biographie einer Grenzgängerin," doctoral thesis, TU Berlin, 2003 and "Taylor - Gilbreth - Ford: aus der Sicht der Rationalisierungsexpertin Irene Witte," *Technikgeschichte* 70, no. 3 (2003): 153-83.

96   Osip Ermanskii, *Sistema Teilora: chto neset ona rabochemu klassu i vsemu chelovechestvu* (Petrograd; Moscow: Kniga, 1918); republished as *Nauchnaia organizatsiia truda i proizvodstva i sistema Teilora* (Moscow: Gos. izd., 1922); Vladimir I. Lenin, "A Fly on the Ointment," in *Lenin on the United States*, 513–14.

97   Aleksei K. Gastev, "Svidanie s Leninym," *Organizatsia truda*, no. 1 (March 1924): 11–13.

98   Ivan V. Rabchinskii, *O sisteme Teilora* (Moscow: Gos. tekhnicheskoe izd-vo, 1921). He also published *Promyshlennyi kapital i novaia shkola NOT v Amerike* (Moscow: Gos. tekhnicheskoe izd-vo, 1925). Sergei F. Glebov, *Teilor i ego raboty* (Moscow: Tsentralnyi Inst. Truda, 1922); Vasilii Sibarov, *O "nauchnosti" i o sisteme Teilora* (Moscow: 1922); Arsenii Mikhailov, *Sistema Teilora* (Moscow; Leningrad: Gos. izd-vo, 1928); id., *Sistema TsIT* (Moscow: Narkomat Tiazh. Prom., 1932).

99   Henri Fayol, *Administration industrielle et générale* (Paris: Dunod, 1916); Iurii Lubovich, *Teilor i Faiol* (Riazan; Izdateltstvo, 1924).

100 Jean-Maurice Lahy, *Sistema Teilora i fiziologia truda* (Moscow: Gos. izd-vo, 1925); originally: *Le système Taylor et la physiologie du travail professionnel* (Paris: Masson, 1916). See also Anson Rabinbach, *The Human Motor: Energy, Fatigue, and the Origins of Modernity* (Berkeley, University of California Press, 1992), 249-53.

101 Kurt Lewin, *Socializatsiia sistemy Teilora* (Leningrad; Moscow: Petrograd, 1925); Eduard Mikhel, *Kak proizvoditsia izuchenie rabochego vremeni (po Teiloru i Merriku)* (Moscow: Gos. Tekhnicheskoe Izd-vo, 1926).

In addition to launching the GOELRO plan, the new government effectively embraced Taylorism, replacing the leaders' elusive aspirations with concrete programmes. In January 1921, Trotsky organized the inaugural Congress of the Union devoted to the scientific organization of labour, or *Nauchnaia Organizatsia Truda* (NOT), a denomination that was officially adopted from that time[87]. The first decade of the Bolshevik era was characterized by an outburst of writings about the field of scientific management. A handbook published in 1925 analyzed several hundred titles to help readers find their way through the labyrinth of books and brochures[88]. This mass of material can be divided into three types of corpora: translations, often recent ones, of Taylor's original works and those of his colleagues; Russian interpretations and transpositions; and European works, namely German or French, usually offering a "critical" left-wing perspective. Taylor's classics were reprinted and issued in several collections[89]. The works of followers of the doctrine, such as Clarence B. Thomson, who taught at the Harvard Business School, were also translated[90]. Among others, Iosif Kan and Z. A. Papernov offered a comprehensive view of the methods devised by "American rationalizers."[91] In Germany, an illustrated overview of the experiments they inspired in Russia was published in 1924 by the psychologist Franziska Baumgarten[92].

Russians were already aware of Frank and Lillian Gilbreth's spatially oriented work before 1914, and many translations accounted for the various aspects of the couple's activity after 1917. They focused on the most basic popularization writings, such as the 1912 *Primer of Scientific Management*, reprised from the German edition and retranslated in 1925[93]. The books centred on motion studies, from bricklaying to factory plan analyses, and were translated and promoted by labour organization experts. Filmmakers, such as Arkadii Ialovoi, Dean of the Faculty of Engineering at the State Cinema Polytechnic, were also interested in the question[94]. During the same period, the bestseller *Taylor, Gilbreth, Ford* gave an overview of American methods. The author, Irene Witte, was employed by a German client of the Gilbreths, who encouraged her to study scientific management[95].

In this mass of production, one work stood out: *The Taylor System*, published in 1918 by the Menshevik Osip Ermanskii. Although the author had criticized the regime in 1921, Lenin felt the 1922 reissue of the book was quite useful despite its "unacceptable [...] verbosity."[96] Lenin's interest might be explained by his own intention, according to Aleksei Gastev, to write a full book on scientific management[97]. Sergei Glebov, Vasilii Sibarov, Arsenii Mikhailov, Ivan Rabchinskii (an expert on electrotechnics and a revolutionary), and many others followed suit by offering their own analyses[98]. Comparisons were made with rival doctrines such as "administration," developed by the French engineer Henri Fayol at the start of the 20th century[99]. The connections between labour organization and physiology, studied by the psychologist Jean-Maurice Lahy, did not go unnoticed[100]. Criticism by German intellectuals such as his colleague Kurt Lewin, also resonated in the USSR[101].

This extraordinary wave of publications encompassed all disciplines and extended to literature, as evidenced by the dystopian novel *We*, by Yevgeny Zamyatin, written between 1919 and 1921, whose plot takes place in such a bureaucratized and technical society that its members are all identified by numbers. The book offers a scathingl critique of Taylorism as seen from an imagined future: "Yes, this Taylor was unquestionably the greatest genius of the ancients. True, his thought did not reach far enough to extend his method

Frank B. Gilbreth and Lillian M. Gilbreth. Factory floor plan with motion study, ca. 1915.
Purdue University Libraries, Frank and Lillian Gilbreth Papers.

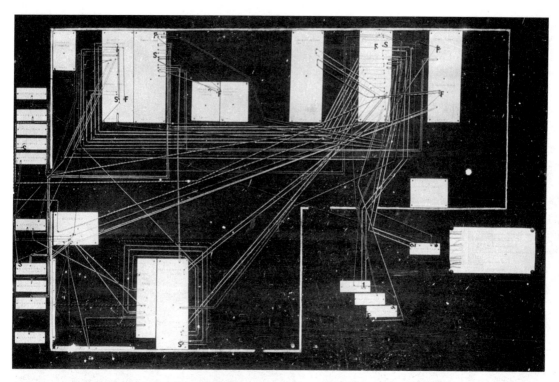

Frank B. Gilbreth. View of a model tracking movements in a factory, 1910.
Purdue University Libraries, Frank and Lillian Gilbreth Papers.

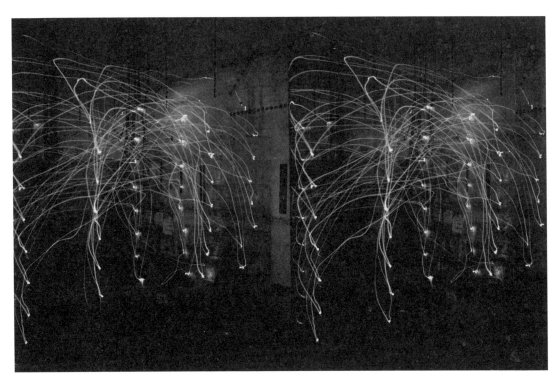

Central Institute of Labour. Motion study, 1921, illustration published in René Fülöp-Miller's, *Geist und Gesicht des Bolschewismus :
Darstellung und Kritik des Kulturellen Lebens in Sowjet-Russland*, Zurich: Amalthea-Verlag, 1926. CCA, PO3807.

to all of life, to every step, to the twenty-four hours of every day. He was unable to integrate his system from one hour to twenty-four. Still, how could they write whole libraries of books about some Kant, yet scarcely notice Taylor, that prophet who was able to see ten centuries ahead?"[102] In this fictional society governed by a vicious hierarchy, Taylor's methods are applied to every undertaking. The organization and efficiency principles are so pervasive that one of the characters becomes, after appropriate psychological treatment, a sort of man-shaped machine. The Soviet regime's recently established censorship prohibited the circulation of the book, but it was published in English in New York. In the face of the incessant flow of publications on Taylorism crossing the Atlantic and permeating Western Europe, this unusual work is a unique case of criticism of the system disseminated in the opposite direction. The novel did not become available to Russian until 1988.

From the most arid technical writings to fiction, Taylorism engulfed Russia's politics, economy, and culture. The movement waned, at least in its most explicit expression, only in the mid-1930s, when Soviet industrial infrastructure was well established. Highly ideological, Stakhanovism retained certain Taylorist traits[103]. The Russian interpretation of Taylorism and the development of NOT were part of a more general movement to establish "scientific" foundations for production, reproduction, and the entire material culture of the USSR. Not only did NOT become an agent of the socialist overhaul of the economy, when piece rates and productivity norms were implemented in April 1918, it also spurred the cultural revolution[104].

After the 1921 Congress, two organizations were contending for hegemony in the field for NOT: the Central Institute of Labour (TsIT) and the League of Time. They were both offsprings of the Proletkult movement—i.e., the Proletarian Culture Organization, founded in 1917 by Aleksandr Bogdanov, who had often clashed with Lenin. Although Proletkult activists were initially hostile to futurism, a term they used in a generic sense to designate all modernist trends, they tirelessly described the future society they envisioned. Several proponents of "left-wing art," such as Boris Arvatov, Sergei Tretiakov, and Aleksandr Rodchenko, got their start and developed their work within the organization. Vladimir Kirillov, an active member of the association and a poet shunned by those same futurists, portrayed in his 1921 poem "The Iron

102   Yevgeny Zamiatine, We [1924], trans. Mirra Ginsburg (New York: Avon Books, 1972), 30.
103   Samuel Liberstein, "Technology, Work and Sociology in the USSR: The NOT Movement," Technology and Culture 16, no. 1 (January 1975): 48–66; Zenovia A. Sochor, "Soviet Taylorism Revisited," Soviet Studies 33, no. 2 (April 1981): 246–64.
104   Stites, Revolutionary Dreams, 144–55.
105   Vladimir Kirillov, Zheleznyi Messia (Moscow: Izdanie moskovskogo Proletkulta, 1921). See also Lynn Mally, Culture of the Future: The Proletkult Movement in Revolutionary Russia (Berkeley, CA: University of California Press, 1990), 99.
106   Mally, Culture of the Future, 172.
107   Bogdanov, Mezhdu chelovekom i mashinoi, 15.
108   Aleksei Gastev, "Rabochii mir; zavod i sindikat. I. Sila mashinizma," Zhizn dlia vsekh, no. 3–4 (1911).
109   Aleksei Gastev, Poezia rabochego udara (Petrograd: Izdanie Proletkulta, 1918), p. 253 of the 1972 edition, in Kurt Johansson, Aleksej Gastev, Proletarian Bard of the Machine Age (Stockholm: Almqvist & Wiksell International, 1983), 27. Nikolai Aseev, "Gastev," in Sobranie stikhotvorenii (Moscow: Gos. Izdat., 1930), vol. 1, 202. For more on Gastev, see Simon Ings, Stalin and the Scientists: Images of Triumph and Tragedy 1905-1953 (London: Faber & Faber, 2016), 68–84; Gastevskie chteniia 2017, Aleksei Tkachenko-Gastev, ed. (Moscow: Izd-vo MPSU, 2019). A remarkable exhibition devoted to Gastev was shown at Moscow's Center of the Avant-garde in 2019.
110   Aleksei Gastev, "O tendentsiakh proletarskoi kultury," Proletarskaia Kultura, no. 9–10, (1919).
111   Idid., 36.
112   Aleksei Gastev, "Vosstanie kultury," in Poezia rabochego udara, 245.
113   Vladimir M. Friche, "Tvorchestvuiushchaia pesnia kovannogo metalla," Tvorchestvo 2 (1918), 17-18.
114   Johansson, Aleksej Gastev, 81.
115   Aleksei Gastev, "Novaia industria," Vestnik metallista 2 (1918): 5–27, in Johansson, Aleksej Gastev, 62.

Messiah", one of the literary classics of the movement, a machine paradise very similar to the United States, where he had lived during his exile[105]. In 1919, the Socialist Education section of Proletkult in Petrograd promoted sending delegations of workers to investigate on American techniques, but Bogdanov had reservations[106]. He remained nevertheless in favour of Taylorism, as he wrote in 1918 in the second edition of his *Mezhdu chelovekom i mashinoi* (Between Man and the Machine)[107].

One of the most prominent members of Proletkult was Aleksei Gastev, a proletarian activist who emigrated to Paris before 1914, where he discovered modern industry and structures such as the Eiffel Tower, which inspired one of his poems. An excellent writer who was influenced by the works of Walt Whitman and Émile Verhaeren, Gastev published poetry in the futurist vein, celebrating the "strength of machinery" and industrial components[108], leaeding his fellow poet Nikolai Aseev to dub him "the Ovid of engineers, miners, and metallurgists." His poetic writings were assembled in the collection *Poeziia rabochego udara* (Poetry of the Worker's Blow), issued in 1918 by the Proletkult. In his poetry, he advocated nothing less than the need to move past the "manufacture [of] things" and to the "thorough manufacture of men."[109] In search of the "lyricism of the Labour Movement," he saw the basis of proletarian culture in the material backbone of the industry: "the main specific trait of the new industrial proletariat, of its psychology and its culture, is industry itself. Buildings, pipes, pillars, bridges, cranes, and all the intricate structures of modern constructions and undertakings—this is what infiltrates the day-to-day conscience of the proletariat. [...] The mechanization not only of gestures, not only of working methods and means of production, but also of daily thoughts, paired with extreme objectivism, admirably standardize the psychology of the proletariat. We confidently declare that no other class, past or present, has such a standardized psychology as the proletariat."[110]

The Proletkult's novel frame of mind originated overseas: "the metallurgy of this new world, the motor car and the airplane factories of America, and finally the arms industry of the whole world—here are the new gigantic laboratories where the psychology of the proletariat is being created, where the culture of the proletariat is being manufactured."[111] Elsewhere, Gastev imagined Russia becoming a "new blossoming America," by way of a "Soviet Americanism,"[112] a vision conveyed by the literary critic Vladimir Friche in the Proletkult journal *Tvorchestvo* (Creation).[113] Revisiting the metals on which Gorky had focused in his essay on America, he used the language of factories to oppose "iron poetry" against that of gold. Odes to the "Hammer," the "Crane," or the "Beam"[114] foreshadowed the factographic literature of the late 1920s and employed free verse in a manner that was new in the realm of Russian poetics.

In a defining 1918 text on the "new industry," Gastev added an urban perspective to his vision: "machinism is gradually saturating not only the purely industrial aspect of human life; it will fuse enterprises together, it will permeate all areas of everyday life, it will give life to the mighty edifices we boldly call machine cities."[115] As Julia Vaingurt has shown, Gastev was entirely opposed to individualism and developed a moralistic discourse leaning towards corporal punishment. He set out to purge Russia of its laziness and improve its efficiency, with the aims of transforming the human species. These ideas were advocated at the end of the nineteenth century by the philosopher Nikolai Fedorov, a prophet of immortality who was at the root of several of the Soviets' "scientific" delusions. Gastev's Americanism is apparent in his short Siberian science fiction tale, *Express: A Siberian Fantasy*, published in 1916, in Krasnoiarsk.

He describes the construction of a train named "Panorama," which would cross Siberia by way of the "steel city" of Novo-Nikolaevsk—renamed Novosibirsk in 1925—and Irkutsk, and would then take an underwater tunnel in the fictional city of Bering, and reach, in Alaska, its coveted destination: America. This city of Bering "knows only two slogans: "To the Pole!" and "To America!"[116] The most obvious inspiration for this narrative is Bernhard Kellerman's novel *Der Tunnel*, whose pre-war acclaim endured well into the 1920s[117]. According to Gastev, Siberia would become, by way of a trans-Pacific and intercontinental connection, a sort of Russian-American territory whose inhabitants would speak a hybrid language[118].

Furthermore, Gastev had played a major part in rallying the unions behind the 1918 decrees. He left behind his work as a writer during the New Economic Policy, fully dedicated to leading the TsIT, which he created in 1921. He took on the appearance of an austere man of science, whose cold stare was reminiscent of that in Taylor's widely circulated portraits. Some saw in his approach, supported by Lenin, a type of Soviet Calvinism, disseminating Max Weber's theories on the "spirit of capitalism" to the east[119]. Caricatures abounded. While Zinovii Tolkachev gave Gastev the face of a lab researcher—a sort of futuristic Frankenstein— [ill. p. 126], the Kukryniksy collective depicted him as an ascetic mechanic screwing humanoid bolts into a machine whose conveyer belt is made of workers trapped in endless motion[120].

Inspired by Filippo Tommaso Marinetti's futurism, already well-known in Russia before his 1914 tour, the TsIT's discourse extended to culture at large; although it addressed the concrete gestures related to production, it also held an aesthetic component, thus surpassing Taylor's scientific management. Motion studies stemming from the Gilbreths' work—namely Gastev's re-enactment of experiments with the chronocyclegraph in his analysis of the use of hammers or chisels [ill. p. 121]—launched the research conducted at the Institute, which fell under the auspices of the Central Council of Trade Unions.[121] Gastev established a cinematographic lab, led by the film director Arkadii Ialovoi, in the spacious offices allocated to the TsIT on 24 Petrovka Street. In 1924, he attended the Conference on Scientific Organization of Labour in Prague, where he heard Lillian Moller Gilbreth's presentation on motion studies. This event, organized by the new Czechoslovak

116   I.I. Dozorov [pseudonym for Aleksei Gastev], "Ekspress, sibirskaia fantazia," *Sibirskie zapiski*, no. 1 (1916); quoted in Johansson, *Aleksej Gastev*, 140–51.
117   This best-seller was republished many times after the revolution. See for example Bernhard Kellerman, *Tunnel* (Moscow: Izd. Krasnaia Noch, 1923), with illustrations by Vladimir N. Taleperovskii.
118   Julia Vaingurt, *Wonderlands of the Avant-garde: Technology and the Arts in Russia of the 1920s* (Evanston, IL: Northwestern University Press, 2013), 42–44.
119   Timothy W. Luke, "The Proletarian Ethic and Soviet Industrialization," *The American Political Science Review* 77, no. 3 (September 1983): 588–601.
120   Zinovii Tolkachev, illustration in *Vosstanie kultury* (Kharkov: Molodoi Rabochii, 1923); Kukryniksy, "Rabotchii i mashina, ustanovka Gasteva," caricature, 1930.
121   See the illustrated collection of ideas inspired by Gilbreth: Boris V. Babin, Aleksei K. Gastev, and Krikor Kha. Kechkeev, *TSIT Issledovania* (Moscow: Izdanie TsITa, 1923).
122   *Report of the Proceedings of the First International Management Congress in Prague (PIMCO), July 20–24, 1924* (Prague: Institute for the Technical Management of Industry, Masaryk Academy of Work, 1925), 45. After emigrating to Germany and then to France, Chakhotin would publish *The Rape of the Masses; the Psychology of the Totalitarian Political Propaganda* [1939], transl. Ernest Walter Dickes (London: Routledge, 1940).
123   Aleksei K. Gastev, "O tendentsiakh proletarskoi kultury," *Proletarskaia kultura*, 1919, n° 9-10, 1919, 35–45.
124   Sochor, "Soviet Taylorism Revisited," 249.
125   Bailes, "Alexei Gastev," 379–80 and 386–87.
126   Platon Kerzhentsev, "2-aia konferentsiia po NOT i TsIT," *Organizatsia truda*, no. 2-3, 2-53, in Johansson, 107.
127   See Ulf Brunnbauer's detailed and nuanced analysis in "The League of Time," 461–95.

state and the Taylor Society, was a milestone in the globalization of the scientific management movement. Heading a delegation of some ten people, Gastev spoke about "the equipment method of the TsIT" during a panel on "the human element in scientific management." Among the envoys were also the physiologist Nikolai Bernstein, who led his Institute's department of biomechanics and addressed the "normalization of motion," Izaak Shpilrein, the director of Narkomtrud's psychotechnical lab, and the Pavlovian psychologist Sergei Chakhotin, who would go on to publish *The Rape of the Masses* in 1939. During the plenary session, Chakhotin praised "our American colleagues who are highly honoured in the new Russia as masters of the scientific management of work" and declared that "in many respects we are imitating them: it is certainly well known to you that people speak of the Amerikanization of Russia."[122]

Gastev openly recognized the impact of America on his vision, and considered its great factories to be "laboratories" where Taylor's methods were applied[123]. When the first Conference on Scientific Organization of Labour was held in Moscow, the Institute, which had just recently launched its operations, measured up against competing approaches in front of 400 attendees. The debates moderated by the psychiatrist Vladimir Bekhterev revealed a clear divide between two factions. The first camp, led by the revolutionary and publicist Platon Kerzhentsev, advocated for a critical and socially discerning application of Taylorism, while the second camp, headed by Gastev, defended a systematic and comprehensive approach. The two competing groups, affiliated with opposing political factions, were locked in fierce debates throughout the 1920s, but nevertheless joined forces to create the League of Labour in 1923[124]. Gastev faced criticism from Bogdanov, who accused him of sacrificing workers' creativity to implement an extreme form of Taylorism. A campaign, whose main agent was the League of Time, created in 1923 by Kerzhentsev, was launched against Gastev in 1922–1923. He defended his views by referencing Bukharin's pro-American writings[125].

After having emigrated to England, Kerzhentsev had lived in New York in 1916, before returning to Russia to work within Proletkult alongside Bogdanov from 1917 to 1921. He accused Gastev of setting out to create a proletarian aristocracy—or a clergy of the scientific organization of labour—sold out to America: "TsIT proposes to turn out the aristocrats of the working class, the priests of scientific management. [...] Oh, Taylor, it is you! The TsIT people have learned well your approach to the worker—from on high, with money in your fist, with obscure formulas and a distrust for his consciousness." According to Kerzhentsev, Gastev relied on the "hypocritical" and "pseudo-scientific" American premium scheme, against the true interests of the working class[126]. Though Gastev had been a member of the board of the League of Time upon its creation, alongside the theatre artist Vsevolod Meyerhold, it was in the name of this association that Kerzhentsev proposed a new approach of the scientific organization of labour. He called for a method based on Taylor's original text and not on its interpretations, and presented this idea at the 1921 Congress in a talk entitled "The Organizational Principles of a Uniform Economic Plan." The League of Time, with its nearly 25,000 members, operated through 800 cells, namely active in the army, in a young Soviet Union suffering a severe decline in production and productivity[127]. It was dismantled in 1926, and Kerzhentsev became ambassador to Italy.

Despite these attacks, Gastev prevailed over his rival. His victory was sanctioned at the second national congress of NOT in March 1924, during which he opened the doors of his Institute to the 383 delegates, predominantly

Aleksei K. Gastev, illustration by Zinovii Tolkachev. Published in *Vosstanie kultury*,
Kharkov: Molodoi Rabochii, 1923.

Central Institute of Labour. Motion Studies, 1920. Illustrations published in René Fülöp-Miller, *Geist und Gesicht des Bolschewismus:*
Darstellung und Kritik des Kulturellen Lebens in Sowjet-Russland, Zurich, 1926. CCA, PO3807.

Images taken with the chronocyclegraph and their geometrical interpretation in Nikolai A. Bernstein, "Studies on strike biomechanics using a light recording system," article published in Boris V. Babin, Aleksei K. Gastev, Krikor Kha. Kechkeev, *TsIT Studies*, Moscow: Izdanie TsITa, 1923. CCA, W.I842.

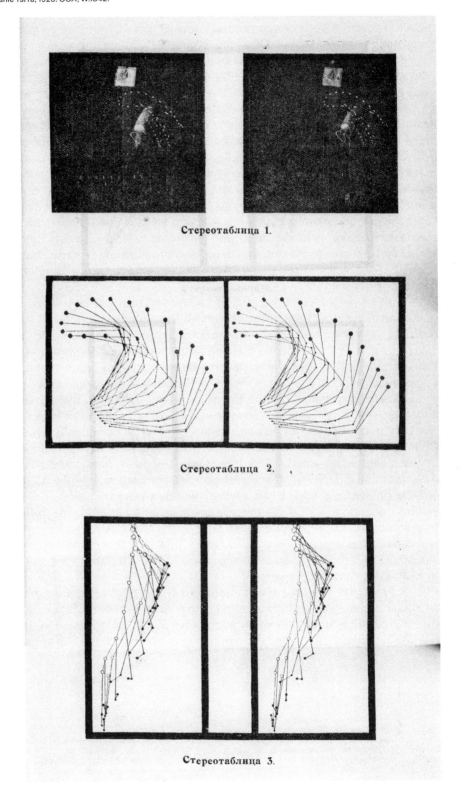

Стереотаблица 1.

Стереотаблица 2.

Стереотаблица 3.

intellectuals and executives rather than proletarians. Open support from Valerian Kuibyshev, then president of the Central Control Commission of the Communist Party, gave Gastev free rein to develop, unhindered, the machinist theory articulated in *Kak nado rabotat* (How to Work Correctly), an instructional book where he writes: "The movement of a working human is a combination of lines, points, angles, and weights, all working with a certain tolerance, with a habitual efficiency"[128] [ill. p. 127]. This view is in line with the idea of the body as a motor, as conveyed by the French physiologist Jules Amar, whose studies were known to Gastev even before their translation into Russian[129]. To Amar, if each body is a machine, the working class as a whole is a megamachine, as he wrote in his 1925 foreword to a new edition of *Poeziia rabochego udara*: "I must work with exceptional energy at creating a social engineering machine, in which I see something I must have spent decades working towards, as an artist and as an organizer of the Revolution. Three more words—trajectory, vector, movement—express in theory the general laws of cinematography but denote in practice the ABCs of all machines. These laws are themselves, it seems to me, now open, unlimited horizons. I apply them, as far as I can, not only to the creation of defined organizational norms, but also to arrive at conclusions concerning a restructuring—a biological restructuring—of present-day man."[130]

At its height, Gastev's Institute employed over 120 people, and became one of the most frequented venues for the countless foreign visitors to Moscow, who described it in the most contradictory ways. René Fülöp-Miller saw it as a place where "anyone entering the front door as a normal living man, issues from the back door, after passing through endless laboratories, as a completely perfected working machine."[131] The German playwright Ernst Toller, the short-lived president of the Bavarian Soviet Republic, described the spectacle of the TsIT's laboratories, and expressed reservations about the threat of mechanization for human creativity[132]. The French novelist Georges Duhamel wrote upon his return from the USSR that "the discipline imposed by the machine is a shackle [...]. It is always imposed, never cherished."[133] After creating a powerful space dedicated to instruction, unique in Europe outside of Germany, where half a million workers were trained before 1931, Gastev continued his activities before being arrested in 1938. The TsIT was then liquidated, its laboratories overtaken by the Moscow Aviation Institute, and Gastev was executed in 1941. His ideas, however, resonated beyond the industrial sphere, giving way to new tendencies in the theatre, such as those from director Vsevolod Meyerhold.

From 1912, Meyerhold was interested in novel performance methods, using pantomime and already working with a certain mechanization of gestures. To position the artistic orientation of his studio, he had chosen to borrow the pen name Dr. Dapertutto, from the character of the evil wizard in

128   Alexei K. Gastev, *Kak nado rabotat* [1922] (Moscow: Ekonomika, 1972), 51.
129   Jules Amar, *Le moteur humain et les bases scientifiques du travail professionnel* (Paris: H. Dunod et
       E. Pinat, 1914). Rabinbach mentions his research in *The Human Motor*, 185-88 and 246-49.
130   Aleksei K. Gastev, preface to *Poeziia rabochego udara*, 6th ed. (Moscow: Izd-vo VSPS, 1926), 30; in English
       in: Jean-Louis Cohen, "America, A Soviet Ideal," *AA Files*, no. 5 (January 1984), 34. See also Walter Süss,
       *Die Arbeiterklasse als Maschine: Ein industrie-soziologischer Beitrag zur Sozialgeschichte des
       aufkommenden Stalinismus* (Berlin: O. Harrassowitz, 1985).
131   Fülöp-Miller, *Geist und Gesicht des Bolschewismus*, 283; *The Mind and Face of Bolshevism*, 211.
132   Ernst Toller, *Quer durch: Reisebilder und Reden* (Berlin: Kiepenheuer, 1926), 121–24.
133   Georges Duhamel, *Le voyage de Moscou* (Paris: Mercure de France, 1927), 188.

Aleksandr A. Vesnin and Liubov S. Popova. Model for the set of G. K. Chesterton's play *The Man Who Was Thursday*, Kamernyi Theatre, Moscow, ca. 1923. General view. Gelatin silver print on paper, 16.1 × 21.4cm. CCA, PH1998:0008:005.

A.A. Temerin. Photograph of Meyerhold's biomechanical exercises. A.A. Bakhrushin State Central Theatre Museum. In Jane Baldwin, "Meyerhold's Theatrical Biomechanics: An Acting Technique for Today," *Theatre Topics* (*ThTop*) 5, no. 2, September 1995: 181-201.

Liubov S. Popova. Stage device for the set of *Earth in Turmoil*, directed by Vsevolod Meyerhold, 1923.
Fragments of silver print on paper, gouache, press clipping on plywood, 49 × 82.7 cm. Costakis Collection, Thessaloniki Museum of Modern Art.

ЧИЧЕРИН

...машина завоевала воду ...здух,

Механизация сельского хозя
...тва завоюет землю

KEROSENE TRACTOR

INTERNATIONAL

Jacques Offenbach's *The Tales of Hoffmann*. After the Revolution, Meyerhold became close to the contributors to the Scientific Organization of Labour and became one of the founding members of the League of Time. As early as 1914, he developed a training programme for actors and theatre directors called "biomechanics," influenced by circus, pantomime, and burlesque. The project was based on the idea of a science of human movement, which would be publicly exhibited through theatrical representations[134] [ill. p. 129]. Meyerhold's eclectic approach drew on William James' philosophy and theory of emotions as well as Gastev's analytical methods, which he assimilated entirely. In his 1922 essay "The Actor of the Future and Biomechanics," Meyerhold noted that "the methods of Taylorism may be applied to the work of the actor in the same way as they are to any form of work with the aim of maximum productivity." He stated that "the spectacle of man working efficiently affords positive pleasure. This applies equally to the work of the actor of the future. [...] The art of the actor consists in organizing his material, that is, in his capacity to utilize correctly his body's means of expression." The productivist undertones are unmistakable: the "Taylorization of theatre" allowed the cast "to perform in one hour that which requires four at present."[135] They can also be found in his version of the play *Le Cocu magnifique* (The Magnificent Cuckold) by the Belgian playwright Fernand Crommelynck, reviewed in 1922 by Sergei Tretiakov, who pronounced the end of the pantomime: "Gesticulatory garbage is discarded—the simplest, most economical, well-aimed gesture is sought—the Taylorized gesture." The constructivist artist Liubov Popova devised a theatrical device in line with this migration from the factory to the stage: a large machine comprised of walkways, cogwheels, and cranes. These elements enabled Tretiakov to remark that "the scenery itself [...] smiles and cracks jokes as the action progresses."[136]

The following year, Meyerhold staged *The Earth in Turmoil*, an adaptation written by Tretiakov of the verse drama *Nuit* [Night] by the French socialist author Marcel Martinet. They play was dedicated to Trotsky, who wrote about it in 1924. Popova was once again in charge of the stage design, producing preparatory collages combining elements from American farming machinery [ill. p. 130-131]. The device can be interpreted, according to her, as a workbench or a construction for the development of actors' performances[137]. Meyerhold's work quickly came to the attention of Western readers, namely thanks to the American theatre artist Huntley Carter, who disseminated images of the plays in 1924, and analyzed their biomechanic features, which to him stemmed from futurism and *commedia dell'arte*, in combination with what he called "constructionism."[138] The People's Commissar for Education, Anatolii Lunacharsky, was greatly in favour of the opening of a theatre adapted to Meyerhold's projects, but insisted on their limitations: "It will be an extraordinary and charming endeavour, where you can go to relax your soul. It will be an expression of Amerikanizm, which we have no intention of avoiding like the devil, to whom we will willingly surrender our own (just as we do not intend to vilify the delightful little imps that are operettas), but all of this will, of course, by no means substitute itself to theatre."[139] While striving to limit the frivolous elements of Amerikanizm, he also recognized that the discipline had extended from the factory to the stage. One might add that it had also extended to the screen, with the reference to the NOT in Aleksei Popov's 1927 film *Dva druga, model i podruga* (Three Friends and an Invention), where two workers in a soap factory are confronted with the Nepmen and their bureaucracy.

Two Soviet Heroes: Ford and the Fordson Tractor

The first Soviet five-year plan, launched in 1928, owed much more, in its con-figuration of industrial infrastructure, to the American model, based on the development of mines, metallurgy, and mechanical manufacturing, than to the German one, based on chemistry and electrotechnics[140]. A great auton-omous power whose quick growth was independent from Europe, the United States provided a prototype for the construction of a new Russia. As Thomas P. Hughes showed in *American Genesis*, the power plants of the US fuelled with the Niagara Falls, Ford's factories, and Gary's steel mills embodied an ideal trinity[141]. These models were transformed in the Soviet rhetoric, where the term *stroika* (construction site), *stroiki* in the plural form, and often short-ened as *stroi*, took on a quasi-incantatory dimension in the propaganda of the regime, both in its internal discourse and in the image it aimed to export. The five-year plan therefore boasted four significant *stroiki*, which received funding and focus from the State apparatus and the Party: Dneprostroi for electricity, Avtostroi and Traktorstroi for automobiles and tractors, and Magnitstroi for the steel industry.

Economic exchanges with America developed throughout the 1920s. Despite the privileged trade agreements established between the USSR and Germany in Rapallo in 1922, over half of economic assistance deals were signed with Americans, a proportion that grew to two thirds in the following fifteen years. To finance these operations, the Soviets did not shy away from selling Saint Petersburg's cultural heritage, including paintings from the Her-mitage Museum, as they had no access to credit for their acquisitions[142]. The American contribution to the Soviet economy was significant, as evidenced by the major projects of the first five-year plan: the construction of a dam on the Dnieper River, the development of the metal and mining industries, me-chanical structures, and the mechanization of agriculture.

In the strategic coal sector, the engineer Charles E. Stuart, from the New York City-based firm Stuart, James and Cooke, developed a stream-lining plan for the Donbass in 1930, where technical issues went hand-in-hand with social guidelines drawn from prolonged on-site observation[143]. Stuart's treatment of the workforce nevertheless sparked criticism from his colleague Willard L. Gorton, who served as a consultant for the Soviet government on irrigation projects in Turkestan[144]. The engineer Zara Witkin, who designed

134 Meyerhold's exercises are discussed in Alma H. Law and Mel Gordon, *Meyerhold, Eisenstein and Biomechanics: Actor Training in Revolutionary Russia* (Jefferson, NC: McFarland, 1996), 95–123. See also the material on Meyerhold's first performances, collected in Jörg Bochow, *Das Theater Meyerholds und die Biomechanik* (Berlin: Alexander Verlag, 1997), especially 61–122.

135 Vsevolod E. Meyerhold, "Akter budushchego i biomekanika," *Ermitage*, no. 6 (1922): 10–11; in English: *Meyerhold on Theatre* (New York: Hill & Wang, 1969), 198–99.

136 Sergei Tretiakov, "Velikodushnyi rogonosets," *Zrelishcha*, no. 8 (1922): 12.

137 Vaingurt, *Wonderlands*, 69.

138 Huntley Carter, *The New Theater and Cinema of Soviet Russia* (London: Chapman and Dodd, 1924), 67–80; Mikhail B. Iampolskii, *Demon i labirint: diagrammy, deformatsii, mimesis* (Moscow: Novoe literaturnoe obozrenie, 1996).

139 Anatolii V. Lunacharsky, 1922, quoted in Annenkov, *Dnevnik*, vol. 2, 65.

140 Bailes, "The American Connection," 429.

141 Thomas P. Hughes, *American Genesis; a Century of Invention and Technological Enthusiasm* (New York: Viking, 1989), 269–84.

142 Robert C. Williams, *Russian Art and American Money* (Cambridge, MA: Harvard University Press, 1980).

143 Hoover Institution Library & Archives, Charles E. Stuart papers, boxes 2 and 3.

144 *Making Things Work*, 100.

the structure for the Hollywood Bowl in Los Angeles, travelled to Russia and became something of a factory "super inspector" for the GPU (the Soviet State police). Witkin later recounted his experience with great disappointment, a response shared by many idealist technicians disenchanted by difficult Soviet conditions[145].

In its forecasting and management, the five-year plan progressively used diagrams for task planning developed by the Taylorist engineer Henry L. Gantt to measure workers' efficiency[146]. In 1917, Gantt contributed to the creation of The New Machine, an association of technocrats wishing to apply the economic principles of industry to policy making[147]. Gantt's diagrams, immediately assimilated as part of the American war effort, were popularized in the United States by Henry Wallace Clark, whose 1922 book, a staple among company executives, was quickly translated into Russian[148]. Gantt's ideas, as articulated by Clark, circulated in the Soviet Union through the latter's former employee Walter N. Polakov, who had left Russia in 1906, but sustained relations there and exchanged letters with Gastev from 1924[149]. Polakov settled in Moscow from December 1929 to May 1931. Known for his writings, which had not yet been put in practice, and also through his social network, he quickly demonstrated the effectiveness of the Gantt diagram, in such varied applications as workshops, mills, and the industrial sector at large[150]. For the American audience, he depicted daily scenes from the Russian factories he was working to streamline: "Everywhere in the plant there was a great stir and bustle, but there were few signs of smoothly organized production. Workers stood about in little groups, talking, while others busied themselves spasmodically at their tasks. There was a complete absence of co-ordinated activity, of systematized routing and planning of work." He provided an explanation that was common among many observers: "The lack of discipline which is so noticeable in Russian industry is not due, then, to any lack of rules and regulations, or to their non-enforcement; it is an inner self-discipline that is wanting. The average Russian worker's background is agricultural. His habits of work, his attitude of mind have been shaped on the farm and inherited from generations of peasants." Polakov advocated for an "aggressive" response to this deficiency through "intensive and unified" worker training—inspired by none other than Gastev[151].

145   Zara Witkin with Michael Gelb, An American Engineer in Stalin's Russia: The Memoirs of Zara Witkin, 1932–1934 (Berkeley: University of California Press, 1991).
146   Henry L. Gantt, Organitsiia truda; razmyshlenia amer. inzh. ob ekonomicheskikh posledstviakh mirovoi voiny, trans. Iu. M. Kaplanskii, preface by S. Chlenov (Moscow: Izd.-vo VSNKh, 1923); Iosif R. Belopolskii, Grafiki Ganta: poiasnitelnyi tekst k postroeniu grafikov (Leningrad: Kult. prosvet. koop. t–vo "Nachatki znanii," 1929); Pavel A. Chernikov, Grafiki Ganta v upravlenii proizvodstvom (Moscow: Standardizatsia i ratsionalizatsia, 1934).
147   Charles S. Maier, "Between Taylorism and Technocracy: European Ideologies and the Vision of Industrial Productivity in the 1920s," Journal of Contemporary History 5, no. 2 (1970): 27–61.
148   Henry W. Clark, Uchet proizvoditelnosti: graficheskii metod Ganta, trans. and preface by E. Papernov (Moscow: Izd-vo NKRKI, 1925); originally The Gantt Chart: A Working Tool of Management (New York: The Ronald Press Company, 1922) (appendices by Walter N. Polakov and Frank W. Trabold); Wallace Clark, Grafiki Ganta (Uchet i planirovanie raboty) (Moscow: Tekhnika upravlenia, 1929).
149   Among Polakov's major works, see Mastering Power Production: The Industrial, Economic and Social Problems Involved and their Solution (London: Cecil Palmer, 1922); Man and His Affairs from the Engineering Point of View (Baltimore: Williams & Wilkins Co, 1925); The Power Age, its Quest and Challenge (New York: Covici & Friede, 1933).
150   Wren, "Scientific Management in the U.S.S.R;" Diane J. Kelly, "Marxist Manager Amidst the Progressives."
151   Walter N. Polakov, "How Efficient Are The Russians?," Harper's Magazine, December 1931, 39, 41, and 42.
152   Walter N. Polakov, "The Gantt Chart in Russia," American Machinist, 13 August 1931, 264.
153   Pearl Franklin Clark, Challenge of the American Know-How (New York: Hillary House, 1957), 110, quoted in Wren, "Scientific Management," 8.
154   Georges Duhamel, Le voyage de Moscou (Paris: Mercure de France, 1927), 105–6.

In 1931, Polakov recounted his on-site experience in the American press, insisting on the strategic significance of tools such as Gantt's diagrams: "Lack of engineering skills shortage of men experienced in technical processes, and even willful sabotage are often referred to by both Russians and foreign visitors as the greatest handicaps. Our personal observations make us believe it to be of secondary importance, since the clean-cut managerial principles and simple mechanism of planning and control, given for instance by the use of Gantt's method, most of the mistakes of inexperience and causes of failure are immediately brought to light, remedy suggests itself, and improvement follows rapidly with attending accumulated experience."[152]

In 1934, in light of the acclaim for Clark's writings, the Supreme Board of the People's Economy (VSNKh) invited the author to continue Polakov's work in the Soviet Union. Clark curtly refused after a short stay in the USSR, coming to the conclusion that the fact that political decisions outweighed economical ones would impede any rationality[153]. However, this failure to entice an American to work in and for the Soviets during the Depression is an exception in the overall industrial ties between the two states, which were strengthened even before Franklin D. Roosevelt's 1933 decision to resume diplomatic relations. During this period of fast-paced growth, wishful Amerikanizm made way for a certain Americanization of production that made an impression on Western visitors. The French novelist Georges Duhamel revealed in his 1927 *Journey to Moscow* that "Russia has once again turned towards America [...], whose example it views with irritation as well as jealousy."[154] Returning to the New World three years later, he noted that "the American system [...] is turning Russia itself into

Russian version of a Gantt chart, in Walter Polakov, "The Gantt Chart in Russia," *American Machinist*, 13 August 1931.

a colony, purely in virtue, if I dare say so, of its so clearly pointing the way."[155] Another famous traveller, the journalist Emil Ludwig, went so far as to declare that "no Russian has ever expressed greater sympathy for the United States than Stalin."[156] Indeed, in a 1929 conversation with Thomas D. Campbell, an American farming industrialist, he declared: "We would like the American scientists and technicians to act as our teachers in the field of technology—and we, as their students."[157] In 1948, the President of the US Chamber of Commerce, Eric Johnston, reported that Stalin, while inquiring about Henry Ford, had this surprising thought for a former seminarian turned atheist: "God save him."[158]

Stalin, in that respect, was channelling public opinion. The attorney Bernhard Knollenberg noted, upon his return from Moscow in 1930, that "if Lenin is Russia's God today, Ford is its St. Peter."[159] In a 1927 article for the New York weekly *The Outlook*, Maurice Hindus wrote of Ford, that "incredible as it may seem, more people in Russia have heard of him than of Stalin, the Commander-in-Chief of the one-million-odd Communists who are governing the destiny of the vast Slavic empire. I visited villages far from railroads, where I talked to illiterate peasants who didn't know of Stalin, or Rykov, or Bukharin, but who had heard of the man who made 'iron horses.'"[160] On his side, Ford saw the potentially enormous Russian market as a means to offset the American downturn, which led him to halt his tractor production in 1928. A sort of mutual attraction developed between the industrialist and the Soviets, who were so taken with him that they overlooked the flaws of his machine, which was too light for Russian conditions[161].

A parallel discourse was thus established in the 1920s, echoed both by the countless publications about Ford, along with translations of his books, and by the intense trade relations between Detroit and Moscow, which gave way to a broad factory building programme based on the American model. In 1924, the year of Lenin's death, the industrialist's memoirs were disseminated almost as widely as the writings of the founder of the Soviet state, demonstrating once again the Russians' admiration for American inventors and entrepreneurs—such as Benjamin Franklin, Robert Fulton, or Thomas Edison— and confirming Hindus's observation[162]. Published in 1922 in the United States, *My Life and Work*, written by the journalist Samuel Crowther based on Ford's remarks, was issued nine times between 1924 and 1928. In his foreword to the 1924 Russian edition, Nikolai Lavrov, a professor of technology and an early expert on the NOT who had propagated Ford's methods before the Revolution, insisted on the benefits for the Soviet industry of the production system he had witnessed when visiting the Dearborn factories[163]. Ford's second book,

155   Georges Duhamel, *Scènes de la vie future* [1930] (Paris: Mille et une nuits, 2003), 176; in English: *America, the Menace; Scenes from the Life of the Future*, trans. Charles M. Thompson (Boston: Houghton Mifflin, 1931), 211.
156   Emil Ludwig, *Stalin* (New York: G.B. Putnam's Sons, 1942), 202.
157   "Zapis besedy s g-nom Campbellom, 28 ianvaria 1929 g.," in Iosif V. Stalin, *Sochineniia*, vol. 13, June 1930–January 1934 (Moscow: Gos. Izd-vo politicheskoi literatury, 1951), 149.
158   Eric Johnston, *We're All in It* (New York: E. P. Dutton & Co, 1948), 81-82.
159   Bernhard Knollenberg, "American Business in Russia," *Nation's Business* 8 (April 1930): 266.
160   Hindus, "Henry Ford Conquers Russia," 280.
161   Christine A. White, "Ford in Russia: In Pursuit of the Chimeral Market," *Business History* 28, no. 4 (1986): 77-104.
162   For more on the reception of these works, see S. Shvedov, "Obraz Genri Forda v sovetskoi publitsistike 1920-1930-kh godov: vospriatie i transformatsiia tsennosti chuzhoi kultury," in Oleg E. Tuganov, ed., *Vzaimodeistvie kultur SSSR i SSA XVIII–XX vv.* (Moscow: Nauka, 1987), 133-42.
163   Nikolai S. Lavrov, preface to Henry Ford, with Samuel Crowther, *Moia zhizn i moi dostizhenia*, trans. V.A. Zorgenfrei (Leningrad: Vremia, 1924), 3-8; originally *My Life and Work* (Garden City, NY: Doubleday, Page & Co, 1922). Lavrov also published *Genri Ford i ego proizvodstvo* (Leningrad; Vremia, 1926) and *Fordizm: uchenie o proizvodstve veshchei* (Leningrad: Avtor. tip. pechatnyi dvor, 1928).

Left: Henry Ford, *My Life and Work*, Leningrad: Vremia, 1925. CCA, BIB 244867.
Right: Henry Ford, *Today and Tomorrow*, Moscow: Gos. Izd-vo, 1927. CCA, BIB 244870.

Left: S. G. Ledenev, *Behind a Ford Workbench (Impressions of a Member of the Delegation Sent to Visit the US Tractor Factories)* Moscow and Leningrad, Gos. Izd-vo, 1927. CCA, BIB 244230. Right: V. M. Vasilev, *One Hundred Days at Ford's*, Moscow: Izd. Trud i kniga, 1927. CCA, BIB 244889.

Today and Tomorrow, published in 1926 with an introduction from the German Communist activist and journalist Paul Frölich, garnered similarly extraordinary acclaim[164].

In the 1920s, the discourse and practices surrounding Fordism were threefold: the cult of personality around Ford as a modern-day hero; *Fordizm*, comprising all the writings about his industrial policy; and *Fordizatsiia*, or "fordization," a term modelled on "electrification," describing the attempts to adapt Ford's methods to the Russian industry. Writings on Ford and Fordism proliferated significantly, at a similar rate to that of Western travel narratives recounting visits to the USSR. The corpus was comprised of theoretical analyses, some more scholarly than others, works of popularization, reports, and brief or lengthy accounts by Russians who had visited Detroit. In contrast with writings about Taylorism, which did not permeate into the broader public, the tireless labour of Ford's biographers and critics reached news kiosks and train stations[165]. The array of authors was eclectic, ranging from the linguist and educator German Genkel, to the former Menshevik Osip Ermanskii[166]. Encyclopedia entries about Ford were written by contributors such as Gastev, who saw the Highland Park Plant as the ideal "training facility,"[167] while others still viewed Ford's approach as a summary of American industrial policy[168]. Just as with Taylor, German authors contributed to the debate, with publications such as *Ford oder Marx* by the oppositional Communist Jacob Walcher and the work of the Socialist sociologist Hilda Weiss, who decried both Ford's industrial utopia and that of Ernst Abbe, the founder of the Zeiss firm in Jena[169].

Several books recount the impressions of Russian visitors to Detroit, home to a large emigrant colony, be it for a short stay or for a longer period. One of the first commentators was Vladimir Mayakovsky, who in 1925 painted

164   Henry Ford, with Samuel Crowther, *Segodnia i zavtra: o SShA*, ed. St. Volskii, preface by Paul Frölich (Moscow; Leningrad: Gos. Izd-vo, 1927); originally *Today and Tomorrow* (Garden City, NY: Doubleday, Page & Co, 1926).

165   N. Asov, *Genri Ford, Amerikanskii korol avtomobilei i traktorov: ego zhizn, dela i mysli, populiarny ocherk* (Leningrad; Moscow: Izd-vo Petrograd, 1925); *Naum Z. Beliaev, Genri Ford* (Moscow: Izd-vo zhurnalno-gazetnykh obedineniia, 1935) (from the series "The life of remarkable people," edited by Mikhail Koltsov and Maxim Gorky).

166   German G. Genkel, *Ford i fordizm (vpechatleniia)* (Leningrad: Kubuch, 1925); Osip Ermanskii, *Legenda of Forde* (Moscow; Leningrad: Gos. Izd-vo, 1925)

167   Aleksei Gastev, "Fordizm," *Bolshaia Sovetskaia Entsiklopedia* (Moscow: OGIZ, 1936), vol. 57, 131–35; "Ford," Ibid, 128–30.

168   Boris S. Shikhman, *Ford i fordizm; ratsionalizatsiia truda v Amerike* (Moscow: Gudok, 1927); Ian Ia. Mutsenek, *Ratsionalizatsiia amerikanskogo khoziaistva* (Moscow: Tekhnika upravlenia, 1929).

169   Jacob Walcher, *Ford ili Marx*, trans. O. Sargorodskaia, preface by E. Lerner (Moscow: Izd-vo Profinterna, 1925); originally *Ford oder Marx: Die praktische Lösung der sozialen Frage* (Berlin: Neuer Deutscher Verlag, 1925); Hilda P. Weiss, *Abbe i Ford: kapitalisticheskie utopii*, trans. St. Volskii, preface by Paul Frölich (Moscow; Leningrad: Krasnyi proletarii, 1928); originally *Abbe und Ford: kapitalistische Utopien* (Berlin: Prager, 1927).

170   Vladimir V. Mayakovsky, *Moe otkrytie Ameriki* (Moscow: Gosizdat, 1926, 131); in English: *My Discovery of America*, trans. by Neil Cornwell (London: Hesperus Press Ltd., 2005), 95–99.

171   V.M. Vasiliev, *Sto dnei u Forda* (Moscow: Izd. Trud i kniga, 1927). For an announcement about the visit, see "50 Russians to Learn Tractor," *Ford News* 6, no. 16 (22 March 1926), 1.

172   S.G. Ledenev, *Za stankom ou Forda*, preface by Lev Varshavskii (Moscow; Leningrad: Gos. Izd-vo, 1927).

173   Stites, *Revolutionary Dreams*, 149.

174   David E. Nye, *America's Assembly Line* (Cambridge, MA: MIT Press, 2013), 42–45.

175   Henry Ford, "Mass Production," *Encyclopaedia Britannica*, 1926, quoted in Hounshell, 217.

176   *Vremia*, no. 15 (1924), quoted in Brunnbauer, "The League of Time," 486.

177   Aleksei K. Gastev, Letter to Henry Ford, 9 June 1928; Ford Company, Letter to Aleksei Gastev, 10 July 1928, in Gastev, *Kak nado rabotat*, 312–314; Johansson, *Aleksej Gastev*, 109.

178   Ford Motor Company, "Report of the Ford Delegation to Russia and the USSR" (1926), 64, Benson Ford Research Center, Henry Ford Collection, acquisition no. 1870, box 1.

179   Hindus, "Henry Ford Conquers Russia," 280.

180   Reynold M. Wik, *Henry Ford and Grass–Roots America* (Ann Arbor: University of Michigan Press, 1972).

181   Hannes Meyer, "Die neue Welt," *Das Werk* 13, no. 7 (July 1926): 205.

182   Maurice Hindus, preface to Margaret Bourke-White, *Eyes on Russia* (New York: Simon and Schuster, 1931), 15.

a fiercely sardonic picture of assembly lines in *My Discovery of America*, remarking, in a nod to Nikolai Lavrov, that "Fordism is the most popular term among our labour organizers."[170] Among the other visitors was a group of some fifty workers and administrators sent to the Ford factory for a three-month visit to study tractor production[171]. The head of the delegation, S. G. Ledenev, published his travel impressions in the 1927 book *Za stankom u Forda*[172] (Behind a Ford Workbench). The same year, V. Vasiliev issued another account, reporting on factories and industrial practices.

As noted by Richard Stites, two opposite forms of worship coexisted: the rural adulation of Ford the magician, and the urban, intellectual cult around Ford's system[173]. Contrary to Taylor, who had deconstructed, coded, and reorganized the working process without resorting to mechanization, Ford fragmented it into even simpler gestures enacted by machine tools that restricted manual intervention and installed time-saving organization throughout the entire factory. The cadence of work was dictated by the assembly line, the first of which was established in August 1913 in Highland Park to produce the T model[174]. In 1926, Ford summarized his venture in the following words: "Mass production is the focusing upon a manufacturing project of the principles of power, accuracy, economy, system, continuity, and speed."[175] It became possible to massively produce consumer goods for enormous markets, owing also to the significant sales and marketing mechanism deployed by the company along with its factories. But Fordism was also based on a compensation policy that allowed workers to acquire the products of their labour, a component that was obviously lacking in Russian post-revolutionary society. Kerzhentsev's League of Time sought to assimilate the positive aspects of Fordism, which consisted in learning from Ford without imitating him[176], while Gastev directly questioned Ford on the relationship between swiftness and working precision[177]. Gastev was unaware that in Detroit, his experiments seemed laughable and that the delegation sent by Ford to the USSR reported, after visiting the TsIT, having uncovered "a circus, a comedy, a crazy house."[178]

The Soviets had begun importing products from Detroit before the visit from the experts, starting with the Fordson tractor—Fordzon, in Russian—, whose popularity was as widespread as its inventor's. In 1930, Maurice Hindus quoted Leon Trotsky's statement that "the most popular word among our forward-looking peasantry is Fordson. The peasant speaks of the *Fordzonishka*—dear little Fordson—gently, lovingly."[179] Thousands of children were named in its honour. Launched on the American market in 1916 by the Henry Ford & Son Tractor Division, the Fordson tractor played a major role in the mechanization of British agriculture after the war, and later in modernizing farming equipment in the United States, with production surpassing 500,000 vehicles a year in the 1920s[180]. Essential to American rural life, the tractor's aura extended worldwide, so much so that the functionalist architect, Hannes Meyer, praised it as a symbol of the "new world" he welcomed in 1926[181]. The Fordson became one of the tools of the mechanization of Russian agriculture, along with equipment produced by the International Harvester, whose factory was never shut down by the regime, and the concession of large model farming plots to Germans or Americans, intended as a way of teaching local farmers modern methods. Hindus noted the tractor's importance to Soviet life in his introduction to the 1931 book of photographs taken in Russia by Margaret Bourke-White, who according to him "has caught the full meaning of its place on the Russian scene. She exhibits to us not a mechanical monster, but a heroic conqueror, as sublime and as alive as the horses in the adjacent fields."[182]

Left: Copy of the Fordson tractor produced by the Krasnyi Putilovets factory. Cover of *Nauka i Tekhnika* [Science and Technology]. April 1930. Private collection. Right: Advertisement for the Fordson tractor, *Sport i Okhota* [*Sports and Hunting*], ca. 1926. Letterpress print and comments typed in red ink. The Henry Ford Collection, Dearborn, Michigan.

After the Council of Labour and Defence decreed the establishment, on 4 March 1924, of a national tractor industry, Ford's machine was chosen over its German and American counterparts as the model to be produced. As of 1923, an unauthorized copy was already in the works at the Putilov Plant, in Petrograd. At first quite chaotic, as shown on the 1931 painting "The Tractor Shop" by Pavel Filonov, Russian production continued until the fifty-thousandth tractor was issued in 1932, though it was hindered by the lack of quality steel. The Soviet tractor reached a certain level of industrial quality only after recurrent crises, thanks to the contribution of engineers having travelled to Detroit, such as the director Mikhail Ter-Asaturov[183]. The circulation of technicians and workers between Detroit and Russia remained intense during the following decade, with many émigrés returning to the motherland for work.

The first contract for American automobile imports into the Soviet Union was signed in March 1919 with Ivan Stacheev's company, while a significant fleet of vehicles was sent to Russia by way of Denmark[184]. A month later, Ludwig Martens addressed Ford on behalf of the Soviet Bureau in New York, paving the

183   On the political significance of the Fordson and the history of its production at the Putilov Plant, see Yves Cohen, "The Soviet Fordson: Between the Politics of Stalin and the Philosophy of Ford, 1924–1932," in *Ford, 1903–2003*, Hubert Bonin, Yannick Lung, and Steven Tolliday, eds. (Paris: P.L.A.G.E., 2003), 531–38. On the tractor's use, see the manual *Fordzon; rukovodstvo k polzovaniu traktorom* (Rostov: Tekhnoimport NKVTT, 1924).

184   Edsel B. Ford, Letter to P.P. Batolin [Ivan Stacheeff & Co. in Petrograd], 20 March 1919, Benson Ford Research Center, Henry Ford Collection, acquisition no. 49, box 1; see also White, "Ford in Russia," 81–82.

Nikolai B. Sokolov. *Lenin is Dead, Leninism is Alive*, calendar for the year 1925, 1924.
Typographic print with collage, 33 × 19.4 cm. Alex Lachmann Collection.

way for a productive relationship: "I have [...] in my mind something else than the purely commercial interest your firm may have in Russian trade. We would like very much to discuss with you the social aspects of the regeneration of Russia and we believe we could make you understand that Soviet Russia is inaugurating methods of industrial efficiency compatible with the interests of humanity and unhampered by the curse of greed and graft."[185] The number of interested parties increased, including the Hammers, father and son. The latter, Armand, had introduced tractors to southern Russia as of 1922. Not unlike Ford himself, he organized a plowing presentation in Rostov-on-Don, in the presence of the local political leader, Anastas Mikoyan[186]. Sometime later, Julius Hammer tried to convince Ford to become interested in the significant Soviet market, despite the latter's zeal in battling Communists within his own corporation. He thus obtained an exclusive concession for his Allied American Corporation, whose stationary was adorned with a bright red Fordson[187].

Between 1925 and 1926, upwards of 20,000 tractors were delivered to the Soviets, before complications at Ford's Irish company halted the process. In 1926, upon returning from a five-month journey in the USSR, from Leningrad to Baku and from Odessa to Saratov, a group of Ford engineers painted a dark portrait of factory working conditions including daily work life, wages and living conditions of workers. Ford's engineers also offered a detailed analysis of the economy and prospects for the tractor market in the Soviet Union[188]. In 1929, Charles Sorensen, one of the masterminds behind the Detroit factories, visited the USSR and advised his hosts to tear down the inefficient Putilov mills and to rebuild plants based on his own American creations, Highland Park and River Rouge[189]. Ford himself was very clearly in favour of trading with the USSR: "Russia [...] is beginning to build. It makes little difference what theory is behind the real work, for in the long run facts will prevail."[190]

Three quarters of the Russian tractor fleet was then comprised of American machines, for the most part built by Ford or his Leningrad imitators[191]. An entry in the Great Soviet Encyclopedia was dedicated to the Fordson, as

185   Ludwig Martens, Letter to Henry Ford, 21 April 1919, Benson Ford Research Center, Henry Ford Collection, acquisition no. 62, box 109.
186   Hammer, *Armand Hammer*, 82–102; see also White, "Ford in Russia," 85. On repression in Ford's factories, see David E. Greenstein, "Assembling Fordizm: The Production of Automobiles, Americans, and Bolsheviks in Detroit and Early Soviet Russia," *Comparative Studies in Society and History* 56, no. 2 (April 2014): 265–67.
187   Julius Hammer, Letters to Russell I. Roberge and Charles Sorensen, 3 June 1923, Benson Ford Research Center, Henry Ford Collection, acquisition no. 38, box 47. On his discussions with Ford about Russia, see Hammer, *Armand Hammer*, 134–38.
188   *Report of the Ford Delegation to Russia and the USSR, April–August 1926*, Detroit, 1926. Benson Ford Research Center, Henry Ford Collection, acquisition no. 1870, box 1. The delegation comprised H.C. Luedtke, W.S. Ostendorf, M.R. Tuban, B.H. Berghoff, and W. G. Collins. See David E. Greenstein, "Assembling Fordizm: The Production of Automobiles, Americans, and Bolsheviks in Detroit and Early Soviet Russia," *Comparative Studies in Society and History* 56, no. 2 (April 2014): 259–89. Boris M. Shpotov, "The Case of US Companies in Russia-USSR: Ford in 1920s–1930s," in Hubert Bonin and Ferry de Goey, eds., *American Firms in Europe, 1880-1980: Strategy, Identity, Perception and Performance* (Geneva: Librairie Droz, 2009), 435–58.
189   Charles E. Sorensen, *My Forty Years with Ford* (New York: W.W. Norton & Co., 1956), 201.
190   Henry Ford, in Henry Ford with William McGarry, "Why I Am Helping Russian Industry," *Nation's Business*, June 1930, 22.
191   Dana Dalrymple, "American Technology and Soviet Agricultural Development, 1924–1933," *Agricultural History* 40, no. 3 (July 1966): 187–206; Dana Dalrymple, "The American Tractor Comes to Soviet Agriculture: The Transfer of a Technology," *Technology and Culture* 5, no. 2 (Spring 1964): 191–214.
192   See the entry for "Fordzon," in *Bolshaia sovetskaia entsiklopedia* (Moscow: OGIZ, 1936), vol. 57, 131.
193   Leonard E. Hubbard, *Economics of Soviet Agriculture* (London: Macmillan 1939), 260–61.
194   Joseph Roth, "Reise nach Russland, XI. Russland geht nach Amerika," *Frankfurter Zeitung*, 13 November 1926, in *Reise nach Rußland: Feuilletons, Reportagen, Tagebuchnotizen 1920–1930*, ed. Klaus Westermann (Cologne: Kiepenheuer & Witsch, 1995), 179.
195   Roland Barthes, *Mythologies* [1957], trans. Annette Lavers (London: Vintage, 1972), 88.
196   Gilbert Simondon, *Du mode d'existence des objets techniques* [1958] (Paris: Aubier-Montaigne, 1969), 9.

if it were a historical figure. It also became a weapon in the ferocious battle waged by Stalin to impose agricultural cooperation by eradicating middle peasantry[192]. The Fordson was used in circumstances where its performance was detrimental to production, that is when the number of necessary spare parts and the tractor's fuel consumption surpassed the value of harvested grains[193]. But western visitors, such as the writer Joseph Roth, took notice of the cry "Tractors! Tractors! Tractors!" resonating countrywide[194].

Given affectionate nicknames, the Fordson rose to a mythical status, despite—or owing to—its primitive form, "no pretensions about being as smooth as cake-icing," as Roland Barthes wrote about the Citroën DS 19[195]. Contrary to its streamlined successors of the 1930s, the Fordson was still, to borrow Gilbert Simondon's expression, an "abstract machine,"[196] meaning a combination of disconnected components resembling a constructivist sculpture. Beyond its political significance, its robust shape found its way into multiple films. Even more than the peasant Marfa Lapkina, the Fordson is the true protagonist of Sergei Eisenstein's 1927 feature film *The General Line*, where tractors engage in a circle ballet to celebrate the victory of collectivization. In *Earth*, a 1930 motion picture directed by Aleksandr Dovzhenko, the peasant Vasyl Opanas defeats the kulaks -or middle peasants, despite their sabotage, thanks to his tractor. In a less lyrical vein, in Esfir Shub and Mark Tseitlin's 1929 film *Today*, which opposes the victorious USSR of the first five-year plan period to the United States, a scene is dedicated to the ceremonious launch of the five thousandth Putilov tractor, displayed onstage in the Proletarskii district's House of Culture in Leningrad.

Vera D. Lotonina. *Energy*, Design for a decorative textile with a tractor pattern, 1931.
Gouache on paper, 36 × 29.9 cm. Alex Lachmann Collection.

At the other end of the food chain, as of 1926, the McCormick Company built three gigantic industrial bakeries to provide daily bread to the citizens of Moscow and Leningrad, in buildings whose constructivist architecture seemed to be dictated by the production process itself. Agreements with Americans were common in many sectors of mechanical fabrication, with a few notable exceptions, including ball bearing manufacturing, which remained dominated by the Swedish firm SKF. As for locomotive construction, Baldwin and General Electric were the main partners, while Singer, nationalized in 1918, regained control of its factories in 1925 and resumed production. The first Russian typewriters were produced under licence from Underwood as of 1930[197]. Furthermore, the old installations prevailed, so much so that in 1928, only 7% of production stemmed from factories created after 1917[198]. Things changed with the first five-year plan, and attempts to introduce Fordism to all sectors proliferated[199].

Amtorg: A Russian Purchasing Office in New York

The Amtorg Trading Corporation or simply Amtorg, an acronym that stands for Amerikanskaia Torgovlia (American trade), based in New York City from May 1924, was one of the main importers of Ford tractors and played a central part in the transatlantic transfer of technology. It centralized negotiations and, more importantly, funded the purchases, replacing a wide network dealing in products, equipment, and information, which included the Association of Russian Engineers in America, headed by Polakov. Amtorg, a private joint-stock company, was born from the union between the Products Exchange Corporation and Armand Hammer's Allied American Corporation, with Arcos-America, a relocated branch of the Soviet organization created to enable trade with Great Britain. Amtorg settled at 165 Broadway, before moving, in 1929, to 261 Fifth Avenue. Its first president was Isai Khurgin, who was quickly replaced by Efraim Sklianskii, a close friend of Trotsky whom Stalin had

197   Sutton, *Western Technology*, vol. 1, 164–184.
198   Brunnbauer, "The League of Time," 467.
199   Kurt Stephen Schultz, "The American Factor in Soviet Industrialization: Fordism and the First Five-Year Plan, 1928–1932," PhD dissertation (Columbus: Ohio State University, 1992).
200   Boris Bazhanov, *Bazhanov and the Damnation of Stalin* [1930], transl. and commentary by David W. Doyle (Athens, OH: Ohio University Press, 1990), 64; Richard B. Spence, "Death in the Adirondacks: Amtorg, Intrigue, and the Dubious Demise of Isaiya Khurgin and Efraim Sklyansky, August 1925," *American Communist History* 14, no. 2 (August 2015): 135–58.
201   Saul G. Bron, "New Head of American–Soviet Trading Organization," *Soviet Union Review* 5, no. 6 (June 1927), 92, in Sonia Melnikova-Raich, "The Soviet Problem with Two 'Unknowns': How an American Architect and a Soviet Negotiator Jump-Started the Industrialization of Russia, Part II: Saul Bron," *Journal of the Society for Industrial Archeology* 37, no. 1–2 (2011): 7. Bron also published *Soviet Economic Development and American Business* (New York: Horace Liveright, 1930).
202   Petr A. Bogdanov, articles in *Pravda* and *Moscow Daily News*, 1935, quoted in Parks, *Culture, Conflict and Coexistence*, 43.
203   J.H. Wilson, "American Business and the Recognition of the Soviet Union," *Social Science Quarterly* 52, no. 2 (1971): 352.
204   Joseph M. Tatcher Feinstein, *Fifty Years of U.S.–Soviet Trade* (New York: Symposium Press, 1974), 43. This book is a eulogy to Amtorg, written by one of its former executives.
205   "Soviet Bridge Construction Engineers Arrive," *Economic Review of the Soviet Union*, 15 November 1927, 5.
206   "1924–1931," *Amerikanskaia tekhnika i promyshlennost* 8, no. 9 (September 1931), 618; "Zhurnal AMTORGa: kak vsestoronnyi popouliarizator dlia SSSR dostizhenii amerikanskoi tekhniki," *Amerikanskaia tekhnika i promyshlennost* 9, no. 9 (September 1932): 556.
207   "Zhurnal AMTORGa:" 556.
208   Walter N. Polakov, "NOTovskoe dvizhenie posle Teilora," *Amerikanskaia tekhnika* 1, no. 1 (November 1924): 6–9.
209   V.V. Chikov, "Standartizatsiia v SShA," *Amerikanskaia tekhnika i promyshlennost* 11, no. 12 (December 1934): 598–602.

ejected from his position as Deputy People's Commissar for Defence. The fact that both presidents drowned on August 27, 1925, in Long Lake, in Upstate New York, was likely not coincidental, as, according to his secretary, Boris Bazhanov, Stalin "hated" Sklianskii[200].

From 1927 to 1930, after Aleksei Prigarin, the corporation was headed by the economist Saul Bron. After completing a PhD in Zurich, Bron had led Exportkhleb, the conglomerate dealing with strategic grain export, and later Roskombank, the foreign trade bank. Shortly after arriving in New York, he declared: "Industrial leaders in the Soviet Union are fully awake to the value of utilizing American technical and industrial skill to assist in developing the rich natural resources of the country and promoting its industrialization."[201] His successor at the head of Amtorg, Petr Bogdanov, pleaded in 1935 for "constant and systematic relationships with American engineering" and for the creation of permanent Soviet "production bases" in the United States to train the necessary workforce[202]. With a significant staff—489 employees in 1930, among whom 305 were American—, Amtorg established a wide range of contracts, from the purchase of printing presses, tractors, and entire factories to the import of live cattle. In 1930, at its height, Russian trade accounted for 3% of total American exports, rising to 4.3% in 1931, but only in particularly strategic sectors[203]. Serving as an unofficial embassy until 1933, the corporation organized American visits for an increasing number of Russian technicians: 66 were hosted in 1926, and 575 in 1930[204]. In 1927, for instance, a group of Soviet engineers spent two months in the United States, studying the construction of metal bridges[205].

In May 1930, Amtorg was accused of harbouring spies, which indeed seemed to be one of its hidden purposes, as it provided legitimate cover to several Soviet intelligence agents. It also controlled the circulation of information through a special service, headed in the early 1930s by the seasoned Bolshevik Petr Voevodin. From 1926 to 1932, it issued the *Economic Review of the Soviet Union*, intended for American readers. For the Russian public, Amtorg joined forces with Polakov's association to publish, from November 1924 to late 1928, the monthly journal *Amerikanskaia tekhnika*, which in January 1929 was renamed *Amerikanskaia tekhnika i promyshlennost* (American Engineering and Industry), whose last issue was printed in 1948. Published in Russian in New York and intended for a readership comprised of Soviet managers and engineers, the periodical boasted its 25,000 Russian readers to potential advertisers. The following year, its circulation was said to reach readers in Moscow (14%), Leningrad (13%), Ukraine (13%), and the Ural Region (7%), mostly in engineering firms and on construction sites[206]. It served as a manner of encyclopedia, with entries on crucial issues for the Soviet economy: 18% on electrotechnics, 10% on metalworking, and 6% on construction[207], and were illustrated with graphs, sectional views, and technical details, as well as photographs taken in major factories. The ever-growing number of advertisements are rather helpful to determine which American firms were dealing with the USSR, or wished to do so.

The question of the NOT was addressed in the very first article of the inaugural issue, in which Polakov assessed the situation of Taylorism after Taylor[208]. The subject remained a continuous thread throughout the publication, offering up-to-date statistics concerning American production, work efficiency in the United States, and interactions with the USSR. The publication was a strong advocate for the use of American standards in Soviet industry at large[209]. In addition to all the energy-related technologies, namely the construction of great dams such as the Boulder Dam and Grand Coulee Dam, there was significant focus on the chemical industry as well as transportation—the automotive, aviation, and rail industries. The creation of high-speed railway lines and the introduction of streamlined trains such as the *Flying Yankee* were thoroughly documented[210]. Civil works and major infrastructural operations like dams, large train stations, and bridges were regularly discussed, while urban technologies such as sanitation were rarely brought up, likely because they were more difficult to import[211]. The programme was quite deliberate regarding construction, as the journal called for the "transfer of advanced American techniques to the USSR[212]." It thus covered themes such as foundations and construction site organization and presented the latest techniques in cooling and lighting systems."[213]

In the field of architecture, the main points of interest were light-frame wooden construction, skyscrapers, and housing, to a lesser degree. There were frequent updates on new skyscraper projects and ongoing high-rise construction sites[214]. Major publications on the economics and aesthetics of skyscrapers, such as the writings of Hugh Ferriss, were discussed and critiqued[215]. Articles on these themes were often written by Viacheslav Oltarzhevskii, a Russian architect who was in New York from 1924[216] and who also designed the journal's title page for the new version published as of 1926, combining various mechanical elements with skyscraper outlines. He used the publication to promote his own projects, including that of a 65-storey skyscraper for Manhattan[217]. As a regular columnist, Oltarzhevskii examined the hotels, schools, and structures such as Grand Central Station, as well as suburban houses[218]. One of several American contributors, the young New York architect Simon Breines wrote pieces on kitchens, bathrooms, stand-alone houses, and new construction materials[219].

210   "Novyi sverkh-skorostnyi poezd 'letaiushchii ianki'," *Amerikanskaia tekhnika i promyshlennost* 12, no. 1 (January 1935): 119–23.

211   The George Washington Bridge was evoked many times, notably in L.S. Moiseev, "Visiashchii most cherez Gudzon," *Amerikanskaia tekhnika i promyshlennost* 4, no. 10 (October 1927): 10–15.

212   "Peredovuiu stroitelnuiu tekhniku SShA perenesem v stroitelstvo Sovetskogo Soiuza," *Amerikanskaia tekhnika i promyshlennost* 9, no. 10 (October 1932): 562–64.

213   A.V. Canney, "Obshchaia teoria i praktika tekhniki konditsirovania vozdukha," *Amerikanskaia tekhnika i promyshlennost* 12, no. 1 (January 1935): 22–33; "Standarty osveshchenia shkol i zavodov," *Amerikanskaia tekhnika i promyshlennost* 12, no. 4 (April 1935): 172–77.

214   P.E. Nikitin, "Radio-gorod," *Amerikanskaia tekhnika i promyshlennost* 8, no. 14 (April 1931): 270 [on the Rockefeller Center]; P.E. Nikitin, "Neboskreby i ikh vozvedenie," *Amerikanskaia tekhnika i promyshlennost* 7, no. 11 (November 1930): 755–64

215   "The Skyscraper: A Study of Its Economic Height," *Amerikanskaia tekhnika i promyshlennost* 7, no. 12 (December 1930): 779–80; "The Metropolis of Tomorrow," *Tekhnika i promyshlennost* 7, no. 5 (May 1930): 304.

216   On the architect's work at the beginning of his American stay, see "Work by W. Oltargevsky [sic], architect, Moscow, Russia and New York," *The American Architect*, 5 September 1926, 210–15.

217   Viacheslav Oltarzhevskii, "Neboskreb rekordnoi vysoty," *Amerikanskaia tekhnika* 3, no. 9 (September 1926): 29–30.

218   Viacheslav Oltarzhevskii, "Proektirovanie otelei v SShA," *Amerikanskaia tekhnika i promyshlennost* 10, no. 6 (June 1933): 190–96; "Amerikanskaia arkhitektura (vokzaly)," *Amerikanskaia tekhnika i promyshlennost* 11, no. 2 (February 1934): 84–90; "Amerikanskaia arkhitektura (zagorodnye doma)," *Amerikanskaia tekhnika i promyshlennost* 11, no. 7 (July 1934): 345–52. On hotels, see also A. Bravin, "Osnovnye printsipy proektirovaniia otelei v Amerike," *Amerikanskaia tekhnika i promyshlennost* 9, no. 8 (August 1932): 481–83.

219   Simon Breines, "Amerikanskie kukhni" and "Amerikanskaia vannaia komnata," *Amerikanskaia tekhnika i promyshlennost* 12, no. 4 (April 1935): 151–54 and 155–58; "Gos. stroitelstvo deshevykh kvartir v SShA," *Amerikanskaia tekhnika i promyshlennost* 13, no. 4 (April 1936): 138–44; "Konstruktsii is stekliannykh kirpichei, *Amerikanskaia tekhnika i promyshlennost* 15, no. 12 (December 1938): 608–11.

220   In advertisements, Hugh L. Cooper presented the Wilson Dam as "the biggest hydroelectric project in America," *Amerikanskaia tekhnika i promyshlennost* 4, no. 9 (September 1927): 7.

221   *Spravotchnik amerikanskoi tekhniki i promyshlennosti* (New York: Amtorg, 1927–1948). See also "Amtorg Issues New Catalog of American Industry," *Economic Review of the Soviet Union*, 15 November 1929, 396–97.

222   Sorensen, *My Forty Years*, 194.

Scarce at first, advertisements proliferated in *Amerikanskaia tekhnika i promyshlennost* as soon as the five-year plan was launched. The advertisers were mostly car manufacturers such as Ford, Packard, or Lincoln—selling trucks, planes, civil engineering equipment, locomotives, machine tools, drilling gear—as well as General Electric, which focused its message on the delights of household electrification. There were also engineers such as Hugh L. Cooper and construction firms like the Austin Company, all involved in the Russian market.[220] Amtorg bound these postings in thick volumes, published between 1927 and 1948 as eight successive issues of a general inventory of American products, widely disseminated among Russian leaders[221]. Each of these *Spravochniki* (Directories) was divided by industry sector and contained over 1,000 pages of advertisements and technical sheets, serving as overseas sales catalogues directed at factory directors wishing to stock up on supplies. The United States thus appeared as a gigantic market catering to the needs and wishes of Soviet managers, though the turnover was tempered by the growing currency shortage and the fact that American companies were forbidden from selling on credit.

In the automotive sector, Amtorg engaged in significant negotiations with the Americans in 1928, with help from the economist Valerii Mezhlauk, vice-president of the VSNKh, whom the Ford executives seemed to particularly appreciate, according to Charles Sorensen[222]. In 1929, these painstakingly prepared deliberations resulted in the signing of several determinant contracts for Soviet architecture and industry. This outcome was reached solely owing to Mezhlauk and Bron's diplomatic savvy and to the efforts of Valerian Obolenskii, also known under his pen name Nikolai Osinskii, within

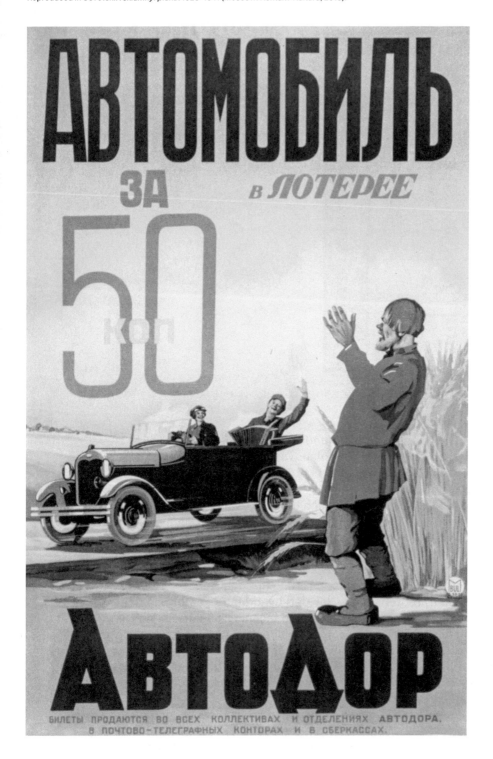

the Soviet leadership. A Bolshevik journalist and economist who had studied in Germany, Osinskii was the first president of the VSNKh in 1917, before he became ambassador to Sweden, and later headed the Central Statistical Directorate. Osinkii was also one of the few high-level Soviet leaders to be fully acquainted with the United States. He travelled there twice and published his critical impressions on his return, which resulted in his failure to obtain a new visa[223]. More importantly, he returned as an automobile fanatic, driving his car during rallies, and presiding the Avtodor corporation, established for the improvement of the Soviet road network.

Osinskii published aspirational articles in the monthly journal *Za Rulem* [At the Wheel], which he created in 1928, demonstrating both his detailed understanding of the American industry and his awareness of the total absence of a real road network in Russia, where the most extravagant infrastructure projects were envisioned, but without any tangible effects[224]. His ideas seemed to enthuse Stalin for a time, who declared in 1929: "We are becoming a country of metal, a country of automobiles, a country of tractors. And when we have put the USSR on an automobile, and the *muzhik (peasant)* on a tractor, let the worthy capitalists […] try to overtake us!"[225] Osinskii's pamphlet *The American Automobile or the Russian Cart?*, initially published as an article in the *Pravda* in 1927, was widely discussed[226]. Unlike most economists who were in favour of a cautious industrial policy, Osinskii, though he was hostile to large projects such as the Dneprostroi, worked with Valerian Kuibyshev to set ambitious goals and prevailed after a relentless battle[227]. While the first version of the five-year plan projected the production of 3,500 cars per year, Osinskii wished to produce 100,000 and in 1928, launched negotiations with General Motors and Ford, resulting in the agreement signed by Valerii Mezhlauk with the latter[228].

Albert Kahn's Factories, From Detroit to the Urals

Before signing the agreement with Ford, Amtorg was already interested in building structures that could house future assembly lines. The course of discussions changed when the organization contacted Albert Kahn Associates, the Detroit architectural firm behind the 1913 Crystal Palace erected for Ford in Highland Park. Kahn's office was particularly productive in the interwar period, designing for instance 20% of all the American industrial structures built in 1938[229]. A Russian delegation visited Kahn in 1928, before his meeting with Bron in New York. Their conversation focused on the giant Ford River Rouge complex, created by the architect in Dearborn, southwest of Detroit,

223   Nikolai Osinskii, *Po tu storonu okeana: iz amerikanskikh vpechatlenii i nabliudenii* (Moscow; Leningrad: Gos. Izd-vo, 1926); *Moi Izheuchenia o Soedinennykh Shtatakh Severnoi Ameriki* (Moscow: Pravda i bednota, 1926).
224   Nikolai Osinskii, "Avtomobilnaia voina v Soedinnennykh Shtatakh," *Za Rulem*, no. 1 (April 1928): 9–11; "O tom, kak udovletvorit blizhaishuiu massovuiu potrebnost v avtomachinakh," *Za Rulem*, no. 2 (May 1928): 2–5.
225   Iosif V. Stalin, "God velikogo pereloma," *Pravda*, 7 November 1929; in English: *Works*, vol. 12, 124–141.
226   Nikolai Osinskii, *Amerikanskii avtomobil ili rossiiskaia telega* (Moscow: Pravda i bednota, 1927).
227   Kurt S. Schultz, "Building the 'Soviet Detroit': The Construction of the Nizhni-Novgorod Automobile Factory, 1927-1932," *Slavic Review* 49, no. 2 (1990): 200–12.
228   Sutton, *Western Technology*, 1, 246–247.
229   Sonia Melnikova-Raich, "The Soviet Problem with Two 'Unknowns': How an American Architect and a Soviet Negotiator Jump-Started the Industrialization of Russia, Part I: Albert Kahn," *Journal of the Society for Industrial Archeology* 36, no. 2 (2010): 60.

that allowed Ford to oversee the entire process of automobile manufacturing. Initiated in 1917 and mostly completed by 1928, the construction site remained active until 1941. On a 1,000-acre (400-hectare) territory furrowed with railroads, all the stages of production were laid out, from the manufacturing of steel, forges, and rolling mills to the fabrication of tires and motors, and to the final assembly of vehicles[230]. In contrast with the architectural principle of Highland Park, which combined a concrete structure with brick and glass fillings, the River Rouge buildings stretched horizontally and struck a rhythm with the angular rooftop profiles. The tension between the smokestacks and the diagonal lines of the conveyer belts inspired Charles Sheeler's most dramatic photographs.

The firm established by Albert Kahn and his brothers, the engineers Louis and Moritz Kahn, the latter a specialist in reinforced steel and based in London for a time[231], built hundreds of structures in Detroit and on the city's outskirts: factories, villas for automobile manufacturers, public buildings, as well as many buildings on the campus of the University of Michigan[232]. The firm's industrial expertise made it indispensable to Soviets, who wished to replicate entire integrated industrial complexes such as those found in the American Midwest. River Rouge became a prototype for the kombinat, a giant facility created on virgin territory that incorporated all the necessary installations for a specific type of production. The River Rouge model also came to symbolize Detroit, as the Soviets equated the factory with the nearby city, setting out to miraculously reproduce it despite the lack of urban complexity on bare Soviet lands[233]. To this end, Amtorg secured several significant agreements over the span of a few weeks. The first one, signed with Kahn on 8 May 1929, concerned the establishment of the tractor plant in Stalingrad, which had been in the works for five years[234].

On August 23rd of the following year, a second contract, devised to accelerate the construction of Avtostroi near Nizhnii Novgorod, was entrusted to The Austin Company, which specialized in the creation of turnkey factories[235]. The firm was to build the plant and its extensions, the agreement stating that "all buildings shall be carried out according to the best methods used by the concern in the United States."[236] The plans were meant to be "understood by workers with an average level of training."[237] The construction site was supervised by two executives from the firm, Harry F. Mitter and Chet Appleton, while Allan S. Austin, also settled in Nizhnii Novgorod, regularly described the daily hardships to his father[238]. Wilbert J. Austin, the president of the firm, travelled to visit his crew and eloquently depicted the competition between the teams using Russian techniques and those operating in the American way, each with its own tools: "The construction sites

230   Lindy Biggs, *The Rational Factory: Architecture, Technology, and Work in America's Age of Mass Production* (Baltimore: Johns Hopkins University Press, 1996), 137–60.
231   Moritz Kahn, *The Design & Construction of Industrial Buildings* (London: Technical Journals Ltd., 1917).
232   Michael H. Hodges, *Building the Modern World: Albert Kahn in Detroit* (Detroit: Wayne State University Press, 2018). Claire Zimmerman, "Albert Kahn's Territories," in Franch, Lawrence, Miljački and Schafer, eds., *Office Us Agenda*, 117–127.
233   See the article "Doroga v sovetskii Detroit", *Krasnaia niva*, no. 28 (1929): 19.
234   Dana D. Dalrymple and Norton T. Dodge, "The Stalingrad Tractor Plan in Early Soviet Planning," *Soviet Studies* 18, no. 2 (October 1966): 164–68.
235   Martin Greif, *The New Industrial Landscape: The Story of the Austin Company* (Clinton, NJ: Main Street Press, 1978), 97ff.
236   Contract between the USSR government and The Austin Company, 23 August 1929, 2, GARF, R5446 11a 446.
237   Ibid., 7.
238   Allan Austin's letters are the foundation for Richard Cartwright Austin, *Building Utopia: Erecting Russia's First Modern City, 1930* (Lanham, MD: Kent State University Press, 2004).

Signing of contract between Albert Kahn Associates and Amtorg, 9 January 1930. At the forefront: Albert Kahn and Saul G. Bron; at the back: Moritz Kahn between L. Olkhovsky and J. Michaels, Amtorg legal advisers. Bentley Historical Library, University of Michigan.

Benjamin Goodwin Seielstad. Diagram of automobile production at the Ford River Rouge Complex, Dearborn, Michigan, spread in *Life*, 19 August 1940. CCA.

Albert Kahn Associates. Automobile plant, Nizhnii Novgorod, 1930-1931. Aerial perspective, drawing by Georgii A. and Vladimir A. Stenberg.
Gelatin silver print on paper, 18 × 24 cm. The Henry Ford Collection, Dearborn, Michigan.

Albert Kahn Associates. KIM automobile plant, Moscow, 1930-1931. View of the Coil Spring Plant, 2 January 1931.
Gelatin silver print on paper, 18 × 24 cm. The Henry Ford Collection, Dearborn, Michigan.

under way represent a combination of American and Russian building methods, for we realized that no one nation has a corner on all the advanced ideas in building."[239] This combination can also be witnessed in the architecture of the complex: while the factory was built according to The Austin Company's plans, a contest was organized in 1930 among Soviet teams for the creation of residential quarters. The rationalists of the ARU and the constructivists of the OSA were locked in competition, along with a team from the Vkhutein and Ernst May's architectural brigade, who had just arrived from Germany[240]. The residential buildings were built by The Austin Company, whose survival during the Depression was insured by the Russian contracts.

On 31 May 1929, Mezhlauk and Bron signed the contract to furnish the Nizhnii Novgorod factory. The plan was to purchase massive quantities of equipment and parts from Ford. After four years, this would provide the USSR with the annual production capacity of 100,000 GAZ-A automobiles—the equivalent of the Ford A model—and AA model trucks. The assembly of parts produced in America would thus progressively make way for the handling of the entire manufacturing cycle[241]. Furthermore, the agreement also included the creation of the KIM (Communist Youth International) factory in Moscow, opened in 1930 to assemble the A models, which became the cradle of the Moskvich automobiles[242].

Assembly of American parts as a starting point for production in Nizhnii Novgorod was also applied to the Stalingrad plant, set to manufacture tractors inspired by those of The International Harvester. Its metal structures were created in the New York workshops of McClintic-Marshall Products before being delivered to Russia, piece by piece[243]. Kahn sent the engineers John K. Calder and Leon A. Swajian, veterans of the River Rouge project, to conduct the operations of 380 technicians and workers and to supervise the Russian work-force in Stalingrad. As this initial operation was launched, Kahn and Ford worked on a second agreement, signed on 9 January 1930. While the first contract did not include patent dedication, Kahn transferred all of his expertise to Moscow, following the industrialist's advice, who recommended he be generous[244]. Kahn's team quickly became skilled in the art of dealing with the Soviets, to the point where they counselled Ford on the terms of his negotiation regarding the living conditions of technicians sent to settle on the banks of the Oka River[245].

The Detroit architecture firm created two other significant projects for tractor manufacturing, one in Kharkov, Ukraine, the other in Cheliabinsk, in the Urals, for which a temporary drawing office was established in Detroit[246].

239   Frederick A. Van Fleet, "Building a Ford Factory in Russia: an Interview with W. J. Austin," *The Review of Reviews*, January 1931, 46. On The Austin Company's engagement in the Soviet Union, see Jeffrey W. Cody, *Exporting American Architecture 1870–2000* (London: Routledge, 2003), 103-6.

240   Vitalii A. Lavrov, "Avtostroi – sotsialisticheskii gorod," *Stroitelstvo Moskvy*, no. 4 (1930): 20–24. See also Marco De Michelis and Ernesto Pasini, *La città sovietica 1925–1937* (Venice: Marsilio, 1976), 60–69.

241   Agreement between Ford and the VSNKh, 31 May 1929, Benson Ford Research Center, Henry Ford Collection, acquisition no. 199, box 1. See also "Ford Company to Aid Development of Soviet Automobile Industry," *Economic Review of the Soviet Union*, 1 July 1929, 230–31. Automobile production would reach 84,000 units per year in 1938, according to German sources quoted in Sutton, *Western Technology*, vol. 1, 248. On Russian Fords, see Robert Scoon, "Those Communist Model A's," *The Restorer; The Magazine for Ford A Enthusiasts 14*, no. 6 (1970): 9–22.

242   Frank Ernest Hills and Allan Nevins, *Ford: Expansion and Challenge 1915–1933* (New York: Charles Scribner's Sons, 1957), 678; Siegelbaum, *Cars for Comrades*, 61.

243   Vasilii I. Kasianenko, "Ispolzovanie amerikanskogo opyta v periode stanovleniia sovetskogo promyshlennogo zodchestva (sotrudnichestvo s firmoi Alberta Kana)", in *Vzaimodeistvie kultur*, 111-120.

244   Contract project between the NKTP and AKA, 14 December 1929, GARF R5446 11a 448.

245   Louis Kahn, Letter to Russell Gnau [Ford Motor Company], 27 February 1932, Benson Ford Research Center, Henry Ford Collection, acquisition no. 531, box 1.

246   Melnikova, "Kahn," 70. On the Kharkov project and its urban environment, as well as Baku's urbanism in this period, see the impressive work of Christina Crawford, "The Socialist Settlement Experiment: Soviet Urban Praxis, 1917-1932," PhD dissertation (Harvard University, 2016), 279-358, as well as her article "From Tractors to Territory: Socialist Urbanization through Standardization," *Journal of Urban History* 44, no. 1 (2018): 54–77.

Ford A model automobiles at the KIM factory assembly line, 6 November 1930.
Gelatin silver print on paper, 18 × 24 cm. Benson Ford Research Center.

6 НОЯ 1

Albert Kahn Associates. Stalingrad Tractor Plan, 1929–1930. Sections, 1929.
Pen and ink, graphite, on drafting cloth, 72.5 × 116.3 cm. Bentley Historical Library, University of Michigan.

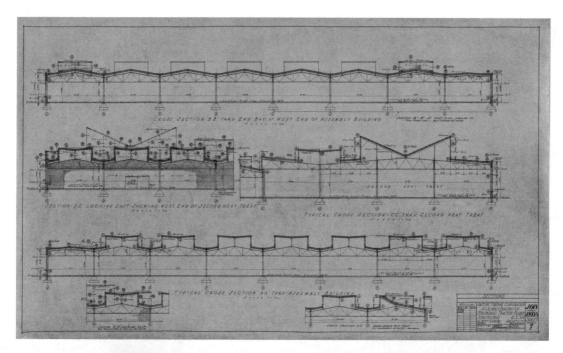

Truss assembly for the tractor factory in Stalingrad designed by Albert Kahn Associates in the McClintic-Marshall shop, New York.
Photograph by Santangelo Studio, 1930. Gelatin silver print on paper, mounted on cardboard, 19.6 × 29.3 cm.
Bentley Historical Library, University of Michigan.

On location, the plans were drawn up by a mixed crew of Russians and Americans overseen by Calder, while Swajian headed the Kharkov site. Most importantly, the second agreement resulted in the relocation of the design hub, with the creation of the Gosproektstroi drawing office in Moscow. Under the leadership of Moritz Kahn, a team of 25 architects and engineers, along with their families, settled in Moscow, where they would operate until 1932. According to available estimates, some 521 to 570 projects were designed in this office, including almost all the Soviet metallurgical and machine factories[247]. Located a few hundred metres away from the Kremlin, on the corner of the Bolshoi Cherkasskii Pereulok and Nikolskaia Street [ill. p. 162], the studio employed 900 Russians at its peak, in 1931: 300 in its Leningrad branch, 100 in Kharkov, and several others in local branches, as far as Novosibirsk[248]. Over 4,000 people, including students and executives, were exposed to Kahn's "Russian-American system" for project management and construction, an experience recounted by some of the participants and a few historians[249].

Anatolii Fisenko, a young and talented engineer, was put in charge of the technical section, and went on to become an architect and the head engineer of the Gosproektstroi, thanks to support from the constructivist architect Viktor Vesnin, who had himself been long involved in factory building. Fisenko oversaw training for engineers and designers, whose initial lack of experience and quick overturn deeply annoyed Kahn[250]. Detained twice, in 1932 and in 1939, in relation with his political past—he was considered as a former member of the Constitutional Democratic Party—, he most likely owed his freedom to Vesnin. He pursued his work as an engineer and a trainer, completing the extension of the factory in Nizhnii Novgorod, renamed Gorky in 1932[251]. Albert Kahn remotely controlled one of the largest project teams ever gathered by the agency, and praised the enthusiasm and perseverance of young Russians, while his brother Moritz described their excellent theoretical knowledge, compensating their lack of pragmatism compared with their American counterparts[252]. The daily newspaper *Izvestiia* reported that upon his return from a ten-week stay in Stalingrad, Moritz spoke of "miracles" accomplished by the Soviet industry and made the case for the benefits that American companies would derive from a diplomatic recognition of the USSR[253]. Confrontation between citizens of both countries extended from offices to construction sites. The periodical *Za Industrializatsiiu* (For Industrialization) commented: "It is very important to note that the American specialists are not just consulting; they are actually supervising the entire construction.

247   According to the Michigan Society of Architects, the number was 521: *Weekly Bulletin* 17, no. 13 (30 March 1943) [a special issue devoted to Kahn], quoted in Melnikova, "Kahn," 75; alternatively, a tally of 570 was asserted by Louis Kahn in a note on 7 February 1944, 2, archives AKA.

248   Gosproektstroi, annual report, RGAE, fund 5741, section 2, file 149, quoted in Melnikova, "Kahn," 63.

249   Mark G. Meerovich, "Arkhitektor v sovetskoi istorii; Anatolii Fisenko i Albert Kahn," *Projekt Baikal*, no. 20 (2009): 156–61; Franch y Gilabert, Lawrence, Miljački and Schafer, *Office Us Agenda*, 117–141. Among the earlier publications, see Anatole Kopp, "Foreign architects in the Soviet Union during the first two five-year plans," in *Reshaping Russian Architecture*, William Craft Brumfield, ed. (Cambridge: Cambridge University Press, 1999), 176–214; Anatole Senkevitch Jr., "Albert Kahn's Great Soviet Adventure as Architect of the First Five-Year Plan, 1929–1932," *Dimensions* 10 (1996): 35–49. On Kahn's work as a whole, see W. Hawkins Ferry, *The Legacy of Albert Kahn* (Detroit: Detroit Institute of Arts, 1970), 24 and 118–119; Grant Hildebrand, *Designing for Industry: The Architecture of Albert Kahn* (Cambridge, MA; London: MIT Press, 1974), 128–30.

250   Albert Kahn, letter to N.P. Komarov, 1930, in *Za Industrializatsiiu*, 5 February 1930, quoted in Meerovich, "Arkhitektor v sovetskoi istorii," 160.

251   See the recollections of Fisenko's son in Mark G. Meerovich, "Interviu s Alekseem Fisenko," *Projekt Baikal*, no. 20 (2009): 161–65.

252   "Disputes of Reds and Americans Revealed," *The New York Times*, 27 October 1929; Melnikova, "Kahn," 64.

253   "'Sovetskoe pravitelstvo sovershaet chudesa v promyshlennosti': amerikanskii arkhitektor o SSSR," *Izvestiia*, 5 July 1930, 1.

Albert Kahn Associates. Tractor Factory, Stalingrad, 1929–1930. Views of the site with Russian and American technicians, including John Calder and Leon Swadjian. Photographs by The Conrad Studio. Gelatin silver prints on paper, mounted on cardboard, 28 × 36.8 cm. Bentley Historical Library, University of Michigan.

356

Albert Kahn Associates. Tractor factory, Cheliabinsk, 1930–1932. Photograph by Leonid M. Surin, 1935.
State Archive of the Sverdlovsk region.

The shortage of our own qualified workers has forced us to increase as much as possible the number of American technical specialists invited to work at the Stalingrad plant."[254]

On the construction sites they oversaw, the engineers from Kahn's crew were surprised by the proactive rhythm of the Russian labourers, who accused them in return, according to Abe L. Drabkin, of behaving like "Italians," which meant refusing to work when it was too cold[255]. In a notable example of technicians travelling between the two countries, John Calder, who moved on to Cheliabinsk from Stalingrad, became the model for Carter, the main character of a four-act comedy by Nikolai Pogodin, *Temp* (Tempo), staged in Moscow in 1930. In the play, the American is constantly outraged by the Russians, all the while declaring himself apolitical: "I do not care for luxurious [sic] desk and office which [sic] were very kindly provided for me. I am neither a businessman nor a theorist. I am a construction engineer and my place is in the field, right on the job, and not at a desk with the sole purpose of answering telephone calls [In English in the original play]." He is frustrated by constantly receiving the answer "next week" to all his questions[256].

Kahn's construction sites were open to distinguished visitors, such as the New York photographer Margaret Bourke-White, who marvelled in 1930 at the "perfection of arrangement" of the Stalingrad factory. She observed: "All the machinery has come new and glistening from Germany and America. The foundry floor is ablaze in the whiteness of its sand. Our factories are largely a product of gradual growth and renovation. But these Russian factories have sprung full-blown from the plan of the Supreme Economic Council plus American skill."[257] She was mostly struck by the swiftness with which the buildings, "designed to embody the latest American ideas of factory construction," were raised from the ground, and remarked that "[t]he Russians, as well as the firm of Albert Kahn, are proud of the fact that only one year after construction was started the first tractor was delivered." According to her, the few Russians who had travelled to America brought back an astonishing number of skills; rather than simply aspiring to the *amerikanskii* rhythm, they had "the feeling for it."[258] American workers employed in Russia also travelled to receive training, like Victor and Walter Reuther, who would lead the United Automobile Workers' union for twenty-five years. The brothers spent two years in Nizhnii Novgorod as of 1933, where they encountered issues with the organization of production, recounted in a lively tone in Victor's memoir, published in 1938[259].

Americans were significantly involved in the Stalingrad, Cheliabinsk, and Kharkov construction projects, but the civil engineering institute Gosstroiproekt, renamed the Promstroiproekt in 1932, designed other ambitious undertakings, such as the enormous railway car factory in Nizhnii Tagil, in the Urals. The project was devised by N. Ia. Belskii as part of the Promstroiproekt and construction was overseen by the engineer Lazar Mariasin, who had been involved in Dneprostroi and Magnitogorsk, and who remained at the helm of the project until 1937[260]. Like Calder, Mariasin inspired writers, namely Valentin Kataev, who modelled his character David Margulies after him in his 1932 novel *Vremia, Vpered!* (Forward, oh Time!).[261] Mariasin was executed for sabotage in 1937, his Trotskyist past serving as a pretext for the accusation[262].

Were the factories of the first five-year plan a mere transposition of their American models—River Rouge for Avtostroi and the Caterpillar plant in Peoria, Illinois for Cheliabinsk? In 1930, the Berlin architect Bruno Taut weighed in on this question upon returning from Moscow, when he described "Russia's architectural situation: the Ford plant in Detroit could just as well have been built in Russia, with minor modifications necessitated by different climatic conditions, and the new plant by Ford in Nizhnii Novgorod will indeed soon confirm this contention."[263] Russian manuals seemed to confirm this idea, documenting Kahn's method for decades to come, namely in the 1932 three-volume work by Vladimir Tsvetaev, *Sovremennaia fabrichno-zavodskaia arkhitektura* (Contemporary Factory Architecture). The author was involved in Gosstroiproekt, and openly mentioned "Albert Kahn's American corporation" among the drawing offices whose practices he reviewed, without hesitating to highlight the fact that the structures, trusses, doors, windows, and many mechanical components

254   Melnikova, Kahn, 68.

255   Abe L. Drabkin, "American Architects and Engineers in Russia," *Pencil Points*, June 1930, 435–40.

256   Maurice Hindus, "Pinch Hitter for the Soviets," *American Magazine*, April 1932, 31–36; see also the text of *Tempo* in Eugene C. Lyons, *Six Soviet Plays* (Boston: Houghton Mifflin, 1934), 157–224.

257   Bourke-White, *Eyes on Russia*, 118.

258   Ibid., 124 and 126.

259   Victor G. Reuther, *The Brothers Reuther and the Story of the UAW: A Memoir* (Boston: Houghton Mifflin, 1938), 88–103.

260   N. Ia Belskii and M.M. Padosek, "Nizhnetagilskii vagononostroitelnyi zavod – Uralvagonstroi," *Proekt i standard* 4, no. 3 (1935): 1–22.

261   Valentin Kataev, *Vremia, vpered !* (Moscow: Federatsia, 1932); in English: *Forward, oh Time!*, trans. Charles Malamuth (London: Victor Gollancz, 1934).

262   On Mariasin's persecution, see Oleg V. Khlevniuk, *In Stalin's Shadow: The Career of "Sergo" Ordzhonikidze*, adapted and prefaced by Donald J Raleigh (Armonk, NY: M.E. Sharpe, 1995): 121–25. On the eventual fate of the factory, see Alexandre Birman, "Liudi ne buksuiut; kak Ouralvagonzavod vkatilsia v ochestvennuiu istoriu," 2015. https://lenta.ru/articles/2015/05/16/ural/ [accessed 2 September 2019].

263   Bruno Taut, « Russlands architektonische Situation », *Moderne Bauformen*, 29, no 2, (February 1930): 57.

ПРОФ. В. Д. ЦВЕТАЕВ

СОВРЕМЕННАЯ
фабрично-заводская
АРХИТЕКТУРА

ГОССТРОЙИЗДАТ

МОСКВА-ЛЕНИНГРАД · 1932

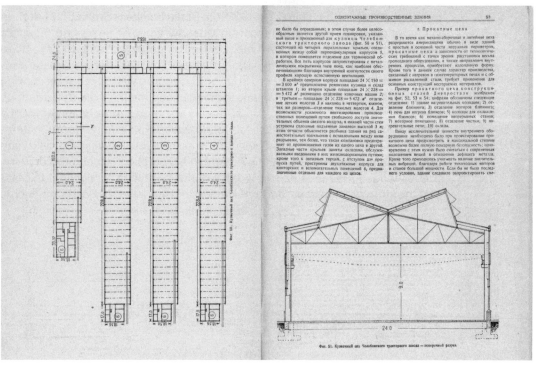

не было бы оправданным; в этом случае более целесо-образным является другой прием планировки, указан-ный выше и примененный для кузницы Челябин-ского тракторного завода (фиг. 50 и 51), состоящий из четырех параллельных крыльев, соеди-ненных между собой перпендикулярным корпусом 5, в котором помещается отделение для термической об-работки. Все пять корпусов запроектированы с метал-лическими покрытиями типа понд, как наиболее обес-печивающими благодаря внутренней конгруэнтности своего профиля хорошую естественную вентиляцию.

В крайнем северном корпусе площадью 24 × 150 = = 3 600 м² предположена ремонтная кузница и склад штампов 1; во втором крыле площадью 24 × 228 = = 5 472 м² размещено отделение ковочных машин 2; в третьем — площадью 24 × 228 = 5 472 м² отделе-ние легких молотов 3 и наконец в четвертом, южном, тех же размеров—отделение тяжелых молотов 4. Для возможности усиленного вентилирования производ-ственных помещений путем свободного доступа значи-тельных объемов свежего воздуха в нижней части стен устроены сплошные подземные заниженной высотой 3 м; этим отчасти объясняется разбивка здания на ряд са-мостоятельных параллельно с оставленными между ними разрывами, тем более, что такая компановка предохра-няет от проникновения газов из одного цеха в другой. Западные части крыльев заняты складами, обслужи-ваемыми введенными в них железнодорожными путями; кроме того к западным торцам, с отступом для про-пуска путей, пристроены двухэтажные корпуса для конторских и вспомогательных помещений 6, предна-значенные отдельно для каждого из цехов.

г. Прокатные цеха

В то время как механо-сборочные и литейные цеха разрешаются американцами обычно в виде зданий с простым в основной части корпусным периметром, прокатные цеха в зависимости от технологиче-ских требований с точки зрения расстановки весьма громоздкого оборудования, а также направлены внут-ренних процессов, приобретают изломанную форму. Кроме того в данном случае характер производства, связанный с нагревом в газогенераторных печах и с об-работкой раскаленной стали, требует применения для основных конструкций несгораемых материалов.

Пример прокатного цеха конструкции особых сталей Днепростали наиболее на фиг. 52, 53 и 54; цифрами обозначены следующие отделения: 1) здание нагревательных колодцев; 2) от-деление блюминга; 3) отделение моторов блюминга; 4) печь для нагрева блюмсов; 5) колодцы для охлажде-ния блюмсов; 6) помещение непрерывных станов; 7) моторное помещение; 8) отделение чистки; 9) на-гревательные печи; 10) склады.

Ввиду исключительной ценности внутреннего обо-рудования необходимо было при проектировании про-катного цеха предусмотреть в максимальной степени возможно более полную пожарную безопасность; одно-временно с этим нужно было считаться с современным положением вещей в отношении дефицита металла. Кроме того приходилось учитывать наличие значитель-ных вибраций, благодаря работе тихоходных моторов и станов большой мощности. Если бы не было послед-него условия, здание следовало запроектировать сме-

Фиг. 50. Кузнечный цех Челябинского тракторного завода — план.

Фиг. 51. Кузнечный цех Челябинского тракторного завода — поперечный разрез.

were sourced in America[264]. In 1936, *Arkhitektura promyshlennykh sooruzhenii* (The Architecture of Industrial Building), another multi-volume design handbook published by Promstroiproekt and edited by Fisenko, unapologetically compared the Stalingrad tractor factory to the Ford plant, designed by Kahn, in Chicago[265].

This operation, a rare case of transmission of a system both technological and architectonic, was reminiscent of the eastward transposition of production equipment sets along with their architectural envelopes. The designers and technicians trained at Gosstroiproekt/Promstroiproekt created countless variations on the projects initially developed in Detroit, from the general plan of the buildings and the structure and lighting principles to heating, ventilation, and energy distribution systems. The generalized use of square modules extending to the size of 12 or even 15 square metres, much larger than in previous constructions, allowed to produce heavy military equipment and to standardize details entirely. This geometrical simplicity enabled uninterrupted work in specialized drawing offices, stemming from Moscow's Promstroiproekt and its regional branches, and echoing Kahn's practices, as he became a "producer of production lines" at the beginning of the Second World War[266].

Articles in the journal *Proekt i Standart* regularly bore witness to the *priviazka* (transfer) of designs and descriptions. In 1933, it stressed the importance of adopting the method used for the Nizhnii Tagil factory plan: "The advanced American project management practice is always focused on establishing 'consolidated' plans in the development of the buildings, including the layout of heating, ventilation, water, electricity, and sanitation ducts, thus allowing them to interlock. Such a method eases the construction and assembly processes from the launch of the site to commissioning. Noting the lack of such a process in most of our drawing offices, the journal wishes to direct their attention to the importance of this dimension in devising implementation plans, the general plan, and buildings themselves, to save resources and improve our socialist construction."[267]

One of the most original indications of Kahn's relations with the USSR is the testimony of the young architect Andrei Burov, who travelled to the United States near the end of 1930. In 1927, he had combined references to Le Corbusier's Parisian villas with nods to Buffalo's grain silo in the *sovkhoz*, or State farm, which served as inspiration for the set of Sergei Eisenstein's *The General Line*. The architect could at last witness his Detroit inspiration in person. He travelled to New York, Chicago, and finally to Detroit, where he joined the team assembled by Kahn Associates to design the Cheliabinsk tractor factory, in addition to investigating housing architecture, as he was also charged with designing the city's new neighbourhoods. In his letters to his wife, Burov expressed his views on the "stupidity" of skyscrapers, leading

264   Vladimir D. Tsvetaev, *Sovremennaia fabrichno-zavodskaia arkkhitektura* (Moscow; Leningrad: Gosstroiizdat, 1933), 8.

265   Anatolii S. Fisenko, ed., *Arkhitektura promyshlennykh zdanii* (Moscow: Glav. red. stroit. literatury, 1936), 149.

266   "Producer of Production Lines," *Architectural Record* 91, no. 6 (June 1942), 40.

267   N.I. Bannikov, "Rabochii generalnyi plan vnov stroiashchegosia zavoda," *Proekt i standart*, no. 1 (1933): 16. The journal also published articles on American practice, such as E. Dzerkovich, "Amerikanskie priemy konstruirovaniia i stroitelstvo stalnykh konstruktsii," *Proekt i standart*, no. 2 (1934): 55–63; G.F. Kuznetsov, "Organizatsia stroitelstva v SShA," *Proekt i standart*, no. 8 (1935): 6–8. V.M. Vakhurkin, "Novye amerikanskie stroitelnye detali i materialy," *Proekt i standart*, no. 11 (1935): 28–29.

to "idiotic city plans," and remained wholly unimpressed with American architecture: "A pure building, contemporary to our architecture, to mine, would seem ridiculous here, in my view, without the rules of urban planning. [...] Architecture outside of, or without, urban planning, cannot be called contemporary, and that is why the purism of contemporary architecture has nothing in common with America. It is too slight. I heard here that the motion picture *The King of Jazz* was just released; the idea is to show music from all ages, from all peoples, and in the end, absorbing, appropriating, and dominating them all, comes jazz. America is jazz; American architecture is also jazz, but the results are poorer than in music. I declare that there is an American architecture, terribly real and specific to America. It is Le Corbusier's architecture, with all its refinement and exceptional talent, as well as its aesthetic snobbery towards cities and its absurd consequences on city planning."[268]

Burov was also harsh in his appraisal of Kahn's architecture, sarcastically dubbing him "the world's greatest architect." Oscar Stonorov, a young architect from Zurich who had settled in Philadelphia, shared a similar point of view, writing in a letter to Le Corbusier in 1932 that Kahn was a "God-engineer," as well as a "pig-architect."[269] Burov recognized the positive qualities of Ford's factories, but criticized their creator's other views: "It's astonishing, he lays claims on History, on Eternity. He has such poor taste, he is so pretentious. He showed me a project for a school and asked me what I thought of it. I told him that he had confused the horizontal and vertical principles. His answer: 'I don't follow principles or theories in architecture, I want it to look beautiful!' Isn't it incredible? A true airhead. We took a tour of the Fisher Building he had built. Before the visit, they told me I would see the greatest building in the world. But the most impressive element was the restroom. [...] If there were no architects in America, it would likely be a less beautiful country, but at least it would be a less twisted one."[270]

Back in Moscow, writing for the magazine *Brigada khudozhnikov* (Artists' Brigade), Burov decried the shapes of the great American city and the regressive eclecticism of its skyscrapers, drawing optimistic conclusions on Soviet architecture's ability to establish new standards: "Our views on this matter are much broader, as our technological development and housing organization policies aren't held back by obstacles such as private property or the despotic artistry and dreary taste of petty-bourgeois Americans."[271] Drawing on his experience, Burov built residential neighbourhoods in Cheliabinsk, complete with a movie theatre and a workers' club, whose housing blocks resembled those of the *Siedlungen* in the Weimar Republic rather than the American suburbs he disparaged.

The completion of the Cheliabinsk factory concluded Kahn's direct involvement in Soviet industrial construction. Despite the *Holodomor*—the extermination of millions of Ukrainians through hunger, by violently robbing them of their wheat for export purposes—, and although Armand Hammer had sold major artworks from the Hermitage Museum, such as Raphael's *Madonna*

268   Andrei K. Burov, Letter to his wife, 30 November 1930, in Raisa G. Burova and Olga I. Rzhekhina,
        Andrei Konstantinovich Bourov, pisma, dnevniki, besedy s aspirantami (Moscow: Iskusstvo, 1980), 33.
269   Oscar Stonorov, Letter to Le Corbusier, 22 March 1932, Fondation Le Corbusier, Paris, 12-5-231.
270   Andrei K. Burov, Letter to his wife, 30 November 1930, in Burova and Rzhekhina, *Andrei Konstantinovich Burov*, 37.
271   Andrei K. Burov, "Arkhitektura sovremennoi Ameriki," *Brigada khudojnikov*, no. 5–6 (1931): 44.

Albert Kahn Associates. Railway wagon factory, Nizhnii Tagil, 1930–1932.
Aerial view, in *USSR in Construction,* July 1936. Private collection.

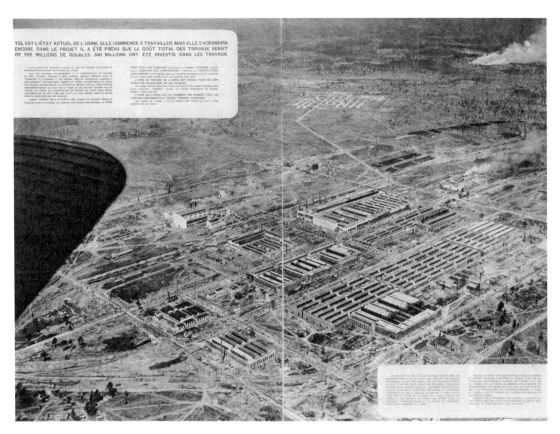

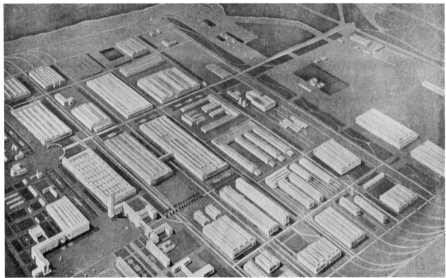

Automobile factory, Gorky, aerial perspective of expansion plan, 1934.
In *Handbook for the designer of industrial buildings*, Moscow and Leningrad: Glavnaia redaktsiia stroitelnoi literatury, 1935.

d'Alba and Titian's *Venus with a Mirror*[272], there was a shortage of currency. Though Kahn received much gratitude from Stalingrad executives, who presented him with a luxurious commemorative album, his attempts during his 1932 trip to Moscow to sign a third contract paid in American dollars proved unsuccessful, and he had to withdraw his crews[273].

The Dneprostroi and the Magnitstroi as American Construction Sites

After the most spectacular and publicized endeavours of the first five-year plan, which enlisted Americans or Russians with experience working in the United States, American expertise excelled in the field of electricity, namely the development of the GOELRO electrification plan. Americans received a considerable portion of the concessions from *tresty* (trusts) created in the early 1920s, alongside the Swedish ASEA, the French CSF and the British Metropolitan-Vickers—a share that would surpass all others after 1930[274]. Although the GOELRO's goals were then drastically reduced—from the hundred plants initially envisioned to only three—, the true importance of the plan and its symbolic significance remained substantial. After the Volkhov hydroelectric plant, the largest site was the Dnieper, in Ukraine, a waterway which had been studied at length before the Revolution, first as a possible connection between Russia and the Black Sea, and later as a resource for electricity production.

The first project was developed under VSNKh president Feliks Dzerzhinskii by the engineer Ivan Aleksandrov, who justified it with articles from the *Electrical World* journal[275]. A feasibility study was conducted in 1926, on Trotsky's initiative, as he was then in charge of industry after having been removed from the People's Commissariat for Defence. That same year, after Aleksandrov's overseas mission, the project was assigned to the American engineer Hugh L. Cooper, who had already completed several dam construction

272 Armand Hammer, *Quest of the Romanoff Treasure* (New York: William Farquhar Payson, 1932); Anne Odom and Wendy R. Salmond, *Treasure into Tractors: The Selling of Russia's Cultural Heritage, 1918–1938* (Seattle: University of Washington Press, 2009).
273 The large-format album is held at the Bentley Research Library. Kahn was optimistic: "Architect Off for Russia to Renew Firm's Contract: Albert Kahn Believes Soviet Will Grant New Business," *Detroit Free Press*, 4 March 1932.
274 Sutton, *Western Technology*, vol. 1, 202–5.
275 Ivan G. Aleksandrov, in *Torgovo-promyshlennaia gazeta*, 20 September 1925, quoted in Rassweiler, *The Generation of Power*, 45.
276 Harold Dorn, "Hugh Lincoln Cooper and the First Détente," *Technology and Culture* 20, no. 2 (April 1979): 322–47. See also Williams, *American Russian Relations*, 214–19.
277 Trotsky admitted to being "deeply interested" by the project: *My Life* [1930] (New York: Grosset & Dunlap, 1960), 519. On American–German competition at the time, see Saul G. Bron, "American and German Technique in the USSR," *Economic Review of the Soviet Union*, 15 March 1929, 113–14.
278 An important contract was signed on 9 October 1928. "Amtorg Concludes Contract with International General Electric," *Economic Review of the Soviet Union*, 1 November 1928, 348; and "Huge Turbines Ordered for Dniepr Power Plant," *Economic Review of the Soviet Union*, 1 April 1929, 131. See also Sutton, *Western Technology*, vol. 3, 203.
279 Rassweiler, *The Generation of Power*, 64–72.
280 Ibid., 200.
281 Louis Fischer, *Machines and Men in Russia* (New York: Harrison Smith, 1932), 33.
282 Dorn published a photo of Cooper and Stalin sitting at the same table. Hughes relies on Dorn's text in *American Genesis*, 264–69.
283 Bourke-White, *Eyes on Russia*, 84.
284 Hugh L. Cooper, "Rezultaty ispytanii koefitsienta poleznogo deistvia raznykh tipov vsasyvaiushchikh trub na ustanovke plotiny Wilsona," in *Dneprostroi, biulleten gosudarstvenno dneprovskogo stroitelstva*, no. 2–3 (January–February 1928): 57–59.
285 Anne D. Rassweiler, "Cooper, Hugh Lincoln," in *American National Biography*, 2000. https://doi.org/10.1093/anb/9780198606697.article.1300338 [accessed 2 September 2019].
286 Rassweiler, *The Generation of Power*, 131–55.

mandates, from Brazil to the United States. His realizations included a dam upstream from Niagara Falls, another one in Keokuk, Iowa, on the Mississippi River, and most notably the Wilson Dam, then the world's largest, built across the Tennessee River in Muscle Shoals[276] [ill. p. 171]. It was decided, after the engineer's first annual trip to Russia—the last one taking place in 1932—, that Cooper would build an even larger structure on the Dnieper, measuring 720 metres long and 51 metres high. As part of Trotsky's goal to establish competition between Western companies, Cooper's team initially contended with Siemens' crew. Each firm began construction from one side of the river, until the American was declared the winner, owing in part to his superior workforce management[277]. In addition to Cooper's spearheading of the project, aided by excellent financial conditions, turbine orders were placed to the Newport News Shipbuilding and Drydock Company, and General Electric was called upon to build five of the plant's power generators[278], while the four others were manufactured in Leningrad. The General Electric contract was negotiated by Solomon A. Trone, a Lithuanian-American communist, one of the many Jewish technicians then working between the United States and the USSR. The design of the structure and its extensions was created by a team of Soviet architects overseen by Viktor Vesnin.

Cooper, however, appointed chief consultant in February 1927, remained the central figure at Dneprostroi. His involvement in the project led him to settle in Russia for periodic two-month stays over the course of nearly seven years, while at least four engineers from his team were permanently on location. He was the highest paid Western expert in the country, his wages totalling 6% of the total cost of construction[279], and he basked in luxury when living in the Soviet Union. He advocated for a series of changes to Aleksandrov's initial project, including a significant shift in building material from backfill to concrete, a more efficient leveraging of topography, and the use of locks meeting existing standards[280]. In *Machines and Men in Russia*, the pro-Soviet journalist Louis Fischer describes this "leading construction engineer," as "a picturesque character whose abilities and personality are very much appreciated by Soviet leaders."[281] Indeed, Cooper had the honour of being invited to Stalin's table, where he appeared during an informal picnic[282]. In 1930, Margaret Bourke-White celebrated the "energy and foresight," of the chief consultant, whom "the engineers fondly call the 'Old Man.'"[283] In addition to his role as an organizer and leader, alongside the Russian construction manager Aleksandr Vinter, Cooper published technical articles on the Wilson Dam in the bulletin of the Dneprostroi organization[284]. On-site, he led his workers in an "American dance" to pack the freshly poured concrete without suitable machinery[285]. Although he played a key role in the launch and execution of the project, he lacked complete control over an operation involving tens of thousands of labourers. Many of these men had not received any training, and their living and working conditions were miserable, a situation that could not be compensated by the Party's calls for revolutionary fervour[286].

The construction of the dam inspired Fedor Gladkov to write his "Letters from the Dneprostroi" as well as the novel *Energiia*, published in 1933. The project was also covered by documentary filmmakers. Dziga Vertov revealed its early stages in his 1928 *Odinadtsatyi* (The Eleventh Year), followed by Aleksandr Medvedkin's *Pusk Dneprostroia* (The Launch of Dneprostroi), where Cooper can be briefly seen; and Aleksandr Dovzhenko's *Ivan*, both shot in 1932. That same year, the final sequence of the Esfir Shub's epic *KShE— Komsomol shef elektrifikatsii* (The Komsomol, champion of electrification), portrayed the delivery ceremony of the Dneprostroi. Among the officials gathered on stage, Cooper addressed the crowd in English, starting his speech with the words "I had a dream"—the dream of speaking Russian to the workers—, and apologetically continued in his own language. A supporter of diplomatic recognition for the USSR and the intensification of its relations with the United States, Cooper obliged the Soviets by providing them services that were commensurate with his high wages. He gave lectures and created the American-Russian Chamber of Commerce, bringing together some of the most powerful export organizations, such as General Electric, General Motors, Chase, Edison, and Westinghouse[287]. In 1932, the Italian critic Pietro Maria Bardi visited several notable sites, including the Dneprostroi, during a study trip for the journal *L'Architecture d'aujourd'hui*. In his book *Un Fascista al Paese dei Soviet* (A Fascist in the Land of the Soviets), he mocked this "American frenzy" and the delusional expectations for industrial growth arising from the dam: "A nation was thus born on the face of this Earth which, in addition to knowing it, has discovered that two plus two equals five, a discovery made in the American school of thought."[288]

Along with the Stalingrad factory and the Dnieper Dam, the third flagship operation of the initial five-year plan was the Magnitogorsk Steel Works, built on an iron ore deposit. Its presence caused a magnetic anomaly and had been detected years prior to 1917. A model for the project had been identified in Gary, Indiana, by the engineer Ivan Bardin during his 1910–1911 stay in the United States. His mandate became to establish a strategic metallurgical industry for the economy and defence of the USSR[289]. The pioneering steel mill designing firm Arthur G. McKee & Co., based in Cleveland, Ohio, was hired to develop a factory complex for the Ural-Kuzbas metal works project based on the United States Steel in Gary, which was then the world's largest industrial facility. Four hundred and fifty engineers and designers adapted the plans and handed them over to Soviet technicians in Moscow. The chief engineer overseeing the project, R. W. Stuck, described it as "finished to the last bolt," stating that "nothing of this magnitude had ever been done before" and that it was nothing less than the best steel project mill ever drawn[290].

For the Kuznetsk Steel Works, the Gipromez—the State Institute for the Design of Metallurgical plants—signed important contracts with the Chicago Freyn Engineering Co. in 1927–1928[291]. Henry J. Freyn stressed in an interview addressed to the Russians that it was best to employ independent consulting engineers rather than firms that would limit them to a certain equipment: "The Soviet government greatly admires American projects and methods, but the main criterion in the choice of American engineers is the fact that the Soviets did not wish to hire consultants related with foreign industrialists and corporations."[292] Bardin himself revealed in 1936 the influence these teams had on his endeavours: "The arrival of Americans was a great event. Until then Gipromez was lame in all four legs. It was a puny establishment, highly liable to

287   Hugh L. Cooper, "Address Before the Society of American Military Engineers," Philadelphia, 25 February 1931, *Engineers and Engineering* 48, no. 4 (April 1931): 76–86.
288   Ibid., 92.
289   Bailes, "The American Connection," 439; Stephen Kotkin, *Magnetic Mountain: Stalinism as a Civilization* (Berkeley: University of California Press, 1995).
290   R.W. Stuck, "American Engineer in Russia," in Sutton, *Western Technology*, vol. 2, 62.
291   "Freyn Makes Russian Deal," *The New York Times*, 2 August 1928. On the experience at the building site, see the memoir of worker John Scott, *Behind the Ural: An American Worker in Russia's City of Steel* (Boston: Houghton Mifflin, 1942), 137–70.
292   Henry J. Freyn, in "American Engineering Firm Assumes Direction of Soviet Russia's Iron and Steel Production," *The Cornell Daily Sun* 47, no. 180 (25 May 1927).

Hugh L. Cooper in front of the Dnieper Dam, 1931. Photograph by Margaret Bourke-White.
Photogravure, 23.5 × 33.1 cm. Library of Congress.

Hugh L. Cooper. Wilson Dam on the Tennessee, Muscle Shoals, Alabama, 1918–1924.
Views of the completed dam. Postcard, ca. 1940, 8.8 × 13.8 cm. CCA.

Dnieper Hydroelectric Power Station and Dam, Zaporozhe, Ukraine, 1928–1932.
Views of the construction site and of the final project. Fold-out in *USSR in Construction*, October 1932. Private collection.

Dnieper Hydroelectric Power Station and Dam, Zaporozhe, Ukraine, 1928–1932. Plans for the entire project as well as
the powered factories, and view of the powerhouse. Fold out in *USSR in Construction*, March 1934. Private Collection.

1932
10 ОКТЯБРЯ

1927

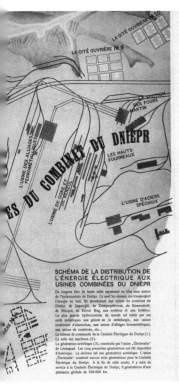

LA CITÉ OUVRIÈRE № 10

LA CITÉ OUVRIÈRE № 9

DES FOURS MARTIN

L'USINE DES ALLIAGES FERROMÉTALLIQUES

ES DU COMBINAT DU DNIÈPR

LES HAUTS-FOURNEAUX

L'USINE DE COKE ET D'ENGRAIS

L'USINE D'ACIERS SPÉCIAUX

SCHÉMA DE LA DISTRIBUTION DE L'ÉNERGIE ÉLECTRIQUE AUX USINES COMBINÉES DU DNIÈPR

De longues files de hauts mâts rayonnent en bleu sous autour de l'hydrocentrale du Dniépr. Ce sont les réseaux qui transportent l'énergie au loin. Ils aboutissent aux usines du combinat du Dniépr, de Zaporojié, de Dniépropétrovsk, de Kamenskoïé, de Nikopol, de Krivoï Rog, aux sovkhoz et aux kolkhoz. La plus grande hydrocentrale du monde est reliée par ses nerfs métalliques aux géants de la métallurgie, aux usines combinées d'aluminium, aux usines d'alliages ferrométalliques, aux usines de combinés, etc...
Le tableau de commande de la Centrale Électrique du Dniépr (1).
La salle des machines (2).
La génératrice soviétique (3), construite par l'usine „Électrosila" de Léningrad. Les cinq premières génératrices ont été importées d'Amérique. La sixième est une génératrice soviétique. L'usine „Électrosila" construit encore trois génératrices pour la Centrale Électrique du Dniépr. À la fin de cette année, il y aura en service à la Centrale Électrique du Dniépr, 9 génératrices d'une puissance globale de 558 000 kw.

empty talk and unprincipled chatter, incapable of elaborating technical ideas either in writing or in drawing. [...] The Americans left behind a serious trace. Our young people learned a lot from the Americans; they had borrowed from them both technical knowledge and—the main thing—a way of working."[293] Mikhail Posokhin, then a young topographer on the Kuznetstroi sites who went on to become Moscow's chief architect, painted in contrast a scathing caricature of Americans who had settled in Russia[294].

In the oil sector, the relationship with America, crucial during the NEP for exports and the rise of heavy industry, was just as essential for the production and transportation of goods, though German and British partnerships were also consequential[295]. In 1924, in one of the first trips to the United States organized by Amtorg, Aleksandr Serebrovskii, then in charge of nationalizing the Baku deposits, revived oil extraction after convincing John D. Rockefeller to sell equipment on credit to the USSR thanks to his rhetorical ability and his modest demeanor[296]. Serebrovskii, nicknamed the "Red Rockefeller" after his expedition and in a nod to his industrial expertise, imported almost everything from the United States[297]. He then launched local production of the same goods: drilling materials, state-of-the-art refining equipment, the arc welding technique used for pipelines, everything up to the kottedzhi (cottages) of oil industry executives. Crowned by his success in Baku, Serebrovskii went on to work in the field of gold extraction, surrounding himself with American technicians, some of whom stayed in the USSR until the late 1930s, before his arrest and his execution in 1938. According to John Littlepage, who had relocated to work under him for the organization tasked with the exploitation of the Tsvetmetzoloto mines, the impetus for gold mining came from Stalin, who had read several books on the 1849 California gold rush[298].

The political leaders proclaimed not only the importance of scientific management, but also the urgent need to assimilate all the resources of American technical culture, in its material and symbolic manifestations. This belief was embodied in the subsequent phases of the construction of Soviet industrial infrastructure: all the sectors that experienced significant growth between 1920 and 1932 owed their rise to Western, and mainly American,

293   Ivan P. Bardin, in Robert W. Davies, *The Industrialization of Soviet Russia*, vol. 3, *The Soviet Economy in Turmoil, 1929-1930* (London: Palgrave, 1989), 216.

294   Mikhail V. Posokhin, *Dorogi zhizni; iz zapisok arkhitektora* (Moscow: Stroiizdat, 1995), 29

295   Sutton, *Western Technology*, vol. 1, 16-44.

296   Aleksandr P. Serebrovskii published, among other books, *Sovetskaia Neft* (Moscow: VSNKh, 1926). See also the volume by the founder of Lukoil Oil Company, Vargit Alekperov, *Oil of Russia: Past, Present, & Future* (Minneapolis, East View Press, 2011).

297   On urban planning in Baku during this period, see Crawford, "The Socialist Settlement," 35-163.

298   John Littlepage, *In Search of Soviet Gold* (New York: Harcourt, Brace and Company, 1938).

299   Parks, *Culture, Conflict and Coexistence*, 25-26.

300   Samuel Lieberstein, "Technology, Work and Sociology in the USSR: The NOT Movement," *Technology and Culture* 16, no. 1 (January 1975): 55-58; Luke, "The Proletarian Ethic and Soviet Industrialization," 588-601; Merkle, *Management and Ideology*, 127-34.

301   Moshe Lewin, *The Making of the Soviet System: Essays in the Social History of Interwar Russia*, (New York: The New Press, 1994), 225.

302   Aleksei K. Gastev, ed., *Organizatsia truda v stakhanovskom dvizhenii* (Moscow: Standartizdat, 1936).

303   Sergo Ordzhonikidze, "Un pays agraire devenu industriel," speech given to the joint meeting of the Central Committee and the Central Control Commission of the USSR, 9 January 1933, in *Du premier au deuxième plan quinquennal: résultats et perspectives* (Paris: Bureau d'éditions, 1933), 159. On representations of this period and agents, see Katerina Clark, "Engineers of Human Souls in an Age of Industrialization: Changing Cultural Models, 1929-41," in *Social Dimensions of Soviet Industrialization*, William G. Rosenberg and Lewis H. Siegelbaum, eds. (Bloomington: Indiana University Press, 1993), 248-64.

304   Arkh. V.A. Feoktistov, "O nekotorykh urokakh vreditelstva trotskistikh agentov v planirovke gorodov," *Proekt i standart*, no. 7 (1937): 4-8.

305   "Industrial Architecture of Albert Kahn, Inc., ed. by George Nelson " *The Architectural Forum*, 69, n° 2 (August 1938).

306   "Khlestakovskie otkrovenia Alberta Kana," *Arkhitektura SSSR* 8, no. 10 (October 1938), 89.

technology and imports. In 1930, taking advantage of the opportunities it had scantily exploited in the 1920s, the government also sent a cohort of students abroad to study technical disciplines in American universities. The transfer of experience was particularly apparent in the field of library studies, as the American cataloguing methods were applied to both the Lenin Library and the National Library of France[299].

Stakhanovism, a movement orchestrated following the supposed feat of the eponymous miner Aleksei G. Stakhanov, who had purportedly extracted fourteen times more coal than the standard norm in a Donbass mine in July of 1935, replicated and amplified certain traits of Taylorism and Fordism, while insisting on individual exploits and selflessness[300]. The technical intelligentsia and the industrial workforce were then in full expansion, as millions of peasants flooded construction sites and factories. In the industry, manpower rose from 10.8 million in 1928 to 20.6 million in 1932, resulting in a violent and sustained social crisis[301]. Even before the introduction of Stakhanovism in 1935, NOT's methods permeated into Soviet production and became the foundation for the development of strict working norms and wage policies, especially after the 1931 decree abolishing income equality. Beyond the public exploitation of Stakhanovism, techniques derived from Taylorism were back in operation. Gastev, put in charge of workforce training by the People's Commissar to Heavy Industry, Sergo Ordzhonikidze, took advantage of the new climate to further promote his methods[302].

Damnatio Memoriae

At the end of the first five-year plan, Soviet leaders declared that the age of concessions and contracts with Westerners was over. In January 1933, Commissar Ordzhonikidze made the following statement: "From now on, there is no machine that our country does not know how to manufacture. As of now, there is no endeavour, factory, or mill that we cannot design and build with our own technical workforce and our own engineers. There is no such endeavour. There is no more going abroad, our suitcases filled with paper, to commission projects for our automobile and tractor plants: this behaviour belongs to the past."[303]

Once the massive import of American industrial equipment was mostly halted, the official Soviet discourse tried to minimize its scope, and went so far as to brazenly deny its past existence. In the second half of the 1930s, the Soviet press raised a storm against those responsible for introducing American factories to the USSR. In 1937, the journal *Proekt i standart* set the pace by condemning the "demolition" enacted by "Trotskyist agents" in urban planning, tarnishing the work of Ordzhonikidze's assistant, Georgii Piatakov, who had been executed at the start of the year[304]. American contribution was outright disavowed, namely in the 1938 review of a special issue by *Architectural Forum* on Albert Kahn published in *Arkhitektura SSSR*[305]. Alleging that the architect-engineer had not built anything in Russia, the text denounced his "Khlestakov-like confessions," alluding to the character of the impostor in Gogol's *Revizor*, and accusing Kahn of adorning himself with "a peacock's feathers": "There was never a 'branch' of Albert Kahn's firm in Moscow [...]. Soviet engineers, architects, and labourers, inspired by the heroic ideals of socialism have created factories surpassing the best American industrial facilities on their own, thus undermining the affairs of Mr. Kahn, to whom architecture is 90% business."[306]

Upon Kahn's death in 1942, Viktor Vesnin—who ten years earlier had been Ordzhonikidze's primary advisor in architectural matters and a mentor to Fisenko, Kahn's main successor—was the only Soviet to send a telegram to his widow Ernestine. He paid a warm tribute to the "talented engineer and architect" who rendered the USSR a "great service in designing a number of large plants and helped [it] to assimilate the American experience in the sphere of building industry."[307] In an utterly Orwellian gesture, the name of the Detroit architect was obliterated from the books for almost sixty years. Even Cooper, who had died two years earlier, was entirely overlooked in the captions on the Dnieper Dam model, one of the great attractions of the Soviet pavilion at the 1939 New York World's Fair.

307   Viktor A. Vesnin, telegram to Ernestine Kahn, 16 December 1942, Archives of American Art, Albert Kahn Papers.

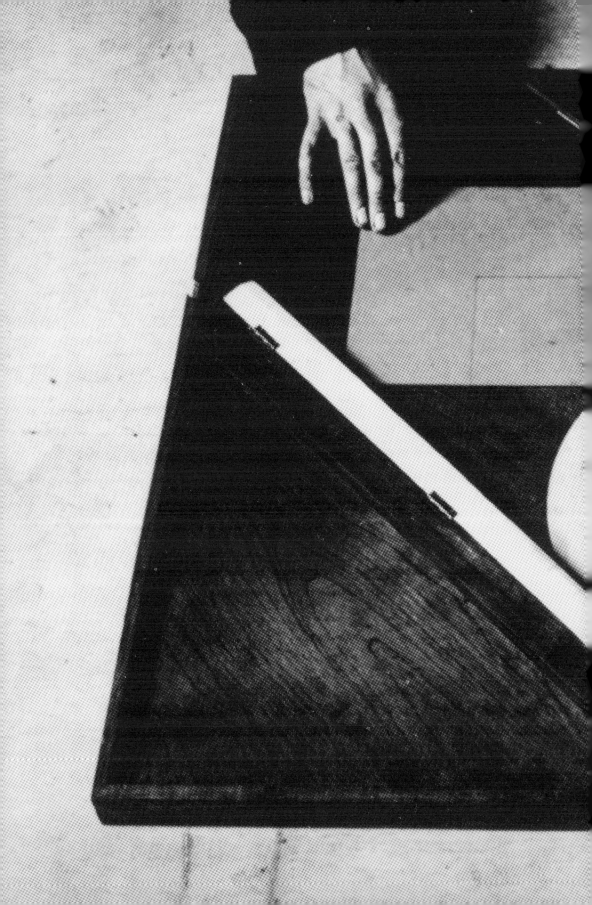

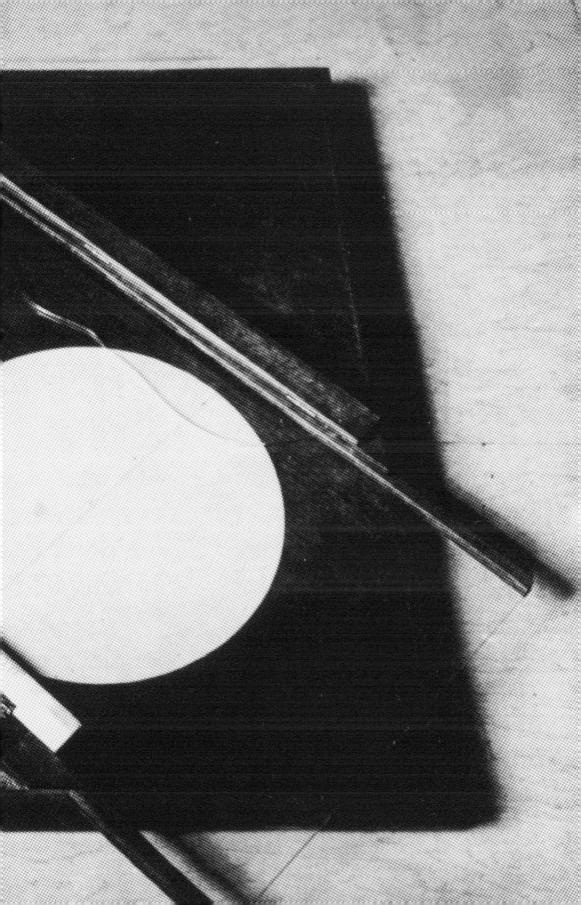

Avant-Garde Amerikanizms

3

Vladimir V. Mayakovsky
(1893-1930). Russian poet.
Travelled to New York in 1925.

Erich Mendelsohn (1887-1953).
German architect. His book
Amerika was met with great
enthusiasm in the USSR.

Eleazar (El) Lissitzky (1890-1941).
Soviet architect and artist.
A vibrant critic of Amerikanizm.

Hugo Münsterberg (1863-1916).
German psychologist who
taught at Harvard. The Soviets
reproduced his experiments.

Nikolai Ladovskii (1881-1941).
Russian architect. Created a
psychotechnical laboratory at
the Vkhutemas.

"European and American industrial buildings of the past decade—the powerful silos, the plants and electrical motors, with their dynamic and monumental modernity, with the pathos of their working conditions, with the lapidary nudity of their shapes—are significant achievements. They represent a unique victory in the search for the modern architectural form."

Moisei I. Ginzburg, "Contemporary Aesthetics," 1923[1].

In 1922, while the NEP was still in full force, the new nation was renamed the Union of Soviet Socialist Republics, in a strong semantic identification with the American model: its four-letter denomination—SSSR in Russian—echoed the one often used to designate the United States of North America at the time: SShSA. Despite the absence of diplomatic relations between the two countries, economic ties were sustained through new channels. While technicians effortlessly crossed the Atlantic—often with the help of Amtorg and other agencies—, intellectuals, artists, and architects were met with greater complications when they attempted the journey. They were thus introduced to American cities, industry, and agriculture by proxy, in a country flooded with Hollywood films.

In 1921, the NEP opened the domestic market to Western cultural products, disseminated through private publishers and projectionists. With the rise of a new class of businessmen—the NEP's outreach was mostly commercial[2]—Russian intellectual life coalesced around institutions and publications closely related to Germany. Left-leaning art theorists, often stemming from Proletkult, were nevertheless aware of Aleksei Gastev's endeavours and mindful of America's tangible as well as symbolic presence in the Russian cultural sphere. In *LEF*, the journal of the Left Front of the Arts, Boris Arvatov welcomed Gastev's newly issued book, *A Packet of Orders*, which he saw as a successful attempt to "socialize poetic forms" by borrowing from technical and military lexicons[3]. In *Art and Production*, Arvatov reflected upon the forces at play at the end of the nineteenth century: "Powerful industrial centres have been created; the latest techniques have emerged, and along with them, the technicist ideology. To the bourgeoisie, the realm of objects has gained a new aura—Americanism,

View of New York, in Ilya Ehrenburg, *And Yet the World Goes 'Round*. Berlin: Gelikon, 1923. Private collection.

the impetus towards a superior material culture (the novels of Wells)."[4] In his 1923 book *From Easel to Machine*, the critic Nikolai Tarabukin laid out his thoughts on the relationship between art and labour, stating that "Taylor was the first to address the issue of the rational use of labour energy."[5]

Writers who had not crossed the Atlantic were nevertheless inspired by America in their poetry and novels. One of these authors was Ilya Ehrenburg, whose 1922 booklet *And Yet the World Goes 'Round*, published in Berlin, was rife with imagery from the New World. A locomotive with its snowplow, an aerial view of Manhattan, a floating dock and a new bridge envisioned for the island can be seen alongside airplanes borrowed from Le Corbusier's *L'Esprit Nouveau* and works by El Lissitzky, Aleksandr Rodchenko, Fernand Léger, and Pablo Picasso. Quoting Aleksandr Blok's 1913 poem "Novaia Amerika," Ehrenburg observed that "new architecture comes from America. There, they have developed an industrial type of house, where one can park a Ford in the driveway without blushing." However, he also noted that "in that same America, so-called pure art is extremely poor. People hang 'sunsets' and 'melancholies' in their beautiful houses. Those same people—Americans—build extraordinary bridges and listen tearfully to nauseating elegies."[6] Ehrenburg's ambivalent positions were revealed the following year, when he published his novel *Trust D.E. or The Fall of Europe*, a tale about an American named Hans Bloot seeking to destroy the Old Continent, where Blok presented jazz and foxtrot as threats to culture[7]. In his 1930 novel, *10 H. P., A Chronicle of Our Times*, he extended his critiques to Fordism, whose workings he witnessed in the Citroën automobile plants in Paris[8].

Esenin and Mayakovsky in New York

In the twenty years following the 1917 Revolution, avant-garde Soviet intellectuals scarcely had any direct contact with America. It is therefore worth examining Vladimir Mayakovsky's 1925 trip in detail. The poet set off to America to meet with his former futurist comrade, David Burliuk, who had emigrated in 1922. Before Mayakovsky, another poet, Sergei Esenin, suffered a disastrous journey from 1 October 1922 to 3 February 1923, travelling with the dancer Isadora Duncan, whom he had previously married to avoid a scandal similar to Gorky's[9]. Upon his return, he published *Iron Mirgorod*, an essay with an evocative title associating metal, already vilified by Gorky, to the imaginary city Gogol had equated with mediocrity and triteness[10]. He had harsh words for the Futurists, sardonically accusing them of being too timid in their depictions of America:

2   Alan M. Ball, *Russia's Last Capitalists: The NEPmen, 1921–1929* (Berkeley: University of California Press, 1994).
3   Boris I. Arvatov, "Aleksei Gastev, '*Pachka orderov*,' Riga, 1921," *LEF* 1, no. 1 (March 1923): 243–45.
4   Boris I. Arvatov, "Iskusstvo v sisteme proletarskoi kultury," in *Iskusstvo i proizvodstvo* (Moscow: Proletkult, 1926), 123.
5   Nikolai Tarabukin, *Ot molberta k mashine* [1923] (Moscow: Ad Marginem, 2015), 39.
6   Ilya G. Ehrenburg, *A vse-taki ona vertitsia*, (Berlin, Moscow: Gelikon, 1923), 74 and 77.
7   Ilya G. Ehrenburg, *Trest D.E., istoria gibeli Evropy*, (Berlin, Moscow: Gelikon, 1923).
8   Ilya G. Ehrenburg, *10 L.S.: khronika nashego vremeni* (Berlin: Petropolis, 1929).
9   Gordon McVay, *Isadora & Esenin* (Ann Arbor, MI: Ardis, 1980), 105–51.
10   Nikolai Gogol, *Mirgorod, Being a Continuation of Evenings in a Village near Dikanka*. [1835] (Moscow: Foreign Language Publishing House, 1958).

"On the sixth day, around noon, we sighted land. An hour later New York appeared before my eyes. Oh, my sainted mother! How untalented Mayakovsky's poems about America are! How can you possibly express this iron and granite might in words? It is a poem without words. To tell about it is worthless. You dear old dumb homegrown Russian urbanists and electrifiers in poetry! Your 'smithies' and your LEFs are like Tula compared to Berlin or Paris. Buildings block out the horizon and almost push against the sky. Over all this extend the most enormous arches of reinforced concrete. The sky is leaden from fuming factory smokestacks. The smoke evokes a feeling of mystery; beyond these buildings something so great and enormous is taking place it takes your breath away."[11]

Though he criticized the annihilation of Indigenous peoples and the practice of slavery, Esenin sang the praises of American achievements: "When you look at that merciless might of reinforced concrete, at the Brooklyn Bridge hanging between two cities at the height of twenty-story buildings, all the same no one will regret that wild Hiawatha no longer hunts deer here. And no one will regret that the hand of the builders of this culture was sometimes cruel. The Indian would never have done what the 'white devil' has done on his continent."[12] Upon his return to Russia, ravaged by bootleg alcohol and disappointed in the American public's tepid welcome—he believed himself to be the next Pushkin, and Isadora introduced him as the "Russian Walt Whitman"—, he delivered a most ambivalent verdict: "'Listen,' one American told me, 'I know Europe. Don't argue with me. I've been all over Italy and Greece. I've seen the Parthenon. But this is all old hat to me. Did you know that in Tennessee we have a much newer and better Parthenon?' Words like this make me want to both laugh and cry. These words characterize everything that comprises America's inner culture remarkably well. Europe smokes and throws away the butts; America picks up the butts, but out of them something magnificent is growing."[13]

Esenin also mocked Mayakovsky's poetry, such as the 1921 poem "Before, Now," which described the GOELRO plan as America's advent in the village, responding to critics who considered electrification a mere "utopia:" "Just you wait, bourgeois, New York will come to Tetyushi, there will be paradise in Shuia," alluding to two modest Russian villages[14]. The previous year, in his poem "150,000,000," he had depicted a victorious America headed by a monstrous Woodrow Wilson, in a vaudevillian Chicago setting[15]. Trotsky sternly criticized this vision for its lack of "class consciousness," mocking the poem's battle scene between Wilson and Ivan in *Literature and Revolution*

11   Sergei Esenin, "Zheleznyi Mirgorod," *Izvestiia*, 22 August and 16 September 1923, in *Sobranie sochinenii v piati tomakh*, (Moscow: Gos. Izd-vo khudozhestvennoi literatury, 1962), vol. 4, 259; in English in Olga Peters Hasty, Susanne Fusso, *America through Russian Eyes: 1874–1926* (New Haven: Yale University Press, 1988), 149. The Forge and the LEF were two avant-garde groupings; Tula is a symbol of the Russian heartland.
12   Esenin, "Zheleznyi Mirgorod," 26; Hasty, Fusso, *America Through Russian Eyes*, 152.
13   Ibid. 268; Ibid. 155.
14   Vladimir V. Mayakovsky, "Ranshe, teper," 1921, in *Polnoe sobranie sochinenii* (Moscow: Gos. izd-vo khudozh. literatury, 1955–1958), vol. 2, 98.
15   Vladimir Mayakovsky, "150.000.000", in *Polnoe sobranie sochinenii*, vol. 2, 113–64; see also Carol Avins, *Border Crossings: The West and Russian Identity in Soviet Literature 1917–1934* (Berkeley: University of California Press, 1983), 48–55.
16   Leon D. Trotsky, *Literatura i revoliutsiia* [1923] (Moscow: Gos. Izd-vo, 1924), 114–15; in English: *Literature and Revolution* [1925] (Chicago, Haymarket Books, 2005), 132.
17   V. Seltsov, "Amerika v voobrazhenii russkogo, lektsia V. Maiakovskogo", *Novyi Mir*, 8 October 1925, quoted in Semen Kemrad, *Maiakovskii v Amerike, stranitsi biografii* (Moscow: Sovetskii pisatel, 1970), 179.
18   Semen Kemrad, *Maiakovskii v Amerike*, 17.

and lamenting "[h]ow out of place, and particularly how frivolous […] these primitive ballads and fairytales sound when hurriedly adapted to the industrial metropolis of Chicago, and to class struggle."[16]

In 1925, Mayakovsky presented the New York public with the following naïve, albeit self-ironic, image, perfectly in line with the stereotypes inspired by Petr Tverskoi's narratives: "The Russian public's understanding of America, particularly that of Russian artists and futurists, manifests itself in several ways, all of which can be summarized as following: it is a vision of grandiosity. In the peasant's imagination, America stretches into endless and prosperous prairies where graze large flocks of well-fed cattle. To the Futurists, it towers as the gigantic puppet likeness of Woodrow Wilson, a symbol of the American bourgeoisie. Chicago is colossal with its 14,000 streets, each complete with 600 alleys, all flooded by a sea of electrical light, next to which sunlight is but a dime candle. All citizens rank as high as generals at the very least."[17]

Arriving in New York on 31 July 1925, after a detour through Mexico, Mayakovsky introduced himself, as he stated upon his return, as "a poet preaching for industrialization, seeking to become acquainted with the country where it reached its most advanced stage of development." In other words, he wrote, "the early stages of Futurism were a cry for industrialization—for the 'Amerikanization' of Russia. It was now time to see with our own eyes what Amerikanizm entailed."[18] Like Konstantin Balmont twenty years before him, Mayakovsky walked on the elevated railway track, but also had his photograph taken and followed its curves:

Left: Vladimir V. Mayakovsky in New York in 1925, in *Contemporary Architecture* 5, no. 1–2, 1930. CCA, W. C6.
Right: Vladimir V. Mayakovsky, *My Discovery of America*, cover by Aleksandr M. Rodchenko, Moscow: Gos. Izd-vo, 1926. Private collection.

"If you want to go underground, just take the subway; for the sky, take the elevated train. the wagons go up as high as the smog, and hang out around the heels of the buildings."[19]

Like Gorky, he described a society under the sway of money, painted a bleak picture of the alienated crowds, and painstakingly listed the many segregated Americas. Observing the skyscrapers, he imagined seeing through their façades, and finding floor after floor filled with decaying bodies[20]. After contemplating the metal structure of the Brooklyn Bridge—built forty years earlier, in 1883, by John and Washington Roebling, who were well known to the Russians through the press as well as through technical journals—, Mayakovsky declared:

"I am proud of just this mile of steel; upon it, my visions come to life, erect— here's a fight for construction instead of style, an austere disposition of bolts and steel."[21]

Mayakovsky's stance was not merely one of admiration, though he immediately saw America as a confirmation of the "futurism of pure technique, of the superficial impressionism of smoke and cables," "tasked with the considerable duty of reforming the dormant and flaccid rural mindset," as he wrote in 1926 in *My Discovery of America*[22]. He marvelled at the stacked layers of Grand Central Station and colourfully described daily life in New York, echoing Gorky in his dismissal of Luna Park and his disapproval of the dollar—at once "God," "Father," and "Holy Spirit." He also diligently noted the changes that had taken place in Manhattan ever since his predecessors' travels. In Chicago, he followed in Vladimir Korolenko's footsteps, including two plates depicting slaughterhouses in this otherwise sparsely illustrated book. Though he was impressed by the pace of construction, he remarked on the precarious and repetitive nature of domestic architecture: "For all the grandiose qualities of America's buildings, and although the American construction rate, the height of American skyscrapers, their facilities and spaciousness are unattainable in Europe—even America's houses give a strangely provisional impression."[23] He also offered a rebuttal to the clichés peddled by his fellow countrymen: "The expression 'an American' brings to mind, for us in Russia, a cross between O. Henry's eccentric hobos, Nick Carter and his inevitable pipe, and the checkered cowboys of the Kuleshov film studio."[24]

19   Vladimir V. Mayakovsky, "Broadway," in *Polnoe sobranie sochinenii*, vol. 7, 56; in English: *Selected Poems* (Evanston: Northwestern University Press, 2013), 112.
20   Vladimir V. Mayakovsky "Neboskreb v razreze," in *Polnoe sobranie sochinenii*, vol. 7, 66–69; in English: Edwards James Brown, *A Poet in the Revolution* (Princeton: Princeton University Press, 2016), 280.
21   Vladimir V. Mayakovsky, "Bruklinskii most," in *Polnoe sobranie sochinenii*, vol. 7, 85. On this engineering feat, see Alan Trachtenberg, *Brooklyn Bridge, Fact and Symbol* (London; New York: Oxford University Press, 1965); *The Great East River Bridge 1883–1983* (New York: The Brooklyn Museum, Harry N. Abrams, 1983).
22   Vladimir V. Mayakovsky, *Moe otkrytie Ameriki* (Moscow: Gos. Izd-vo, 1926), 139; in English: *My Discovery of America*, trans. by Neil Cornwell (London: I lesperus Press Ltd., 2005), 102.
23   Mayakovsky, *My Discovery of America*, 77.
24   Ibid. 83. O. Henry is William Sydney Porter's pseudonym.
25   [Le Corbusier] "Finds American Skyscrapers 'Much Too Small'," *New York Herald Tribune*, 22 October 1935, 21; Le Corbusier, *When the Cathedrals Were White; a Journey to the Land of Timid People* [1937] (London: Routledge, 1947), 51.
26   "Russia's Dynamic Poet Finds New York Tame: We're Old Fashioned, Unorganized, to Mayakovsky," *New York World*, 9 August 1925; in Wiktor Woroszylski, *The Life of Mayakovsky* (New York: The Orion Press, 1970), 368-369.
27   Mayakovsky, *My Discovery of America*, 52.
28   Bengt Jangfeldt, *Mayakovsky: a Biography* [2007], trans. Harry D. Watson (Chicago: The University of Chicago Press, 2014), 331-33. Patricia J. Thompson, *Mayakovsky in Manhattan: A Love Story with Excerpts from the Memoir of Elly Jones* (New York: West End Publications, 1993).
29   Vladimir V. Mayakovsky, *Pro eto* (Moscow: Gos. Izd-vo, 1923), photomontages facing pages 30 and 36.

In an interview with the communist writer Michael Gold published in *New York World*, Mayakovsky, in a rather futuristic mindset, allowed himself to disdain the eclectically decorated Manhattan skyscrapers. He presaged Le Corbusier's deliberately provocative statements, when the Paris architect deemed them "too small" during his 1935 trip[25]: "No, New York is not modern, [...] New York is unorganized. Mere machinery, subways, skyscrapers and the like do not make a real industrial civilization. These are only the externals. America has gone through a tremendous material development which has changed the face of the world. But the people have not yet caught up to their new world... Intellectually, New Yorkers are still provincials. Their minds have not accepted the full implications of the industrial age. That is why I say New York is unorganized—it is a gigantic accident stumbled on by children, not the full-grown, mature product of men who understood what they wanted and planned it like artists. When our industrial age comes in Russia it will be different—it will be planned—it will be conscious. [...] Take these selfsame skyscrapers of yours. They are glorious achievements of the modern engineer. The past knew nothing like them. The plodding hand-workers of the Renaissance never dreamed of these great structures that sway in the wind and defy the laws of gravity. Fifty stories upward they march into the sky; and they should be clean, swift, complete, and modern as a dynamo. But the American builder, only half-aware of the miracle he has produced, scatters obsolete and silly Gothic and Byzantine ornaments over the skyscrapers. It is like tying pink ribbons on a steam dredge, or like putting Kewpie figures on a locomotive."[26]

In his 1926 poem "Broadway," Mayakovsky once again described the New York skyscrapers and the human tide they swallowed in the morning and released at night. The *Great White Way* was his "very favourite street, the only one that capriciously and brazenly butts through streets and avenues as regulars as prison bars."[27] He roamed Broadway with Burliuk and regularly met with Isai Khurgin, the first head of Amtorg, who helped him obtain a visa, and later perished in a suspicious boating accident. He developed a romantic relationship with Elly Jones, a model of Russian descent, who would later join him in Moscow[28], and embarked for his return on 28 October 1925.

Pickfordism and Pinkertonitis

In *My Discovery of America*, Mayakovsky expressed admiration for certain technical realizations such as the Brooklyn Bridge and Ford's streamlined production, but without going so far as to celebrate an industrial civilization that, compared to Russia, was deficient in terms of culture. The book cover image was by Aleksandr Rodchenko, who had illustrated the ten fascicles of the 1924 serial novel *Mess-Mend: Yankees in Petrograd*, using collages of people and building fragments mostly cut out from German magazines, but reminiscent of American imagery. These photomontages were akin to the more complex ones he had created in 1923 for Mayakovsky's "About That," a poem with both verbal and graphic references to America. For instance, one of the montages combines a Jazz Band banner with scattered dancers and liqueur bottles; another shows Mayakovsky sitting atop the Ivan the Great Bell Tower, the Kremlin's tallest structure, and crushing a miniature Equitable Building[29].

The protagonist of the serial "tale-novel" *Mess-Mend*, which bore the enigmatic signature Dzhim Dollar, is Arthur Rockefeller. In a quasi-cinematographic pace, he discovers a proletarian Russia on the rise and joins

Dzhim Dollar (pseudonym for Marietta Shaginian). *Mess Mend, or the Yankees in Petrograd,* vol. 7.
Cover design by Aleksandr M. Rodchenko, Moscow: Gos. Izd-vo, 1924. CCA, BIB 249322.

Mess-Mend—a group of workers who "mend messes" with makeshift and almost magical electrical equipment and weapons—in their fight against capitalism. At the helm of the faction is the American labourer Mick Thingsmaster, whose name expresses the idea that the true owners of industrial merchandise are those who manufacture it[30]. The first fascicle of the series contained Dzhim Dollar's fictional life story as an abandoned child whose biological family had traced him later in life and restored his fortune, allowing him to publish the adventures of ingenious and optimistic workers. These characters were written as polar opposites to Upton Sinclair's miserable proletarians. Marietta Shaginian, the true author of the biography as well as of the entire series and of two other serial novels to come, was only uncovered in 1926, when Fedor Otsep and Boris Barnet directed the film adaptation, entitled *Miss Mend*[31]. Despite this discovery, for a time, many thought Nikolai Bukharin, an avid reader of adventure novels, was the author of the series. This theory was made plausible by the fact that the Bolshevik leader had called, in a 1922 article in the *Pravda*, for the publication of affordable popular novels, "red Pinkertons," as he dubbed them[32]. At the time, the USSR was indeed flooded with cheap American series.

30   Dzhim Dollar, *Mess-Mend, ili ianki v Petrograde, roman-skazka* (Leningrad; Moscow: Gos. Izd-vo, 1924–25); in English: *Mess-Mend, Yankees in Petrograd*, trans. and introduction by Samuel D. Cioran (Ann Arbor, MI: Ardis, 1991).

31   Marietta S. Shaginian, *Lori Len Metallist* (Leningrad; Moscow: Gos. Izd-vo, 1924); *Doroga v Bagdad* (Leningrad; Moscow: Gos. Izd-vo, 1925).

32   Nikolai Bukharin, "Kommunisticheskoe vospitanie molodezhi v usloviakh NEPa", *Pravda*, 14 October 1922; see Boris Dralyuk, "Bukharin and the 'Red Pinkerton'," in *The NEP Era: Soviet Russia 1921–1928*, vol. 5 (2011): 3–21.

Maurice Hindus, for instance, found *The Adventures of Tarzan* being sold in pamphlets at every train station kiosk[33].

Bukharin's calls were soon answered, and many other American-style narratives were dedicated to dark conspiracies ultimately thwarted by fearless Soviet detectives. The literary theorist Viktor Shklovskii and the writer Vsevolod Ivanov fed into the generalized *Pinkertonovshchina*, or Pinkertonitis, with their 1925 novel *Iperit* (Mustard gas)[34]. Around the same time, Aleksei Tolstoi exploited the genre in *The Garin Death Ray*, a novel first published as a series, and as a book in 1927, where the Old World weaponizes technology to conspire against the New World, embodied by Russia[35].

Filmmakers also answered the regime's call for "Red" adventures. While Sergei Eisenstein, formerly of the Proletkult theatre, was inspired by David Wark Griffith's films, starting with his 1925 movie *Strike*, his peers relished in shooting adventure films. Some of them were closely tied to literary works, such as Barnet and Otsep's *Miss Mend*, which was deemed contaminated by American models in 1926. That same year, Lev Kuleshov shot *Dura Lex*, adapted by Shklovskii from Jack London's short story "The Unexpected." Kuleshov had already directed the 1924 comedy *The Extraordinary Adventures of Mr. West in the Land of the Bolsheviks*. In this rollicking tale, an American businessman is terrorized and hounded by counterrevolutionaries and ends up getting rescued by the Reds, who turn out to be rather charming. This largely popular film is striking both in its plot, which suggests a parallel between America and Russia, and in its cinematography, which borrows its gags, pantomimes, and acrobatics from Hollywood slapstick comedies by extracting their tropes from suburban Los Angeles and repurposing them in Russian cities[36] [ill. p. 195].

33   Maurice Hindus, "American Authors in Russia," *Saturday Review of Literature*, 1, 16 August 1925, 50–51.
34   Viktor B. Shklovskii and Vsevolod V. Ivanov, *Iprit* (Leningrad; Moscow: Gos. Izd-vo, 1925).
35   Aleksei N. Tolstoi, *Giperboloid inzhenera Garina* (Moscow: Gos. Izd-vo, 1927). See also Julia Vaingurt, *Wonderlands of the Avant-Garde: Technology and the Arts in Russia of the 1920s* (Evanston, IL: Northwestern University Press, 2013), 182–223.
36   This film has been the subject of many analyses, such as Peter G. Christianson "Contextualizing Kuleshov's *Mr. West*," *Film Criticism* 18 (1993): 3–15; Greta Matzner-Gore "A Copy of a Copy (of a Copy): The Search for Authenticity in Mess-Mend and The Extraordinary Adventures of Mr. West in the Land of the Bolsheviks," *Ulbandus Review* 5 (2013): 153–69; Nancy Yanoshak, "Mr. West Mimicking 'Mr. West': America in the Mirror of the Other," *The Journal of Popular Culture* 41 (2008): 1051–68.
37   Lev V. Kuleshov, "Amerikanshchina," *Kino-fot* 1, no. 1 (25–31 August 1922), 14–15; in English: Ron Luvaco, ed., *Kuleshov on Film: Writings* (Berkeley: University of California Press, 1974), 127. See also Denise J. Youngblood, "'Americanitis': the *Amerikanshchina* in Soviet Cinema," *Journal of Popular Film & Television* 19 (1992): 148–63.
38   Dziga Vertov, 'We. A Version of a Manifesto,' August 1922, as quoted in Richard Taylor and Ian Christie, *The Film Factory: Russian and Soviet Cinema in Documents* (Cambridge, MA: Harvard University Press, 1988), 69.
39   Dziga Vertov, "My", *Kinofot* 1, n° 1 (25–31 August 1922), 11; in English: "We." In *Kino-Eye; the Writings of Dziga Vertov*, trans. Kevin O'Brien, intro. Annette Michelson (Los Angeles: University of California Press, 1985), 7–8.
40   Sergei M. Eisenstein and Sergei Io. Iutkevich "Vosmoe Iskusstvo: ob ekspressionizme, Amerike i, konechno, o Chapline," *Ekho*, no. 2 (1922): 20–21. I would like to thank François Albera for leading me to this text, which he translated. On Chaplin's popularity and the feature of "Americanness," see Owen Hatherley, *The Chaplin Machine: Slapstick, Fordism and the International Communist Avant-Garde* (London: Pluto Press, 2016), 35–63.
41   Vance Kepley Jr. and Betty Kepley, "Foreign Films on Soviet Screens, 1922–1931," *Quarterly Review of Film Studies* 4, no. 4 (Fall 1979): 431.
42   Leon S. Zamkovov [Amkino director] *New York Times*, 19 December 1926, sect. 7, 2, quoted in J.D. Parks, *Culture, Conflict and Coexistence*, 19.
43   Richard Taylor, *The Politics of the Soviet Cinema, 1917–1929* (Cambridge: Cambridge University Press, 1979), 183.
44   "'Quelque chose de grand croît sur ce sol'... Ainsi parlent du régime soviétique Douglas Fairbanks et Mary Pickford," *L'Humanité*, 20 August 1926. This article was brought to my attention by François Albera.

In 1922, Kuleshov detected widespread "Americanitis" among Soviet movie-goers, noting that "of the foreign films, all the American ones and detective stories appeal most. The public especially 'feels' American films. When there is a clever maneuver by the hero, a desperate pursuit, a bold struggle, there is such excited whistling, howling, whooping, and intensity that interested figures leap from their seats, so as to see the gripping action better."[37] At the opposite end of the spectrum in Soviet cinema theory, Dziga Vertov, though claiming to share this positive appraisal of the swift and dynamic montage of American films, considered them filled with jumbled and reductive clichés, making each one seem like "a copy of a copy."[38] In his essay, he calls for the recording of machines as an alternative to the disappointing human gestures, an idea in line with Gastev's manifestos. The filmmaker writes: "The machine makes us ashamed of man's inability to control himself, but what are we to do if electricity's unerring ways are more exciting to us than the disorderly haste of active men and the corrupting inertia of passive ones?" Fascinated with the idea of man as a machine, Vertov proposes to reframe cinema as a "factory of facts" rather than a narrative medium, through the observation of working rhythms: "For his inability to control his movements, we temporarily exclude man as a subject for film. Our path leads through the poetry of machines, from the bungling citizen to the perfect electric man."[39]

In an article published the same year, Eisenstein and Sergei Iutkevich discussed "expressionism, America, and, of course, Chaplin." They criticized Hollywood's use of matte painted sets, praised the "new possibilities for genuine Eccentrism" offered by "detective, adventure, comedy films", and noted the general craze around Charlie Chaplin[40]. The "Americanitis" Kuleshov and Vertov diagnosed in Soviet cinema was tangible, as evidenced by the overwhelming preference of Soviet mass culture consumers for American productions. Film reels from the United States ranked first in terms of imports. Between 1918 and 1931, 944 American motion pictures were distributed, against only 684 Russian productions[41]. In 1926, the director of the Soviet association Amkino, created in New York to ensure the circulation of films between the United States and the USSR, wrote in the New York Times that "America [...] represents to the Russians a land of incredible efficiency, and in his desire to imitate its ideas the Russian is eager for every bit of news of life in this country."[42] In such a context, the popularity of stars like Douglas Fairbanks Sr.—a remarkable actor, according to Eisenstein—and Mary Pickford was at its peak, while Raoul Walsh's 1925 The Thief of Bagdad, starring Fairbanks, was the greatest commercial success of the decade. When Eisenstein's Battleship Potemkin was released at the end of 1925, the Pravda used quotes from the two actors to promote the picture[43]. The pair was met with tremendous acclaim during their Soviet tour the following year and declared to the press that "something great is growing in this soil, something solid as an oak."[44] The filmmaker Sergei Komarov shamelessly exploited their success in A Kiss From Mary Pickford, or the Story of the Fight Between Douglas Fairbanks and Igor Ilinskii about Mary Pickford, where the two American stars appear in a quick cameo from footage filmed during their triumphant Soviet tour in 1926. Fairbanks' co-star played a movie usher.

Comedies were just as popular as adventure films; Buster Keaton, Harold Lloyd, and especially Charlie Chaplin were the stars of the Soviet silver screen. Chaplin was portrayed in dozens of portraits and caricatures, notably by Rodchenko and Fernand Léger, along with studies by Shklovskii. Grigorii Kozintsev and Leonid Trauberg, the founders of the FEKS—the Factory of the Eccentric Actor—, were especially interested in him as an inspiration for their synthetic stage performances, as Trauberg would later explain: "Our ideal actor was Chaplin. We considered that Eccentrism was the surest way to 'Americanize' theatre, to give the theatrical action the dynamics required by the twentieth century—the century of unheard of velocities."[45] And while Mr. West's innocent face was borrowed from Harold Lloyd, Buster Keaton inspired Barnet in his caustic 1927 comedy The Girl with a Hatbox.

In his 1929 book on the Art of Cinema, Kuleshov explained that American cinematography was a question of rhythm and cutting up the narrative in short sequences, in a process reminiscent of Taylor's organization of labour: "Thanks to the commercial determinant of the American film, thanks to the very tempo of American life, much more accelerated than the tempo of Russian or European life, thanks to all of this, what struck the eye watching the American films is that they consist of a whole series of very short shots, of a whole series of short sequences, joined in some determined order of priority—as opposed to the Russian film, which at that time consisted of a few very long scenes, very monotonously following each other."[46] In his own films, he hurried the pace, inspired by the rhythm of directors such as David Wark Griffith.

The writers and critics of the Left Front of the Arts (LEF) reclaimed the themes of Amerikanizm more overtly. They promoted Vertov's machinist perspective rather than Kuleshov's narrative view, in the name of an "authentic" portrayal of Americans, as advocated by the publicist Mikhail Levidov. In a 1923 article published in LEF's journal, he denounced the "hysteria" of Amerikanizm, which he saw as a "tragicomedy" when reduced to the celebration of "muscle" in body as well as in spirit, as expressed by Baudelaire[47]. Sergei Tretiakov, a proponent of "factual literature" and a regular contributor to the publication, harshly criticized Soviet studios for their production. In 1923, in a most Gastevian gesture, he launched a crusade against those depicting "the sorrows of off-duty proletarian Werthers," arguing in favour of "standardized activists." Tretiakov supported "left-wing artist workers, turning art into a factory producing precise tools of the revolutionary imperative, elaborating the 'Americanized' man in an electrified country."[48] In a 1928 article, he lamented that "motion pictures dream of 'Pickfordizing' labourers' daily lives instead of 'Fordizing' them."[49] In Petrograd as well as in Moscow, several fictional and theatrical "factories" took part in this programme. In 1922, in the old capital, Iurii Annenkov designed a set for Konstantin Khokhlov's staging of the play Gaz by Georg Kaiser[50], comprised of fragments from an industrial landscape painted over a backdrop, in a static and decorative version of Meyerhold's performances.

45   Leonid Z. Trauberg, in Konstantin Rudnitsky, Russian and Soviet Theatre: Tradition and the Avant-Garde (London: Routledge, 1994), 124; quoted in Hatherley, The Chaplin Machine, 81.
46   Lev V. Kulechov, Iskusstvo kino, (Moscow: Teatr–Kino pechat, 1929), 14; in Screen, Winter 1971-1972, 110-111.
47   Mikhail Levidov, "Amerikanizm tragifars," LEF 1, no. 2 (April–May 1923): 45–46.
48   Sergei M. Tretiakov, "LEF i NEP," LEF 1, no. 2, 1923, 77.
49   Sergei M. Tretiakov, "S novym godom, s novym LEFom," Novy LEF (January 1928) 2, no. 1.
50   Iurii P. Annenkov, Dnevnik moikh vstrech, tsikl tragedii (Moscow: Khudozhestvennaia literatura, 1991), vol. 2, 59.

Semen Semenov-Menes. Movie poster for *A Kiss from Mary Pickford,* directed by Sergei Komarov, produced by Mezhrabprom-Rus, 1927. Lithographic print on paper, 72 × 102.5 cm.

Iakov T. Rukhlevskii. Poster for the movie *A Sailor Made Man* (1921), by Fred C. Newmeyer, with Harold Lloyd, produced by Hal Roach, 1929. Lithographic print on paper, 68.5 × 97.7 cm. Merrill C. Berman collection.

Red Skyscrapers

The effects of Americanism were most visible in the fields of art and architecture. American culture was referenced on the silver screen, on stage, as well as in journals. *LEF*, for instance, issued excerpts from Sinclair Lewis's satirical novel *Babbitt* as of 1922, a tale met with extraordinary acclaim when it was published in book form two years later[51]. Artists and architects were interested in skyscrapers as emblematic constructions of the New World. Their interpretations of these structures were particularly inventive, as there were practically no commissions for such endeavours in the USSR.

In Petrograd—renamed Leningrad following the revolutionary's demise, echoing the commemoration of the main hero of the Independence in the US capital name—, Kazimir Malevich opposed the views of LEF's constructivists and intellectuals. He thus abandoned his pictorial approach, which had peaked with his 1915 *Black Square*, in favour of three-dimensional objects. He moulded plaster prisms from 1923 to 1929, using the evocative term "arkhitektons" to describe them. The *Alpha*, *Beta*, *Gota*, and *Zeta* pieces were a reversal of Malevich's former technique, where he projected three-dimensional spaces onto the canvas[52]. These works were recreated in the late 1970s based on their original elements, though no scale had been specified by the artist. They can be interpreted as skyscraper models clustered in an interchangeable and informal way, evoking a beaming white American city centre on the black-and-white photographs. Though it is unlikely that Malevich had heard of the zoning by-law passed in New York City in 1916, which favoured receding tiers and was already shaping the Manhattan skyline, the *Beta* arkhitekton seems to be based on the same principle, with its clusters of vertical square prisms flanked by smaller ones, as if escorting them in their rise. The hierarchy between the components is not as obvious in *Gota*, but it also follows the principle of successive setbacks.

Malevich's considerations on architecture were as scarce as they were disjointed. The title of his 1928 article "Painting and the Problem of Architecture" conveys his struggle to articulate a true programme. Though the "small avant-garde" heralding the new European architecture succeeded, according to him, to "move towards artistic form," he accuses it of being incapable of surpassing "two-dimensionality." As for present-day architects, they are "cowardly," and "have been unable to rise up and abandon the speculative building demanded by life's speculators in order to extend the front of new architecture. One might say that to this day they remain on the front of naked utilitarianism, hindering with all the means at their disposal the movement of new architecture as an artistic form."[53]

In the photomontage "Suprematist Structure Among American Skyscrapers," Malevich apposed an image of one of his arkhitektons to an aerial photograph of New York City, presenting it on the scale of the American metropolis. The montage was first published in 1926, in the inaugural issue of the *Praesens*, a journal created by Szymon Sirkus on the occasion of the first International Exhibition of Modern Architecture in Warsaw, where Malevich displayed his work[54]. The buildings used as a backdrop are perfectly recognizable on the photograph, which is practically identical to the one printed in a 1925 edition of Le Corbusier's *Urbanisme*. The Woolworth and Singer buildings can be seen on the left, and the Bankers Trust Tower, on the right. The A11 arkhitekton, pictured horizontally in its other representations, appears upright, wiping out both Trinity Church and part of the Equitable Building[55]. The monolith is floating in mid-air, standing out against the background not only because of the outline of its orthogonal volumes, but also owing to the strong contrast between the black and white elements. New York City, as a canvas for Malevich's architectural ideal, seems to be sanctioning the relevance of a previously floating proposition [ill. p. 202-203]. This photomontage is exceptional in all respects: previous skyscraper designs such as Mies van der Rohe's glass structures or Le Corbusier's Plan Voisin towers were represented against the cityscapes of Paris and Berlin, these symbols of European Americanism.

Before Malevich, tall building projects had already begun spreading in post-revolutionary Russia, either off-ground or rooted in concrete locations. The most abstract projects, without any urban context, were developed in 1919–1920 by members of Zhivskulptarkh (Committee for the Synthesis of Painting, Sculpture and Architecture), a working group created within the People's Commissariat for Education. The collective, comprised of rationalist and constructivist artists and architects driven by various beliefs, attempted to materialize projects such as the Peoples' Communion Temple, the communal house, or the House of the Soviets. Among the most ambitious endeavours were those of Nikolai Ladovskii, whose communal houses were designed to move upward. One of them was crowned with a crane, as if to evoke the construction of the Babel Tower by Pieter Bruegel the Elder. Another one sat atop a double base, in a nod to the Colossus of Rhodes, and stacked shifting volumes topped with a long, sharp spire [ill. p. 204]. Georgii Mapu erected a tower by juxtaposing and stacking cylinders, and another by superposing twenty storeys worth of prisms and cubes [ill. p. 205]. They all worked with the accumulation and combination of elementary volumes, whose structures remained as unfathomable as their intended location[56].

In the early 1920s, the active members of the group became instructors at the Higher State Artistic and Technical Studios (Vkhutemas), and pursued their research with their students, fulfilling the government's initial demands. In 1923, Vladimir Krinskii developed a skyscraper project for the Supreme Council of the National Economy (VSNKh), then headed by Aleksei Rykov, one of Nicolai Bukharin's allies. Located on Lubianka Square, on a corner lot with Miasnitskaia Street—the subject of one of the Futuristic 1912 postcards—the project was launched by Ladovskii as part of the architects' working group at the Institute of Artistic Culture (Inkhuk)[57]. The geometry of Krinskii's subversive project, initially oblique and dynamic, espoused a more orthogonal and concise shape during its inception. Its variants appear in a half-dozen sketches, a photomontage, and several model photographs. In his most accomplished projection for the structure, Krinskii imagined a superposition of prisms whose volume shrank as it grew taller, with an exposed framework weaved into various patterns.

51 Sinclair Lewis, "Mister Bebbit – amerikanets," LEF 1, no. 2 (1923): 55–64.
52 Jean-Hubert Martin, Malevitch, architectones, peintures, dessins (Paris: Centre George Pompidou, 1980).
53 Kazimir S. Malevich, "Maliarstvo v problemi arkhitektury," Nova generatsiia 3, no. 2 (1928): 116–32;
    in English: K. S. Malevich, "Painting and the Problem of Architecture," Essays on art 1915-1933, trans.
    Xenia Glowacki-Prus and Arnold McMillin, ed. Troels Andersen (New York: George Wittenborn, Inc. 1972),
    Volume 2: 15.
54 Kazimir S. Malevich, "Budowla suprematyczna pośród amerykánskich drapaczy nieba," Praesens 1, no. 1
    (1926): 28. The arkhitekton in the photomontage is the item A 11 in the nomenclature established by Martin,
    Malevitch, architectones, peintures, dessins, 122.
55 Le Corbusier, Urbanisme (Paris: G. Crès & Co, 1925), 174.
56 Selim O. Khan-Magomedov, Zhivskulptarkh, 1919-1920: pervaya tvorcheskaia organizatsiia sovetskogo
    arkhitekturnogo avangarda (Moscow: Arkhitektura, 1993).
57 Selim O. Khan-Magomedov, "Neboskreb VSNKh v Moskve, proekty 1922-1925 godov," Arkhitektura i
    stroitelstvo Moskvy, no. 11 (November 1988): 4–6.

Kazimir S. Malevich. *Suprematist Building Among American Skyscrapers.*
Collage published in *Praesens* 1, no 1, June 1926. Reprinted in 1994. W.P71. CCA, W.P71.

Nikolai A. Ladovskii. Project for a communal house, 1919.
Elevation. Graphite and ink on paper, 58 × 42.3 cm. Alex Lachmann Collection.

Georgii M. Mapu. Project for a communal house, 1920.
Perspective. Graphite on tracing paper, 24.4 × 17.2 cm. Alex Lachmann Collection.

The plan shows a slanted six-storey base, more massive than the rest of the construction, topped with the layout of the six following levels and the horizontal shapes of the eight top storeys. A lattice mast stiffens the structure. Disproving Mies van der Rohe's glass prisms and the abomination of eclectic façades, the project served as a critique of American precedents, with their standardized floors. Located on one of the capital's central intersections, it was meant to become a landmark for the entire city.

In 1926, Ladovskii introduced this project as a response both to the German approach, which he deemed too psychological and intricate, and to American solutions, which he considered dishonest, as they dissimulated their frameworks: "Despite the apparent technical courage displayed in skyscraper construction in New York, broadly speaking, their structural solutions are far from reaching the level that could be attainable with contemporary means. This is evidenced by the laments of young architects who have acquired their taste for innovation in America. As we can see, the most talented engineers find no interest in designing structures destined to be completely hidden, and leave to build bridges, planes, and automobiles."[58] As for Krinskii, he would later justify his project by recalling having "remembered a verse from a poem by Mayakovsky, whose pathos dictated the tenacity of [his] work," referencing the line from the 1919 poem "We March": "To keep lowly natures from soiling our squares, we toss reinforced concrete into the skies."[59]

As of 1920, those same architects extended their interest for skyscrapers to their pedagogical activities at the Vkhutemas studios in Moscow. The students of the "space" discipline explored "vertical rhythms," following Krinskii's own work, and presented various solutions, such as isolating the building's different blocks and tying them together with lattices or spiral frameworks or suggesting more realistic, albeit acrobatic, structural layerings[60]. In 1924, during their first semester, Vkhutemas students Aleksandr Silchenkov and Gleb Glushchenko, in keeping with the former approach, offered a solution to an exercise on "the revelation of the (vertical) dynamics, rhythm, relationships, and proportions."[61] It consisted of stacked parallelepipeds barely attached to each other, with structures so thin they seemed impossible to build [ill. p. 208-209].

More convincing propositions were made as part of the same exercise a few months later, when Ladovskii submitted the VSNKh programme to his students, a call that Krinskii had answered alone in 1923. This time, the ventured solutions were more realistic, though they were presented as elevation views and axonometric perspectives concealing their structural principles. Ladovskii and Krinskii developed different projects, seemingly inspired by some of the contestants of the 1922 *Chicago Tribune* competition, whose images were published in German journals distributed in Moscow[62]. Glushchenko submitted a proposition to connect two rectangular-shaped towers—one vertical, the other with setbacks—with a vertical glass circulation shaft. He projected it in

58 Enael [Nikolai A. Ladovskii], "Neboskreb na Lubianskoi ploshchadi, proekt V. F. Krinskogo, 1923," *Izvestiia ASNOVA* 1, no. 1 (1926): n. p.
59 Vladimir V. Mayakovsky, "My idiom" [1919], in *Polnoe sobranie sochinenii* (Moscow: Khudozhestvennaia literatura, 1956), vol. 2, 30. Vladimir F. Krinskii, "Vospominania," manuscript, private collection, quoted in Khan-Magomedov, "Neboskreb VSNKh," 6.
60 Muzei MArkhI, KP 501/171-176.
61 *Arhitektura, raboty arkhitekturnogo fakulteta Vhutemasa 1920-1927* (Moscow: Izd-vo Vkhutemasa, 1927), 4.
62 Gerhard Wohler, "Das Hochhaus im Wettbewerb der Chicago Tribune," *Deutsche Bauzeitung*, 5 July 1924, 325-30 and 16 July 1924, 345-47; Werner Hegemann, "Das Hochhaus als Verkehrsstörer und der Wettbewerb der Chicago Tribune: mittelalterliche Enge und neuzeitliche Gotik," *Wasmuths Monatshefte für Baukunst* 8, no. 10-11 (1924): 297-310.

Studies of vertical rhythms, exercise for the discipline "Space" at Vkhutein, 1927.
MArkhI Museum, KP 501/172 – KP 501/175.

an axonometric worm's eye view as introduced by Auguste Choisy. Six other known projects were in line with Krinskii's perspectives, but distinguished more clearly between the assembled volumes, following the accumulation principle, in some cases evocative of Malevich's architectones. Among these, Sergei Lopatin's project, presented as an aerial view, was the only one set in an urban context. Ivan Volodko and Izaak Iosefovich emphasized the vertical lines and limited the number of setbacks, especially the former, who created the most towering effect. Vitalii Lavrov, on the other hand, emphasized the expressive nature of the stacked volumes, whose tectonics, strong at the bottom and thinner towards the top, was in line with Krinskii's teachings. As for Iurii Mushinskii and Valentin Popov, they set the four constituent prisms of their project so far apart from each other that they seemed to form an urban complex rather than a single structure[63].

In 1923, Ladovskii, Krinskii, and their fellow teacher Nikolai Dokuchaev founded the Association of New Architects (ASNOVA). The cover of the single eight-page issue of the association's news bulletin, published in 1926 with a layout by El Lissitzky, an independent member of the association, was illustrated with a head-to-toe coupling of Volodko's project and an upside-down Ivan the Great Bell Tower. Commenting on his students' plans, Ladovskii announced that "the skyscraper is no longer a problem for the USSR, but rather a reality." He offered concrete propositions for hoistways and skyscraper fire safety, and most importantly, he advocated for a Ruskinian truthfulness principle: "Architecture must not conceal the structure, as per the American practice, it must be 'sincere.' But it would be naïve to think that showing the structure in an 'honest' way is sufficient to achieve architectural goals."[64] Ladovskii stated that "the expression of height is the first problem of the skyscraper," paraphrasing Louis Sullivan. He had likely been acquainted with the latter's work through the long excerpts published by Fiske Kimball in Berlin the previous year[65]. But Ladovskii rejected the American "gothic" solutions, considering that the medieval "mysticism" on which they were based was outdated: "When a bank, a newspaper headquarters or a department store are adorned with gothic shapes, it seems as though a banker has dressed up as a cardinal. Height can only be treated like a bold upward movement, like a victory over weight and a technical achievement."[66]

As the NEP led to a trade revival and state companies grew more prosperous, office building construction became a central issue, and many architects began offering their solutions to the skyscraper problem. In his first project for the headquarters of the daily newspaper *Izvestiia* in Moscow, Grigorii Barkhin, who could see the site from his apartment in the Nirnzee building[67], used several components borrowed directly from another press-related project: Walter Gropius and Adolf Meyer's submission to the 1922 *Chicago Tribune* competition. After the regulation limiting the height of Chicago's

63   Volodko and Lopatin's projects were published in *Arkhitektura, raboty arhitekturnogo fakulteta Vkhutemasa 1920-1927*, 10 and 12; see Selim O. Khan-Magomedov, *Arkhitektura sovetskogo avangarda* (Moscow: Stroiizdat, 1996), vol. 1, 254–55.
64   Enael [Nikolai A. Ladovskii], "Neboskreby SSSR i Ameriki," *Izvestiia ASNOVA* 1, no. 1 (1926): n. p.
65   Fiske Kimball, "Alte und neue Baukunst in Amerika: der Sieg des jungen Klassizismus über den Fonktional-ismus der neunziger Jahre," *Wasmuths Monatshefte für Baukunst* 9, no. 9 (1925): 225–39; originally: "Louis Sullivan: An Old Master," *The Architectural Record* 57, no. 4 (1925), 289–304.
66   Enael, "Neboskreby SSSR i Ameriki.".
67   Vladimir Besonov and Rachid Yangirov, *Dom Nirnzee, Bolshoy Gnezdikovskii pereulok 10* (Moscow: Intellekt-Tsentr, 2012), 35.

Left: Ivan Io. Volodko. Project for a skyscraper, student work at Vkhutemas, 1923, elevation. In *Architecture,*
Works of the Architectural Faculty of Vkhutemas, 1920–1927, Moscow: Izd-vo Vkhutemasa, 1927. CCA, ID:90-B3489.

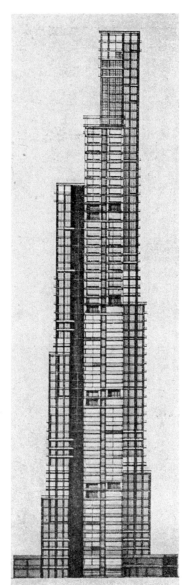

Right: Sergei A. Lopatin. Project for a skyscraper, student exercise at Vkhutemas, 1923, perspective.
In *Architecture, Works of the Architectural Faculty of Vkhutemas, 1920–1927*, Moscow: Izd-vo Vkhutemasa, 1927. CCA, ID:90-B3489.

Left: Walter Gropius and Adolf Meyer. Project for the *Chicago Tribune* competition, 1922. Perspective in *The International Competition for a New Administration Building for the Chicago Tribune,* Chicago: The Tribune Company, 1923. CCA, NA2340.C5 1923.

Right: Grigorii B. Barkhin. Project for the headquarters of *Izvestiia,* Moscow, 1926. Photomontage with the site in El Lissitzky, *Rußland: Die Rekonstruktion der Architektur in der Sowjetunion,* Vienna: A. Schroll & Co, 1930, 81. CCA, NA44.L772.A35 1930.

skyscrapers was abolished, the newspaper developed a plan uniting an office building and a printing press, and launched a worldwide call for submissions, excluding Russia. The number of German contestants was particularly high: 37 on a total of 229[68]. The winning project, by Raymond Hood and John M. Howells, was a perfect illustration of Ladovskii's greatest phobias.

Barkhin praised Gropius and Meyer's unique design—which was already circulating in Berlin journals, but had arrived too late to be judged in Chicago— in a 1924 article on the new German architecture, then on display in Moscow: "Delicate steel and glass framework. Excellent prismatic masses. Absence of any ornaments, except a few protruding horizontal balcony slabs, elegantly breaking the monotonous surface of the glass planes. Nothing superfluous in the treatment, no compromise made to architectural design for its own sake. In its elevated and perspective views, the project is simple yet convincing, and sketched with a stable and energetic hand using a few light touches of monochrome ink. The contrast between the colossal front tower and the small prismatic tower in the back is quite striking."[69]

A single photomontage remains from Barkhin's first project for *Izvestiia*, showing a dozen-storey tower, flanked by two lower wings. Its cantilevered balconies are reminiscent of his beloved Gropius and Meyer's entry, while the exposed framework, whose most salient components are vertical beams surrounding the glass façades, echoes the explorations of Ladovskii's students[70]. Unfortunately for Barkhin, in a movement contrary to Chicago's initiative, a 1926 Moscow regulation instated the height limitation of structures to six floors within the Sadovoe Koltso (Garden Ring), which encompassed the site chosen for the project. The completed *Izvestiia* building kept its balconies, but the only trace of the abandoned vertical structure is the staircase skylight, while a row of oculi hints at a modern interpretation of Doric metopes[71]. Other skyscraper projects were impeded by the regulation, like Boris Velikovskii's design for the Gostorg, one of the first modern office complexes in Moscow, which lost its tower and became a compact glass-clad block on Miasnitskaia Street.

Before the 1926 regulation, few structures had pierced the capital's ceiling, the most notable being the 11-storey Mosselprom Building erected in 1924 by David Kogan, immediately popularized by Rodchenko's supergraphics conveying slogans written by Mayakovsky. Its likeness had spread through advertisements, turning it into a beaming monument, rising above a pile of colourful goods and crushing the dark outline of the city with its imposing presence. The illustrated magazine *Krasnaia niva* described it as an actual "skyscraper," comparing it to office buildings in Cologne and Düsseldorf[72]. The most original projects were conceived for newspapers such as *Izvestiia*, playing a similar role to those of the dailies for the creation of the early New York

68   *The International Competition for a New Administration Building for the Chicago Tribune, MCMXXII* (Chicago: The Tribune Company, 1923); Katherine Solomonson, *The Chicago Tribune Tower Competition: Skyscraper Design and Cultural Change in the 1920s* (Chicago: University of Chicago Press, 2001).

69   Grigorii B. Barkhin, "Arkhitektura na vystavke nemetskikh khudozhnikov v Moskve, " *Stroitelnaia promyshlennost 2*, n° 11 (1924), 736. The project had been published in *Wasmuths Monatshefte für Baukunst 7*, no. 11–12 (1922–23): 344–45.

70   El Lissitzky, *Rußland: Die Rekonstruktion der Architektur in der Sowjetunion* (Vienna: Anton Schroll & Co, 1930), 81.

71   On the successful restoration of the building, see Natalia Melikova, "Constructive Renewal," *The Architectural Review*, October 2017, 68–74.

72   "Neboskreby," *Krasnaia nlva 2*, no. 2 (11 January 1925): 41.

Ivan I. Leonidov, Project for a skyscraper (*Izvestiia VTsIK*), student exercise at Vkhutemas, 1926, in *Architecture, Works of the Architectural Faculty of Vkhutemas, 1920–1927*, Moscow: Izd-vo Vkhutemasa, 1927. CCA, ID:90-B3489.

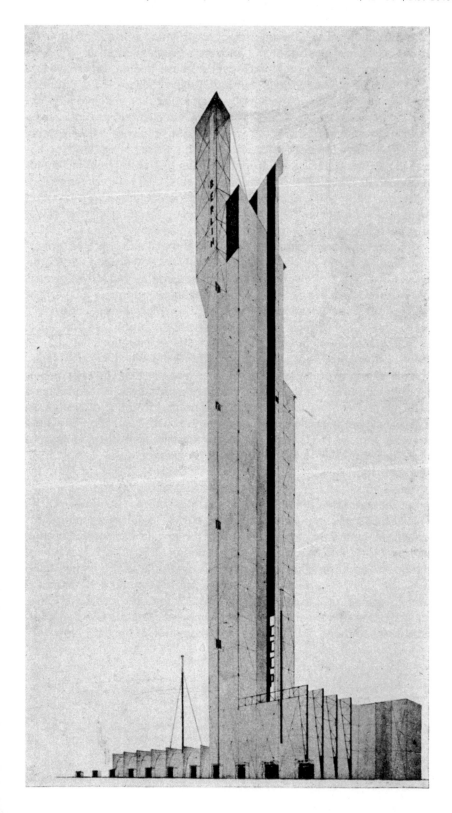

City skyscrapers. Though modest in stature, the submissions to the 1924 competition for the *Pravda*'s Moscow headquarters were varied in their exploration of form. Compared to Konstantin Melnikov's unusual kinetic device, the Vesnin brothers' tower seems timorous at first, but it is actually quite dynamic, with its external elevator and luminous rotating newspapers. The tower, serving propagandist purposes with its large dials and projectors, can also be viewed as a printing press extending into space, embodying the machinist prophecies articulated in Aleksandr Vesnin's 1922 "Credo."[73] His Vkhutemas student, Ivan Leonidov, followed in his footsteps in 1926, with a project for a "newspaper [*Izvestiia VTsIK*] 'printing press'. The offices stretch vertically into a narrow tower, along which elevators glide up and down, while a low volume is used as a factory whose structure, made of metal lattice porticos, houses the presses. This duality is reminiscent of most of the submissions to the *Chicago Tribune* competition, as if to outshine not only the winners but also the modern contestants[74]. In 1926, confirming the popularity of skyscrapers, an article in the second volume of the *Great Soviet Encyclopedia* was devoted to "American buildings," with their typical standardized framework construction, illustrated by an etching of the Woolworth Building[75].

The Eye of the Architect: Erich Mendelsohn and Richard Neutra

Engaged without delay by Hood & Howells, the Tribune Tower construction site was photographed in the fall of 1924 by the Berlin architect Erich Mendelsohn, whose album *Amerika, das Bilderbuch eines Architekten* (America, the Picture Book of an Architect), found perhaps its most devoted public in Moscow[76]. Indeed, ever since the signature of the 1922 treatise in Rapallo by Georgii Chicherin and Walther Rathenau, Russia fostered close industrial, military, and cultural ties with Germany. While few Russians crossed the Atlantic, the rest of the country turned to Germany to contemplate its refracted images of America.

Mendelsohn captured sights from his visit to the eastern United States after a crossing with the filmmaker Fritz Lang, whose impressions of the country later found their place in *Metropolis*. Remotely familiar with the works of Frank Lloyd Wright and with grain silos, the architect took dozens of photographs, printed along with those of his Danish colleague Knud Lonberg-Holm in a large volume, accompanied by rather critical commentary. Focusing on the "grotesque" he witnessed in urban situations, Mendelsohn echoes Gorky, lamenting the "lack of culture" of this "nouveau riche" country and describing Manhattan as the "golden mountain" of the world. The intensity of his reactions is apparent in the letters he sent back to Europe, where he evokes, in a sort of stream of consciousness, his impressions of downtown New York City: "the tragedy of insanity, insane power, powerful space, the infinite exhilaration of victory."[77]

73 Aleksandr A. Vesnin, "Credo," 1922, in *Mastera sovetskoi arkhitektury*, Mikhail G. Barkhin, ed. (Moscow: Iskusstvo, 1975), vol. 2, 14.

74 *Arkhitektura, raboty arkhitekturnogo fakulteta Vhutemasa*, 32; also in Alessandro de Magistris and Irina Korobina, *Ivan Leonidov 1902–1959* (Milan: Electa, 2009), 141.

75 Vladislav K. Dmokhovskii (engineer specializing in foundations), "Amerikanskie postroiki," *Bolshaia sovetskaia entsiklopedia*, vol. 2 (Moscow: Aktsionernoe obshchestvo Sovetskaia Entsiklopedia, 1926), 469.

76 Erich Mendelsohn, *Amerika, das Bilderbuch eines Architekten* (Berlin: Rudolf Mosse, 1926).

77 Erich Mendelsohn, "New York, 11. Oktober 1924; an Bord der *Deutschland*," in Oskar Beyer, *Erich Mendelsohn; Briefe eines Architekten* (Munich: Prestel, 1961), 60.

Closely observing the skyscrapers of New York and Chicago, the silos of Buffalo, and the industrial landscapes of Detroit, Mendelsohn assembled a series
of images allowing his readers to feel as though they were walking the city
streets. To him, "to see America today causes a giddiness of perspective. It is
only here that we recognize the entire monstrosity of the nay-saying civilization; but at the same time we can already perceive in the midst of this magma
the first solid foundations of a new era. Only very rarely does history allow
itself such perspectives. But this extravagance has always worked to the advantage of history up to now. Whirlwinds are only harbingers. This country
gives everything: the worst strata of Europe, abortions of civilization, but also
hopes for a new world."[78]

Beyond this dialectic perspective, Lissitzky was moved by the visual
approach characteristic of this album, which resembled no other. He promptly published an article entitled "The Architect's Eye" in a Moscow paper, analyzing Mendelsohn's method. He had met the architect in Berlin in 1925 and
seems to have remained under the impression of his in-person account of his
journey[79]. He compared the album to a "dramatic film," depicting an "America

78   Mendelsohn, *Amerika*, IX; in English: Erich Mendelsohn, *Erich Mendelsohn's "Amerika": 82 Photographs*
      (New York: Dover, 1993), xi.
79   El Lissitzky, Letter to Sophie Küppers, Moscow, 18 October 1925, in Sophie Lissitzky-Küppers, *El Lissitzky:
      Life, Letters, Texts* (London: Thames & Hudson, 1967), 69.

Erich Mendelsohn, street scene in Detroit, 1924, in *Amerika: Bilderbuch eines Architekten,* Berlin:
Rudolf Mosse, 1926. CCA, NA44.M537.A35 1926.

El Lissitzky. *Runner in the City*, ca. 1926. Gelatin silver print on paper, 13.1 × 12.8 cm. The Metropolitan Museum of Art.

not from a distance but from within," much more tangible in this book than in any other lacklustre volume, as "in order to understand some of the photographs you must lift the book over your head and rotate it."

Lissitzky celebrated Mendelsohn's point of view and declared that one had to "commend the eye of the architect, showing us familiar things in a deeper way, allowing us to reflect upon them."[80] However, he was disappointed to find empty streets, devoid of "crowds" on the pavements of *Amerika*, highlighting Mendelsohn's disenchantment towards a country that had lost its spirit, as revealed by his photographs: "What then does the architect see, whose sight is clearer than his understanding? This eye is not blinded by the eccentricity of the sensations of the city that surround it; it sees and ascertains that real

80 El Lissitzky, "Glaz arkhitektora", *Stroitelnaia promyshlennost*, n° 2 (1926), 144-146; in English: Christopher Phillips, *Photography in the Modern Era: European Documents and Critical Writings, 1913-1940* (New York: Metropolitan Museum of Art, 1989) 221-222.

81 Lissitzky, "Glaz arkhitektora", p. 145; Phillips. *Photography in the Modern Era*, p. 222.

82 Mendelsohn, *Amerika*, 45; *Erich Mendelsohn's America*, 52.

83 On the neologism *fotopis*, see Margarita Tupitsyn, "After Vitebsk: El Lissitzky and Kazimir Malevich, 1924-1929," in *Situating El Lissitzky: Vitebsk, Berlin, Moscow*, Nancy Perloff and Brian Reed, eds. (Los Angeles: Getty Research Institute, 2003), 186-88.

84 Maria Gough, "Lissitzky on Broadway," in *Object: Photo. Modern Photographs: The Thomas Walther Collection 1909-1949. An Online Project of The Museum of Modern Art*, eds. Mitra Abbaspour, Lee Ann Daffner, and Maria Morris Hambourg (New York: Museum of Modern Art, 2014) http://www.moma.org/interactives/objectphoto/assets/essays/Gough.pdf [accessed 2 September 2019]; Margarita Tupitsyn, *El Lissitzky: Beyond the Abstract Cabinet: Photography, Design* (New Haven: Yale University Press, 1999), 32-34.

85 El Lissitzky, "Chelovek mera vsekh portnykh", *Izvestiia ASNOVA* 1, n° 1 (1926), 8; See Alla G. Vronskaya, "The Productive Unconscious: Architecture, Experimental Psychology and Techniques of Subjectivity in Soviet Russia, 1919-1935," PhD dissertation (Massachusetts Institute of Technology, 2014), 141-44.

progress — really profound change in the very principles and forms of spatial division — is still very rare. On the other hand one finds much energy and very large dimensions. Everything grows elementally, like a tropical forest, depriving itself of light and air, consuming itself."[81]

Though he agreed with Mendelsohn's criticism, Lissitzky used the double exposure photograph of Broadway by night for one of his projects. In the 1928 edition of his book, Mendelsohn credited the image to Fritz Lang and described it as an expression of the American grotesque, "still disordered, because exaggerated, but at the same time full of fantastic beauty, which will one day be completed."[82] Lissitzky used it as a backdrop for a *fotopis* (photographic painting), adding hurdles and a runner, in a photomontage entitled *Record*. The print was destined to become part of a fresco for the Red Sport International Stadium, in the Southwest of Moscow, designed by his friends from the ASNOVA[83]. Maria Gough has offered a detailed analysis of various versions of this work, where the visual stutter of the duplicated incandescent New York landscape matches the athlete's stride[84]. Eagerly repurposing Mendelsohn's photographic materials, Lissitzky drew inspiration from his worm's eye shots and some of his compositions, namely in his rendering of the building he erected with Ladovskii on Sivtsev Vrazhek Lane in Moscow, in 1925. He also used a similar shot of the Equitable Building in the enigmatic 1926 montage "Man is the Measure of All Tailors," published in *Izvestiia ASNOVA*, inviting the readers to "tilt [their] heads backwards and to lift the page to see," as he had suggested for *Amerika*[85]. In *Russland*, a publication issued in Vienna in 1930 as a testament to Soviet inventions of the past decade, Lissitzky printed one of Malevich's arkhitektons, some views from the first project of the *Izvestia*

Aleksandr L. Pasternak, "America", article on *Amerika, das Bilderbuch eines Architekten* by Erich Mendelsohn in *Contemporary Architecture* 1, no. 4, 1926. CCA, W.C6.

building and others of the Gostorg building, whose façade and interiors nod at an Americanized modernity inspired by Mendelsohn's visual patterns[86]. Among other notable uses of Mendelsohn's photographs were the photomontages and eight frontispieces of the catalogue of works on America, created by the graphic designer Elizaveta Lavinskaia and disseminated by the state publisher[87].

The *Sovremennaia arkhitektura* editorial team was also interested in Mendelsohn's book. In the journal's first issue, the constructivist theorist Moisei Ginzburg praises Mendelsohn's investigation. He cautiously states that the choice of illustrations does not "lack interest" and that "it paints quite a brilliant general picture of today's America, with its negative and positive aspects. It depicts the chaotic piling and completely tasteless eclecticism of New York skyscrapers, the magical transformation of the city at night with its colourful advertisements and lighting, Chicago and Buffalo's admirable silos as well as the rhythm of urban America itself." However, Ginzburg turns his nose on the layout, too "luxurious" with its excessive margins and blank pages."[88]

In a later issue, Aleksandr Pasternak noted that "the West is better informed than us" about what goes on in America, but that to a certain extent, news headlines were "infiltrating" Russia. As an example, he cited the exhibition *Neue amerikanische Baukunst*, organized in 1926 in Berlin and in several other German cities by the Akademie der Künste, describing the events and deploring Frank Lloyd Wright's absence[89]. He opposed the exhibit to Mendelsohn's book, whose photographs showed a "quintessential" America, but whose commentary was, according to him, useless to Russian readers, who could draw "their own conclusions."[90] He retraced the history of New World architecture since its discovery by the Europeans, recognizing "the voice of authentic creation growing on the firm ground of social relations, promoting its ideas and its language. [...] Industrial America has already given brilliant examples of this new style. We have known it for a long time, as the lapidary and powerful shapes of the silos, factories, and plants have been discussed, commented upon, and illustrated at length in our country. In the case of these constructions, it is not just a matter of dilating shapes and details. They are characterized by simple volume arrangements, clear structures, and logical, slender shapes. The fact that such solutions first appeared in this industry is no coincidence. By unveiling machines that had previously been hidden, the sector has acquired the qualities of these precision tools. Just like the machine is now an emblem of our times, with its precise and calculated movements, these structures are modern at their core. Along with America, Europe is also working in this direction. The building standards, the mechanization of labour, the energy savings, the NOT, and everything that followed suit—it all rose from the machine and submerged the whole world."[91] Pasternak also drew a parallel between Le Corbusier's constructions—stemming from the ocean liner—, Dutch architecture—inspired by

86   El Lissitzky, *Rußland*, 72, 77, 84, and 85.
87   *Amerika, katalog knig* (Moscow; Leningrad: Gos. Izd-vo, 1927).
88   Moisei Ia. Ginzburg, "Erich Mendelsohn, Amerika," *Sovremennaia arkhitektura* 1, no. 1 (1926): 38.
89   Aleksandr L. Pasternak, *Neue amerikanische Baukunst* (Berlin: Akademie der Künste, 1926).
90   Aleksandr L. Pasternak, "Amerika," *Sovremennaia arkhitektura* 1, no. 4 (1926): 92.
91   Ibid., 94.
92   Ibid., 94.
93   Fotograf, "Illiustrirovannoe pismo v redaktsiiu: nashi i za granitsa," *Sovetskoe Foto* 3, no. 4 (April 1928): 176; in English: "A 'Photographer'; an Illustrated Letter to the Editor: At Home and Abroad", *Sovetskoe Foto*, n° 4, April 1928, in Phillips, *Photography in the Modern Era*, 243-244.

the speed of automobiles—, and American structures—dictated by Ford's factories, where it was easier to build an additional story than to manufacture another car. He saw the promise of an "urbanized" city in the "vertical monoliths" envisioned by Hugh Ferriss, in those captured by Mendelsohn's lens as well as in the developments of the New York regional plan[92].

 Amerika's illustrations were bound to catch Rodchenko's eye, though he was not as interested in the American city as he was in Mendelsohn and Lonberg-Holm's photographic approach. He opposed their visual schemes to the static images printed in most previous books on New York City architecture, where the "reactionary points of view" remained similar in framing and composition to European urban landscape paintings from the seventeenth century. In 1928, the journal *Novy LEF* published open letters exchanged between Rodchenko and the poet and essayist Boris Kushner, after the former had been accused of plagiarizing Western photographers such as Ira W. Martin, László Moholy-Nagy, and Albert Renger-Patzsch[93]. Entitled "Pathways of Contemporary Photography," Rodchenko's response was based on binary comparisons, contrasting two of *Amerika*'s images to more common depictions of the same subject matter. To a heavily edited commercial photograph of the Woolworth Building, shot from afar and stripped of its context, with perfectly straightened vertical lines, he opposed Mendelsohn's snapshot, showing the building in a worm's eye close-up, in a vantage point that excludes its cornice, thus attenuating its historicist undertones. Similarly, Rodchenko contrasted a distant view of the Equitable Building, barely visible against the backdrop of Trinity Church, to Mendelsohn's dramatic rendering, where the skyscraper's vertical surge is accentuated by dark neighbouring masses.

Reviewing Kushner's recent book[94], Rodchenko stated that "[t]he modern city with its multi-storey buildings, the specially designed factories and plants, the two- and three-storey store windows [...] have redirected (only a little, it's true) the normal psychology of visual perceptions."[95] Hence, the "belly-button view" no longer makes sense, especially when the centre of a 68-storey building like the Woolworth is at the 34th floor, meaning that the photograph must be straightened "to ensure the correct projectional perspective." He thus revisited his comparison between the representations of both buildings, criticizing the conventional perspectives, which "were difficult to shoot, because the adjacent buildings got in the way; that's why they were touched up." They therefore conform to the generally internalized "laws of correct perspective." By contrast, "the second set of photographs of the same building is by the German leftist architect Mendelsohn. He photographed them in an honest way, just as the man in the street could see them."[96] "To sum up," he writes, "[i]n order to accustom people to seeing from new viewpoints it is essential to take photographs of everyday, familiar subjects from completely unexpected vantage points and in completely unexpected positions. New subjects should also be photographed from various points, so as to present a complete impression of the subject."[97] Rodchenko used his indirect observation of scenes from urban New York as a form of experimentation through which to theorize his own practice of photographic composition. Since 1925, he had indeed been creating Moscow cityscapes and photographs of buildings such as the radio broadcasting tower built by Vladimir Shukhov for the Komintern.

Mendelsohn developed his considerations from a privileged point of view: invited to build a textile factory in Leningrad, he had the opportunity to compare his memories of America with impressions gathered during his regular trips to the USSR. Observing young Russian architects in 1927, he posed the rhetorical question: "Can Russia be constructive in form?" He also remarked that the architects' "constant feeling of polarity with America is instinctive. The enthusiasm of the young Russians to combine the two is understandable. Is only courage in experiment, in self-sacrifice, in ecstasy, a part of it? Do not the inward-turning of creative industry and sustained effort, as opposed to the intuition of a moment, belong to it above all?"[98]

In 1929, Mendelsohn published a second album drawing on his experience, in the same format as *Amerika*, illustrated with many of his photographs, where he portrayed a sort of "cross-section" between Russia, Europe,

94   Boris A. Kushner, *103 dnia na Zapade, 1924–1926 gg* (Moscow; Leningrad: ZIF, 1928); see his previous article "Otkrytoe pismo," *Novy LEF* 2, no. 8 (August 1928): 34; in English: "Open letter to Rodchenko, " in Phillips, *Photography in the Modern Era*, 249–251.
95   Aleksandr M. Rodchenko, "Puti sovremennoi fotografii," *Novyi LEF* 2, no. 9 (September 1928): 34; in English: "The Paths of Modern Photography," in Phillips, *Photography in the Modern Era*, p. 258–59.
96   Rodchenko, "The Paths of Modern Photography," 262.
97   Ibid. 261.
98   Erich Mendelsohn, Letter to Luise Mendelsohn, 11 July 1927, 3, Getty Research Institute, Erich and Luise Mendelsohn papers, box 1, file 11, document 17; in English: Beyer, *Erich Mendelsohn*, 96.
99   Erich Mendelsohn, *Rußland, Europa, Amerika: ein architektonischer Querschnitt* (Berlin: Rudolf Mosse, 1929), 217.
100   Richard Neutra, Letter to Frances Toplitz, 26 November 1924, quoted by Thomas Hines, *Richard Neutra and the Search for Modern Architecture* (Oxford: Oxford University Press, 1983), 55.
101   Nikolai V. Markovnikov, "Wie baut Amerika?," *Stroitelnaia promyshlennost*, n° 5 (May 1927): 366–69.
102   "Kak stroiat v Amerike," *Sovremennaia arkhitektura* 2, no. 3 (1927): 86.
103   Akad. arkh. Aleksei V. Shchusev, [untitled article], *Stroitelnaia promyshlennost* 2, n° 12 (1924), 760–762.
104   Aleksei V. Shchusev, preface to Richard Neutra, *Kak stroit Amerika?*, trans. L.A. Olisovaia (Moscow: MAKIZ, 1929), 5–8; originally: *Wie baut Amerika?* (Stuttgart: Julius Hoffmann Verlag, 1927).

and America, in a manner of geographical feedback. He highlighted the contrast between Russian intellectualism and American idealism: "For Russia and America alike, technique is the common ground. Certainly America says: I am the world; I myself am life. But Russia says: I still have to make the world; my life belongs to all men. [...] Feverishness and overemphasis in any transitional period lead easily into the danger of romanticism. Consequently Russia, still technically primitive, seeks its salvation in an excess of intellectual effort which is strange to it. The technically highly developed America, on the contrary, seeks its salvation in an excess of idealism which is strange to it.[99] However, Soviet critics seemed uninterested in the book, unanimously ignoring it.

At the time in which Mendelsohn grappled with his Leningrad construction project, his former Viennese schoolmate Richard Neutra, who had emigrated to Los Angeles after working with Frank Lloyd Wright in Wisconsin, published the Russian translation of *Wie baut Amerika?* (How Does America Build?) in Moscow in 1929, two years after its original publication in Germany. The book was illustrated with his own photographs and based on his own experience working with the Holabird and Roche agency in Chicago. With this publication, Neutra wished to respond to his former employer, whose judgment he deemed "as negative as it [was] superficial." To him, it was impossible "to get a correct idea" of the United States "without paying the price as I do; to know it by patiently working here."[100] As soon as it was issued, Neutra's book was appraised by housing technicians, such as Nikolai Markovnikov[101], as well as by constructivists, who compared it to Martin Wagner's work, considering that "what is most interesting for us is the part, which must be discussed in further detail, where many photos taken on location describe the design and construction of the Palmer House skyscraper hotel in Chicago. The project plans, construction site views, and data gathered by the author provide us with a clear vision of the organization and technical level of American construction."[102]

While the constructivists' remarks and their reprinting of several of Neutra's illustrations were predictable, Aleksei Shchusev's patronage of the translation is more surprising, as five years earlier, he had proved to be definitely anti-American[103]. An influential figure among his Moscow peers, Shchusev had designed the plan for the "new Moscow" in 1924 and built, with Markovnikov, the Sokol garden district in the capital. With his introduction to Neutra's book, he positioned himself as a modern architect. During the same period, he erected Lenin's definitive mausoleum, made of black and red granite. Shchusev was particularly interested in the description of "giant cities with their grandiose street traffic, inevitably bringing to mind a gridlock of ideas." He commended the zoning regulations devised to mitigate the most detrimental effects of vertical structures, but was perplexed by Neutra's interest in "the Indians' cubic constructions with flat roofs." One of the indisputable innovations of the book was the fact that it showcased Southern California's architectural scene and its vernacular precedents. Shchusev offered a nuanced analysis of American projects, stating that he did not find them all to be "convincing." Specifically, he did not share Neutra's conclusions, according to whom architecture had to be based only on the "raw data" of the programme and structure. Shchusev deplored the fact that the "engineer-builder" seemed to be replacing the "architect-designer" in the United States, and though he ultimately called for an emulation of American planning and technical "feats," he warned against a blind imitation of their architecture[104]. The success of Neutra's first publication contrasted strongly with the indifference towards

Richard Neutra, *How America Builds?* [1927], Moscow: Makiz, 1929.
Cover and views of the construction site of the Palmer House Hotel, Chicago, 1923–1924. CCA, NA44.N497.A35 1980a.

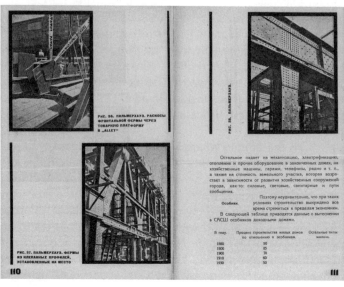

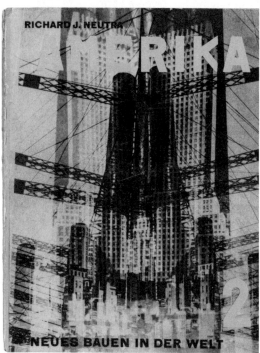

Richard Neutra, *Amerika: Die Stilbildung des neuen Bauens in den Vereinigten Staaten*,
Vienna: A. Schroll & Co, 1930. Cover photomontage by El Lissitzky. CCA, NA44.N497.A35 1930.

his second book, *Amerika*, published in Vienna in 1930 with a cover montage by El Lissitzky, which superimposed Brett Weston's photograph "Stacks" onto a view of the brand new Chanin Building in New York City[105].

American urban and architectural production reached Russia in various and often indirect ways. Thirty years after the Chicago Fair, as the new state launched more substantial labour housing programmes around factories, Pavel Mizhuev continued to spread information on American company towns, such as those of the National Cash Register Company in Dayton, Ohio, the Apollo Iron & Steel Company in Vandergrift, Pennsylvania, East Aurora in New York State, and Ludlow in Massachusetts[106]. Workers' clubs served as "social condensers," which Ginzburg associated with collective housing developed in the late 1920s. They were created using the information gathered by the architect and educator Aleksandr Zelenko in 1923 on American people's houses. Zelenko had worked for the People's Commissariat for Education and became close to Ladovskii. He had discovered these public institutions during his two American exiles, in 1903–1904 and in 1908. In a book published in Russian by the YMCA in Prague, Zelenko described with infinite details the facilities established by religious institutions—namely the YMCA and the Salvation Army—, cities, and "various classes of society," as well as the different programmes offered by each of them. Though he himself had replicated these achievements in Moscow in particularly original buildings before the Revolution, he readily admitted that some of his examples were not relevant for Russia. He nevertheless advocated in favour of establishing the widest possible network of collective equipment, as a sort of "skeleton" for a social organization that would have to stem from a grassroots movement[107]. He continued his investigation in a second book on *The Americans and Their Clubs*, published in 1927[108].

The Russians were also aware of the American experience of Martin Wagner, the social-democratic deputy mayor and chief city planner for Berlin and a significant figure in architecture and urban planning in the Weimar Republic. A keen observer of the United States, where he borrowed many of his planning methods, Wagner published *Amerikanische Bauwirtschaft* (The American Building Industry) two years after his 1923 investigative trip. The constructivists showed interest in the book and printed excerpts on industrial housing in *Sovremennaia arkhitektura*[109]. The work was issued in its entirety in 1928, under the patronage of Nikolai Bogdanov, a construction union organizer who had become one of the directors of Dneprostroi. He considered that despite his "head [being] stuffed with social-reformist muck," Wagner offered a series of solutions that could be put in practice in the USSR, provided that the "necessary amendments" were made[110]. One of the activists behind the introduction of the NOT in the construction sector, Bogdanov headed the journal *Stroitelnaia promyshlennost* (The Construction Industry) from 1923.

105   Richard Neutra, *Amerika: die Stilbildung des neuen Bauens in den Vereinigten Staaten* (Vienna: Anton Schroll & Co, 1930).
106   Pavel G. Mizhuev, *Obraztsovye rabochie poselki v Anglii i Amerike* (Leningrad: Vremia, 1925).
107   Aleksandr U. Zelenko, *Obshchestvennye tsentry i narodnye doma v Severnoi Amerike* (Prague: YMCA Press Ltd., 1923).
108   Aleksandr U. Zelenko, *Amerikantsy v svoikh klubakh i obshchestvennykh tsentrakh* (Moscow: Rabotnik prosveshcheniia, 1927).
109   "Amerikanskoe stroitelnoe khoziaistvo," *Sovremennaia arkhitektura* 2, no. 3 (1927): 87–88.
110   Nikolai P. Bogdanov, "O broshiure Dra. Wagnera," in Martin Wagner, *Amerikanskaia stroitelnaia promyshlennost*, trans. S.I. Orshanskii (Moscow: Gos. tekhnicheskoe izd-vo, 1928); originally, *Amerikanische Bauwirtschaft* (Berlin: Vorwärts Buch-Druckerei, 1925). See also "Amerika nakanune krisisa (o broshiure M. Wagnera *Amerikanische Bauwirtschaft*)," *Stroitelnaia promyshlennost* 6, no. 5 (May 1928): 354–60.

The journal's first editorial declared that "Russian technical progress would not be strong enough if our technical thinking was not in touch with Western European and American accomplishments."[111] The monthly publication devoted a regular column to "America in construction," an expression modelled after the largely used syntagm "USSR in construction." The column was illustrated with excerpts from German publications, and its main themes were large construction projects and innovations in the field of mechanization.

El Lissitzky's Horizontal Skyscrapers

El Lissitzky had served as an informal messenger between the USSR and the West since the early 1920s and played a significant and multifaceted role in the transmission of American motifs to the changing Soviet architectural scene by way of Germany. He made critical remarks on American architecture and contributed to the debate on skyscrapers with his 1924–1925 *Wolkenbügel.* In 1925, he distanced himself from the manifestations of "Americanism in European Architecture," the title of an article published in the popular journal *Krasnaia niva,* where he wrote that "[i]n the Old World—in Europe—, the words 'America' and 'American' conjure up ideas of something ultra-perfect, rational, utilitarian, universal" and that "[t]o the European mind, New York became the new Athens, Manhattan the Acropolis, and the skyscrapers the Parthenon." His goal was to refute this widespread notion: "It is true that New York itself knew nothing of this discovery. There they continue to build their temples to the Greek gods over subway stations, with the firm conviction that they are more beautiful than the original ones because they are ten times bigger. In New York and Chicago, engineers invented and constructed the fantastic steel skeletons of skyscrapers fifty storeys high, but the artist-architects, trained at the ancient Paris academy, clothed this living skeleton so skillfully with ostentatious embellishments that it was twenty years later before Europe recognized the crux of the matter"[112] [ill. p. 228].

Lissitzky's emphasis on the clash between the structural rationality of skyscrapers and the retrograde futility of their ornamentation is not unprecedented. Mayakovsky also made snide remarks on the theme in his New York impressions. The first to highlight this problem was Le Corbusier, in *Towards an Architecture,* with the following watchword: "Let us listen hear the advice of American engineers. But let us fear American architects."[113] However, the idea that the only true innovation hub in the New World was located in the western United States was a new one. To Lissitzky, "there in the West originated the works of Frank Lloyd Wright, America's only architect, who dared to discard all textbook precepts and to create a new type of dwelling, which has revealed him as the father of contemporary architecture."[114] He wrote that "Europe is now more American than America itself," in terms of its use of new materials. Though it "adopt[ed] American principles," the Old World developed them in new directions, which he attempted to demonstrate by replicating the Lonberg-Holm project for the *Chicago Tribune,* the concrete office building by Ludwig Mies van der Rohe, and Eugène Freyssinet's hangars in Orly.

The following year, Lissitzky followed up on his analysis in *Stroitelnaia promyshlennost,* writing on the topic of industrial building and skyscraper structures. Borrowing images from Mendelsohn, he tried to offer a critical framework for the then popular "isms": "Functionalism, constructivism, horizontalism, verticalism, and, above all, Americanism, these are the slogans and pivotal points of today's architecture," he declared[115]. In this essay, he retraced the history of the skyscraper, recounting the transition from load-bearing masonry to steel frame construction, which lightened the weight of the building and allowed to cover it with various cladding materials, from terracotta to stone. He stressed the importance of standardizing components and only recognized Sullivan's and Wright's innovations to state that the "gravity centre" of the new architecture was no longer in America, but rather in the work of Bruno and Max Taut, Mies van der Rohe, and Auguste Perret. Above all, he considered that the skyscraper issue was henceforth raised in "our Union."[116]

A few weeks after this declaration, Lissitzky published an article entitled "A Series of Skyscrapers for Moscow" in *Izvestiia ASNOVA*, presenting a project he had been designing since his 1923 exile in Switzerland. The idea was to provide Moscow with a network of vertical constructions, dubbed WB, from the German neologism *Wolkenbügel*, or "cloud pressers."[117] These reinforced concrete structures, already exhibited in other forms in Berlin and Mannheim, served as a dual critique of Americanism, both in terms of urban design and architecture. The site plan accounts for the implementation of eight *Wolkenbügel* at the main gates of the White City, as the Moscow centre was nicknamed, at the intersection of the Boulevard Ring and the major radial thoroughfares: "Here were born the squares that can be used without slowing down traffic, which is particularly dense around here. This is the location of central equipment. This is where the proposed idea was born."[118] This vast open space, adapted to the capital's urban form, is, of course, contrasted with the capitalist skyscrapers piling up along the tip of the Manhattan Island.

Lissitzky was also in favour of horizontal expansion, as featured by buildings oriented towards the Kremlin, shaped more like railway switching posts than skyscrapers. He criticized the typically North American obsession with verticality: "The first tall buildings were created in America, replacing the horizontal hallway of European constructions with a vertical hoistway, the central point for the surrounding floors. This type of construction has developed erratically, without any general urban planning. The only concern was to surpass one's name in height and in opulence."[119] He intended to return to the Old Continent's solutions: "We considered that until we invent the ability to float freely in mid-air, it remains appropriate to move horizontally, not vertically. Therefore, if there is no space to implement a horizontal dwelling on a given lot, we elevate the required surfaces on pillars, allowing them to serve as pathways between the sidewalks and the building's horizontal hallways.

111   "Ot redaktsii," *Stroitelnaia promyshlennost* 1, no. 1 (September 1923): 1.
112   El Lissitzky, "Amerikanizm v evropeiskoi arkhitekture," *Krasnaia niva* 2, no. 49 (29 November 1925): 1188; in English: "'Amerikanism' in European Architecture," in Lissitzky-Küppers, *El Lissitzky*, 373.
113   Le Corbusier, *Vers une architecture* (Paris: G. Crès & Cie, 1923), 29; in English: *Toward an Architecture*; transl. John Goodman (Santa Monica: Getty Research Institute, 2007), 117.
114   Lissitzky, "'Amerikanism' in European Architecture," 374.
115   Lissitzky, "Arkhitektura zheleznoi i zhelezobetonnoi ramy," *Stroitelnaia promyshlennost* 4, no. 1 (January 1926): 59.
116   Ibid. 62.
117   The term "cloud-presser" had been used in Chicago before "skyscraper" became mainstream: Paul Bourget, *Outre-mer, Impressions of America* [1894)] (London: T. Fisher Unwin, 1895), 32. The first mention of the Wolkenbügel was made in a letter to Sophie Küppers on 29 December 1924, Getty Research Institute, Lissitzky Archive, box 1, file 1, 34.
118   El Lissitzky, "Seriia neboskrebov dlia Moskvy", *Izvestiia ASNOVA 1*, no. 1 (1926): 2.
119   Ibid.

El Lissitzky, "Americanism in European Architecture", article in *Krasnaia niva* 2, no 49, 29 November 1925. Private collection.

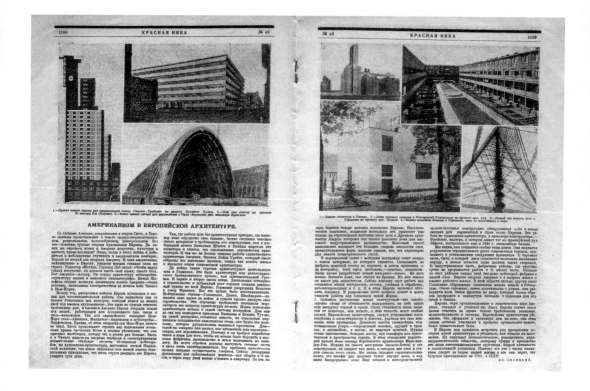

The goal is to create the most useful surface with the smallest possible footprint. The consequence: a clear functional coordination"[120] [ill. p. 230-231].

The most detailed *Wolkenbügel* in this 1926 article brings together three pillars containing the hoistways, connecting the elevators to subway stations, as shown on the designs kept at the Tretiakov Gallery. They are topped with a horizontal volume, comprised of a rectangular prism and an L-shaped one, which seems to be the three-dimensional version of Lissitzky's own 1923 *Proun 88*[121]. A perspective published in *Izvestiia ASNOVA*, against a roughly sketched urban backdrop, unveils the project's tectonics: the pillars have glass corners and the horizontal volumes are placed on reinforced concrete cantilevers. According to its creator, this solution, meant to be erected without scaffolding, offered "immense benefits in terms of light and air circulation compared with the American tower-shaped skyscraper."[122] In that sense, the *Wolkenbügel* can be seen as a counter-skyscraper, in echo to Vladimir Tatlin's "counter-reliefs." Furthermore, Lissitzky stressed that the stark contrast with the existing urban fabric was deliberate, declaring that "a) a city is comprised of ancient, static parts and sections that are growing, lively, and new"; and that "b) he meant to provide the building with a spatial balance borne out of the tensions between its surrounding vertical and horizontal shapes."[123]

Starting in November 1924, Lissitzky was in contact with the Zurich architect Emil Roth, who designed the structure of the orthogonal version published in 1926[124]. It was detailed with technical drawings and options were traced in coloured pencil and watercolour. The Dutch Functionalist architect Mart Stam developed a version where a stretched out horizontal volume is placed on two inclined pillars and four trusses serving as crutches[125]. Lissitzky never completed the second design, announced as WB2, which would have served as a response to Roth's suggestion to rest the building on three slanted and intercrossed pillars. This solution was expected to be more stable, or at least more dynamic in its upward movement[126] [ill. p. 232]. The most convincing depiction of the WB1 remains a photomontage showing the buildings in the urban setting of Nikitskii Gate in Moscow, reminiscent of those produced by Mies van der Rohe in 1921 for his Friedrichstraße skyscraper in Berlin.

120   Lissitzky, Ibid.
121   Alan C. Birnholz, "El Lissitzky's 'Prouns', Part II," *Artforum* 7 (November 1969): 68–73.
122   Lissitzky, "Seriia neboskrebov dlia Moskvy," 3.
123   Ibid.
124   J. Christoph Bürkle and Werner Oechslin, *El Lissitzky: der Traum vom Wolkenbügel: El Lissitzky, Emil Roth, Mart Stam* (Zurich: Eidgenössische Technische Hochschule, 1991), 35–40.
125   Ibid., 50–52 and 74–75. These undated drawings are held in the Deutsches Architekturmuseum in Frankfurt.
126   Samuel Johnson, "El Lissitzky's Other *Wolkenbügel*: Reconstructing an Abandoned Architectural Project," *The Art Bulletin* 99, no. 3 (September 2017): 147–69.

Серия небоскребов для Москвы. ШВ1 (1923—25)

Проект эль лисицкого

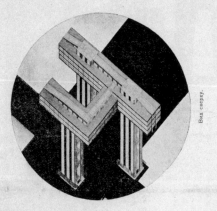

Вид сверху.

Предпосылки

Предлагаемый здесь новый тип постройки можно отнести к роду небоскребов. Он предназначается не для жилья, а для размещения центральных учреждений.

Тип высокого дома создала Америка, превратив европейский горизонтальный коридор в вертикальную шахту лифта, вокруг которого нанизаны ярусы этажей. Рос этот тип совершенно анархично, без какой бы то ни было заботы об организации города в целом. Единственная его забота была перещеголять высотой и пышностью соседа.

При выработке нашего типа мы исходим из противоположных предпосылок:

1) Мы считаем, что часть подчиняется целому и система города определяет характер его сооружений

2) Мы говорим „сооружения", а не „дома", считая, что новый город должен преодолеть понятие индивидуального дома.

3) Мы считаем, что пока не изобретены возможности совершенно свободного парения, нам свойственней двигаться горизонтально, а не вертикально.

Поэтому, если для горизонтальной планировки на земле в данном участке нет места, мы подымаем

Конструкция небоскреба.

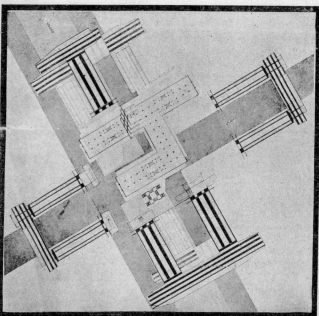

требуемую полезную площадь на стойки и они служат коммуникацией между горизонтальным тротуаром улицы и горизонтальным коридором сооружения. Цель: максимум полезной площади при минимальной подпоре. Следствие: ясное членение функций.

Но есть-ли надобность строить в воздухе? „Вообще"—нет. Пока есть еще достаточно места на земле.

Но... „в частности"?

Происхождение

Мы живем в городах родившихся до нас. Тему и нуждам нашего дня они уже не удовлетворяют. Мы не можем сбрить их с сегодня на завтра и „правильно" вновь выстроить. Невозможно сразу изменить их структуру и тип. Москва относится по своему плану к концентрическому средневековому типу. (Париж, Вена). Структура ея: центр — Кремль, кольцо А, кольцо Б и радиальные улицы. Критические места: это точки пересечения, больших радиальных улиц (Тверская, Мясницкая, и т. д.) с окружностью (бульварами). Здесь выросли площади, которые требуют утилизации без торможения движения, особенно сгущенного в этих местах (см. план). Здесь место центральных учреждений. Здесь родилась идея предлагаемого типа.

Конструкция

Для устойчивого положения свободно балансирующего тела, необходимы и достаточны 3 точки опоры*). Поэтому мы ограничились тремя стойками с открытыми каналами лифтов и патерностеров, между ними застекленный канал лестничных клеток. Стойки опираются системой катков и ребер на фундамент. (Принцип упругих ферм и мостовых конструкций). Одна стойка заключена под землей между линиями метрополитена и служит ему станцией. У других двух остановки трамвая. Структура верхней рабочей части (бюро, учреждения): скелетная центральная труба, открытая от пола до верхнего света внутри, несет балконы коридоров; т. е. выйдя из лифта в первом этаже можно читать №№ на дверях помещений 2-го и 3-го этажей. На этой центральной раме консолями держатся горизонтальные площади этажей. Все тело, как вагон положено на стойки.

Материал

Скелет из новых сортов нержавеющей и выдерживающей высокия напряжения стали (Крупп). Легкие и хорошо изолирующие на тепло-и звукопроводность материалы для междуэтажных перекрытий и перегородок. Стекло химически обработанное для пропуска световых и задержки тепловых лучей.

Каче-

Все элементы скелета нормированы и поэтому, по мере потребности застройки новой площади по линии кольца А или Б, остается лишь провести

*) Одна ножка четырехногого стола висит в воздухе.

План центра Москвы с небоскребами по кольцу А.

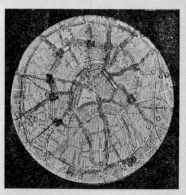

таж готовых частей. Монтаж может производиться 3 ЛЕСОВ: до наводки верхних форм стойки держатся на троссах. Поэтому стройка может итти не прерывая движения площади. Затем по отношению существующим постройкам то качество, что их ти не нужно сносить. Огромные преимущества наличии света и воздуха по отношению к американскому башенному типу небоскреба.

1. При пластическом оформлении этого сооружения, я учитывал конструкцию лишь как один первичных элементов в достижении необходимого десаного действия (механического эффекта). Я бы той-же логической последовательностью, так же удовлетворяя всем утилитарным требованиям мог брать другую конструкцию*), если-б хотел достигнуть другого эстетического эффекта.

2. Я считаю, что в своей основе сила эстетического эффекта определяется не качеством и не ничеством,—это есть, состояние, температура.

3. Я исходил из равновесия двух пар контрастов:
   а) Город состоит из атрофирующихся старых частей и растущих живых, новых. Этот контраст мы хотим углубить.
   б) Дать самому сооружению пространственное равновесие, как результат контрастных вертикальных и горизонтальных напряжений.

4. Дать новый масштаб городу, в котором человек более не мерит собственным локтем, а сотни метров.

5. Элементарно организовать сооружение из ребер, плоскостей и объемов, сквозных, прозрачных плотных, вместе составляющих однозначную пространственную систему.

Перспектива вдоль бульвара.

6. Со всех основных 6-ти точек зрения данное сооружение однозначно характеризовано:

Схема формы при виде:

По направлению:

1. Сверху	2. Снизу	3. К Кремлю	4. От Кремля	5. Вдоль бульвара	6. В обратную сторону:

Такая характеристика делает ориентировку по этим сооружениям в городе совершенно ясной. При установке всей серии, введение цвета для отметки каждого небоскреба в отдельности послужит к усилению его ориентировочных качеств.

*) В выработке и расчете конструкции мне помогал ЭМИЛЬ РООТ (Цюрих), которому я рад и здесь выразить свою признательность.

В следующей серии (W B 2) будет показана совершенно другая конструкция.

Этот проэкт (Wolkenbügel) был впервые демонстрирован на выставке Ноябрьской группы в Берлине, затем на международной выставке современной архитектуры в Мангейме.

ACHOBASNOWACHOBASNOWACHOBASNOWACHOBASNOWACHOBASNOWACHOBASNOWACHOBASNOWACHOBASNOWACHOBASNOWACHOBASNOWA

Основы построения теории Архитектуры

(Под знаком рационалистической эстетики)

Н. ЛАДОВСКИЙ

Архитектурная рациональность зиждется на экономическом принципе так же, как и техническая рациональность. Разница заключается в том, что техническая рациональность есть экономия труда и материала при создании целесообразного сооружения, а архитектурная рациональность есть экономия психической энергии при восприятии пространственных и функциональных свойств сооружения. Синтез этих двух рациональностей в одном сооружении и есть рацио-архитектура.

Часть I. О ФОРМЕ.

1. При восприятии материальной формы как таковой мы одновременно можем усмотреть в ней выразительность качеств:

1) геометрических — отношения сторон, ребер, углов, характер поверхностей и т. д.
2) физических — весомость, плотность, массу, и т. д.
3) физико-механических — устойчивость, подвижность,
4) логических — выразительности поверхности как таковой и ограничивающей объем . . . . . .

В зависимости от выразительности величины мы можем говорить о:
   а) мощи и слабости,
   б) величии и низменности,
   в) конечности и бесконечности. . .

2. Архитектура оперирует этими „качествами" как определенными величинами. Архитектор конструирует форму внося элементы, которые не являются техническими или утилитарными в обычном смысле слова и которые можно рассматривать как „архитектурные мотивы". В архитектурном отношении эти „мотивы" должны быть рациональны и служить высшей технической потребности человека **ориентироваться в пространстве** . . . .

Для иллюстрации одного из видов работы над геометрической выразительностью формы рассмотрим

Черт. № 1.

Пример 1.

3. Две проекции параллелопипеда дают о нем точное геометрическое п. едставление – образ (черт. № 1).

Реальная перспектива его, представленная в ряде статических моментов 1. 2.. . черт. № 2, дает приближенный образ, стремящийся к геометрическому, выраженному в двух проекциях, как к своему пределу.

1,   2,....

Черт. № 2.

4. Работа архитектора над геометрической выразительностью формы, которую мы всегда воспринимаем в перспективе, заключается в приближении образа получчаемого от восприятия реальной перспективы к образу, данному в проекциях.

Степенность приближения зависит от количества и качества, входящих в конструируемую архитектором систему определения — элементов-признаков. Материалом этой системы элементов-признаков, обычно служит в сооружении видимая техническая конструкция. Там, где она может быть использована полностью создается синтез техники и архитектуры, где этого

El Lissitzky. *Wolkenbügel* (cloud-pressers) project for Moscow, variant with oblique supports, 1924–1925. Elevation.
Graphite on paper, 50 × 39 cm. Sprengel Museum.

The Vkhutemas and their post-1927 avatar, the Vkhutein (Higher State Artistic and Technical Institute), deeply infiltrated by ASNOVA members, were among the institutions where the most explicit inclination towards American architecture took shape, both in studio exercises and in the previously mentioned graduation projects. In February 1927, Ladovskii opened his psychotechnical research laboratory at the School on Rozhdestvenka Street. The laboratory focused on spatial perception, which was at the heart of his teaching and was one of around a hundred centres devoted to psychotechnics initiated by Isaak Shpilrein, who had created the first one within Gastev's TsIT, before distancing himself from the latter's rigid Taylorism and privileging a psychological approach[127]. Having revealed his intentions as of 1921, Ladovskii unveiled his psychotechnical research programme in 1926, in the *Izvestiia ASNOVA*, alluding to Hugo Münsterberg's research, familiar to all Russians then working in the field of scientific management, to justify resorting to this "young science": "Large industrial and commercial American firms were the first to apply it as a way of selecting their workforce; brokers for advertising, education specialists for school admissions and student evaluations. As of now, psychotechnics can be used in all spheres of human activity. The well-known psychologist Hugo Münsterberg applies it to the field of aesthetics for years in his Harvard laboratory. The following studies in relation to architecture are being conducted there: equilibrium of simple forms ([George] Pierce [Baker]); unequal division (Anquier); symmetry ([Ethel] Puffer); repetition of spatial forms ([James] Rowland [Angell]); vertical division (Davis), simple rhythmical forms, etc."[128]

   Seemingly unaware that Münsterberg, his role model, had died in 1916, Ladovskii quoted one of his analyses using the present tense: "Psychotechnics cannot create artists […], but it can provide them with solid grounds to achieve their goals in the most scientifically correct way, and more importantly to avoid certain dangers […]. The future rise of psychotechnics could bring solutions to creators, even though it seems that genius always discovers intuitively what science arrives to painstakingly."[129] Notably, in analyzing various professions, and distinguishing between motivations, information, and abilities, Münsterberg studied architects' thought patterns and skills, highlighting their aesthetic inclinations. He stated that "all these activities must be guided by a sense of beauty, by a constructive imagination, by a feeling for the needs of the time, by a sociological understanding of the architect's function, in short, by a high cultivation that demands more than a mere specialized training and that is to take its energy from all sides of human life."[130]

127   Isaak N. Shpilrein is the author of *Prikladnaia psikhologia: psikhologia truda i psikhotekhnika* (Moscow: Izdanie B.Z.O. pri M. P. I., 1930).

128   Nikolai A. Ladovskii, "Psikho-tekhnitcheskaia laboratoria arkhitektury (v poriadke postanovki voprosa)," *Izvestiia ASNOVA* 1, no. 1 (1926): 7. See the early study by Selim O. Khan-Magomedov, *Psikhoanaliticheskii metod N. Ladovskogo vo Vkhutemase-Vkhuteine: Obedinennye levye masterskie, psikhotekhnicheskaia laboratoriia*, (Moscow: Architectura, 1993). The list of experiments is an abridged version of that given by Münsterberg in *Grundzüge der Psychotechnik* (Leipzig: J.A. Barth, 1914), 615; in Russian: Hugo Münsterberg, *Osnovy psikhotekhniki*, trans. and preface V.N. Severnyi and V.M. Ekzempliarskii (Moscow: Russkii knizhnik, 1922). Ladovskii relies on volume 3.

129   Hugo Münsterberg, quoted in Ladovskii "Psikho-tekhnicheskaia laboratoria," 7. See also Margarete Vöhringer, *Avantgarde und Psychotechnik: Wissenschaft, Kunst und Technik der Wahrnehmungsexperimente in der frühen Sowjetunion* (Göttingen: Wallstein, 2007).

130   Hugo Münsterberg, "The Vocation of the Architect," in *Vocation and Learning* (Saint-Louis: Press of the People's University, 1912), 252–55. See also Vronskaya, "The Productive Unconscious"; and id., "Composing Form, Constructing the Unconscious: Empiriocriticism and Nikolai Ladovskii's 'Psychoanalytical Method' of Architecture at Vkhutemas," in *Architecture and the Unconscious*, eds. John S. Hendrix and Lorens E. Holm (Farnham: Ashgate, 2016), 77–96; James Graham, "The Psychotechnical Architect: Perception, Vocation, and the Laboratory Cultures of Modernism, 1914–1945," PhD dissertation (Columbia University, 2018).

Münsterberg, who had taken over as the head of the Harvard psychology laboratory in 1892, following its founder, William James, was highly acclaimed in the USSR, as evidenced by the many translations of his works and the widespread success of his equipment demonstration at the 1893 Chicago Fair. Having read his *Americans* before 1914, Russian readers were now discovering his major writings on experimental psychology[131]. It is surprising how widely the works of this scholar working to fulfill the capitalist market's needs were applied to build socialism[132]. His lucid reflections on the limits and resources of psychotechnics were determinant for the Vkhutemas, whose many students came from working-class backgrounds, often without high school diplomas. The laboratory's primary goal was thus to assess their capacities in fields like the perception of architecture and to register their results in administrative forms[133] in order to tailor the learning activities to their abilities[134].

Before it was shut down in 1930, the tools used in Ladovskii's facility were inspired, as described by his closest assistant, Georgii Krutikov, by those employed by Münsterberg in Emerson Hall, a building inaugurated in 1905 on the Harvard campus. Münsterberg's laboratory occupied there forty rooms painted in black, where he led basic experiments isolating components of action and perception[135]. In its Moscow derivation, each tool installed at the Vkhutemas was placed on a wooden pedestal and contained fixed frames as well as specific mobile components. The main ones were the *liglazometr*, for line perception, the *uglazometr*, for corners, the *ploglazometr*, for surfaces, the *oglazometr*, for volumes and shapes, and the *prostrometr*, for space and movement. Though they explored all ranges of vision studied by Münsterberg and his German peers, these tools were relatively in line with the basic experiments conducted in the Western world since 1920[136].

Furthermore, Ladovskii tried to gauge his students' creative abilities using the Alpha test developed during the war by the American psychologist Robert Yerkes, a method also applied by his Soviet colleague Petr Rudik[137]. Georgii Krutikov established a series of similar tests destined to assess the imagination demonstrated by groups of pupils and their ability to combine shapes, explicitly referencing German and American capability measuring systems, as well as the NOT, as practised by Gastev's Central Institute of Labour[138]. Ladovskii's psychotechnics laboratory had likely forged ties with that of the People's Commissariat for Labour, headed by Isaak Shpilrein after his departure from the TsIT.

131   Hugo Münsterberg, *Psychology of Life* (Boston: Houghton Mifflin, 1899); *Psychology and the Teacher* (New York: D. Appleton & Co, 1909); in Russian: *Psikhologiia i uchitel*, trans. A.A. Grombakh (Moscow: Mir, 1910); *Psychologie und Wirtschaftsleben* (Leipzig: J.A. Barth, 1912); in Russian: *Psikhologiia i ekonomicheskaia zhizn*, trans. M. Kruchinin (Moscow: Sovremennye problemy, 1914); *Sbornik statei po prikladnoi psikhologii* (Moscow: Gostekhizdatelstvo, 1922). See also the biography written by his daughter, Margarete Münsterberg, *Hugo Münsterberg, His Life and Work* (New York: D. Appleton & Co, 1922).

132   Matthew Hale, Jr., "Industrial Efficiency," in *Human Science and Social Order: Hugo Münsterberg and the Origins of Applied Psychology* (Philadelphia: Temple University Press, 1980), 148–63.

133   Vronskaya, "Composing Form," 150–54.

134   Anna Bokov, "Teaching Architecture to the Masses: Vkhutemas and the Pedagogy of Space, 1920–1930," PhD dissertation (Yale University, 2018).

135   Graham, "The Psychotechnical Architect," 42–44.

136   For more on these devices, see Vronskaya, "Composing Form," 134–40, and Graham, "The Psychotechnical Architect," 92–96. They were reconstructed by Aleksandra Selivanova for a 2017 exhibition at the Center of thr Avant-Garde at the Shabolovka in Moscow.

137   Petr A. Rudik, *Umstvennaia odarennost i eio izmerenie* (Moscow: Izd-vo Kommunisticheskogo Universiteta, 1927); Vronskaya, "Composing Form," 150–56.

138   Georgii T. Krutikov, "Arkhitekturnaia nauchno-issledovatelskaia laboratoriia arkhitekturnogo fakulteta Vkhutemasa. Laboratornaia rabota v 1928–1929 godakh," *Arkhitektura i Vkhutein* 1, no. 2 (1929): 2; "Arkhitekturnaia nauchno-issledovatelskaia laboratoriia pri arkhitekturnom fakultete moskovskogo Vysshego Khud-Tekhnich. Instituta," *Stroitelnaia promyshlennost* 8, no. 5 (1928): 372–75.

Psychotechnical Laboratory of Vkhutemas. Top: prostometr, apparatus to measure spatial depth, in *Arkhitektura i Vkhutein* 1, no. 2. Reproduced in Selim O. Khan-Magomedov, *Vhutemas*, Paris: Éditions du Regard, 1991. CCA, N332.S65.M675 (ID:93-B1002).

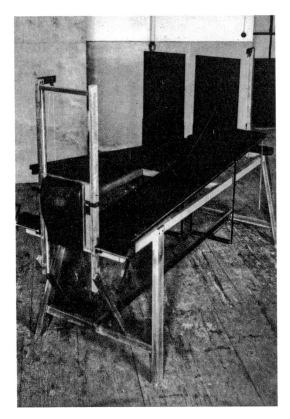

Bottom: Ploglazometr, apparatus to measure areas. Illustrations in *Arkhitektura i Vkhutein* 1, no. 2, 1929.
Reproduced in Selim O. Khan-Magomedov, *Vhutemas*, Paris: Éditions du Regard, 1991. CCA, N332.S65.M675 (ID:93-B1002).

To the eyes of observers, these institutions seemed quite different from the American ones, precisely because of their political engagment. Upon returning from a trip to the USSR in 1934, Gregory Razran, who emigrated in 1920 and had recently received a doctorate from Columbia University, wrote that "[u]nlike most of his American colleagues, the Soviet psychologist is really not just a laboratory experimentalist, a fact finder who finds facts to be used somewhere, by someone, some time. He is above all a scientific worker who is to further and promote the cause of socialist construction."[139] He noted that Soviet psychologists, starting with Ivan Pavlov, were perfectly aware of American research, and declared that in the realm of psychotechnics and industrial psychology, "American psychologists may, indeed, envy their Soviet colleagues the greater possibility of carrying theory into practice and laboratory ideas into life actuality."[140]

America According to Ginzburg and the Constructivists

In 1927, Ivan Lamtsov and Fedor Shalavin, both members of the ASNOVA along with Lissitzky and Ladovskii, criticized the "leftist phraseology in architecture" and accused their competitors at the OSA (Union of Contemporary Architects), the constructivist organization created in 1925, of falling prey to the siren song of Americanism[141]. Their critique was met with a thoroughly argued response in *Sovremennaia arkhitektura*, the journal of the OSA, firmly rejecting their conclusion that constructivism "stems from idealism, and its motherland is not the Soviet Union, but rather the United States," and deriding their claim that the movement saw "new life forces" in capitalist America[142]. Indeed, the philosophy of OSA members was more nuanced.

America was a frame of reference both for the constructivists' theoretical considerations and their architectural projects. Though the term had been used by the sculptors Naum Gabo and Antoine Pevsner in their 1920 manifesto, the constructivist movement was born out of Vladimir Tatlin's impulsion. Its principles were articulated in discussions between painters and sculptors within the Obmokhu, the Society of Young Artists, and the first working group assembled as part of the Inkhuk (Institute of Artistic Culture)[143]. The initial position, however, was not exactly one of adoration. In his 1922 manifesto

139   Gregory H.S. Razran, "Psychology in the USSR," *Journal of Philosophy* 32, no. 1 (3 January 1935): 19.
140   Ibid. 22.
141   Ivan V. Lamtsov and Fedor Shalavin, "O levoi fraze v arkhitekture: (k voprosu ob ideologii konstruktivizma)," *Krasnaia nov* 7, no. 8 (1927): 226–39.
142   "Kritika konstruktivizma," *Sovremennaia arkhitektura* 3, no. 1 (1928): 1 and 14.
143   On the origins of constructivism, see Maria Gough, *The Artist as Producer: Russian Constructivism in Revolution* (Berkeley: University of California Press, 2014).
144   Aleksei M. Gan, *Konstruktivizm* (Tver: Tverskoe Idz-vo, 2ia Tipografia, 1922), 61; in English: Aleksei M. Gan, *Constructivism*, ed. and transl. Christina Lodder (Farnham: Ashgate, 2014) 61.
145   Platon M. Kerzhentsev, *Tvorcheskii teatr* [1918] (Moscow: Gos. Izd-vo, 1923), 18–20; Percy MacKaye, *The Civic Theatre* (New York: Mitchell Kennerly, 1912).
146   Aleksei A. Gvozdev, "Massovye prazdnestva na zapade: grazhdanskie prazdnestva v sovremennoi Amerike," in Gosudarstvennyi Institut istorii ikusstv, *Massovye prazdnestva* (Leningrad: Akademiia, 1926), 47–50.
147   Reyner Banham, *A Concrete Atlantis: US Industrial Buildings and European Modern Architecture, 1900–1925* (Cambridge, MA: MIT Press, 1986).
148   Moisei Ia. Ginzburg, "Estetika sovremennosti," *Arkhitektura* 1, no. 1–2, 1923, 5.
149   Ibid., 6.
150   Moisei Ia. Ginzburg, *Stil i epokha, problemy sovremennoi arkhitektury* (Moscow: Gos. Izd-vo, 1924), 68; in English: Moisei Ginzburg, *Style and Epoch*, transl. Anatole Senkevitch, Jr. (Cambridge, MA: MIT Press, 1982), 70.

Constructivism, the graphic designer Aleksei Gan, who viewed the revolutionary impulse as part of the movement, expressed disdain for pre-revolutionary apartment houses, both in Russia—likely referring to the Nirnzee House—and in America: "They were decorated haphazardly, for commercial effect, according to the eclectic caprice of the private owner or the fancy of the builder himself, and speculatively clothed in a mixed style, but was most frequently modernistic. In America, these buildings were simply multiplied numerically, cutting vertically into space."[144] Tectonics, one of the three constitutive components of constructivism, according to Gan, which denoted the revolutionary energy, could be related to the mass celebrations in Petrograd and in Moscow. Among its organizers was Platon Kerzhentsev, who was interested in the pageants of the American theatre director Percy MacKaye[145]. The first analyses of these events credited the "national celebrations of current day America" as their inspiration[146].

In 1923, Moisei Ginzburg, the main theorist of architectural constructivism, tackled American industrial buildings, as Walter Gropius and Le Corbusier had done before him[147]. In an article for the Moscow journal *Arkhitektura*, created by Aleksandr Vesnin, the founding members of the movement, Ginzburg applied the principles of "contemporary aesthetics" to the Midwestern grain elevators, already described by Aleksandr Dmitriev in Saint Petersburg in 1905. In discussing their aesthetics, he used the term "contemporary" rather than "modern," which was irrevocably tainted by its association with Art Nouveau. Ginzburg purposely illustrated his claims with various photographs by his predecessors and with a drawing whose writing seems offset compared to the abstract geometry of the elevator it portrays. He also established clear principles: "The wise frugality of materials and energy, the precise movement and interrelation of parts, the concise language of their shapes, the unvarnished bluntness of their composition and the clear resolve in the axis of their motion, such is the aesthetic of the modern machine, which clearly encompasses several orientations for the artists' work."[148] Elsewhere, his writing becomes lyrical, in a mode reminiscent of his first book *Rhythm in Architecture*, published a year earlier and permeated by the German *Kunstwissenschaft*: "European and American industrial buildings of the past decade—the powerful elevators, the plants and electrical motors, with their dynamic and monumental modernity, with the pathos of their working conditions, with the lapidary nudity of their shapes—are significant achievements. They represent a unique victory in the search for the modern architectural form."[149]

Ginzburg's thinking evolved with his second book, *Style and Epoch*, published in 1924. Carefully avoiding the use of images and terms employed by Le Corbusier in *Toward an Architecture* the previous year, he nevertheless accused American architects of similar wrongdoings: "A new national power that has not yet had the time to accumulate its own traditions and artistic experience quite naturally turns to Europe for assistance; Europe, true to the stodgy ideals of its classical system, begins transporting its products across the ocean. However, the life of North America as a vital new power cannot, despite its own wishes, proceed along a course well-trodden by that of Europe—businesslike, dynamic, sober, mechanized, devoid of any romanticism—and this intimidates and repels a placid Europe. Nevertheless, wishing to be 'as good as' Europe, America continues to import European aesthetics and romanticism as though they were commodities that had stood the test of time and been 'patented,' as it were. Thus, there emerges a single aspect of America: a horrifying mechanical mixture of new, organic, purely American elements with the superficial envelopes of an outlived classical system 'made in Europe.'"[150] To this "horrifying mixture," Ginzburg opposed American "industrial constructions," illustrating them with previously unpublished photographs of the Buffalo silos[151].

Seeking a way to re-establish the architectural harmony of the Renaissance, obsessively referenced throughout the book, Ginzburg called for an emulation of American industrial buildings, or constructions inspired by them, such as Fiat's Lingotto factory in Turin: "The factory envelops this monumental movement, representing a grandiose envelope for it, and must certainly express all of its characteristic aspects. On the other hand, it already represents a kind of housing –true, a housing more for labour and machines than for man but housing nevertheless– i.e., a veritable work of architecture, with all its spatial characteristics; hence, an analysis of such industrial structures should be of great importance to us. [...] In the industrial structures of the last decade in the largest cities of Europe and America we see already realized not only the foundations of a modern aesthetic, but even individual elements of architecture, systems of supports, joints, spans, openings, terminations, flashes of compositional schemes and flashes of new form, which can already be transferred to domestic architecture, can already serve as the concrete and profoundly practical material that will be able to help the architect find a true course for creative work and help transform the language of abstract aesthetics into a precise lexicon of architecture."[152]

The impact of Ginzburg's reproductions was confirmed when his images were repurposed by the philosopher Aleksei Toporkov in his 1928 book *Technical Life and Contemporary Art*[153]. As for the reference to America, it took on a new form when Ginzburg articulated the OSA position in several doctrinal articles published in *Sovremennaia arkhitektura* as of 1926[154]. He positioned the

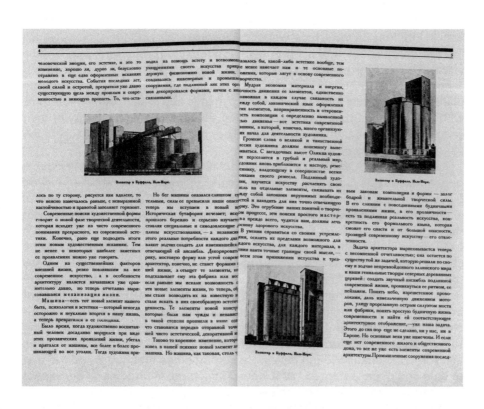

constructivist project as part of an "international front of contemporary architecture," including figures such as Walter Gropius, Bruno Taut, Ludwig Mies van der Rohe, Erich Mendelsohn, Auguste Perret, Le Corbusier, J. J. P. Oud, and Theo van Doesburg, as well as a "young America," though without naming any of its architects: "When America follows in the footsteps of European art, it obviously despairs and loses its vitality. Where America stays America, meaning where it expresses it pragmatism, free from the weight of tradition, employing the rational minds of inventors unrestricted by aesthetic considerations, that is where the unique manifestations of its practicality emerge, setting new benchmarks for a humanity in search of life and establishing outposts for the international front of contemporary architecture."[155]

For the editors of *Sovremennaia arkhitektura*, borrowing from an authentic America was not enough: Russian factories had to be "better than American ones,"[156] calling for a radical shift in Ginzburg's design method, as proposed in *Style and Epoch*. Rather than observing the exterior aspect of plants, conclusions needed to be drawn from the industrial processes they housed. The architect ceased to be a "decorator of life" to become a "manager," meaning a technician similar to the Taylorist "methods engineers," which were increasingly pervasive in Russian factories. Some constructivists turned to mathematical methods to establish the basis for a new method, where the architectural manifestation of the plan explicitly mimicked the search for unknown variables in an algebraic equation[157].

According to Ginzburg, design solutions had to be determined by the trajectories traced within the buildings, which would guide the structure as per Frank and Lillian Gilbreth's observations. However, the architects were less concerned with analyzing the necessary gestures for bricklaying or secretary work than with shaping the space around repetitive motions and circuits. Motion studies had spatial implications, as they accounted for the routes followed by workers and fabricated goods amid the machines in the factory workshops. Ginzburg therefore brought two distinct, but related, types of representation to the forefront of "functional design," a method he defined in 1927: the *grafik dvizheniia*, or motion graph, and the *skhema oborudovaniia*, or equipment scheme. The confrontation between these two representations served to determine the "most radical" architectural envelope for the project. Both techniques were based on a spatial analysis of Ford's factories, with Ginzburg quoting a lengthy passage from *My Life and Work* to describe the layout of machines in the workshop and to indicate his intentions[158]. In fact, he used the factory model as a guide to analyze any type

151   Banham, *A Concrete Atlantis*, 231–36. On the theoretical origins of Ginzburg's statements, see Anatole Senkevitch, Jr., introduction to Ginzburg, *Style and Epoch*, 10–33.
152   Ginzburg, *Style and Epoch*, 108–109.
153   Aleksei K. Toporkov, *Tekhnicheskii byt i sovremennoe iskusstvo* (Moscow; Leningrad: Gos. Izd-vo, 1928), 175–78.
154   On OSA as an organization, see S. Frederick Starr, "OSA: The Union of Contemporary Architects," in George Gibian, H.W. Tjalsma, *Russian Modernism, Culture and the Avant-Garde, 1900–1930* (Ithaca, NY: Cornell University Press, 1976), 188–208.
155   Moisei Ia. Ginzburg, "Mezhdunarodnyi front sovremennoi arkhitektury," *Sovremennaia arkhitektura* 1, no. 2 (1926): 41.
156   "Kritika konstruktivizma," *Sovremennaia arkhitektura* 3, no. 1 (1928): 14. This anonymous article was most likely written by Ginzburg himself. Ginzburg's emphasis.
157   On the methods constructivists employed in their "objective" projects, see Catherine Cooke, "'Form is a Function X': The Development of the Constructivist Architect's Design Method," *Architectural Design*, no. 53 (1983): 34–49.
158   Henry Ford, with Samuel Crowther, *Moia zhizn, moi dostizheniia* (Leningrad: Vremia, 1924), 134; originally *My Life and Work*, (Garden City, NY: Garden City Publishing Co., 1923), 113.

of plan: "The end result, sometimes described with a single word—factory, club, dwelling, etc.—must, after careful analysis, materialize through the architect's use of a specific system of *social and productive processes: productive or working processes* are usually associated with what we imagine as a mill, a factory; while *social processes* apply to housing and collective buildings. There is no fundamental difference here. The production process in any individual endeavour results in a given product. It is dynamic, consistent, and its movement follows a specific route from the beginning to the end of operations. It is a unit, ideally uninterrupted, but nevertheless clearly divided into various sequences. The dynamics of the production process can easily be illustrated by a *motion graph*. The division of the process into different phases helps stabilize its dynamic in a *static system* of separate and interrelated production operations, revolving around the appropriate equipment. In the contemporary factory, the *motion graph* is the trajectory of the assembly line, describing the entire process from beginning to end and from one machine to the other. The *equipment scheme* is the system of tools and machines that facilitate the various steps of the production process. The method used to lay out the equipment determines the entire spatial configuration of the motion graph, according to production specificities and the principle of workforce economy."[159]

While he based his reflections on Ford, Ginzburg made a point of distinguishing his utilitarian approach from the American one. In his view, when Americans built "for people," they used old European recipes, and it is only when building "for machines," such as with elevators, that they "brilliantly" used the functional method. According to him, Soviet architects were rooted in more complex social foundations than their American peers. However, he saw "a resemblance between American engineering and our architecture, in that contemporary [modern] architects based their work on the latest and most advanced techniques. Just like them, we do not count on craftsmanship, though unfortunately we must deal with it in practice. And we are unafraid of using American technical achievements, of importing and adopting them, just as the USSR is considering importing American tractors and machines."[160]

A few months later, as he evaluated the "assessment and perspectives" of the past decade's developments during the contemporary architecture exhibit hosted by OSA in Moscow, Ginzburg revisited his analogy. He contrasted the Vesnin brothers' "social" approach for the 1923 Palace of Labour competition in Moscow with the nearly contemporary project by Gropius and Adolf Meyer for the *Chicago Tribune*, which was simply "the usual type of business building."[161] A few pages later, he showcased his own apartment building created for the Gosstrakh, photographed according to Mendelsohn's patterns. He then stated that the "true purpose" of the constructivists' work was to design "social condensers" meant to hasten the creation of the new society. Communal houses were meant to fulfill this mission, with an internal OSA competition established in 1927 to explore potential solutions. This programme allowed to implement several fundamental ideas, like the reduction of minimal

159   Moisei Ia. Ginzburg, "Tselevaia ustanovka v sovremennoi arkhitekture," *Sovremennaia arkhitektura* 2, no. 1 (1927): 4.
160   Untitled anonymous editorial, *Sovremennaia arkhitektura* 2, no. 1 (1927): 2.
161   Moisei Ia. Ginzburg, "Itogi i perspektivy," *Sovremennaia arkhitektura* 2, no. 4–5 (1927): 112.

Motion diagrams, in Moisei Ia. Ginzburg, "The Functional Method in Modern Architecture", *Contemporary Architecture* 2, no. 1, 1927. CCA, W.C6.

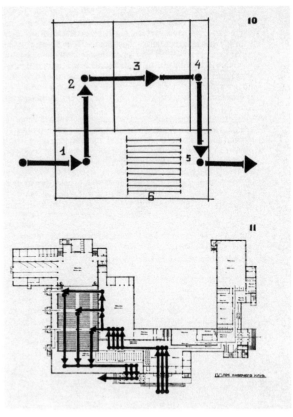

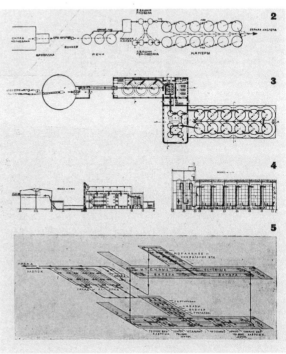

Andrei K. Burov. Study sketches for the set of Sergei M. Eisenstein's film *The General Line*, 1926.
Ink on paper, 22.2 × 47.2 cm. Shchusev State Museum of Architecture, Pla 15019/1.

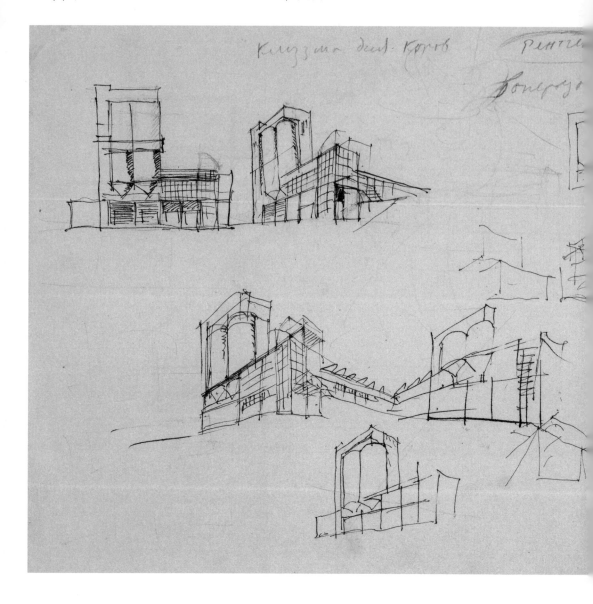

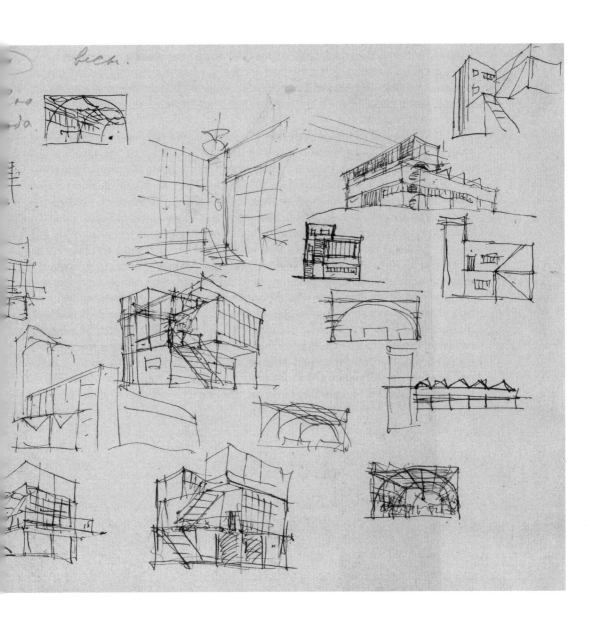

243

living space, which Ginzburg illustrated with transatlantic ocean liner cabins or American hotel rooms with foldaway beds. Ivan Nikolaev created the large communal living complex for the students of the Textile Institute in 1930 in keeping with this Spartan ideal. As for Ginzburg, he revisited his research in a 1934 book on housing and provided an overview of his completed buildings, namely the two emblematic communal houses built in Moscow and Sverdlovsk, while keeping their industrial origins hidden and expunging any reference to America[162].

At the end of the decade, the teachings of the NOT were implemented as part of the research conducted under the auspices of the typification section of the Construction committee of the Economic Council of the Russian Soviet Federative Socialist Republic, known as Stroikom. Among these were the studies led by Mikhail Barshch and Viacheslav Vladimirov, who examined the economy of trajectories and movements as a way of establishing a rational typology of collective housing. They referenced the work of Ernst May's Frankfurt team as well as Ginzburg's previous writings and his reproductions of flow charts by the American economist Christine Frederick, disseminated by Bruno Taut in Germany, the country that remained the prism through which the Russians could contemplate visions of America. Barshch and Vladimirov presented examples of American kitchenettes and shower cubicles to justify their proposed densification of living space, and drew a dining hall where meals were provided to residents on a conveyer belt, a mechanism straight out of a Ford factory[163]. This idea for the mechanization of food supply, irresistibly reminiscent of the famous sequence from Charlie Chaplin's 1928 film *Modern Times*, is akin to those mocked by the writer Andrei Platonov

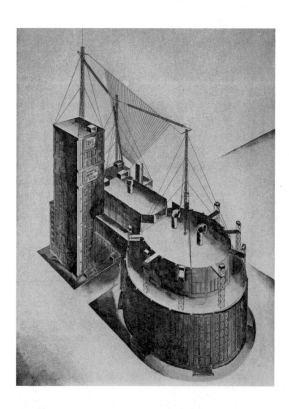

Aleksandr A. Vesnin and Leonid A. Vesnin. Competition project for a Palace of Labour in Moscow, 1923.
Perspective, plate from *L'architecture vivante*, Spring 1926. CCA, W.A778.

in his 1930 play *The Barrel Organ*, where a kolkhoz director distributes filthy meals by way of a complex machine[164].

American themes widely circulated among the members of the following generation. Andrei Burov, one of Aleksandr Vesnin's students, illustrated this circulation in his set for Sergei Eisenstein's 1926 film *The General Line*, coupling long windows and pilotis borrowed from Le Corbusier to vertical cylinders inspired by the Buffalo grain elevators [ill. p. 242-243]. For his graduation project from Vkhutemas, Burov designed a train station topped with a skyscraper with an exposed frame and an external elevator, echoing his mentor's project for the *Pravda*. But attempts to send students to the United States were relatively unsuccessful, as many were unable to cross the border, as for instance the young Mikhail Ginzburg (a namesake of Moisei), who was held back in Mexico[165].

De-Urbanism: With Ford Against Cities

The hastened industrialization of the Soviet Union was combined with an ambitious yet contradictory urban policy, giving way to lively disputes between economists, sociologists, and architects. Be it for the creation of entirely new cities, the transformation of existing ones by enslaving them to production needs, or their complete eradication, American experiments lingered on the horizon.

They also remained present in popular imagery, as evidenced by travel narratives by Western visitors. In 1927, René Fülöp-Miller recounts having found "a fanatic veneration for Chicago and 'Chicagoism'"[166] in Bolshevik literature. After his 1930 trip, the writer Franz Carl Weiskopf wrote in an article for the German daily paper *Berlin am Morgen*, that the population of Novosibirsk "half-seriously and half-ironically" nicknamed the town "Sib-Chik" or "Sibirskoe Chikago," the Siberian Chicago[167]. Ilya Ehrenburg confirmed this, but noted that its muddy ground evoked "groundscrapers" rather than "skyscrapers" to its inhabitants[168]. Sib-Chik's urban ideal was undoubtedly difficult to achieve, as evidenced by panoramic views of the city taken in the late 1920s, more akin to a Midwestern township established on Asian soil.

Other urban metonymies were born: after the establishment of Avtostroi, the press described Nizhnii Novgorod as a fledgling "Soviet Detroit."[169] Ukraine's new capital, Kharkov, where the leading teams of the Donbass industrial development were settled, was dubbed a Soviet "City," in reference to London.[170] In this town, with its nearby Kahn tractor plant, a House of State

162   Moisei Ia. Ginzburg, *Zhilishche* (Moscow: Gosstroiizidat, 1934).
163   Vladimir I. Velman, ed., *Tipovye proekty i konstruktsii zhilichnogo stroitelstva*, (Moscow: Gos. tekhnicheskoe izd-vo, 1929).
164   Andrei I. Platonov, *Sharmanka* [1935] (Ann Arbor, MI: Ardis, 1975). See also Avins, *Border Crossings*, 64–68.
165   Hugh D. Hudson, Jr., *Blueprints and Blood, the Stalinization of Soviet Architecture* (Princeton: Princeton University Press, 1994), 102.
166   René Fülöp-Miller, *The Mind and Face of Bolshevism: An Examination of Cultural Life in Soviet Russia* (New York: G.P. Putnam's Sons, 1927), 23.
167   Franz Carl Weiskopf, quoted in *Sovetskaia Sibir*, 7 December 1932, picked up again in "Pechat za borbu za sotsialisticheskie goroda," *Za Soregor*, no. 1 (1933): 37.
168   Ilya G. Ehrenburg, *Den vtoroi* [1934], in *Sobranie sochinenii v vosmi tomakh* (Moscow: Izd. khudozhestven-naia literatura, 1990), vol. 3, 243. See also Ivan Nevzgodin, *Konstruktivizm v arkhitekture Novosibirska* (Novosibirsk: Upravlenie po gos. okhrane kulturnogo nasledia Novosibirskoi obl., 2013), 18 and 14.
169   "Doroga v sovetskii Detroit," *Krasnaia niva*, no. 28 (7 July 1929): 19.
170   G. Burshtein, "Sovetskii City," *Krasnaia niva*, no. 16 (17 April 1927): 17.

Industries, or Gosprom was erected as of 1926 based on plans by the Leningrad architects Mark Felger, Samuil Kravets, and Sergei Serafimov, and the engineer Pavel Rotert. The team was selected in a competition whose other participants included Andrei Belogrud, Aleksandr Dmitriev, and the émigré Nikolai Vasilev, who submitted an expressionist skyscraper[171]. The Gosprom housed the offices of twenty-two ministries, stretching parallelepiped-shaped volumes of varying heights connected by aerial galleries around a circular square. From the other side of the square, the resulting effect was that of a horizontally compressed skyline. The construction site of the "first Soviet skyscrapers" was photographed according to visual tropes reminiscent of the erection of New York towers, as seen on the cover of the journal *Vokrug Sveta* (Around the World), showing a carpenter suspended in mid-air above the site[172] [ill. p. 248].

After performing in Kharkov in January 1929, Béla Bartók described in a letter to his wife back in Budapest how struck he was by the Gosprom's architecture: "Then I saw a new building, a real skyscraper, in the new Dessau-ish style, without ornament and grouped in blocks."[173] Its powerful appearance inspired a scene from Eisenstein's *General Line*, where the peasant Marfa Lapkina turns to bureaucracy to obtain a stamp to acquire a Fordson tractor for her kolkhoz. Both the outline as seen from the square and the buildings, shot in a vertical panorama, evoke a New World metropolis.

When the journalist and art critic Pietro Maria Bardi visited the Gosprom in 1932, he saw in it, along with the Dneprostroi, another example of the "Soviet Americanisms" he condemned: "Russia never misses an opportunity to parrot America: in all fields of activity, from industry to the planning of civil and economic life, this country aims to 'catch up to and surpass the capitalist countries.' It builds and acquires anything that can help it reach the seriousness and substance of a capitalist nation. With this sort of mimesis, the colour of the flower ends up rubbing off on the butterfly that insists on sitting upon it."[174]

In a 1926 article in *Sovremennaia arkhitektura*, the constructivist architect Aleksandr Pasternak broached the theme of *gradostroitelstvo* (urban planning), a term denoting both the impetus for urban growth and the practice of regulating urban development, based on the German *Städtebau*, or construction of the city. Apparently ill-informed, Pasternak addressed the lack of urban planning in the United States and focused on the American metropolis and its most emblematic constructions. He saw the skyscraper as a prototype for the "social condenser" promoted by the avant-gardists as a way of transforming the Soviet way of life as quickly as possible, a goal that Ginzburg considered to be the main item on the constructivist agenda. For Pasternak, "the 'social condenser' cannot, by definition, be dispersed or scattered in space: it must be as concentrated as possible in a single area.

171   Ia. Kenski, "Budinok derzhavnoi promislovosti v Kharkivi," *Naukovo-tekhnichnii visnik*, no. 2 (1926): 26, quoted in Vladimir G. Lisovski and Richard Gachot, *Nikolai Vassiliev, ot moderna k modernizmu* (Saint Petersburg: Kolo, 2011), 302–3.
172   "Gorod vydvijzhenets," *Vokrug sveta*, no. 45 (1929). See also V. Mikhels, "Sovetskii neboskreb," *Krasnaia niva*, no. 1 (1926): 15. On the Gosprom, see Hatherley, *The Chaplin Machine*, 136–39.
173   Béla Bartók, Letter to Edith Pásztory, 7 January 1929, in János Demény, *Béla Bartók Briefe*, collected and trans. Klara L. Brüll et al. (Budapest: Corvina, 1973), 71. I would like to thank Juliet Koss for bringing this text to my attention.
174   Pietro Maria Bardi, *Un fascista al paese dei Soviet* (Rome: Le Edizioni d'Italia, 1933), 89.
175   Aleksandr L. Pasternak, "Urbanizm," *Sovremennaia arkhitektura* 2, no. 2 (1926): 4–7.
176   Leonid M. Sabsovich, *Sotsialisticheskie goroda* (Moscow: Moskovskii rabotchii, 1930).
177   Leonid M. Sabsovich, *Sovetskii Soiuz cherez 10 let* (Moscow: Moskovskii rabotchii, 1929); in French: *L'URSS dans dix ans* (Paris: Bureau d'éditions, 1930), 57. He had already published *Sovetskii Soiuz cherez 15 let* (Moscow: Planovoe Khoziaistvo, 1929).
178   Sabsovich, *L'URSS dans dix ans*, 98.

This area is the skyscraper. […] Our readership is certainly aware of the detailed programme of the skyscraper, so we will not explain it here. It is a perfect match for the American character, for which any waste of time is unbearable. In our daily lives, because of our habits and lifestyle, this will be different, but the concept remains the same. Americanism will also influence our future cities, where, in addition to the usual rules of construction, we will have to obey another crucial rule, the most important one of all: respecting the principles of urban planning."[175]

In the late 1920s, the "socialist city" was an object of heated polemics, opposing the proponents of a rapid urbanization of the nation and those in favour of eradicating the existing cities. The idea of "catching up" to America was articulated by both factions, as well as by those who were against this dichotomy. Among the "urbanists" was the economist Leonid Sabsovich, who advocated for the creation of a wide network of new cities. His 1930 work *Socialist Cities* was mostly concerned with collectivized forms of housing and food supply, compared in many cases to American examples, in a plea for urban density[176]. Sabsovich published two books a few months apart, *The USSR in Fifteen Years* and *The USSR in Ten Years*, claiming, based on myriad statistics, that the Soviet economy would surpass the American one before the end of the decade, because of its superior working productivity and lower costs of production[177]. According to him, "the fast-paced rhythm of all of economic life will require a proliferation of cars. […] Very quickly, the automobile will become a vital part of our work and our lives, even more so than for the Americans."[178]

Carpenter at work in the sky above Kharkov's Gosprom scheme, cover of *Around the World*, no. 45, 1929. CCA, W.V635.

Particularly active in this debate, Georgii Puzis, also an economist, gave a detailed assessment of various forms of urbanization and advocated for the collective housing scheme introduced by Neutra in *Wie baut Amerika?*[179]

The constructivist positions reached a turning point in 1929, when Ginzburg spoke out against the extremism of the communal houses designed by his young colleagues, claiming to have "heard" the critiques. The OSA doctrine began advocating for individual dwellings and a strong decentralization[180]. These positions were heralded by the economist Mikhail Okhitovich, who had already faced troubles because of his pro-Trotskyist views. He synthesized the de-urbanization ideas articulated by OSA as part of its 1929 competition for the "Green City" on the outskirts of Moscow, in a project he designed in 1930 with Mikhail Barshch, Viacheslav Vladimirov, and Nikolai Sokolov for the Magnitogorsk contest[181]. The plan was dedicated to David Riazanov, the founder of the Marx-Engels Institute, who was committed to democratic values. He was deported in 1931 for Menshevism because of his opposition to Stalin's authoritarian mode of government.

Okhitovich made no secret of his Fordist inspiration: "De-urbanization is a centrifugal process, a motion of rejection. It is based on an identically centrifugal movement in the technical field. Ford, despite unfavourable conditions related to private ownership of land, extended his production in a space characterized by specialized manufacturing based on the proximity of source materials: the finished product is a result of an 'encounter' between spare parts in a workshop, and the workshops themselves obey a centrifugal rule."[182] In his 1924 introduction to Ford's *My Life and Work*, Nikolai Lavrov had already insisted on the "extraordinary importance" of the Tennessee experiment in urban decentralization[183]. He commented on Ford's project, which was discussed at length in the Senate and in the press in 1921–1922, for a vast industrial urban and rural territory, which would be powered by the Wilson Dam. The idea was to create "a 75-mile long city" with a land concession, flanked with farms where factory workers, living alongside mills built in the wilderness, would practise farming[184]. A road network would have been its core framework, making it "A City All Main Street," as coined by the *Literary Digest*[185]. In his second bestselling book *Today and Tomorrow*, also widely read among the Russians, Ford called for "turning back to village industry," citing the example of the River Rouge factory near Detroit, which combined "the benefits of industry to those of agriculture" thanks to the dissemination of the purchasing power of wages across a vast territory and the workers' participation in agricultural production[186]. In the United States, Frank Lloyd Wright took an interest in Ford's projects, remarking in a 1930 talk that "his

179   Georgii B. Puzis, "Sotsialisticheskii sposob rasselenia i sotsialisticheskii tip zhilia," *Vestnik komunisticheskoi akademii*, no. 37–38 (1930): 344–88.
180   Moisei I. Ginzburg, "Slushali: problemy tipizatsii zhilia v RSFR," *Sovremennaia arkhitektura* 4, no.1 (1929): 4–6.
181   "Magnitogore, k skheme genplana," *Sovremennaia arkhitektura* 5, no. 1–2 (1930): 38–56.
182   Mikhail A. Okhitovich, "K probleme goroda," *Sovremennaia arkhitektura* 4, no. 4 (1929): 130–34. On the whole of his de-urbanization projects, see Selim O. Khan-Magomedov, *Mikhail Okhitovich* (Moscow: Fonds Russkii Avangard, 2009). On Okhitovich's end, see the discussions of the Communist Party architects: RGALI, fonds 674, op. 2, d. 13 and 14; and Hudson, *Blueprints and Blood*, 147–65.
183   Nikolai S. Lavrov, preface to Ford, *Moia zhizn i moi dostizhenia*, trad. V. A. Zorgenfrei, (Leningrad: Vremia, 1924), 8.
184   Littell McClung, "The Seventy-Five Mile City," *Scientific American* 127, no. 3 (1922): 156–57 and 213–14. On this project, see Reynold M. Wik, *Henry Ford and Grass-Roots America* (Ann Arbor, MI: University of Michigan Press, 1973), 107–125.
185   "A City All Main Street," *The Literary Digest* 73 (8 April 1922): 72–74.
186   Henry Ford, with Samuel Crowther, *Segodnia i zavtra: o SShA* (Moscow; Leningrad: Gos. Izd-vo, 1927), 145; English in *Today and Tomorrow* (Garden City, NY: Doubleday, Page & Co, 1926), 141.

proposition for Muscle Shoals was one of the best things that I have heard of as a solution to the excess machine increment."[187] He considered this new approach based on "ruralism as distinguished from urbanism" to be "American, and truly democratic."[188]

The de-urbanists intended to base their territorial planning on the Ford factory organizing principle, adapting it to the expectations of Russian society by building a layered network of collective infrastructure along the roads. Contrary to the series of large blocks submitted by the other contestants for Magnitogorsk[189], they proposed low-density urbanization, rooted in the American suburban model mentioned by Okhitovich[190]. The key was a sprawling road network, requiring extensive car use, at least for a given period of time. According to Okhitovich, the automobile developed better outside the city and was "a temporary requirement between the existence of the city and its disappearance, linking it to the countryside in a single unit: the automobile is the essential companion to an industry that has yet to spread territorially."[191] The optimism of this hypothesis can be measured against Soviet automobile manufacturing during the completion of the Nizhnii Novgorod factory: 1,766 cars were made in 1929, and 4,226 in 1930[192]. However, during the assemblies on urban planning organized by the Communist Academy on 31 October and 5 November 1929, many participants supported de-urbanism, citing the American model. Sabsovich stood out by wondering whether Okhitovich was a "wandering salesman" for a car company – obviously Ford[193]. Elsewhere, he dubbed him "the stupidest" of the constructivists and disparaged his ideas as "garbage."[194]

Among the alternative solutions discussed at the assembly, those offered by the economist Nikolai Miliutin were especially noteworthy. As People's Commissar of Finance for the RSFSR, he commissioned a communal house to Ginzburg, completed in Moscow in 1928–1929, before studying architecture under his guidance in the late 1930s. A disgruntled architect, Miliutin rebuffed the black-and-white choice between urbanism and de-urbanism and suggested a third solution. In his 1930 book *Sotsgorod*, he presented his submissions to the urban planning competitions around the three celebrated *stroiki* that were Nizhnii Novgorod, Stalingrad, and Magnitogorsk, according to the principle of the linear city. Inspired by an article published in 1928 by Vitalii Lavrov on Charles Gide's interpretation of the concept, as well as by the idea of the assembly line, Miliutin argued for the replacement of traditional Russian radial-concentric agglomerations with a fabric stretched out along roads and railways. He contended that the old town structures had

187   Frank Lloyd Wright, lecture given to the National Terra Cotta Society, 1930, in *On Architecture, Selected Writings 1894-1940* (New York: Duell, Sloan and Pearce, 1941), 144.
188   Frank Lloyd Wright, "Modern Architecture 6: The City" [1930] in *The Future of Architecture* (New York: The Horizon Press, 1953), 175.
189   On Okhitovich and the Magnitogorsk contest, see Christina Crawford, "The Socialist Settlement Experiment: Soviet Urban Praxis, 1917–1932," PhD dissertation (Harvard University, 2016), 192–93 and 255–57.
190   See Mikhail Barshch's recollections in *MArkhI — XX vek* (Moscow: MArkhI, 2008), vol. 1, 108–10.
191   Mikhail A. Okhitovich, "Zametki po teori rasselenia," *Sovremennaia arkhitektura* 5, no. 1–2 (1930): 7–16.
192   Central Administration of Economic and Social Statistics, *Socialist Construction of the USSR* (Moscow: Soyouzorgouchet, 1936), 236.
193   Leonid M. Sabsovich, in Boris V. Lunin, *Goroda sotsializma i sotsialisticheskaia rekonstruktsia byta* (Moscow: Rabotnik prosveshchenia, 1930).
194   Sabsovich, *Sotsialisticheskie goroda*, 42.

Aerial view of the Tennessee Valley in the Muscle Shoals area, showing the Wilson Dam and its surroundings, in "The Seventy-Five Mile City", *The Scientific American* 127, no. 3, 1922.

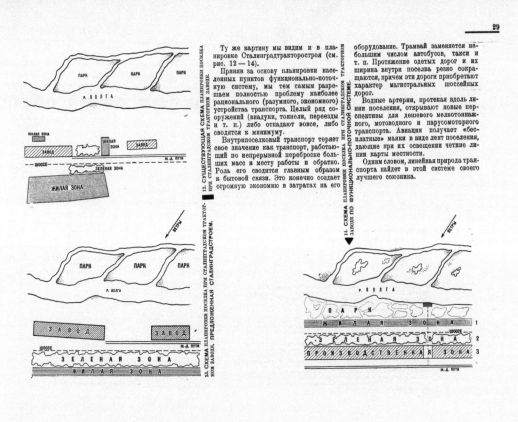

Ту же картину мы видим и в планировке Сталинградтракторостроя (см. рис. 12 — 14).

Приняв за основу планировки населенных пунктов функционально-поточную систему, мы тем самым разрешаем полностью проблему наиболее рационального (разумного, экономного) устройства транспорта. Целый ряд сооружений (виадуки, тоннели, переезды и т. п.) либо отпадают вовсе, либо сводятся к минимуму.

Внутрипоселковый транспорт теряет свое значение как транспорт, работающий по непрерывной переброске больших масс к месту работы и обратно. Роль его сводится главным образом к бытовой связи. Это конечно создает огромную экономию в затратах на его оборудование. Трамвай заменяется небольшим числом автобусов, такси и т. п. Протяжение одетых дорог и их ширина внутри поселка резко сокращаются, причем эти дороги приобретают характер магистральных шоссейных дорог.

Водные артерии, протекая вдоль линии поселения, открывают новые перспективы для дешевого мелкотоннажного, мотоводного и парусомоторного транспорта. Авиация получает «бесплатные» маяки в виде лент поселения, дающие при их освещении четкие линии карты местности.

Одним словом, линейная природа транспорта найдет в этой системе своего лучшего союзника.

12. СУЩЕСТВУЮЩАЯ СХЕМА ПЛАНИРОВКИ ПОСЕЛКА ПРИ СТАЛИНГРАДСКОМ ТРАКТОРНОМ ЗАВОДЕ.

13. СХЕМА ПЛАНИРОВКИ ПОСЕЛКА ПРИ СТАЛИНГРАДСКОМ ТРАКТОРНОМ ЗАВОДЕ, ПРЕДЛОЖЕННАЯ СТАЛИНГРАДСТРОЕМ.

14. СХЕМА ПЛАНИРОВКИ ПОСЕЛКА ПРИ СТАЛИНГРАДСКОМ ТРАКТОРНОМ ЗАВОДЕ ПО ФУНКЦИОНАЛЬНО-ПОТОЧНОЙ СИСТЕМЕ.

Nikolai Miliutin. Projects for linear industrial cities in Stalingrad and Nizhnii Novgorod, 1930, in *Sotsgorod: The Problem of Building Socialist Cities*, Moscow: Gos. Izd-vo, 1930. CCA, 0003875.

Mikhail O. Barshch, Mikhail A. Okhitovich, et al. Competition project for the plan of Magnitogorsk. Plan of one of the centrifugal roads and diagram of the frequency of collective infrastructure, foldouts in *Contemporary Architecture*, vol. 5, no. 6, 1930. CCA, W.C6.

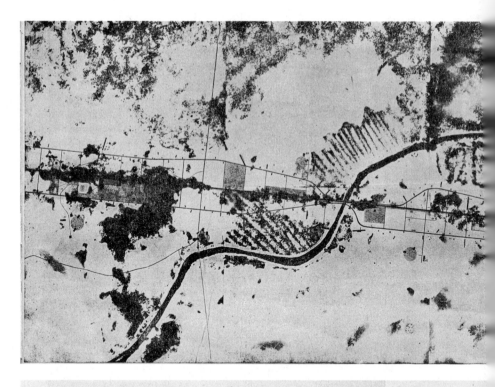

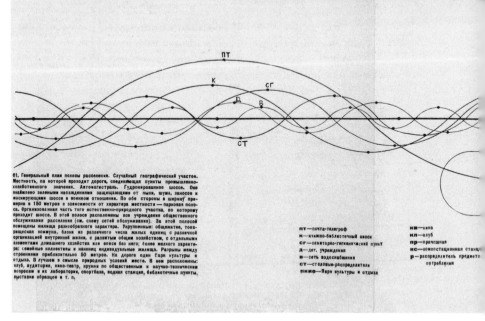

схема сетей обобщес

61, Генеральный план полосы расселения. Случайный географический участок. Местность, по которой проходит дорога, соединяющая пункты промышленно-хозяйственного значения. Автомагистраль. Гудронированное шоссе. Оно окаймлено зелеными насаждениями защищающими от пыли, шума, заносов и маскирующими шоссе в военном отношении. По обе стороны в ширину примерно в 150 метров в зависимости от характера местности — парковая полоса. Организовавшая часть того естественно-природного участка, по которому проходит шоссе. В этой полосе расположены все учреждения общественного обслуживания расселения (см. схему сетей обслуживания). За этой полосой помещены жилища разнообразного характера. Укрупненные: общежитие, товарищеская коммуна, блоки из различного числа жилых единиц, с различной организацией внутренней жизни, с развитым общим хозяйством, с отдельными элементами домашнего хозяйства или вовсе без него; более мелкого характера; семейные коллективы и наконец индивидуальные жилища. Разрывы между строениями приблизительно 50 метров. На дороге один Парк культуры и отдыха. В лучшем в смысле природных условий месте. В нем расположены: клуб, аудитория, кино-театр, кружки по общественным и научно-техническим вопросам и их лаборатории, спортбаза, водная станция, библиотечные пункты, выставки образцов и т. п.

пт—почта-телеграф
к—книжно-библиотечный киоск
сг—санитарно-гигиенический пункт
д—дет. учреждения
в—сеть водоснабжения
ст—столовые-распределители
пкио—Парк культуры и отдыха

ки—кино
кл—клуб
пр—прачешная
ис—компостационная станция
р—распределитель предмето потребления

нного обслуживания (к генеральному плану)

not been affected by the large industrial projects, which according to him had simply substituted their *kremlins* for factories, providing a new centre to preexisting clusters.

In Stalingrad, the "residential zone" devised by Miliutin was modelled after its bordering "production zone," located across from a green stretch of land. This continuous system, without pacing, had nothing in common with Vladimir Semenov's 1929 plan for the same area, where industrial and urban centres, designed as separate entities, were laid along the Volga River[195]. At the start of the year 1930, Miliutin, along with Anatolii Lunacharsky, presided over the jury for the Magnitogorsk competition, whose contestants included a crew from the Vkhutein, led by Rudolf Brilling, a contingent from the OSA, headed by Ivan Leonidov, and a team formed by Barshch and Okhitovich[196]. No first prize was awarded. Miliutin printed a graphic representation of his own solution in *Sotsgorod*, which combined production and housing in a linear layout stretching on the west side of the proposed site, contrary to most competing projects, who had chosen the east side. There, stripes intended for parks and housing were bordered by factories and the Ural River[197].

The Nizhnii Novgorod project was the most radical of the three published in *Sotsgorod*. The competition organized for the living quarters, to be built by The Austin Company, was secured by a crew led by Arkadii Mordvinov, from the Moscow State Technical University[198]. Miliutin opposed the most methodical version of his linear arrangement to the strict zoning of the official projects. He redesigned the automobile plant according to a longitudinal plan, with no relation to the chosen matrix structure borrowed from the River Rouge factory, painstakingly identifying the various workshops, from foundry to painting. The plan clearly defines the "flowing" sequence of production that would regulate the living quarters, with each point of entry aligned with a canteen, and the row of houses surrounded by a park and a forest along the Oka River[199] [ill. p. 251].

The deconstructivists' projects for the Soviet city as well as Miliutin's solutions, which gained significant exposure in the West, were rejected during the June 1931 meeting of the Communist Party's Central Committee. Lazar

195   Nikolai A. Miliutin, *Sotsgorod: problema stroitelstva sotsialisticheskikh gorodov* (Moscow: Gos. Izd-vo, 1930), 29; in English: *Sotsgorod, the Problem of Building Socialist Cities*, transl. Arthur Sprague, ed. by George R. Collins and William Alex (Cambridge, MA: MIT Press, 1974), 72; Semenov's scheme can be found in Maurice F. Parkins, *City Planning in Soviet Russia* (Chicago: University of Chicago Press, 1953), fig. 6.

196   On the jury, see Nikolai V. Dokuchaev, "Konkurs na planirovku Magnitogorska," *Stroitelstvo Moskvy*, no. 4 (1930): 25–28; Elke Pistorius, "Das Sozgorod-Ideal," *Bauwelt*, no. 48 (29 December 1995): 2764–69. Harald Bodenschatz and Christiane Post, *Städtebau im Schatten Stalins: die internationale Suche nach der sozialistischen Stadt in der Sowjetunion 1929-1935* (Berlin: Braun, 2003), 45–63; see also Marco De Michelis and Ernesto Pasini, *La città sovietica 1925-1937* (Venice: Marsilio, 1976), p. 76-90.

197   Miliutin, *Sotsgorod, the Problem of Building Socialist Cities*, 70.

198   Vitalii A. Lavrov, "Avtostroi -sotsialisticheskii gorod," *Stroitelstvo Moskvy*, no. 4 (1930): 20–24. See A.A. Gordin and E.V. Radchenko "Sotsgorod gorkovsgo avtozavoda i kontseptsiia goroda-sada," (Nizhnii Novgorod: Nizhnenovgorodskii gosudarstvennyi arkhitekturo-stroitelnyi Institut, 2017); see also De Michelis and Pasini, *La città sovietica*, 60-69.

199   Miliutin, *Sotsgorod, the Problem of Building Socialist Cities*, p. 72.

200   Lazar M. Kaganovich, *The Socialist reconstruction of Moscow and other cities in the U.S.S.R.*, (New York: International Publishers, 1931), 87 and 97-100.

201   F. Linde and A. Esukhukov [VOKS], Letter to Albert Kelsey, 3 July 1928, Columbus Memorial Library, Organization of American States, Washington, DC, quoted in Robert Alexander Gonzalez, *Designing Pan-America: U.S. Architectural Visions for the Western Hemisphere* (Austin: University of Texas Press, 2011), 117. Albert Kesley, Letter to F. Linde, 12 June 1928, Columbus Memorial Library, Organization of American States, Washington, DC, Ibid., 117.

202   Gonzalez, *Designing Pan-America*, 116.

Kaganovich declared that the discussion around the "socialist" city was henceforth pointless: to him, if the production relations were socialistic, Soviet cities were also socialistic by default. He specifically overruled Sabsovich and Miliutin's solutions, rebuking the "idiocy" of the de-urbanists' "drivel" on the disappearance of cities. Instead, he oriented the efforts of urban planners towards rebuilding existing cities while limiting the creation of new agglomerations[200].

Fantastic Amerikanizms: Three Albums and a Competition

Alongside the documentary or pragmatic Americanism of the various movements and their publications, a fantasized America emerged, whose designs were usually presented against a New World backdrop. One of its most notable manifestations was the Russian architects' contribution to the 1929 competition for a memorial lighthouse to Christopher Columbus, made possible by funding from the Carnegie Foundation, which the Pan-American Union decided to establish in Santo Domingo. Since December 1917, the absence of diplomatic relations impeded Russian architects' contact with the United States, preventing them from participating in various international competitions. Their outreach was also stunted by the post-civil war disorganization in the network of professional institutions. There were no Russian participants to the 1922 competition for the *Chicago Tribune* headquarters, though the main developing projects had caught their attention. The Russians were also *de jure* barred from participating in the 1927 Geneva Palace competition, as the USSR was not a member of the League of Nations. Frustrated by this absence of global reach, they eagerly seized the opportunity awarded by the Santo Domingo call. When the ASNOVA contacted the organizers for information, the head of the contest, the architect, Albert Kelsey, readily claimed that his problem would "appeal mightily to the Russian imagination."[201] In the end, 26 of the 84 registered Russians sent a project, of the 455 total submissions[202].

The Soviet proposals, in their more or less faithful interpretations of the memorial lighthouse programme, can be seen both as a cross section of Russian architectural culture and as an x-ray view of its Americanism. Ivan Leonidov's project was at once the most concise and the most innovative in terms of technology: furthering research he had begun as part of his 1927 thesis project for the Lenin Institute, he submitted a cable-stayed metal antenna along with a small sphere, forgoing the idea of a lighthouse and leading the monument into the age of wireless telegraphy [ill. p. 256]. The leaders of ASNOVA applied principles developed as part of their teachings at Vkhutemas/Vkhutein. Ladovskii imagined a skyscraper, some sixty storeys tall, on a cross-shaped plan, sitting in a sort of crater and divided into alternating filled and hollowed sections, drawn from a striking bird's-eye view. Partnering with Aleksei Rukhliadev, Krinskii was more faithful to the lighthouse theme, expressing it through a stack of curtailed pyramids. Andrei Bunin, Georgii Krutikov, and Trifon Varentsov seemed to elaborate on a notion developed in the Institute's studios, with the lighthouse spire piercing a sphere crossed by a triangular veil.

Not all submissions were sent in by radical moderns. Vladimir Tarasov divided the lighthouse into two towers facing each other and emitting a singular glow, as if an electric arc was binding their crystalline peaks. One of the Leningrad traditionalists, Andrei Belogrud, drew a single tower, whose angulations echoed the Art Deco patterns that were then beginning to permeate

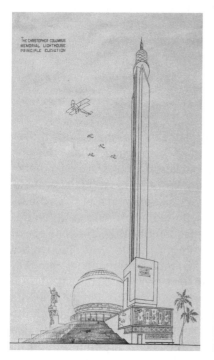

into Soviet architecture. The eccentric artist Nikolai Lanceray, a former member of the World of Art movement, submitted a massive block topped with three caravels. As for Shchusev, he reprised the theme of the sphere and the tower, but clearly separated them, placing the first on a layered pedestal and rooting the second in a granite parallelepiped. Like Leonidov, he included the image of a blimp in the remarkable perspective sent to the jury in Madrid, to convey the modernity of his project.

The most original response came from the idyosincratic Konstantin Melnikov, who drew a gigantic windmill made of two cones which intersected each other vertically. When the wind blew in the right direction, the rotating wings propelled the rain into a turbine, making the entire construction revolve. This kinetic principle was strongly reminiscent of Vladimir Tatlin's project for a monument to the Third International, but Melnikov's discourse was purposefully different. Rather than celebrating the communist movement, he wished to magnify the beneficial flow of American civilization, as stated in the manuscript, written in English and printed in the publication consecutive to the first phase of the competition: "Two worlds (two cones) mutually support one another. Amidst two worlds is Christopher Columbus's monument, which in uniting them awakened the vital of America. The juices rush in a mighty downpour from the summit of the cone and over the crown of Spain along the crystal coros of the monument of Columbus and into the Old World. The American culture, whose base was the European civilization, grows more and more independent and original in its creations. The supporter of the Old World's (the lower cone) is gradually substituted by new powerful supporters: two flyaway wings. These mechanized supporters cut

Konstantin S. Melnikov. Competition project for Christopher Columbus Memorial Lighthouse in Santo Domingo, 1929. Plate in Albert Kelsey, *Program and Rules of the Second Competition [...] for the Monumental Lighthouse [...] to the Memory of Christopher Columbus*, Washington, DC: Pan-American Union, 1931. CCA, NA2335.C5.

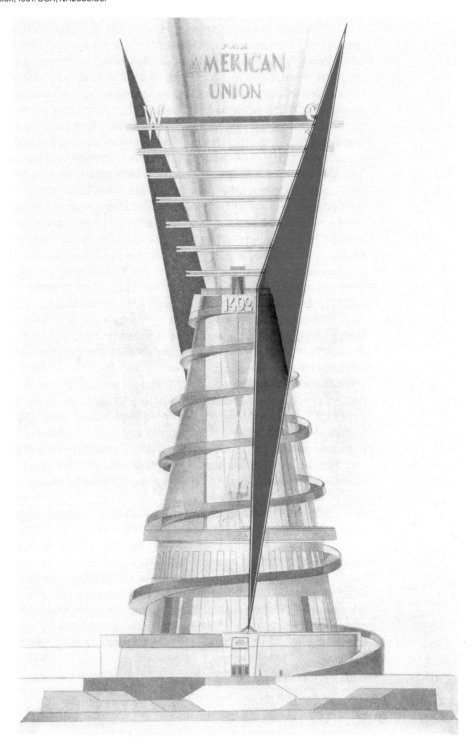

down the wind and occupy a favourable position for supporting the cupola of the Pan-American Union leaving each time a new impression on the inhabitants of Santo Domingo."[203]

Though Kelsey was interested in the Russian contributions, namely Melnikov's, this last one was too outrageous—and not Hispanic enough—to be chosen by the jury, on which sat Raymond Hood and Eliel Saarinen. Ten projects were selected for a second turn, and ten honourable mentions were awarded, one to Nikolai Lanceray and another to Nikolai Vasilev, a Saint Petersburg architect who emigrated to the United States in 1923. Among the ten winning teams was the New York team, comprised of Robert P. Rogers and Albert E. Poor and the firm Helmle, Corbett and Harrison firm, whose project was designed by the Russian Manhattanite Viacheslav Oltarzhevskii. The design showed a stone-clad tower with setbacks—modelled on the post-1916 zoning regulation skyscrapers in New York City—set on a seaside square decked with arches and enclosed in a ribbed fortress. Chosen after the second round, the pre-Columbian-inspired project by the young British architect Joseph Lea Gleave remained unfinished until 1992. Submissions by Bunin, Krutikov, Varentsov, and Shchusev did not, however, remain unnoticed. Their propositions for a combination between a large hollow sphere and a slender tower were among the sources for the Trylon and Perisphere project created by Wallace Harrison and André Fouilhoux for the 1939 New York World's Fair.

Among the Russians who were most passionate about the Santo Domingo competition was the Leningrad architect Iakov Chernikhov, though it is unclear whether he actually submitted a project to the jury in Madrid. Chernikhov was obviously inspired by the idea of a project for a monumental structure with the single goal of offering a luminous compass for navigation. He designed several solutions for such a function: in figure 197 of his *Foundations of Contemporary Architecture*, one of the three illustrated volumes featuring his amazing graphic inventions, Chernikhov drew a Neo-Suprematist composition with rectangular prisms, stacked horizontally for the base, and then vertically. In another figure from the same collection, the project was treated like a composition of cylinders wrapped into thin spirals and adorned with little masts[204] [ill. p. 260].

Chernikhov's Americanizm was mostly inspired by industry, so much so that it seemed to illustrate some of Gastev's foresights. Contrary to the constructivists, who deplored his predominantly graphical approach, Chernikhov overlooked Taylorism, equipment design, and spaces arranged to resemble Ford's manufacturing plants. However, some of his designs assembled industrial-looking structures over whose vast territories, strewn with conveyer belts, such as in Composition 311 of *Construction of Architectural and Machine Forms* or in figure 28 of *Architectural Fantasies*[205]. Chernikhov often included grain silos as building blocks for his designs, dilated or arrayed to

203   Konstantin S. Melnikov, manuscript reproduced in Albert Kelsey, *Program and Rules of the Second Competition for the Selection of an Architect for the Monumental Lighthouse Which the Nations of the World Will Erect in the Dominican Republic to the Memory of Christopher Columbus. Together with the Report of the International Jury, the Premiated and Many Other Designs Submitted in the First Contest* (Washington, DC: Pan-American Union, 1930), 99.

204   Iakov G. Chernikhov, *Osnovy sovremennoi arkhitektury: experimentalno-issledovatelskie raboty* (Leningrad: Izd-vo Leningradskogo ob-va arkhitektorov, 1931).

205   Iakov G. Chernikhov, *Konstruktsiia arkhitekturnykh i mashinnykh form* (Leningrad: Izd-vo Leningradskogo ob-va arkhitektorov, 1931); *Arkhitekturnye fantazii* (Leningrad: Mezhdunarodnaia kniga, 1933).

Viacheslav K. Oltarzhevskii, for the firm of Helmle, Corbett and Harrison. Competition project for the Christopher Columbus Memorial Lighthouse in Santo Domingo, 1929. Plate in Albert Kelsey, *Program and Rules of the Second Competition [...] for the Monumental Lighthouse [...] to the Memory of Christopher Columbus*, Washington, DC: Pan-American Union, 1931. CCA, NA2335.C5.

Iakov G. Chernikhov. Competition project for the Christopher Columbus Memorial Lighthouse in Santo Domingo, 1929.
Plate in *The Foundations of Contemporary Architecture*, Leningrad: Izd-vo Leningradskogo ob-va arkhitektorov, 1930. CCA, ID:87-B3573.

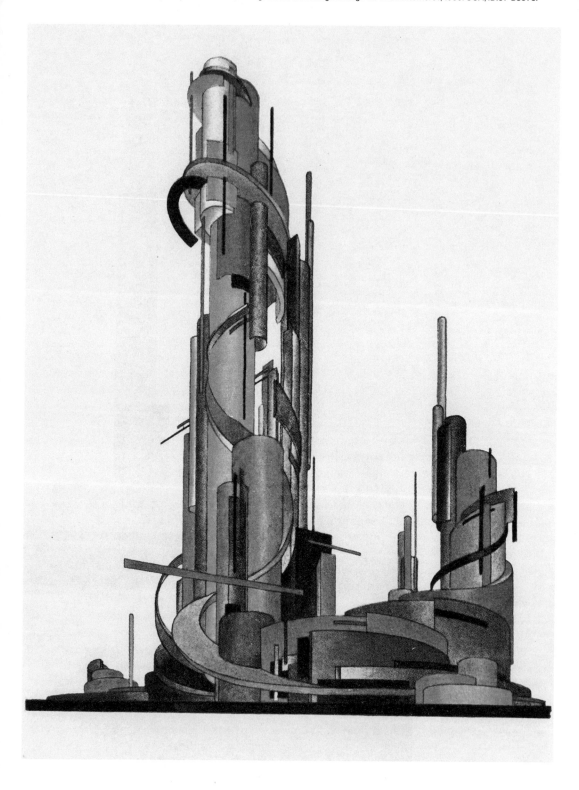

create greater ensembles, while other projects reprised the configuration of Neutra's theoretical plans in *Rush City Reformed*, known to Russians through the translation of *Wie baut Amerika?*

Chernikhov's Amerikanizm is also eloquent in his interpretations of skyscrapers, which frequently appear in his books as separate entities or as part of complex ensembles. Incidentally, Chernikhov designed numerous structures vast or compartmentalized enough to form entire cities. In the *Foundations*, for example, there are several versions of a "house-city" or a "factory-city," in addition to an illustration of a cluster of buildings called a "skyscraper city."[206] He revisited this theme with his "giant skyscraper city" in his *Fantasies*, where streamlined towers can be seen, as though ready to head for a distant horizon. These skyscrapers are much more radical than all the overseas structures existing at the time[207] [ill. p. 263]. Chernikhov went as far as to imagine his own contribution to the American urban landscape with a Suprematist-inspired "giant house in New York" depicted in *Foundations*[208] [ill. p. 262].

An eclectic creator, Chernikhov was able to employ elementarist components inspired by Malevich as well as the dynamics and sense of contrast characteristic of ASNOVA's design strategy. Elsewhere, some of his skyscrapers, despite their thoroughly geometrical treatment, are symmetrical and pyramid-shaped—such as the "skyscraper palace," figure 122 in *Foundations*—, making them genuine forerunners for the tall structures of the late 1940s. Several of Chernikhov's projects, though not explicitly described as skyscrapers, are assembled from the aggregation of vertical elements. Engaged in industrial construction in Leningrad, Chernikhov did not return to his *Fantasies* until the forced idleness of the Second World War, after a decade that saw an overhaul of the workings and perspectives of Soviet Americanism.

206   "Gorod neboskrebov," in Chernikhov, *Osnovy*, ill. 100.
207   "Gorod gigantskikh neboskrebov," in Chernikhov, *Fantazii*, ill. 10.
208   "Dom-gigant v Niu-Iorke", in Tchernikhov, *Osnovy*, ill. 223 a.

Iakov G. Chernikhov. "Giant house in New York", in *The Foundations of Contemporary Architecture*,
Leningrad: Izd-vo Leningradskogo ob-va arkhitektorov, 1930. CCA, ID:87-B3573.

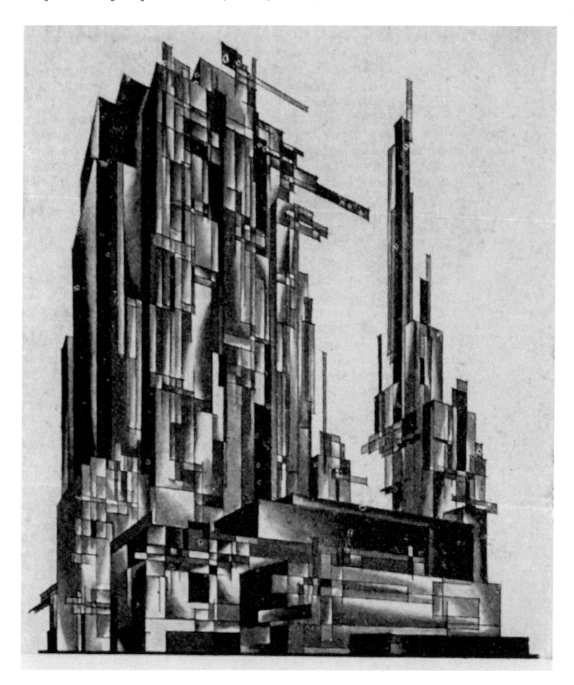

Iakov G. Chernikhov. "Lattice space construction for an industrial building", ca. 1928, preparatory drawing for plate 2 of the *101 Architectural Fantasies* (1933). Gouache on paper, 30 × 24 cm. Alex Lachmann Collection, Drawing 17 - Tsch 006.

Iakov G. Chernikhov. "Giant skyscraper city", plate in *101 Architectural Fantasies*, Leningrad: Mezhdunarodnaia kniga, 1933. Plate 10. CCA, W12242.

Architectural Amerikanizm in the Early Phase of Stalinism

4

Sergei M. Eisenstein
(1898-1948). Soviet film director.
Stayed in Hollywood in 1930.

Viacheslav K. Oltarzhevskii
(1880-1966). Russian architect.
Practiced in New York from
1924 to 1935.

Boris M. Iofan (1891-1976).
Soviet architect. Designed the
Palace of Soviets in Moscow.

Anastas I. Mikoyan (1895-1978).
Communist leader and
statesman. Traveled to America
in 1936.

Ilia A. Ilf (1897-1937) and Evgenii P. Petrov (1903-1942).
Satirical writers from Odessa. Their travelogue through the United
States became a best-seller.

"One can imagine how quickly the material state of the country would improve if district secretaries could see for themselves the significance of services offered to the population and what a gas station, a cafeteria, a hotel, standard furniture, clean tablecloths, bathrooms, showers, highways, […] and hundreds of other essential things look like. But we also believe that the matter of taste and its development among those who are building on the ground the new world every single day is of utmost importance. Therefore, well-organized trips to America for party leaders could be greatly beneficial to the country."

Ilia Ilf, Evgenii Petrov, letter to Joseph Stalin, February 1936[1].

1   Ilia A. Ilf and Evgenii P. Petrov, Letter to Joseph V. Stalin, [late February – before the 26th] 1936, APRF, f. 3, op. 34, ed. khr. 206, l. 54–63, published in *Iskusstvo kino*, no. 11 (1992): 87–89.

In June 1937, the aviators Valerii Chkalov, Georgii Baidukov, and Aleksandr Beliakov undertook the first non-stop Moscow-New York flight, by way of Vancouver, in the State of Washington, aboard a Tupolev ANT-25 aircraft, which was greeted by swarms of reporters upon landing. At a meeting in honour of the crew held on 1 July, in the 71st Regiment Armoury in Manhattan, Chkalov, a star Soviet pilot, declared: "Our country, which established its independence twenty years ago, is marching forward from victory to victory. We ask forgiveness of our American friends if within a few years we even surpass them in some ways. [...] We have overcome the hardships, the freezing and the storms of the Arctic to bring greetings to this country on the red wings of our plane. And when the first plane from this country lands in Moscow, then we shall know our friendship has been accepted by the American people."[2] The flight of Chkalov's crew was known to all Russian children thanks to a book illustrated by Aleksandr Deineka[3]. Following up with this programme a few weeks later, another flight, from Moscow to San Jacinto, California, was completed by Mikhail Gromov, Andrei Iumashev, and Sergei Danilin.

While Chkalov, Gromov, and their crew flew across the Pole, almost all the proponents of Americanization who had been active in 1928–1932 were eliminated. Aleksei Gastev, Isaak Shpilrein, Eleazar Gurevich—the director of the Cheliabinsk factory—, Valerii Mezhlauk, Saul Bron, Mikhail Okhitovich, Nikolai Osinskii (Valerian Obolenskii), and hundreds of thousands of other executives disappeared. The purges reached the highest ranks of the Soviet economic leadership with the 1938 execution of Aleksei Rykov, following that of Georgii Piatakov, the kingpin of the People's Commissariat of Heavy Industry, who drove his superior, the Commissar Sergo Ordzhonikidze, alledgedly opposed to the abuses of repression, to commit suicide in 1937[4]. After Stalin had firmly established his power by eradicating his opponents and violently exterminating the remaining loyal executives, and despite the departure of most experts recruited as part of the first five-year plan, Amerikanizm lived on in various forms.

After some initial hurdles, large Soviet factories mastered Western techniques, and the focus moved from heavy industry to other fields such as food supply. A new generation of managers, arising from peasantry and the working class, took charge of the state apparatus, the party, and state-owned companies. These hastily trained *vydvizhentsy* (promoted workers) were more attached to the values of industrial production than to European intellectual heritage[5]. In terms of urban planning, new concrete measures included the transformation of major cities, starting with Moscow, whose general plan integrated explicitly American themes, among other sources. In the architectural field, programmes for the creation of houses of industry proliferated, specifically targeting skyscrapers. The pull towards high-rise structures was particularly apparent in the programmes promoted by the regime, such as the

2   Valerii P. Chkalov, quoted in Jessica Smith, "America Welcomes the Flyers," *Soviet Russia Today*, August 1937, 9. The first flight between Moscow and New York (with stops) was celebrated by Amtorg in 1929: *Aviation Supplement Issued in Recognition of the First Moscow-New York Flight of the Soviet All-Metal Monoplane "Land of the Soviets,"* 23 August–1 November 1929 (New York: Amtorg Pub. Division, 1929).
3   Georgii F. Baidukov, *Cherez polius v Ameriku* (Moscow: Detizdat, 1938), illustrations by Aleksandr A. Deineka.
4   On the purges within the Commissariat, see Oleg V. Khlevniuk, *In Stalin's Shadow: The Career of "Sergo" Ordzhonikidze*, adapted and preface by Donald J. Raleigh (Armonk, NY: M.E. Sharpe, 1995), 116–20.
5   Sheila Fitzpatrick, *The Cultural Front: Power and Culture in Revolutionary Russia* (Ithaca, NY: Cornell University Press, 1992), 14ff.

Unknown artist from the village of Palekh. Urn commemorating the first direct flight between the USSR and the United States, 1938. Painted and lacquered wood, h: 45 cm. Alex Lachmann Collection.

Dans ce tas d'automobiles usagées il y en a qui sont encore bonnes. On les a entassées là à l'aide de grues, puis détruites par bombes jetées d'un avion. La scène s'est passée à Chicago.

Automobiles withdrawn from the American market and destroyed by airplanes, illustration in Mikhail Ilin, *L'épopée du travail moderne : la merveilleuse transformation de l'Union soviétique*, Paris: Éditions sociales internationales, 1932. Private collection.

Palace of the Soviets. Simultaneously, the dream factory of Soviet cinema remained transfixed by Hollywood, whose infrastructures it attempted to emulate.

After the stock market crash of 1929, the Russians' perception of America was deeply altered. Images of new cars being destroyed to be taken off the market, an unthinkable spectacle for the Soviets, and long lines filled with unemployed men became a familiar sight. Soviet publicists took advantage of the situation to contrast what seemed to signal the twilight of capitalism with the rigorously organized projects of the five-year plan. Mikhail Ilin's best-selling book *Moscow Has a Plan*, printed in several British and American editions in 1931, was among the bluntest, insisting on the absence of a general plan in the West. Condemning the impact of advertisements on the landscape, in a tone announcing what Peter Blake would critique thirty years lated in *God's Own Junkyard*, this rather simplistic poem delights in the differences between American wastefulness and Soviet exploits—Ilin wrote: "America has many large factories, many more than we have. There, factories turn out four automobiles a minute; there, some buildings are sixty storeys high; there, a huge steel bridge was recently constructed in one day; there, a million tractors work in the fields. The Americans are proud of their machines, of their factories. But how do these factories work? According to some general plan, do you suppose? No, they work without a general plan. […] In a country boasting millions of machines, storerooms are bursting with goods, corn is burned in place of coal, milk is poured into the rivers, and at the very same time in this very same country thousands of people go hungry."[6]

Street scene in New York, illustration by William Kermode, in Mikhail Ilin, *Moscow Has A Plan: A Soviet Primer*, London: Jonathan Cape, 1931. CCA, ID:87-B7018.

Most importantly, Ilin distinguished between the manifestations of machinism in the United States from those characterizing Soviet industrialization: "In America, the machine is not a helper to the worker, not a friend, but an enemy. Every new machine, every new invention, throws thousands of workers out upon the streets. [...] But how is it with us? The more machines we have the easier will be the working day, the lighter and happier will be the lives of all. We build factories in order that there may be no poverty, no filth, no sickness, no unemployment, no exhausting labour—in order that life may be rational and just. We build factories in order that we may have as many mechanical helpers as possible, machines in order that these mechanical helpers may belong to all and work for all equally."[7] While railing against the American machinist nightmare, Mikhail Ilin failed to mention that the young Soviet industry owed much of its success to the United States.

America in the Lens of Filmmakers

As negative images of America proliferated, interactions in the field of filmmaking reversed its course. The eastbound circulation of American films, obtained directly in the United States or through Germany, almost comes to an end, as begin the first trips of Soviet filmmakers and film industry executives to the United States, on the grounds of Hollywood's advance in the field of talking pictures: the first Soviet sound film, Nikolai Ekk's Road to Life, came out in 1931, four years after Alan Crosland's The Jazz Singer. Sergei Eisenstein's 1930 expedition was the most notable. He travelled to Hollywood with his assistant Grigorii Aleksandrov and the cameraman Eduard Tisse, upon an invitation from Jesse L. Lasky, one of the founders of Paramount Pictures. On his way to California, he discovered New York City. At first, he wondered why the skyscrapers "don't seem high,"[8] but he enjoyed watching the spectacle from an airplane: his "rebellious spirit" made him wish to "see those stone giants not from the ground, but... from the sky." Luckily, the technical crew "obliged and chartered an airplane," allowing him to "see from above that which had to be viewed from below." Eisenstein summed up the experience with the following observation: "It is extraordinary to have such an 'itch' for skyscrapers!"[9]

Major Frank Pease, the president of the Hollywood Technical Directors Institute, led a violent press campaign against Eisenstein, calling for the expulsion of this "communist agitator." After meeting the canine actor Rin Tin Tin, an encounter he described as his first with an American star, the filmmaker sent a photograph to his partner Pera Atasheva, captioning it with a caustic nod to the insults that were being hurled at him: "Red dog meets Hollywood movie star."[10] During the weeks he spent in Hollywood, Eisenstein

6   Mikhail Ia. Ilin [pseudonym of Ilia Ia. Marshak], Rasskaz o velikom plane, graphic design by Mikhail I. Razulevich (Moscow: Gosizdat, 1930), 16; in English: Moscow Has a Plan, A Soviet Primer, trans. G.S. Counts and N.P. Lodge, illustr. by William Kermode (London: Jonathan Cape, 1931), 22 and 28.
7   Ilin, Rasskaz o velikom plane, 21; Moscow Has a Plan, 32–33.
8   Marie Seton, "'An American Tragedy'," in Sergei M. Eisenstein, a Biography [1952] (London: Dennis Dobson, 1978), 158. Ivor Montagu, who travelled with him, wrote his own memoir: With Eisenstein in Hollywood (New York: International Publishers, 1969).
9   Serge M. Eisenstein, Mémoires (Paris: Julliard, 1989), 356.
10 Document held in the Eisenstein collection, RGALI, quoted in Ronald Bergan, Sergei Eisenstein: A Life in Conflict (New York: Overlook Press, 1999), 194. See Mason Ham, "Rin-Tin-Tin Does His Tricks for Noted Russian Movie Man," Boston Herald (27 May 1930).

"Red dog meets Hollywood movie star" [Eisenstein's own caption], 1930. Gelatin silver print, 25.4 × 20.5 cm. Alamy.

jumped from one film project to another. While he had intended to direct a film inspired by Blaise Cendrars' *Gold*, for which he scouted several locations, Paramount offered him the adaptation of *An American Tragedy* by Theodore Dreiser, who had visited him in Moscow, a screenplay he ended up declining[11]. He met David Wark Griffith, Charles Chaplin, and Robert Flaherty, as well as Walt Disney. In a 1941 essay, the director penned a deep dive into the first Mickey Mouse pictures, which he saw as a playful compensation for Fordist standardization. To him, "the 'grey wolf'" which, "in America is behind every corner, behind every counter, on the heels of every person" was a personification of capitalist unemployment."[12] In Stalin's Moscow, Eisenstein was alone in having a drawing by Disney in his interior.

Eisenstein was in Berlin when he got the idea for "a satirical film on America drawing on the visual and dramatic possibilities offered by glass skyscrapers,"[13] an unfinished project titled *Glass House*. According to him, the concept was born at the Kessler Hotel, on Kantstrasse in Berlin, where he felt "the influence of glass architecture." In 1927, he wrote: "A view of America as seen through its walls; embodied in the parody of the true American material—the America of Hollywood clichés; reality presented as a parody, as if Hollywood clichés were factual."[14] This project can be seen as a response to Fritz Lang's dystopian film *Metropolis*, as the Soviet filmmaker was aware of its existence since the movie's production. But the parallel with Germany goes further. Eisenstein's America was mediated through Berlin projects, particularly through Mies van der Rohe's glass skyscrapers, widely known in the USSR, where they served to illustrate popular books, rather than through Bruno Taut's crystalline compositions, inspired by the poet Paul Scheerbart[15]. Eisenstein imagined the New World before even setting foot there, drawing, for instance, the "glass balcony above a busy street" as of January 1927. After crossing the Atlantic, he discovered the plans for Frank Lloyd Wright's St. Mark's-in-the-Bouwerie Towers project, published on 29 June 1930 in the *New York Times Magazine*. Upon seeing them, he recognized his own project, captioning the clipping he enclosed in an album: "This is the skyscraper I invented in Berlin!"[16] Eisenstein's idea therefore owes nothing to the work of Soviet architects, whom he pointedly fails to mention.

His considerations on the film led him to work on glass as a material and the gazes it invites—or obstructs[17]. He strove to "cover all attempts at finding new points of view both in terms of filming and performance" and to "build a general plotline around the progressive mutual 'discovery' of its inhabitants, who start seeing each other, which, in a capitalist system, leads to

11   Useful observations about this visit can be found in Grigorii V. Aleksandrov, *Epokha i kino* (Moscow: Izd-vo politicheskoi literatury, 1976), 128–38.
12   Sergei M. Eisenstein, "Notes on Walt Disney" [1941], in *Eisenstein on Disney*, ed. by Jay Leyda (London: Methuen, 1988), 4.
13   Sergei M. Eisenstein, "notes on the Glass House project," RGALI, quoted in *Glass House: du projet de film au film comme projet*, intro. by François Albera, trans. Valérie Pozner, Michail Maiatsky, and François Albera (Dijon: Les Presses du réel, 2009), 26. See also François Albera, "Glass House: Note pour un film," *Faces*, no. 24 (Summer 1992): 43–52; Oksana Bulgakowa, *Sergei Eisenstein: Drei Utopien – Architekturentwürfe zur Filmtheorie* (Berlin: Potemkin Press, 1996), 109–23.
14   Sergei M. Eisenstein, work journal, 13 January 1927, quoted in *Glass House*, 69.
15   See Mikhail Razulevich's book cover for D. Mikhailov, *Novy gorod* (Moscow: OGIZ, 1931).
16   Sergei M. Eisenstein, work journal, 29 June 1930, quoted in *Glass House*, 79.
17   Antonio Somaini, "Utopies et dystopies de la transparence: Eisenstein, Glass House, et le cinématisme de l'architecture de verre," *Appareil* [online], no. 7 (2011): http://journals.openedition.org/appareil/1234 [accessed 2 September 2019]; id., *La Glass House de Serguei Eisenstein: cinématisme et architecture de verre* (Paris: B2, 2017); Mikhail Iampolskii, "Mifologia stekla v novoevropeiskoi kulture," *Sovetskoe isskustvoznanie*, no. 24 (1988): 314–47.

chaotic hatred, misdemeanours, abuses, and catastrophes. Passions will run high until the house shatters into a million pieces." Eisenstein meant to contrast the "ideal village commune" to this glass house that ends up destroying itself. The fragile material is also, when smooth, a pure "nightmare," the symbol of the "coldness of objects," except for a pool located at the centre of the building, above a "dining room with *girls* diving and swimming on the ceiling," in an inverted take on American musicals. A "black, metallic elevator" would have circulated in the glass prism of the "transparent house," with "dark lights like all-seeing eyes," like "a fishbone or a key in a pocket seen on an x-ray."[18]

As he came into contact with America, the screenplay became more intricate, with the added characters of a poet and a robot—or "artificial man"—who plays a "human role (he is the only being to express something human, with his mechanical gestures)" and who ultimately destroys the glass house. Besides positioning itself in the Soviet discussion on art and architecture, the film also served as a critique of technology, surveillance, and social control in America, despite the explicit reference to Russia. According to film historian Naum Kleiman, its depiction of the United States represented humanity in general, from the fundamental viewpoint of European Americanism[19]. Beyond America itself, Eisenstein was attempting to undermine its representations, namely in films[20]. Paramount's hesitation drove him to abandon the project. Having befriended Upton Sinclair, which allowed him to extend his stay in the United States, he began filming one of the writer's pictures in Mexico. However, the director was not in charge of the final cut, and Sinclair kept the film reels[21]. Eisenstein returned to the USSR upon an order from Stalin, who threatened to consider him a "deserter" if he remained abroad any longer.

In the economy of film production, Soviet pictures were dominating the market since the end of the 1920s, though they were produced at a slow rate. The seasoned Bolshevik Boris Shumiatskii, president of Soiuzkino—the State Committee for Cinema—and later head of the General Directorate of the Film and Photo Industry between 1930 and 1937, who was extremely hostile to Lev Kuleshov and Eisenstein, was interested in Western methods used to boost an idle production[22]. In 1935, he led an investigative trip to Paris, London, Berlin, and Hollywood, with the filmmaker Fridrikh Ermler, the cameraman Vladimir Nilsen, and the sound engineer Aleksandr Shorin. They met filmmakers like Frank Capra and Rouben Mamoulian, and the émigrés Georg W. Pabst and Erich von Stroheim[23]. Ermler and Shumiatskii also held the compulsory photo opportunity with Charlie Chaplin, a meeting recounted in the *Pravda*[24].

Upon his return, Shumiatskii wrote an extremely detailed report on American film production, describing studios, post-editing techniques, and theatre distribution. He focused on the cartoons produced in Disney's studios

18   Sergei M. Eisenstein, notes on the *Glass House* project, 26.
19   Naum I. Kleiman, "Stekliannyi dom S. M. Eisensteina: k istori zamysla," *Iskusstvo kino*, no. 3 (1979): 94.
20   Julia Vaingurt, *Wonderlands of the Avant-garde: Technology and the Arts in Russia of the 1920s* (Evanston: Northwestern University Press, 2013), 217.
21   Harry M. Geduld and Ronald Gottesman, *Sergei Eisenstein and Upton Sinclair: The Making and Unmaking of Que Viva Mexico!* (Bloomington: Indiana University Press, 1970).
22   Boris F. Bagaev, *Boris Shumiatskii: ocherk zhizni i deiatelnosti* (Krasnoiarsk: Kn. Izd-vo, 1974), 200–1; Richard Taylor, "Ideology as Mass Entertainment: Boris Shumyatsky and Soviet Cinema in the 1930s," in *Inside the Film Factory*, Richard Taylor and Ian Christie, eds. (London: Routledge, 1991), 193–216.
23   Echos of this trip appear in *Kino*, 17 July 1935, 1 and *Kino*, 23 July 1935, 1; see Taylor, "Ideology as Mass Entertainment," 213 and note 96.
24   Boris Z. Shumiatskii, "U Charli Chaplina," *Pravda*, 20 and 21 August 1935.

А. РОЗЕНБАУМ

ГОЛЛИВУД
АМЕРИКАНСКИЙ КИНО-ГОРОД

Изд-во КИНОПЕЧАТЬ

and the first uses of colour, noting that a single Hollywood studio produced more than the total Soviet output. To reach the goal of releasing 800 films a year, attainable only with on-location shooting, Shumiatskii stressed "the necessity of building a single film centre in the southern, sunniest part of the Soviet Union, close to the sea and the mountains, in short, a productive *kino-gorod* [film city]."[25] He quickly began fulfilling the already existing idea of a "southern base" on the shores of the Black Sea. Its first description, published in 1936, was illustrated by multiple aerial and terrestrial views of Hollywood. These facilities had already been presented to the Russian public as a *kino-gorod* by Alisa Rozenbaum, aka Ayn Rand, in a book published in 1926, before she emigrated to the United States[26] [ill. p. 283]. The complex was developed with support from the People's Commissar of Heavy Industry Sergo Ordzhonikidze, and was similar to the industrial giants developed in the beginning of the decade. Owing to a favourable context, the premises were meant to contain four studios operating simultaneously[27]. The proposed working method would have borrowed from the American model, which was apparent in the use of the term *produsery*, a transposition of Hollywood's producers. Shumiatskii commended this approach in his report, which he presented at the end of 1935 at a national filmmakers meeting[28]. It was illustrated with images from Hollywood and detailed the project's goals and timeline. An economic trust was then formed, and detailed studies were conducted in 1936, with the contribution of the engineer Pavel Rotert and Moisei Ginzburg, then in charge of developing the landscape plan for the southern coast of Crimea. These studies resulted in the choice of a site in Laspi, near Sebastopol, on a bluff overlooking the Black Sea, whose economical and technical details were thoroughly examined, including potential anti-aircraft defence[29]. The plan called for a city centred on a rectangular square, flanked by a culture and leisure park, located at a significant distance from the studios, and designed to house some 12,000 film workers as of 1940 [ill. p. 286].

Stalin being a movie enthusiast, the project received his explicit approval [30]. In a meeting recounted by Shumiatskii, he declared: "Of course we need a city. Its detractors are incredibly short-sighted. Can our cinema be based on dwarf-sized headquarters?" His counterpart replied that he had "identified the conditions required for the location and the grounds: maximum sunlight, limited rainfall, the sea, mountains, a plateau, a mild climate, without sudden shifts."[31] In July 1936, Shumiatskii informed Viacheslav Molotov that he had completed a report that had called for a lengthy correspondence with Hollywood and European filmmakers[32]. But the project was not as successful as the Roman Cinecittà, also Hollywood-inspired, inaugurated by Benito Mussolini in April 1937. Those who opposed the highly ambitious endeavour insisted on its extravagant cost, despite the expected economies of scale, and Stalin grew tired of it. Strongly criticized by the press in 1937, the *kino-gorod* project on the Black Sea turned into a modest filming base in the south of the USSR. Shumiatskii and Nilsen were executed the following year.

In addition to technical and economic issues, Shumiatskii was engaged in a campaign against intellectual cinema. He contrasted its concern with montage with the importance of storytelling and political relevance and insisted on unearthing Soviet stars that would be as hostile to elitist films as the Hollywood kingpins. He condemned Eisenstein's circle and prevented him from finishing his picture *Bezhin Meadow*, after compelling him to change the screenplay. In his programmatic 1935 book *A Cinema for the Millions*, Shumiatskii claimed that "the victorious class wishes to laugh with joy. It is quite justified in this desire, and Soviet cinema must provide its audiences with joyous Soviet laughter."[33] The best example of such productions is Grigorii Aleksandrov's 1934 musical *Jolly Fellows*, one of the greatest and most durable successes of Soviet cinema, instigated by Shumiatskii. It features the adventures of the shepherd Kostia Potekhin, who travels from his village to an extravagant finale set in Moscow, where an orchestra fills the streets and leads up to the stage of the Bolshoi. Off-screen, the real jazz orchestra was that of Lazar Vaisbain, aka Leonid Utesov, whose revue *The Music Store* served as the movie's soundtrack[34] [ill. p. 287].

In *Jolly Fellows*, Aleksandrov used his direct knowledge of Hollywood, beginning with his discovery of Walt Disney films. He had composed a *kartoteka*, a card catalogue filing system where he gathered his notes on various cinematographic effects, namely gags, which had caught his attention in the United States. In his memoir, he makes no secret of these sources, declaring Mickey Mouse to be his "favourite hero": "The Disney method of filming was of great interest to us. The famous cartoonist began with the phonogram. The carefully prepared phonogram became, as it were, the carcass of the film. In the Disney studios, we discovered that sound pictures required a director with a rich musical culture and an ability for composition."[35] The opening scene of the film, where Potekhin uses any object he can find to play music, was directly copied from *Steamboat Willie*, Disney's first sound cartoon. The film was determinant in establishing the career of Liubov Orlova, Aleksandrov's wife, the first star who could make the Russian public forget about Mary Pickford[36]. The movie was promoted with an advertisement campaign inspired by those Aleksandrov had seen in Hollywood.

Aleksandrov's following film was even more explicit in its ties to America. In the 1936 feature *Circus*, Orlova plays Marian Dixon, an American acrobat who flees to Russia with Jimmy, the child she had with a Black man, causing a widespread scandal. Despite those who conspire against her and try to sabotage her, she is met with warm welcome, and the picture ends with a choir of all the Soviet nationalities surrounding her. The first screenplay was written by the satirists Ilia Ilf and Evgenii Petrov, who would later distance themselves from its staging after their visit to the United States, which will be discussed further on. In 1938, Orlova starred in *Volga-Volga*, another of Aleksandrov's great hits. In 1940, in *Tania* (or *The Radiant Path*), she played a housekeeper, Tania Morozova, who became a Stakhanovist labourer, and later an engineer and a deputy of the Supreme Soviet[37]. In a fairy-tale-like ending, her trajectory leads her to fly across Moscow in a GAZ 11-40 cabriolet taking her to the Agricultural Fair,

25   GUKF pri SNK SSSR, *Doklad komissii B. Z. Shumiatskogo po izucheniiu tekhniki i organizatsii amerikanskoi i evropeiskoi kinematografii* (Moscow: Kinofotoizdat, 1935), 150.
26   Alissa Rozenbaum aka Ayn Rand, *Gollivud, amerikanskii kino-gorod*, preface by B. Filippov (Moscow: Izd-vo Kinopechat, 1926). The future novelist's first book also dealt with cinema: *Pola Negri* (Moscow: Kino-Izd-vo RSFSR, 1925).
27   SNK SSSR, VKI, *Iuzhnaia baza sovetskoi kinematografii (Kinogorod)* (Moscow: Tip Iz-va. Der Emes, 1936).
28   Boris Z. Shumiatskii, *Sovetskaia kinematografia segodnia i zavtra* (Moscow: Kinofotoizdat, 1936), 49.
29   SNK SSSR, VKI, *Osnovnye polozheniia planovogo zadaniia po iuzhnoi baze sovetskoi kinematografii (Kinogorod)* (Moscow: Tip. Iskra Revoliutsii, 1936).
30   On Stalin's reception of the movies and his policies, see: Grigori B. Mariamov, *Kremlevskii tsenzor: Stalin smotrit kino* (Moscow: Kinotsentr, 1992).
31   Shumiatskii's notes following a conversation with Stalin and Molotov, 25 December 1935, in Kirill M. Anderson, ed., *Kremlevskii kinoteatr. 1928–195. Dokumenty* (Moscow: Rosspen, 2005), 1032.
32   Boris Z. Shumiatskii, note to Viacheslav Molotov, 15 July 1936, in Anderson, *Kremlevskii kinoteatr*, 327.
33   Boris Z. Shumiatskii, *Kinematografiia millionov* (Moscow: Kinofotoizdat, 1935), 249.
34   Rimgaila Salys, *The Musical Comedy Films of Grigori Aleksandrov: Laughing Matters* (Bristol; Chicago: Intellect, 2009), 24.
35   Aleksandrov, *Epokha i kino*, 131.
36   For more on the couple, see Mark Kushnirov, *Svetly put, ili Charli i Spencer* (Moscow: Terra Knizhnyi Klub, 1998).
37   Maria Enzensberger, "'We were born to turn a fairy tale into reality': Grigori Alexandrov's *The Radiant Path*," in *Stalinism and Soviet Cinema*, Richard Taylor and Derek Spring, eds. (London: Routledge, 1993), 97–108.

View of Fox Studios in Century City, CA, in Boris Z. Shumiatskii, *Soviet Cinematography Today and Tomorrow*,
Moscow: Kinofotoizdat, 1936. Private collection.

Постоянная натурная декорация „Фоксфильм"

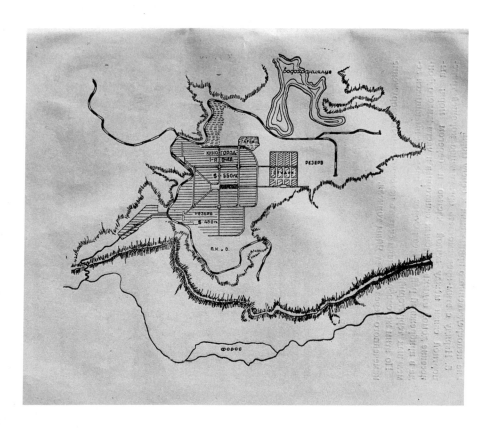

Moisei Ia. Ginzburg. General plan for the southern base of cinema production, 1936,
in *The Southern Base of Cinema Production*, Moscow: Tip. Izd-va Ter Emes, 1936. Private collection.

Boris A. Zelenskii. Poster of the film *Circus* by Grigorii Alexandrov, produced by Mosfilm, 1936.
Lithographic print on paper, 43 × 33.7 cm. Alamy.

set in an environment inspired by Boris Iofan's Palace of the Soviets, then in construction. These picturesque finales are reminiscent of the crowd scenes featured in grandiose settings on Broadway stages and Hollywood sets.

With their synchronized movements, the musicals produced in American theatres and studios were also a source of inspiration for the great parades organized to celebrate the regime. On the first of May or on the anniversary of the Revolution, soldiers, athletes, and artists marched by the official tribunes, in a Soviet rendition of the mass ornament as described by Siegfried Kracauer[38]. One of the main stages was, of course, the Red Square, where successive tableaux, sometimes perched on trucks, were reminiscent of Broadway's revolving stages[39]. Come nightfall, the place was lit up by five red stars on the Kremlin's towers. Between 1935 and 1937, the towers replaced the empire's double-headed eagles and introduced the theme of illuminated spires to Moscow, following the example of the Chrysler Building[40].

Soviet Swing

Shumatskii's proposed title for Jolly Fellows, Jazz-Comedy, speaks to the immense popularity of the musical genre in the USSR. After the early stages in the Russian discovery of jazz at the beginning of the century, it had reached the Soviet NEP through Germany, namely when Sam Wooding's orchestra performed in Moscow in 1926, in addition to its Berlin tour, following Sidney Bechet and Frank Whiters, who had also both toured Russia a few months earlier. The Stenberg brothers designed a memorable poster for Wooding's staging of Chocolate Kiddies, scored by Duke Ellington and presented under the title Negro-Operetta at the Moscow State Circus. These imported shows competed with performances by Aleksandr Tsfasman's Moscow orchestra as well as Leopold Teplitskii's Leningrad ensemble, both created in 1927[41]. The previous year, Teplitskii was sent on a mission to the United States by the People's Commissariat for Education, to study silent film scores, and had been delighted by Paul Whiteman's orchestra. At the same time, Leonid Utesov, already famous for his contributions to many films, discovered Jack Hilton's and Ted Lewis's ensembles while travelling in Paris. Upon his return, Utesov created his first orchestra, Tea-Jazz, and went on to dominate the Soviet screens and stages[42].

These imported rhythms, which Maxim Gorky labelled as "music for thugs" in a 1928 article[43], were far from unanimously appreciated among Soviet leaders, and fiery controversies surrounded them in the press. In the Communist Party's daily Pravda, Shumiatskii rejected the criticism expressed in 1936 in Izvestia, the government's daily. Attacks targeted, among others, jazz orchestras comprised of American Marines dressed in uniform. Platon Kerzhentsev, the former leader of the League of Time, who had become the

38   Siegfried Kracauer, The Mass Ornament: Weimar Essays [1963], transl., ed., and with an introduction, by Thomas Y. Levin (Cambridge, MA: Harvard University Press, 1995).
39   See Richard Stites, "The Origins of Soviet Ritual Style: Symbol and Festival in the Russian Revolution," in Lars Erik Blomqvist, Claes Arvidsson, Symbols of Power: The Esthetics of Political Legitimation in the Soviet Union and Eastern Europe (Stockholm: Almqvist & Wiksell International, 1987), 23-42.
40   The red stars on the Kremlin towers were a highlight. See Julia Bekman Chagada, "Light in Captivity: Spectacular Glass and Soviet Power in the 1920s and 1930s," Slavic Review 66, no. 1 (Spring 2007): 82-105.
41   Aleksei N. Batashev, Sovetskii dzhaz: istoricheskii ocherk (Moscow: Muzyka, 1972), 25-43.
42   On his trip to Paris, see Leonid O. Utesov [1976], Spasibo, serdtse! Vospominania, vstrechi, razdumia (Moscow: Tsentrpoligraf, 2016), 187-88.
43   Maxim Gorky, "O muzyke tolstykh," Pravda, 18 April 1928.

president of the State Committee for Artistic Affairs was vehemently opposed to the avant-gardes. He strongly criticized the decadent aspects of jazz, but refrained from issuing a global condemnation[44]. Following Stalin's horrified reaction, the *Pravda* also denounced Dmitrii Shostakovich's opera *Lady Macbeth of the Mtsensk District*, staged in Moscow and in Leningrad in 1934. Its score was deemed an example of "Meyerholdism": "Dissonant, confused stream of sounds [...] copying its nervy, convulsive, epileptic music from jazz as to give 'passion' to its heroes. [...] The music shouts, quacks, explodes, pants, and sighs, so as to convey the love scenes in the most naturalistic manner."[45] These violent attacks against Shostakovich notwithstanding, Sovietized jazz was widely disseminated on the screen and on the radio until the war. As for more "serious" music, Sergei Prokofiev's ballet *Romeo and Juliet*, written in 1934 upon the composer's return to the USSR, received a chilly welcome from Leningrad and Moscow dancers because of its complexity. The machinist inspiration, stemming from Prokofiev's American experience, is tangible in the composition. While he was not allowed to stage his ballet in Russia until 1940, the composer presented it in Chicago as part of his last American tour. He returned to Moscow in 1937 with a Ford automobile, in a rare case of an individual owning a vehicle, a material tribute to his relationship with the American industry.

Towards a Realistic Amerikanizm

The events surrounding film policy were among the many ways in which socialist realism was imposed onto all artistic disciplines. The final conquest of the doctrine came with the "reconstruction" of artistic associations in 1932, followed by the inaugural writers' congress in 1934 and the First Congress of architects in 1937. In the architectural field, longstanding conflicts between constructivists and rationalists became obsolete when the Party, upon request from the young Vkhutemas graduates, put an end to the debate and established a clear line of conduct. This form of centralized control resulted in the creation of the Union of Soviet Architects. However, the union maintained a certain pluralism for a time[46]. The constructivist journal *Sovremennaia arkhitektura* (Contemporary Architecture) published its last issue in 1930, as Nikolai Miliutin created and headed *Sovetskaia arkhitektura* (Soviet Architecture), which was replaced in its turn in 1933 by the new official publication of the Union, *Arkhitektura SSSR* (Architecture of the USSR). The realistic turn of Soviet cultural production, far from abating the general interest for America, opened a new phase of *Amerikanizm*, characterized by a reframing of publications and its themes, but also by a certain intensification of Russian architects'

44   A. Berlin and A. Brun, "Dzhaz ili simfonia," *Izvestiia*, 21 November 1936; Boris Z. Shumiatskii, "Protiv khandzhei i spiatok," *Pravda*, 24 November 1936; Platon M. Kerzhentsev, "O muzike," *Pravda*, 4 December 1936. On this controversy, see S. Frederick Starr, *Red & Hot: The Fate of Jazz in the Soviet Union 1917–1980* [1983] (New York: Limelight Editions, 1994), 164–69.

45   Anon., "Sumbura vmesto muziky," *Pravda*, 28 January 1936. This unsigned editorial has been attributed to Andrei Zhdanov: Fitzpatrick, *The Cultural Front*, 187–88.

46   The principal analyses of this shift can be found in Hugh D. Hudson, Jr., *Blueprints and Blood, the Stalinization of Soviet Architecture* (Princeton: Princeton University Press, 1994); Danilo Udovički-Selb, "Between Modernism and Socialist Realism: Soviet Architectural Culture Under Stalin's Revolution From Above, 1928–1938", *Journal of the Society of Architectural Historians* 68, n° 4 (December 2009), 466–95; and *Soviet Architectural Avant-Gardes: Architecture and Stalin's Revolution from Above, 1928–1938* (London: Bloomsbury, 2020).

The Rockefeller Center in New York, cover of *Architecture Abroad* 2, no. 2, 1935. CCA, W.A7937.

The skyline of New York as seen from the East River, cover of *Architecture Abroad* 3, no. 5, 1936. CCA, W.A7937.

direct ties to the United States. New heroes appeared or were referenced more often, as they provided breeding ground for the Party line.

In these circumstances, American voices were sometimes invited to join peculiar choirs. For instance, in 1933, *Arkhitektura SSSR* published an article by Paul Philippe Cret, an eminent professor at the University of Pennsylvania, who taught a composition method adapted from a modernized Beaux-Arts tradition and was the chief architect for the international exposition *A Century of Progress*, on display in Chicago the same year. The newly minted journal seized the opportunity to claim that Nazis were not the only ones to criticize "constructivist" and "functionalist" architecture, and that similar ideas were put forth in a democratic nation like the United States. But the authors of the editorial did not hide their perplexity regarding Cret's "new classicism," associating it with typically capitalistic "neoclassical imitations."[47] In addition to the writings of this journal, whose scope narrowed in the second half of the 1930s, *Arkhitektura za rubezhom* (Architecture Abroad) dedicated a large portion of its articles to America between 1934 and 1937, and two of its front covers featured images of the Rockefeller Center and the Midtown Manhattan landscape[48] [ill. p. 291].

The executives who had once lived in the United States reported on their experience, like Petr Bogdanov, who returned to Moscow after being at the helm of Amtorg from 1930 to 1934 and recounted his observations from the company offices: "From my office window on the seventeenth floor of one of the skyscrapers along Fifth Avenue I was able to observe the daily construction of the biggest building in the world—the Empire State. Every day at specified hours, trucks brought separate metal structures that had been previously bolted together. A simplified derrick picked them up and raised them to the required height. The building grounds were never cluttered up, and the construction in no way interfered with the stream of pedestrians on the sidewalk."[49] Bogdanov's remarks focused on construction site organization rather than architecture, as though only technical lessons remained to be learned from the United States. In keeping with this attitude, Buckminster Fuller's Structural Studies Associates were met with indifference by the Soviets when they offered them a collapsible scientific shelter, a structure made of cover fabric and a pillar strapped with cables[50].

Iofan's Palace of the Soviets and the American Experience

Along with the political reform of professional practices, the regime's architectural turn coincided with the events surrounding the competition for the Palace of the Soviets, organized between 1930 and 1934, and with the evolution of the winning project until 1941. During this long process, American expertise was

47   "O state P. F. Cret," *Arkhitektura SSSR* 1, no. 5 (November 1933): 49. This was followed by the article "Desiat let novoi arkhitektury," 51–52; originally: "Ten Years of Modernism," *Architectural Forum* 59, no. 2 (August 1933): 91–94.
48   *Arkhitektura za rubezhom* 2, no. 2, 1935 [Rockefeller Center] and 3, no. 5, 1936 [Midtown Manhattan].
49   Petr A. Bogdanov, quoted in "As Others See Us: A Russian on American Efficiency," *The Living Age*, September 1935, 88.
50   "Scientific Shelter for USSR," *Shelter* 2, no. 5 (November 1932): 94–95.
51   David E. Arkin, "Dvorets Sovetov – proletarskaia vyshka, sintezuiushchie vyrazhenie sovetskoiarkhitektury," *Sovetskoe iskusstvo*, 23 July 1931, 2.
52   "Programma proektirovaniia Dvortsa Sovetov SSSR v Moskve," in *Dvorets Sovetov*, no. 2–3 (October 1931) 123ff.
53   Selim O. Khan-Magomedov, "K istori vybora mesta dlia Dvortsa Sovetov," *Arkhitektura i stroitelstvo Moskvy*, no. 11 (1988): 21–23.
54   Yuri Slezkine, *The House of Government: a Saga of the Russian Revolution* (Princeton: Princeton University Press, 2017).

continually sought out. After the end of the Civil War, the idea of erecting a monument in the centre of Moscow to celebrate the city's recovered status as capital and to symbolize the new State had begun to take shape. Its first embodiment was the unfinished Palace of Labour project. A Palace of the Soviets was then imagined in 1928 as a "crowning" of the five-year plan, and was initially labelled a "proletarskaia vyshka" (proletarian tower)[51]. The plan, whose scope varied incessantly, contained no specifications concerning the structure of the tower, though it mentioned two halls, containing respectively 15,000 and 5,900 seats, intended for the regime's large assemblies[52]. After considering several proposals that required the demolition of many dwellings, the authorities settled on destroying the Cathedral of Christ the Saviour, built in commemoration of the Russian victory over Napoleon, on the banks of the Moskva River[53]. It was dynamited in December 1931.

As such an operation required a qualified architect, a four-phase competition was organized by the USDS—the Directorate for the Construction of the Palace of the Soviets, an operational entity created in 1931 by a political committee that was presided by Viacheslav Molotov since 1928. Its chief architect was Boris Iofan, who had studied in Italy, where he befriended Aleksei Rykov, the president of the Council of People's Commissars of the Soviet Union, in 1924. Thanks to this privileged connection, as Iofan was building a gigantic House of Government in front of the Kremlin, destined to house the State's elites across 500 apartments, the leaders trusted him[54]. He was subordinated to the head of the project, the party executive Vasilii Mikhailov, who had demonstrated his own abilities during the Dneprostroi, and was also in charge of completing the House of Government.

Деталь башни
Дворца Советов
Проект
архитектора
Б. М. Иофана

Фото
М. Ярнуш

Boris M. Iofan. First project for the Palace of the Soviets, 1931. Illustration in *Soviet Art*, 23 July 1931. Private collection.

Appointed as Mikhailov's assistant, chief architect, and head of construction all at once, Iofan was also in charge of organizing the competitions[55]. A closed preliminary phase, restricted to Russian teams, was established in February 1931. Fifteen projects, including 12 by architects invited by the USDS, were submitted five months later, and were evaluated by a technical commission presided by the electrical engineer and economist Gleb Krzhizhanovskii. Interpreting the request for a tower in the literal sense, Iofan designed a skyscraper with setbacks, similar to those prescribed by the 1916 New York zoning regulation[56] [ill. p. 293]. At his suggestion, an international competition was launched in July 1931, whose deadline, initially set for 20 October, was postponed to 1 December, most likely to encourage American participation. After the competitions for the Chicago Tribune in 1922 and the League of Nations in 1927, which had held the Russians at bay, and after the rather hypothetical one launched in 1929 for the Christopher Columbus monument, the Palace of the Soviets carried high political and symbolic stakes: the idea was to gather the best global experts, especially American ones. In total, 160 proposals were submitted by the end of the year, including 24 from abroad. One hundred and twelve others came from workers' collectives[57]. These projects were widely circulated and have since been largely discussed, but the significant American input has not yet received the attention it deserves[58].

American participation was no coincidence, as the nation's expertise in the construction of large venues was considered exceptional and unparalleled in Russia; the Udarnik cinema, located in Iofan's House of Government, had no more than 2,000 seats, as did the Bolshoi Theatre. The first administrator of the USDS, Mikhail Kriukov, recalled Albert Kahn's advice, who had suggested that he send his executives to meet with American experts[59]. Amtorg, called upon to recruit participants, asked the American Institute of Architects for the names of "five well-known architects, men in whom you have great confidence, to whom we might entrust the designing of the Palace of the Soviets," specifying that they would not be part of the competition[60]. Robert D. Kohn, the president of the Institute, submitted two lists. The first included six architects "whose tendency in design is classic," who created government buildings in Washington, among whom were Delano & Aldrich, John Russell Pope, and Zantziger, Borie and Medary. The second listed nine men who were "more modern in their tendencies" and created "more or less progressive designs," such as Raymond Hood, Howe and Lescaze, Ely Jacques Kahn, Albert Kahn, Richard Neutra, and Shreve, Lamb & Harmon[61]. Ultimately, Amtorg did not invite any of these firms and turned to the theatre specialists Joseph Urban and Thomas W. Lamb, recruited along with the

55   Transcript of a Council session on the construction of the Palace of the Soviets [meeting chaired by Klim E. Voroshilov], 5 February 1931, OKhaD, f. 694, op. 1, d. 3, l. 66–67.

56   There is a mediocre reproduction of the project in Sovetskoe iskusstvo, 23 July 1931, 2.

57   Peter Lizon, The Palace of the Soviets: The Paradigm of Architecture in the USSR (Colorado Springs: Three Continents Press, 1995); Karine N. Ter-Akopyan, "The Design and Construction of the Palace of the Soviets of the USSR in Moscow," in Jörn Merkert, Vladimir A. Rezvin et al., Naum Gabo and the Competition for the Palace of Soviets Moscow 1931–1933 (Berlin: Berlinische Galerie, 1992), 185–96; Helen Adkins, "International Participation in the Competition for the Palace of Soviets," Ibid., 197–201; Yuya Suzuki, "Konkurs na dvorets Sovetov 1930-kh gg. v Moskve i mezhdunarodnyi arkhitekturnyi kontekst," PhD dissertation (Moscow: Gosudarstvennyi Institut Istorii Iskusstv, 2014).

58   The remarkable work of Virginia Corbin Brown is an exception: "The American Contribution to the Palace of the Soviets," MA thesis (Charlottesville: University of Virginia, 1996).

59   Mikhail V. Kriukov, Letter to Avel S. Enukidze, 16 September 1931, GARF, f. R-3316, op. 64, d. 564, l. 65.

60   P.E. Nikitin [representative of the USSR construction industry], Letter to the American Institute of Architects, 11 September 1931, AIA Archives, Washington, DC, quoted in Brown, The American Contribution, 31.

61   Robert D. Kohn [AIA], Letter to P.E. Nikitin, 15 September 1931, AIA Archives, Washington, DC, quoted in Brown, The American Contribution, 32–33.

Joseph Urban. Project for the Palace of the Soviets, 1932. View of the Great Hall with demonstration. Graphite, watercolour, coloured ink and spray paint on paper, 74 × 64 cm. Joseph Urban Papers, Butler Library, Rare Book & Manuscript Library, Columbia University.

Thomas W. Lamb. Competition project for the Palace of the Soviets, 1932. General view from the Moskva River. Graphite and watercolour on paper, 54 × 102 cm. Shchusev State Museum of Architecture.

Percival Goodman. Competition project for the Palace of the Soviets, 1932. Plan and axonometries. Gelatin silver print on paper, 75 × 56.5 cm. Percival Goodman Architectural Records and Papers, Avery Architectural & Fine Arts Library, Columbia University.

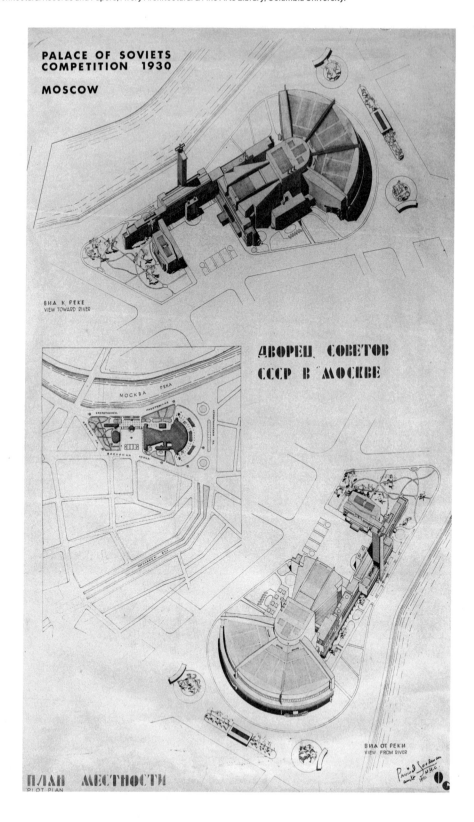

Europeans Armando Brasini, whom Iofan had met in Rome, Walter Gropius, Le Corbusier, Erich Mendelsohn, Auguste Perret, and Hans Poelzig. The fact that the two New Yorkers were explicitly asked to apply American standards of construction goes to show that their contribution was viewed mostly as that of technical experts[62]. In addition to them, several other firms sent their designs.

After the verdict was made public on 28 February 1932, the American presence was overall palpable. The invited projects received honourable mentions. Lamb gathered the halls in a compact and withdrawn volume [ill. p. 295]. Thomas E. Hibben's heavy façades and pyramidal cladding were reminiscent of the Milano Centrale railway station, then recently completed. In contrast to these massive proposals, Urban drew a scattered composition, dominated by the quarter cylinder of the great hall, complete with mobile stages, and whose precise technical devices were developed with New York firms serving as consultants. His work was based on experience acquired since 1915 on Broadway, as a scenographer for all the Ziegfeld Follies theatrical revues[63]. Despite Urban's efforts of expressing symbolism by including the colour red in the hall—with a perspective showing a parade with flags floating in the wind—, his project was deemed too "utilitarian," resembling "an industrial exhibition building," and therefore inadmissible[64] [ill. p. 295]. The other proposals were more imaginative and experimental. Drawing on the motto "The Ship of State," the Russian émigré Nikolai Vasilev drew two aerodynamic volumes resembling giant beetles, interacting by way of a slender tower[65]. An avid admirer of Le Corbusier and politically in favour of the Soviet Union, Percival Goodman connected the two halls with a long spine, reminiscent of his hero's project for the League of Nations as well as of one of his sketches for the Palace. He used ramps for the main pathways, in a nod to the Centrosoyuz Building[66]. Following the competition, Percival Goodman sent to Moscow a project for a "Palace of Music" as a "gift to the Soviet Union[67]."

Alfred Kastner and Oscar Stonorov, radical moderns who had recently immigrated from Europe and had developed a joint project for the Kharkov Theatre competition in 1931, obtained a second prize for a pile of cascading volumes assembled by cables [ill. p. 298-299]. Grigorii Barkhin praised their "scientific and technical analysis of all the questions raised by this grandiose building." Skeptical regarding the use of escalators to access the great hall, he deplored that the "industrial nature" of the project prevailed over its "artistic form," while applauding the quality of the rendering of its façades, designed by master perspectivist Hugh Ferriss[68]. Simon Breines, a 26-year-old New Yorker, proposed a hall with details reminiscent of Le Corbusier's work, coupled with a cylinder covered with a bicycle-wheel roof[69]. As a member of Fuller's

62 P.E. Nikitin, Letter to Joseph Urban, 31 October 1931, Joseph Urban Collection, Butler Library, Columbia University, quoted in Brown, *The American Contribution*, 38.
63 See the drawings held in the Joseph Urban Collection, Butler Library, Columbia University
64 "Critic Russ"[sic], 1932, Joseph Urban Collection, quoted in Brown, *The American Contribution*, 47.
65 Vladimir G. Lisovskii and Richard Gachot, *Nikolai Vasilev, ot moderna k modernizmu* (Saint Petersburg: Kolo, 2011), 351–55.
66 Percival Goodman, "General Observations," undated text [1931], Percival Goodman Collection, Avery Library, quoted in Brown, *The American Contribution*, 51–53.
67 Albert Coates, "Postroika dvortsa muzyki v Moskve" and Percival Goodman, "Proekt dvortsa muzyki," *Amerikanskaia tekhnika i promyshlennost* 9, no. 10 (1932): 577–80.
68 Grigorii B. Barkhin, "Innostrannye arkhitektory na konkurse dvortsa Sovetov," in Soyuz Sovetskikh Arkhitektorov, *Dvorets Sovetov, vsesoyuznyi konkurs 1932 g.* (Moscow: Izd-vo Vsekokhudozhnika, 1932), 85–86.
69 Brown, *The American Contribution*, 55–57. Kept in the collection of Moscow's Museum of Achitecture, the projects of Kastner and Stonorov, Urban, Vasilev and Hamilton are reproduced in Merkert and Rezvin, *Naum Gabo*, 128–35.

Oscar Stonorov and Alfred Kastner. Competition project for the Palace of the Soviets, 1932. Perspectives from the Moskva River and the Kremlin. Drawings by Hugh Ferriss. Graphite, watercolour and spray on paper, 70.1 × 126.7 cm. Shchusev State Museum of Architecture.

299

Simon Breines. Competition project for the Palace of the Soviets, 1932. Exploded axonometry.
Heliographic print and ink on paper, 76 × 104 cm. Shchusev State Museum of Architecture.

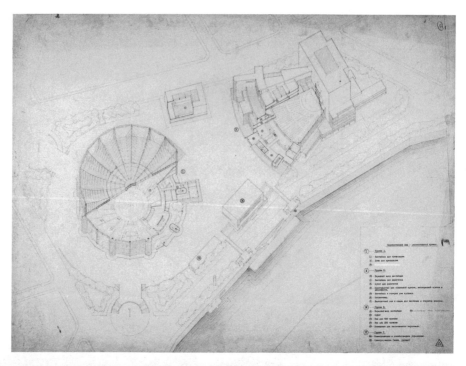

Hector Hamilton. Competition project for the Palace of the Soviets, 1932. Longitudinal elevation.
Graphite and watercolour on paper, 182 × 541 cm. Shchusev State Museum of Architecture.

Structural Study Associates, he was fond of tensile structures, and soon distanced himself from the growing propensity for "grandiosity" among the judges of the Moscow competition[70].

Indeed, on 28 February 1932, discarding all the modern submissions, the jury attributed three grand prizes to the proposal by the elegant neo-Palladian architect Ivan Zholtovskii, to Iofan, and to Hector Hamilton—a then unknown 29-year-old British architect based in New Jersey, where he had created several buildings. In the first of many pieces featuring him in *The New York Times*, his project was described as an "American skyscraper design."[71] But in an article published right before the verdict, the writer Aleksei Tolstoi claimed that making the Palace "the eighth wonder of the world" would involve rejecting "Americanism and Corbusianism," which "have found many admirers among us to this day, despite the hostile (and useless)—to us— nature of both styles." As the skyscraper was deemed "the enchanted castle of the servants of the capital," it was considered unusable for the Palace project[72].

Off the record, Barkhin was unenthused with Hamilton's design, which was difficult to understand, as it was presented without cross sections. Though the idea of establishing a train station under the Palace was ingenious, he regarded the symmetry of the scheme as "artificial" and noted that it did not account for the differences between the programme's components. As for its exterior shape, it did "not lack a certain imposing presence," but it did "not entirely meet the requirements for the building's purpose."[73] The mediocrity of Hamilton's project, who distanced himself from "modernistic"[74] forms in the press, did not justify the grand prize, nor was it warranted by any exceptional technical contribution. The fact that his rendering was submitted past the due date is further proof that Hamilton enjoyed special treatment[75]. Some have seen in Hamilton's participation and victory the proof of an intervention from Albert Kahn, who had allegedly advised the organizers of the USDS[76]. However, is it possible that the Soviet leaders had any reason to placate the Detroit architect, who in March 1932 travelled to Moscow for ultimately failed negotiations towards a third contract? Hamilton followed him shortly after, arriving to take part in the third round of the competition, from March to June 1932, after claiming to *The New York Times* that he had been named chief architect for the project and that Zholtovskii and Iofan would be his "assistants."[77] Hamilton likely made his requests public to compel the Russians and to obtain the most luxurious treatment possible. Through Amtorg, he demanded living expenses and significant wages from the USDS[78]. Mikhailov was thus

70   Simon Breines, "SSA to USSR," *Shelter* 2, no. 5 (November 1932): 84–85.
71   "Jersey Architect Wins First Soviet Palace Prize: His Skyscraper Design Shares Prize,"
        The New York Times, 1 March 1932, 5, 1.
72   Aleksei N. Tolstoi, "Poiski monumentalnosti," *Izvestiia*, 27 February 1932, reprinted in *Putechestvie v drugoi mir; zarisovki i stati* (Moscow: Gospolitizdat, 1932), 41.
73   Barkhin, "Innostrannye arkhitektory na konkurse dvortsa Sovetov," 85.
74   Hector Hamilton, statement reported in "Soviet Palace Competition," *Architectural Forum* 56, no. 3 (March 1932): A.
75   "Jersey Architect Wins First Soviet Palace Prize," *New York Times*, 1 March 1932.
76   On the American invitation, see the correspondence held at TsGAORSS, f. 694, op. 1, d. 10, l. 149;
        Ter-Akopyan, "The Design and Construction of the Palace of the Soviets of the USSR in Moscow," 291.
77   "Red Palace to Fill Site 7 Blocks Long," *The New York Times*, 13 April 1932, 40;
        reprinted in *Izvestiia*, 28 April 1932.
78   Mikhailov took care to write to Molotov to explain that Hamilton came on his own initiative: Vasilii M. Mikhailov to Viacheslav M. Molotov, 13 July 1932, TsMAM, f. 694, op. 1, d. 19, l. 301, quoted in Sona S. Hoisington, "'Ever Higher': The Evolution of the Project for the Palace of Soviets," *Slavic Review* 62, no. 1 (Spring 2003): 53.

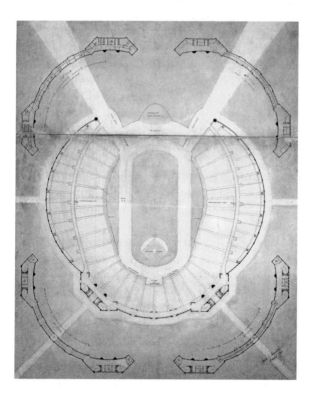

removed from the negotiations and had to ask Bogdanov, the head of Amtorg, for Hamilton's prerequisites to continue his work. Bogdanov deemed his requests unreasonable and urged Molotov to decline them[79].

Described in the Moscow press as the "main consultant," Hamilton confirmed the initial claims of *The New York Times* by placing, between both halls, a small, forty-storey office skyscraper with Art Deco details, aimed at enticing the Soviets, especially since it was meant to contain murals resembling those of the Rockefeller Center[80]. In July 1932, Hamilton asked Mikhailov for permission to continue developing his project, but his submission was erased from the official reviews of the third round[81]. Possibly to keep him busy during his visit, the organizers of the second competition for the Stalin Stadium—then projected to be built on a site in Izmailovo, on the eastern outskirts of Moscow—invited him to compete against Dmitrii Iofan, Ilia Golosov, and Nikolai Kolli, who ultimately won the bid. Hamilton drew a U-shaped arena containing a baseball field, a most exotic addition for Moscow[82]. He later boasted in *The New York Times* about what he claimed was a firm commission presaging considerable contracts for American firms. He so crudely patted himself on the back for the large sums in American dollars he received in Moscow and for the fact that "1,200 labourers were working on the foundations of the Palace" that he was derided in Fuller's journal *Shelter*[83]. Ultimately fired in November 1932, Hamilton grew resentful and vindictive, going as far as to sue Amtorg. In 1934, back in Great Britain, where he continued his work, he claimed that the Russians had stolen his ideas[84]. Knud Lonberg-Holm, a member of the Structural Studies Associates along with Breines, denounced

Hamilton's "romantic skyscraper" in *Shelter*, declaring that "the Russian desire for the feudal and static American skyscraper reveals a lack of clarity and direction."[85]

One last round was organized between August 1932 and February 1933, with the participation of Karo Alabian, the Vesnin brothers, Shchusev, in association with Zholtovskii, and Iofan. Iofan was put in charge of implementation along with the Leningrad architects Vladimir Shchuko and Vladimir Gelfreikh, who were then working on the Lenin Library in Moscow. Their vision was adopted in February 1934 and presented to the public, before serving as an inspiration for all subsequent versions. In order to stay in the race, Iofan never ceased to transform his project. He presented the tower he had submitted to the initial closed competition in a taller and slenderer version as a response to the 1931 international competition. Shchusev criticized this design, claiming it was "reminiscent of American skyscrapers, which [could] in no way contribute to embellishing the project."[86] Everything changed when Stalin became personally involved in the competition. After getting acquainted with the projects during a holiday in Sochi, he wrote in August 1932 to Kaganovich, Molotov, and Voroshilov, that "of all the plans for the 'Palace' of the Soviets, Iofan's is the best." He gave very clear guidelines for the architect: "We should (according to me) force Iofan: a) not to separate the small hall from the large one, but rather to unite them following the government's programme; b) to give shape to the top of the 'Palace' by stretching it upward with a tall column (I'm thinking of a column shaped like the one Iofan had in his first project); c) to place a sickle and hammer on top of the column, illuminated with electricity from the inside; d) if, for technical reasons, it is impossible to elevate the column above the 'Palace,' set it down near (next to) the 'Palace,' ideally making it as tall as the Eiffel Tower or a little taller; in front of the 'Palace,' place three monuments (to Marx, Engels, Lenin)"[87]. The General Secretary thus plainly expressed the wish to see the building grow as unified and as tall as possible, expressing an aim for the sublime, in what Katerina Clark interprets as a sign of both the edification and the representation of the "Fourth Rome."[88]

In something of a telescopic effect, Iofan's Palace grew progressively taller, with the configuration of the lower levels serving as a hybrid of Saint Peter's Square and the Victor Emmanuel II Monument, two Roman landmarks with which he was familiar[89]. His successive sketches reflected a process of

79   "American Asked to Be Architect of Soviet Palace," *The New York Times*, 22 March 1932, 1.

80   "400-Ft Tower Projected for Soviet Palace," *The New York Herald Tribune*, 13 April 1932.

81   Hector Hamilton, Letter to Vasilii M. Mikhailov, 20 July 1932, GARF, f. R–3316, op. 64, d. 563, l. 152–53.

82   Shchusev Museum of Architecture, drawings Rla 15 and 52. See also Eduard S. Akopian and Alisa Gorlova, "Concepts of the Central Stadium in the Architecture of the USSR 1920–1950s," in *Arkhitektura stadionov*, Eduard S. Akopian, ed. (Moscow: Kuchkovo Pole, 2018), 119–20 and 188–89.

83   "Hamilton Leaves Moscow for Home," *The New York Times*, 18 August 1932, 5; "Happy Hamy Keynotes," *Shelter* 2, no. 5 (November 1932): 79–80.

84   "USSR: American Says Soviets Stole 'Idea' for Huge Palace," *New Masses*, 17 March 1934, 15.

85   Knud Lonberg-Holm, "Monuments and Instruments," *Shelter* 2, no. 4 (May 1932): 5.

86   Aleksei V. Shchusev, "Mezdunarodnyi konkurs dvortsa sovetov," in Soyuz Sovetskikh Arkhitektorov, *Dvorets Sovetov*, 76.

87   Joseph V. Stalin, Letter to Lazar M. Kaganovich, Viacheslav M. Molotov and Klim E. Voroshilov, 7 August 1932, RGASPI, f. 81, op 3, d. 99, l. 132–37, in *Stalin i Kaganovich; perepiska. 1931–1936*, O. Khlevniuk, R. Devis, L. Koseleva, E. Ris, and L. Rogovaia, eds. (Moscow: Rosspen, 2001), 269.

88   Katerina Clark, "The Imperial Sublime," in *Moscow, the Fourth Rome: Stalinism, Cosmopolitanism and the Evolution of Soviet Culture, 1931–1941* (Cambridge, MA: MIT Press, 2011), 276–306.

89   Hoisington, "'Ever Higher'," 41–68.

Boris M. Iofan. Project for the Palace of the Soviets in Moscow, 1933. Telescopic variant with avant-corps and without monumental sculpture. Parallel projection. Graphite and ink on paper, 43 × 53 cm. Alex Lachmann Collection.

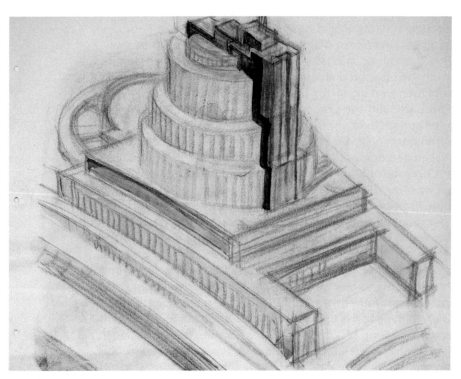

Boris M. Iofan. Project for the Palace of the Soviets in Moscow, 1933. Telescopic variant without monumental sculpture. Axial perspective. Graphite on paper, 53 × 43 cm. Alex Lachmann Collection.

Boris M. Iofan. Project for the Palace of the Soviets in Moscow, 1933. Telescopic variant with monumental sculpture. View from the Moskva River. Graphite and ink on paper, 50 × 64 cm. Alex Lachmann Collection.

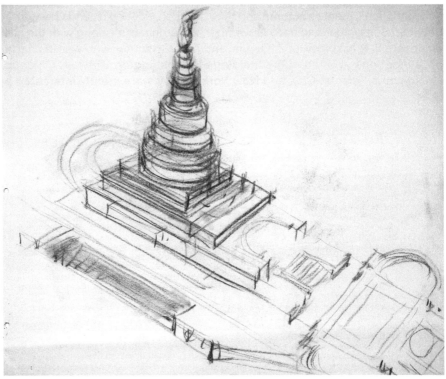

Boris M. Iofan. Project for the Palace of the Soviets in Moscow, 1933. Telescopic variant with monumental sculpture. Parallel projection. Graphite on paper, 43 × 53 cm. Alex Lachmann Collection.

verticalization, with increasingly taller cylinders superimposing themselves to the stocky figure from the winning project of the third competition, in a partial return to the 1931 proposition [ill. p. 304-305]. The "technical reasons" cautiously brought up by Stalin were dismissed, and the "column" was placed vertically over the hall. Presented as a final version, the design exposed in March 1934 at the Moscow Museum of Fine Arts, assembled three New York landmarks: a Radio City Music Hall whose capacity was almost tripled, an office skyscraper, and a statue of Lenin designed according to the principle of Auguste Bartholdi's *Liberty Enlightening the World*: a metal frame covered in thin cladding. A comparison between the Palace's skeleton structure and that of the "American skyscraper," published in 1940, exposed the device and, in doing so, demonstrated its absurdity: there was no need to be an expert in civil engineering to understand that there was excessive pressure on the foundations[90] [ill p. 313]. This parallel was depicted in numerous illustrations comparing the winning project with the Empire State Building and the Eiffel Tower.

Though American architects had been excluded from the final Palace project, acquiring construction expertise from New York remained essential. As of March 1934, Mikhailov, who understood the importance of American skills ever since his stint at the Dneprostroi, organized an investigative trip to the United States with help from the head of Amtorg, Bogdanov. The journey was generously funded thanks to the efforts of Avel Enukidze, the Kremlin's chief administrator[91], and was meant to allow the designers of the Palace to visit recent constructions and to meet with technical consultants. Accompanied by the engineer Vasilii Nikolaev, Iofan, Gelfreikh, and Shchuko were sent across the Atlantic as part of an "architectural and technical commission" to study construction sites, meet with firms, and consult compensated experts on foundations, steel structures and their erection, acoustics, and elevators[92]. Between September and early November, the architects—along with the civil engineers V. P. Nikolaev, L. Z. Osnas, and A. T. Gridunov, who was in charge of foundations—visited many buildings in Washington, Detroit, Chicago, Philadelphia, Atlantic City, and New York[93]. They were mostly interested in

90   Nikolai S. Atarov, *Dvorets Sovetov* (Moscow: Moskovskii rabochii, 1940), 85.
91   The decisions about financing the $30,000 mission, including $12,500 towards the consultants' fees, were taken at the highest level, as shown in Sovnarkom's internal memos: GARF, f. R-5446, d. 997, l. 1-15.
92   Vasilii M. Mikhailov, mission program, 28 March 1935, OKhaD, f. 694, op. 1, d. 39, l. 2.
93   The precise list is in the program: Ibid., l. 22.
94   Note to Vasilii M. Mikhailov about the mission program, 28 March 1935, Ibid., l. 16.
95   "Russia to Have World's Tallest Public Building," *The American City* 49 (December 1934): 68-69; Ralph W. Barnes, "Soviet Changes Palace Designs after Look at Skyscrapers Here," *The New York Herald Tribune*, 31 May 1935.
96   Council decision on construction of the Palace of Soviets, 29 June 1935, GARF, f. R-5446, d. 560, l. 15-16.
97   Isaac Hathaway Francis, letter to Boris M. Iofan, 29 May 1935, OKhaD, f. 694, op. 1, d. 50, l. 82.
98   On consultations with New York firms, see Viacheslav K. Oltarzhevskii, *Avtobiografia*, dactyl., 1964, MUAR, 3. On the use of trucks, see Viacheslav K. Oltarzhevskii, Letter to Boris Iofan, 2 January 1935, OKhaD, f. 694, op. 1, d. 50, l. 5-7. Iofan supports this proposition in a letter to Mikhailov on February 1st, OKhaD, f. 694, op. 1, d. 50, l. 9.
99   "Soviet Architects Hailed: New York League Entertains at Tea for Iofan and Aides," *New York Times*, 26 October 1934, 13.
100   Address of Boris Iofan, chief architect of the Palace of Soviets, at the Museum of Modern Art, 15 October 1935, MoMA Archives, REG 34d.
101   Moran & Proctor Archives (New York), project 647, 0044, quoted in Katherine E. Zubovich, "Moscow Monumental: Soviet Skyscrapers and Urban Life under High Stalinism," PhD dissertation (Berkeley: University of California, 2016), 30. On the firm's contribution, see "Huge Palace Held Feasible in Moscow: Bedrock 90 Feet Below Surface," *New York Times*, 30 May 1935, 2. On the engineer's visit, see "Proctor Back, Praises Soviet for Palace Plans," *New York Herald Tribune*, 5 July 1935, 13.
102   Sovnarkom SSSR, decision to allot $18,000 toward payment of Moran & Proctor's services, 15 September 1935, GARF, f. R-5446, d. 1186.
103   Albert Kahn, Letter to Boris M. Iofan, 16 April 1935, OKhaD f. 694, op. 1, d. 50, l. 34. Kahn puts him in contact with an expert suggested by General Electric: Albert Kahn, Letter to Iofan, 7 May 1935, OKhaD, f. 694, op. 1, d. 50, l. 54-56.

skyscrapers, such as the Empire State Building, and ensembles like the Rocke-feller Center, which Iofan tirelessly sketched in his notebook [ill. p. 308-309]. They focused more specifically on the foundations, metal structures, and cladding of high-rise buildings. To perfect the acoustics and lighting of the Palace's halls, they also investigated several theatres and cinemas, such as the Earl Carroll Theater, the Paramount, and the Roxy, which, with their 3,000, 3,600, and 6,000 seats, respectively, were akin to one of the projected halls. Following the detailed programme devised by Iofan in June 1934, they also visited the Chrysler Building and Woolworth Building, the Capitol, the Chicago Tribune, and Kahn's General Motors headquarters[94].

The six envoys "studying American architecture, methods of con-struction and city planning" did not go unnoticed by the press, which report-ed the changes made to the Palace project after their travels[95]. They were especially determined to sign an agreement with the firm Moran & Proctor, specialized in soil mechanics and foundations. Created in 1910, the office had built the George Washington Bridge in New York, and was at work on the Lincoln Tunnel and the Golden Gate Bridge in San Francisco. As a precedent for the Palace's foundations, the firm could rely on those created for the 1910 project developed by Guy Lovell for the New York County Court, which had a circular plan. It was determined in the summer of 1935 that the firm would contribute the required digging equipment, labour organization, and engi-neering[96]. Isaac Hathaway Francis, a Philadelphia expert on fluids and me-chanical systems, was also consulted[97].

Beyond the visits and negotiations that were closely related to the Palace project, the delegation met with several New York stakeholders and institutions thanks to Viacheslav Oltarzhevskii's connections. He organized consultations with engineers and continued to advise Iofan and his colleagues upon their return, specifically on New York's experience with trucking con-struction equipment to supply major sites[98]. The visitors held discussions with Oltarzhevskii's friend Harvey Wiley Corbett and with Ely Jacques Kahn, two key figures of the New York profession. The members of the commission were also invited by Ralph T. Walker, the regional president of the American Institute of Architects to visit the Architectural League[99]. On 15 October, at a reception hosted by the Museum of Modern Art, Iofan addressed the new orientations of the Soviet policy, stating that "the emphasis has been shifted from the architecture of façades to that of the mass, with fullest use of the art of site planning." In carefully chosen terms, he stated: "Our commission has come to the United States to make a study of the achievements in the field of construction in this country. What we have seen here has been of the greatest interest to us and will undoubtedly be of great help in the solu-tion of some of the problems presented by the construction of the Palace of the Soviets."[100]

Upon the delegation's return to the USSR, Carleton Proctor visited Moscow in 1935, in a rare instance of an expert travelling from west to east at that time, and signed several agreements with the USDS[101]. A note penned by Molotov approved the funding for his services on 15 September 1935[102]. Iofan went on to exchange letters with Albert Kahn, whom he had met in Detroit, to remain up to date on the latest developments in lighting system technolo-gies[103]. Different conclusions were drawn from the expeditions depending on the Soviet reader being addressed. For instance, in his official report to his commissioners, Iofan claimed that "specifically American technology is the most applicable" to the Palace of the Soviets, owing to "its pace, its approach to problem solving, to the precision of the model for carrying out work, and

in the businesses that serve construction."[104] These remarks were largely based on his visit to the Rockefeller Center site, for which he thanked John R. Todd, director of construction for the project[105]. In 1939, he once again wrote about the complex, which never ceased to fascinate him, in a *Pravda* article paraphrased by *The New York Times*[106].

To the general public, Iofan addressed his more subjective travel impressions, published in the *Pravda*. In this text, he gave a detailed description of the "gigantic streams" of automobiles in New York City, their noise and traffic, highlighting the convenience of the Holland Tunnel and Riverside Drive. However, his depiction of the subway was apocalyptic, opposing it to Moscow's underground palaces[107]. To his peers, in a 1936 issue of the Academy of Architecture's journal, he discussed "materials on American and Italian contemporary architecture", as the 1934 mission returned to Moscow by way of Rome, with which Iofan was familiar. Using photographs taken during his trip, he introduced the skyscraper, with its historical and present-day context. He commended the solution used for the Empire State Building façades, which he considered "reserved, even austere," but criticized the details and the crown of the Chrysler Building, too influenced by publicity according to him. He had high praise for the tectonics and materials employed by Howe and Lescaze for the Philadelphia Saving Fund Society (PSFS) building, though the interior of the bank looked to him like a "sanctuary of the dollar."

Interested in structures built like "small cities," Iofan took note of the merits of the Cornell Medical Center and focused mainly on the Rockefeller Center: "This group of buildings was designed by seven architects […]. As opposed to others, it was designed like a single architectural complex using the proven principles of classical architecture. Two six-storey buildings—dedicated to France and England—act as propylea. They frame the entryway to the central building, a 72-floor skyscraper, and highlight the grandiose scale of the whole operation. […] Radio City seems to be the first of the new skyscrapers to use sculpture as a way of shaping the façades. Inside, it is more interesting than the other skyscrapers, particularly in the use of painting and other cladding materials such as metal-reinforced glass."[108] To Iofan, the Rockefeller Center was an exceptional example in a capitalist city where skyscrapers were built "independently from one another." However, he declared, "in our country, the city is a grandiose ensemble comprised of wholly interdependent parts. In this context, which is fundamentally different from the setting of capitalistic cities, isolated high-rises can play an important role in shaping the skyline and highlighting the city's architecture. They can thus acquire new architectural qualities."[109] Iofan felt obligated to distinguish between the virtues of American architecture, which he attributed to its workers, whose "energy, business savvy, and practical sense" he admired, and the result of production imperatives enslaved to the capital, whose crisis also affected the architects. This was obviously not the case for him, and he was able to return to the USSR with his newly acquired Buick. His admiration for the Rockefeller

104   "Theses of the report to the Concil for the construction of the Palace of Soviets," OKhD f. 694, op. 1, d. 39, l. 3.
105   Boris Iofan, letter to John R. Todd, 22 May 1935, OKhaD, f. 694, op. 1, d. 50, l. 48.
106   "Moscow Architect Finds New York Is Depressing," *New York Times*, 12 February 1939, 33.
107   Boris M. Iofan, "Na ulitsakh gorodov Evropy i Ameriki," *Pravda*, 13 March 1935, 2.
108   Boris M. Iofan, "Materialy o sovremennoi arkhitekture SShA i Itali," *Akademia arkhitektury* 3, no. 4 (1936): 18–19.
109   Ibid., 23.

Photographs of skyscrapers collected by Boris M. Iofan in New York and brought back to Moscow in 1934.
Gelatin silver prints on paper, 27 × 20 cm. Alex Lachmann Collection.

Top across from left: Corbett, Harrison & MacMurray, Hood, Godley & Fouilhoux and Reinhard & Hofmeister.
Rockefeller Center, New York, 1930-1936; Raymond Hood and John M. Howells. Chicago Tribune, 1922-1925;
bottom across from left: Sloan & Robertson. Chanin Building, New York, 1929, general view and worm's-eye view.

Center was apparent in the pavilion he designed for the 1937 Paris World's Fair, carefully composing the photographs published in order to mimic the New York complex[110].

While Gelfreikh seems to have left no written account of his visit, Shchuko drew sketches of the Cornell Medical Center and Manhattan, as seen through the bridge structure and from Brooklyn. He also drew several portraits of Iofan on the deck during their crossing, and followed his example by writing in the *Pravda*, making rather conventional remarks on New York's urban fabric, the subway, and the ubiquitous cars. Regarding the skyscrapers, he spoke only of the opulence of their lobbies and the efficiency of their elevators, and was also impressed with the PSFS Building[111]. In an article published in *Arkhitektura SSSR* and written in a particularly obscure and stale language, he marvelled at the Italian part of his trip and described the United States in even more predictable terms than Iofan: "America can bring a lot to our architects in terms of building techniques, the use of construction materials, and more generally in their quest for bold solutions to architectural problems."[112] This reluctant accolade served only to warn his readers of the Americans' aesthetic shortcomings, which he could not help highlighting as an admirer of the Italian Renaissance.

110   David E. Arkin, "Sovetskii pavilion," *Arkhitektura* SSSR 5, no. 9 (September 1937): 4.
        See also Udovički-Selb, "Between Modernism and Socialist Realism," 484.
111   Vladimir A. Shchuko, "Planirovka i arkhitektura, iz zagranichnykh vpechatlenii," *Pravda*, 20 April 1935, 2.
        Reprinted in Mikhail G. Barkhin and Iurii S. Iaralov, eds., *Mastera arkhitektury ob arkhitekture* (Moscow: Iskusstvo, 1975), vol. 1, 268–72.
112   Vladimir A. Shchuko, "Tvorcheskii ochet," *Arkhitektura SSSR* 3, no. 6 (June 1935): 19–20.

Structural section of the Palace of the Soviets and of an American skyscraper, in *Palace of the Soviets*, Moscow:
Moskovskii rabochii, 1940. Private collection.

Boris M. Iofan, Vladimir G. Gelfreikh, and Vladimir A. Shchuko. Project for the Palace of the Soviets, Moscow, 1934.
Wood, 52 × 35.3 × 58.7 cm. Alex Lachmann Collection.

A three-month mission involving the engineers B. P. Popov, A. T. Gridunov, and A. L. Rubinshtein was organized in 1935, namely to negotiate with Moran & Proctor and to acquire the necessary equipment for the foundations. They travelled to Chattanooga, Boston, Chicago, and San Francisco[113]. Conversely, the minister of Foreign Affairs, Viacheslav Molotov, denied an investigative tour to Andrei Prokofiev—who succeeded to Mikhailov and was executed in 1937—and also one requested by Iofan in 1939[114]. In Moscow, the American example was still explicitly mentioned in technical literature and propaganda. A 1939 book on steel frame high-rises mentions the contribution of American consultants to the groundwork for the assembly of the Palace of the Soviets structure, which was completed using derrick cranes[115]. Nikolai Atarov's popular 1940 book about the Palace is a poetic depiction of this method of construction. With an elegant design by Solomon Telingater, Atarov published not only the previously mentioned confrontation between cross sections, but also between the Statue of Liberty and the monument to Lenin, adding a view of Manhattan and musings on "the way Americans build." He also advocated for the necessity to borrow the best of what America had to offer[116]. It seems that Le Corbusier—the most illustrious figure to lose the 1931 competition for the Palace—was mistaken when, upon his return to America in 1937, he wrote in *When the Cathedrals Were White*: "During these ten years New York raised itself into the sky; but the Soviets in Moscow denounced the skyscraper as 'capitalist.' A denaturing of the objects in question."[117] The open pit excavation in Moscow's soft soil was indeed intended for an American skyscraper, from the foundations to the crown, or rather for a skyscraper that would have swallowed a theatre, like the snake consuming an elephant in Saint-Exupéry's *Little Prince*.

The People's Commissariat of Heavy Industry

While the architects who were to build the Palace of the Soviets were visiting America, the newfound passion for verticality sparked other Moscow projects, starting with that of the People's Commissariat of Heavy Industry, for which a competition was opened in 1934. The idea of accommodating industry executives in stately buildings, like those of the General Motors headquarters in Detroit, which Iofan and his colleagues had visited, was not a new one, as Krinskii had developed a similar project as early as 1923 for the VSNKh. The fourteenth Congress of the Communist Party in 1925, which launched the policy for heavy metallurgical production, sparked several regional houses of industry projects. The first was Kharkov's Gosprom, built between 1925 and 1927. Houses of Industry were also envisioned in Novosibirsk, Irkutsk, and Novokuznetsk—Stalinsk as of 1932, and one of them was established in Samara[118]. The most ambitious one was in Sverdlovsk, with a call for submissions launched in 1927. The winning entry, by Grigorii Simonov, Aleksandr Gegello, and David Krichevskii, was eventually abandoned, and the operation was relaunched in 1931 based on a plan by Daniil Fridman, featuring a long office block, which would have been topped with a 34-storey tower. This was the first high-rise building to be undertaken in the USSR. It reached its fifth floor in 1935 before being destroyed in a fire and construction never resumed[119] [ill. p. 317].

Between 1932 and 1935, Arkadii Langman erected the headquarters of the Council of Labour and Defense in a central Moscow location, on the corner of Tverskaia Street and Okhotnyi Riad. This parallelepiped with strongly emphasized vertical lines seemed to please Stalin. Not all undertakings of that period were conducted with such efficiency. In 1929, the VSNKh had organized a competition for a nine-storey House of Industry, to be located in Zariadie, near the Red Square. Though El Lissitzky had developed an impressive project, the winner was Panteleimon Golosov. Ivan Leonidov submitted a much taller, prismatic glass skyscraper. The volume was interrupted by an open floor providing a lookout and had an exterior elevator [ill. p. 316]. Heavily criticized in the press, the project was withdrawn from the competition[120]. A new competition was launched for the same lot in 1934, this time enlarged to include the GUM, or Main department store, a masterly structure from the end of the nineteenth century. Among the participating architects were Daniil Fridman, Ivan Fomin, Moisei Ginzburg, Panteleimon Golosov, Ivan Leonidov, Konstantin Melnikov, and Aleksandr and Viktor Vesnin. The location of the building and its plan inspired countless inventions, many of which summoned industrial and American imagery.

Golosov submitted a project with linear office units with a spindly tower. Fridman, who had no qualms about recycling the Sverdlovsk design, aligned his New York-style structure, with setbacks, on Lenin's mausoleum. In an alternative version, he proposed a wall of skyscrapers along the Red Square, shaping a vertical fragment of the city with a single building, in a manner reminiscent of the Gosprom in Kharkov [ill. p. 317]. In a more industrial style, the surprisingly similar projects by Ginzburg and the Vesnin brothers seemed to derive from a cross between the offices Kahn had built for General Motors and a row of blast furnaces. Fomin and Melnikov both submitted ensembles that were just as overpowering, but also porous: the former organized his project according to towering classical orders, while the latter orchestrated a staggering ascent, having the employees and visitors circulate through the stator of a large turbine similar to those of the Dnieper Hydroelectric Station[121].

Leonidov, the child prodigy of constructivist architecture, who had been the first target of attacks from the "proletarian" movement, developed the most complex and promising solution, elevating three clustered towers above the Red Square, each with its own tectonics[122]. The first, a rectangular prism entirely clad with glass, reenacted the 1929 House of Industry theme on its side walls; the second was a triangular prism covered in glass bricks illuminating the place at night; and the third had a round cross section and was shaped like a stretched out hyperboloid of revolution, reminiscent of factory cooling towers, and covered with stone and glass[123]. The three towering elements were connected with walkways. Leonidov drew his perspectives reproducing Erich Mendelsohn's

113   Council decision on the construction of the Palace of Soviets, 29 June 1935, GARF f. R-5446, op. 16a, d. 560, l. 14-16.
114   Andrei N. Prokofiev, "O komandirovkakh za granitsu spetsialistov Dvortsa Sovetov i obsluzhivaiushchikh stroitelstv o postroronnikh organizatsii," 2 December 1937, RGASPI f. 82, op. 2, d. 505, l. 6. Andrei N. Prokofiev, "Spravka o tselevom naznachenii zagranichnykh komandirovok spetsialistov Dvortsa Sovetov i ego postavshchikov," 2 December 1937, RGASPI f. 82, op. 2, d. 505, l. 7; "Postanovlenie Soveta stroitelstva Dvortsa Sovetov," March 1937, RGASPI f. 82, op. 2, d. 504, ll. 86, 103; Boris M. Iofan, Letter to Viacheslav M. Molotov, 27 October 1938, RGASPI, f. 82, op. 2, d. 505, l. 134. See Zubovich, "Moscow Monumental," 47.
115   V.A. Baldin, ed., Stalnye karkasy mnogoetazhnykh zdanii (Moscow: Gostroiizdat, 1939), 291.
116   Atarov, Dvorets Sovetov, 97-98.
117   Le Corbusier When the Cathedrals Where White; a Journey to the Land of Timid People [1937] (London: Routledge, 1947), 58.
118   Igor A. Kazus, "Doma promyshlennosti v istorii arkhitektury Sibiri 1920-1930-kh godov," Balandinskie chneniia (2018) https://cyberleninka.ru/journal/n/balandinskie-chteniya [accessed 2 September 2019].
119   Liudmila Tokmeninova, Dom promyshlennosti i torgovli (Ekaterinburg: Tatlin, 2013).
120   Ivan I. Leonidov, "Dom Promyshlennosti, Moskva, 1929 g.," Sovremennaia arkhitektura 5, no. 4 (1930): 1-2.
121   See David M. Aranovich's analysis of the projects, "Arkhitekturnaia rekonstruktsiia tsentra Moskvy," Stroitelstvo Moskvy, no. 10 (1934); see also Alexei Tarkhanov and Sergei Kavtaradze, Stalinist Architecture (London: Laurence King, 1992), 33-43.
122   Andrei P. Gozak, Narkomtiazhprom Leonidova (Moscow: Russkii Avangard, 2011).
123   Rem Koolhaas and Gerrit Oorthuys, "Ivan Leonidov's Dom Narkomtjazjprom, Moscow," Oppositions 1, no. 2 (1974): 95-102.

Ivan I. Leonidov. Competition project of the House of Industry, Moscow, 1930.
Ink on paper and collage of gelatin silver prints, laid down on cardboard, 32 × 19 cm. CCA DR1995:0002.

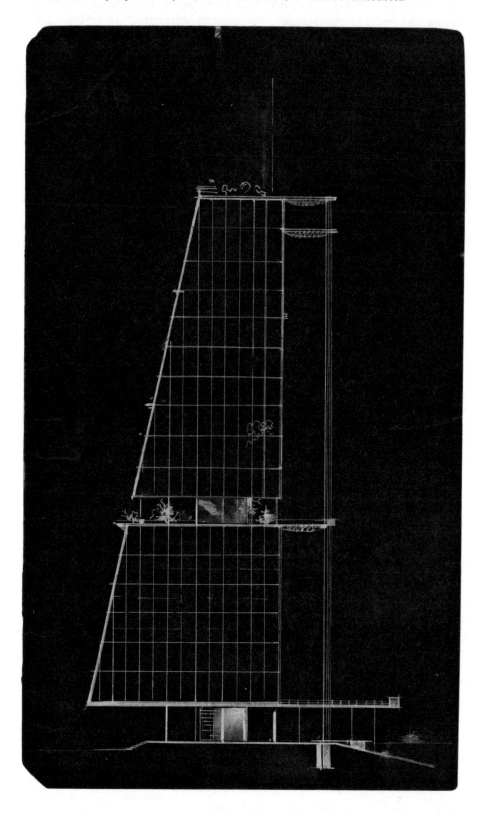

Daniil F. Fridman and Gleb I. Glushchenko. House of Industry, Sverdlovsk, 1931–1935. Model view.
Gelatin silver print on paper, 23.2 × 17 cm. CCA, PH1993:0221.

Daniil F. Fridman, A.M. Kogan, and S. Vlasiev. Competition project for the People's Commissariat of
Heavy Industry (Narkomtiazhprom), Moscow, 1936. Perspective from the Red Square.
Graphite, ink and watercolour on paper, 108.2 × 149.3 cm. Shchusev State Museum of Architecture, RIa 3708.

Moisei Ia. Ginzburg and Solomon A. Lisagor. Competition project for the People's Commissariat of Heavy Industry (Narkomtiazhprom), Moscow, 1934. Perspective. Ink on tracing paper, 23 × 31.5 cm. Alex Lachmann Collection.

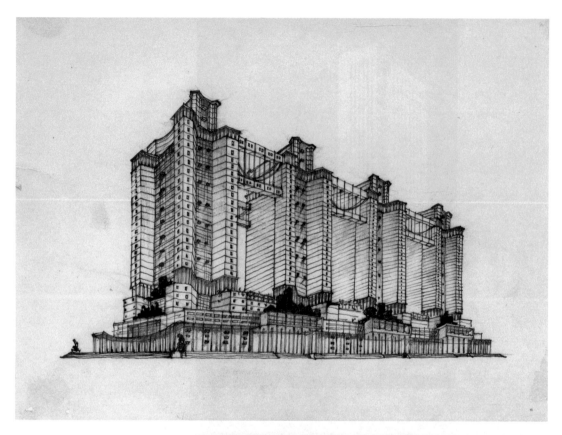

Ivan I. Leonidov. Competition project for the People's Commissariat of Heavy Industry (Narkomtiazhprom), Moscow, 1934. Model view. Gelatin silver print on paper, 23.8 × 30.2 cm. CCA, PH1987:0268.

Ivan I. Leonidov. Competition project for the Narkomtiazhprom, Moscow, 1934. Two views of a tower.
Graphite, ink and gouache on paper, 162 × 45 cm and ink on paper, 50 × 50 cm (modeled on Mendelsohn's photograph below).
Shchusev State Museum of Architecture, Rla 3725 and Rla 4676/3.

Saint Basil's Cathedral, worm's-eye view, in Erich Mendelsohn, *Rußland, Europa, America: ein architektonischer Querschnitt*. Berlin: Rudolf Mosse, 1929. CCA.

visual schemes, portraying his tall prismatic structures in a striking worm's eye
view, reminiscent of *Amerika*'s depiction of skyscrapers and of Moscow's landscape as revealed in *Rußland, Europa, Amerika*. Leonidov's structure, taller than
the Manhattan skyscrapers, rose like a rocket above Saint Basil's Cathedral, in
a composition and a perspective modelled after the Berlin architect's photographs [ill. p. 319]. Without resorting to mimicry, he nevertheless remained
much more aware of the surrounding historical buildings—the Kremlin's Ivan the
Great Bell Tower—than all the other contestants. In a rare commentary on
contemporary architecture, El Lissitzky's most positive remarks were about
Melnikov and Leonidov's proposal, whose theatricality he nevertheless criticized, condemning what he called the "American-skyscraperesque eclecticism" and the lavish monumentality in the work of the other contestants[124].

    The second competition was launched in 1935, and submissions were
received from Blokhin, Shchusev, Fridman, Iofan, Mordvinov, Shchuko, Gelfreikh,
the Vesnin brothers, and an internal team from the Commissariat. This time,
the proposals were even more pompous. Shchuko raised a wall with indents
reminiscent of those of the General Motors headquarters in Detroit, which
he had visited in 1934. Fridman surrounded the simplest version of his initial
project with a nauseating profusion of colonnades and arcades. Mordvinov
and the Vesnin brothers drew overbearing pyramidal compositions, extending their tentacles to the entire neighbourhood. Iofan remained fixated on the
Rockefeller Center, drawing a dominant structure similar to the RCA Building,
though vertically compressed into a more compact shape. As in New York,
his building was flanked by two propylaea, but gave way to a platform that
could serve as a tribune rather than to a half-buried courtyard.[125] This proposition

seems to have been the closest to Stalin's desires, as he respected American architecture and was open to seeing it as a legitimate source of inspiration[126]. At the beginning of 1937, Sergo Ordzhonikidze's death led to the cancellation of this undeniably megalomaniac project, which would also have diverted resources from the Palace of the Soviets.

The 1935 Moscow Plan and its American Inspiration

Since 1930, Soviet leaders had been deeply concerned with the planning and expansion of Moscow, but five years passed before they could produce and agree upon a coherent document on the matter. During this difficult fruition process, they massively drew upon European experiments, inspired not so much by publications and investigative trips abroad, but mainly by the contributions of Western architects working in the USSR. Le Corbusier's theories were rejected as of 1930, but in 1932, Ernst May and Hannes Meyer took part in a competition for the expansion of the capital city and the reconstruction of existing neighbourhoods. Opposed to the idea of an extensive decentralization, Kurt Meyer, the former urban planner for Cologne under Konrad Adenauer, advocated in favour of a dense agglomeration, radial-concentric in structure, and ventilated with parks expanding from the periphery to the very centre[127]. Incidentally, the Party's *Politbiuro* criticized at the same time the overwhelming presence of German experts, deploring the fact that they represented half of the foreign consultants, while Americans accounted for only 10%, even though "America ha[d] surpassed Germany in the field of large-scale construction."[128]

The development of Moscow's plan was diligently overseen by Lazar Kaganovich, who took it upon himself to advise the architects in astonishing discussion sessions. On 31 July 1932, at the Mossoviet, he presided over a meeting devoted to the restructuring of Moscow, during which, while reviewing the proposed projects, he moved to dismiss "ultra-urbanism" and grandiose expansion for Moscow, condemning the widespread "infatuation with Americanism."[129] His address coincided with the departure of a large proportion of American specialists from the USSR, while specialized publications started criticizing the theories and projects developed in the United States, though sometimes in a nuanced manner.

Contradictory tendencies nevertheless emerged among those interested in American experiments. In 1931, the Chicago engineer Jacob L. Crane and the renowned American urban planner John Nolen were invited to visit Moscow and Nizhnii Novgorod and to present their thoughts on the future of

124   El Lissitzky, "Forum sotsialisticheskoi Moskvy," *Arkhitektura SSSR* 2, no. 10 (October 1934): 4–5.
125   "Dom narodnogo komissariata tiazheloi promyshlennosti v Moskve," *Arkhitektura SSSR* 4, no. 6 (June 1936): 1–27.
126   On this point and the relation between Iofan's project and the Rockefeller Center, see Udovički-Selb, "Between Modernism and Socialist Realism," 480 and 483.
127   Harald Bodenschatz and Thomas Flierl, *Von Adenauer zu Stalin: der Einfluß des traditionellen deutschen Städtebaus in der Sowjetunion um 1935* (Berlin: Edition Gegenstand und Raum, 2015); Harald Bodenschatz and Christiane Post, *Städtebau im Schatten Stalins: die internationale Suche nach der sozialistischen Stadt in der Sowjetunion 1929–1935* (Berlin: Braun, 2003).
128   Central Control Commission of CP(b)US, "Report of the supreme economic council of the USSR and the NKPS on the use of overseas missions and foreign experts," 25 December 1929, RGASPI, "appendix to the transcript to the 175th meeting of the organizing office of the Central Committee on 25 December 1929", 6 January 1930, RGASPI, f. 17, op. 113, d. 811, 44. See also Elisabeth Essaïan, "L'Amérique des architectes russes et soviétiques: miroir et projection des ambitions urbaines 1876–1953," *Espaces et sociétés*, no. 107 (2001): 53.
129   "Po povodu rekonstruktsii Moskvy," transcript of a meeting at 31 July 1932, RGASPI, fonds 81, op. 3, delo 181, 68, quoted in Elisabeth Essaïan, *Le prolétariat ne se promène pas nu: Moscou en projets* (Marseille: Parenthèses, 2020), 225.

Vladimir N. Semenov, Sergei E. Chernyshev. General Plan of Moscow, 1935. Layout of new roads and reconstruction of the existing ones, foldout in Aleksandr M. Rodchenko, Varvara F. Stepanova. *Moscow is being reconstructed*, Moscow: Izostat, 1938. CCA NA9211.M6 (9463).

Daniel H. Burnham and Edward H. Bennett, Plan for Chicago, 1909. In *Plan of Chicago: prepared under the direction of the Commercial Club during the years MCMVI, MCMVII, and MCMVIII*, Chicago: Commercial Club, 1909. CCA, NA44.B966.25.C4 1909.

Soviet cities[130]. Two years later, Ludwig Hilberseimer's theoretical projects for Berlin and the New York regional plan were both criticized in an article published in *Planirovka i stroitelstvo gorodov* (The Planning and Building of Cities)[131]. The book, *Outline of Town and City Planning*, written by Thomas Adams, the author of the plan, was nevertheless translated upon publication, in 1935[132]. While Germany, the homeland of urban planning, was overrun by Nazism, the United States was the object of a longstanding focus, as shown by the detailed analysis proposed by Harland Bartholomew's 1932 book *Urban Land Uses*. The surface area standards recommended in these publications were considered as "exclusively informative," but it was noted that the Harvard University faculty of urban planning was "one of the best in America, perhaps even in the world."[133] The urban planning treatises shaping Soviet thought also featured a large proportion of American projects. Shchusev and Zagorskii, in their considerations on urban composition based on a comparative and historical approach, were interested in the notions of contrast and architectural ensemble. They extolled the compositional virtues of the National Mall in Washington, dominated by the Capitol Building, and those of the Fairmount Parkway, designed by Jacques Gréber, oriented towards the Philadelphia Museum of Art, as though they were seeking models for the street layout leading up to the Palace of the Soviets[134]. Accomplishments useful to the modernization of Moscow were also regularly featured in *Amerikanskaia tekhnika i promyshlennost* (American Industry and Technology), with articles on themes like New York's subway and underground tunnels[135].

The general structure of the plan, whose final version emphasized Moscow's historical radial-concentric configuration, was officially attributed to Vladimir Semenov, the founding father of Russian urban planning and Sergei Chernyshev. At first glance, it seemed to exhibit no American traits. However, several urban figures, familiar to the Russians, pointed to the opposite. Firstly, the radial passageways leading to the Palace of the Soviets and its cross-linking with the general road network was modelled, apart from Washington and Philadelphia, after Daniel Burnham and Edward Bennett's 1909 plan for Chicago[136] [ill. p. 322]. Secondly, the orthogonal grid of the main urban expansion in the proposition, the south-west neighbourhood, evoked both the structure of Otto Wagner's unlimited metropolis and those of large American cities. And lastly, the vast green spaces of the proposed parks system were connected with parkways, according to a principle—familiar to the Russians[137]—devised by Frederick Law Olmsted in 1870, and later adapted to the automobile.

130   Jacob L. Crane, "City Planning in the Soviet Union," *Economic Review of the Soviet Union* 5 (January 1932): 36; John Nolen, "Problems in the Planning of Moscow," Ibid., 37–38. See also the earlier, more substantial article by Robert Whitten, "City Planning in Soviet Russia," *Economic Review of the Soviet Union* 7, no. 3 (July 1931): 147–60.

131   S.N. and V.V. Pokchichevskie, "V tupike (planirovochnaia mysl na zapade)," *Planirovka i stroitelstvo gorodov*, no. 10 (1933): 25–29.

132   Thomas Adams, *Noveishie dostizheniia v planirovke gorodov* (Moscow: Izd-vo Vses. Akad. Arkhitektury, 1935); originally: *Outline of Town and City Planning: A Review of Past Efforts and Modern Aims* (New York: Russell Sage Foundation, 1935).

133   V. Mirer, "Zemelnyi balans gorodov Ameriki," *Planirovka i stroitelstvo gorodov*, no. 9 (1935): 40–41.

134   Aleksei V. Shchusev and L.E. Zagorskii, *Arkhitekturnaia organizatsiia goroda* (Moscow: Gosstroiizdat, 1934), 47.

135   S. Perlin, "Nekotorye dannye po postroike metropolitena v g. Niu-Iorke," *Amerikanskaia tekhnika i promyshlennost* 9, no. 3 (March 1932): 159–65, (5 May 1932): 296–97, and (6 June 1932): 358–60.

136   This parallel was suggested in, among other sources, Bodenschatz and Post, *Städtebau im Schatten Stalins*, 191–92.

137   A. Zilbert, "Planirovka goroda v strane 'neogranichnennogo individualizma'," *Stroitelstvo Moskvy*, no. 1 (1931): 35–39.

Upon his return from America, Iofan had rejoiced at the appearance of these new promenades in New York and Chicago, which he considered relevant for the Soviet capital[138]. In Moscow, the road system originated in the Gorky Central Park of Culture and Leisure, established on the location of the 1923 Agricultural Fair, and unraveled along the Moskva loop line, while other large parks were built according to composition principles established in a 1934 manual by Leonid Lunts[139].

According to the plan attributed to Semenov, the Moscow city centre was to be lined with wide treeless roads, punctuated with large building complexes comparable to high-rise structures in Chicago and New York. The first complex established at the beginning of Gorky Street by Arkadii Mordvinov, complex "A," is indeed reminiscent of the Belnord Building erected on New York's Upper West Side by H. Hobart Weekes in 1908[140]. They are similar in length, and share the general shape of a palazzo, with its rusticated plinth and entablature. The main difference is of course that the New York building has no statues of workers or peasants on its cornice. The Moscow doors seem to be inspired by Carlo Rossi's General Staff Building arch in Saint Petersburg, while those of the Belnord evoke the Palazzo Medici in Florence. The apartment buildings on Park Avenue North also come to mind. The rusticated bases were one of the distinctive marks of the newest tall buildings in Moscow. Without directly referencing the Tuscan palaces, they echo the interpretations of some of their elements in Saint Petersburg and in the United States. For instance, Dankmar Adler and Louis Sullivan's Auditorium Building or Daniel Burnham's Monadnock Building both alluded to Chicago's past, as opposed to the new metal architecture[141]. In Moscow, these solid foundations were the sign of a refusal to use modernist pilotis.

Gorky Street, heralding the new Moscow, was born from the transformation of the historical Tverskaia Street, which was enlarged from 20 to 60 metres with the destruction of certain buildings on its western side and the displacement of some fifty others. The houses were moved back from their original alignment using American methods, as reported by technical journals and Amtorg publications[142]. The idea was not new in itself—New York's "travelling" houses had been mentioned as early as 1893 in *Nedelia Stroitelia*[143]—, but the operation remained notable: it was, so to speak, a double transfer, as not only were the buildings mimicked, but the transfer technique itself was also reproduced. In its lower portion, Gorky Street leads to Okhotnyi Ryad, where Aleksei Shchusev erected the Hotel Moskva between 1932 and 1935, which can be interpreted as a dilated version of the International House

138   Iofan, "Materialy o sovremennoi arkhitekture SShA i Italii," 30–31.
139   Leonid B. Lunts, Alexandre Ia. Karra, "Rekonstruktsiia moskovskikh parkov", *Problemy sadovo-parkovoi arkhitektury*, eds. Mikhail P. Korzhev et al. (Moscow: Izd-vo Vses. Akademii Arkhitektury, 1936), 45–80. Leonid B. Lunts, *Parki kultury i otdykha* (Moscow: Gosstroiizdat, 1934), *passim*.
140   Greg Castillo, "Gorky Street and the Design of the Stalin Revolution," in *Streets: Critical Perspectives on Public Space*, Zeynep Çelik, Diane Favro, and Richard Ingersoll, eds. (Berkeley: University of California Press, 1994), 57–70; Monica Rüthers, "The Moscow Gorky Street: Space, History and Lebenswelten," in *Late Stalinist Russia, Society Between Reconstruction and Reinvention*, ed. Juliana Fürst (London: Routledge, 2009), 247–68.
141   Ross Miller, *American Apocalypse: The Great Fire and the Myth of Chicago* (Chicago: University of Chicago Press, 1990), 110–11.
142   A. Pozdnev, *Doma peredvigaiutsia* (Moscow: Gazeta tekhnika, 1934); A. Ling, "Moving Buildings in the USSR," *Architect's Journal*, no. 2 (1944): 155. The techniques used for moving buildings are described at least twice: A. Ia. Brailovskii, "Praktika peredvizhki zdanii v SShA," *Amerikanskaia tekhnika i promyshlennost* 12, no. 9 (September 1935): 414–21; Simon Breines, "Opyt peredvizhki zdanii v SShA," *Amerikanskaia tekhnika i promyshlennost* 13, no. 11 (November 1936): 454–60.
143   "Stranstvuiushchii dom v New Yorke," *Nedelia Stroitelia* 21, no. 21 (23 May 1893): 102.

Gorky Street in the 1930s; on the right, Arkadii G. Mordvinov's apartment block, in *Moscow*,
Moscow: State Art Publishers, 1939. CCA, DK601 .M6 1939.

H. Hobart Weekes. The Belnord Apartments, New York, 1908. General view, 1915.
Gelatin silver print on paper, 27.9 × 35.9 cm. Museum of the City of New York, Photo Archives.

built on Riverside Drive in New York for John D. Rockefeller by Louis E. Jallade and Marc Eidlitz & Son in 1924. The resemblance was not lost on Frank Lloyd Wright, who, during his 1937 trip, described it as the very manifestation of what he was struggling to overcome in America[144]. While the appeal of the Upper West Side resonated at the heart of Moscow, the focus on New York took on an unexpected form in the second half of the 1930s. Le Corbusier, who was a persona non-grata, but who nevertheless remained popular, published his last article "What is America's Problem?" before a long period of silence, David Arkin welcomed his harsh critique of New York City, initially issued in *American Architect and Architecture*[145].

In the subsoil of the new Moscow, the construction of the metro, launched in November 1931, represented a *stroika* comparable to the great projects of the first five-year plan, resulting in the opening of the first line on 15 May 1935. The first contract for a circular line was signed in 1929 with the underground works entrepreneur and New York émigré Samuel Rosoff, but the agreement was never honoured[146]. Ultimately, the machines used to dig the tunnels were British, while the American contribution was limited to a small portion of the workforce involved in the project. However, one figure stood out: the engineer George Morgan, a concrete construction consultant who published a particularly pompous propagandist pamphlet in 1935[147]. It was immediately printed in the journal *Modern Mechanix*, as evidence of "America's Part in Soviet Engineering Triumphs."[148]

The new plan and its major buildings, like the Palace of the Soviets, were celebrated in all forms of Soviet media, especially in film. Eisenstein abandoned his 1933 movie project to present Moscow "as a concept [of] the concentration of the socialist future of the entire world."[149] In 1938, Aleksandr Medvedkin wrote and directed *Novaia Moskva* (The New Moscow), a film centred on an animated diorama showing the avenues, bridges, and palaces promised to the people. Certain shots seemed to be modelled after Fritz Lang's *Metropolis*, whose success had been considerable in the USSR, with the Palace of the Soviets replacing the towering city of the plutocrats in the German film. Medvedkin's triumphalist picture was banned because of a subversive sequence wherein the diorama is inadvertently interrupted and retreats towards Moscow's czarist past instead of portraying its glorious future.

Oltarzhevskii, Between New York City, Moscow, and the Gulag

Viacheslav Oltarzhevskii, whom Iofan and his travelling companions had met in New York in the fall of 1934, returned to Moscow when the general plan was approved. He arrived too late to contribute to the document but took part in the development of one of its components: the Agricultural Exposition project. Before travelling to the United States in 1924 to "get acquainted with foreign architecture and building techniques," as he wrote in his 1947 official biography, Oltarzhevskii had already left behind a substantial body of work[150]. For instance, between 1909–1911, he had designed the office buildings of the Northern Insurance Society on Moscow's Ilinka Street, along with Marian Peretiakovich, Ilia Golosov, and Ivan Rerberg. He had also partnered with Rerberg between 1912 and 1917 to build the Kiev train station in Moscow. Serving as an engineer for the Red Army during the Civil War, he had been deputy chief architect for the 1923 Agricultural Exposition under Shchusev and built several of its pavilions. Oltarzhevskii emigrated in April 1924; in 1928, he obtained permission to practise from the State University of New York;

and in 1929, he entered the American Institute of Architects[151]. He associated both with the White émigré circles and with the Amtorg offices, designing the title page of their monthly publication *Amerikanskaia tekhnika i promyshlennost* (American Engineering and Industry), as previously mentioned.

Oltarzhevskii created a fairy-tale-like neo-Russian villa for the model and designer Sonia Levienne, in Oyster Bay, on Long Island[152] [ill. p. 328]. In the same high-profile émigré circles, he converted a building for the Russian financier George Schlee, who was married to Levienne's business partner, Valentina Sanina, and who was also involved in an affair with Greta Garbo. Another émigré, the adventurer and comic book publisher Benjamin W. Sangor, commissioned him to build a housing complex in Pinewald, New Jersey, including his vast, Italian-inspired home, and the luxurious Royal Pines Hotel, inaugurated in 1929, which infamously served as Al Capone's headquarters. Oltarzhevskii designed several remarkable hypothetical projects and became close with his employer Harvey Wiley Corbett. Echoing his mentor's long-running influential projects for the modernization of New York's transit system, he imagined his own version of the "City of the Near Future," printed in 1927 in *The American City Magazine*. The editors marvelled at its "elevated sidewalks" and its "gargantuan skyscrapers that would make the pyramids of Egypt picayune beside their colossal bulk" [ill. p. 328]. This "amazing drawing" was viewed as an attempt to "approach [...] nature's most striking work of architecture, a mountain range."[153] He also proposed a "Coast to Coast City," where the "homes of the future" were pyramidal and mobile skyscrapers, whose orientation would change according to sunlight. These images were widely disseminated in the press[154].

Oltarzhevskii drew colour renderings for the projects developed by Corbett's firm, as he excelled in tracing pencil perspectives, like the one he created for the Chanin Construction Company's skyscraper. Partnering with Helmle, Corbett and Harrison's team as part of the competition for the Christopher Columbus monument [ill. p. 259], he drafted all the plans for their submission[155]. His connections in the Parisian-Russian émigré circles also allowed him to take part in the competition organized by Léonard Rosenthal for the Porte Maillot, where his project for a pair of towers was appraised against those of Auguste Perret, Le Corbusier, and Robert Mallet-Stevens[156].

144   Frank Lloyd Wright, "Architecture and Life in the USSR," *Soviet Russia Today*, October 1937, 14–19.
145   Le Corbusier, "Chto takoe amerikanskaia problema?," *Arkhitektura za rubezhom* 3, no. 5 (1936): 46–47; originally: "What is America's Problem?," *American Architect and Architecture*, no. 2648 (March 1936): 17–22.
146   "Moscow Signs Agreement with Rosoff for $40,000,000 Water Works," press release from the Jewish Telegraphic Agency, 23 May 1929. On Rosoff, see "A Master Digger," *The New Yorker*, 4 June 1927, 19–21.
147   George Morgan, *Moscow Subway is the Finest in the World* (Moscow: Moskovskii rabotchii, 1935).
148   "America's Part in Soviet Engineering Triumphs," *Modern Mechanix* (July 1935): 82–84 and 130.
149   Sergei M. Eisenstein, "Moskva vo vremeni," *Literaturnaia gazeta*, 11 July 1933, 3. On this project, see Katerina Clark, "Eisenstein's Two Projects for a Film about Moscow," *Modern Language Review*, no. 101 (Spring 2006): 188–204.
150   RGALI, f. 2466, op. 8, d. 832, 2. This biographical piece written in 1947 is limited to architectural business. See Catherine Cooke, "Oltarzhevsky, Viacheslav," *Oxford Art Online*, 2003; Olga A. Nikologorskaia, *Oltarzhevskii* (Moscow: Molodaia Gvardia, 2013).
151   US Department of Labor, Certificate of Arrival, 24 April 1930, and Petition for Citizenship, 26 August 1930, National Archives, and Oltarzhevskii files, MUAR.
152   "Russia in America: The Residence of Mrs Sonia Levienne at Oyster Bay, N.Y." *Country Life*, no. 60 (April 1929); *The American Architect*, 5 August 1928, 152, 171 and 172.
153   "Must We Come to This: City of the Near Future," *The American City Magazine*, June 1927, 801.
154   "Quest for Sunshine May Revolutionize Our Cities," *Brainerd Daily Dispatch*, 7 September 1929; "When We All Live in 'Merry-Go-Round' Skyscrapers," *Ogden Standard Examiner*, 29 September 1929. I thank Sam Omans for bringing these articles to my attention.
155   MUAR, Oltarzhevskii collection, drawings Rla 7472/1 to 12.
156   MUAR, Oltarzhevskii collection, drawing Rla 7488/1 and 2. On this contest, see Henri Descamps, "La démolition des fortifications de Paris, aménagement de la porte Maillot," *La Construction moderne* 6, no. 51 (21 December 1930): 187–91; Raymond Fischer, "Concours pour l'aménagement de la porte Maillot," *L'Architecture d'aujourd'hui* 2, no. 9 (December 1931): 13–19.

Viacheslav K. Oltarzhevskii. Project for Sonia Levienne's house, Long Island, 1926. Elevation. Graphite and colour pencil on paper, 31.1 × 32.4 cm. Shchusev State Museum of Architecture, RIa 7475. "The City of the Near Future," 1927. Aerial perspective published in *The American City Magazine*, June 1927. Harvey Wiley Corbett Architectural Drawings and Papers, 1914–1949, Avery Architectural & Fine Arts Library, Columbia University.

Viacheslav K. Oltarzhevskii. Project for a high-rise complex with stores, hotels, exhibition halls, New York, ca. 1929. Perspective, 50.8 × 40.7 cm. Graphite and watercolour on paper. Shchusev State Museum of Architecture, RIa 9797.

In 1931, he designed an Art Deco building at 116 bis, avenue des Champs-Élysées for the same adventurous developer[157]. In the meantime, all his ambitious projects in the United States fell through following the Depression, including the small skyscraper he had designed for the Pennsylvania Power & Light in Allentown[158].

In this dire professional situation, Oltarzhevskii resorted to his graphic skills to draw a set of New York views, which he exhibited in 1932, and later published in his portfolio *Contemporary Babylon*[159]. Patiently composed in various stages, these plates depict the entire Manhattan skyline with the most notable buildings of the time and offer picturesque views of the urban landscape[160]. The analogy between New York and Babylon was not a new one[161], but Oltarzhevskii used it to describe the "city in a city" that was the Rockefeller Center, "the potential focal point of New York cultural and commercial life," "with its international buildings, forums, theatres, office and radio buildings, and landscaped roofs and terraces reminiscent of the hanging gardens of Ancient Babylon."[162]

In a brief introduction, Oltarzhevskii commented on his drawing technique, the pencil stump, which allowed him "to produce the desired effect through the intersection of shaded planes without contour lines," a method long used by the celebrated illustrator Hugh Ferriss, whose work shared many similarities with his own. He recalled his first impressions from the boat of the "colossus hewn from rocky sierras," and how he was struck by the cliffs and the deserted streets. Most notably, he saw in the vertical city the result of a cooperative mode of production: "The builders of Babylon demonstrated their inability to cooperate in their work; both in their organization and technical problems. The skyscrapers of New York are symbols of exceptionally skillful coordination of manifold interests and products of hundreds of different professions united in one creative effort."[163]

In his introduction to the work of the "noted Russian architect," Corbett identified the elements that characterize New York's "incredible splendour": the steel frameworks, the elevators, and the subway, the density and the zoning regulations, and especially the fact that the city has become the world's financial centre, which lends its architecture a "worldwide significance." He praised the visual acuteness of Oltarzhevskii, the "trained foreigner." To him, New York was "a mixture of the splendid and the sordid. [...] It forms a picture with an enormous surface enriched by the play of light and shadow, a picture of contrast of old and new; [...] when first sighted from the sea in the mists of the early morning or with the myriad twinkling lights at sunset, it becomes a veritable fairy panorama. What was once the dream of Babylon has here become reality." Oltarzhevskii's choice to make "the building masses [...] the dominant note" of his drawings is "true to the real character of New York architecture," as "only an architect could have kept so

157   MUAR, Oltarzhevskii Collection, Ria drawings 9800. Today the building houses the UGC Normandie Cinema.
158   MUAR, Oltarzhevskii Collection, Ria drawings 7480/1–4. See Léonard Rosenthal's comments in
       Mémoires d'un chasseur de perles (Paris: Éditions des Deux-Rives, 1949), 197.
159   On the exhibition, see Helen Appleton Read, "New York as Art," *Brooklyn Daily Eagle*, 15 May 1932.
160   Wiacheslav K. Oltar-Jevsky, *Contemporary Babylon in Pencil Drawings* (New York: Architectural Book
       Publishing Company, Inc., 1933). The original drawings are held at MUAR, Oltarzhevskii collection, Ria 9807
       (sketches); Ria 7504 (published versions).
161   Thomas A.P. van Leeuwen, *The Skyward Trend of Thought: Five Essays on the Metaphysics of the
       American Skyscraper* (Cambridge, MA: MIT Press, 1988), 42–52.
162   W. Oltar-Jevsky, *Contemporary Babylon*, cover notes, n. p.
163   W. Oltar-Jevsky, "Contemporary Babylon," in *Contemporary Babylon*, n. p.

Viacheslav K. Oltarzhevskii, Plates in *Contemporary Babylon*, New York: Architectural Book Publishing Company, Inc., 1933. Private collection.
Left: "Highway Across the River". Right: "Framing Central Park."

faithfully to the essential character of the structures while at the same time treating them in so dramatic fashion."[164]

While he was developing the collection, Oltarzhevskii frequently wrote articles for Amtorg's monthly publication, *Amerikanskaia tekhnika i promyshlennost*, where he gave detailed descriptions of the organization of labour in the firms and the cooperation with other professions, based on his own experiences[165]. He also discussed the general situation in the United States as well as various types of buildings[166]. Back in Moscow in 1935, he published several analyses on the specific professional practices in *Arkhitektura SSSR* and *Arkhitektura za rubezhom*[167]. The reasons for this successful return remain mysterious and are not elucidated in any of his autobiographical notes. One possible reason for this smooth homecoming could be that he had relations in the Soviet secret services, for which Amtorg was often used as a cover.

Legend has it that Nikolai Bulganin, the president of the Executive Committee of the Moscow Soviet, was so impressed with Oltarzhevskii's project for the porte Maillot that he invited him to return to the motherland[168]. It seems more likely, however, that in discussions held in the fall of 1934, Iofan and Shchuko managed to convince the architect that he had a better professional future in Stalin's USSR than in an America still reeling from the Depression. This theory can be confirmed by the fact that a similar offer was made to Nikolai Vasilev[169]. Oltarzhevskii immediately found a position as chief architect in the Promstroiproekt, the offspring of the firm established by Kahn. Other architects who had stayed in the United States were then also returning to Russia. One of them was Aleksei Chiniakov, who had studied at MIT

Left: Viacheslav K. Oltarzhevskii. General plan for the All-Union Agricultural Exposition in Moscow, 1935. Aerial perspective. Gelatin silver print on paper, 45.1 × 70.5 cm. Right: Project for a thermal power plant, Vorkuta, 1941. Pencil on tracing paper, 28.2 × 22.2 cm. Shchusev State Museum of Architecture, RKhl 7455/1 and Rla 9817.

from 1931 to 1934 and later worked at the People's Commissariat of Oil Industry under his brother-in-law Aleksandr Vesnin's supervision[170].

An exhilarating experience awaited Oltarzhevskii with the preparation of the Soviet Agricultural Exposition, decreed on 17 February 1934. Meant to be inaugurated in 1937, for the twentieth anniversary of the Revolution, it was to remain open for one hundred days. After several lengthy discussions, a location was chosen in Ostankino, in the north of the capital, and an ad hoc committee was created in mid-1935, under the leadership of Mikhail Chernov, People's Commissar of Agriculture, who was assisted by Izaak E. Korostashevskii, formerly in charge of construction at the 1923 Fair. Quite naturally, Korostashevskii recruited his former colleague Oltarzhevskii as chief architect for the project[171]. An invited competition was held between 11 teams—several of which included students, including those of Grigorii Barkhin, Mikhail Siniavskii, and Leonid Teplitskii—along with Oltarzhevskii's in-house brigade, which was ultimately put in charge of developing the final plan[172]. His first sketch arranged the pavilions around two squares connected with a single circulation path, following a broken line, which was simplified and amplified in the final version, approved in April 1936. The opening of the Exposition was scheduled for 6 July of the following year[173].

Oltarzhevskii designed both entrances to the complex, whose main access, the southern gate, seemed to be inspired by Rome's Città universitaria, its portico flanked with two blind walls. He also designed the administration building and oversaw its construction, as well as the pavilion of mechanization, which was particularly important in a structure intended as a celebration of Soviet agricultural accomplishments. Foregoing all classical elements, Oltarzhesvkii imagined a building with sharp angles and bare walls, topped with a clerestory spire. The structure was vaguely reminiscent of the Carillon Tower, in Chicago, built in 1933 as part of the exposition *A Century of Progress*, where Corbett chaired the architecture committee. A perspective of the projected interior dome reveals obvious Art Deco elements. The pavilion was finished by mid-August 1937, but due to various delays, its opening was postponed until

164   Harvey Wiley Corbett, "Introduction," in Oltar-Jevsky, *Contemporary Babylon*, n. p.
165   Viacheslav K. Oltarzhevskii, "Stroitelstvo Ameriki i arkhitektor," *Amerikanskaia tekhnika i promyshlennost* 6, no. 6 (May 1929): 245–47.
166   Viacheslav K. Oltarzhevskii, "Problemy ognestoikogo stroitelstva SShA," *Amerikanskaia tekhnika i promyshlennost* 5, no. 2 (1928), 55-58; "Proektirovanie otelei v SShA," *Amerikanskaia tekhnika i promyshlennost* 10, no. 6 (1933), 190-196; "Proektirovanie zdania uchebnogo kombinata na osnove opyta shkolnogo stroitelstva v SShA," *Amerikanskaia tekhnika i promyshlennost* 10, no. 8 (1933), 276-285; "Amerikanskaia arkhitektura," *Amerikanskaia tekhnika i promyshlennost* 1, no. 2, 7 and 10 (1934), 8-14, 84-90 and 345-352.
167   Viacheslav K. Oltarzhevskii, "Zarozhdenie kolonialnogo stilia v Amerike," *Arkhitektura za roubezom* 2, no. 5 (1935); 1–6; "Arkhitektura Soedinennykh Shtatov Ameriki," *Arkhitektura SSSR* 3, no. 9 (September 1935); 52–59. "Amerikanskie neboskreby," *Arkhitektura za rubezhom* 3, no. 5 (1936); 11–20. "Stroitelnaia industria i arkhitektor: iz amerikanskogo opyta organizatsii proektirovaniia i stroitelstva," *Arkhitektura SSSR* 4, no. 3 (March 1936); 52–59; "Sanitarno–tekhnicheskoe oborudovanie zhiloi iacheiki," *Arkhitektura SSSR* 4, no. 5 (May 1936): 24–27. "Sanitariia zhilogo doma," *Arkhitektura SSSR* 5, no. 3 (March 1937): 43–48; "Amerikanskii zagorodnyi dom," *Arkhitektura SSSR* 5, no. 7–8 (July–August 1937): 94–101.
168   Recollections of I.I. Korovin, Oltarzhevskii's cellmate in Vorkuta, reported in "Sudby intelligentsii v zaprovo-lochnom mire," in E.V. Markova et al., *Sudby intelligentsii v vorkutinskikh lageriakh 1930–1950-e gody* (Moscow: Stroiizdat, 2002), 110.
169   Lissovskii and Gachot, *Nikolai Vasilev*, 355.
170   RGALI, answer to a question by the author, 10 April 2018.
171   Alexandr Zinovev, *Ansambl VSKhV, arkhitektura i stroitelstvo* (Moscow: self-published, 2014), 19; A.V. Rogachev, *Velikie stroiki sotsializma* (Moscow: Tsentrpoligraf, 2014), 295–334.
172   "Proekty planirovki selskokhoziaistvennoi vystavki 1937 goda," *Akademia arkhitektury*, no. 6 (1935): 43–51 [on the projects by applicants to the Architecture Academy]. Viacheslav K. Oltarzhevskii, "Vsesoiuznaia selskokhoziaistvennaia vystavka, forproekty," *Arkhitektura SSSR* 4, no. 1 (1936): 22–29. On these projects, see Irina V. Belintseva, "Vsesoiuznaia selskokhoziaistvennaia vystavka 1930–kh godov – pervye zamysli," in *Arkhitektura stalinskoi epokhi: opyt istoricheskogo omyshlenia*, ed. Iuliia L. Kosenkova (Moscow: Komkniga, 2010), 162–70.
173   Viacheslav K. Oltarzhevskii, "Generalnyi plan Vsesoiouznoi selskokhoziaistvennoi vystavki," *Arkhitektura SSSR* 5, no. 2 (February 1937): 28–31.

1 August 1938. Accusations of sabotage led to the arrest of several members of the exhibition committee, followed by Chernov and Korostashevskii, who were later executed. They were criticized for having created a construction that seemed too frail and transient, not at all representative of the greatness of socialism.

Also accused of sabotage, Oltarzhevskii was scolded for speaking English too often on the construction site. Worse, his general plan, "entirely deprived of a festive character," displayed an orthodox cross symbol, while statues of Lenin and Stalin were nowhere to be found. The main door, too horizontal, "resemble[d] a palisade." In an even more twisted reproach, he was accused of having sculpted the Soviet symbol in such a way that the hammer seemed to be hitting the blade of the sickle, as though alluding to a conflict between workers and peasants[174]. In June 1938, Oltarzhevskii was arrested and his buildings were immediately ostracized. The northern entrance to the Exposition was transformed by Leonid Poliakov, while the administrative pavilion was reconfigured by Ivan Sobolev. As for the mechanization pavilion, after being criticized for "closing the perspective of the longitudinal axis of the exhibition and thus giving a misleading impression of its scale and scope,"[175] it was simply destroyed and replaced by a large hall with a metal structure.

Eluding the fate met by his sponsors, Oltarzhevskii was deported to Vorkuta, where he quickly found a position as head of construction within the Vorkutstroi led by Leonid Raikin[176]. A popular figure among his fellow detainees and well respected by some of the technical executives from the local industry, he enjoyed a certain freedom, drawing and building several administrative buildings in a classical style for the regional administration and the Kapitalnaia coal mine in 1940 and 1941. He also designed an electrical plant in a decidedly modern fashion, free from the compromises made for the Agricultural Exposition, as if, against all odds, the Gulag were a space of architectural freedom[177] [ill. p. 334].

Ilf and Petrov and the American Heartland

After the stock market crash of 1929, depictions of the United States in Soviet culture underwent a deep transformation. Readers of Russian magazines became accustomed to seeing images of American wastefulness and working

174   S.A. Alekseev, "Istoriia stroitelstva i proektirovaniia Vsesoiuznoi selskokhoziaistvennoi vystavki 1939 g.," typoscript, private collection, quoted in Vladimir Paperny, Architecture in the Age of Stalin: Culture Two (Cambridge; New York: Cambridge University Press, 2002), 199. I thank Vladimir Paperny for sending me this document.

175   A. Taranov, V. Andreev, N. Bykova, and N. Umanskii, "Vsesoiuznaia S.-Kh. Vystavka 1939 g., ploshchad i pavilion mekhanizatsii," Arkhitektura SSSR 7, no. 5 (May 1939): 34.

176   Markova et al., Sudby intelligentsia, 109–11. On this workhouse-town, see Alan Barenberg, Gulag Town, Company Town: Forced Labor and Its Legacy in Vorkuta (New Haven: Yale University Press, 2014).

177   MUAR, Oltarzhevskii collection, RIa 9810, 9812 and 9816.

178   Ilin, Rasskaz o velikom plan, 16–17; Moscow Has a Plan, 22–33.

179   Upton Sinclair, Avtomobilnyi korol, povest o fordovskoi Amerike (Moscow: 1938); originally: The Flivver King: A Story of Ford-America (Pasadena: self-published, 1937).

180   Aleksandr G. Tyshler, Sakko i Vantsetti, oil on canvas, 1927, Tretiakov Gallery, Moscow.

181   Christina Kiaer, "Sotsrealizm i amerikanskii modernizm. Deineka v SShA," Pinakotheke 22–23, no. 1–2 (2006): 455–64; Id., "African Americans in Soviet Socialist Realism: The Case of Aleksandr Deineka," The Russian Review 75, no. 3 (July 2016): 402–33; Id., "Modern Soviet Art Meets America, 1935," in Totalitarian Art and Modernity, eds. M.B. Rasmussen and J. Wamberg (Åhrus: Åhrus University Press, 2010), 241–82.

182   Meredith L. Roman, "Forging Soviet Racial Enlightenment: Soviet Writers Condemn American Racial Mores, 1926, 1936, 1946," The Historian 74, no. 3 (Fall 2012): 528–50; Katerina Clark, "The Representation of the African American as Colonial Oppressed in Texts of the Soviet Interwar Years," The Russian Review 75, no. 3 (July 2016), 368–85; V.N. Sushkova, Otkrytie Ameriki sovetskimi pisateliami 30-kh godov (ot putevykh ocherkov k dokumentalnomu romanu) (Vladivostok: Izd-vo Dalnevostochnogo Universiteta, 1986).

183   "Calls Artists Richest of Russia's Classes," The New York Times, 13 March 1931, 3.

184   Boris Pilniak, The Volga Falls to the Caspian Sea [1930] (New York: Cosmopolitan Book Co., 1931).

class children starving[178]. Popular American heroes such as Ford were portrayed in a harsher and less romanticized light. The Detroit industrialist was now viewed as the ruthless capitalist described in *The Flivver King*, Upton Sinclair's 1837 biographical novel, translated into Russian a year after its publication. According to Walter Reuther, this book had become a powerful recruitment tool for unions[179]. Several indices reveal the unfolding of a new discourse. In 1927, the artist Aleksandr Tyshler was moved by the execution of the anarchist activists Niccola Sacco and Bartolomeo Vanzetti and painted two men detained in a prison passage dominated by a flock of ominous skyscrapers observing them from a distance, as if they were the guardians of the capitalist order[180]. The theme of racism and oppression faced by African-Americans, which was scarcely discussed in the 1920s, made its appearance in paintings, such as those of Aleksandr Deineka, who travelled to the United States in 1935[181]. Some writers compared their condition to the plight of colonized peoples[182].

In the new context of Stalin's growing supremacy and with the imposed artistic canon of socialist realism, very few writers were able to cross the Atlantic. Among the exceptions was Boris Pilniak, who had become famous in the USSR and the Western world with his 1921 novel *The Naked Year*. Stalin personally allowed him to travel to America to collect material for a book that was deemed necessary following those of Gorky and Mayakovsky. Shortly after arriving, Pilniak expressed his "thirst for knowledge about America and [his] desire to learn from this country" to *The New York Times*[183] His host was Ray Long, the editor of *Cosmopolitan*, who was working on the publication of Charles Malamuth's translation of his 1930 book *The Volga Falls to the Caspian Sea*[184].

Boris A. Pilniak. *Okay, An American Novel*, Moscow: Federatsiia, 1933. Private collection.

After a six-month voyage, Pilniak's discovery of an America in the throes of the Great Depression led to the 1933 publication of *O'kei, Amerikanskii roman* (Okay, an American Novel). Filled with American expressions, his travelogue was written in an intimate tone[185] [ill. p. 337]. He was struck by the global electrification and decried the tyranny of advertising and the hegemony of Ford, ice cream, and Coca-Cola, echoing Gorky in his descriptions of Sunday scenes on Coney Island[186]. But he also looked further back in the history of Russian travel narratives, quoting Pavel Svinin on the theme of Native Americans, and agreeing with his observation on the "tyranny of the dollar."[187]

"Seen from the sixtieth or hundredth floor, New York is a baffling city—unspeakable, unusual, sinister, with an ominous beauty…a city of triumphant industry, of impulse, of human capacity. Neither Tatlin nor any other European poet-urban planner could imagine this exceptional grandeur, these constructions, these lines, and this unrivalled grandiosity. To the European, New York, with its skyscrapers, is closer to a dream than to reality, a dream like no other, except perhaps the fantastical and biblical childhood memory of the mysterious city of Babylon. [...] New York is an inhuman and lavish city, a disturbing and bewildering construction. From the top of the Empire [State Building] or from the eagles of the Chrysler Building, the Atlnatic ocean, the Hudson River, the East River, the New Jersey Hills become brothers. A ten- to sixteen-storey New York lies at your feet, in the smoke, the fog, and the buzzing streets. And beside you, the skyscrapers—your brothers, your equals—rise among or above the clouds. The man standing on the roof of the Empire State Building, who is held by the Empire, finds himself at the level of the inhuman beauty and uniqueness of New York. But if one walks, drives, or rides the subway at the ground level, it is an ugly city, the ugliest in the world, from Park Avenue to the Bowery. The city is dazed with noise. It breathes not air, but gasoline. It deceives you with the whorish beauty of its electrical ads. It is a vast gas hotplate with suffocating grime. Blessed is the city that is crushed by iron, concrete, stone, and steel. An unlivable city where you cannot drive, unless the cars roll on each other instead of on the streets, though this city has the most of the world's best makes and models."[188]

185   V. N. Sushkova, "Amerikanizmy Borisa Pilniaka v romane "Okei"," *Iazyk i kultura*, no. 1 (2014): 63–69.
186   Boris A. Pilniak, *Okei, amerikanski roman* (Moscow: Federatsia, 1933), 35–44. To date this book has not been translated.
187   Pilniak, *Okei*, 293.
188   Ibid., 91-92.
189   Ibid., 145–153; Harlow Robinson, *Russians in Hollywood, Hollywood's Russians: Biography of an Image* (Boston: Northeastern University Press, 2007), 52–58; Frank Capra, *The Name Above the Title: an Autobiography* (New York: Bantam Books, 1971), 161.
190   Pilniak, *Okei*, 56.
191   Ibid., 18.
192   Garry Browning, *Boris Pilniak: Scythian at a Typewriter* (Ann Arbor, MI: Ardis, 1985), 54–57. On Pilniak's road trip in the USSR, see Eugene Lyons, *Assignment in Utopia* (New York: Harcourt, Brace and Co., 1937), 440–44.
193   On the original order, see RGASPI, f. 17, op. 3, d. 970, l. 63. On this talented duo, see Alain Préchac, *Ilf et Petrov, témoins de leur temps: Stalinisme et littérature* (Paris: L'Harmattan, 2001).
194   Ilia A. Ilf [pseudonym for Fainzilberg] and Evgenii P. Petrov [pseudonym for Kataev], *Odnoetazhnaia Amerika, putevye ocherki* (Moscow: Sovetski Pisatel, 1937).
195   Ilia Ilf, Evgueni Petrov, *Lettres d'Amérique - Correspondance et journaux*, trans. and ed. Alain Préchac (Paris: Parangon, 2004). The first post-Stalin edition was Ilia A. Ilf., *Rannie ocherki i feletony: pisma iz Ameriki* (Moscow: Izd-vo Pravda, 1961).
196   Ilia A. Ilf, "Luchshaia v mire strana (Amerika)," *Zhelezodorozhnik*, no. 3 (February 1924), in Ilf, *Rannie ocherki i feletony*, 35.
197   Ilya Ilf and Evgeny Petrov, *Little Golden America* (New York, Farrar & Reinhart, 1937), 23.
198   In 2009, Michael Chanan dedicated to Trone (1872-1969) his film, *The American Who Electrified Russia*.

Pilniak also discovered Hollywood, where he met the famous radio evangelist Aimee McPherson. He was recruited as a consultant by MGM, for a movie produced by Irving Thalberg and directed by Frank Capra, meant to enthuse the American public with the Soviet industrial boom. Its main character was Morgan, an engineer working in Moscow faced with the devious ploys of the GPU (State Political Directorate). Pilniak felt the initial screenplay was too hostile towards the USSR and quit before the end of his ten-week contract[189]. Having purchased a car, he drove to New York through the southwestern deserts, Texas, Louisiana, Detroit, Washington, and Boston. Throughout his trip, he was struck by the constant presence of automobiles, noting that "the roads looked more like assembly lines," an analogy he repurposed in his other travel accounts[190]. His harshest remarks were about Ford's plants in Detroit and Dearborn. He also mocked the industrialist's alleged humanism, puritanism, and moralism. He also tried, unsuccessfully, to visit Al Capone when he stopped in Chicago, expressing a genuine fascination for the gangster throughout the book. Studded with striking accounts of daily life and his encounters, Pilniak's narrative ends with a montage of tabloid headlines, leaving the reader with the impression of a damaged civilization. Nonetheless, he drew the conclusion that "the USSR and the USA are now locked in a decisive chess game for the future of humanity."[191] Returning to Moscow with his Chevrolet, he published his text as a series in *Novyi Mir*, and later as a book issued in three editions between 1933 and 1935[192]. Boris Pilniak was executed in 1937.

Four years after Pilniak's trip, two of his most distinguished colleagues, the satirists Ilia Ilf and Evgenii Petrov, embarked on their own American journey and upon their return, published a book that was met with both instant and durable acclaim. After the resounding success of their novels, *The Twelve Chairs* (1928) and *The Little Golden Calf* (1931), in the USSR and the Western world, Ilf and Petrov stepped off the brand new *Normandie* liner on 7 October 1935. The *Politbiuro* had commissioned a report from them on the "Soviet man abroad."[193] They set sail on the way back to the USSR on 22 January 1936, bringing with them a Ford automobile. Ilf and Petrov were more effusive than Pilniak in recounting their travels and, over the course of that same year, published their impressions in the weekly paper *Ogonek* (Little Light), illustrated with Ilf's photographs taken with a Leica camera. The following year, they published a full story entitled *Odnoetazhnaia Amerika* (One-Storied America; also translated as Little Golden America)], which was later reissued in several other editions in the USSR[194]. In addition, Ilf's regular letters to his wife give a more intimate and uncensored glimpse into the satirists' travels to the United States[195].

In 1924, when he was living in his hometown in Odessa, Ilf wrote that it was imperative to "Americanize life" in Russia, but without the workers being dominated by machines[196]. He finally had the opportunity to witness daily life in America, following a more rigorously planned itinerary than Pilniak's spontaneous one. Passing through Buffalo, Detroit, Chicago, Oklahoma City, and Santa Fe, Ilf and Petrov travelled to San Francisco and Los Angeles, and came back through San Antonio, New Orleans, Charleston, and Washington. The pair toured these cities while being guided—and supervised—by a certain "Mister Adams," whom they describe as having worked in the USSR for seven years and who helped them survive "in a country filled with gangsters, gasoline pumps, and ham and eggs."[197] The man was actually Solomon A. Trone, who had negotiated the 1920 agreement between the USSR and General Electric, and who had remained involved in Amtorg[198]. His wife Florence served as their driver.

Ilia A. Ilf. Photographs shot in the United States, October 1935 – January 1936. Gelatin silver prints on paper. Russian State Archive of Literature and Art.

Top left to right: Times Square, New York; view of a road in the West;
Bottom left to right: view of a road in the West; a group of men in a street in the West.

Ilia A. Ilf. Photographs shot in the United States, October 1935 – January 1936. Gelatin silver prints on paper. Russian State Archive of Literature and Art.

Top left to right: view of a motel in Los Angeles; view of a street in Los Angeles.
Bottom left to right: view of a store in Los Angeles; view of Hollywood Boulevard, Los Angeles.

343

Ilf and Petrov give often hilarious insights into small town America, while remaining ambivalent about the extravagance of New York, "the city where live two million automobiles and seven million persons who serve them."[199] Along with conventional depictions of the eastern metropolis and Chicago, they painted an original portrait of the Midwest and California, particularly Hollywood. They drew perfectly pragmatic conclusions from their trip, unsurprisingly criticizing the American political system, but praising the "democracy in intercourse between people," "which should interest us no less than a new machine model."[200] To them, there were lessons to be learned in terms of economy and daily life: "America does not know what will happen with it tomorrow. We know, and we can tell with definite accuracy, what will happen with us fifty years from now. Nevertheless, we can still learn much from America. We are doing that. But the lessons which we learn from America are episodic and too specialized. To catch up with America! That task which Stalin set before our people is immense, but in order to carry out this task we must first of all study America, study not only its automobiles, its turbine generators and radio apparatuses (we are doing that), but likewise the very character of the work of American workers, engineers, business people, especially the business people, because if our Stakhanovites sometime outstrip the norms of American workers, while the engineers are no worse at times than the American engineers (about that we heard frequently from Americans themselves), still, our business people or economists are considerably behind American business people and cannot compete with them in any way."[201]

The first version of the travelogue, along with selected photographs among the thousand or so Ilf had taken with his Leica, was met with great acclaim in the widely distributed illustrated paper *Ogonek*. Quite different from the images that were circulating in the USSR beforehand, Ilf's snapshots crystallized the authors' observations about the American heartland[202]. Aleksandr Rodchenko was critical of them, writing that they comprised a "motley collection of photographs" with "elements of naturalism, enthusiasm for formalism, and work of an almost applied character." In other words, Ilf's photographs lacked style and were a mere "first experiment." "In the future, the writer [would] find his own style, just as he found his own style in literary work." More importantly to him, the images failed to communicate satire and humour, though they exuded "much naïve charm, which reflects the writer's good taste." Overall, Rodchenko encouraged Ilf to pursue his still amateurish

199   Ilf and Petrov, *Little Golden America*, 234.
200   Ibid.
201   Ibid., 232.
202   Erika Wolf, "Ilf and Petrov's American Photographs," *Cabinet*, no. 14 (2004): 77–81; Id., ed., *Ilf and Petrov's American Road Trip: The 1935 Travelogue of Two Soviet Writers* (New York: Princeton Architectural Press, 2007). On the writer's photographic work, see *Ilia Ilf - fotograf: fotografii iz sobrania Aleksandry Ilf, Moskva: 1930-e gody*, (Moscow: Moskovskii Tsentr Iskusstv, 2002); Aleksei Loginov, *Ilia Ilf i fotografia* (Moscow: Punktum/Trilistnik, 2007).
203   Aleksandr M. Rodchenko, "Amerikanskie fotografii Ili Ilfa," *Sovetskoe foto* 11, no. 8 (1936): 26–27.
204   Prints of these photographs in 6 × 9, 9 × 12, or 12 × 18 cm formats are held at RGALI, f. 1821, opis 1, d. 180. The negatives have been destroyed: Wolf, ed. *Ilf and Petrov's American Road Trip*, 147.
205   Ilf and Petrov, *Little Golden America*, 20.
206   Robert Venturi, *Complexity and Contradiction in Architecture* (New York: Museum of Modern Art, 1966), 102.
207   Ilia A. Ilf and Evguenii P. Petrov, *Odnoetazhnaia Amerika, putevye ocherki* (Moscow: Molodaia gvardiia, 1947).
208   "Beseda s Erskinom Kolduellom," *Internatsionalnaia literatura*, no. 6 (1941): 190. The American edition is *Little Golden America*, trans. Charles Malamuth (New York: Farrar & Rinehart, 1937).
209   Ilia A. Ilf and Evgeni P. Petrov, Letter to Joseph V. Stalin, [late February – before the 26th] 1936, APRF, f. 3, op. 34, ed. khr. 206, l. 54–63; published in *Iskusstvo kino*, no. 11 (1992): 87–89.
210   Boris Z. Shumiatskii, Letter to Joseph V. Stalin, 27 March 1936, APRF, f. 3, op. 63, d. 63, l. 23–36, published in *Kremlevskii kinoteatr*, 312–14.

work with this "new and sharp" approach[203]. Unfortunately, the latter died in April 1937, before he could put in practice the former's patronizing advice.

These photographs, taken by a gifted amateur, reveal a diverse America. Ilf espoused Mendelsohn's worm's-eye view in his compositions with New York skyscrapers,[204]. His nocturnal Broadway landscapes show electricity being "brought down (or brought up, if you like) to the level of a trained circus animal."[205] Far from the large metropolis, Ilf portrayed the sublime horizons he discovered through the windshield of his Ford, or while parked on a roadside in desolate expanses. The viewer can catch glimpses of Native reserves and African-American neighbourhoods. The milestones of the road trip were recorded as raw data, from southwestern motels to small towns whose idle inhabitants roamed the streets. The highlight of the duo's road journey, Los Angeles, can be seen with its palm tree-lined streets and boulevards. Some of the portraits of haphazardly encountered men are reminiscent of stills taken in the same time period by Walker Evans, with whom Ilf shared an interest for signs and advertisements. To some extent, their focus on mundane scenes observed in the public space foreshadows Robert Venturi's interrogation, coined thirty years later: "Is not Main Street almost all right?"[206]

Ilf's photographs, excluded from the 1930s editions and already edited for their publication in *Ogonek*, were terribly retouched and printed in a 1947 publication, at the beginning of the Cold War[207]. Meanwhile, the book's success spread to the American public, and Erskine Caldwell told Russian reporters in 1941 that it was "the most popular book in the United States."[208] Encouraged by their successful trip, Ilf and Petrov wrote directly to Stalin in February 1936, describing the comfortable living conditions they encountered even in the remotest places. They recommended sending Soviet executives to witness this for themselves: "One can imagine how quickly the material state of the country would improve if district secretaries could see for themselves the significance of services offered to the population and what a gas station, a cafeteria, a hotel, standard furniture, clean tablecloths, bathrooms, showers, highways, […] and hundreds of other essential things look like." Their conclusion was even clearer: "We understand that the concept of quality of life is based on the overall increase in production of consumer goods and in the improvement of their quality. But we also believe that the matter of taste and its development among those who are building the new world every single day is of utmost importance. Therefore, well-organized trips to America for party leaders could be greatly beneficial to the country." Ilf and Petrov also criticized Shumiatskii's *kino-gorod* project based on their impressions of Hollywood, believing sunlight to be a marginal factor and, more importantly, claiming that film production could only develop in a major capital such as London[209]. Shumiatskii, sensing a threat to his project, condemned the writers' "superficial approach," objecting that they visited Hollywood in the dark month of December. In a nod to Stalin's expression, and to support his rebuttal, he claimed that British cinema was a "dwarf" and that the Italians were hurrying to build their own *kino-gorod* near Rome[210].

Mikoyan and the Americanization of Russian Food Supply

In the summer of 1936, seemingly following Ilf and Petrov's recommendations, a peculiar investigative tour was organized with the blessing of the highest authorities. The regime began promising relative plenty to the population, after putting an end to bread rationing the previous year, and new technologies had to be imported to help supply cities[211]. A delegation comprised of a dozen engineers spent two months in the United States and travelled some 21,000 kilometres across the country to study food production and supply. The mission was led by Anastas Mikoyan, People's Commissar of Food Industry as of 1934; he was therefore away from Moscow when the Great Purge trials began, but played a major part in the 1938 trial against Bukharin and Rykov, and 19 other alleged saboteurs[212]. Mikoyan's political longevity was exceptional: according to a popular saying, he served "from Ilich [Lenin] to Ilich [Brezhnev] without suffering a stroke." As he wrote in his memoir, the 1936 trip was instigated by Stalin himself, who put his full weight behind the project, funding it and selecting its participants. Indeed, he explicitly asked Mikoyan to bring along the engineer V. V. Burgman, head of the Commissariat's construction service[213]. The 1936 operation, exceptional in all respects in the history of Russian explorations of the American industry, resulted in a technological transfer involving consumer goods instead of heavy industry like during the first five-year plan.

Ilf and Petrov were very critical towards the industrialized produce they had to ingest throughout their trip. They quoted a speech by Mikoyan, who said that "food in a socialist country must be palatable—that it must bring joy to people—and it sounded like poetry to us."[214] Nevertheless, the industrial production of food was the focal point of interest in the Russians' investigation of Chicago, Cleveland, Detroit—where they met Henry Ford—, Gary, and Los Angeles. They visited some hundred firms listed by Mikoyan in a 1971 text: "Tin can manufacturers, beer and non-alcoholic beverage factories, ice cream, crouton, biscuit, and bread makers, refrigerators for fish and meat preservation, a crushed ice factory, a conglomerate for chocolate and candy production, coffee, tea, and cocoa packaging, a duck freezing plant, metal roof manufacturers for chicken coops, milk, and canned produce factories, the Chicago slaughterhouses, farms and factories for the deep-freezing of cereal flakes and grains, mayonnaise and powdered milk manufacturers, fruit and vegetable juice and wine factories, including champagne makers, beet sugar factories, etc."[215] The People's Commissar was particularly interested in refrigeration technologies and recommended an action plan for the acquisition of entire chains of production. The Soviet technical apparatus pursued its work in the vein of Mikoyan's delegation. At the same time, the monthly journal *Amerikanskaia tekhnika i promyshlennost* published reports on the food industry along with the usual articles on dams and airplanes. They covered processes from refrigeration to deep-freezing, products such as mayonnaise, ice cream, and sliced bread, and services like dry cleaning[216].

211   Sheila Fitzpatrick, *Everyday Stalinism; Ordinary Life in Extraordinary Times: Soviet Russia in the 1930s* (Oxford: Oxford University Press, 1999), 90–91.

212   Mikhail Iu. Pavlov, *Anastas Mikoian: politicheskii portret na fone sovetskoi epokhi* (Moscow: Mezhdunarodnye otnosheniia, 2010), 90–107.

213   Anastas I. Mikoyan, *Tak bylo: razmyshlenia o minuvshem* (Moscow: Tsentrpoligraf, 2014), 302. Mikoyan wrote a detailed account in "Dva mesatsa v SShA," *SShA Ekonomika, politika, ideologiia* 2, no. 10 and 11 (1971): 68–77 and 73–84. See Frederick Barghoorn, *The Soviet Image of the USA*, 30.

214   Ilf and Petrov, *Little Golden America*, 27.

215   Mikoyan, "Dva mesatsa v SShA," no. 11 (1971): 73.

216   "Metody bystrogo zamorazhivaniia v sviazi s kontsentratsei proizvodstva pishchevykh produktov," *Amerikanskaia tekhnika i promyshlennost* 13, no. 1 (January 1936): 32–42; G.S. Margolin, "Proizvodstvo margarina, kompaunda i maioneza v SShA," *Amerikanskaia tekhnika i promyshlennost* 13, no. 4 (April 1936): 151–54; C.D. Dahle, "Proizvodstvo morozhenogo v SShA," *Amerikanskaia tekhnika i promyshlennost* 13, no. 7 (July 1936): 285–91; A. Julian, "Sovremennye khlebozavody v SShA," *Amerikanskaia tekhnika i promyshlennost* 13, no. 9 (September 1936): 354–66; Frigidaire Corp., "Praktika kholodilnogo dela v SShA," *Amerikanskaia tekhnika i promyshlennost* 13, no. 10 (October 1936): 404–13; A. Ia. Brailovskii, "Organizatsiia i postanovka prashechnogo dela v SShA," *Amerikanskaia tekhnika i promyshlennost* 13, no. 6 (June 1936): 264–74.

Top left to right: Boris A. Zelenskii. "Ask for sausages everywhere", 1937; Aleksandr N. Zelenskii. "Hot Moscow-style cutlets with a bun - 50 kopeks", 1937. Bottom left to right: Aleksandr N. Pobedinskii. "Ice cream, both in winter and summer: delicious and healthy", 1937; Stepan Prokoptsev. "Mayonnaise sauce", 1938.

Theses encounters had a significant effect on Soviet industry and daily life[217]. A new type of bread roll—*bulochki*—was introduced, destined to be sometimes filled with minced meat, as Mikoyan waxed lyrical about hamburgers and aimed to develop their consumption. Upon his return, he imported 25 grills that would allow to produce two million hamburgers a day. Renamed *moskovskye kotlety* (Moscow cutlets), they were sold in kiosks in Moscow, Leningrad, Kharkov, Kiev, and Baku[218]. Other factories were repurposed to produce "the doctor's sausages," the popular nickname for a meat product meant to fight malnutrition. Notably, industrial production of ice cream was initiated in 1938. This cause was so dear to Mikoyan's heart that Stalin reportedly teased him by quipping: "You, Anastas, care more about ice cream than about communism."[219] Soviet consumers also discovered products such as corn flakes, ketchup, industrial mayonnaise, tomato juice—which Mikoyan loved—, and all types of canned foods. As for drinks, though the Coca-Cola licence proved too expensive, American carbonation technologies were acquired to massively produce champagne, a craving of Stalin's, who liked it sweet, according to Mikoyan[220].

Returning to Moscow with gifts for his family, such as Mickey Mouse pens, immediately stolen from his children in school, the People's Commissar started planning detailed menus for the population[221]. In 1939, he inspired the publication of the the thick volume *The Book of Tasty and Healthy Food*, bearing on its cover a dedication to "housewives" and listing the newly imported industrial products, along with recipes for their simple use[222]. The book often explicitly referenced Mikoyan's trip, citing the "American habit" of serving fruit at breakfast and discussing the production of tenderloin, ketchup, and whisky[223]. This classic was reissued dozens of times until the 1980s, each time more lavishly illustrated. At the same time, massive publicity campaigns were launched to popularize unknown foods with posters produced by the Pishchepromreklama firm, stemming from the People's Commissariat, which employed talented graphic designers such as Mariia Nesterova-Berzina, Aleksandr Pobedinskii, Stepan Prokoptsev, and Aleksandr and Boris Zelenskii[224]. Though Stalin normally supported his lieutenant, he seemed to have reservations regarding the production of refrigerators, which were essential in the American food chain, citing the long Russian winters to contend their uselessness. The machines were produced at an extremely slow pace, and mostly owing to the automotive industry[225]. After Mikoyan's mission, a 1937 agreement was made between the two States to normalize product circulation and foster commercial negotiations. Licences were also acquired to manufacture aviation equipment, while reverse engineering of American automobiles continued[226]. The first Soviet luxury car, the ZIS-101, inspired by a Buick model,

217 See the information collected in Katya von Bremzen, *Mastering the Art of Soviet Cooking: A Memoir of Food and Longing* (New York: Random House, 2013).
218 Mikoyan, "Dva mesatsa v SShA," no. 11 (1971): 77.
219 Joseph V. Stalin, statement reported in Irina Glushchenko, *Obshchepit: Mikoian i sovetskaia kukhnia* (Moscow: Izd-vo dom Gos. Univ. Vysshei Shkoly Ekonomiki, 2010), 93.
220 Mikoyan, *Tak bylo*, 313–15. On this point, see Annette Henry, "Cuisine capitaliste, cuisine communiste," *Médium*, no. 3 (2011): 78–91.
221 Stepan Mikoyan, in Glushchenko, *Obshchepit*, 99.
222 *Kniga o vkusnoi i zdorovoi pishche*, Evgenii L. Khudiakov, ed. (Moscow: Pishchepromizdat, 1939).
223 Ibid., *passim*, quoted in Glushchenko, *Obshchepit*, 95.
224 *Sovetskii reklamnyi plakat 1923-1941* (Moscow: Kontakt-Kultura, 2013).
225 Mikoyan, *Tak bylo*; Harrison Evans Salisbury, *Anatomy of the Soviet Union* (London: Nelson, 1968), 13.
226 On Soviet industrial property practices, see Antony C. Sutton, "Copying as a Development Mechanism," in *Western Technology and Soviet Economic Development, 1930–1945* (Stanford: Hoover Institution Press, 1971), 299–317.

was mass-produced as of 1939 with equipment purchased from the Budd Company in Gary. It was pictured on two covers of the journal *Za rulem*, photographed against the backdrop of the Kremlin towers and in the fictional setting of the Palace of the Soviets[227].

Mumford and Wright in Moscow

As of 1933, the restoration of diplomatic relations with the United States contributed not only to technical missions like the one conducted by Mikoyan, but also led to a certain dissemination of American architecture. In October 1934, Aleksei Neiman, a Soviet diplomat in charge of Soviet Affairs in Washington, gave voice to one of Iofan's ideas by suggesting that the Union of Soviet Architects organize an exhibit to showcase "the best and most interesting" aspects of American architecture "in the most concrete way, with models, drawings, and photographs."[228] The Union readily accepted to organize such an exhibition and replied with a list of themes to be presented. The organization of the first architects' Congress, planned for 1935, but postponed to 1937, seems to have prevented this project from materializing. The art historian David Arkin, who has most probably penned the response to Neiman and was then acting as the Union's scholarly secretary, would go on to become one of the main agents of the USSR's remote relationship with the United States.

In his 1932 *Architecture of the Contemporary West*, a book on architectural and urban issues according to certain European figures, Arkin printed a translation of Richard Neutra's *Amerika* in a section entitled "Some Specificities of Recent American Architecture." The book was illustrated with images from *Rush City Reformed* and with a montage by El Lissitzky based on a Brett Weston photograph, similar to the one used in 1930 for the cover of Neutra's book [ill. p. 224]. Arkin devoted more space to a selection of writings by Frank Lloyd Wright, who was increasingly acclaimed in Moscow[229]. Being on the receiving end of the entire foreign correspondence with the Union of Soviet Architects and the VOKS (the Union Society for Cultural Relations with Foreign Countries), Arkin published an overview of American architecture in 1934, claiming that "nowhere else has technical industrial progress, until recently a pipe dream, shown so much potential as in America." He listed not

227   *Za rulem*, no. 7 et 13 (1939).
228   Aleksei F. Neiman [USSR embassy in the US], Letter to the Architects' Union, 22 October 1934, RGALI, f. 674, op. 1, d. 14, l. 10.
229   David E. Arkin, *Arkhitektura sovremennogo zapada* (Moscow: OGIZ–IZOGIZ, 1932, 86–92 [Wright] and 118–124 [Neutra].
230   David E. Arkin, "Zametki ob amerikanskoi arkhitekture," *Arkhitektura SSSR* 2, no. 1 (January 1934): 43–52.
231   David E. Arkin, *Iskusstvo bytovoi veshchi* (Moscow: Izogiz, 1932), 42–43 and 81. Lewis Mumford's text is "'Modern' als Handelsware," *Die Form*, no. 8 (1930): 322–26.
232   Sergei M. Eisenstein, "Organichnost i obraznost," in *Izbrannye proizvedenia v shesti tomakh* (Moscow: Iskusstvo, 1964[1934]), vol. 4, 652–72. I thank François Albera for bringing this text to my attention.
233   Lewis Mumford, *Vom Blockhaus zum Wolkenkratzer, eine Studie über amerikanische Architektur und Zivilisation* (Berlin: Bruno Cassirer Verlag, 1926). Originally: *Sticks and Stones: A Study of American Architecture & Civilization* (New York: Norton, 1924). Iofan, "Materialy o sovremennoi arkhitekture SShA i Italii," 23. I am restating here my own analyses from *Scenes of the World to Come* (Paris: Flammarion, Montreal: Canadian Centre for Architecture, 1995): 153–54.
234   David E. Arkin, "Amerikanskaia arkhitektura i kniga Mumforda," preface to Lewis Mumford, *Ot brevenchatogo doma do neboskreba, ocherk istorii amerikanskoi arkhitektury* (Moscow: Izd-vo vses. Akademii Arkhitektury, 1936), 15–16.
235   Ibid., 4–5. Arkin republished his preface shortly thereafter as "The Skyscraper": "Neboskreb," in *Obrazy arkhitektury* (Moscow: Gos. arkhitekturnoe izd-vo, 1941): 313–30.
236   Arkin, "Amerikanskaia arkhitektura i kniga Mumforda," 7.

only the recent skyscrapers, but also the major hospitals, park systems, and the works of Frank Lloyd Wright, whom he considered the most representative figure in a field filled with potential teachings, despite all of its contradictions.[230] In another book from the same period on *The Art of Everyday Objects*, Arkin quoted Wright's discourse on the "Arts and Craft of the Machine" and adopted Lewis Mumford's critique of the American impetus to excessively replace furnishings, which he saw as a typical example of capitalist wastefulness[231]. Remarkably, in a 1934 lecture, Sergei Eisenstein also discussed Mumford, whose *Technics and Civilization* he had seemingly recently read, and wondered what shape the Soviet heavy industry had to take to emerge from the "paleotechnic" age[232].

Arkin issued in 1936 his translation of the German version of Lewis Mumford's 1924 *Sticks and Stones*, whose positions Iofan had referenced in one of his travel narratives[233]. In this compact, critical history of American architecture, Mumford endorsed Louis Sullivan's retrospective condemnation of the "white plague" embodied by the 1893 Chicago colonnades, a position that Arkin obviously could not sanction as the Soviet aesthetic was veering back to classicism. He somewhat distanced himself from Mumford's critique, in what he considered a "tract" against the consequences of machinism, inspired by Oswald Spengler's historical pessimism. However, he made sure to discard this hostile attitude and the "fetishism of the machine," an accusation then commonly made against Le Corbusier in Moscow[234]. Arkin's discourse was mainly comprised of blanket praise of American architectural culture, advocating for it despite its social context. He wrote that "only in America has the capitalist city raised such complex and contradictory issues for the architect, and no other place has seen such profound transformations of architectural project methods and the work of the architect himself."

Arkin reserved special treatment for skyscrapers. To him, these building types were the most representative of capitalist inconsistency, an opinion he stressed to placate the Soviet censors: "The same skyscraper, which in our minds, is the dominant, even exclusive, type of construction in America, contains a series of complex and fundamentally novel architectural components, whose meaning extends far beyond the confines of the American experience. [...] Stemming directly from competition and ground rent—as if ground rent itself was hurled into the sky—and thus expressing the very contradictions of the capitalist city, the skyscraper has also allowed the architect, faced with unprecedented problems, to considerably expand his thinking and methods."[235] Likely drawing on Iofan's narrative, Arkin analyzed the urban nature of the then relatively unknown structure, mentioning how its shape was determined by the street grid and the setback rules of the 1916 zoning regulation. He also noted—as Iofan and Neutra, in *Wie baut Amerika?*, before him—, that American skyscrapers were not only intended for offices or, more rarely, for dwellings, but could also house "venues with the most varied purposes." This variety of uses embodies the flexibility theorized by Rem Koolhaas, who sees it as one of the positive traits of New York's culture of congestion.[236]

Though Arkin, who appreciated the categorization of venues and equipment, acknowledged that this functional generosity was "very interesting," he highlighted the shortcomings of the "culture of details, furnishings, and cladding" of the buildings. In a militant text, he reprised 1920s critiques of skyscraper shapes, paraphrasing El Lissitzky's discourse from a decade earlier: "American architecture, which has solved, with the skyscraper, a series of extremely complex technical, constructional, and organizational problems, has clothed this entirely new type of building in a tight breastplate of traditional stylistic forms, both busy and incoherent in its eclecticism." Arkin mocked the "naïve" gesture of applying the classical structure of the column, made of a base, a pillar, and a capital, to the skyscraper, a practice already criticized by Louis Sullivan. He incidentally deplored the lack of appreciation for this pioneer, as well as for "the most recent visionary," Frank Lloyd Wright, whose criticism of the metropolis he endorsed almost word for word: "Architecture has created new giant structures, but it has lost its sense of scale; it has worked with enormous masses and volumes, but has considered them without relation to the fundamental unit of any architectural scale: man himself. [...] By erecting vertical constructions into space, builders have failed to account for the horizontal coordinates required for the perception of the whole, they have made these gigantic architectural masses inaccessible to the mere mortal."[237]

Arkin's mentioning of Wright is no coincidence. The two kept regularly in touch ever since the American architect contributed, in 1934, to the series "How I Work" published by *Arkhitektura SSSR*, along with André Lurçat, Robert Mallet-Stevens, Hannes Meyer, and J. J. P. Oud. Questioned on the theme of "composition," Wright unequivocally distanced himself from the notion: "In organic architecture composition, as such, is dead. We no longer compose. We conceive the building as an entity. Proceeding from generals to particulars by way of some appropriate scheme of construction, we try to find the equation of expression best suited, that is to say most natural, to all the factors involved."[238] He also categorically refused to see the past as a source of architectural invention, claiming that "the only way classical or modern architectural monuments can be helpful to us is to study that quality in them which made them serviceable or beautiful in their day and be informed by that quality in them. As ready-made forms, they can only be harmful to us today."[239] Wright's figure was used to attack capitalism well beyond architectural circles. In 1932, and once again the following year, the *Pravda* asked him about the effects of the Great Depression on American intellectuals. He replied that they had been the "hapless beneficiaries of a success system they have never clearly understood, but a system that has worked miracles for them while they slept." He also had positive, even friendly things to say about the Soviet system, but without going as far as to endorse it: "I view the USSR as a heroic endeavour to establish more genuine human values in a social state than any existing before. Its heroism and devotion move me deeply and with great hope. But I fear that machine worship to defeat capitalism may become inverted capitalism in Russia itself and so prostitute the man to the machine."[240] In 1935, Arkin turned to Wright once again to commission an essay for the first issue of the Union's bimonthly publication, *Arkhitekturnaia gazeta*[241].

Several factors dictated Wright's attitude towards Russia. First, he was flattered to be taken seriously by the Soviets, as he was then overlooked by American politicians. Furthermore, his wife Olgivanna Lazović, a disciple of the mystic philosopher Georges Gurdjieff, spoke Russian and was a Slavophile. Lastly, he never ceased to see Russia as a possible pool of apprentices for his school in Taliesin, Wisconsin, as evidenced by a telegram sent to Arkin in December 1934: "Hope to see an organic architecture by Russians for Russia and several young Russians working at Taliesin to help the matter forward."[242]

As the idea of an inaugural Congress of Architects to be held in 1937 materialized, Arkin and his colleagues worked tirelessly to establish a list of American participants, which kept fluctuating according to the available resources and selection criteria. The initial list, developed by the Union of

Architects and by VOKS, included Wright, Eliel Saarinen, Joseph Urban, Lonberg-Holm, Fellheimer & Wagner—on the basis of their participation to the 1933 Chicago Exposition, Frederick Kiesler, Paul Philippe Cret, the German critic and urban planner Werner Hegemann, who was living as a refugee in New York, Neutra, and the historian Fiske Kimball[243]. The list was then divided into four categories to establish a final selection: "1. Renowned architects, active in institutions (presidents of national associations, institute directors, chief architects of great cities)—12 pers. 2. Masters of the previous generation, who strive to combine traditional elements with new principles, as well as specialists of new construction techniques—7 pers. 3. Representatives of the so-called 'new architecture' (constructivists, functionalists, and related movements)—7 pers. 4. Representatives from left-wing architectural organizations, close to the Popular Front and friends to the USSR—4 pers."[244]

A second list was then written with the same participants, with Simon Breines replacing Urban, who had died in 1933. A margin note was jotted down as a reminder to ask comrade [Hannes] Meyer about his opinion of America[245]. Finally, the last list, annotated by Arkin, contains Wright ("the main representative of the elder generation of modern architects, with a worldwide reputation as the creator of original works, exerting a great influence on American architecture. His recent books and articles have been strongly critical of the contemporary capitalist city. He has often expressed sympathy for the USSR"); Breines ("a young architect, who has openly shown his support to the USSR and who took part in the competition for the Palace of the Soviets"); William F. Lamb ("one of the main practising architects in the United States; created many buildings and co-created the world's tallest skyscraper, the Empire [State] Building); Richard Neutra ("the author of a book series on American architecture. Well-regarded practitioner, close to constructivism. Author of the book *Wie baut Amerika?*, translated into Russian"); Walter Gropius, who had recently settled in America; and Saarinen ("a very famous Finnish architect, a master of the older generation, living and working in America. Created the Helsinki Central Station and other major buildings.") In the meantime, Hegemann had died[246]. This cunning diversity was short-lived: in the end, only Wright, Breines, and Lamb—who declined—were invited to the State-mandated spectacle in June 1937[247].

The purpose of the Congress was to reaffirm the centralized system that had been in place since 1932, and to establish a consensus around socialist realism[248]. According to Arkin, who commented candidly on the debates,

237   Ibid., 10-11.
238   Frank Lloyd Wright, "Kak ia rabotaiu," *Arkhitektura SSSR* 2, no. 2 (February 1934): 71. In English: "Categorical Reply to Questions by 'Architecture of the USSR'," in Frank Lloyd Wright, *Collected Writings, vol. 3, 1931–1939*, ed. Bruce Brooks Pfeiffer (New York: Rizzoli, 1993), 145.
239   Ibid., 145.
240   Frank Lloyd Wright, "First Answers to Questions by *Pravda*," 19 October 1933, in *Collected Writings, vol. 3*, 141–42.
241   David E. Arkin, Telegram to Frank Lloyd Wright, 1 January 1935, Frank Loyd Wright Collection, Avery Library.
242   Frank Lloyd Wright, Telegram to David E. Arkin, 11 December 1934, RGALI, f. 674, op. 1, ed. khr. 14, l. 21.
243   List of foreign guests to the Congress of Architects, 1936, RGALI, f. 674, op. 2, ed. khr. 22, l. 10-11.
244   Ibid., l. 30
245   Ibid., l. 34.
246   Ibid., l. 100, 113 and 135–36.
247   Karo S. Alabian, Aleksei V. Shchusev, and Viktor A. Vesnin, Letters to Frank Lloyd Wright, Simon Breines, and William F. Lamb, 10 May 1937, RGALI, f. 674, op. 2, ed. khr. 22, l. 167–69.
248   On the Congress, see Richard Anderson, "The Future of History: the Cultural Politics of Soviet Architecture, 1928–41," PhD dissertation (Columbia University, 2010), 186–240; Hudson, *Blueprints and Blood*, 185–202; Udovički-Selb, "Between Modernism and Socialist Realism," 479–80.

matters were decided beforehand, and there was no space for discussions about architectural language: "The first Congress of Soviet architects did not engage in a academic war of words on the relative merits of one architectural style or another, it did not waste time and words trying to find subtle and rhetorical interpretations of the meaning of socialist realism in architecture. Yet still this meaning prevailed in all the work of the Congress in every multi-day discussion of the creative questions of Soviet architecture."[249] Though communists were a very small minority in the profession, the assembly was decidedly in favour of the imposed doctrine, with constructivists publicly and ruthlessly criticizing their own movement. References to America were focused on technical issues, as Aleksei Shchusev declared, for example, that a lot remained to be learned from the United States about construction materials and interior design[250]. On the theme of industrialized housing, Ginzburg praised the productivity of American construction sites, and was commended for his statement by the press[251].

Wright was undoubtedly the guest of honour at the Congress, where he enjoyed special treatment. He was chaperoned by Olgivanna, who served as his interpreter. He was afforded the opportunity to visit the latest creations of the constructivists. Viktor Vesnin, who had delivered one of the most nuanced speeches at the Congress, introduced him to the Palace of Culture and the ZIL factories. Wright was also taken to the Union of Architects' resthouse in Sukha-novo, in a suburb south of Moscow. He presented drawings and a film about his work to a select audience and offered to train three dozen Soviet appren-tices in Taliesin. The highlight of the trip was his speech in the Pillar Hall of the House of Unions, where the Congress was held. Wright fervently praised the successes of Soviet industry and took care to avoid positioning himself in the debate between moderns and conservatives, advocating for a rather vague "scientific" approach: "The USSR must now construct buildings on a scientific basis, guided by common sense and making the most efficient use of high quality building materials. The left wing of the so-called "new" architecture also advocated the principles of creating an organic architecture but, to all intents and purposes, did not proceed beyond plain wall panels, flat roofs, and ornamental corner windows; and the right wing of said "new" architecture turned the buildings into ornaments. Both tendencies are generated by decaying old cultures. The correct path to the creation of organic architecture consists of the scientific organization of building activity and animating it with a genuine spirit of humanity."[252]

In parallel to this uncontentious discourse and despite the warm rap-port established with Iofan, Wright made no secret of his opposition to the Palace of the Soviets project, which he criticized by comparing it to the eclec-tic American skyscrapers he despised: "This palace—only proposed I hope— is good if we take it for a modern version of Saint George slaying the dragon:

249   David E. Arkin, "Tvorcheskie uroki," *Arkhitektura SSSR* 5, no. 7–8 (July–August 1937): 51.
250   Aleksei V. Shchusev, Address to the Congress of Soviet Architects, June 1937, RGALI, fonds 674,
        pop. 2, d. 30, 10.
251   Moisei Ia. Ginzburg, "Industrializatsiia zhilishchnogo stroitelstva," *Arkhitekturnaia gazeta*, 28 June 1937, 2;
        Nikolai P. Bylinkin, "Voprosy zhilishchnoi arkhitektury na sezde," *Arkhitektura SSSR* 5, no. 7–8 (July–
        August 1937), 54.
252   "Frank Lloyd Wright," *Arkhitektura SSSR* 5, no. 7–8 (July–August 1937): 49–50. At least four versions of this
        text were published, including two in Moscow. See also Brian A. Spencer, "Frank Lloyd Wright and Russia:
        First All-Union Congress of Soviet Architects, Moscow, Russia, Soviet Union, June 1937,"
        Journal of the Taliesin Fellows, no. 51 (October 2017): 12–38.

Frank Lloyd Wright with David E. Arkin and his wife. Sukhanovo, 1937. Silver gelatin print on paper, 6.5 × 10.5 cm.
Frank Lloyd Wright Foundation Archives, Avery Architectural & Fine Arts Library, Columbia University.

Frank Lloyd Wright with Boris M. Iofan and Olga F. Sasso-Ruffo. Moscow, 1937. Silver gelatin prints on paper, 9 × 14 cm
Frank Lloyd Wright Foundation Archives, Avery Architectural & Fine Arts Library, Columbia University.

that is to say the leonine Lenin stamping the life out of a capitalistic sky-scraper."[253] Needless to say, this part of his speech was censored by the official newspapers and the Russian architectural press[254]. Upon Wright's return to Taliesin, the journal *Soviet Russia Today*, published in New York since 1932 by the Friends of the Soviet Union, solicited his allocution for publication. He titled it "Architecture and Life in the USSR" and tried to compensate his light criticism of the official Soviet architecture with high praise for "comrade Stalin."[255] Viewed as a "travel companion," Wright continued to be invoked in the Soviet media through the Amkino, an organization operating in parallel to Amtorg as a channel for cinematographic exchange, which often loaned him film reels[256]. He felt free to lecture the Russians in an *Izvestiia* article on organic architecture and democracy: "Study Russian nature for your forms, my Russians. Throw the must textbooks away. Close these morgues you were taught to call museums. Learn the basic principles of the new reality you profess as these principles apply to buildings, sculpture, painting, planting and closing."[257] In a more political vein, as reported in the communist newspaper *Daily Worker* in August 1937, he lauded the new Soviet constitution declared in December 1936[258]. For almost a decade, while all European architects were systematically discarded, Wright was thus used both by the architectural hierarchy and by the leaders of the regime to show that the USSR had a loyal friend in the person who was the most famous architect in America.

The 1939 World's Fair

Following in the footsteps of their *Politbiuro* colleague Mikoyan, two of Stalin's main lieutenants, Lavrentii Beria and Lazar Kaganovich, landed in New York in April 1939 to attend the unprecedented inauguration of a Soviet building in the United States. After the 1925 and 1937 exhibitions in Paris, the USSR intended to showcase the new face of its great industrial power at the World's Fair held in Flushing Meadows[259]. The pavilion was designed by Karo Alabian and Boris Iofan in response to a commission launched—shortly before he was arrested—by Ivan Mezhlauk, the brother of the previously mentioned economist. The structure was built according to a circular plan, centred on a mast holding the statue of a man carrying a red star in his outstretched arm, in a

253   Frank Lloyd Wright, "Address to the Architect's World Congress – Soviet Russia 1937," in *An Autobiography* [1943] (New York: Horizon Press, 1977), 573.
254   Excerpts from Wright's speech were published in *Izvestiia*, 26 June 1937, and in *Arkhitektura SSSR* 5, no. 7-8 (August 1937): 49–50.
255   Frank Lloyd Wright, "Architecture and Life in the USSR," *Soviet Russia Today*, October 1937, 14–19; also published in *Architectural Record* 82, no. 4 (October 1937): 58–63; and in *An Autobiography* (1943), 549–56.
256   Vladimir Verlinskii [Amkino], Letter to Frank Lloyd Wright, 21 October 1937, Frank Lloyd Wright Collection, Avery Library.
257   Frank Lloyd Wright, "For 'Izvestiia'," 1937, in Frank Lloyd Wright, *Collected Writings*, vol. 3, 214–15.
258   Paul Romaine, "Wright Praises New Soviet Constitution," *Daily Worker*, 12 August 1937.
259   Anthony Swift, "The Soviet World of Tomorrow at the New York World's Fair, 1939," *Russian Review* 57, no. 3 (1998): 364–79.
260   Fabien Bellat, "Mission à l'étranger, appropriations et dénis tacites dans l'architecture soviétique," in *L'étranger dans la littérature et les arts soviétiques*, ed. Marie-Christine Autant-Mathieu (Villeneuve-d'Ascq: Presses universitaires du Septentrion, 2014), 174–75.
261   Igor V. Riazantsev, *Iskusstvo sovetskogo vystavochnogo ansamblia 1917–1970* (Moscow: Sovetskii khudozhnik, 1976), 110–14.
262   "World's Tallest Building," *Mechanics Illustrated*, September 1939, 34.

nod to the Statue of Liberty. The two lateral pavilions shaped like bookends were reminiscent, in their tectonics, of the Rockefeller Center, while the walls enfolding the main body paid homage to the pavilion Albert Kahn had built for Ford as part of the 1933 Chicago exhibit, and which had been rebuilt in Dearborn[260].

Inside this ostentatious palace built with help from Simon Breines, another palace was featured: the one Iofan had started building in Moscow. A giant model of the building was presented in front of Iurii Pimenov's painting *The Sportsmen's Parade* . Other models showed the Dnieper dam and the Kuibyshev dam, the Magnitogorsk iron and steel works, and the Red Army Theatre designed by Alabian. A life-size replica of a section of the Maiakovskaia subway station and two ZIS-101 automobiles—the most luxurious cars manufactured in the USSR, using American techniques—were exposed to the public[261]. A sequence from Mikhail Kaufman's film *Our Moscow* was screened in a gallery, showing the Council of People's Commissars building on Okhotnyi Ryad, as seen from the Moskva Hotel. Its entablature was left off-screen to make it appear like a skyscraper. The film also showed grid crossings—railway and road—above the Moscow-Volga Canal, echoing the American highway interchanges shown in Norman Bel Geddes's *Futurama* within Albert Kahn's General Motors pavilion, and, of course, the "tallest and largest building in the world," the Palace of the Soviets, which the American press compared to the Eiffel Tower and the Empire State Building[262]. The pavilion's entire rhetoric was based on dimensional excess, aiming to show that the USSR was henceforth capable of competing with the United States.

Karo S. Alabian and Boris M. Iofan. Pavilion of the USSR at the New York World's Fair. Perspective, 1939.
Graphite, ink and watercolour on paper, 39 × 62 cm. Alex Lachmann Collection.

Propaganda booklets on the USSR, produced for distribution at the New York World's Fair.
Moscow: Foreign Languages Publishing House, 1939. CCA.

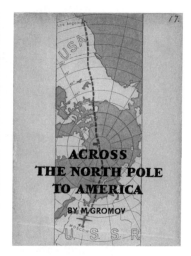

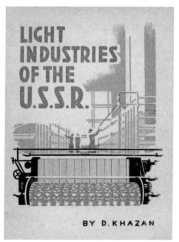

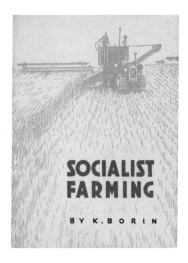

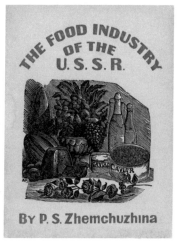

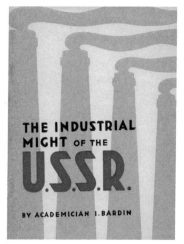

In charge of overseeing construction, Alabian stayed in New York for a long period of time, and Wright, still eager to host Russian apprentices, invited him to visit Taliesin[263]. Iofan was once again able to cross the Atlantic for the occasion[264]. The pavilion was met with genuine popular acclaim, but the American public opinion, which was favourable at first, was overturned by the war between the Soviet Union and Finland, and the pavilion remained closed for the 1940 season of the Fair. It was destroyed along with almost all its buildings, though it was briefly considered recreating it in Gorky Park[265]. The Soviet press sparsely covered the Fair itself, discussing only the general plan before its inauguration[266]. Spectacular displays depicting the "World of Tomorrow" such as Norman Bel Geddes' *Futurama* and Henry Dreyfuss' *Democracity* were ignored entirely[267].

    The USSR was meant to embody a tangible future and an attractive social system for the American people. This claim was repeated in articles published in Moscow and expressed in artworks such as those of Veniamin

263   Frank Loyd Wright, Telegram to the USSR consulate in New York, 15 June 1939, Avery Library;
    Leonid B. Karlik, *Arkhitektor Karo Alabian* (Erevan: Izd-vo Aiastan, 1966), 28–29.

264   According to Simon Breines, Iofan visited New York a total of three times: Breines, interview with Virginia
    Corbin Brown, 13 March 1996, in Brown, *The American Contribution to the Palace of the Soviets*, 77.

265   Swift, "The Soviet World of Tomorrow," 379.

266   Pier Balter, "Mezhdunarodnaia vystavka 1939 goda v Niu-Iorke ('Stroitelstvo mira zavtrashnego dnia',
    voprosy planirovki)," *Arkhitektura SSSR* 6, no. 9 (September 1938): 85–88. "Mezhdunarodnaia vystavka
    1939 goda v Niu-Iorke (Arkhitekturno-prostranstvennaia traktovka)," *Arkhitektura Leningrada*, no. 5
    (November 1938): 70–71.

267   On the event as a whole, see Rosemarie Haag Bletter et al., *Remembering the Future: The New York
    World's Fair from 1939 to 1964* (New York: The Queens Museum, 1989); Helen A. Harrison, *Dawn of a New
    Day: The New York World's Fair, 1939/40* (New York: The Queens Museum, 1980).

Kremer, the resident painter at the pavilion, showing a group of African-American visitors laying down flowers in front of Lenin's statue seemingly guarding the hall of the pavilion[268]. When the *Great Soviet Encyclopedia* published its 51st volume for the letter "S" in 1945, the entry for SShA—the United States—was illustrated with the by-then dismantled pavilion[269]. Back in Moscow, Tania Morozova's flight over the Soviet capital and the Agricultural exposition in her GAZ 11-40, which concluded Grigorii Aleksandrov's 1940 film *The Radiant Path*, could be seen as providing the evidence that what the *Futurama* depicted as a city still to come in America had already materialized in the USSR, in a stage set initially designed by former New Yorker Viacheslav Oltarzhevskii.

268 M. Olgin, "Otkrytie mezhdunarodnoi vystavki v Niu-Iorke," *Pravda*, 3 May 1939; "Pavilion SSSR na vsemirnoi vystavke v Niu-Iorke," *Pravda*, 18 May 1939; "Uspekh sovetskogo paviliona na Niu-Iorkskoi vystavke," *Pravda*, 7 September 1939; *Literaturnaia gazeta*, 10 May and 26 September 1939; *Sovetskoe iskusstvo*, 1 May and 11 June 1939; *Komsomolskaia pravda*, 14 June 1939. See the complete list in Swift, "The Soviet World of Tomorrow," 376.

269 Anon., "Kulturnye sviazi SShA i SSSR," *Bolshaia sovetskaia entsiklopedia*, vol. 51 (Moscow: Gos. Nauchnyi institut Sovetskaia Entsiklopedia, 1945), 829.

ПО ВОДЕ: МЫ СВЯЗЫВАЕМ АТЛАНТИЧЕСКИЙ ОКЕАН С В
ЛИКИМ ОКЕАНОМ И С РЕКОЙ МИССИСИПИ.

ВРЕМЯ И РАССТОЯНИЯ ВЛИЯЮТ НА НАШУ КУЛЬТУРУ.

ЖЕЛЕЗНОЙ ДОРОГЕ:
МОДАВАСКА В ШТАТЕ МЕЙН МЫ ПОПАДАЕМ В САН ДИЕ-

ПО ВОЗДУХУ: МЫ ЛЕТИМ В МОСКВУ, РИО ИЛИ МАНИЛ

ПО ШОССЕЙНЫМ ДОРОГАМ:
ПРОХОДЯТ 33,000,000 АВТОМАШИН.

НАШИ ОТЕЛИ ПРЕДОСТАВЛЯЮТ ПУТЕШЕСТ

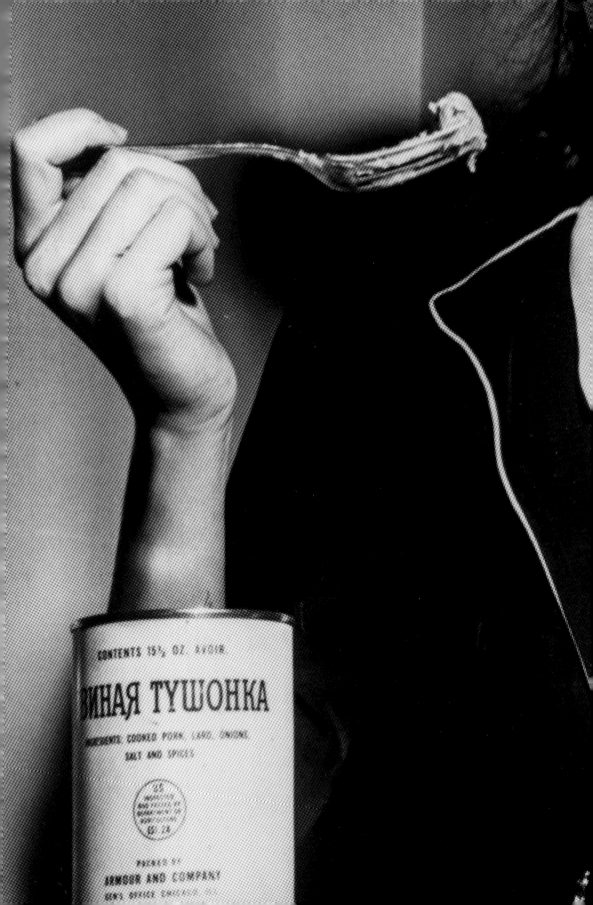

War and Peace: From Alliance to Competition

Aleksandr N. Tsfasman
(1906-1971). Jazz pianist and
composer. He was forbidden to
perform after 1947.

Leonid O. Utesov (1895-1982).
Jazz musician, singer and
comedian. Had to adjust
after 1947.

Andrei K. Burov (1900-1957).
Constructivist architect.
Was criticized for his
"cosmopolitanism."

David E. Arkin (1889-1957).
Critic and architecture
historian. Was criticized for
his "cosmopolitanism."

Lev V. Rudnev (1885-1956).
Soviet architect. Designed the
Moscow State University.

"We have won the war and are recognized the world over as the glorious victors. We must be ready for an influx of foreign visitors. What will happen if they walk around Moscow and find no skyscrapers? They will make unfavourable comparisons with capitalist cities."

Joseph V. Stalin, circa 1948, as quoted by Nikita S. Khrushchev[1].

1   Nikita S. Khrushchev, *Khrushchev Remembers: The Last Testament*, trans. Strobe Talbott (Boston: Little, Brown, 1974), 98.

The Wehrmacht invasion of the USSR on 22 June 1941 and the defeat of the Soviet forces that followed had immediate consequences on Russia's relationship with the United States. The military leadership, wiped out by the purges, was further weakened by Stalin's disbelief regarding the true intentions of the Nazis, though he was informed on the impending menace by multiple sources. Losing no time, the Soviets tried to rally the American public opinion in response to the German offensive, and to obtain primary resources as well as civil and military equipment.

On 6 July, four years after the 1937 Congress of the Architects in Moscow and merely two weeks after the invasion, Boris Iofan penned a call to his "American colleagues," namely to Frank Lloyd Wright, reminding them that in 1939, "[t]he Soviet Union [had] enthusiastically accepted the hospitable invitation of the United States and endeavoured in its pavilion at the World's Fair to show to the American people its achievements in science, technique, art and economy." He implored them to rise against "fascism and barbarism."[2] Earlier, Wright had written a pacifist statement, without overtly condemning Hitler: "The soul of Russia is great but misunderstood. Faithful to democracy I say end these wars of the rulers now by letting peace declare itself."[3] The filmmaker Joseph Losey called upon the architect on behalf of the Russian War Relief, unsuccessfully attempting to have him participate in a second meeting set for 27 October in Madison Square Garden[4]. Wright wrote him a letter intended for Iofan, where he reaffirmed his position: "We take our stand together against the Fascist barbarian. But let our stand be against all forms of 'barbarism.' The time is now. War itself is the foremost barbarism. [...] The people do not want to make war but rulers see no other way. Russia was once a great new hope but, under a ruler, was desperately arming for war. So war came. The United States is a great hope now under a ruler desperately arming for war. So war will come."[5]

Solidarity ties became stronger after the attack on Pearl Harbor on 7 December, and after the United States subsequently joined the war effort. On the media front, Hollywood began producing realistic films—shot in California—to provide audiences with an idyllic picture of daily life in the USSR and to introduce the heroes of the resistance against the Nazis. Metro Goldwyn Mayer produced Lewis Milestone's 1943 picture *The North Star* and Gregory Ratoff's 1944 *Song of Russia*, while Michael Curtiz directed *Mission to Moscow* for Warner Brothers in 1943, inspired by the memoirs of the ambassador Joseph E. Davies. The general press, for instance *Life* magazine, reported on the widespread mobilization of the USSR and the efforts to support it.[6] In this pro-Soviet atmosphere, filmmakers were among the main leaders of the National Council of American-Soviet Friendship, which in 1941 replaced the Friends of the Soviet Union, created in 1929, whose operations later extended to the architectural field.

In terms of military support, the decisive American contribution to the Soviet war effort came from the factories built in the 1930s, which were now fully dedicated to manufacturing weapons. On 15 July 1929, when the major

2   "Statement of Boris Iofan, architect, to his American colleagues," 6 July 1941. A message from TASS was also sent to Frank Lloyd Wright on 30 June 1941, Frank Lloyd Wright Collection, Avery Library.
3   Frank Lloyd Wright, untitled statement, 4 July 1941, Frank Lloyd Wright Collection, Avery Library.
4   Joseph Losey [Russian War Relief], Letter to Frank Lloyd Wright, 14 October 1941, and telegram, 24 October 1941, Frank Lloyd Wright Collection, Avery Library.
5   Frank Lloyd Wright, letter to Boris Iofan, 23 October 1941, Frank Lloyd Wright Collection, Avery Library.
6   Special issue of *Life* on the USSR, 29 March 1943.

agreements of the first five-year plan were signed, the *Politbiuro* had brought up the possibility of converting tractor factories to tank manufacturers. General Mikhail Tukhashevskii who, like Charles de Gaulle understood the impending importance of armoured forces, developed a production plan for tanks on the assembly lines.[7] In 1933, during the inauguration of the Cheliabinsk Tractor Plant, the head of state, Mikhail Kalinin declared that "crawler tractors [would] play a significant role in the strengthening of the country's defensive capacity."[8] Kahn's factory became strategically important in 1941, when the Leningrad Kirov plant and the Kharkov diesel engine manufacturer, evacuated and displaced eastward as a result of German advances, settled on its premises, leading to the creation of "Tankograd," an industrial base overseen by General Isaak Zaltsman[9]. The Cheliabinsk factory produced the JS heavy tanks, named after Joseph Stalin, while the uralvagonzavod, another great achievement of the Promstroiproekt in Nizhnii Tagil, manufactured T-34s. During the war, it became obvious that the use of tractors as carrier platforms paid off: the Soviet tanks, which were heavier and ran on diesel engines, turned out to be more powerful than their German counterparts, manufactured by automobile plants. The union organizer Victor Reuther reported that, in the beginning of the war, his brother Walter had tried, on behalf of the United Automobile Workers' Union, to convince Charles Erwin Wilson, the president of General Motors, to adapt his lines to tank production following the Soviet example[10]. If he had not failed, Soviet expertise could have been, for once, put to use in the United States.

The Lend-Lease Act and the American Contribution to the Russian War Effort

In the late 1920s, the Russians had begun directly purchasing military equipment through covert contacts established by Amtorg with the tank manufacturer John Walter Christie. They acquired two M1931 tanks whose suspensions were carefully examined by Soviet engineers[11]. They had conducted advanced research in the aviation sector prior to 1917, namely with the large aircraft designed by the engineer Igor Sikorsky, who emigrated to America after the Revolution. The Imperial Army also purchased American Curtiss Model F and Model K seaplanes, as well as French and British airplanes. In the second half of the 1930s, the USSR imported a significant amount of materials and continued the technology transfers initiated during the previous decade, for instance the production of the M-5 engine, derived from Packard's Liberty L-12 airplane. The research effort led at the prompting of the Central Aerodynamic Institute (TsAGI; founded in 1918 by Nikolai Zhukovskii) was remarkably original, but did not suffice to replace proven Western technologies.

7   RGVA, f. 33097, op. 3, d. 155, l, 91, quoted in Sonia Melnikova-Raich, "The Soviet Problem with Two 'Unknowns': How an American Architect and a Soviet Negotiator Jump-Started the Industrialization of Russia, Part I: Albert Kahn," *Journal of the Society for Industrial Archeology* 36, no. 2 (2010): 72–73.
8   Mikhail I. Kalinin, in *SSSR na stroike* 4, no. 8 (1933): 13.
9   Lennart Samuelson, *Tankograd: The Formation of a Soviet Company Town: Cheliabinsk, 1900s–1950s* (Basingstoke: Palgrave Macmillan, 2011).
10   Victor G. Reuther, *The Brothers Reuther and the Story of the UAW: A Memoir* (Boston: Houghton Mifflin, 1938), 102–3.
11   Mikhail Mukhin, "Amtorg: amerikanskie tanki dlia RKKA," *Otechestvennaia istoriia*, May 2001, 51–61.

Transportation routes for equipment shipped under the Lend-Lease Act. In United States Department of State, *Report on War Aid Furnished by the United States to the USSR,* 28 November 1945. Hoover Institution, Stanford University.

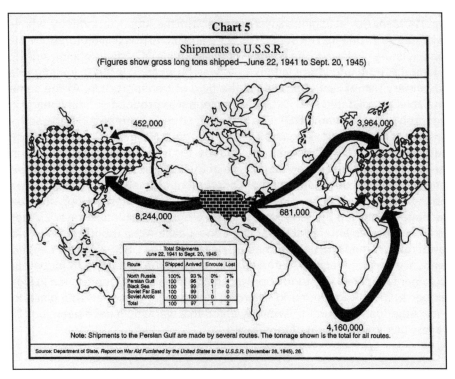

Chart 5

Shipments to U.S.S.R.
(Figures show gross long tons shipped—June 22, 1941 to Sept. 20, 1945)

452,000

3,964,000

8,244,000

681,000

Total Shipments June 22, 1941 to Sept. 20, 1945				
Route	Shipped	Arrived	Enroute	Lost
North Russia	100%	93 %	0%	7%
Persian Gulf	100	96	0	4
Black Sea	100	99	1	0
Soviet Far East	100	99	1	0
Soviet Arctic	100	100	0	0
Total	100	97	1	2

4,160,000

Note: Shipments to the Persian Gulf are made by several routes. The tonnage shown is the total for all routes.

Source: Department of State, *Report on War Aid Furnished by the United States to the U.S.S.R.* (November 28, 1945), 26.

Bell P-39 Airacobra fighter aircraft in Edmonton, Canada, on their way to Siberia, 1944.
Gelatin silver print on paper, 20 × 25.3 cm. National Archives and Records Administration.

Therefore, Polikarpov's I-15 fighter aircraft, used extensively during the Spanish Civil War, was equipped with a M-25 engine, the Russian version of the Wright Cyclone. By the mid-1930s, the USSR accounted for 20% of American aviation exports. Many Soviet engineers were familiar with the American industry, whose sway was so strong that its standards were applied to Russian factories for the nomenclature of alloys[12]. The licence for the Douglas DC-3 twin-engine airliner, renamed PS-84, and later Lisunov Li-2, was purchased in 1940, leading to a momentary halt of Soviet studies in the field of transportation. At the same time, the Consolidated PYB Catalina seaplane was produced under licence in Taganrog under the name GST. Restrictions to Russian-American trade activities were established in August 1939, following the Molotov-Ribbentrop Pact; they were waived by Roosevelt on 24 June 1941, two days after Operation Barbarossa had started. The magnitude of Russian losses called for massive material support, but the framework agreement between the United States and the Soviet Union materialized only on 11 June 1942, following long debates and negotiations led by Harry Hopkins, the programme administrator[13]. After the United States entered the war, the Lend-Lease Act supported the entire Soviet military machine and permeated daily life in the USSR. Indeed, beyond weaponry and war-related materials, the programme extended to industrial equipment, apparel, and food supply. During the Teheran Conference in December 1943, in Roosevelt and Churchill's presence, Stalin raised a glass to toast "American production, without which this war would have been lost,"[14] in a rare acknowledgment of foreign aid.

American and Soviet officers on an unidentified airfield. The American white star of the Curtiss P-40 has been repainted red. Gelatin silver print on paper, 20 × 25.3 cm. National Archives and Records Administration.

The first shipments—namely those of the Curtiss P-40 fighter planes, which were prone to frequent engine failures— slowly began after the attack on Pearl Harbor. Roosevelt had ratified the principle in July 1941, when the swift progression of German troops deprived the USSR from a major part of its industrial and agricultural capacity. After this prelude, 18 million tons of material were shipped to the Russians between 1941 and 1946[15]. The main routes to the USSR were seaborne, such as the one leading to Arkhangelsk and to Murmansk across a danger-filled Atlantic Ocean, as evidenced by the misfortunes of the convoy PQ-17, located by the Germans, who sank 26 of its 37 ships in July 1942. A second route led to Abadan, in Iran, and arrived in Baku and in Ashkhabad by road and by rail, with the help of railway workers lent by the New York Central Railroad and Pennsylvania Railroad. A third route led to Vladivostok by way of the Pacific, while many aircraft reached Siberia across Canada and Alaska [ill. p. 375].

During the war, the United States transferred 14,000 airplanes to the USSR, while the Russians built 115,000, among which many were manufactured with US equipment, though not as modern as the American ones[16]. The US supplied large quantities of models that were unpopular among its own aviators, such as the Bell P-39 Airacobra, nicknamed *Kobrushka* on the front, and the P-63 Kingcobra, as well as the medium bombers Douglas A-20 Boston and North American B-25 Mitchell[17]. The Lend-Lease programme also involved electronic equipment, such as radars and Norden bombsights, which later became significant for the aviation industry and flight operations. However, the Americans refrained from providing heavy bombers, despite the Russians' repeated requests. Fifteen thousand Soviets travelled to the United States to oversee the shipments and to receive training for the use of the equipment, as the USSR refused to authorize large contingents of Allies to come into prolonged contact with its units, officially stating that it feared the "perfectionism" of American instructors[18].

In what appeared to be a miracle, the equipment showcased in Amtorg's catalogues for the past 15 years was finally delivered to the USSR[19]. In addition to the ready-to-use material, the Soviets received machine tools, namely metal presses. As for the uranium shipped to help build hardened munitions, it was likely used for nuclear research. The transferred goods were classified into 500 categories, with a significant part comprised of industrial gear (such as electric power plants, oil refineries, and alloy steel and ball bearing factories), fuel, and raw materials (such as copper, rubber, and aluminum, which accounted for 42% of Russian industrial consumption)[20]. Tires were among the most

12   Robert A. Kilmarx, *A History of Soviet Air Power* (New York: Frederick A. Praeger, 1962), 163 et seq.
13   George C. Herring, *Aid to Russia, 1941–1946; Strategy, Diplomacy, the Origins of the Cold War* (New York: Columbia University Press, 1973).
14   Pierre Mélandri, "La Seconde Guerre mondiale: 'Au sommet du monde'," in *Le siècle américain, une histoire* (Paris: Perrin, 2016), 151.
15   Henri Dunajewski, "Le lend-lease américain pour l'Union Soviétique," *Revue d'études comparatives est-ouest* 15, no. 3 (1984): 36–37. In parallel to Russian studies on specific industry branches, an overview is given in Natalya Butenina, *Lend-liz, sdelka veka* (Moscow: Izd-vo Vyschei Shkoly Ekonomiki, 2004).
16   Richard C. Lukas, *Eagles East: The Army Air Forces and the Soviet Union 1941–1945* (Tallahassee, Florida State University, 1970).
17   Hubert P. van Tuyll, *Feeding the Bear: American Aid to the Soviet Union, 1941–1945* (New York: Wesport, Greenwood Press, 1989), 112ff.
18   Ibid., 11.
19   The best synthesis is Foreign Economic Section, Office of Foreign Liquidation, Department of State, *Report on War Aid Furnished by the United States to the USSR June 22, 1941–September 20, 1945*, 28 November 1945. The appendices to this report give a clear quantitative image of American deliveries.
20   Robert Huhn Jones rightly stresses the strategic importance of certain suppliers: *The Roads to Russia: United States Lend-Lease to the Soviet Union* (Norman: University of Oklahoma Press, 1969), 237–39.

critical areas of shortage facing the USSR, as the country's only factory, located in Leningrad, was inoperative. The United States shipped 3.8 million units and, more importantly, transferred all the machines from the Ford River Rouge Complex to the USSR, where the plant, which had launched production in 1937, was fully rebuilt. Its promised output was one million tires per year, but it did not become operational until 1945[21].

In addition to rail material—essential to supply the war front—, airplanes and over 700 naval units, the Russians received some 410,000 land vehicles, including 44,000 *Uilis* (Willys) Jeeps, well-regarded among the troops. *Stiudbaker* (Studebaker) became a household term to designate the majority of the 350,000 shipped trucks, and also, incidentally, young women with appealing figures...[22] The remarkable mobility with which the Red Army conquered Eastern Europe in 1944–1945 was partly due to American motor vehicles. For the population, the provision of apparel as well as the 5.5 million tons of food aid had more significant impact than military support. American food items became an integral part of combat zones as well as civil canteens, including products developed specifically for the USSR, such as canned pork (*svinnaia tushonka*)[23]. Long after the war and the fall of the Soviet Union, the writer Vasilii Aksenov recalled, in his 2008 autobiographical novel *Lend-Leasing*, the significance of these American products in his teenage years. He described the appearance of Douglas bombers on the front line, which were vital to Soviet Air Forces which had been decimated during the first months of the war, and also food, which not only "saved millions of children from rickets, but also lifted everyone's spirits." He also recounted how the young men wondered at the jeans arriving from the "United Pants of America," in a pun on the words "shtany" (pants) and "shtaty" (States)[24].

Despite its military, cultural, and economic significance—which, in absolute terms, represented only a third of the resources sent to Great Britain—, the strategic contribution of the Lend-Lease Act was officially downplayed by Moscow, during and after the war[25]. After being announced in the press in 1941, the programme was partly censored until 1943, and Soviet authorities worked hard to mask the labels indicating the source of the materials, for example by applying sham logos from Russian factories to convey the impression that the equipment was made in the USSR [ill. p. 376]. In its subsequent statistics, the government claimed that the Lend-Lease goods accounted for only 4% of industrial production during the war, which clearly underestimated its actual contribution[26], as the actual proportion fell somewhere between 18%

21   "Ford Ships Tyre Factory to Russia," *Ford News*, December 1942, 12–30; "Ford Tyre Plan is Shipped to USSR," *Life* 4, no. 13 (29 March 1943): 16; Charles E. Sorensen, *My Forty Years with Ford* (New York: W.W. Norton & Co., 1956), 212–15. On the difficult acclimatization of the factory, see John R. Deane, "The Strange Alliance," *Life*, 20 January 1947, 104 and 107.

22   Frederick C. Barghoorn, *The Soviet Image of the United States: A Study in Distortion* (New York: Harcourt Brace, 1950), 240. Barghoorn spent part of the war on American air bases in the USSR. Specialized literature facilitated the use of American vehicles. See for example O. E. Kotovich, *Konstruktivnye i eksploatatsionnye osobennosti avtomobiliei Ford, Dodge, Chevrolet i Studebaker* (Moscow: Zagotizdat, 1945).

23   Food aid to Russia was, for example, 2% of total American production in 1944: Albert L. Weeks, *Russia's Life-Saver, Lend-Lease Aid to the USSR in World War II* (Lanham, MD: Lexington Books, 2004), 123.

24   Vasilii Aksenov, *Lend-lizovskie: Lend-Leasing* (Moscow: Eksmo, 2010), 33, 39 and 96. Aksenov also published among his other works the short story "Zavtraki 43–go goda," in *Na polputi k lune: kniga rasskazov* (Moscow: Sovetskaia Rossiia, 1966), 33–42.

25   Jones, *The Roads to Russia*, 252–50.

26   Roger Munting, "Lend-Lease and the Soviet War Effort," *Journal of Contemporary History* 19, no. 3 (1984): 495–510. Among recent Russian analyses, see Petr I. Petrov, "Fakticheskaia storona pomoshchi po Lend-lizu," *Voenno-istoricheskii zhurnal*, no. 6 (1990): 34–42. Nicolas Voznesensky gives the figure of 4% in *L'économie de guerre de l'URSS 1941–1945* (Paris: Librairie de Médicis, 1948), 57.

An American woman tastes the canned pork stew shipped by the thousands of tons to the USSR at a press conference in New York, ca. 1944. Gelatin silver print on paper, 25.3 × 20 cm. National Archives and Records Administration.

and 27%[27]. As Stalin himself admitted, after the Lend-Lease programme and the first five-year plan, "about two-thirds of all the large industrial enterprises in the Soviet Union had been built with United States' help or technical assistance."[28] The spontaneous celebration of American friendship in the streets of Moscow upon the announcement of the German surrender is a testament to the popular sentiment towards the great ally. But the Lend-Lease shipments were suddenly withheld as of 12 May 1945 and resumed in August strictly as part of the Russians' involvement in Japan. New orders were irrevocably blocked when the Japanese surrendered on 2 September. The final settlement of the Soviet debt did not take place until 1972, as returning the ships—a third of the Russian fleet—proved to be a particularly lengthy process.

  In early 1945, in the wake of the Lend-Lease programme, the Soviets requested American aid for reconstruction. Restating calls already made by Mikoyan, Viacheslav Molotov asked Averell Harriman, ambassador to Moscow, for a $6 billion dollar loan. Some American officials saw the USSR as a potential market for industrial equipment and considered extending the Lend-Lease Act, like Secretary of the Treasury Henry Morgenthau and Secretary of Commerce Henry Wallace. The United States Congress, however, prohibited any agreement, refusing to pursue its aid policy beyond the end of the war in Europe. President Harry Truman's advisors were also reticent, as they were worried about Russian policy regarding Poland[29]. As soon as the war ended, the Soviet press labelled the United States the main foreign threat, a title previously reserved for Great Britain, while the Americans established their doctrine of containment and cut aid that might have partially helped avoid the massive depletion of Eastern European resources towards Russian deconstruction. The stage was thus set for the Cold War.

Towards a Single-Storey Russia?

Between June 1941 and September 1945, as planes, trucks, and major shipments of supplies travelled across the oceans, American music—made more acceptable thanks to allied relations—became immensely popular. Aleksandr Tsfasman and Leonid Utesov's bands —as well as that of the Berlin musician Eddie Rosner, who had fled to Bielorussia in 1939—played continuously on the front line, in uniform or in evening dress, as a musical backdrop for military exercises, while several bands formed within the army ranks. An enthusiastic

27 Dunajevski, "Le lend-lease américain," 56.
28 Statement by Stalin to a top American official, in W. Averell Harriman, State Department, file 033.1161, Johnston/6-3044, telegram on 30 June 1944, quoted in Antony C. Sutton, *Western Technology and Soviet Economic Development, 1930–1945* (Stanford: Hoover Institution Press, 1971), 3. Khrushchev reported a similar statement from Stalin in his memoir: Nikita Khrushchev, *Khrushchev Remembers: The Glasnost,* trans. Jerrold L. Schecter and Viacheslav V. Luchkov (Boston: Little, Brown, 1990), 84.
29 Herring, *Aid to Russia,* 144–78.
30 Aleksandr A. Troianovskii, "Muzika v Soedinennykh Shtatov," *Sovetskoe Iskusstvo,* 18 September 1941, quoted in S. Frederick Starr, *Red & Hot: The Fate of Jazz in the Soviet Union, 1917–1980* [1983] (New York: Limelight Editions, 1994), 192.
31 Vladimir G. Grossman, "Stroitelstvo voennogo vremeni v SShA i v Anglii," *Arkhitektura SSSR,* no. 1 (1942): 26–32; L. Vrangel, "Novoe v arkhitekturnoi praktike SShA," *Arkhitektura SSSR,* no. 2 (1943): 31–36. In 1943-1944, Vrangel designed courtyard house projects for central Asia with Andrei K. Burov.
32 Karo S. Alabian, preface to Roman Ia. Khiger, *Maloetazhnye doma v SSA* (Moscow: Izd-vo Akademii Arkhitektury, 1944), 2; Jean-Louis Cohen, *Scenes of the World to Come* (Paris: Flammarion, Montreal: Canadian Centre for Architecture, 1995), 160.

article by Aleksandr Troianovskii, the first Soviet ambassador to Washington, was published in 1941, calling for the dissemination of jazz[30]. At the same time, architects were locked in endless discussions on the reconstruction of the western part of the country. Their deliberations were recorded in largely hypothetical plans for the duration of the war, as well as in forecasting exercises on the state of building production and construction after the armistice. Evacuated to the Kazakh city of Chimkent, the Union of Architects and the Academy of Architecture were interested in American housing methods for armament workers and in their new light wood construction techniques, turning away for a time from grandiose embellishing projects for Moscow. An ad hoc periodical, titled *Stroitelstvo voennogo vremeni* (Wartime Construction), and the journal *Arkhitektura SSSR*, published sporadically and in a very crude form, showed a renewed interest for American techniques, shifting their primary focus from England[31].

These publications primarily studied various types of individual American dwellings, namely those developed to house factory workers. The former constructivist Roman Khiger devoted a booklet to the matter, the first in a series entitled "American Housing Construction Expertise," with a foreword by Karo Alabian. Appointed president of the Academy's commission on scientific and technical issues, Alabian was eager to revisit his first-hand knowledge of American architecture. He stated that "during this preparatory phase, architects, engineers, and economists must absolutely make a detailed study of and become familiar with the best American examples in terms of construction."[32] Reversing the canon of Americanism, previously associated with skyscrapers, Khiger wrote that the "bold experimentation, organization,

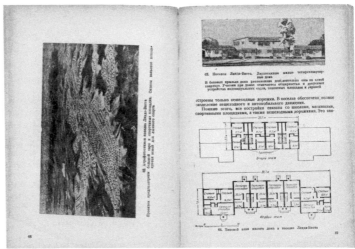

Roman Ia. Khiger, *City Planning in the United States*, Moscow: Izd-vo Akademii Arkhitektury, 1944. Cover and spread devoted to a workers' housing scheme in Linda Vista, California. CCA, BIB247257.

architectural merits" deployed in low-density ensembles were a "worthy and able competitor to the skyscraper, which until quite recently had embodied the most advanced building practices and technologies in the USA."[33] Another publication, on *Low-Rise Structures in the United States*, presented the ordinary balloon frame, bricklaying solutions, and new systems such as Cemesto, whose panels used sugarcane stalks, asbestos, and cement[34]. Khiger also published a booklet on American urban planning, where he documented the layout of the Greenbelt Towns, designed in the 1930s for workers and built during the war. He explained the guiding principles of their composition and presented realizations selected mainly from the West Coast, including trailer parks. With its plans on various scales and cost tables, this document is a rather technical read[35]. Khiger wrote a third volume on collective housing[36]. The series was completed with a booklet compiling materials reprinted from journals on *Built-In Equipment in Apartments*, a particularly developed field in the United States according to Alabian[37].

Most architects seemed to agree on the idea of a "single-storey" Russia comprised of horizontal neighbourhoods and villages, as articulated by the urban planner Andrei Bunin, seemingly in a nod to Ilf and Petrov's book[38]. This idea did not necessarily imply that Wright's principles would be reprised, even though the Old Master exchanged letters with Arkin and Alabian in 1943[39]. Upon returning from America, Iofan had described Broadacre City as a "utopian project for an agricultural village" that fostered the illusion of "rescu[ing] humankind from capitalism."[40] In the months preceding both countries' involvement in the war, the Union of Architects' press outlet indirectly criticized Wright's 1939 London talks on "organic architecture." The publication gleefully reported that the "very nebulous thoughts of this idealist architect," namely Broadacre City, had been "bitterly attacked by the progressive component of the British architectural youth, which underlined the unreality of his plans in the conditions of capitalism."[41]

33   Roman Ia. Khiger, *Maloetazhnye doma v SSA*, 8, quoted in Richard Anderson, "USA/USSR: Architecture and War," *Grey Room*, no. 34 (Winter 2009): 97.
34   Vitalii N. Gornov, *Konstruktsii maloetazhnykh domov v SShA* (Moscow: Izd-vo Akademii Arkhitektury, 1944).
35   Roman Ia. Khiger, *Planirovka poselkov v SShA* (Moscow: Izd-vo Akademii Arkhitektury, 1944). A summary was published under the same title: "Planirovka poselkov v SShA," *Arkhitektura SSSR*, no. 5 (1944): 23–29.
36   Roman Ia. Khiger, *Mnogokvartirnye doma v SShA* (Moscow: Izd-vo Akademii Arkhitektury, 1945).
37   Karo Alabian, introduction to Olga G. Boiar, *Vstroennoe oborudovanie kvartir* (Moscow: Izd-vo Akademii Arkhitektury, 1945), 4.
38   Andrei Bunin, Statement reported in Alexey Tarkhanov and Sergey Kavtaradze, *Stalinist Architecture* (London: Laurence King, 1992), 106.
39   Frank Lloyd Wright, Letter to David E. Arkin and Karo S. Alabian, 20 January 1943, in *Letters to Architects* (Fresno: California University Press, 1984), 101–3.
40   Boris M. Iofan, "Materialy o sovremennoi arkhitekture SShA i Itali," *Akademiia Arkhitektury* 2, no. 4 (1936): 34.
41   "Organicheskaia arkhitektura Franka Lloyda Wrighta," *Arkhitektura SSSR* 9, no. 2 (February 1941): 70.
42   Andrei K. Burov, "Na putiakh k novoi russkoi arkhitekture," *Arkhitektura SSSR* 4 (1943): 34.
43   Andrei K. Burov, "Iz vystupleniia arkhitektora A. Burova na XI plenume pravleniia SSA SSSR, 16 avgusta 1943 g.," in *Iz istorii sovetskoi arkhitektury 1941–1945 gg.: Dokumenty i materialy: khronika voennykh let: arkhitekturnaia pechat,* Tatiana Malinina, ed. (Moscow: Nauka, 1978), 88.
44   Ignatii Milinis, address to the administration of the Union of Soviet Architects in Moscow, February 1942, RGALI, f. 674, op. 2, d. 80, 39, in Malinina, *Iz istorii sovetskoi arkhitektury 1941–1945 gg.*, 26.
45   Alexei Shchusev, "Fascism Is My Personal Enemy: A Russian Architect Looks Upon Destruction," *California Arts & Architecture* 59, no. 12 (December 1942): 30.
46   Clarence Stein, *The Writings of Clarence S. Stein: Architect of the Planned Community* (Baltimore: Johns Hopkins University Press, 1998), 427–28.
47   David E. Arkin, Letter to John Howard Stevens, 1944, GARF f. R–5283, op. 14, d. 170, quoted in Katherine E. Zubovich, "Moscow Monumental: Soviet Skyscrapers and Urban Life under High Stalinism," PhD dissertation (Berkeley: University of California, 2016), 45.
48   NKVD, certificate attesting the annulment of the Oltarzhevskii "case," 5 August 1943, Oltarzhevskii archive, MUAR.

To Andrei Burov, who had erected buildings using manufactured concrete panels before the war, the quest for the "new path for Russian architecture" had to draw on the progress made by the United States, as "in America new architectural ideas—freed from the nihilism of proselytes and arising from industry—have begun to show the first sprouts of new organic architectural forms." To him, these ideas called for not only an educational reform, but also for a shift "from a conception of the unique to a conception of the mass."[42] Speaking during an executive meeting of the Union, he called for "the acquisition from the USA of a series of factories for the production of prefabricated low-rise houses from ready-made components; a complex of factories that produces everything necessary—from the foundations to the door handles."[43] In the winter of 1942, during another meeting of the Union of Architects, the former constructivist Ignatii Milinis announced the "study of American expertise regarding prefabricated housing plants" as the first step of his programme[44].

In a country protected from bombings by its surrounding oceans, American architects expressed strong sympathy for the destruction facing their Russian colleagues. Aleksei Shchusev appealed to them in his condemnation of Nazi vandalism in an article published in *California Arts & Architecture*[45]. Some of them turned to listen to the Russians, such as Clarence Stein, who was involved in designing satellite towns like Greenbelt, well known to the Soviets, in the 1930s. An aerial view of the towns was used to illustrate Khiger's *Planirovka poselkov v SShA*. Stein wrote: "I have heard that when the Russian architects were criticized for the barrenness of their early architecture they answered that these buildings were not permanent—they did not yet know what forms of structure will be required to house the activities of the future; [...] there is probably a good deal we are going to learn from the Russians during this war, but we are not going to tell Congress about it."[46]

The ties formed in the 1930s were being rekindled. David Arkin, the secretary of the architecture section of VOKS, exchanged letters with several correspondents, stressing the importance of urban planning in Soviet reconstruction: "Here an architect must be able to design not only separate residential and public buildings but entire streets, whole blocks and towns. We aim at achieving integral architectural 'ensembles' in our cities. This is especially important now when many of our towns and cities have been razed to the ground by the Nazi aggressors."[47] Viacheslav Oltarzhevskii, had also returned at last to Moscow. His American peers, worried by his silence, had called upon Ambassador Harriman to enquire about the architect by addressing Stalin himself. Careful to preserve his precious connections in light of a possible extension of the Lend-Lease Act, Stalin quickly ordered the repatriatation of the former émigré, clearing him of all charges with a certificate from the NKVD dated 5 August 1943, after five years in the Gulag[48].

Upon returning to Moscow, Oltarzhevskii was appointed head of the Scientific and Technical Information Bureau of the Council of Ministers' architectural committee, bearing witness both to the fact that he had returned to favour and to the importance of America for the leaders of the construction field. He immediately turned to his old friend Corbett, who headed the Architects Committee of the National Council of American-Soviet Friendship, stating that his "brilliant and well-deserved reputation as an architect and a public figure serves as the best guarantee to the success of the commission." Oltarzhevskii asked Corbett to keep him regularly informed about the latest changes to American legislation and regulations and enquired about the "blueprints and specifications" of a series of systems and products useful to reconstruction. He provided his American colleague with a specific list, including the use of plaster as a structural material, drywall in general, prefabricated toilets, ceramic ovens, and the "by-products" of industry and agriculture."[49]

American Exhibits for Moscow

As of 1943, Corbett presided over this committee created within the National Council of American-Soviet Friendship, in cooperation with the American Institute of Architects. He worked to promote the exchange of information on urban planning and construction, to disseminate the expectations of the Soviet building industry among American architects and to acquaint the Russians with recent developments in American construction, in a friendly atmosphere of mutual understanding[50]. The NCASF's intense activity in the fields of art, music, publishing, and science was sponsored by distinguished characters such as Albert Einstein and Charlie Chaplin, and supplemented the work of the American Russian Institute in San Francisco. The architectural committee initially included a most diverse group of men: Simon Breines, Serge Chermayeff, Antonin Raymond, and Lorimer Rich, as well as Talbot Faulkner Hamlin, director of the Avery Architectural and Fine Arts Library at Columbia University[51]. They were joined by the architects Vernon DeMars, Philip L. Goodwin—then active at MoMA—, Knud Lonberg-Holm, Joseph Hudnut, Hugh Pomeroy, John W. Root, Henry R. Shepley, and William Wurster, the journal editors George Nelson, Kenneth Reid, and Kenneth K. Stowell, and the urban planner Hans Blumenfeld, who had worked in the USSR for seven years and had helped Breines draw the 1939 pavilion plans in New York City[52]. The American architect Hermann H. Field served as secretary.

Apart from a very small exhibition in New York devoted to the European monuments destroyed by the Nazis, the committee was far from engaging in the "two-way flow" of exchanges it had promised, focusing almost entirely on conveying materials to the USSR. In 1944, with help from Lonberg-Holm, Field prepared the publication of a newsletter destined to Soviet architects[53].

49   V.K. Oltar-Jevsky [he comes back to the spelling used in the US], Letter to Harvey Wiley Corbett, n.d. [1943], Knud Lonberg-Holm Archives [documents shared by the late Marc Dessauce].
50   Architects Committee National Council of American-Soviet Friendship, "Statement of Purpose," n.d. [Winter 1943-1944], NCASF Records, f. 6, b. 5, Tamiment Library, New York University. The founding of the Committee was announced in the media: "Architects' Committee for American-Soviet Friendship," *Journal of the American Institute of Architects*, May 1944, 250-51. "American-Soviet Architects Committee," *Magazine of Art* 37, May 1944, 194-95. On the National Council, see J.D. Parks, *Culture, Conflict and Coexistence: American-Soviet Cultural Relations, 1917-1958* (Jefferson, NC; London: McFarland, 1983), 65-69.
51   Antonin Raymond, Letter to Simon Breines et al, 28 September 1943, Breines Papers, Avery Library, Columbia University.
52   Harvey Wiley Corbett, Letter to Karo Alabian, 2 May 1944, Lonberg-Holm Archives. Hans Blumenfeld, *Life Begins at 65: The Not Entirely Candid Autobiography of a Drifter* (Montreal: Harvest House, 1987), 188 and 197.
53   Hermann H. Field, Letter to Knud Lonberg-Holm, 3 May 1944, Lonberg-Holm Archives. The first issue was published on 29 May 1944.
54   Karo S. Alabian, Viktor A. Vesnin and Igor E. Grabar, Letter to Harvey Wiley Corbett, 25 April 1944, Lonberg-Holm archives.
55   Karo S. Alabian, Letter to the Architects Committee, National Council of American-Soviet Friendship, 25 April 1944, Lonberg-Holm archives.
56   Architects Committee, National Council of American-Soviet Friendship, *News Bulletin*, no. 3 (26 June 1944): 3.
57   Harvey Wiley Corbett, Letter to Karo S. Alabian, 2 May 1944, Lonberg-Holm archives.
58   Architects Committee, National Council of American-Soviet Friendship, *News Bulletin*, no. 9 (25 July 1945): 1-5.

He orchestrated the response given by the members of the committee to the incessant and insistent requests arriving from Moscow. In a letter apparently written by Oltarzhevskii, Karo Alabian, Viktor Vesnin, the president of the Academy of Architecture, and the head of the Academy of Fine Arts, Igor Grabar requested documents on "methods of rapid construction such as projects, models, samples of building materials, literature, etc."[54] Alabian detailed the request, signalling his interest for American legislation, the regulations relative to green spaces and density, and the ways in which these rules were applied[55]. A solemn reunion organized by VOKS celebrated the Soviets' reception of the documents sent by their American counterparts[56]. Corbett turned to Alabian to introduce the members of the committee and request specific information on reconstruction[57].

The year 1945 marked the peak of the committee's activities, with several exhibitions exported to the USSR and a Russian-American conference on construction—an unprecedented event bringing together 300 participants to the New York Engineers' Club on 4 and 5 May[58]. Organized under the auspices of Amtorg and the American Institute of Architects, the conference tackled five different themes: the organization of the building industry, prefabrication, industrial buildings, mechanical systems, and single-housing equipment. Each theme was discussed in roundtables with both American and Soviet experts. A certain imbalance can be noted among the participants. Several renowned American architects were in attendance, such as Marcel Breuer, Serge Chermayeff, André Fouilhoux, José Luis Sert, Roland Wank—a veteran of social housing then working at Albert Kahn Associates—, and Henry Wright. They were accompanied by representatives from the industry and its

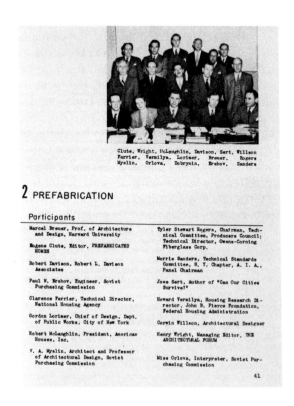

Clute, Wright, McLaughlin, Davison, Sert, Willson
Farrier, Vermilya, Lorimer, Breuer, Rogers
Myslin, Orlova, Dobrynin, Ershov, Sanders

2 PREFABRICATION

Participants

Marcel Breuer, Prof. of Architecture and Design, Harvard University

Eugene Clute, Editor, PREFABRICATED HOMES

Robert Davison, Robert L. Davison Associates

Paul N. Ershov, Engineer, Soviet Purchasing Commission

Clarence Farrier, Technical Director, National Housing Agency

Gordon Lorimer, Chief of Design, Dept. of Public Works, City of New York

Robert McLaughlin, President, American Houses, Inc.

V. A. Myslin, Architect and Professor of Architectural Design, Soviet Purchasing Commission

Tyler Stewart Rogers, Chairman, Technical Committee, Producers Council; Technical Director, Owens-Corning Fiberglass Corp.

Morris Sanders, Technical Standards Committee, N. Y. Chapter, A. I. A., Panel Chairman

Jose Sert, Author of "Can Our Cities Survive?"

Howard Vermilya, Housing Research Director, John B. Pierce Foundation, Federal Housing Administration

Corwin Willson, Architectural Designer

Henry Wright, Managing Editor, THE ARCHITECTURAL FORUM

Miss Orlova, Interpreter, Soviet Purchasing Commission

41

Roundtable on prefabrication. In *Proceedings, American–Soviet Building Conference*, held on 4 and 5 May 1945. New York: Architects Committee of the National Council of American–Soviet Friendship, 1945. CCA, HD9715.A2 A5 1945.

unions. Conversely, the Soviet contingent was entirely comprised of engineers, most of whom worked at the Soviet Purchasing Commission, except the architects A. V. Ivanov and Vladimir Myslin, formerly from the ASNOVA and the designer of several industrial buildings[59]. The most contentious theme of discussion was prefabrication. Breuer, Sert, and Wright explained their positions, the former insisting on trailers, while the president of Albert Kahn Associates, George Miehle, spoke of the expertise acquired with war factories. The technically precise and engaged landscape portrayed by the Americans stood in stark contrast with the dry and institutional presentations given by the Soviets. The journal *Pencil Points* thus noted a "schism" between the two groups, as they disagreed on the notions of "profit," more social for the Russians, and centralized planning, which they put forth as a solution to all their problems[60]. After the conference, the committee widened its composition to become the Building Industry Committee, tackling a wider range of technical issues[61].

Along with this conference, whose impact on the USSR is impossible to measure, the committee focused on organizing an exhibition on American contemporary architecture in Moscow, a project that was brought up in 1934 by the Washington embassy but had not been followed through. The exhibition, described by Arkin in 1944, opened on 26 June at the House of the Architects, under the title *The Architecture of the USA*, and presented a collection of diverse materials obtained through the American embassy in Moscow or found in Soviet archives. Arkin noted that Moscow's "architectural circles" were interested in "new methods of prefabrication, town and city plans, as well as in the work of notable American architects," but showed disappointment in the poor quality of the featured "photo-illustrations." He explicitly asked the committee to send better documents, and the response lived up to his expectations[62].

First, the NCASF committee sent a section of the travelling exhibition *US Housing in War and Peace* to Moscow. The exhibit was initially designed for the Royal Institute of British Architects in London, based on materials presented at the MoMA in 1942 by Janet Henrich O'Connell, as part of the larger *Wartime Housing* show. The selection made by Vernon DeMars, and renamed *Rapid Construction in the USA*, included a series of large montages depicting the variety of construction systems used since 1941, from traditional processes to complete factory prefabrication, including Konrad Wachsmann and Buckminster Fuller's experimental prefabricated systems, and made considerable space for mobile or portable dwellings[63]. Given the relevance of the issue in a country embattled and in ruins, the exhibition was met with resounding success and thoroughly praised. At the inauguration, Alabian

59   Louise Cooper and Louis Fitch, Jr., *Proceedings, American–Soviet Building Conference / Published in Collaboration with the Architectural Forum* (New York: Architects Committee of the National Council of American–Soviet Friendship, 1945).

60   "Russian attending the American–Soviet Building Conference early last month in New York must have been mystified to some degree by the mixture of viewpoints, facts, and emotions that constituted the American contribution to the two-day program," *Pencil Points* 26, no. 6 (June 1945): 16. "American–Soviet Building Conference," *Architectural Record* 97, no. 6 (June 1945): 20 and 128.

61   Architects Committee, National Council of American–Soviet Friendship, *News Bulletin*, no. 12 (28 February 1946): 3.

62   David E. Arkin, Letter to Harvey Wiley Corbett (Moscow: n. d. [after June 1944]), Lonberg-Holm Archives.

63   "The Museum Goes Abroad," *Museum of Modern Art Bulletin* 12, no. 2 (1944): 2. "Exhibit for the USSR," *Architectural Forum* 81, no. 3 (September 1944): 194. See the photographic prints held in Vienna at the Austrian Frederick and Lillian Kiesler Private Foundation.

US Housing in War and Peace Exhibition. Panels displayed at the Central House of the Architect, Moscow, 1945.
Two gelatin silver prints on paper, 21.4.x 27.9 cm. Austrian Frederick and Lillian Kiesler Private Foundation, Vienna.

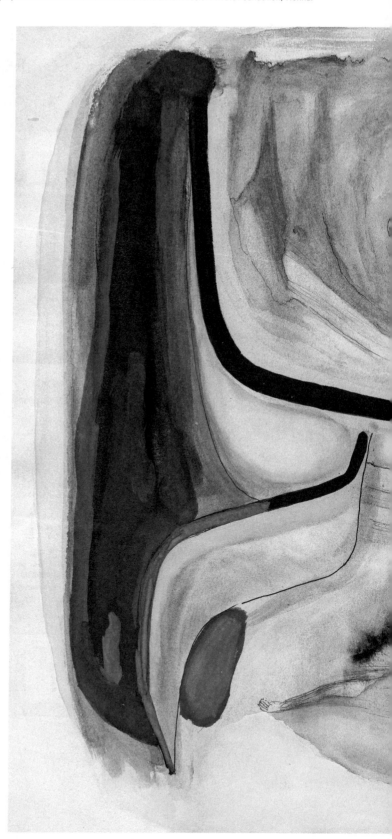

Frederick Kiesler. Exhibition on American architecture sent to the USSR by the National Council of American–Soviet Friendship, 1945. Initial concept. Tempera and Indian ink on paper, 43.8 × 57.7 cm. Austrian Frederick and Lillian Kiesler Private Foundation, Vienna.

Frederick Kiesler. Exhibition on American architecture sent to the USSR by the National Council of American–Soviet Friendship, 1945. Study for the assembly of the panels. Austrian Frederick and Lillian Kiesler Private Foundation, Vienna.

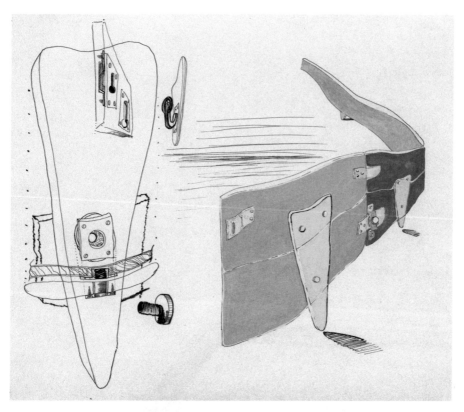

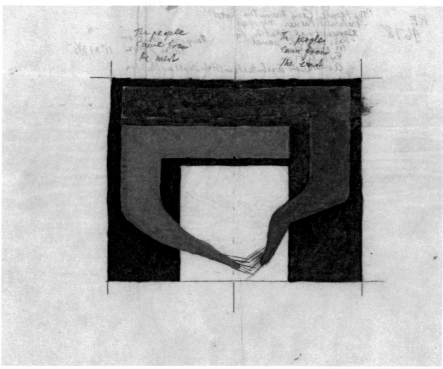

Top: Study of panel assembly and detail, 1944. Tempera and Indian ink on tracing paper, 27.9 × 34.3 cm.
Bottom: Study for the first panel, "The people came from the West…", Graphite and tempera on tracing paper, 57.8 × 72 cm.

Exhibition on American architecture sent to the Soviet Union by the National Council of American–Soviet Friendship, 1945. The team at work in New York. Left to right: Hermann H. Field, Frederick Kiesler, and Harvey Wiley Corbett. Gelatin silver print on paper, 19 × 22 cm. Douglas Putnam Haskell Papers, Avery Architectural & Fine Arts Library, Columbia University.

declared: "It is natural that Soviet architects and builders have a lively interest in the valuable lessons of their American colleagues, whose achievements in this area undoubtedly have exerted a positive effect."[64] In an article on Soviet prefabrication published by the committee in *Prefabricated Homes* with two images from the exhibition, Arkin spoke of the "very great interest" it sparked "on the part of Moscow architects, engineers and large sections of the public." He saw in "the excellent section of photographs" the expression of a "friendly cooperation between America and the Soviet Union in the field of creative effort."[65]

Starting in the summer of 1944, in collaboration with the United States Office of War Information, the committee prepared an exhibit specifically targeted at the USSR, and much more ambitious in scope. It had two working titles: *The Development of Building Types in North America* and *The American Architectural Scene*. The curator was Douglas Haskell, associate editor of *Architectural Record*, after a first version had been developed in May by Hermann Field, who noted that the project would be "the first real picture that the Russian public at large will get of this aspect of American life." He affirmed: "it is therefore doubly important that it should be handled competently and

64   Karo S. Alabian, Speech for the opening of the exhibit *Skorostnoe stroitelstvo v SShA*, RGALI, f. 674, op. 2, d. 129, 14. Some of the reactions written in the public guest book are reproduced in "Exhibition of Prefabricated Houses in the United States," *VOKS Bulletin*, no. 3–4 (1945): 76

65   David Arkin, "Prefabrication in the USSR," *Prefabricated Homes* 6, no. 3 (January 1946), 15 and 26.

with great caution in the telling so as to avoid it becoming simply a propaganda show or an unrepresentative angle, more of the Museum of Modern Art type. Our objective will be to try to give a picture of average America in the building field as a basis, making it clear when we show advanced examples in the various fields that this is not characteristic of the whole."[66]

Based on the first draft, mostly typological in structure, Haskell developed a more detailed project, discussed by the most active members of the committee. Breines alone considered the Russians' potential expectations regarding wood construction and landscaping.[67] In September, on a suggestion from Lonberg-Holm, the exhibition design was assigned to Frederick Kiesler, whom Corbett knew well, as the artist had worked for him in the 1920s, on his arrival from Europe[68]. Kiesler built upon his legendary 1942 installation for the *Art of This Century* show at the Peggy Guggenheim Gallery in New York. For the Moscow exhibition, he initially designed a system of panels with fluid and sculptural mounts, which he placed on bases made of anthropomorphic and zoomorphic shapes, combining disjointed Atlantean limbs with bovine hoofs and tails. Large photographic prints were set to present a flowing and lyrical narrative of the origins of modern American architecture. However, the committee's resources did not allow for such an imaginative and ambitious project. Haskell wrote that he was "sorry not to have been able to cajole or master this vastly expanded and wounded ego," expressing his hope that "the exhibit will be found useful or entertaining in return for all the work that went into it from so many people." He noted: "It was no doubt for the good of the soul that fate made me work with a spirit such as Kiesler, but I fervently hope to be spared a repetition of the discipline, and of the frustration."[69]

Kiesler's studio completed the design and executed it according to a simpler principle, using flat panels, with a photo mosaic vaguely reproducing some of the figures from the initial project. The final installation was comprised of 40 photographic montages set against a black backdrop, each mounted on a rectangular six feet by four feet panel (1,82 by 1,22 metres). The panels were striped with large grey figures running from one to the other, with the idea of a continuous display from beginning to end. Excerpts from the presentation written by Talbot Faulkner Hamlin were reprised as an introduction[70]. Haskell went out of his way to ensure that the captions remained his own, without edits from the Russians, who had wished to review the copy, and without interventions from the committee. This was especially important as Kiesler

66   Hermann H. Field [NCASF], Letter to Douglas Haskell, 5 September 1944, "Exhibit of American architecture to be sent to the Soviet Union: Tentative plan," 9 May 1944; "Subject index for the exhibit of American architecture to be sent to the Soviet Union," 27 p., n.d. [May 1944], Haskell Papers, Avery Library.
67   Simon Breines, "Memo on exhibit," 26 January 1945; Untitled summary of a discussion on the project, 15 January 1945; Douglas Haskell, "Exhibit of American architecture; Proposed general outline of materials," 43 p., n.d. [1944], Haskell Papers, Avery Library.
68   Harvey Wiley Corbett, Letter to Friedrich Kiesler, 21 September 1944, Austrian Frederick and Lillian Kiesler Private Foundation.
69   Douglas Haskell, Letter to Harvey Wiley Corbett, 19 May 1945; Haskell Papers, Avery Library; Douglas Haskell, Letter to Talbot Faulkner Hamlin, 4 August 1945, Hamlin Papers, Avery Library.
70   Marion Lowndes [OWI], Lettor to Talbot Faulkner Hamlin, 23 June 1945, Hamlin Papers, Avery Library.
71   Douglas Haskell, Letter to Frances Dodge [NCASF], 4 August 1945, Hamlin Papers, Avery Library.
72   Negatives and prints in the Douglas Haskell Papers, box C222, Avery Library.
73   Invitation to the presentation of the exhibit at the consular offices, Douglas Haskell Papers, Avery Library. Architects Committee, National Council of American-Soviet Friendship, *News Bulletin*, no. 11 (5 December 1945), 3; "Architecture Exhibit Presented to Russia," *Architectural Record* 98, no. 6 (December 1945), 134.
74   "American Architecture Exhibit Arrives in Moscow," *News Bulletin*, no. 14 (8 January 1947), 1.
75   Stenogram of the meeting of the Architecture section of VOKS devoted to discussing the exhibit, *Arkhitektura SShA*, 4 March 1947, RGALI, f. 674, op. 2, ed. khr. 232.

wanted the descriptions to be concise and confined to black ribbons with white lettering contrasting with the photographs[71]. Rather than an explanatory document—a brochure providing useful information to the visitors—Haskell's captions formed a narrative leading from the brief history of an architectural type to the other, while presenting the technical systems and different types of urban fabric. The images were carefully selected among the most eloquent illustrations published in American magazines since 1940, and portrayed diverse works from various architects, sometimes of opposing views, while accounting for a pluralistic modern stance that went beyond the "international style" popularized by MoMA since 1932. The panels thus presented, without naming their creators, constructions by Richard Neutra (Channel Heights), Frank Lloyd Wright (Goetsch-Winckler House), Louis I. Kahn and George Howe (Carver Court), and Clarence Stein (Baldwin Hills Village), some of Albert Kahn's factories, Philip Goodwin and Edward Durell Stone's Museum of Modern Art in New York, and the Sears department store by Skidmore, Owing & Merrill in Los Angeles. Inevitable views of the Empire State Building, Rockefeller Center, and the Los Angeles County General Hospital alternated with highways, power plants, and theatres. Though a certain part of the discourse described the destitute slums and the hardships of the displaced peasants, the overall copy was more lyrical than documentary, emulating 1930s persuasion techniques used by *USSR in Construction*[72].

The panels were shipped to Moscow in November 1945, after Corbett presented them to the Soviet Consul Pavel P. Mikhailov, on 26 October[73]. However, their arrival in the USSR was not confirmed until January 1947[74]. After having opened in the Great Hall of the House of the Architect, the exhibit was vigorously debated within VOKS in a discussion sparked by Alabian, who justified the delay with the absence of an adequate space. Vladimir Myslin explained that in 1945, he had contributed to translating the exhibition notes in New York, and claimed that they were "biased," not allowing for an understanding of constructivist techniques, too focused on individuals—namely on Wright—, and lacked materials on ordinary housing meant for the general population. Others also deemed the narrative too close to journal illustrations, but not Arkin, who highlighted the instructional aspects of the exhibit and stressed that its role was to restore the "face" of American architecture. In a discourse reminiscent of Mumford's analyses, he deplored the deadly grip of the construction industry—as though, as he put it, "a mummy could give birth to a child" —and compared Wright, a prophetic figure huddled in a remote Taliesin villa, to Tolstoy and his Iasnaia Poliana. Alabian closed the debate by admitting that American architecture was in a "deadlock" due to its excessive focus on function and structure, as it failed to consider architecture as "art." Nonetheless, he deemed the event instructive for a time when the Soviet Union was striving to "catch up to America and surpass it," and called for the development of a critique of the American architectural press. Most importantly, he sent the organizers, whom he warmly congratulated, a series of questions to pursue further discussions[75].

Shortly before the exhibition opened, Amtorg released *American Construction*, a special edition of its *spravochniki*, following up on the 1945 publication, already devoted to the building industry. Most texts were written by participants to the 1945 conference held in New York City, making the volume a direct result of the event. The 682 pages of content and the 282 pages of advertisements were mostly focused on building materials and the mechanization of construction sites, while several chapters presented material on architecture gathered by the Pomerance & Breines firm. The volume

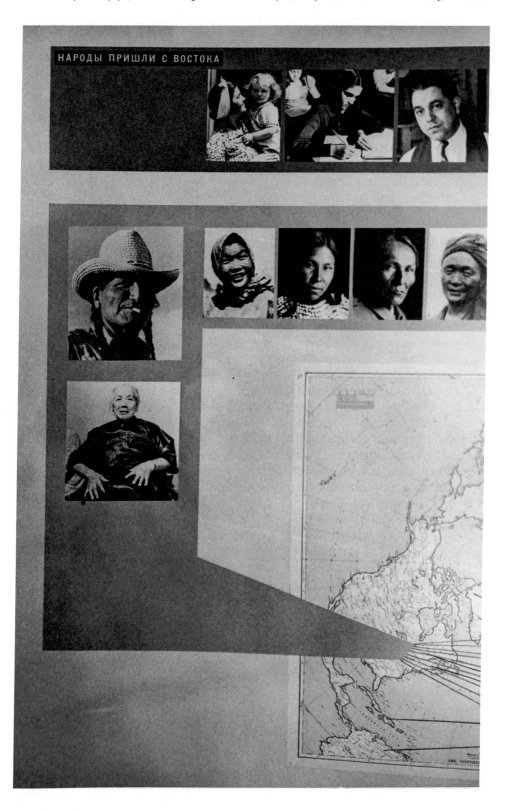

"People came from the East."

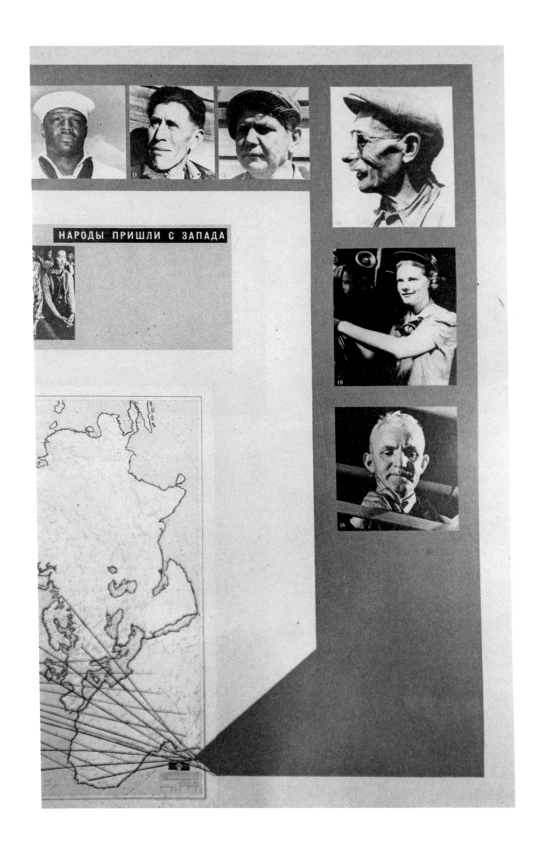

НАРОДЫ ПРИШЛИ С ЗАПАДА

Panels of the exhibition on American architecture sent to the USSR by the National Council of American–Soviet Friendship, 1945.
Gelatin silver prints on paper, 24 × 18 cm. Douglas Putnam Haskell Papers, Avery Architectural & Fine Arts Library, Columbia University.

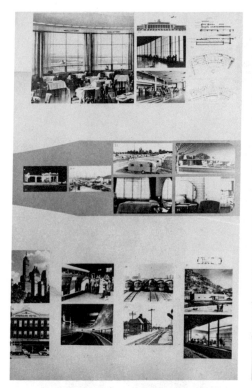

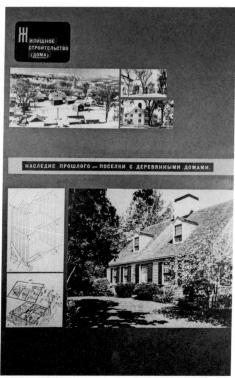

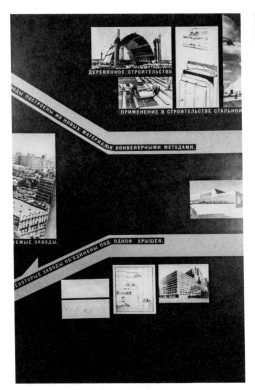

ДЕРЕВЯННОЕ СТРОИТЕЛЬСТВО

ПРИМЕНЕНИЕ В СТРОИТЕЛЬСТВЕ СТАЛЬНОЙ

...ОДЫ ПОСТРОЕНЫ ИЗ НОВЫХ МАТЕРИАЛОВ КОНВЕЙЕРНЫМИ МЕТОДАМИ.

...ЕМЫЕ ЗАВОДЫ.

...ЕКОТОРЫЕ ЗАВОДЫ ОБ'ЕДИНЕНЫ ПОД ОДНОЙ КРЫШЕЙ.

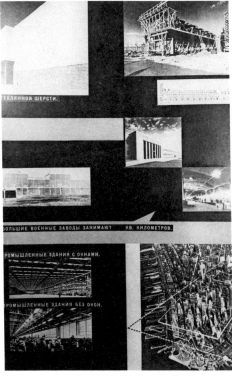

...ЕКЛЯННОЙ ШЕРСТИ.

...БОЛЬШИЕ ВОЕННЫЕ ЗАВОДЫ ЗАНИМАЮТ ... КВ. КИЛОМЕТРОВ.

...РОМЫШЛЕННЫЕ ЗДАНИЯ С ОКНАМИ.

...РОМЫШЛЕННЫЕ ЗДАНИЯ БЕЗ ОКОН.

ОБРАЗЦЫ ИНДУСТРИАЛЬНОЙ АРХИТЕКТУРЫ ОТЛИЧАЮТ...

......И ПРЕДУСМАТРИВАЮТ БЫТОВОЕ ОБСЛУ...
...ВАНИЕ РАБОЧИХ.

...ЛЬШИМ РАЗНООБРАЗИЕМ.

ЗАМЕТНО НАЧАЛО ДИФФЕРЕНЦИАЦИИ КРУП...

ОТОПЛЕНИЕ ЖИДКИМ ГОРЮЧИМ.

ОТОПЛЕНИЕ УГЛЕМ.

...ЭЛЕК...

Panels of the exhibition on American architecture sent to the USSR by the National Council of American–Soviet Friendship, 1945. Gelatin silver prints on paper, 24 × 18 cm. Douglas Putnam Haskell Papers, Avery Architectural & Fine Arts Library, Columbia University.

"Here are examples of contemporary houses. ...Our contemporary architects like trees,"

"open spaces and straight lines."

Panels of the exhibition on American architecture sent to the USSR by the National Council of American–Soviet Friendship, 1945.
Gelatin silver prints on paper, 24 × 18 cm. Douglas Putnam Haskell Papers, Avery Architectural & Fine Arts Library, Columbia University.

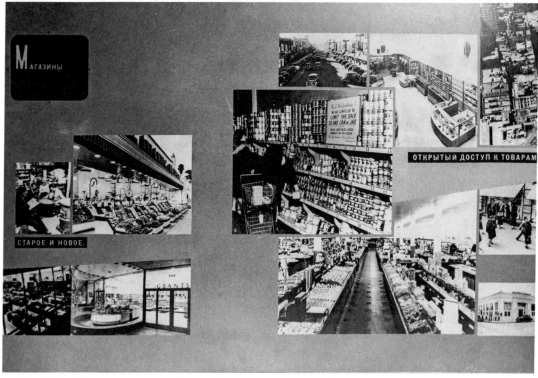

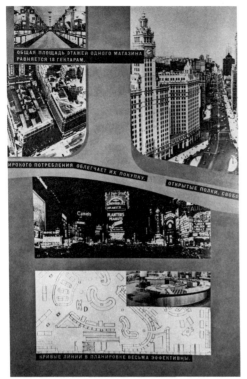

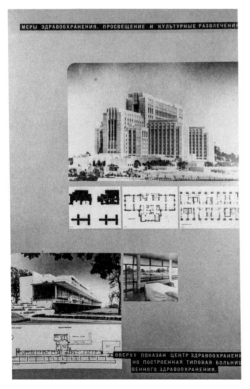

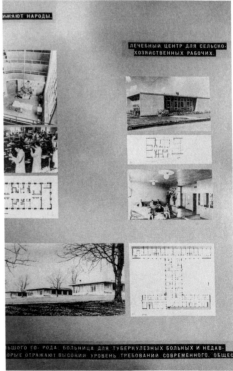

Panels of the Exhibition on American architecture sent to the USSR by the National Council of American–Soviet Friendship, 1945.
Gelatin silver prints on paper, 24 × 18 cm. Douglas Putnam Haskell papers, Avery Architectural & Fine Arts Library, Columbia University.

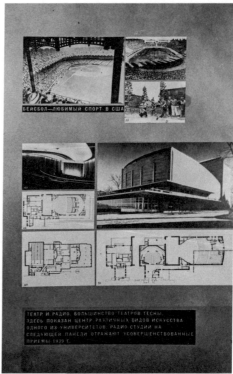

American Construction, manual published by Amtorg, New York, 1946.
Left: Chrysler Tank Arsenal by Albert Kahn Associates, 1941. Right: Residential neighbourhood in Clifton, N. J.. CCA, BIB 244229.

also introduced transportation infrastructure and major factories built during the war, without naming their architects and with some semantic caution. In an ironic reversal of the Cheliabinsk Tractor Plant's fate, Albert Kahn's Chrysler Tank Arsenal in Warren was thus called a "tractor factory."[76] The New Deal housing complexes and workers' towns built during the war were studied much more seriously than Khiger had done using printed sources. Vertical hospitals and campuses were also analyzed, likely a first for Russian readers. Fundamentally descriptive, the heavy volume embodied the fantasies of American industrial managers, still tempted by a market they continued to view as accessible, and condensed the Russian technicians' investigations, as they would soon be called back to Russia.

Though he failed to import American building systems and equipment, Oltarzhevskii provided Soviet designers with dimensional standards, easier to transfer on paper, in a 1947 album published by the Academy of Architecture and sponsored by Alabian, who had attained a pivotal role in the dissemination of American practices. The *Architect's Guide to Dimensions* was filled with illustrations meant to standardize architectural projects, much like the *Architectural Graphic Standards* published by Charles G. Ramsey and Harold D. Sleeper in 1932, and continually reissued thereafter[77]. Covering several scales,

76   N.P. Remizov and A.N. Popov, eds., *Amerikanskoe stroitelstvo* (New York: Amtorg, 1946), 35.
77   Charles G. Ramsey and Harold R. Sleeper, *Architectural Graphic Standards for Architects, Engineers, Decorators, Builders and Draftsmen* (New York: J. Wiley & Sons, 1932).

Viacheslav K. Oltarzhevskii, *Dimensional Handbook for the Architect*, Moscow, 1947.
Plates on hospitals, restaurant counters, service stations, and road widths, 34 × 26 cm. CCA, ID:94-B2323.

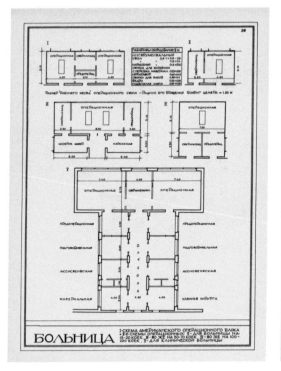

БОЛЬНИЦА

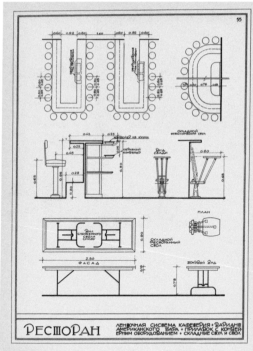

РЕСТОРАН

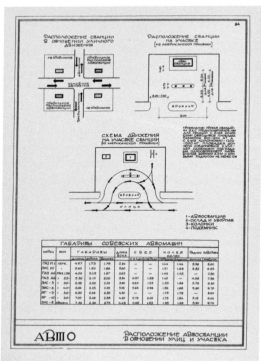

АВТО

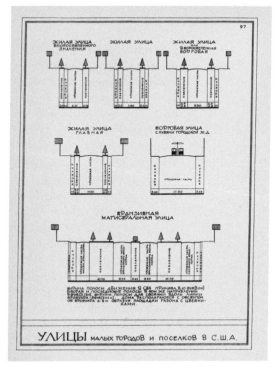

УЛИЦЫ малых городов и поселков в С.Ш.А.

from the general plan to details, Oltarzhevskii's handbook presented many of the dimensions and modules used in the building industry. In his foreword, Corbett's former employee took care to cautiously highlight that "the examples taken from foreign practices (American and British) are given as cases of solutions found abroad, and can by no means be used without being critical towards the issues they raise."[78] The explicit sources of the illustrations were reference books regularly used by American designers: the *Time Saver Standards*, a source for the main measurements, Philip G. Knobloch's *Good Practice in Construction* and Sweet's architectural catalogue, the regularly updated information database on materials and techniques, with Lonberg-Holm serving as its technical director[79]. Information was also derived from the *Information Book* written by the London architect John Burnet and, covertly, from the *Bauentwurfslehre*, a 1936 manual published in Berlin by Ernst Neufert, whose mention was likely frowned upon in the USSR after 1945[80].

A comparative analysis helps identify almost all the sources of the types featured: kindergartens, schools, stadiums, hospitals, farm buildings, hotels, and stores. Street dimensions and gas station designs were clearly "inspired by the American practice." As for interiors and furnishings, the focus was on bathrooms, kitchens, and luncheonettes as well as other businesses, all of which were blatantly plagiarized from the *Architectural Graphic Standards*. The light fixtures were borrowed from Knobloch; Neufert inspired the escalators and bleachers; while the pianos and pool tables were based on the work of Burnet. Oltarzhevskii's loose plates —essential supplements to the denser volumes of the *Architect's Guide* published as of 1946, where the Western sources were obscured[81]—served as a reference for architects throughout the 1950s, underhandedly introducing the fabric of America into the material aspects of Soviet construction. Oltarzhevskii once again appeared in the press with an article on the "Contemporary American Hotel," where he described his own Pinehurst, New Jersey building[82].

While American measurement standards infiltrated the Soviet practice and as American construction techniques remained out of reach, Russian reconstruction plans applied similar principles to those of the turn-of-the-century City Beautiful Movement. The only exception was Burov's project for the reconstruction of Yalta, developed between 1944 and 1946, as part of the general plan for the Crimean south shore established by Ginzburg in the 1930s[83]. To imagine the future seaside resort, after studying its landscape from above from an airplane, Burov discarded the traditional design, centred on the intersection of two monumental avenues, and drew a two-level urban highway, clearing the ground for pedestrians. The skyline would have been transformed by the projected construction of five hotels, each around ten

78   Viacheslav K. Oltarzhevskii, Preface to *Gabaritny spravochnik arkhitektora* (Moscow: Izd-vo Akademii Arkhitektury SSSR), n.p. A thorough analysis of sources was done by Sam Omans, "Vyacheslav Oltarzhevksky's Dimensional Handbook for the Architect: Architectural Standards, Reconstruction, and Americanizm in the USSR c. 1947," seminar paper (Institute of Fine Arts, 2016).

79   *Time-Saver Standards: A Desk Manual of Architectural Practice* (New York: American Architect, 1935); *Sweet's Indexed Catalogue of Building Construction* (New York: Architectural Record Co., 1906 [first edition, followed by annual update]); Philip G. Knobloch, *Good Practice in Construction* (New York: Pencil Points Press, 1923).

80   Sir John Burnet, Thomas Tait, and Francis Lorne, *The Information Book of Sir John Burnet, Tait and Lorne* (London: The Architectural Press, 1933); Ernst Neufert, *Bauentwurfslehre* (Berlin: Bauwelt-Verlag, 1936).

81   Karo S. Alabian, Nikolai P. Bylinkin, Viktor A. Vesnin et al., eds., *Spravochnik arkhitektora* (Moscow: Izd-vo Akademii Arkhitektury, 1946–1960).

82   Viacheslav K. Oltarzhevskii, "Sovremenny amerikanski otel," *Arkhitektura SSSR*, no. 13 (1946): 42–47.

83   For his reflections on the architectural context, see Andrei K. Burov, "Voina i arkhitektura," *Znamia*, no. 5 (1945): 100–14.

storeys tall, whose tectonic solutions varied from arcades to façades made entirely out of glass[84]. This plan likened the city to Miami Beach, Florida, which Burov had discovered during his 1930 trip and described in rather simplistic terms in his notebooks and contemporary writings: "A palm tree-lined avenue separates the beach from the street. On the other side of the road, there is a park filled with palm trees. [...] In the park and closer to the road, approximately 200 metres away from each other, there are 42 tower hotels, each 10 to 15 storeys tall, all built in the same year."[85] The Crimean shore, where the destiny of the world was decided during the February 1945 Yalta Conference, had thus been successively reimagined as California—with Shumiatskii's Kinogorod—and as Florida, which was then becoming a place of refuge for East Coast Jewish retirees. Notably, Burov developed his plan while Stalin was considering creating a Jewish republic in Crimea, a project supported by the Jewish Antifascist Committee. The United States promised to support the project financially, namely during Solomon Mikhoels and Itzik Fefer's 1943 mission to America as representatives of the Committee[86]. The idea was abandoned when the impending creation of the State of Israel materialized, with the Soviets instead helping the Zionists attain their goal. In 1948, officials such as Grigorii Simonov, president of the Council of Ministers' Architectural Committee, rejected Burov's plan, which had been criticized as of June 1945 for its failure to analyze the location and the "mechanical solution" proposed for the shore. The officials stated that the plan "ignored the practical aspects of architecture while focusing on its most formal aspects."[87] With the onset of the Cold War, any overt reference to the United States became incriminating.

Andrei K. Burov. Project for the reconstruction of the city of Yalta, 1944-1945.
Pencil, ink and watercolour on paper, 19.6 × 78.1 cm. Shchusev State Museum of Architecture, Ria 6120/2.

The meeting of the Soviet and American troops at the Elbe River, near Torgau, symbolic of a fraternity that would not come to last, happened only a few months before the beginning of the Cold War, with the atomic bombs dropped on Hiroshima and Nagasaki. The industry leaders' hopes of pursuing American exports to the USSR—a vast potential market for equipment and consumer goods—had crumbled[88]. The US maintained political ties with the Soviets in the shadow of the anti-Nazi alliance for a time, but a hostile discourse against the agents of Amerikanizm was soon implemented, along with a monumental construction programme set to fulfil Stalin's ambition to compete with the United States.

After 1946, the travels of architects and experts were put to a halt. Some never came back, like Sergei Kozhin, an architect from Ivan Zholtovskii's school who was attuned to western architecture, having visited the Bauhaus and met Le Corbusier in 1928. He was held prisoner by the Germans and freed by the United States Army. He then reached Los Angeles, where he got in touch with Richard Neutra, who was very popular in the USSR; in the 1950s, he became a partner in his firm, where he remained for 17 years[89]. In New York, Nikolai Basov sat for two years on an expert committee tasked with choosing a location for the UN headquarters and with the development of its programme[90].

Conversely, one of the most telling transfers from West to East was that of some 200 Hollywood films seized by the Red Army in Berlin and distributed little by little in Soviet movie theatres over the course of several years. Audiences thus discovered "foreign films"—a euphemism used to avoid stating their origin—in their original subtitled versions, including the latest musicals and four episodes of the adventures of Tarzan, which became immensely popular[91]. According to Dmitrii Shostakovich, they were among Stalin's favourites[92]. Another great success was the illustrated, large-format monthly *Amerika*, whose inaugural issue, published in March 1945, had an initial print run of

84   "Eskiz proekta novogo Ialty," *Sovetskoe Iskusstvo*, 28 November 1944. A manuscript titled *O Ialte i eio tsentre* [On Yalta and its centre] is held in the Burov family archives: Raisa G. Burova, Raisa N. Blashkevich, and Olga I. Rzhekhina, *A.K. Burov* (Moscow: Stroiizdat, 1984), 98–106. See also Tarkhanov and Kavtaradze, *Stalinist Architecture*, 99, 105, and 106.

85   Andrei K. Burov, *Ob arkhitekture* (Moscow: Stroiizdat, 1960), 142–43. See also *Andrei Konstantinovich Burov: pisma, dnevniki, besedy s aspirantami, suzhdenia sovremennikov*, texts collected by Olga I. Rzhekhina and Raisa G. Burova (Moscow: Iskusstvo, 1980), 102.

86   On this mission, see Shimon Redlich, *War, Holocaust and Stalinism: A Documented Study of the Jewish Anti-Fascist Committee in the USSR* (Luxembourg: Harwood Academic Publishers, 1995), 305-13.

87   Resolution of the Architecture Committee on the Yalta plan, 15 June 1945, RGAE, f. 432, op. I, d. 257, 89, reprinted in Iuliia L Kosenkova, *Sovetskii gorod 1940-kh: pervoi poloviny 50-kh godov* (Moscow: URSS, 2000), 378; and Grigorii Simonov, "Preodolet sereznye nedostatki v arkhitekture," *Sovetskoe Iskusstvo*, 26 March 1948.

88   David S. Foglesong, *The American Mission and the Evil Empire: The Crusade for a Free Russia Since 1881* (New York: Cambridge University Press, 2007).

89   Gulya Kozhina [wife of S. Kozhin], letter to Vera and Nikolai Troitskii, 12 March 1975, GARF. f. 10015 op. 1, d. 757, l. 1–2. See the biographic note by Boris A. Iakovlev in support of the request for naturalization, 4 January 1955, GARF, f. 10015 op. 1, d. 757, l. 1–2. Barbara Lamprecht, "Architect Sergei N. Koshin (1898–1971)," unpublished study for the Christ Cathedral Catholic Corporation, Los Angeles, 2014. I thank Barbara Lamprecht for sharing the document with me.

90   George A. Dudley, *A Workshop for Peace: Designing the United Nations Headquarters* (New York; Cambridge, MA: Architectural History Foundation, MIT Press, 1994), 143–48.

91   Kristina Tanis, "'This Film Was Captured as a Trophy…': the International Context of Trophy Films," *Studies in Russian and Soviet Cinema*, no. 3 (2019): 1-15; id., "Trofeinye filmy v SSSR v 1940-1950-e gody: k praktikam kinoprokata," *Artikult*, no. 34 (2019): 79-88.

92   Dmitri Shostakovich, *Testimony; The Memoirs of Dmitri Shostakovich* (London: Faber, 2005), 193, quoted in David Caute, *The Dancer Defects: The Struggle for Cultural Supremacy During the Cold War* (Oxford: Oxford University Press, 2003), 117.

10,000 issues and immediately became a sought-after item on the Moscow black market. Created by William Averell Harriman based on the same model as *Life* and *Look*, it was launched with the approval of the Minister of Foreign Affairs, Viacheslav Molotov, so long as the Russians could disseminate a similar publication in the United States. They used a revamped version of *USSR in Construction*, renamed *Soviet Union*, plagiarizing the American magazine's layout to paint everyday life in the Soviet Union in a flattering light. *Amerika* became increasingly influential in the circulation of exotic representations of the New World and had a print run of 50,000 issues in 1947[93]. That same year, the *Voice of America* began airing in the USSR from Munich, and later became a global network whose channels were consistently jammed on the east side of the Iron Curtain[94].

Among the representatives of the Soviet press sent to the United States was Ilya Ehrenburg, who finally discovered the sights he had described twenty years earlier in *And Yet the World Goes 'Round*. Accompanied by his young colleague Konstantin Simonov—made famous by his war stories—and General Mikhail Galaktionov, he set off on a propaganda tour in 1946. The tour failed because of the Russians' wariness of an American nuclear attack and his hosts' suspicions regarding Soviet claims on Europe[95]. After the NCASF welcomed the three envoys, Ehrenburg published his impressions, first in *Izvestiia*, and later in a book that was promptly translated in Paris and East Berlin. Along with the usual clichés about New York's magnitude and multi-ethnicity, he described a uniformity of thought and general lack of culture, denouncing the latent anti-Semitism and the racial segregation he witnessed in the South, where he was chaperoned by Bill Nelson, the editor of *Amerika*. Quoting Le Corbusier, his old acquaintance encountered during the trip, on the "fairy catastrophe" of New York City, he also commented on Mayakovsky's impressions: "He understood the threat of New York; he also understood its anguished charm." He considered that in New York, "not only were there great skyscrapers, but there was also great fear, anger, cupidity, labour, and great fatigue."[96] More critical of the automobile— "the American's first love"—than Ilf and Petrov, Ehrenburg condemned the standardization of the main streets he visited[97]. Paraphrasing Goethe, he noted that America "lacked ancient stones" and mocked the fact that the citizens contemplated their monuments with "love and devotion."[98] Along with literature and film, he considered architecture to be one of America's useful contributions: "Though dry, sometimes lacking in humanity, it has blood ties to our era; it is also a contribution to world culture." He drew an analogy between architecture

93 *The New York Times*, 25 October 1945, 12; "The Press. The Voice of America," *Time*, 6 June 1949; Creighton Peet: "Russian 'Amerika', a Magazine about US for Soviet Citizens," *College Art Journal 11, no. 1 (Fall 1951)*: 17–20. See also Parks, *Culture, Conflict and Coexistence*, 87–88. On the sabotaging of the magazine's distributions, see Amanda Wood Aucoin, "Deconstructing the American Way of Life: Soviet Responses to Cultural Exchange and American Information Activity during the Khrushchev Years," PhD dissertation (Fayetteville: University of Arkansas, 2001), 45–47.

94 Walter L. Hixson, *Parting the Curtain: Propaganda, Culture, and the Cold War, 1945–61* (New York: St. Martin's Press, 1997), 29–55.

95 This is the explanation provided in Anatol Goldberg, *Ilya Ehrenburg: Writing, Politics and the Art of Survival* (London: Weidenfeld & Nicolson, 1984), 219–23. See also Ewa Bérard, *La vie tumultueuse d'Ilya Ehrenbourg: juif, russe et soviétique* (Paris: Ramsay, 1991), 267–69.

96 Ilia Ehrenbourg, *Retour des États-Unis* (Paris: Nagel, 1947), 17–19. See what he disclosed to the American press: "Visiting Russian Sums Up His Trip: Taking Home His UNRRA Bread," *The New York Times*, 26 June 1946.

97 Ehrenbourg, *Retour des États-Unis*, 32.

98 Ibid., 64.

Left: Ilia G. Ehrenburg, *In America,* 1947, German edition, East Berlin: SWA Verlag, 1947. Private collection.
Right: Maxim Gorky. *In America,* 1949, French edition. Moscow. Foreign Languages Publishing House. Private collection.

and culture to describe the divide between mass consumption and superior works, such as those of "Hemingway, Faulkner, Steinbeck, and others," noting that "in America, there are no four- or five-storey houses. Throughout the country, there are thousands of little cottages (veranda, rocking chair) and a few sky-scrapers. The same can be said of literature: both very good and very bad."[99]

In the following years, intellectuals scarcely travelled to the United States. When they were sent across the Atlantic, it was no longer to report back but rather to defend the Soviet political line. This was the case for Shostakovich, who in 1949 took part in the Cultural and Scientific Conference for World Peace at the Waldorf Astoria Hotel along with the writer Aleksandr Fadeev and the filmmakers Sergei Gerasimov and Mikhail Chiaureli[100]. The tables had turned as soon as Simonov returned from America, as a resolution from the Central Committee on 26 August 1946 called for anti-American performances. Simonov contributed to launch the new policy with his play *The Russian Question*, pub-lished in December in *Zvezda* (The Star)[101]. In the play, a New York publishing mogul tries to force a reporter to write a book condemning the USSR, despite the favourable opinion the journalist acquired while travelling in Russia. It was performed in 500 theatres, as far as in East Berlin, where it launched a cultural Cold War. It was adapted for the screen by Mikhail Romm, but with a rather nuanced portrayal of the United States[102]. The same cannot be said for Grigorii Aleksandrov's 1949 *Encounter on the Elbe*, in which the 1930s musical director painted the American soldiers in the worst possible light.

There was occasionally a strong backlash against American films. In February 1946, a screening of *Casablanca* by Michael Curtiz at the Actors Club was interrupted and the film reels were confiscated[103]. In 1947, the Rus-sians deserted the previously beloved weekly screenings at the American Embassy in Moscow[104]. As the second instalment of Eisenstein's *Ivan the Terrible* was censored and he was unable to jump-start the filming of *Mos-cow 800*—his triumphalist picture on the history of the capital[105]—, the famed director channelled his bitterness towards Hollywood by supporting Simonov's play and denouncing the rising anti-Soviet sentiment in Hollywood in an article titled "Dealers in Spiritual Poison."[106]

99   Ibid., 162.
100   Terry Klefstad, "Shostakovich and the Peace Conference," *Music and Politics* 6, no. 2 (Summer 2012): http://dx.doi.org/10.3998/mp.9460447.0006.201.
101   Konstantin M. Simonov, "Russkii vopros," *Zvezda*, no. 12 (December 1946): 74–112.
102   Caute, *The Dancer Defects*, 92–116.
103   Parks, *Culture, Conflict and Coexistence*, 93.
104   Ibid., 90–103.
105   Katerina Clark, "Eisenstein's Two Projects for a Film about Moscow," *Modern Language Review*, no. 101 (Spring 2006): 188–204.
106   Sergei M. Eisenstein, "Postavshchiki dukhovnoi otravy," *Kultura i zhizn*, 31 July 1947. See Caute, *The Dancer Defects*, 124.
107   "O zhurnalakh 'Zvezda' i 'Leningrad': iz postanovlenia TsK VKP(b) ot 14 avgusta 1946 g.," *Kultura i Zhizn*, 20 August 1946. See also David Brandenberger, *National Bolshevism: Stalinist Mass Culture and the Formation of Modern Russian National Identity, 1931–1956* (Cambridge, MA: Harvard University Press, 2002).
108   Starr, *Red & Hot*, 216.
109   Natalia Sazonova, *Red Jazz ou la vie extraordinaire du camarade Rosner* (Paris: Parangon, 2004).
110   Leonid O. Utesov, statement reported in Yuri Krotkov, *I Am From Moscow: A View of the Russian Miracle* (New York: Dutton, 1967), 5.
111   Maria Mileeva, "Utopia in Retreat: The Closure of the State Museum of Western Art in 1948," in *Utopian Reality: Reconstructing Culture in Revolutionary Russia and Beyond*, eds. Christina Lodder, Maria Kokkori, Maria Mileeva (Leyde: Brill, 2016), 203–17.
112   "Diadia Sam risuet sam," in *Krokodil*, 30 November 1948, and "Iskusstvo liudoedov," *Krokodil*, 30 September 1949, quoted in Mileeva, "Utopia in Retreat," 216.
113   Maxim Gorky, *In America* [1906] (Moscow: Foreign Languages Publishing House, 1949).

The starting point for the Central Committee's policy, associated with Andrei Zhdanov, was the condemnation, in August 1946, of the journals *Zvezda* and *Leningrad*. The poet Anna Akhmatova and the satirist Mikhail Zoshchenko were personally attacked and accused of being amoral and apolitical. Russian nationalism was thus reaffirmed and "foreign" tendencies were incriminated[107]. Soviet *djazmeny* (jazzmen) were also repressed, along with, in a fetishistic approach, the musical instruments symbolizing American music, like the saxophone, which was banished from orchestras and whose sale was prohibited[108]. Deported to the Kolyma, the trumpet player Eddie Rosner was able to recreate an orchestra in Magadan, in an outcome similar to Oltarzhevskii's, who had practiced as an architect in Vorkuta.[109] As for Leonid Utesov, he disguised his concerts as demonstrations of the toxic nature of American jazz through the tongue-in-cheek performance of numerous pieces, most likely in front of knowing audiences[110]. In 1948, the State Museum of Western Art in Moscow was closed, and the paintings from Shchukin and Morozov's former collections were scattered[111]. The satirical paper *Krokodil* mocked American abstract art, calling it "cannibalistic" in a discourse reminiscent of the Nazi offensive against "degenerate" art in the 1930s[112].

The most negative visions of America such as Maxim Gorky's 1906 account were reissued, printed with terrifying covers and translated for foreign publication[113], while painters, among whom Boris Prorokov, based frightening street scenes and monstrous portraits upon them, resulting in the 1949 series *Vot ona, Amerika* (Here it is, America). Photomontage techniques, used by John Heartfield in his anti-Nazi imagery, were perfected by his follower

Mikhail M. Cheremnykh. "The American way of life: every 21 seconds a serious crime is committed in the United States". Lithographic print on paper, 59.5 × 78 cm, 1949. Alamy Images, ID: R90GKE.

Aleksandr A. Zhitomirskii. Photomontages for *Literaturnaia gazeta*, Gelatin silver prints. Ne boltai! Collection.

Top: "The Right to Hang and the Right to be Hanged," July 3, 1948. 60 × 47 cm;
Bottom: "In the American Ring: Knockout", with Harry Truman and the Rockefeller Center, 23.5 × 21.5 cm.

Aleksandr Zhitomirskii in evocative illustrations. They gave appalling images of Harry Truman, turned the skyscrapers into ominous giants, and portrayed the Statue of Liberty as monumental gallows[114]. Each week, these themes were featured in *Krokodil*[115].

Secretly Borrowing American Technology

In this context, it had become dangerous to praise American technology, and though millions of Soviets had witnessed the quality of the Lend-Lease equipment, they were strictly punished for expressing their appreciation for the imported products. As Alexander Solzhenitsyn wrote in *The Gulag Archipelago*, ad hoc articles of the penal code sanctioned three attitudes, summarized in easy-to-report abbreviations used in indictments: VAT, "praise of American technology;" VAD, "praise of American democracy;" and PZ "toadyism toward the West."[116] To establish a new political and historical truth, the Soviet leaders minimized the massive provision of equipment through the Lend-Lease Act, which was labelled in retrospect as a "weapon of imperialism."[117] Despite the official law banning any mention of American involvement, the Soviet military-industrial complex began openly copying transportation equipment and weaponry from this definitively dry well of materials, reprising—25 years later and at an infinitely more intricate level—the method used after the revolution to plagiarize the Fordson tractor.

The most spectacular example was the Tupolev Tu-4 long-range bomber, an exact copy of the Boeing B-29 Superfortress, which had been deliberately omitted by Roosevelt from the Lend-Lease Act. Miraculously, five B-29 airplanes that ran out of fuel or were damaged after raids over Japan, had to make an emergency landing in the Russian Far East at the end of the war. Stalin ordered the airplane designer Andrei Tupolev to abandon the development of his own project for the heavy bomber n° 64—made problematic by the Russians' technological backwardness—and clone the Boeing aircraft in the space of two years[118]. Tupolev directed all his energy towards studying the captured airplanes, whose components were exhibited in Moscow before being reproduced by some 900 different firms under his leadership. He accomplished a truly phenomenal feat, having to manufacture materials previously unknown in the USSR—such as plastics—and adapt the sizing to the metric system. This reverse engineering principle was also applied to Wright R-3350 engines, copied by the Shvetsov engineering firm—with some metallurgy-related difficulties—and renamed ASh-73TK, and to the advanced electronic systems used on the first high-altitude bomber ever produced[119]. Tupolev's initial prototypes

114   Erika Wolf, *Aleksandr Zhitomirsky: Photomontage as a Weapon of World War II and the Cold War* (Chicago: The Art Institute of Chicago, 2016).

115   William Nelson, *Out of the Crocodile's Mouth: Russian Cartoons about the United States from "Krokodil," Moscow's Humor Magazine* (Washington, DC: Public Affairs Press, 1949).

116   Alexander Solzhenitsyn, *The Gulag Archipelago 1918-1956, An Experiment in Literary Investigation* (New York: Harper & Row, 1973) vol. 1, 91.

117   A. Alekseev, "Lend-liz, – oruzhie agresivnogo amerikanskogo imperializma," *Voprosi ekonomiki*, no. 4 (April 1951), 81–93.

118   Leonid Kerber and Maximilian Saukke, "Ne kopia, a analog (o samolete Tu-4)," *Krylia rodiny*, no. 1 (1989), 24–25; in English: "The Tupolev Tu-4 Story", *Bulletin of the Russian Aviation Research Group of Air-Britain*, vol. 30, n° 107, p. 43–50. Yefim Gordon and Vladimir Rigmant, *Tupolev Tu-4. Soviet Superfortress* (Hinckley: Midland Publishing, 2002).

119   Kurt Rand, "Russia Steals the Superfort," *Flying* 42, no. 6 (June 1948): 73–79; L.C. Kappel, "The American Legacy to Russian Air Power," *Aviation Age* 18 (December 1952): 12–13; Robert Jackson, *The Red Falcons: The Soviet Air Force in Action 1919-1969* (Brighton: Clifton Books, 1970), 158–59; Walter J. Boyne, "Carbon Copy Bomber," *Air Force Magazine*, June 2009, 52–56.

were flown over the public during the Tushino air show on 3 August 1947, convincing Western observers that they were no longer the American machines seized in 1944. This aircraft restored the Soviet Union's strategic parity with American aviation and the apparatus used to build it became the foundation for the entire Soviet post-War aviation industry.

The unwitting technology transfers from America also affected the cargo destined for the Tu-4, i.e. the atomic bomb. Without dismissing the input of outstanding Soviet physicists, there is evidence that Igor Kurchatov and Iulii Khariton could not have developed the Soviet bomb—launched on 18 October 1949, five years after the Enola Gay B-29 dropped its bomb on Hiroshima—so rapidly without help from supporters and Soviet agents in the United States[120]. Stalin trusted foreign researchers more than his own, though it has been shown that Russian scientists would have been able to develop the bomb by themselves[121]. Fittingly, the bomb was hauled by an airplane that was copied from its original carrier, the B-29. In the strategic field of computer science, the engineers Joel Barr and Alfred Sarant, who illegally entered the Soviet Union after the war, made a considerable contribution to the development of the first Soviet computers[122]. Americans became increasingly paranoid after such instances, with tangible consequences. Amtorg's New York executives, whose ties with the Secret Services had always been close, were arrested and accused of being foreign agents[123]. Its last *Spravochnik* was issued in 1948, having lost all practical usefulness in terms of equipment purchases, as trade had come to nothing. As of the previous year, *Amerikanskaia tekhnika i promyshlennost* was no longer published. Its latest issues had increasingly focused on military technology and economic issues involving construction[124].

In the automotive sector, which Amtorg continued to monitor, there were fewer challenges regarding defence, but American models, among others, remained a major source of inspiration. The AZLK (formerly KIM) plant thus launched its production of the Moskvich 400, a copy of the pre-war Opel Kadett. But the ZIS-110 limousine model that the ZIS (formerly ZIL) began to manufacture in 1945 to drive around Stalin and his colleagues was derived from the 1940 Packard 180. Roosevelt had given a few of these vehicles to Stalin, who took a great liking to them[125]. As of 1946, the GAZ factory in Gorky, built between 1929 and 1932 by The Austin Company for Ford's machines, manufactured the M-20 *Pobeda* (Victory), designed by the engineer Andrei Lipgart, head of the firm's engineering division since 1933. The streamlined vehicle, a hybrid between the 1942 Ford sedan and the Nash of the same year, was produced until 1958. A Polish version was also manufactured. Following production delays, Lipgart, a remarkable designer, was dismissed and demoted to design trucks in a ZIS branch near Cheliabinsk.[126]

Anti-Amerikanizm and Anti-Cosmopolitism

The Soviet engineers' borrowing of technical systems and forms from the United States reveals a pursuit of a pragmatic approach to Amerikanizm, the covert flipside of a coin whose front was openly and aggressively anti-American. This hypocrisy was made obvious in 1949 by the fact that the campaign against Arkin, who was accused of being "the most active ideologue of bourgeois cosmopolitism," occurred two years after the launch of a programme for the construction of a high-rise complex based on American examples in Moscow. The attack against Arkin was just one aspect of the offensive against the Union of Architects and its secretary, Alabian, but its reach was all-encompassing. Arkin's entire career was scrutinized, from his 1932 book *Architecture of the Contemporary West* to his allegedly favourable attitude towards the architecture under fascism after his 1935 trip to Rome. In November 1947, he had already been sentenced by a court of honour presided by Viacheslav Shkvarikov for having published an article deemed "slavish" towards the West in *The Architectural Review*. The jury had been notably harsher to him than to his fellow defendants, Andrei Bunin and Nikolai Bylinkin[127]. The historian's main crime was to have promoted a positive vision of America: "Over the last few

120   On Vasilii Zarubin, who managed Soviet Agents in the United States from 1941 to 1945, see Robert K. Baker, *Rezident: the Espionage Odyssey of Soviet General Vasily Zarubin*, (Bloomington: Universe Inc., 2015) and Pavel Sudoplatov, *Special Tasks: the Memoirs of an Unwanted Witness: a Soviet Spymaster* (Boston; Toronto: Little - Brown, 1995).
121   David Holloway, *Stalin and the Bomb: The Soviet Union and Atomic Energy, 1939–1956* (New Haven: Yale University Press, 1994).
122   Steven T. Usdin, *Engineering Communism: How Two Americans Spied for Stalin and Founded the Soviet Silicon Valley* (New Haven, CT: Yale University Press, 2005); John Earl Haynes and Harvey Klehr, *Early Cold War Spies: The Espionage Trials that Shaped American Politics* (Cambridge: Cambridge University Press, 2006).
123   For a contemporaneous American perspective, see Henry L. Zelchenko, "Stealing America's Know-How: The Story of Amtorg," *American Mercury* 74, no. 338 (February 1952): 75–84.
124   B. V. Osin, "Puti korennoi ekonomii osnovnykh stroitelnykh materialov v SShA," *Amerikanskaia tekhnika i promyshlennost* 24, no. 7 (July 1947), 220-237.
125   Lewis H. Siegelbaum, *Cars for Comrades: The Life of the Soviet Automobile* (Ithaca: Cornell University Press, 2008), 26–27.
126   Ibid., 54–56.
127   See the excellent analysis of this episode by Steven Harris in "Two Lessons in Modernism: What the Architectural Review and America's Mass Media Taught Soviet Architects About the West," *Trondheim Studies on East European Cultures and Societies* 31 (August 2010): 1–44.

years, Arkin's cosmopolitanism has taken a particularly acute form that is harmful to the best interests of the Soviet people, namely through his re-newed advocacy for architectural 'Americanism.'" For the architect Aleksandr Peremyslov, the author of these violent remarks, the "cosmopolitans" were guilty in two ways, as they "cause the best and most progressive elements of the people's past and present to wither, by trying to 'show' them that America is the land where humanity's new culture is being created. Propaganda on the 'merits' of American art and architecture is one of the most acute manifes-tations of the corruptive ideology of cosmopolitanism, and its Soviet agents are direct accomplices to American imperialism in its efforts for world dom-ination. The 'activity' of stateless cosmopolitans within our art world serves precisely this purpose."[128] The "stateless" label is significant here, demon-strating that this tirade was part of the campaign launched against Jewish intellectuals as of 1948, assimilating them to the Western Foe, which would soon lead to murder[129].

From this perspective, Arkin's 1936 foreword to Lewis Mumford's *Sticks and Stones* became retrospective evidence against him, in a rationale charac-teristic of the Stalin-era indictments: "Arkin has tried to show in all possible ways that 'America has created a series of remarkable examples of architec-tural achievements,' that nowhere else have the achievements of modern indus-trial technology opened so many possibilities for architecture than in 'America, with its remarkable accomplishments and no less remarkable archaisms.' [...] Using his favourite tactic by expressing reluctant reservations to better hide his true beliefs, disguising his deep anti-patriotic thoughts in purely contrived patri-otic phrasing, Arkin tirelessly restates that 'the innovative American practices in countless contemporary architectural issues are indisputable.' In American ar-chitecture, he sees mostly 'remarkable examples,' 'exemplary solutions,' and 'great progress in terms of architectural and technical findings.'"[130]

Arkin's colleagues from the History and Theory Institute of the Academy of Architecture, Aleksei Nekrasov, Nikolai Brunov, Aleksandr Gabrichevskii, Roman Khiger, and Ivan Matsa, were also accused of practicing the "formalist methodology of cosmopolitan 'science'" by Mikhail Rzianin, who thus earned

128   Aleksandr A. A. Peremyslov, "Ideolog kozmopolitizma v arkhitekture D. Arkin," *Arkhitektura i stroitelstvo* (March 1949): 8.
129   Konstantin Azadovsky and Boris Egorov, "From Anti-Westernism to Antisemitism: Stalin and the Impact of the 'Anti-Cosmopolitan' Campaigns on Soviet Culture," *Journal of Cold War Studies* 4, no. 1 (2002): 66–88.
130   Peremyslov, "Ideolog kozmopolitizma," 8.
131   Mikhail M. Rzianin, "Uluchit rabotu nauchno–isledovatelskogo instituta istorii i teorii arkhitektury Akademii Arkhitektury SSSR," *Arkhitektura i stroitelstvo*, no. 3 (1949): 5. On the context of architectural research after the war, see Dmitrii Khmelnitskii, "Arkhitekturnaia nauka," in *Arkhitektura Stalina; psikhologia i stil* (Moscow: Progress-Traditsia, 2007), 251–78.
132   Grigorii Simonov, "O polozhenii v arkhitekturnoi nauke," *Sovetskoe iskusstvo*, 18 September 1948.
133   Grigorii Simonov, address to the enlarged meeting of the Union of Architects of the USSR, 4 February 1949, RGAE, f. 9432, op. l, d. 177, 4, in Kosenkova, *Sovetski gorod 1940-kh – pervoi poloviny 50–kh godov*, 224.
134   Aleksandr A. Peremyslov, "Protiv kozmopolitizma v arkhitekturnoi nauke i kritike," *Sovetskoe Iskusstvo*, 19 March 1949; "Burzhuaznie kosmopolity v arkhitekturnoi teorii i kritike," *Kultura i zhizn*, 22 March 1949, 4.
135   Andrei K. Burov, "Na putiakh k novoi russkoi arkhitekture," *Arkhitektura SSSR*, no. 4 (1943): 34.
136   Anon., "Za dalneishii podiom zavodskogo domostroenia," *Arkhitektura i stroitelstvo* 4, no. 3 (March 1949): 1.
137   Aleksandr V. Vlasov, "Nazrevchie voprosy sovetskogo zodchestva," *Pravda*, 28 September 1948, 2.
138   Andrei Bunin, Lev A. Ilin, Nikolai Kh. Poliakov, Viacheslav A. Shkvarikov, *Gradostroitelstvo* (Moscow: Izd-vo Akademii Arkhitektury, 1945), 259–77. On discussion of the book, see RGALI, f. 2466, op. 1, d. 148.
139   Iuliia Kosenkova, "Konkurs na sostavlenie eksperimentalnykh proiektov zhilogo mikroraiona goroda. 1945-1946 gg.", *Arkhitekturnoe nasledstvo* no. 40 (1996): 177–84.
140   Natan A. Osterman, RGAE, f. 293, op. 3, d. 232. See the excellent analysis by Daria Bocharnikova, "A History of the Architectural Profession in the USSR, 1932–1971," PhD dissertation (Florence: European University Institute, 2014), 120–37.
141   Nikolai Bylinkin, "Gradostroitelnye utopii zapadnykh arkhitektorov," *Arkhitektura i stroitelstvo*, no. 1 (1947): 16.
142   "Gradostroitelnaia osnova sovetskoi arkhitektury," *Arkhitektura SSSR*, no. 15 (1947): 1.

his stripes as director of the Institute[131]. A similarly acrimonious treatment was reserved for Burov, whose plan for Yalta was criticized in 1948. Though he was considered "active and talented," he was unfortunately "influenced by contemporary American architecture," which caused him to make "serious mistakes."[132] During a meeting of the Union of Architects in Moscow, he was also accused of having remained "imbued with the disgraced doctrine of constructivism."[133] The attacks became more targeted the following year, as Peremyslov condemned "cosmopolitanism in architectural science and criticism," with a use of scare quotes characteristic of Stalin's prosecutions: "The architect Burov, who has extolled the virtues of American technology in his 'literary' works, is a cosmopolitan. Burov's writings are a perfect example of a confirmed cosmopolitan who looks down on Soviet architecture and its representatives while playing footsie with the decadent culture of American imperialism."[134] Burov's most scandalous statement dated back to 1943: "In America, new ideas in the realm of architecture, free from nihilistic proselytism and tested in the industry, have started to bud, setting the stage for a new organic architecture. A simple and precise language, with minimal words, but sophisticated and rational ones that help mould the form."[135] Peremyslov's article also vehemently attacked Moisei Ginzburg, the "infamous" constructivist, "apologist of Western European and American architecture" and his accomplice Khiger, also Jewish, whose wartime works he demonized. Alabian was condemned for supporting them, while Khiger and Arkin were criticized for their positive appraisal of wood construction when the technology was discussed in 1949[136].

Aleksandr Vlasov took part in the campaign against the History and Theory Institute, strongly opposing Burov's views, which he saw as a "clear expression of an anti-national ideology and neo-constructivism—an example of servile worship of the decadent art of architecture in America, a slander on Soviet art and on our building industry."[137] In 1948, in *Pravda*, he accused Viacheslav Shkvarikov, Andrei Bunin, and two of their colleagues for having underestimated Russian historical precedents and favoured Western examples in their urban planning textbook, published the previous year. They allegedly overstated the merits of theoretical plans such as Thomas Adams' regional plan for New York, as well as those for Norris, Tennessee and for Greendale, Wisconsin, while failing to describe the miserable living conditions of American city dwellers[138]. The Academy nevertheless authorized the publication of some pieces that were responsive to the Anglo-American experience, namely as part of deliberations centred on neighbourhoods around the notion of *mikroraion* (microdistrict), which became the basic unit in Soviet urban planning immediately after the war[139]. In three doctoral dissertations submitted in 1946, Natan Osterman, Aleksei Galaktionov, and Evgenii Iokheles discussed the relevance of the "neighbourhood unit" for the Soviet context. The concept, which allowed to design the scale and structure of housing complexes and their communal equipment, had been developed in 1927 for New York City by Clarence Perry, an economist working in Adams' team[140]. Osterman, a student of Burov's who was highly critical of the West, thoroughly examined this notion in his dissertation. In an article vilifying "the urban planning utopias of western architects," Nikolai Bylinkin drew on Perry's 1937 claim that the first new Soviet cities had used the neighbourhood unit principle to declare that the USSR had been a trailblazer in the matter[141]. In an anonymous article published in *Arkhitektura SSSR*, the creators of these utopias—Frank Lloyd Wright, José Luis Sert, and Eliel Saarinen—were explicitly condemned, while also being praised for their criticism of the capitalist city[142].

The American press promptly covered the Soviet "purge" against architects. Peter Blake, a young curator at MoMA, wrote an article on the topic, illustrating it with a VOKS exhibition poster, with the targeted architects' names crossed out, including Alabian, Arkin, and Burov. Blake mentioned Burov, "renowned for his excellent work on prefabrication," and his condemnation as part of a group "denounced as the 'Titos' of architecture."[143] Shortly after, while the FBI investigated those who had taken part in technological aid to the USSR in the 1930s—such as Walter Polakov—, a campaign was launched in the United States against the National Council of American-Soviet Friendship. In 1945, the Council was accused by William Randolph Hearst's yellow press of being a satellite organization of the Communist Party[144]. While many of the initial patrons stepped down, the NCASF was continuously sued, which led to the detainment of its director, Richard Morford, in 1948. Some members of the Architects' Committee were approached by the House Un-American Activities Committee, such as Vernon DeMars, who reported this to Douglas Haskell. The latter justified his participation in the 1944–1945 exhibit with Corbett's unquestionable sponsorship, and while he conceded that the Architects' Committee might have been used as a cover for "dirty work," he firmly defended its activities: "Surely the fact that a group of Americans set out to help their own government through its own official agency to present American ideals to Russians who had been listening only to distorted Communist interpretations cannot conceivably be held against these Americans."[145] The secretary of the Committee, Hermann H. Field—brother of the Soviet agent Noel Field detained in Prague as part of Stalin's post-war purges—was imprisoned for five years in Poland[146].

Further evidence of the rising hostility between the United States and the Soviet Union surfaced in 1952, as the distribution of *Amerika* was discontinued. The Russians sent back half the copies, declaring them "unsold," while the journal was notoriously nowhere to be found in news kiosks, in addition to being attacked by radio propaganda[147]. In response to this sabotage, the

143   Peter Blake, "The Soviet Architecture Purge," *Architectural Record* 106, no. 3 (1949): 129.
144   Parks, *Culture, Conflict and Coexistence*, 131–33. On Polakov's fate, see Diana J. Kelly, "The Scientific Manager and the FBI: The Surveillance of Walter Polakov in the 1940s," *American Communist History* 15, no. 1 (2016): 35–57.
145   Donald Haskell, Letter to Vernon DeMars, 26 March 1952, Haskell Papers, Avery Library.
146   See his recollections in Hermann Field and Kate Field, *Trapped in the Cold War: The Ordeal of an American Family* (Stanford: Stanford University Press, 1999).
147   "The Press: A Red Victory," *Time*, 23 June 1952, 42; "The Press: The Death of *Amerika*," *Time*, 28 July 1952, 51. On the magazine's reception, see Konstantin V. Avramov, *Soviet America: Popular Responses to the United States in Post-World War II Soviet Union*, PhD dissertation (Lawrence: University of Kansas, 2012); and Aucoin, *Deconstructing the American Way of Life*, 48–53.
148   See the interviews by S. Frederick Starr in *Red & Hot*, 236–23. See also Vasilii Aksenov," Loving the States," in *In Search of 'Melancholy Baby*,'trans. Michael Henry Heim and Antonina W. Bouis (New York, Random House, 1987), 12-19. Valerii Todorovskii's 2008 film *Stiliagi* depicts a fictional version of the Moscow scene of the 1950s. See Graham H. Roberts, "Revolt into Style: Consumption and its (dis)contents in Valery Todorovsky's film *Stilyagi*," *Film, Fashion & Consumption* 2, no 2 (June 2013): 187-200.
149   Iosif V. Stalin, Telegram to Joseph Kingsbury-Smith [Hearst's International News Service, Paris], 2 February 1949, *Izvestiia*, 2 February 1949.
150   Khrushchev, *Khrushchev Remembers: The Last Testament*, 98.
151   Stenogram of the meeting of the Moscow committee of the Party on the issue of "Construction of 16, 26, and 32-storey residential buildings in Moscow," 20 January 1947, OKhDOPIM, f. 3, op. 67, d. 12, 47, quoted in Zubovich, "Moscow Monumental,"48.
152   Among the earlier analyses, see Marina Astafeva-Dlugach, Iurii Volchok, "Rol proekta v razvitii obshchest-vennogo soznania, k 40-letiu postanovlenia soveta ministrov SSSR 'o stroitelstve v Moskve mno-goetazhnykh domov'," *Arkhitektura i stroitelstvo Moskvy*, February 1987, 20–22; Catherine Cooke, "La Mosca di Stalin," *Domus*, no. 840 (September 2001): 88–101.
153   USSR Council of Ministers, "O stroitelstve v Moskve mnogoetazhnykh zdanii," *Sovetskoe iskusstvo*, 28 February 1947. The original text is OKhD f. 694, op. 1, d. 421, 1–3.
154   Georgii M. Popov, "Vospominania," in *Partinyi gubernator Moskvy: Georgii Popov*, ed. Evgenii V. Taranov, (Moscow: Izd-vo Glavarkhiva Moskvy, 2004), 63.
155   Boris M. Iofan, "Prospekt i ploshchad dvortsa Sovetov," *Arkhitektura SSSR* 3, no. 10–11 (1935): 28.

United States Information Agency (USIA) halted its publication. At the same time, a spontaneous form of Amerikanizm emerged among Moscow's youth, with the appearance of *stiliagi*—style chasers—who spoke to each other in code. They called themselves *Tarzantsy*, in a nod to Johnny Weissmuller's films, addressed each other as "Bob" or "Jane," and roamed the sidewalks of Gorky Street, which they renamed "Broadway."[148] Copies of jazz albums smuggled across the border were burned on x-ray films, giving way to the very popular *Rentgenizdat* (X-ray Publishing).

A Ring of High-Rises

In 1949, with the Cold War in full swing, Stalin refused an invitation from President Truman, whom he had last met in 1945, all the while expressing interest for the American capital: "To travel to Washington is one of my oldest wishes, as I told President Roosevelt in Yalta and President Truman in Potsdam. Unfortunately, at the moment, I cannot fulfill this wish, as my doctors have prohibited me from any prolonged journeys, especially by sea or by air."[149] Stalin thus never crossed the Atlantic, but after 1945, he took a personal interest in skyscraper construction in Moscow according to Nikita Khrushchev, who attributed the following statement to the leader: "We have won the war and are recognized the world over as the glorious victors. We must be ready for an influx of foreign visitors. What will happen if they walk around Moscow and find no skyscrapers? They will make unfavourable comparisons with capitalist cities."[150] The president of the Moscow Soviet – in other terms the mayor of the capital, Georgii Popov, enjoyed repeating Stalin's words: "As Stalin put it, people go to America and return impressed: 'oh, what gigantic buildings!' Let them come to Moscow to see our buildings, let them marvel at their sight!"[151]

The vast open spaces of the 1935 plan for Moscow, designed to accommodate popular and military parades, could be likened to a stage set for celebrations of the triumphant revolution. After the victory over Germany, celebrated on 9 May 1945 with memorable fireworks across the Moscow sky, along with beams from the many searchlights shining from the Kremlin towers, the rhetoric of this new triumph over Nazism turned to the vertical sublime[152]. As part of this upward trajectory, the Council of Ministers resolved to "build high-rise buildings in Moscow" on 13 January 1947, after a meeting held the previous December. It was clearly stated that these structures would owe nothing to American skyscrapers: "The architects and builders will be faced with a great challenge: to create a series of high-rise buildings unprecedented in our country by their scale, their technique, and their architecture. [...] The proportions and outline of these buildings must be original in their architectural and artistic composition. They must be integrated to Moscow's historical development and to the outline of the future Palace of the Soviets. These new buildings cannot, therefore, be copies of already existing foreign high-rises."[153] Popov recounts having received a pencil drawing at the Kremlin depicting "a structure adorned with a spire holding a red flag, bearing the inscription: 26–32 storeys."[154]

In 1935, Boris Iofan had articulated the idea of a squad of high-rise buildings that would escort the Palace of the Soviets: "I believe it would be useful to implement, in a certain order and at a certain distance from the Palace of the Soviets, a few high-rise buildings that would support and help harmonize its outline with the general cityscape."[155] He thus shaped the idea, possibly inspired by the Manhattan skyline, of a holistic approach to the capital's silhouette.

Henryk Dąbrowski. Panorama of Moscow with four high-rise buildings, the Palace of the Soviets, and the Kremlin, ca. 1953, fold-out in Edmund Goldzamt, *The Architecture of City Centres and the Problems of Heritage*, Warsaw: Państwowe Wydawnictwo Naukowe, 1956. CCA, NA9183.G5 1956.

He further developed this notion in 1940, noting that "there are remarkable cities, like Leningrad or Venice, that are settled on flat locations. How was their outline shaped? In Venice, above all, by bell towers, and in Leningrad, by spires. The situation is different in Moscow and in Rome, where architects have used the various elevations of the city's topography. In a city such as Moscow, we must use both differences in levels and high-rise buildings."[156]

The former ASNOVA members Andrei Bunin and Mariia Kruglova also advocated for an urban skyline contrasting with the cynical and inharmonious American practices. Their handbook *The Architectural Composition of the City* served mainly to promote the classical Parisian ensembles of the 17th and 18th centuries as a model for contemporary urban planning. To them, the arrangement of the Manhattan skyscrapers was a transgression of classical composition rules, resulting in an "abysmal mess" typical of the capitalists' individual quest for profit. Their point of view was reminiscent of the one expressed by Le Corbusier in *Urbanisme*, which was translated into Russian in 1933, and incidentally quoted by Bunin and Kruglova[157]. Their main criticism of the American city, with its "entirely new silhouette," was its lack of culture: "It started taking shape in the last 30 to 35 years, a period of major regression in urban planning as an artistic medium. Furthermore, American cities have no artistic heritage. In skyscraper construction, engineering takes precedence over architecture, with the former serving as a blind weapon of capitalism. All this goes to show that in today's capitalist cities, and especially in the American ones, the question of the urban landscape is devoid of any creative perspectives."[158]

Bunin and Kruglova criticized New York's 1916 zoning ordinance. They deemed the variation in height between the skyscrapers on the Manhattan shoreline insufficient and the gap between the height of the Chrysler Building, the Empire State Building, and the surrounding neighbourhoods—excessive. Luckily, in Moscow, the city's topography could be put to good use: "In certain areas of the city, not chosen at random, but specifically selected, the levels can be much higher, creating striking vertical compositions. They will serve as the vertical markers necessary to any city's architecture to create contrasts with the regular buildings."[159] Iofan detailed this point of view in 1947, aspiring to become the mastermind of the government programme. He agreed with the refusal to repeat foreign examples and articulated his own critique of Manhattan: "At a distance, New York is striking, with its almost fantastic silhouette. But when one approaches, the city's lack of unified architectural composition and the chaotic scatter of its high-rise buildings become increasingly apparent. Narrow ravine-like streets that never receive sunlight create a distressing impression." [160]

The authors also saw the alternative to this detrimental planning in America itself, in the ideal city designed in 1929 by Hugh Ferriss, the extraordinary architectural renderer, as a vision for "the metropolis of tomorrow."

156   Boris M. Iofan, Speech at the VII plenary session of the Union of Architects, in *Arkhitekturnye voprosy rekonstruktsii Moskvy* (Moscow: Izd-vo Akademii Arkhitektury SSSR, 1940), 84–85.
157   Le Corbusier, *Planirovka goroda* (Moscow: OGIZ–IZOGIZ, 1933); originally: *Urbanisme* (Paris: G. Crès & Cie, 1925).
158   Andrei V. Bunin and Maria G. Kruglova, *Arkhitekturnaia kompozitsiia gorodov* (Moscow: Izd. Akademii Arkhitektury SSSR, 1940), 88. Their analyses of American cities are based on, among other sources, on *The American Vitruvius* and *Amerikanische Architektur und Stadtbaukunst*, published in the 1920s by Werner Hegemann in New York and Berlin respectively.
159   Bunin and Kruglova, *Arkhitekturnaia kompozitsiia gorodov*, 89.
160   Boris M. Iofan, "Arkhitekturnye problemy stroitelstva mnogoetazhnykh zdanii," *Arkhitektura i stroitelstvo*, no. 3 (1947): 15.

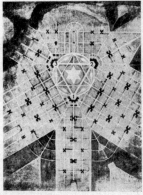

10. Арх. Х. Феррис — Схема нового города.

11. Арх. Х. Феррис — Деловой центр.

шахматном порядке кварталы застройки с симметрично расставленными среди них небоскребами.

Широкие зеленые массивы вклиниваются в деловую часть города, почти достигая его центра.

Аналогичным приемом решены научная и художественная зоны, заключающие в себе комбинаты драмы, музыки, архитектуры и институты чистой науки, техники, инженерии.

Схема Х. Феррисса — продукт мышления и творчества зодчего капиталистической страны и поэтому она имеет свои специфические черты. Тем не менее нельзя не отметить то ценное новое, что найдено им в области архитектурных обликов города и выявлено в многочисленных иллюстрациях его книги. Над подобной проблемой необходимо вдумчиво работать каждому градостроителю.

По Феррису деловой, художественный и научный центры города имеют свой отличный друг от друга архитектурный облик.

Небоскребы делового центра (рис. 11 и 12) представляют собой монументальные сооружения, скомпанованные из простых геометрических объемов. Раскинутые на значительном расстоянии друг от друга они являются хорошо ориентирующими четкими маяками.

12. Арх. Х. Феррис — Архитектура делового центра.

18

3*

19

In their 1934 essay on *The Architectural Organization of the City*, which opens on a panoramic view of Manhattan, Aleksei Shchusev and L. E. Zagorskii considered Ferriss's ideas "far from uninteresting"—as opposed to those of Le Corbusier and Ludwig Hilberseimer—, though his plan was "the product of the creative and thought process of an architect from a capitalist country." The city was shaped like an equilateral triangle whose angles formed its centres, comprised of giant skyscrapers surrounded by lower clusters and isolated towers. The authors insisted on the fact that the three vertical centres— "artistic, scientific, and commercial"—had to differ from one another. Accordingly, "the business centre skyscrapers are monumental constructions made of simple geometrical volumes. Built at a considerable distance from each other, they are separate lighthouses allowing for good orientation." As for the "scientific centre," its "isolated volumes, located on intersecting streets, are perfectly adapted to their function. The scientific centre is larger than the others. Its skyscrapers are taller towers housing laboratories, and the buildings themselves are closer to each other." Finally, "the artistic centre also has its own face. Its buildings are not typical contemporary skyscrapers. They are terraced buildings, with light and circular towers that shrink as they rise." Though according to the two authors, Ferriss's project was "based on the American skyscraper and its penchant for symmetry" and though it was thus "unthinkable to base the general plan of a city on this solution," they nevertheless considered that "in his quest for the shape of the 'metropolis of tomorrow,' he had undoubtedly garnered results."[161] The principles of skyscraper specialization and spacing were thus firmly justified.

Times had changed. The critic Mikhail Tsapenko, in his 1952 book *On the Realist Foundations of Soviet Architecture*, claimed that skyscrapers were a weapon in the "battle against American imperialism" and a sign of maturity for the land of socialism. With highly xenophobic undertones, he wrote that "the socialistic development of the USSR has now reached such heights that a solid base has been built for new and decisive advances in our architectural field, for more in-depth research of new artistic models and ideals. What architects merely dreamed of many years ago, unable to translate their imaginings into appropriate artistic principles, is now within our reach."[162] On 12 February 1947, exactly one month after the Council of Ministers reached its decision, Oltarzhevskii wrote in a polite reminder to Popov that the problem of high-rise buildings was not a new one and had been raised for the past fifty years, as "architects interested in foreign practices" were well aware. He presented its main technical issues, namely those related to foundations, structure, and elevators, assessing their total required amount between 150 and 175 for the entire programme, and insisting on the importance of creating a centralized organization and a strong material base. He also reminded him of the need to train hundreds of executives and, of course, to develop "plans of the highest quality."[163] Oltarzhevskii then wrote numerous technical notes on behalf of the Bureau of Scientific and Technical Information of the Council of Ministers' Architectural Committee, and commissioned the translation of American articles on high-speed elevators, specifically those of the Rockefeller Center, and on heating and ventilation[164]. This rhetoric was similar to the one he used in his presentation of the various aspects of skyscraper construction upon returning to Moscow in 1935: "The American architects have taught us an important art: the art of total construction, which takes into account not only all of the building's components, but also its technical elements. Attention to all these aspects is apparent even at a glance in any contemporary American building."[165]

In a perfect example of doublespeak, the former New York practitioner, who organized technology transfers and embodied the American experience, was charged with devising the discourse around the Soviet high-rise building programme, whose premise was the absence of all foreign influence. He wrote that "the construction of high-rise buildings is part of a long and enduring Russian architectural tradition. In the various golden periods of classical Russian architecture, remarkable examples of high-rise buildings, extremely varied in their nature and purpose, were created. The menacing towers of the defensive ensembles of the kremlins and monasteries, the majestic 'pillar' of Ivan the Great in Moscow's Kremlin, the baroque bell towers of the 17th and 18th centuries, and the outstanding civilian architecture of Russian classicism, including Leningrad's Admiralty Building with its famous spire, which deserves honourable mention, all of these monuments of Russia's national architecture are a testament to the wide range of high-rises developed in this country." Oltarzhevskii connected these constructions with great historical events, calling for a return to this tradition after the 1945 victory. He envisioned the creation of buildings in Russia as "a significant event for global contemporary architecture," highlighting the "crucial role of Moscow, a beacon for the progress of humanity."[166]

Oltarzhevskii thus showed symptoms of what Sona Hoisington has called a form of "schizophrenia" regarding the American experience, with which he was the only Soviet to be perfectly acquainted[167]. He praised the "remarkable success of Soviet construction techniques" towards which he had previously shown reticence, and insisted on the "free" arrangement of buildings in the city: "The construction principles of Soviet high-rise buildings are radically opposed to those of American 'skyscrapers,' which are the product of raging capitalist competition, an attempt to make as much profit as possible from each parcel of the city's land. [...] [The Soviet] buildings are freely arranged in the most strategic points in the city and are surrounded with sufficient open space; they serve the entire city, and the Soviet population as a whole."[168]

Oltarzhevskii's expertise was also leveraged in the field of education. Under his supervision, the students of the Moscow Institute of Architecture developed projects initially referred to as "skyscrapers." In 1947, with his nephew Dmitrii, he supervised graduation projects by Iurii Baranskii, for a building on an unspecified location, and Nikolai Kostoshkin, for a structure intended for Smolenskaia Square. The pencil drawings of the former and the clay model of the latter show an assembly of orthogonal prisms with flat and smooth façades, whose minimal sculpted ornamentations are limited to the entry gates[169] [ill. p. 428]. In accordance with Oltarzhevskii's message, the technical components were carefully studied. In 1948, however, graduation projects

161   Aleksei V. Shchusev and L.E. Zagorskii, *Arkhitekturnaia organizatsiia goroda* (Moscow: Gosstroiizdat, 1934), 17–20.
162   Mikhail T. Tsapenko, *O realisticheskikh osnovakh sovetskoi arkhitektury* (Moscow: Gos. Izd-vo. Lit. po stroitelstvu i arkhitekture, 1952), 352.
163   Viacheslav K. Oltarzhevskii, Letter to Georgii M. Popov, 12 February 1947, MUAR, f. 24, op. 1, d. 31.
164   Viacheslav K. Oltarzhevskii, Technical notes, various dates, MUAR, f. 24, op. 1, d. 25.
165   Viacheslav K. Oltarzhevskii, "Za rubezhom: arkhitektura Soedinnennykh Shtatov Ameriki," *Arkhitektura SSSR* 3, no. 9 (1935): 59.
166   Viacheslav K. Oltarzhevskii, *Stroitelstvo vysotnykh zdanii v Moskve* (Moscow: Gos. izd-vo Lit. po stroitelstvu i arkhitekture, 1953), 3.
167   Sona S. Hoisington, "Soviet Schizophrenia and the American Skyscraper," in *Russian Art and the West: A Century of Dialogue in Painting, Architecture and the Decorative Arts,* eds. Rosalind Blakesley and Susan E. Reid (DeKalb, IL: Northern Illinois University Press, 2007), 156–71.
168   Oltarzhevskii, *Stroitelstvo vysotnykh zdanii*, 3.
169   Muzei MArkhI, Moscow, drawings DP 10/3, 6 and 34; Silver gelatin prints KP 161/10.

by I. V. Leibova (supervised by the former constructivist Mikhail Barshch), N. V. Petunina, and Iu. S. Artamonova (both overseen by Iu. N. Sheverdiaev) were focused on a "high-rise building" devoid of any American connotation. Photographs of the projects developed between 1947 and 1949 show that the use of historicist elements and sculpted ornamentations remained cautious[170].

The plan for Moscow devised by a January 1947 decree was initially connected to the much-awaited construction of the Palace of the Soviets, and was launched by the USDS, created for this purpose before the war. The programme specified that "the proportions and outlines of the buildings must be original and their architectural composition must be inspired by the historical nature of the city's architecture and by the outline of the Palace of the Soviets."[171] The decree also prescribed specific dimensions: one 32-storey building, two structures with 26 floors, and five with 16 floors. But once these initial measurements were set, the rest of the programme evolved, namely regarding the location of the buildings in the city and their plans, except for the tallest among them: the new university established on the Lenin Hills following an explicit instruction from Stalin[172]. An initial list of architects drawn up on 7 May 1947 showed considerable open-mindedness on the leaders' part, as it included Aleksei Shchusev, Aleksandr and Viktor Vesnin, and Nikolai Kolli[173]. On 17 August, a second decree defined concrete measures to complete the programme, drafting five ministers under the exceedingly powerful—and bloodthirsty—Lavrentii Beria. The initial idea to send engineers to investigate the West—including the United States—as a secret complementary measure, was not followed through[174].

The head of the State Committee for architecture, Arkadii Mordvinov, and the chief architect of the capital, Dmitrii Chechulin, oversaw the development of the projects, which were then judged by a commission led by Grigorii Simonov, whose anti-cosmopolitan views have been mentioned. The initial projects were met with strong resistance, even before the final list of architects was set. Oltarzhevskii's project for the Vosstaniia Square building, whose upper section occupied only a corner of the large allotted space [ill. p. 429], was discarded in favour of the plan submitted by Mikhail Posokhin and Ashot Mndoiants, from Shchusev's office, showing a central tower flanked by two terraced volumes. Finally, on 15 March 1948, construction was launched for four of the envisioned buildings, including the university[175]. Popov was ousted the following year for being too politically ambitious, and replaced at the helm of the Party's Committee for Moscow by Nikita Khrushchev. Chechulin, who was close to the former, was deemed suspicious for his supervision of the Kotelnicheskaia Embankment Building site, for his overall leadership style, and

170   Muzei MArkhI, Moscow, album "Vysotnoe zdanie," projects from 1947 to 1952.
171   USSR Council of Ministers, "O stroitelstve v Moskve mnogoetazhnykh zdanii."
172   Katherine Zubovich gives a compelling view of these ambiguities: "Moscow Monumental," 86.
173   Lavrentii I. Beria, "Spisok arkhitektorov, namechennykh v kachestve avtorov proektov vysotnykh zdanii v Moskve," RGAE, f. 9432, op. 1, d. 89, 135–36. Yuliia Kosenkova, Sovetskii gorod 1940-kh–pervoi poloviny 150-kh godov (Moscow: URSS, 2000), 237.
174   USSR Council of Ministers, secret appendices to the decree of 17 August 1947, GARF, R 5446, op. 49a, s. 4608, 67–68, quoted in Zubovich, "Moscow Monumental," 91.
175   A nine-volume series was published to highlight the ongoing projects: Vysotnye zdaniia v Moskve (Moscow: Gos. Izd-vo lit. po stroitelstvu i arkhitekture, 1951).
176   See Zubovich, "Moscow Monumental," 106–11.
177   The drawing was published as a fold-out plate by Edmund Goldzamt, Architektura zespołów Śródmiesjsich i problemy dziedzictwa, Varsovie, Państwowe Wydawnictwo Naukowe, 1956. See Michał Murawski, Palace Complex: A Capitalist Skyscraper, Stalinist Warsaw and a City Transfixed (Bloomington: Indiana University Press, 2019), 36.
178   Nikolai B. Sokolov, "Kompozitsiia vysotnykh zdanii," Sovetskoe iskusstvo, 18 June 1947. On American sources for these buildings, see Polina P. Zueva, "Niu-Iorkskie neboskreby kak prototypy 'stalinskikh vysotok'," in Arkhitektura stalinskoi epokhi: opyt istoricheskogo omyshleniia, ed. Iuliia Kosenkova (Moscow: Komkniga, 2010), 435–51.

the many commissions he monopolized. Also dismissed, he was replaced with Aleksandr Vlasov[176].

Six of the seven buildings completed between 1948 and 1957 were scattered across Moscow's centre. Five of them formed a system, as shown in the plans distributed in the press. The buildings were those of the Ministry of Foreign Affairs on Smolenskaia Square, the Ukraina and Leningradskaia hotels, two housing complexes on Kotelnicheskaia Embankment and Voss-taniia Square, and a tower combining dwellings and offices at the Krasnye Vorota metro station. All located near or at a short distance from the Sadovoe koltso (Garden Ring), these buildings line Moscow's main ring road, reprising El Lissitzky's arrangement of his *Wolkenbügel* at a larger scale. While he had oriented the horizontal part of his buildings towards the Kremlin, their spires dialogued with the bell towers of the historical structure. A seventh 32-storey building meant to house the Ministry of Heavy Industry was projected in Zariadie, near the Kremlin, in the centre of the quasi-circular figure traced by the other buildings, which was completed with the solitary construction of the State University. It was pushed further out to the south-east, where it would rise above the new neighbourhood projected in the 1935 Plan. After a period of uncertainty, the structures became clearly specialized: science dominated the south-east, politics was in the centre and in the south, and housing settled in the farthest points, as if Ferriss's model for the "metropolis of tomorrow," discussed by Shchusev and Zagorskii, had taken on a polygonal shape. Con-versely, many plans were drawn to highlight the specifically Russian, even Moscovian, nature of the programme. Elevations served to compare their out-lines to various stages of the Old City depicting its transformation starting in the seventeenth century.

One of the most surprising depictions of the ensemble was a drawing published in 1956 by the Polish artist Henryk Dąbrowski, in support of the Warsaw Palace of Culture and Science [ill. p. 420-421]. This wide-angle aerial view of Moscow, seen from the top of the Zariadie Building, shows a strangely remodeled landscape, minimizing the height of the university and three other buildings to make them seem dwarflike next to the Kremlin's bell towers, invert-ing the views usually printed in journals[177]. In addition to the statue of Lenin topping the Palace of the Soviets, the drawing shows four spires crowning the buildings, a supplement initially designed by Chechulin for the Kotelnich-eskaia Embankment Building. This element, a nod to the superstructures of the Peter and Paul Fortress and especially to the Admiralty Building in Leningrad, was present in the sketch Popov credits to Stalin, who expressed a desire to highlight Moscow's status as a capital. Oversized spires became an essential detail for the other structures, replacing the initial group of sculptures Iofan proposed for the top of the university. A spire would also crown the Ministry of Foreign Affairs, initially meant to be topped with a horizontal line [ill. p. 434]. While the high-rise buildings revisited the historical repertoire of Russian archi-tecture, American precedents were not eliminated, but simply reassessed with a critical stance. For instance, in 1947, Nikolai Sokolov referred to New York towers to justify the construction of typically Moscovian superstructures, though he continued to view them as cupolas: "American skyscrapers usually have a horizontally levelled crown with a flat roof. In a few exceptional cases, the roof is pyramid-shaped (the Manhattan Bank). Only the Singer Company's skyscraper, used as an advertisement, resembles a cupola, but an unsightly one. The Chrysler company skyscraper is also crowned with a rounded peak. From up close, one can see that the shape of this monumental advertisement is reminiscent of two automobile tires similar to those sold by the firm."[178]

Iurii A. Baranskii, Skyscraper. Diploma project at the Moscow Architectural Institute, 1947. MArkhI Museum.
Tutors: Grigorii A. Simonov, Ivan S. Nikolaev, Viacheslav K. Oltarzhevskii, Dmitrii G. Oltarzhevskii.

Top: Perspectival sketches. Pencil and charcoal on paper, 70 × 145 cm.
Bottom: Elevation. Pencil and colored pencil on paper, 44 × 62 cm.

Viacheslav K. Oltarzhevskii. Project for a residential building on Vosstaniia Square, Moscow, 1947.
Shchusev State Museum of Architecture.

Top: Version with self-standing tower. Perspective, pencil on paper, 55.3 × 59.7 cm. RIa 7525/5.
Bottom: Second version. Perspective. Gelatin silver print on cardboard, 61.8 × 55 cm. RXI 7463.

The university complex housed teaching premises, laboratories, as well as dwellings for students and professors. Iofan had to harmonize a dominant vertical structure with lower buildings, leading him to revisit the Rockefeller Center he so admired, and to invoke it once again: "The Radio City high-rise complex, despite the narrowness of its occupied space, stands out with its expressiveness and monumental quality. In this case, the attempt to ensure an architectural transition between the general urban fabric and the high-rise building has yielded tangible results. The outcome is an architectural ensemble playing an essential role in the spatial organization of a significant portion of the neighbourhood."[179] In terms of tectonics, Iofan invoked the specificity of Moscow to justify the need to work on the central part of the buildings. According to him, Americans neglected that portion because they "operate with the idea that the most important parts of the skyscraper are the top and the bottom. These are indeed the most visible parts of the buildings in the context of the American city. But in Moscow, high-rise buildings are built in such a way that they can be seen from a great distance. Beyond the 'top' and the 'bottom,' the entire structure must be a true architectural work."[180]

Fittingly, Iofan's thoughts on skyscraper composition is akin to Adolf Loos's approach in shaping his *Chicago Tribune* competition project as a pillar. Thirty-five years later, Aldo Rossi still shared Iofan's point of view, writing: "Loos is one of the very few architects who understood American architecture (this was also the case later with certain Soviet architects)."[181] Each of the seven buildings of the 1947 programme for Moscow was dictated by the same fundamentally pyramidal composition principle, where buildings or secondary volumes serve as supporting bases or as buttresses for towers crowned with lanterns or spires. Except for the university, built on mostly vacant ground, the architects were mindful of the interplay between the new buildings and the adjacent streets and blocks. Issues of perception were raised rather astutely, based on rules Bunin and Kruglova had articulated in 1940, which were in turn founded on the notion of "optical scale" defined by Hermann Maertens in 1877[182].

The Ministry designed by Vladimir Gelfreikh and Mikhail Minkus, established on Smolenskaia Square, on the corner of Arbat Street and the Garden Ring, was the most subtle of the "seven sisters." With its assembly of lower volumes and its orchestrated progression towards the 170-metre tall vertical volume, the Ministry building was reminiscent of Cornell University Medical College, built by Coolidge Shepley Bulfinch & Abbott in 1934, but without the ornamentation. In its initial version, the building had a flat roof and a crown indented with obelisks, while the façades were ribbed with many vertical beams. The cornice, added later, was adorned with purely decorative flying buttresses in a mock-Gothic style and a spire similar to that of Cass Gilbert's Woolworth Building. The lateral avant-corps extended towards the Square, like the base of the Palace of the Soviets, which Gelfreikh had helped design in the 1930s. The plan also involved a private elevator for the minister, which would reach his office on the top floor of the tower. Andrei Gromyko, an expert on the United States and an ambassador in Washington in the 1940s, was its exclusive user from 1957 to 1985.

The Ukraina Hotel was built between the Dorogomilovskaia Embankment of the Moscow River and Mozhaiskoe Highway, renamed Kutuzovskii Prospekt in 1957. The project was officially overseen by Mordvinov, though Oltarzhevskii, who had considerable experience in the hotel industry, played a significant part in its development. The lower parts of the main building, 170-metre tall, were designed on a H-shaped plan, with the most rational configuration of the entire programme, dictated by Oltarzhevskii's expertise. The hotel rose above a rectangular lot flanked with apartment buildings. The edicules and the crowning spire seemed to be added as an afterthought to the prismatic volume of the tower, similar to the superstructures of the 1920s buildings built along Central Park by Emery Roth. In the original sketches, the interiors had a certain Art Deco flair. In nostalgic watercolour, Oltarzhevskii painted the Ukraina Hotel rising above an inordinately large Moskva River, like the figurehead of an imaginary city modeled after the views of eighteenth century Petersburg [ill. p. 435].

The Leningradskaia Hotel, by Leonid Poliakov and Aleksandr Boretskii, was much simpler in its general shape and its architectonics. Its stand-alone 138-meter tower was simply placed on a larger base, and rose above Kalanchevskaia Square, renamed Komsomolskaia, and its three railway stations. It faced the Kazan station, designed by Aleksei Shchusev in 1912 and built during the Bolshevik regime, echoing the spire of its superstructure as well as the arch in the middle of its plinth. The building seemed isolated from all urban fabric, almost huddled in its solitary posture on the edge of the wide square. Its exterior decor was an elegant variation on Russian themes and Venetian figures such as the obelisk.

The apartment building on Vosstaniia Square, also isolated on its site, west of the Garden Ring, rose above the Presnia working-class neighbourhood. Facing a large rectangular square, it was comprised of three articulated buildings, each with its own elevator system, on a H-shaped plan. Flanking the 159-metre tower like bookends, the two lateral buildings were reminiscent of the Rockefeller Center towers—with their setbacks and despite their excessive ornamentation—, which had been familiar to the Soviets for fifteen years[183]. With its cone-shaped roof and its four corner pinnacles, the tower's crowning looked like an overdecorated version of the New York Life Building, built in 1928 by Cass Gilbert on Madison Square. Combining figures borrowed from two skyscrapers built in a widely different language is a telling example of the eclectic and hypocritical manifestations of Amerikanizm in the high-rise construction programme [ill. p. 438].

Contrary to the six other buildings, Aleksei Dushkin and Boris Mezentsev's structure was built on a cramped site without much clearance. It was located right by the Garden Ring and close to the Leningradskaia Hotel, on the site previously occupied by a triumphal arch—the Red Gate— and the Church of Three Saints, destroyed in 1927–1928. Its 139-meter tower, housing the offices of the Ministry of Transportation, was bordered by two lower buildings, extended with two L-shaped apartment complexes, surrounding a large rectangular courtyard. The basement contained the vestibule of the Lermontovskaia metro station, which has now recovered its original name, Krasnye Vorota. This was the only completed example of the projected connection between the underground network and the high-rise buildings, in another nod to Lissitzky's 1925 project. The Ministry's hall was punctuated with

179   Iofan, "Arkhitekturnye problem:" 15.
180   Boris M. Iofan, "Mnogoetazhnye zhdaniia stolitsy," *Moskovskii komsomolets*, 19 August 1947.
181   Aldo Rossi, introduction to Adolf Loos, *Spoken into the Void: Collected Essays 1897–1900*
        (Cambridge, MA: MIT Press, 1982), x.
182   Bunin and Kruglova, *Arkhitekturnaia kompozitsia gorodov*, 92–100. Their source is Hermann Maertens,
        Der optische Maßstab oder die Theorie und Praxis des ästhetischen Sehens in den bildenden Künsten
        (Bonn: Max Cohen & Sohn, 1877).
183   Mikhail V. Posokhin, *Dorogi zhizni: iz zapisok arkhitektora* (Moscow: Stroiizdat, 1995), 48–52.

Boris M. Iofan. Project for the Moscow State University, Moscow, 1947.
Elevation. Color pencil on tracing paper, 75.7 × 118 cm. Shchusev State Museum of Architecture, RIa 10755/161.

Vladimir G. Gelfreikh and Mikhail A. Minkus. Ministry of Foreign Affairs on Smolenskaia Square, Moscow, 1948-1953.

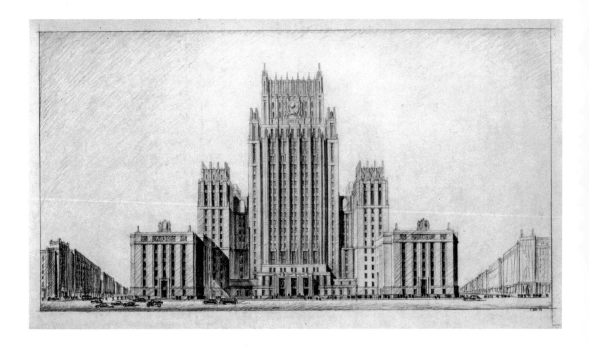

Top: Elevation of the first version, sanguine on paper, 70.3 × 130.1 cm. Shchusev State Museum of Architecture, Ria 6973/131.
Bottom: Site view of the skeleton. *URSS in Construction*, November 1949, CCA.

Arkadii G. Mordvinov and Viacheslav K. Oltarzhevskii. Ukraina Hotel, Moscow, 1953–1957.

Top: Perspective. Pencil, gouache and watercolour on paper, 124.4 × 126.7 cm. Tchoban Foundation, Museum for Architectural Drawing.
Bottom: View from the shore of the Moskva River. Pencil, color ink and watercolour on paper, 56.5 × 102 cm.
Shchusev State Museum of Architecture, Rla 5799

a series of square pillars with aluminum fluting, reminiscent of the ribs traced by Dushkin on his pre-war Maiakovskaia metro station, in an elegant contrast with the ornamental exhuberance of the other structures.

The Kotelnicheskaia Embankment scheme, probably the most complex of the seven built, was designed by Dmitrii Chechulin and Andrei Rostkovskii at the junction of the Moskva and Iauza rivers. The highest of the apartment buildings, 176 metres tall, it echoed the Kremlin towers located nearby. A vertical signal on the river bend, it also served as an angle joint between the two housing rows along each river. The equilateral Y-shaped tower housed 344 of the 540 apartments intended for the regime's cultural and scientific elite, starting with several writers[184]. Two housing blocks designed around the tower were later abandoned. The plinth plated with red granite was higher and more massive than those of the other structures, while the open angles of the main building and the crown were comparable to those of the Manhattan Municipal Building, erected between 1909 and 1912 by McKim, Mead & White near the Brooklyn Bridge. In Moscow, its obligatory spire was substituted to the Civic Fame statue crowning the New York building. A parallel can also be drawn with the siting of the Wrigley Building, built in 1924 in Chicago by Graham, Anderson, Probst & White at the corner of Michigan Avenue and Wacker Drive, right by the river; or with the Terminal Building built in Cleveland in 1928 by the same firm. The Kotelnicheskaia Embankment Building provided the setting for Vasilii Aksenov's novel *Moskva kva-kva*, where the building's occupants, high-ranking officials of the *nomenklatura*, are trapped in a delirious ballet engulfing the entire city, and where a fictitious Stalin meets a ludicrous death. This book, dictated by the author's personal experience of living in the famous complex, mocks its interior, with its sculptures and stone draperies, while offering a critique of the pervasive spy mania of the time[185].

The university's design was initially entrusted to Boris Iofan, who in 1947 still harboured hopes of creating the Palace of the Soviets, a project whose continuation he defended with utmost energy. Stalin had decided to postpone its construction until after the completion of the high-rise buildings, and the project was abandoned after the dictator's demise. Over the course of Iofan's successive projects, the initial Rockefeller Center inspiration subsided and the main building became thicker, forming a wall overlooking the Moskva in one of its half-dozen known versions. However, Iofan kept insisting on the importance of terracing: "The building's terraces, which enrich its outline, offer the possibility to create a more logical and expressive structure, which is essential in light of its large dimensions. We must seek to imbue the entire volume as well as its façades and details with the highest visual expressiveness. It is imperative to create significant chiaroscuro effects [...] and to find a clear architectural treatment that will prevent it from appearing overbearing"[186] [ill. p. 432-433].

Following a decree issued on 3 July 1948, Iofan was dismissed from the project under pressure from Popov, who wished to replace him with a "more capable group of architects and engineers," despite the former's pleas to Stalin[187]. It is hard to tell whether this eviction was motivated by personal reasons, by

184   Anne Nivat, *La maison haute* (Paris: Fayard, 2002).
185   Vasilii Aksenov, *Moskva kva- kva* (Moscow: Eksmo-Press, 2006).
186   Iofan, "Arkhitekturnye problemy," 15; and "Budushchee zdanie Moskovskogo universiteta," *Trud*, 31 March 1948.
187   Georgii M. Popov, "Vospominania," 230; Zubovich, "Moscow Monumental," 87. On the building, see Roman Iankovskii, *Vysotka nomer odin* (Moscow: Startap, 2018).

Leonid M. Poliakov and Aleksandr B. Boretskii. Leningradskaia Hotel, Moscow, 1949–1954.
Graphite and watercolour on paper, 132 × 77.5 cm. Tchoban Foundation, Museum for Architectural Drawing.

Mikhail V. Posokhin, Ashot A. Mndoiants. Residential building on Vosstaniia Square, Moscow, 1948-1954. Perspective. Watercolor on paper, mounted on linen, 127.6 × 168.7 cm. Shchusev State Museum of Architecture, RIa 10032/9.

Dmitrii N. Chechulin and Andrei Rostkovskii. Residential building on Kotelnicheskaia embankment, Moscow, 1949-1952, in *URSS in Construction*, no. 5, May 1953. Private Collection.

the fact that Iofan had questioned the authority of the local potentate, by his persistent Amerikanizm, or by his friendship with the late Aleksei Rykov, still considered then as an enemy of the people. The complex, as designed by Lev Rudnev, with Pavel Abrosimov and Aleksandr Khriakov, was moved several hundred metres away from the location projected by Iofan. The programme was expanded, and the articulation between its components became more complex, while retaining some of the figures from the previous project. While all the other high-rise buildings assembled compressed or deliberately lower wings around a dominant vertical structure, and while Iofan had clearly separated the adjoining buildings from the tower, Rudnev's octopus-shaped plan allowed for continuity between the various edifices. The dominant structure of the ensemble grew taller during the design process, reaching 239 metres at the end of the project. However, it kept its four adjacent towers, expanding into lateral wings and forming a fragment of the future urban fabric of the neighbourhood. In 1953, Boris Rubanenko highlighted the "national" character of the ensemble, writing that "the rich visual interplay between volumes and the outline of the university ensemble as well as its symphonic nature is one of the most instructive and brilliant examples of the inventiveness of the Russian urbanistic tradition."[188] American accents nevertheless became perceptible, be it in Iofan's cherished terracing, reminiscent of great American vertical hotels, or in the crowning, a distorted replica of the Manhattan Municipal Building, made even more similar to the original by the fact that for a time, Rudnev intended to place one or two statues at its helm.

Chechulin designed the Zariadie building on his own. On the banks of the Moskva River and near the Kremlin, he devised a massive office building project, initially intended for the Ministry of Heavy Industry. In 1934–1935, its predecessor, the Narkomtiazhprom, had considered settling on the neighbouring site. The footprint of its maze-like lower components would have been tremendous, as they would have served as the base of a tower with a thicker cross-shaped section than that of the other high-rises. The building was meant to be 25 metres higher than the university, and its visual impact on the banks of the Moskva would have been overpowering if the project had not been abandoned after Stalin's death. The project had already led to the eviction of numerous inhabitants, who were relocated far from the centre, and its foundations, as well as a part of the lower floors, had already been built[189].

The activities of the construction sites were overseen by Aleksandr Komarovskii, who replaced Andrei Prokofiev at the head of the USDS in October 1948. The civil engineer had become major general as a result of his service at the head of the Gulag divisions tasked with factory construction, after leading that of the Moskva-Volga Canal before the war. He played a significant role in the development of Soviet nuclear infrastructure. Under Komarovskii's tenure, the population of Zariadie was displaced and camps were created on the university campus and on the premises of the Kotelnicheskaia Embankment Building for the thousands of prisoners working on the construction sites[190].

188   Boris R. Rubanenko, "Khudozhestvennye osnovy arkhitektury vysotnykh zdanii stolitsy," *Sovetskaia arkhitektura* 4 (1953): 16.
189   Zubovich, "Moscow Monumental," 117–25.
190   Ibid., 126–34. The general's memoirs are sparse on this point: Aleksandr N. Komarovskii, *Zapiski stroitelia* (Moscow: Voenizdat, 1972). Aksenov mentions the presence of prisoners in *Moskva kva–kva*, 254–62.

Boris M. Iofan and Evgenii M. Stamo. Project for an office building in Zariadie, Moscow, late 1940s. View from the Moskva River. Graphite and watercolour on paper, 42.3 × 69 cm. Tchoban Foundation, Museum for Architectural Drawing.

The technical efforts to erect the high-rise structures, façades, and mechanical systems were also decisive in the modernization of Soviet technologies, as a host of engineers cut their teeth on these projects[191].

This new *stroika* was surrounded with an extensive propaganda campaign celebrating the heroic deeds of the builders in songs and newspaper articles. The visual schemes printed in the press were similar to those used in New York in the 1920s. A 1949 cover of *The USSR in Construction* showed assembly workers suspended in the Moscow sky to erect the headquarters of the Ministry of Foreign Affairs, thus literally illustrating the title of the journal[192]. Reprised by Mikhail Kalatozov in his 1954 film *True Friends*, this depiction of nonchalantly weathered danger is unmistakably reminiscent of Lewis Hine's Empire State Building site photographs. The image served as a motif in Fernand Léger's 1950 painting *The Builders*, where a protagonist is modelled after one of the workers featured on the magazine's cover[193]. These troubling resemblances concurred with the self-satisfied propaganda surrounding the completion of the initial projects, striving to show not only that the Soviet buildings owed nothing to the Americans, but also that they were more humane and structurally tougher, as two victims of the anti-cosmopolitan campaign wrote in a desperate effort to redeem themselves.

Indeed, in 1953, Arkin wrote that "the American 'skyscraper' has become the symbol of the decline of architecture and urban planning as forms of art. Devoid of harmonious proportions, skyscrapers reveal the deep divide between knowledge and people, between isolated buildings and cities. The mass of skyscrapers in Manhattan and Chicago has become the symbol of man's slavery to the soulless machine of business." Arkin based his condemnation on declarations by Lewis Mumford, whose writings he knew well, highlighting the "fundamentally different" principles of the Moscow buildings, "which do not deprive existing neighbourhoods of air and light." They were "implemented so as to create a new landscape" and "to serve the city as a whole," and not to profit capitalist speculation[194]. Alabian spoke in more technical terms in a 1952 issue of the largely circulated magazine *Ogonek*, drawing on Maxim Gorky's writings to criticize New York and Chicago skyscrapers, while praising the sturdiness of Moscow's high-rises: "Many of those living in American skyscrapers can feel the building swaying even with light winds. Contrary to the USA, where the oscillation of the tower tops reaches 1/300 of the height, in the USSR, this variation has been limited to 1/1000, and even less in certain cases."[195]

Lauded in this way, the Moscow skyscrapers crystallized the architectural principles condemned by Nikolai Ladovskii, Moisei Ginzburg, and El Lissitzky in the 1920s. Images of their bare metallic structures were printed for documentary purposes[196], but their creators used information gathered by Oltarzhevskii to tile, in thick ceramic cladding, the "living skeleton" of the buildings[197]. There remained a resemblance between the Moscow ensemble and the American corpus—used for architectural and technical inspiration, and later discarded with disdain. This likeness, which in certain cases was akin to plagiarism, though not as literally as in the case of the Tupolev Tu-4, was apparent in the buildings' architectural syntax as well as their ornamental lexicon. Occupying a larger footprint on their sites than their American counterparts, contained within the strict limits of the city grid, the Russian buildings nevertheless borrowed their vertical composition and even their decorative themes, adding copious socialist-realist sculptural motifs and heraldic symbols of the regime—sickles, hammers, wheat sheaves, flags, and stars. The architecture of Moscow's high-rises became an export product, as the Soviet Union "fraternally" offered to provide buildings designed on the same model to other socialist capitals. These structures served various programmes, such as the Palace of Culture and Science in Warsaw, designed by Rudnev, the Družba Hotel in Prague, and the headquarters for the *Scînteia* publishing house in Bucharest[198]. While Americanization affected all of Western Europe—which as of 1948 received subsidies from the European Recovery Program (the Marshall Plan), whose conditions the USSR had refused—, American stereotypes could thus be found in the monumental programmes of the East, where they were introduced in a derivative form with these Soviet-related schemes. The movement reached the People's Republic of China, where the Shanghai Exhibition Centre, "gifted" by the USSR, followed the Moscovian example. There, a 1954 poster illustrated the slogan "The Soviet

191   Oltarzhevskii, *Stroitelstvo vysotnykh zdanii*, 171–202; Nikolai N. Kruzhkov, *Vysotki stalinskoi Moskvy: nasledie epokhi* (Moscow: Tsentrpoligraf, 2014), 132–251.
192   "Montage de la carcasse métallique d'un grand édifice place de Smolensk à Moscou," cover of *URSS in Construction* 13, no. 11 (1949).
193   This similarity was remarked on by, among others, Valérie Nègre in "Contempler ou agir: Quelques manières de représenter les activités techniques," in *L'Art du chantier: Construire et démolir du XVI au XXIe siècle*, ed. Valérie Nègre (Paris: Cité de l'architecture et du patrimoine, 2018), 103–5.
194   David E. Arkin, "Zavoevanie vysoty," *Literaturnaia gazeta*, 12 February 1953, 1.
195   Karo Alabian, "Vysotnye zdania stolitsy," *Ogonek* 30, no. 37 (7 September 1952): 6.
196   *URSS in construction*, vol. 13, n° 11, 1949.
197   El Lissitzky, "'Amerikanizm' v evropeiskoi arkhitekture," *Krasnaia niva* 2, no. 49 (29 November 1925): 1188. The skeleton of the Ministry of Foreign Affairs was published in *URSS in Construction* 13, no. 11 (1949).
198   On Warsaw's building and its link to Moscow, see *Palace Complex*, 47–49. On Soviet Block architecture as a whole, see Anders Åman, *Architecture and Ideology in Eastern Europe During the Stalin Era: An Aspect of Cold War History* (New York: Architectural History Foundation; Cambridge, MA: MIT Press, 1992).

Vladimir G. Gelfreikh and Mikhail A. Minkus. Ministry of Foreign Affairs on Smolenskaia Square, Moscow, 1948-1953.
View of the construction site on the cover of *L'URSS en construction*, no. 11, November 1949. Private collection.

Lewis W. Hine, Riveters working on mooring mast of the Empire State Building, New York City, 1931.
Top: Gelatin silver print on paper, 24.2 × 19.1 cm. CCA PH1984:0075. Bottom: Gelatin silver print on paper, 34.4 × 26.7 cm. CCA PH1987:0421.

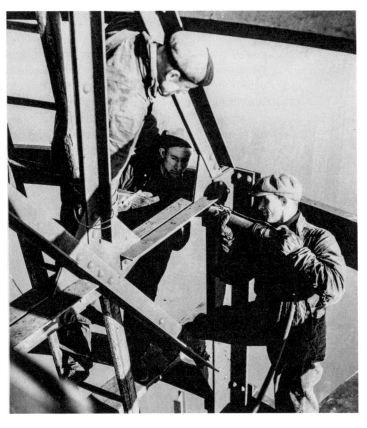

Union Is Our Model" with the image of a worker laying bricks in front of the Ministry of Foreign Affairs, adorned with a portrait of Stalin.

An undated Tekhpromimport advertisement shows a perfect example of two fundamental registers of covert post-war Americanism under Stalin: a greenish M-20 Pobeda sedan is pictured against a cityscape comprised of seven differently shaped buildings, as though Moscow's "seven sisters" had been rearranged in Manhattan. The displacement (from one continent to the other) and the condensation (of an entire city into a vertical neighbourhood) depicted on this image amount to what Sigmund Freud has defined as the dream work[199]. Indeed, the automobile, still reserved to a narrow, privileged elite, remained for nearly the entire Soviet population a dream as unattainable as the individual apartments contained in Moscow's high-rise buildings.

199   Sigmund Freud [1899], *The Interpretation of Dreams*, New York: MacMillan, 1913.

GAZ M-20 Pobeda sedan set against the backdrop a condensed Moscow skyline with the high-rise buildings.
Moscow: Tekhpromimport, ca. 1955.

Khrushchev and His Successors: Reaching, Surpassing, and Forgetting America

6

Nikita S. Khrushchev
(1894-1971). First Secretary of
the CPSU. Visited the United
States in 1959.

Willis Conover (1920-1996).
Radio host of the program
"Music USA" on *The Voice
of America* radio channel.

George Nelson (1908-1986).
Industrial designer. Conceived
the American National
Exhibition in Moscow in 1959.

Victor Gruen (1803-1980).
American architect and urban
planner. Inventor of the
shopping mall.

Raymond Loewy (1893-1986).
American industrial designer.
Worked in the USSR from 1973
to 1976.

Vasilii Aksenov (1932-2009).
Russian novelist. He wrote
many accounts of everyday
Amerikanizm.

"Your exhibition has many interesting things. I do not want to conceal the fact that during my inspection of your exhibits, I not only experienced a feeling of satisfaction, but also, to a certain degree, a feeling of envy. But this is a good envy, in the sense that we should like to have all this in our country as soon as possible. […] We can learn something. We regard the American exhibition as an exhibition of our own achievements in the near future […] when our plans have been realized."

Nikita S. Khrushchev, *Pravda*, 25 July 1959[1]

1   Nikita S. Khrushchev, *Pravda*, 25 July 1959, quoted in Amanda Wood Aucoin, "Deconstructing the American Way of Life: Soviet Responses to Cultural Exchange and American Information Activity during the Khrushchev Years," PhD dissertation (Fayetteville: University of Arkansas, 2001), 111.

In the months following Stalin's death on 5 March 1953, Moscow's high-rise building programme was put to a halt. The area excavated for the foundation of the Palace of the Soviets was later turned into an outdoor swimming pool by Dmitrii Chechulin, likely to make up for his abandoned high-rise project in Zariadie. Between 1964 and 1967, Chechulin used the building's substructures to build the Rossiia Hotel, conservatively limited to 12 floors, topped with a small tower. The antagonism of the Cold War decreased with the 1953 Korean Armistice Agreement and the Austrian State Treaty, signed in 1955. This new global climate was favourable to the development of cultural relations between the United States and the Soviet Union and conducive to the revival of investigative travels, exhibitions, and publications as part of the "peaceful coexistence" advocated in 1956 by Nikita Khrushchev, First Secretary of the Communist Party since March 1953. In the USSR itself, the authoritarian grip was loosened with the political reforms known as de-Stalinization. The effects of the "Thaw," as Ilya Ehrenburg called this political phenomenon in his marking 1954 novel[2], were soon apparent in the realm of architecture.

The second half of the 1950s also saw a resurgence of Americanism, stemming both from this shift in politics and diplomacy and from the new orientation given to Soviet architecture. During the Soviet Builders' Conference held in December 1954, Khrushchev chose this very discipline to announce his new policies, which would be instated only in 1956, during the 20th Congress of the Communist Party of the Soviet Union. In a widely disseminated speech, Khrushchev berated the designers of the "seven sisters," drawing on existing criticism within the profession to direct the sector towards industrial housing[3]. Khrushchev specifically addressed Moscow's spires: "Some architects are keen on designing spires on the buildings, so that they resemble churches. Do you like a church silhouette? I do not want to argue about taste,

2   Ilya G. Ehrenburg, *Ottepel: povest* (Moscow: Sovetskii Pisatel, 1954); in English: *The Thaw*, trans. Manya Harari (London: Harvill, 1955).
3   Catherine Cooke, with Susan E. Reid, "Modernity and Realism: Architectural Relations in the Cold War," in *Russian Art and the West: A Century of Dialogue in Painting, Architecture, and the Decorative Arts*, eds. Rosalind P. Blakesley, Susan E. Reid (DeKalb, IL: Northern Illinois University Press, 2007), 172–94.
4   Nikita S. Khrushchev, "O shirokom vnedrenii industrialnykh metodov, ulushchenii kachestva i snizhenii stoimosti stroitelstva," *Moskovskii stroitel*, 28 December 1954.
5   Ibid.
6   Nikita S. Khrushchev and Nikolai A. Bulganin, "Postanovlenie TsK KPSS i Soveta Ministrov SSSR ob ustranenii izlishchestv v proektirovanii i stroitelstve," 4 November 1955; *Vechernaia Moskva*, 10 November 1955.
7   Beginning in 1953, Arkin taught at the Moscow School of Applied Arts, as indicated in the obituary by Aleksei G. Chiniakov, "D.E. Arkin," *Arkhitekturnoe nasledstvo* 10 (1958) 206–8.
8   Olga Smirnova, "Obostrenie krisisa arkhitektury i gradostroitelstva v poslevoennoi Amerike," *Sovetskaia arkhitektura* 4 (1953): 111–19.
9   R. Kostylev and G. Perestoronina, "Karkasno-panelnoe stroitelstvo v SShA," *Arkhitektura SSSR*, no. 9 (September 1955): 36–39.
10   Fedor V. Konstantinov [head of the agitprop department of the Central Committee CPSU], "O rasprostranenii v SSSR zhurnala "Amerika"," 30 July 1956, Lamont Library, Harvard University, fond 89, Declassified Documents of the Communist Party, 1956, no. 191, op. 46, d. 11, quoted in Yale Richmond, *Cultural Exchange and the Cold War: Raising the Iron Curtain* (University Park, PA: Penn State University Press, 2003), 150.
11   Ilia Lezhava, "Istoria gruppy NER, in Andrei Nekrasov, Aleksei Shcheglov, ed., *MARKhI XX vek: sbornik vospominanii v piati tomakh* (Moscow: Moskovskii arkhitekturnyi institut, Salon-Press, 2006), vol. 3, 87, quoted in Daria Bocharnikova, "A History of the Architectural Profession in the USSR, 1932-1971," PhD dissertation (Florence: European University Institute, 2014), 165.
12   Steven Harris, "Two Lessons in Modernism: What the Architectural Review and America's Mass Media Taught Soviet Architects about the West," *Trondheim Studies on East European Cultures and Societies* 31 (August 2010): 45–93; Greg Castillo, *Cold War on the Home Front: The Soft Power of Midcentury Design* (Minneapolis: University of Minnesota Press, 2010), 130–36; Fabien Bellat, "Missions à l'étranger, appropriations et dénis tacites dans l'architecture soviétique," in *L'étranger dans la littérature et les arts soviétiques*, ed. Marie-Christine Autant-Mathieu (Villeneuve-d'Ascq: Presses universitaires du Septentrion, 2014), 179–81.
13   Don Stetson, "Enroute with the Russians," press release, n.d. [1955], Washington, DC, National Association of Home Builders, quoted in Castillo, *Cold War on the Home Front*, 133–34.

but residential buildings do not require such a look. One should not transform a modern house into a church or museum silhouette by means of architectural decoration. It does not offer any additional conveniences to the residents and it only makes the exploitation of the building more difficult and its cost—higher[4]. Based on a letter sent to the Central Committee by the architect Georgii Gradov on behalf of a group of architects, Khrushchev admonished the creators of the buildings for having produced an excessively dense "building space" in terms of structure and walls, a space that was "only for looking at," "not for working in or living."[5] The condemnation of decorative "excesses" was the most compelling message of the speech, which a joint decree by the Central Committee and the Council of Ministers ratified in November 1955[6].

In this new climate, the "cosmopolitans" were rehabilitated, including the supposed "doctors-assassins" targeted in 1952 as part of Stalin's anti-Semitic "Doctors' plot" as well as more modest protagonists such as David Arkin[7]. Articles criticizing America were no longer relevant, such as the 1953 paper still printed in *Sovetskaia arkhitektura* that denounced the "deepening American architectural crisis" and condemned towers deprived of all context and institutions like MoMA, calling it a "centre for the history of reactionary art."[8]

As of 1955, the professional community became aware of American post-war realizations, chiefly from a technical perspective. For instance, the first images of Ludwig Mies van der Rohe's buildings on Lake Shore Drive, in Chicago, were published as part of a study focusing on construction methods[9]. Owing to an intergovernmental agreement signed on 9 October 1956, the United States Information Agency resumed the publication of *Amerika*, in exchange for the dissemination of *USSR*, its Soviet counterpart, through the Washington embassy. Despite the stringent monitoring of its distribution, limited to a specific number of institutions, the journal was able to reach the architectural world[10]. Ilia Lezhava, then a student at the Moscow Institute of Architecture, recalled its significance: "A big format, a glossy cover, wonderful pictures, a smattering of knowledge. This journal, however, was a great rarity, and only one professor, the father of [Andrei] Baburov subscribed to it. At his home we sucked it dry."[11]

Architects and Political Leaders in America: from 1955 to 1959

While the print publications resumed their circulation and the first delegation of reporters visited the United States, architects and engineers were once again sent overseas by Soviet institutions and tasked mainly with studying industrial methods of construction to fulfill Khrushchev's programme. In 1955, for the first time in a decade, a dozen Soviets set out for the United States, on an invitation from the National Association of Home Builders, which was staking out the opening of a tremendous market for its services[12]. The delegation was headed by the Minister of Urban and Rural Construction, Ivan Koziulia, who had taken part in the 1945 conference on construction in New York, and included the architect Aleksandr Vlasov and the engineer Petr Spyshnov. Equipped with an arsenal of photo cameras, the delegates set out on a five-week itinerary taking them from New York to Boston, Washington, Cleveland, Fort Wayne, Chicago, Seattle, San Francisco, Los Angeles, Tucson, Austin, Houston, and New Orleans, under the watchful eye of each city's local press. The Soviets were chiefly interested in prefabrication and in all the technical aspects of construction and housing equipment[13]. They focused more specifically on the kitchens they discovered in dwellings or at the National Housing

Center in Washington. In addition to visiting factories and construction sites, the delegates bought equipment—such as a pneumatic concrete nail guns and standardized windows—and technical literature[14]. Most importantly, in San Pablo, in the San Francisco Bay area, they purchased a prefabricated split-level home intended for the Rollingwood development from the real estate developer Andres Oddstad. It was shipped to the USSR disassembled, with its fixtures, furnishings, curtains, and cushions. Its whereabouts remains unknown to this day[15].

The delegation's journey was tarnished by an unforeseen incident that put a "grim end" to their tour, as quipped by *Architectural Forum*[16]. Misinterpreting information from the USSR about a new decree on "the excesses in construction and projects," the Associated Press announced that Aleksandr Vlasov had been removed from his position at the head of the Academy of Architecture while he was still in Washington. In truth, Vlasov had been dismissed from his role as Moscow's chief architect by Khrushchev, who had witnessed his work in Kiev and disapproved of his indifference regarding mass housing. In 1948, he had published a stinging critique of western-oriented architects and their admiration for the United States, while commending Frank Lloyd Wright's criticism of America[17]. Taking advantage of the newfound flexibility afforded by the political climate, Vlasov left the group behind for an impromptu visit to Taliesin, in Wisconsin, to meet with his idol Wright, whom he had briefly encountered in Moscow in 1937. As reported in the *Practical Builder*, the visit was a "meeting of the minds," a lively discussion uniting both architects in their hatred of Le Corbusier and Mies van der Rohe. On his way back, Vlasov told the reporter who chaperoned him that he was "genuinely thrilled with the experience." She recounted that he "spoke of Wright's home, commenting not only on the architecture, but that everything in it, the furniture, even the placing of a book, or a vase, or a flower, were expressive of the genius and inspiration of the man," and that he had admitted the following: "Until today I had seen only the technical phase of architecture in America. Today I saw the other phase which is the artistic side, and now I feel that I'm getting a rounded picture."[18]

The American press saw in Vlasov's apparent firing a punishment for his solitary excursion and hinted at the fact that he had been forcefully summoned back to the USSR while his companions continued their tour[19]. As he was heading to Moscow, Vlasov held a press conference in Paris, where he was greeted by anti-Soviet protesters. His talk was covered by French and

14   Harrison E. Salisbury, "Touring Soviet Aide Pictures US as Christmas Dream Come True," *The New York Times*, 29 October 1955.
15   "Russia Buys a House," *The New York Times*, 30 October 1955. See also "Russians to Get a US Dwelling," *The New York Times*, 26 July 1956 [on the late delivery of the house]. See also Castillo, *Cold War on the Home Front*, 134.
16   "Purge Report Puts Grim End to Soviet Experts' US Tour," *Architectural Forum* 103, no. 6 (December 1955): 16.
17   Aleksandr V. Vlasov, "Nazrevchie voprosy sovetskogo zodchestva," *Pravda*, 28 September 1948, 2.
18   Claudia Boynton, "Visiting Russian Architect A.V. Vlasov Pilgrimages to Frank Lloyd Wright," *Practical Builder*, December 1955, 21.
19   "Soviet Dismisses Top Architects," *The New York Times*, 10 November 1955; "Soviet Architects Lose Posts," *Christian Science Monitor*, 10 November 1955; "Moscow Raps Plush Building: Fires Top Men," *Chicago Tribune*, 10 November 1955.
20   "Au cours d'une conférence de presse à l'ambassade de l'URSS, l'architecte soviétique Vlassov se dit victime d'une 'provocation'," *L'Aurore*, 18 November 1955; Jean de Castellane, "M. Vlassov dément et accuse," *Le Figaro*, 19–20 November 1955; "Delo Vlasova," *Russkaia Mysl*, 19 November 1955; *Newsweek*, 17 October 1955, 84; *Time*, 21 November 1955, 16. The incident was commented on by David Caute, *The Dancer Defects: The Struggle for Cultural Supremacy During the Cold War* (Oxford: Oxford University Press, 2003), 537–38.
21   "Wright Fears Russ Architect Sacked for Admiring Him," *The Milwaukee Sentinel*, 15 November 1955, 6.
22   "Beseda s arkhitektorom A. V. Vlasovym," *Pravda*, 5 December 1955.

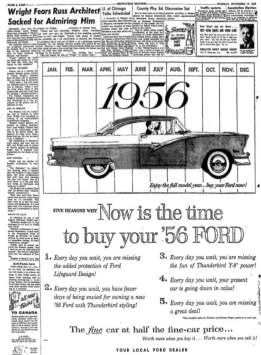

White émigré newspapers, while American outlets offered various interpretations of the incident[20]. Wright recounted Vlasov's visit to Taliesin in an interview with *The Milwaukee Sentinel* and declared that "he believed he could learn something from me. He was too good to be a Russian."[21] Beyond the tribute to Wright, then completely ignored by the Russian architectural community, Vlasov's excursion can be viewed, namely in light of his remarks quoted in *Practical Builder*, as an attempt to defend the figure of the architect as creator, at a time when Khrushchev's policies exclusively advocated for techniques and economics. Back in Moscow, in an article printed by the *Pravda*, Vlasov accused the Americans and the French of using entrapment to undermine the strengthening of Soviet-American ties[22]. Two months later, he presented the Union of Architects with a comprehensive report on "the practice of housing construction in America," partly inspired by the Midwestern landscape he had discovered, and illustrated with his own slides. He deplored having been unable to visit multi-dwelling buildings and described the "single-storey" America of individual houses, whose proliferation he attributed to their inhabitants' thirst for private property. Vlasov also explained the phenomenon of urban sprawl with the threat of a nuclear attack. He praised the American gardens and, taking stock of the equipment, furnishings, and decoration, noted the size of the kitchens and the puzzling fact that they contained televisions for housewives cooking meals or feeding their children. He showed a certain disappointment in the limitations of prefabrication, but recognized the relevance of experimental approaches to construction. In terms of culture, Vlasov condemned the "horrible" pervasiveness of television, aghast at the female wrestling matches he witnessed on the small screen.

During his lecture, Vlasov also mentioned his visit to Wright, reminding his audience that the American architect had signed the 1950 Stockholm Appeal against nuclear weapons. "Here is the house that he drew and built for himself and that seems to me an example of good architecture. The walls are made with local natural stone. The windows reach the floor. There are exposed ceiling trusses and the interior architecture is very simple. But Wright seems to collect unique objects from around the world: he brought back interesting things from India, Burma, China, and our country. [...] They are tastefully disposed in his home."[23] In his speech, Vlasov recalled that during their meeting, this "true friend" of the USSR had spoken of Karo Alabian, Nikolai Kolli, Vladimir Shchuko, Vladimir Gelfreikh, and Boris Iofan. He also marvelled at Wright's studio, with his 60 apprentices, while lamenting the lack of interest for the issue of mass housing on his colleagues' part, with a touch of self-criticism. Following Vlasov, Spyshnov, in charge of the Gosstroi, broached the theme of "methods and techniques for housing construction." He recounted how closely the press followed the group's discoveries and described the American professional context, without mentioning the encountered structures. Spyshnov spoke mostly of the lift slab process, which he found fascinating. However, he gave extensive details on construction sites and tools, praising the practical nature of the procedures and home furnishings. An expert in buildings' mechanicals, he was struck by the plumbing systems, sanitary facilities, and air conditioning, while stressing that, similarly to Vlasov, he had only witnessed a "single-storey" America[24].

In May 1956, another delegation spent two weeks in the United States to attend the congress of the New York State Home Builders Association and the International Home Building Exposition, but did not explore the country beyond Levittown, Long Island[25]. Upon his return, Nikolai Baranov, Leningrad's chief architect, gave a talk on "American construction practises" to the Union of Architects, illustrated by a film shot by the travellers. His impressions of Manhattan, whose plan he deemed "primitive," were rather close to Gorky's remarks, made fifty years earlier, and his comments on Broadway can be read like a prose version of Mayakovsky's. Baranov's observations on dwellings, such as those he saw at the New York exhibition, where he commented on the strong female presence, were very similar to those of his companions. In the suburbs, apart from the Levittown site, he praised the shopping malls. He was especially interested in road traffic, marvelling at highways and parking meters, and lectured his peers on the necessity for such developments, which he considered inevitable in the USSR[26].

23   Aleksandr V. Vlasov, "Praktika zhilishchnogo stroitelstva v Amerike," lecture at the Union of Architects, 19 January 1956, dactyl., RGALI, f. 2466, op. 1, d. 459, 26.
24   Petr A. Spychnov, "Izuchenie amerikanskikh metodov i tekhniki stroitelstva zhilykh domov," lecture at the Union of Architects, 3 March 1956, dactyl., RGALI, f. 2466, op. 1, d. 460, 34.
25   "5 Building Experts Arrive from Russia," The New York Times, 11 May 1956.
26   Nikolai V. Baranov, "Amerikanskaia praktika stroitelstva," lecture at the Union of Architects, 3 March 1956, dactyl., RGALI, f. 2466, op. 1, d. 470.
27   Vasilii I. Svetlichnyi, ed. Opyt stroitelstva za rubezhom: v Soedinennykh Shtatakh Ameriki (Moscow: Gos. Izd-vo literatury po stroitelstvu i arkhitekture, 1956). Other volumes focus on the study missions to England, Western Europe, and the "people's democracies."
28   On this intense year, see Kathleen E. Smith, Moscow 1956: The Silenced Spring (Cambridge, MA: Harvard University Press, 2017).
29   Boris N. Polevoi, Amerikanskie dnevniki (Moscow: Sovetskii Pisatel, 1956).

Upon returning from his second mission, Vasilii Svetlichnyi edited a joint publication derived from both trips. An expert on industrialization, which he had practiced since the early 1950s, Svetlichnyi assembled and combined contributions from nine of the travellers, including the three aforementioned architects. With a print run of 15,000 copies, it was the first overview of American architecture published since Amtorg's 1945 volume, which had been printed ten years earlier without any engaged analytical commentary. This collective work introduced not only post-war construction techniques, but also several architectural innovations. Beyond the detached, mass-produced suburban houses and a few multi-dwelling buildings, Russian readers discovered the latest designs for schools and movie theatres, office buildings—including Skidmore, Owings and Merrill's Lever House and Inland Steel and Wallace Harrison's United Nations Headquarters—, and the more exotic shopping malls, like Roosevelt Field shopping mall in Long Island, created by I. M. Pei. However, almost all the featured works were uncredited. Close attention was paid to sanitary facilities and kitchens, which were unusual as seen from the USSR in 1956[27]. The year of the publication, at the 20th Congress of the CPSU, Khrushchev made his secret speech denouncing the "personality cult" of Stalin, a euphemism to describe the dictator's violent repression practices. The reforms he announced took time to materialize, but the shift in the political and cultural climate of the Soviet Union was palpable[28].

While the architectural community began filling its information gap, sanctioned Soviet writers and journalists travelled across the Atlantic[29]. Arkadii Mordvinov took part in the 1957 convention of the American Institute of Architects. In his brief account of the event, he announced that he was "preparing a few propositions to improve housing construction in Moscow, based on his observations on American building techniques."[30] In 1958, a large contingent of Americans took part in the congress of the International Union of Architects, in Moscow. Foreign experience was thus disseminated through various channels and resonated in the new competition launched in 1957 for the Palace of the Soviets, whose projected location had been moved south-westward, aligned with the new university campus. For the first round, Iofan submitted a barely updated version of his previous project, replacing Lenin's statue with a cupola topped with an antenna, a minimalistic manifestation of Stalin's spires. Like many of his competitors, Vlasov, who won the second round, submitted a simple rectangular box wrapped in glass, with three elliptical halls arranged on the inside[31]. The project never materialized.

The young architects hired by Vlasov to design his competition project were part of a generation that was open to American culture, despite its limited distribution. Literary translations resumed, as shown by the 1956 publication of Ray Bradbury's *Fahrenheit 451*, three years after the original version—though admittedly, the book could be read as a critique of McCarthyism[32]. Truman Capote wrote a hilarious account of the 1955 staging of George Gershwin's *Porgy and Bess* in Leningrad and in Moscow, an event that was remarkable in every respect[33]. The post-war generations started listening to *Voice of America*, the state-owned international radio station. In 1955, Willis Conover started hosting its *Music USA* program, which targeted young Soviet and Eastern European audiences, making him the most popular American in the entire socialist bloc. Vasilii Aksenov's novels are filled with references to pieces discovered on the fuzzy VOA airwaves and printed on "bones"—that is on x-ray films, as customary in the *Rentgenizdat* practice mentioned in the previous chapter[34]. Musicians freed from the camps, such as Eddie Rosner, revived their performances, and hundreds of bands were formed throughout the country. One of them was *Vosmerka* (The Eight), which played cover versions of the pieces broadcast by Conover. These ensembles were revealed during the summer of 1957, at Moscow's World Festival of Youth and Students[35]. The renewed eagerness for American music gave way to the creation of youth cafés, on an initiative from the Komsomol, and reached its peak in 1962, with the Benny Goodman Orchestra's triumphant tour in the USSR. Nevertheless, Khrushchev had harsh words about jazz, declaring: "When I hear jazz, it is as if I had gas in the stomach" during an exhibit opening at the Moscow Manege on 1 December 1962, where he also vilified several painters. This hostile reaction put a temporary halt to the cultural openness of the late 1950s[36].

The USSR scored a significant political and symbolic point in 1957 by placing into orbit Sputnik, the planet's first artificial satellite. Nonetheless, Soviet post-war industrial plagiarism practices prevailed well past Stalin's death. In 1953, the Gorky Automobile Plant's engineers began designing a replacement for the Pobeda, the GAZ M21. Based on a 1952 Ford model, it was manufactured that same year as the "Volga." However, this mid-sized vehicle did not meet the expectations of the high-ranking bureaucracy. Two large limousines were produced to serve the apparatchiks: at the end of 1956, the ZIL factory in Moscow presented its ZIL-111 model, derived from the previous year's Packard Caribbean, which also inspired the Chaika, released in 1959 by the GAZ in Gorky[37]. The Soviet versions of American models, which were rapidly evolving to meet the public's tastes and the changing fashions, often had a lifespan of several decades: the scarcity was such that all copies, fashionable or not, were immediately sold. This practice of copying outdated products for several years in a row increased, as Kendall Bailes has demonstrated for earlier periods, the technology gap between Soviet designs and the American consumer system, which was more developed[38].

In June 1957, Khrushchev, shortly after establishing his power by declaring that he had thwarted a conspiracy hatched by an "antiparty" group comprised of Lazar Kaganovich, Georgii Malenkov, Viacheslav Molotov, and Klim Voroshilov, expressed a new goal. In a May 1957 speech made in Leningrad in front of food industry representatives, he had reprised the ambitious motto that had been often articulated by both Lenin and Stalin: "To catch up with and to surpass" America."[39] [ill. p. 468] At the same time, he infused the restoration of business relations with the United States with the sense of a personal mission. In 1961, in conversation with John F. Kennedy, he recalled his fond memories of Hugh L. Cooper's actions during the Dneprostroi and Russia's relationship with America at the time[40]. That same year, Khrushchev effusively welcomed the industrialist and philanthropist Armand Hammer to Moscow, encouraging him to visit his former pencil factory, which was relaunching its activities after a 25-year halt. According to the boastful billionaire, Khrushchev even thanked him for organizing Ford's imports to the USSR[41].

Khrushchev was the first supreme leader to travel to America. In charge of establishing preliminary contacts, the Deputy Premier Minister Anastas Mikoyan preceded him in January 1959, interspersing impromptu visits with official conversations that were mainly focused on the German question and yielded no results. He discovered a motel, a highway diner, and the Super Giant mall in White Oak, Maryland, where he was seen examining meat cuts in their plastic packaging[42]. The journal *Amerika* eagerly shared images from these travels with its Soviet readers[43]. A few months later, photographs from the First Secretary's tour, which took him from New York to Los Angeles in late September, gave the Soviet public the impression of a prosperity that was completely at odds with the propagandist discourse. Often prone to joking

30 Arkadii G. Mordvinov, "Kratkii ochet o poezdke v Washington na torzhestvennuiu konferentsiu v sviazi s stoletnei godovshinoi Instituta amerikanskikh arkhitektorov," n.d. [1957], RGALI, f. 674, op. 3, ed. khr. 1386.
31 L.I. Kirillova, G.B. Minervin, and G.A. Shemiakin, *Dvorets Sovetov: materialy konkursa 1957–1959 gg.* (Moscow: Gos. Izd-vo literatury po stroitelstve, arkhitekture i stroitelnoi tekhnike, 1961), 58.
32 Ray Bradbury, *451° po Farengeitu* [1953], trans. T. Shinkar (Moscow: Izd-vo Inostrannoi literatury, 1956).
33 Truman Capote, "Porgy and Bess in Russia: When the Cannons Are Silent," *The New Yorker*, 20 October 1956, 38; reprinted in *The Muses Are Heard* (New York: Random House, 1956). See also Faubion Bowers, *Broadway, USSR: Ballet, Theatre, and Entertainment in Russia Today* (New York: Nelson, 1959).
34 This was where he found inspiration for the title of his book about his exile across the Atlantic: Vasilii Aksenov, *In Search of Melancholy Baby*, trans. Michael Henry Heim and Antonina W. Bouis (New York, Random House, 1987). On Conover's popularity, see Walter L. Hixson, *Parting the Curtain: Propaganda, Culture, and the Cold War, 1945–61* (New York: St. Martin's Press, 1997), 115–17.
35 S. Frederick Starr, *Red & Hot: The Fate of Jazz in the Soviet Union 1917–1980* [1983] (New York: Limelight Editions, 1994), 243–51. On the official response to imported culture, see Gleb Tsipursky, "Fighting Western Fashion in the Soviet Union: The Komsomol, Westernized Youth, and the Cultural Cold War in the Mid-1950s," *Euxeinos. Governance and Culture in the Black Sea Region*, 8, no. 25-26 (December 2018): 11-19.
36 "Khrushchev on Modern Art", *Encounter*, 20 April 1963, 102.
37 Valentin Brodskii, "Forma avtomobilia," and Iurii Limanov, "Konstruktor-khudozhnik," *Dekorativnoe iskusstvo SSSR*, no. 7 (1958): 23–27 and 28–29; Vladimir Ariamov, "Ot 'Pobedy' do 'Tchaiki'," *Dekorativnoe iskusstvo SSSR*, no. 10 (1959): 14–19. On these vehicles, see Lewis H. Siegelbaum, *Cars for Comrades: The Life of the Soviet Automobile* (Ithaca: Cornell University Press, 2011), 30 and 68.
38 Kendall E. Bailes, "The American Connection: Ideology and the Transfer of American Technology to the Soviet Union," *Comparative Studies in Society and History* 23, no. 3 (July 1981): 445.
39 Nikita S. Khrushchev, "Dlia tesnuiu sviaz literatury i iskusstva s zhiznu naroda," *Pravda*, 28 August 1957; in English: *Khrushchev Speaks: Selected Speeches, Articles, and Press Conferences, 1949-1961* (Ann Arbor: University of Michigan Press, 1963), 274.
40 Nikita S. Khrushchev, conversation with John F. Kennedy, 3 June 1961, *Foreign Relations of the United States, 1961–1963*, Washington, DC, United States Government Printing Office, 1998, vol. V. *Soviet Union*, doc. 84.
41 Geoffrey T. Hellman, "Hammer and Khrushchev," *The New Yorker*, 1 December 1962, 52–53; Armand Hammer, with Neil Lyndon, *Hammer* (New York: G.P. Putnam's Sons, 1987), 320.
42 "Mikoyan Goes Shopping," *Washington Post*, 9 January 1959.
43 On Mikoyan's visit, see *Amerika*, no. 34, 1959; Norman K. Winston, "Six Things Mikoyan Envied Most in America," *This Week Magazine*, 29 March 1959. See also the very funny note from the French ambassador, Hervé Alphand to Maurice Couve de Murville, French foreign minister, 23 January 1959, La Courneuve, Archives du Ministère des Affaires étrangères, B 0000493, 1.

Aleksei A. Kokorekin, "Let's Catch Up with America regarding meat, milk, and butter production per capita".
Poster, 1957. Lithographic print on paper, 55.5 × 84 cm. Alamy.

Nikita S. Khrushchev and IBM Chairman Thomas J. Watson, Jr. visit the cafeteria of the IBM factory, San José, California,
22 September 1959. Photograph by Carl Mydans/The LIFE Picture Collection via Getty Images.

around, Khrushchev sometimes feigned indifference, declaring about the Empire State Building: "If you have seen one skyscraper, you have seen them all." He did, however, write in his memoirs, that Ilf and Petrov's descriptions of skyscrapers were perfectly accurate[44]. Khrushchev met the union organizer Walter Reuther, a former worker from the Gorky Automobile Plant, who shared with him his memories from the USSR, and visited Roswell Garst's farm in Iowa, marvelling at the size of the corn cobs[45]. To his chagrin, Khrushchev was not able to visit the Walt Disney studios—as Sergei Eisenstein and Boris Shumiatskii had done before him—because the Los Angeles chief of police, William Parker, refused to provide him with protection. Certain moments of Khrushchev's trip were significant, such as his visit to the IBM factory in San José, California, where he was surprisingly more interested in the cafeteria than in the computers manufactured by the firm[46].

1959: An American Exhibition in Moscow

While Khrushchev was visiting the United States, preparations for the American National Exhibition, which was to open in Moscow in June 1959, were in full swing. Major post-war exhibits became the new battleground for the competition between the Soviets and the Americans. The juxtaposition of their pavilions was reminiscent of the face-off between Albert Speer and Boris Iofan's buildings in Paris, in 1937. At the 1958 Brussels World's Fair, positioned side by side Edward Durell Stone's rotunda and the parallelepiped designed by the Russians Aleksandr Boretskii, Iurii Abramov, Viktor Dubov, and Anatolii Polianskii, offered significantly different visions: daily life for the former and spatial technology (among other types) for the latter[47]. This signalled a notable reversal, with the USSR embodying scientific and technical progress related to the launch of the first Sputniks, while the United States displayed all the registers of consumerism and prosperity.

The political confrontation of the Cold War was channelled in this clash between science and consumerism, which the sociologist David Riesman dubbed in 1951 the Nylon War, noting that the arms race was juxtaposed with the nylon stocking craze[48]. The American Pavilion in Brussels can be viewed as the dress rehearsal for the 1959 American National Exhibition, an unprecedented endeavour spearheaded by the USIA and its architect Jack Masey.

44 Sergei N. Khrushchev, *Memoirs of Nikita Khrushchev: vol. 3, Reformer, 1945–1964* (University Park: Pennsylvania State University, 2004), 132.

45 Harold Lee, *Roswell Garst: A Biography* (Ames: Iowa State University Press, 1984). See also Roswell Garst, *Remarques d'un fermier américain à propos du développement de l'agriculture en Union soviétique et aux États-Unis* (Paris: Centre culturel de l'association France–URSS, 1964). These speeches are reprinted in *Khrushchev in America* (New York: Crosscurrents Press, 1960). On the trip as a whole, see Peter Carlson, *K Blows Top: A Cold War Comic Interlude, Starring Nikita Khrushchev, America's Most Unlikely Tourist* (New York: Public Affairs, 2010); Gary John Tocchet, "September Thaw: Khrushchev's Visit to America, 1959," PhD dissertation (Stanford University, 1995).

46 This is what his son Sergei N. Khrushchev reports in *Nikita Khrushchev and the Creation of a Superpower* (University Park: Pennsylvania State University Press, 2001), 334. The account presented at the time to the Soviets was *Litsom k litsu s Amerikoi: rasskaz o poezde N.S. Khrushcheva v SShA* (Moscow: Gospolitizdat, 1960); in English: *Face to Face with America: The Story of the Trip of N.S. Khrushchev to the USA* (Moscow: Foreign Languages Publishing House, 1960).

47 Susan E. Reid, "The Soviet Pavilion at Expo '58," in *A History of Russian Exposition and Festival Architecture, 1700–2014*, Alla Aronova and Alexander Ortenberg, eds. (London: Routledge 2018), 203–26. See also Rika Devos, "'Let Us Now Invest in Peace': Architecture at Expo 58 in Resonance of War," in *Architecture of Great Expositions 1937–1959: Messages of Peace, Images of War*, Rika Devos, Alexander Ortenberg, and Vladimir Paperny, eds. (London: Routledge, 2015), 133–59.

48 David Riesman, "The Nylon War," *ETC: A Review of General Semantics* 8, no. 3 (Spring 1951): 163–70.

This event stemmed from the agreement on cultural, technical, and educational exchanges signed on 27 January 1958 by the ambassadors Georgii Zarubin and William S. B. Lacy, which reaffirmed "the usefulness of exhibits as an effective means of developing mutual understanding between the peoples of the Soviet Union and the United States."[49] The initial project for two parallel exhibitions on nuclear energy was abandoned in September 1958 in favour of a symmetrical organization, wherein an American exhibit, to be held in Moscow in the summer of 1959, would be mirrored by a Soviet display at the New York Coliseum. The terms of the contract were established in November 1958, with the Russians allowing the USIA to build a set of structures designed and assembled in the West, which were to be acquired subsequently by them[50]. After considering a lot in Gorky Park, land was selected in Sokolniki, north of the capital, and the design began at a frenetic pace to allow the general Soviet public to discover the American civilization for the first time[51].

This significant event can be seen as a continuation of the Cold War, particularly because communications between Khrushchev and Vice President Nixon were captured by microphones and television cameras in a vast, uncensored spectacle. American landscapes and daily life in the United States, until then known only to experts and the odd traveller, were brought to the attention of a widely larger audience. The land, cities, and architecture were displayed throughout the exhibition, whose pavilions themselves served to model American culture. The organizers' intentions were clear: "The U.S. government should utilize to the fullest extent this opportunity to implement approved national policy with respect to the USSR (i.e., to stimulate evolutionary

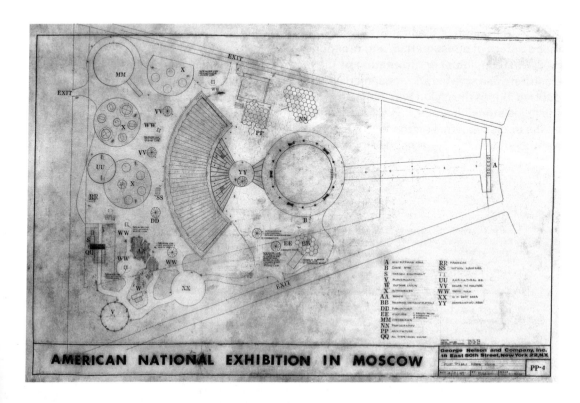

George Nelson. American National Exhibition, Moscow, 1959. General plan.
Heliographic print on paper, 19.6 × 24.4 cm. Vitra Design Stiftung GmbH.

processes which will reduce the aggressive nature of the Soviet Union). We can do this most effectively by contributing to the ferment in Soviet society, particularly among the intelligentsia, rooted in dissatisfaction with Soviet life and methods, and a deep desire for greater freedom of action, well-being, and security."[52] The aim was to embody the watchword of "People's capitalism" coined by the advertisor T. S. Repplier, an adviser to Eisenhower, to "brand" the American system[53].

Specific groups were targeted as such: "The exhibit is certain to attract particular interest among middle and upper bureaucrats including factory managers, intelligentsia in the arts and sciences (including students and teachers), youth, party officials, military personnel, and skilled workers. These groups include the relatively more politically alert and potentially more influential Soviet citizens."[54] According to the government, this "extraordinary opportunity" had to be seized to put together "a propaganda exhibit, not a trade fair."[55] The experts consulted in preparation of the event recommended the creation of innovative buildings. According to Leo Grullow, the former head of the American War Relief in Russia, "Official Soviet architecture ha[d] just taken a lambasting from the government as being wasteful, over-ornate. They will be interested in our use of new materials—steel, aluminum, glass— and more economical use of men, materials and time."[56]

Placed under the supervision of Harold McClelland—a businessman, former deputy secretary of Commerce and the president of the National Association of Manufacturers, whose connections allowed him to enlist the commercial elite—, the designer George Nelson was recruited to develop both the programme for each section and its spatial envelopes. He later recalled his initial idea: "Let us have somewhere in this show a kind of information machine. A place where the Russians can go if they want any information and can get all the poop about the U.S."[57] At two ends of a triangular four-hectare site, he placed two geodesic domes based on the designs of Buckminster Fuller. A semicircular "glass pavilion," created by Welton Becket's Los Angeles firm, stood between them. Nelson sought out the assistance of Eero Saarinen, and later that of Frei Otto, for the sections of the exhibit exceeding the main buildings, but in the end, he had to improvise fibreglass modular sunshades whose transparent roofs sheltered independent displays[58].

49   "Text of the Joint Communique of U.S. and Soviet Union on Cultural Exchanges," *The New York Times*, 28 January 1958.

50   Jack Masey and Conway Lloyd Morgan, *Cold War Confrontations: US Exhibitions and Their Role in the Cultural Cold War, 1950–1980* (Baden: Lars Müller, 2008), 154–58.

51   On the overall configuration of the exhibit, see Castillo, *Cold War on the Home Front*, 139–70; Jochen Eisenbrand, *George Nelson – ein Designer im kalten Krieg: Ausstellungen für die United States Information Agency 1957–1972* (Zurich; Park Books, 2014), 243–49; Masey and Morgan, *Cold War Confrontations*, 162–245. On the politico-cultural project, see Aucoin, "Deconstructing the American Way of Life," 89–135.

52   "Gorky Park Exhibit, Basic Considerations and Approach," n.d. [Fall 1958], 1. NARA, Record Group 230, box 2/2.

53   "People's Capitalism: This *is* Amerika," *Collier's*, 6 January 1955, 74. See also Hixson, *Parting the Curtain*, 133–42.

54   "Gorky Park Exhibit, Basic Considerations and Approach," Appendix 1.

55   Ibid., 2.

56   Conversation with Leo Grullow [former head of American War Relief in Russia], 6 January 1959, Charles and Ray Eames Archives, Library of Congress, box II:130, file 7.

57   George Nelson, in Charles Eames and George Nelson, "What happens when one nation tells its story to another nation," public conversation in front of the Southern California Chapter of the American Institute of Architects, Los Angeles, 10 November 1959, 4, Vitra Design Museum, Nelson Papers, 10414.

58   Eisenbrand, *George Nelson*, 250, 322–24.

Around these structures, Robert Zion and Harold Breen's firm designed land-scaped areas, while remaining mindful of the existing birch tree plantations and without dictating a specific itinerary to the visitors[59]. Each building showed different aspects of American society, in what Nelson called a "baby world's fair."[60] The smallest dome hosted a projection of *A Tour of the West*, a film displayed in 360-degree circle on 11 screens, in a replica of the Circarama inaugurated in 1955 in Disneyland's Tomorrowland. Though it opened the audience to previously unseen images—except for the rare pictures that had made their way into the USSR—, *A Tour of the West* failed to impress the Soviets from a technical standpoint, as on 25 April of the previous year, they had inaugurated their own circular 22-screen cinema, called the Krugorama, at the VDNKh – the Exposition of the Achievements of the National Economy. Similarly, the glass pavilion, with its light structure and its pleated roof reminiscent of an airport terminal, was far from a novelty to Soviet architects. The main interest it presented was the fact that it housed an unprecedented installation, the Jungle Gym, a three-dimensional structure designed by Nelson where hundreds of everyday items were loosely displayed.

Nelson was constantly railing against Welton Becket's untimely decisions, calling on Masey to try to rally him to his cause, but in the end, he achieved his goal[61]. This open maze "jammed with stuff," as Nelson described it, spread its cubic units (3 metres per side, stacked on two levels) across 5,000 square metres and right up to the curved walls of the space, forming a free-range circuit where the visitors were invited to roam, as though swinging from branch to branch in Tarzan's forest. The Jungle Gym's cubes were inspired by the modular *Storagewall* units created by Nelson in 1945 and were designed by Richard Barringer. The structural elements, made of extruded aluminum, akin to those used in 1956 for the OMNI wall system, were built with the help of industrialists from the field. Twenty thousand linear metres of aluminum profile were manufactured in Italy[62]. Inside the labyrinth, speckled with a few patios, products selected among those advertised by the *Industrial Design* journal were displayed. Provided by over 700 manufacturers, the items were duly labelled to demonstrate their availability to American families. An exhibit on schools was featured, as well as a fully furnished "young New York designer's" apartment, complete with Herman Miller and Knoll furniture and a Westinghouse kitchen by Lucia DeRespinis. The domestic marvels foreseen for a near future were mostly displayed in the "miracle kitchen" sponsored by RCA and Whirlpool, also implemented within the Jungle Gym and in the General Electric unit.

59   Robert Zion, Harold Breen, "American Landscape Architecture in Moscow (American National Exhibition),"
        13 March 1959, NARA, Record Group 230, box 2/2.
60   George Nelson, in Eames and Nelson, "What happens when one nation tells its story to another nation," 10.
61   George Nelson, note to Jack Masey, 3 December 1958, Vitra Design Museum, Nelson Papers, MAR-00629.
62   Eisenbrand, *George Nelson*, 252–55. On the structure, see "Designing the Moscow Exhibit," *Architectural Record* 126, no. 5 (November 1959): 169–76.
63   "Be Kind to Americans," *Time*, 18 May 1959, 20. Fuller mentions the order in "Continuous Man" [1960], in James Meller, *The Buckminster Fuller Reader* (London: Jonathan Cape, 1970), 335–36.
64   Peter Blake, "Research & script for the eight exhibits to be located in dome area: American National Exhibition in Moscow," NARA, Record Group 40, box 11.
65   Jack Masey, Note to George Nelson, 31 December 1958, Vitra Design Museum, Nelson Papers, MAR-10970.
66   Eisenbrand, *George Nelson*, 322–30. See "Plastic Parasols for Moscow," *Architectural Record* 126, no. 5 (November 1959): 238–41.
67   "American Architectural Display Set for US–Moscow Exhibition," 5 May 1959, 1, NARA, Record Group 230, box 4. Aline R. Saarinen welcomes it: "Moscow Plans Expand: American Art for Exhibition Includes Photography and Architecture," *The New York Times*, 8 March 1959.

The 200-foot (61-metre) golden metal dome developed by Donald L. Richter based on Fuller's principle, whose building plans were signed by Becket, was manufactured by the Kaiser Aluminum and Chemical Corproration. It enchanted Khrushchev, who pocketed a bolt during his visit of the construction site[63]. Inside, Nelson installed an exhibit focused on science, the only glimpse offered to the visitors of the major issues in the fields of knowledge and technology. The architect and publicist Peter Blake developed the initial script for this presentation, which was placed on the edges of the circle, forming a "donut" shape, in Nelson's eyes, or a "bagel," according to Eames. In its initial version, the exhibit covered eight domains: the exploration of space, labour and education, agriculture, public health and medicine, nuclear energy, chemical research and fundamental research in the United States[64]. In its final version, organized by Nelson, sections were added on transportation and urban planning, illustrated with a scale model of Philadelphia, then seen as the city of the future[65].

This rather limited and reticent presentation—both in content and in form—of science and technology was set alongside several other thematic sections arranged throughout the premises. Automobiles and recreational craft were strewn across the park, where sat a fully furnished ranch-style suburban house designed by Stanley H. Klein for Long Island-based firm, All States Properties with furniture provided by Macy's and a General Electric kitchen. A pathway was laid between both parts of the house, making it easier to visit, which led the American press to dub it Splitnik, in a playful reference to the space race. The plastic sunshades, designed by the MIT engineer Albert Dietz to shelter the visitors from the rain, had been thoroughly tested on a military airfield, where they were exposed to the blast of a B-25 propeller[66]. Arranged in three clusters, they housed an updated version of the momentous *Family of Man* exhibit curated in 1955 by Edward Steichen at the MoMA; a contemporary art exhibition, which sparked outrage among the Russians, developed by Mildred Constantine, curator at the same museum; as well as a fashion exhibit designed by Eleanor Lambert.

Nelson also commissioned an exhibit from Peter Blake, his former collaborator at *Architectural Forum*, who curated it with his associate Julian Neski, and which seemed seemed rather peripheral, despite the 1,000 square metres it occupied. It was nevertheless a significant milestone in the Soviet reception of American post-war production, being the first to target a non-expert audience. Based on *Amerika Baut*, which Blake had created for the USIA at the Interbau in Berlin in 1957, it presented life-sized reproductions of façade fragments. The installation brought together a hundred black-and-white, 12-foot-tall photographs (3,5 metres), giant slides, scale models, and stereoscopes, showing three-dimensional views of the buildings. A dark vestibule showed a panoramic view of New York as seen from a skyscraper, against a soundscape of street noise. The idea was to "give Soviet visitors the impression of actually walking into and through the buildings, rather than the feeling of merely looking at photographs."[67] The installation was based on the dichotomy between the city, showcased on straight walls, and the suburbs and countryside, displayed on curved ones. Though emphasis was meant to be made on "facts and figures" surrounding the mass production of housing, no individual houses were shown. Exceptional structures were given the lion's share, from Frank Lloyd Wright's Johnson Wax Headquarters to Wallace Harrison's United Nations, as well as Lever House, displayed as a scale model, and the Seagram Building. SOM's Connecticut General Life Insurance Building and several other buildings created by the firm were exposed along with Louis I. Kahn's Yale University Art

Photographer unknown. American National Exhibition, Moscow, 1959.

Top: Russian workers in front of George Nelson's Jungle Gym model. Gelatin silver print on paper, 20.3 × 25.8 cm. Vitra Design Stiftung GmbH
Bottom: Visitors inside George Nelson's Jungle Gym. Gelatin silver print on paper, 25.5 × 20.7 cm. Vitra Design Stiftung GmbH.

Photographer unknown. American National Exhibition, Moscow, 1959.
George Nelson photographs his plastic umbrellas. Gelatin silver print on paper, 6 × 6 cm. Vitra Design Stiftung GmbH.

Photographer unknown. R. Buckminster Fuller standing in front of one of the geodesic domes at the American National Exhibition, Moscow, 1959. Stanford University Libraries, Department of Special Collections, M1090, Series 13, box 16, folder 36.

Peter Blake and Julian Neski. American National Exhibition, Moscow, 1959. Architecture exhibition. General plan.
Graphite and coloured ink on tracing paper, 50 × 65 cm. Avery Architectural and Fine Arts Library, Peter Blake Papers, roll A084.09.

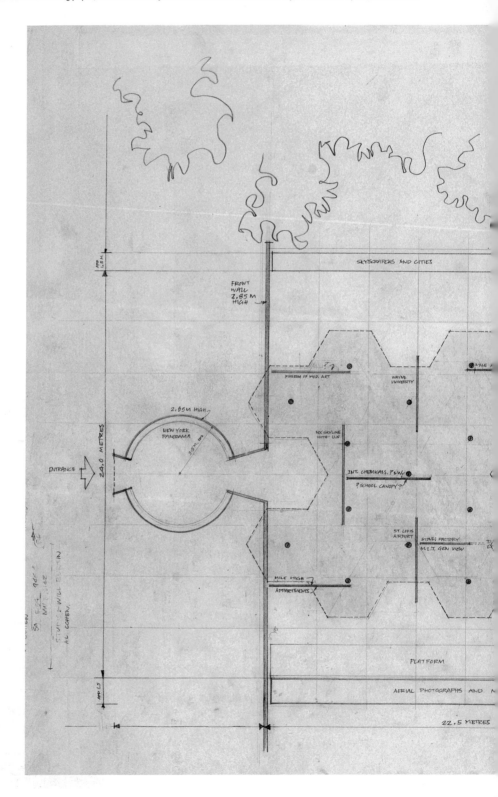

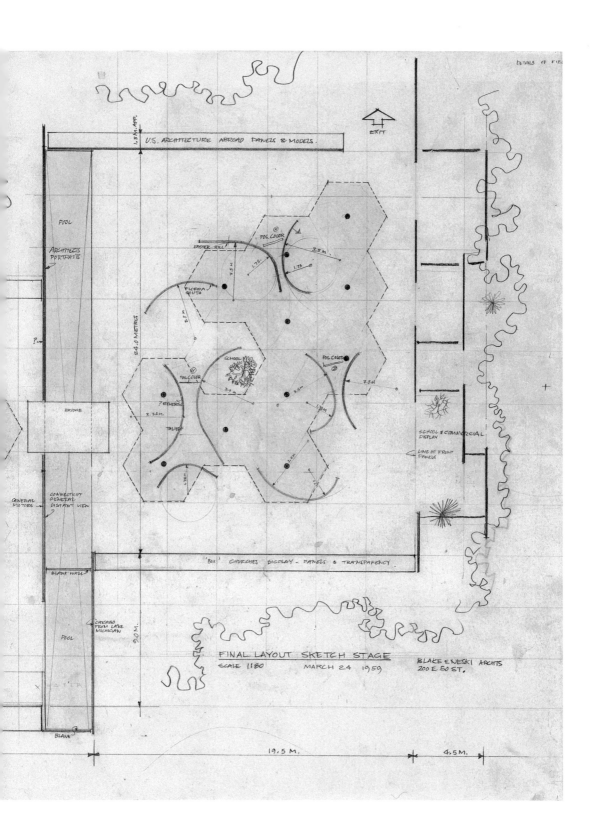

U.S. ARCHITECTURE ABROAD PANELS & MODELS

EXIT

POOL

ARCHITECTS
PORTRAITS

1.5 M. APP.

EASTER HILL

POS. COLOR

3.5 M.

1.75.

1.75

FLORIDA
SOUTH

24.0 METRES

SCHOOL

POS. COLOR

POS. COLOR

7.5 M.

3.5 M.

1.75 M.

BRIDGE

R. 3.5 M.

TALIESIN

? REVERSE

3.5 M.

GENERAL
MOTORS

CONNECTICUT
GENERAL
DISTANT VIEW

SCHOOL & COMMERCIAL
DISPLAY

LINE OF FRONT
PANELS

BLANK WALL

POOL

'BOX' CHURCHES DISPLAY - PANELS & TRANSPARENCY

CHICAGO
FROM LAKE
MICHIGAN

9.0 M.

BLANK

FINAL LAYOUT SKETCH STAGE
SCALE 1:80   MARCH 24 1959

BLAKE & NESKI ARCHTS
200 E 50 ST.

19.5 M.

4.5 M.

DETAILS OF FIE...

Peter Blake and Julian Neski. American National Exhibition, Moscow, 1959. Architecture exhibition. Model view.
National Archives and Records Administration, NARA 59-10673.

Photographer unknown. American National Exhibition, Moscow, 1959. Pastry demonstration,
Gelatin silver print on paper, 20.7 × 25.5 cm. Vitra Design Stiftung GmbH.

Gallery and Eero Saarinen's MIT chapel. Blake's exhibit showed mostly educational and religious buildings, such as Philip Johnson's synagogue in Portchester, as housing was extensively represented everywhere else in Sokolniki[68].

Far from being a passive display to be explored by the wandering public, the exhibit offered several activities. Rigorously trained Russian-speaking guides greeted the visitors, some of whom gave them written messages intended for the organizers. Both men and women were fascinated with the fashion shows, while mostly female visitors marvelled at Ann Anderson's cooking demonstrations in the Miracle Kitchen and those presented in the General Electric kitchen by Barbara Sampson, an executive at General Foods, using processed foods and a microwave oven. Pepsi-Cola was distributed for free at a kiosk in cardboard cups, which were quickly stashed away as souvenirs along with publications offered for consultation to the public: 8,000 of the 15,000 displayed documents were gone as of the first day[69]. The organizers subtly encouraged these appropriations throughout the exhibition. Nelson recalled that "[t]he eagerness with which these people came and felt things, tried to operate them, stole them, broke them, etc., was something the likes of which we had never seen."[70]

As soon as he was selected for the project, Nelson started regularly exchanging letters with Charles Eames to develop his general vision for the exhibit. They spent four days in Pacific Palisades in December 1958 with filmmaker Billy Wilder—a close friend of Eames's—, considering the possibility of making a film that would summarize the American civilization, to be presented under Fuller's large dome. Nelson recalled that Washington officials "kept saying that there ought to be a real impressive thing in that dome. Movies? You know Khrushchev has seen movies. He knows all about them. We've got to show him something real great, so that when he walks into the dome, that Panama hat he wears will fall right off."[71]

Following lively discussions with Hollywood representatives, Eames pitched the idea of a slide presentation projected on several screens, arranged according to an orthogonal and diagonal principle similar to tic-tac-toe. After toying with the titles "Glimpse of the USA" and "A Glimpse of America,"[72] "Glimpses of the USA" was finally chosen for this timed sound installation, presented simultaneously to 5,000 people located inside the donut/bagel. Charles Eames opposed the approach behind *Glimpses* to that of the Circarama, its counterpart, as he explained to the critic Henry Hart of *Films in Review*: "Our objective was to, in twelve minutes, give the Russian viewers the broadest background of credibility against which to view the rest of the Moscow exhibition. The coverage is broad—the land, the people, the weekday,

68   "Architectural Exhibit at Moscow Fair: Blake and Neski Conjure Convincing Illusions of the American Scene," *Interiors* 119, no. 3 (October 1959): 16. "Moscow Looks at US Architecture," *Architectural Forum* 111, no. 3 (September 1959): 110–12.
69   Max Frankel, "Pravda Reports Flaws in US Fair," *The New York Times*, 27 July 1959.
70   George Nelson, in Eames and Nelson, "What happens when one nation tells its story to another nation," 12.
71   Ibid., 5–6. A summary of the origins of the exhibit's features can be found in Stanley Abercrombie, *George Nelson: The Design of Modern Design* (Cambrige, MA: MIT Press, 1999), 159–76.
72   Charles Eames, Handwritten note, n.d., Charles and Ray Eames Archives, LOC, box II:135, file 15.
73   Charles Eames, letter to Henry Hart, *Films in Review*, 19 June 1959, Charles & Ray Eames Archives, LOC, box II:135, file 7.
74   Charles Eames, in Eames and Nelson, "What happens when one nation tells its story to another nation," 14.
75   Eric Schuldenfrei, *The Films of Charles and Ray Eames: A Universal Sense of Expectation* (London: Routledge, 2016), 50–96.
76   Max Frankel, "Image of America at Issue in Soviet: Russians Get Varying Views from Films at US Fair and Moscow Theatres," *The New York Times*, 23 August 1959.

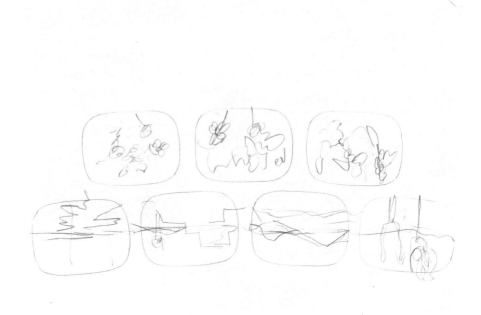

the weekend." Rather than to show details of a "few things," they wished to show "many things" using "multiple, but related" images that were always shown "horizontally and vertically."[73] He noted that "the idea was to show that ours is not a static culture but a culture in development, that we had not arrived where we were going and that we were not satisfied nor ever had intended to be satisfied with where we were."[74]

Before his final installation involving seven synchronized Technicolor films, Eames made several attempts with up to nine screens. He decided to show both urban and rural spaces and their uses at various moments of the day or the week, seeking out what he deemed "usual," as opposed to the images provided by the media, which he also intended to use. Echoing *Berlin, Symphonie einer Großstadt,* filmed in 1927 by Walther Ruttmann, and Dziga Vertov's contemporary pictures, the montage accounted for the passage of time as well as of space[75]. With quick-paced editing, he contrasted the macrocosm of natural and artificial landscapes to the microcosm of dwellings and rituals surrounding family life, in an idyllic portrayal of an America inhabited only by a wealthy middle class. In a montage whose swiftness was noted in the press, the condensation effect characteristic of dream work was once again apparent: "Perhaps fifty clover-leaf highway intersections are shown in just a few seconds. So are dozens of housing projects, bridges, skyscrapers scenes, supermarkets, universities, museums, theatres, churches, farms, laboratories and much more."[76] The dream then became a fantasy with photograms of Marilyn Monroe in scenes from *Some Like It Hot,* recently shot by Billy Wilder.

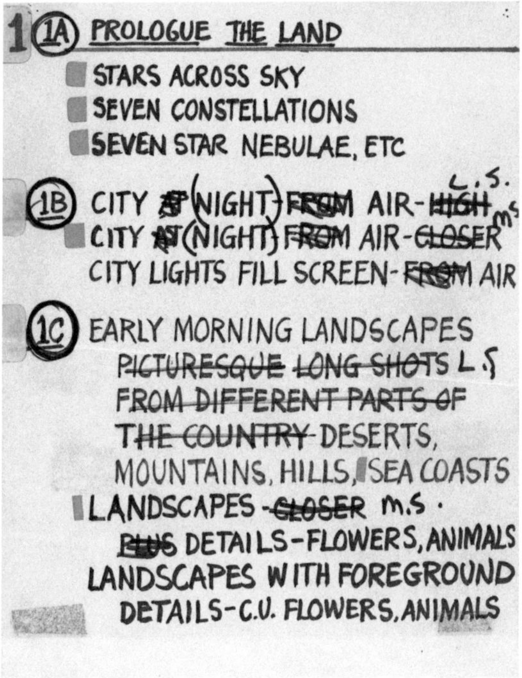

1 (1A) PROLOGUE THE LAND

- STARS ACROSS SKY
- SEVEN CONSTELLATIONS
- SEVEN STAR NEBULAE, ETC

(1B) CITY ~~IS~~ (NIGHT) ~~FROM~~ AIR-~~HIGH~~ L.S.
CITY ~~AT~~ (NIGHT) ~~FROM~~ AIR-~~CLOSER~~ M.S.
CITY LIGHTS FILL SCREEN-~~FROM~~ AIR

(1C) EARLY MORNING LANDSCAPES
PICTURESQUE ~~LONG SHOTS~~ L.S
FROM ~~DIFFERENT PARTS OF~~
~~THE COUNTRY~~ DESERTS,
MOUNTAINS, HILLS, SEA COASTS
LANDSCAPES -~~CLOSER~~ M.S.
~~PLUS~~ DETAILS-FLOWERS, ANIMALS
LANDSCAPES WITH FOREGROUND
DETAILS-C.U. FLOWERS, ANIMALS

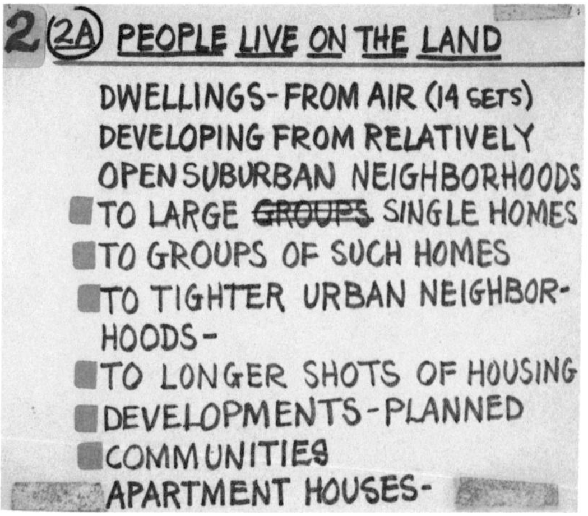

2 (2A) PEOPLE LIVE ON THE LAND

DWELLINGS-FROM AIR (14 SETS)
DEVELOPING FROM RELATIVELY
OPEN SUBURBAN NEIGHBORHOODS
- TO LARGE ~~GROUPS~~ SINGLE HOMES
- TO GROUPS OF SUCH HOMES
- TO TIGHTER URBAN NEIGHBOR-
  HOODS-
- TO LONGER SHOTS OF HOUSING
- DEVELOPMENTS-PLANNED
- COMMUNITIES
- APARTMENT HOUSES-

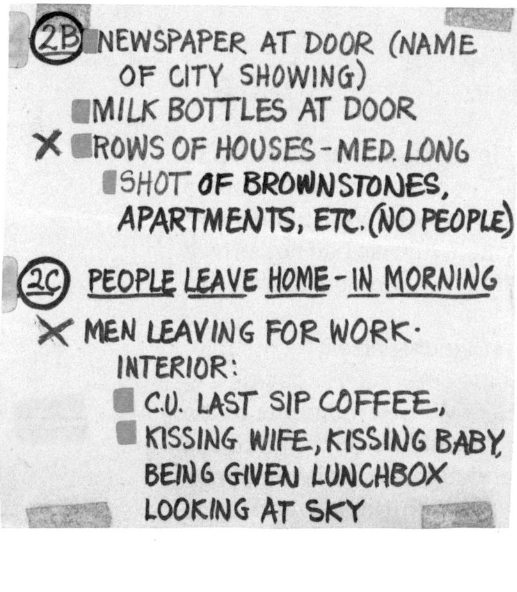

(2B) NEWSPAPER AT DOOR (NAME
OF CITY SHOWING)
- MILK BOTTLES AT DOOR
X - ROWS OF HOUSES-MED. LONG
- SHOT OF BROWNSTONES,
APARTMENTS, ETC. (NO PEOPLE)

(2C) PEOPLE LEAVE HOME-IN MORNING
X MEN LEAVING FOR WORK.
INTERIOR:
- C.U. LAST SIP COFFEE,
- KISSING WIFE, KISSING BABY,
BEING GIVEN LUNCHBOX
LOOKING AT SKY

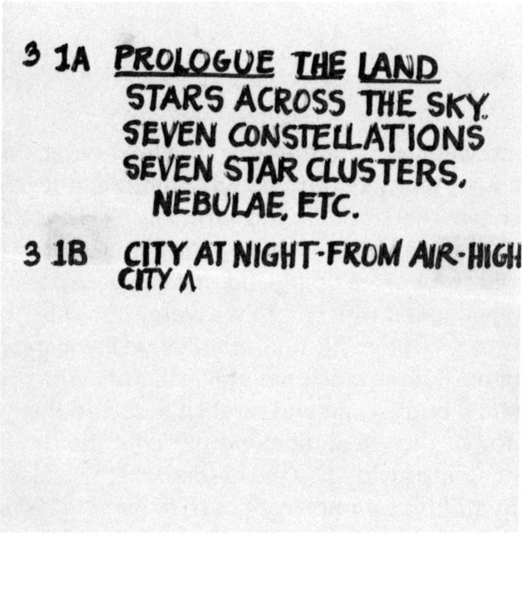

3 1A **PROLOGUE THE LAND**
STARS ACROSS THE SKY.
SEVEN CONSTELLATIONS
SEVEN STAR CLUSTERS,
NEBULAE, ETC.

3 1B CITY AT NIGHT-FROM AIR-HIGH
CITY ∧

Charles and Ray Eames Audiovisual presentation *Glimpses of the USA,* American National Exhibition, Moscow, 1959. Template for the screens. Ink on cardboard. 26.5 × 37.5 cm. Library of Congress, Manuscript Division, Charles and Ray Eames Collection, II:135, OV 26, Folder 1.

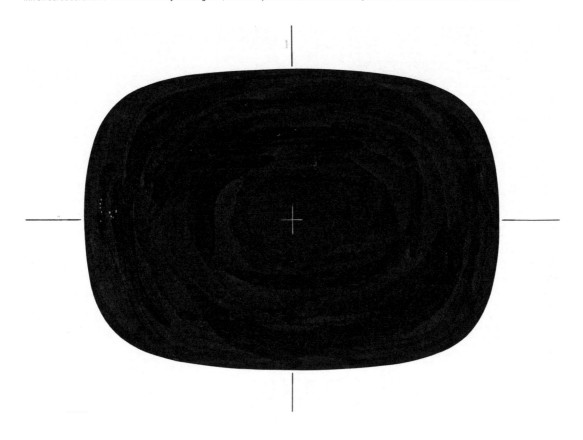

Charles and Ray Eames. Audiovisual presentation *Glimpses of the USA*, American National Exhibition, Moscow, 1959.
View of the seven screens installed in the dome. Gelatin silver print on paper, 22 × 27,5 cm. Library of Congress, Manuscript Division,
Charles and Ray Eames Collection, Box II: OV 26, Folder 1.

485

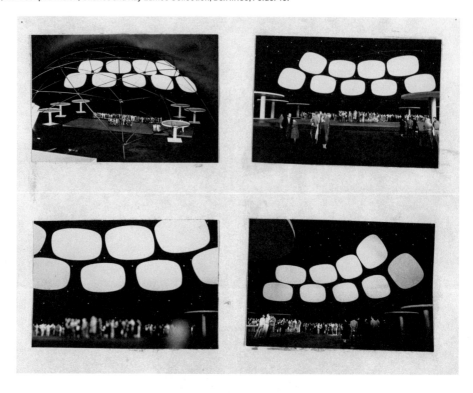

According to Eames, the accumulation of comparable images made the message particularly convincing, as he later explained: "The role of seven screen films was not necessarily one to build up dramatically where we were but rather to give credibility to the show that George was really putting on with all these other elements of accomplishment. We tried to figure out what we could do to make this story really believable. For example, in the area of overpasses and superhighways, we could imagine having either a film that showed the development of an overpass or a magnificent photograph of an overpass. If you showed this to a Russian he might say, 'well, you know, we are planning one in Smolensk and we are going to have two in Minsk. We will have three and you have only one' [77]".

Eames chose half of the 2,200 photographs to be used from his personal collection, as well as among the works of photographers such as Julius Shulman, Ezra Stoller, and Elliott Erwitt, and in magazines like *Life*, *Look*, or *Time*. To set the films to music, he commissioned a score from Elmer Bernstein, Hollywood's star composer. The spatial configuration of the projection was significant. The seven screens, measuring 20 by 30 feet (6 by 9 metres), with their rounded angles likening them to aircraft or train windows, were reminiscent, in their juxtaposition, of the situation rooms created during the war for American army commanders. This resemblance was all the more meaningful considering that Fuller's domes were initially used in the military. With their tiers parallel to the curved bottom part of the structure, they also produced a wraparound effect, loosely inspired by the construction Herbert Bayer imagined for the Deutscher Werkbund exhibit in Paris, in 1930[78]. Fuller himself expressed his admiration for the structure: "The thing was so moving

486

in [the] orchestration of forms and colours and sounds that I thought it was incredible to me that anyone could have been master enough of those frames to make this whole thing really work together like orchestra instruments."[79] Indeed, the screening ended in a manner of jazz concert, surpassing the audience's unspoken expectations. According to the filmmaker Julian Blaustein, a mesmerized Khrushchev went as far as to tell Eames: "I want you to do the same thing for us that you just did for the United States."[80]

Mutual Impressions of the Exhibition

The American National Exhibition was met with resounding and suprising success. While 250,000 visitors were expected from 25 June to 4 September, 2.7 million people rushed to the event. Ticket distribution was initially very restrictive, as it was closely monitored by the party, the Komsomol, and mass organizations, but loosened during the exhibition, likely after it was announced that Khrushchev and Eisenhower would travel to each other's country. While the Russians witnessed an America embodied by objects and framed by screens, Americans were able to delve into the Soviet public opinion. The Moscow exhibit, directed at a specific social group, contained a mechanism developed to capture and interpret visitor reactions[81]. Its most traditional components were the many thoroughly trained guides and presenters who offered detailed reports of any exchanges with visitors. Additionally, diplomats from the American embassy scoured the press and sent a weekly digest to Washington. The true novelty was the IBM 305 RAMAC computer installed under the Kaiser Dome to answer questions that could be chosen from a list of no less than 3,500 enquiries[82]. These questions were then analyzed to gain a relatively precise understanding of the Soviets' main themes of interest. Visitors were also invited to vote for their favourite attraction, in a mock display of direct democracy.

Through these operations, the USIA managed to conduct the first opinion poll ever to be led by a Western power in the USSR. As of September 1959, a thick volume documented visitor reactions, namely the comments left in guest books[83]. The psychologist Ralph K. White, head of the USIA's Communist Analysis Division, issued a summary of the 15,000 votes and the 2,000 remarks gathered in the crowd. Both these measures showed the same results: 85% of the votes and 65% of the comments were in favour of the

77   Charles Eames, in Eames and Nelson, "What happens when one nation tells its story to another nation," 14–15.
78   Beatriz Colomina, "Enclosed by Images: The Eameses' Multimedia Architecture," *Grey Room* 2, no. 2 (Winter 2001): 5–29.
79   R. Buckminster Fuller, in *Eames Celebration: Several Worlds of Charles and Ray Eames*, film directed by Perry Adato, 1977; quoted in Schuldenfrei, *The Films of Charles and Ray Eames*, 72.
80   Julian Blaustein, interview with Eames Demetrios in *Eames Visual Oral History*, video-disk 1, n.d., quoted in Schuldenfrei, *The Films of Charles and Ray Eames*, 89.
81   Susan E. Reid, "Who Will Beat Whom? Soviet Popular Reception of the American Exhibition in Moscow, 1959," *Kritika: Explorations in Russian and Eurasian History* 9, no. 4 (2008): 855–904; also in Györgi Péteri, ed., *Imagining the West in Eastern Europe and the Soviet Union* (Pittsburgh: University of Pittsburgh Press, 2010), 194–236. See also Laura A. Belmonte, *Selling the American Way: U.S. Propaganda and the Cold War* (Philadelphia: University of Pennsylvania Press, 2008), 87–93.
82   On this computer and its very political use, see Evangelos Kotsioris, "Electronic 'Ambassador': The Diplomatic Missions of IBM's RAMAC 305," in *International Communities of Invention and Innovation*, Arthur Tatnall and Christopher Leslie, eds. (Cham: Springer, 2016), 165–80.
83   USIA, Office of Research Analysis, "Report on American Exhibition in Moscow: Visitors Reactions to the American Exhibit in Moscow: A Preliminary Report," Washington, DC, USIA, 28 September 1959, NARA, Record Group 306, box 7.

exhibition, with the four most popular sections being *The Family of Man*, automobiles, colour television, and the Circarama[84]. Among the least popular were the architecture exhibit—because of its static images—and the art exhibition, which sparked the liveliest commentary. A visitor declared that "[i]t is necessary to forget the national dignity of one's people, of one's country, to be able to exhibit this filthy and revolting abstract art."[85] This sentiment also prevailed in the angry press coverage of the art exhibit[86]. As for housing, the most popular showing of household appliances initially obtained 26% of the votes, while the Splitnik got 22%[87]. Some visitors cracked jokes about the lack of bookcases in the homes, while another pitied the "poor little house," criticized for being "too expensive" and "not typical of American conditions."[88] These reactions invalidated *Time* magazine's claim that "watching the thousands of colourful glimpses of the U.S. and its people, the Russians were entranced, and the slides are the smash hit of the fair."[89] Many of the comments, which came in part from duly delegated party supporters, criticized the emphasis on consumer goods in this "transplanted slice of the American way of life," as well as the lack of scientific and technical information[90].

In a letter to *Izvestia*, the writer Marietta Shaginian, who had imagined the adventure-filled America of *Mess Mend*, criticized the "Miracle Kitchen," in a discourse completely at odds with Khrushchev's praise: "The countless domestic conveniences of the Americans [...] anchor the woman in perpetuity to her mission as 'housewife,' wife and cook. They make this role easier for her, but the very process of alleviating individual housework as it were eternalizes this way of life, turning it into a profession for the woman." She claimed to prefer "innovations that actually emancipate women," such as collective kitchens and laundromats, echoing the communal housing of the 1920s[91]. The press was generally critical of the exhibit, though the reporters' zeal dwindled as the weeks went by. The usual attacks against the "American way of life" continued, namely from *Krokodil*, whose June issue associated the American National Exhibition with the pervasive violence in children's literature[92]. The Central Committee of the Party issued guidelines to newspaper editors, informing them that the exhibit was to be described "in a calm and controlled tone, without any kind of display of interest toward the exhibition as a whole or any part of it."[93]

84   Ralph K. White, "Soviet Reactions to Our Moscow Exhibit: Voting Machines and Comment Books," *The Public Opinion Quarterly* 23, no. 4 (Winter 1959–1960): 462–63; Walter L. Hixson, *Parting the Curtain*, 185–213.

85   USIA, "Report on American Exhibition in Moscow," 27; "Sovremennoe iskusstvo SShA na vystavke v Sokolnikakh," *Sovetskaia kultura*, 11 August 1959.

86   See also Gretchen Simms, "The 1959 American National Exhibition in Moscow and the Soviet Artistic Reaction to the Abstract Art," PhD dissertation (University of Vienna, 2007).

87   Max Frankel, "Russians' Votes Support US Fair," *The New York Times*, 1 August 1959.

88   USIA, "Report on American Exhibition in Moscow," 27. On Splitnik, see Cristina Carbone, "Staging the Kitchen Debate: How Splitnik Got Normalized in the United States," in *Cold War Kitchen: Americanization, Technology, and European Users*, Ruth Oldenziel and Karin Zachmann, eds. (Cambridge, MA: MIT Press, 2009), 59–81.

89   "The U.S. in Moscow: Russia Comes to the Fair," *Time*, 3 August 1959, 14.

90   Reid, "Who Will Beat Whom?"

91   Marietta S. Shaginian, "Razmyshnenia na amerikanskoi vystavke," *Izvestiia*, 23 August 1959, quoted in Susan E. Reid, "'Our kitchen is just as good': Soviet responses to the American kitchen," in *Cold War Modern: Design 1945–1970*, David Crowley and Jane Pavitt, eds. (London: Victoria & Albert Museum, 2008), 160. "Russian views Kitchen as Enslaving US Wife »," *New York Times*, 24 August 1959.

92   "On American Lifestyle: Save our Souls!," *Krokodil*, no. 18 (22 June 1959): 12.

93   "Resolution of the Central Committee on Advertising the American Exhibition," 27 June 1959, TsKhSD, f 5, op. 23, d. 95, quoted in Aucoin, "Deconstructing the American Way of Life," 103.

Elliott Erwitt, photographer. American National Exposition, Moscow, 1959.

Top: Fashion show under the umbrellas. Bottom: Visitors in front of a furniture demonstration and woman resting.
Gelatin silver prints on paper, 30.9 × 45.5 cm. Harry Ransom Center, The University of Texas at Austin,
Erwitt no 59-38-41/2 and 59-38-22/13.

Elliott Erwitt, photographer. American National Exposition, Moscow, 1959. Visitors in front of Goodyear tires.
Gelatin silver print on paper, 30.9 × 45.5 cm. Harry Ransom Center, The University of Texas at Austin, Erwitt No. 59-38-45/22.

In the United States and the rest of the Western world, the highlight of the exhibition was the "kitchen debate" on 24 June a widely televised discussion between Khrushchev and Vice-President Nixon in the "Miracle Kitchen," with the First Secretary refusing to see it as a significant achievement for women's liberation[94]. The trajectory of the two leaders throughout the exhibit was peppered with lively exchanges in front of the press, establishing the first worldwide transmission of a verbal confrontation between state leaders of such stature. Khrushchev reaffirmed his plan to surpass America in the space of seven years and to shift the competition between the two nations to the field of household appliances and sectors such as colour television[95]. In his speech for the official inauguration of the exhibit, that same day, Khrushchev articulated the watchword, "We will outdo America." He did not hide his "envy" towards the American way of life, adding: "But this is a good envy, in the sense that we should like to have all this in our country as soon as possible. [...] We can learn something. We regard the American exhibition as an exhibition of our own achievements in the near future [...] when our plans have been realized."[96] As for Nixon, the debate earned him the cover of *Time* magazine and bolstered his presidential campaign, which he lost by a short margin to John F. Kennedy the following year.

While the first five-year plan promised the future of Soviet industry, Khrushchev's seven-year plan for the years 1959 to 1965 was no longer devoted to building steel factories or chemical plants and focused instead on producing fast-moving consumer goods[97]. The First Secretary expected the "achievements" of the new plan to occur chiefly in the field of construction and housing equipment, with the overt goal of doing away with communal apartments. The quickest and most targeted response focused on kitchens, with the development of prototypes and modular furnishings[98].

The architects who worked on the exhibition also recounted their Moscow experience, namely for the American press. Fuller recalled finding out, in July, that "Khrushchev had looked at my dome in May, and said that he liked it and wanted me to talk to his engineers." He thus met with the instructors of the Moscow Institute of Civil Engineering to demonstrate his geodesic structures and the tensegrity principle but declared that he would not carry on unless the USSR bought his patents. Fuller was overjoyed that architects he met at the Sukhanovo dacha, twenty years after Wright's picnic, considered him "one of the pioneers, if not *the* pioneer, in applying aircraft technology to architecture," and that they had been following his work for nearly three decades[99]. He recalled that as of 1933, an "emissary of the USSR planning authority" had told him how well regarded his "industrially-to-be-produced, service-rented, deliverable, scientific dwelling machines—the Dymaxion houses" were among the Soviets[100]. Finally visiting Moscow, he praised the "good planning" of the new housing quarters but noted the poor construction materials and was shocked to find out that the Russians "ha[d] never heard of refrigeration."[101]

Nelson was particularly prolix in writing about his Moscow experience, recalling his ideas, their execution, as well as his impressions of the Soviet Union. Drawing on his own considerable experience in journalism, he published several analyses of his own work in architecture and design journals, while Donn Pennebaker and Albert Maysles' film Opening in Moscow broadcast the experience to American audiences[102]. Nelson also offered a rebuttal to the Soviet press, mocking its attitude in front of a Los Angeles audience: "They couldn't find enough things to tell their readers about what a bad show it was. We didn't have enough heavy machinery. But if we had had enough heavy machinery, they would have said that we hadn't enough culture, and if we had had enough culture (whatever that is) we didn't have enough science."[103]

On a more positive note, Nelson praised the prefabrication systems he encountered in Moscow, noting that the Soviets "are going right from primitive construction to straight industrial production of constantly more improved and advanced types of building. It's that rocket story all over again."[104] He also drew

94   "Moscow Debate Stirs U.S Public," The New York Times, 27 July 1959. The witnesses included William
        Safire, who fifty years later published "The Cold War's Hot Kitchen," The New York Times, 24 July 2009.
95   The text of the dialogue was published the next day in Harrison E. Salisbury, "Nixon and Khrushchev Argue
        In Public As U.S. Exhibit Opens; Accuse Each Other Of Threats," The New York Times, 25 June 1959.
        A full transcript can be found at http://www.foia.cia.gov/sites/default/files/document_conversions/16/
        1959-07-24.pdf [accessed 2 September 2019].
96   Nikita S. Khrushchev, Pravda, 25 July 1959, quoted in Aucoin, "Deconstructing the American Way of Life," 111.
97   Susan Buck-Morss, Dreamworld and Catastrophe: The Passing of Mass Utopia in East and West
        (Cambridge, MA: MIT Press, 2000), 204.
98   See the insightful analyses in Susan E. Reid, "The Khrushchev Kitchen: Domesticating the Scientific-Tech-
        nological Revolution," Journal of Contemporary History 4, no. 2 (2005): 289–316. "Cold War in the Kitchen:
        Gender and the De-Stalinization of Consumer Taste in the Soviet Union Under Khrushchev," Slavic
        Review 61, no. 2 (Summer 2002): 211–52. Reid, "'Our kitchen is just as good'." "Soviet Responses to the
        American Kitchen," in Crowley and Pavitt, Cold War Modern, 154-161. "Soviet Responses to the American
        Kitchen," in Oldenziel and Zachmann, Cold War Kitchen, 83–112.
99   "Buckminster Fuller Chronofile," in Meller, The Buckminster Fuller Reader, 34–35. In any case, his geodesic
        domes were well known before 1959: K. Kartashova, "Kupola v zdaniakh obshchestvennogo naznacheniia,"
        Arkhitektura SSSR, no. 11 (1958): 58.
100   R. Buckminster Fuller, Critical Path (New York: St. Martin's Press, 1981), 138.
101   Geoffrey T. Hellman, "Fuller Revisited," The New Yorker, 10 October 1959, 34–36.
102   George Nelson, "Designer's Comments and Extracts from "Log"," Industrial Design 6, no. 4 (April 1959): 49.
        "In Sokolniki Park," Interiors 119, no. 2 (September 1959): 154–57; "Designing the Moscow Exhibit," 169–76;
        "Moscow Exhibition – In Retrospect," Display World 78, no. 1 (January 1961): 52–53 and 60.
103   George Nelson, in Eames and Nelson, "What happens when one nation tells its story to another nation," 27.
104   Ibid., 41.

upon what he saw as the Russians' reticence to fall prey to the siren call of changing trends to condemn the "public perversion" of the planned obsolescence of American products[105]. He became something of an authority on Soviet material culture, which he described in his Moscow travelogue. In a letter of protest sent to *The New York Herald Tribune*, Nelson called out the main press outlets' distorted coverage of the USSR, remarking that Americans and Russians share the same "blind, smug, pigheaded self-righteousness."[106]

In Moscow, the 1959 exhibit made its strongest professional impact on designers[107]. Immediately following the event, foreign Soviet exhibits and the VDNKh—where the proportion of mass consumer goods was increased— were modernized. The architect Rudolf Kliks became Masey's counterpart by taking charge of all the projects for the following years[108]. The exhibit also had long-term effects, still palpable fifty years later, as demonstrated by the commemoration of the exhibit in 2009[109]. The widely popular television series *The Optimists*, aired in 2017, whose characters are young Soviet diplomats in the 1960s, opens in a replica of the Sokolniki spaces, where the protagonists can be seen chatting while drinking from Pepsi cups[110].

The cooperation agreement on 27 January 1958 also led to the USSR Exhibition of Achievements in Science, Technology and Culture. Its design was assigned to Konstantin Rozhdestvenskii, who had worked on Alabian and Iofan's pavilion at the World's Fair twenty years earlier, and whose relationship with Nelson was most amicable[111]. Perfectly familiar with Nelson's project, the Soviets developed a programme where emphasis was made not on consumer goods, but on peaceful nuclear research, space exploration, and aviation. Contrary to the Sokolniki exhibit, the New York show was contained on two levels in the closed space of the Coliseum, built in 1956 by Leon and Lionel Levy at Columbus Circle. It was inaugurated on 29 June 1959 by Nixon, immediately after his return from Moscow, and Frol Kozlov, a rising star of the *Politbiuro*. The journal *Dekorativnoe iskusstvo* (Decorative Arts) covered it simultaneously with the Sokolniki exhibit and devoted the opening of its issue to the Soviet exhibition[112]. The headliner was the Sputnik 3, rising in the middle of a series of tall photographic panels, echoing El Lissitzky's installations. A scale model of the University of Moscow sat in the section devoted to education rather than construction, as though it was no longer worthy of being considered an aesthetic achievement. A Tupolev Tu-114 four-engine jet was parked at Idlewild Airport—which would become in 1963 John F. Kennedy International Airport, in a separate section of the exhibit. Derived from the Tu-20 bomber, the Tu-114 had the longest range of all the civil aircraft. It gave the American public an idea of the Soviet aviation industry's evolution since its plagiarism of the B-29.

105	George Nelson, quoted in Barbara Williams, "We Could Take a Lesson from Russia," *Detroit News*, 8 January 1960.
106	George Nelson, "Letter to the Editor," *New York Herald Tribune*, 25 October 1959; George Nelson, "Impressions of Moscow," *Holiday Magazine* (January 1961), 91.
107	B. Vilenskii, "Amerikanskaia vystavka v Moskve," *Dekorativnoe iskusstvo SSSR*, no. 12 (1959): 7–10.
108	Rudolf R. Kliks, *Khudozhestvennoe proektirovanie ekspozitsii* (Moscow: Vysshaia Shkola, 1978). On his work, see Maria T. Maistrovskaia, "Rudolf Kliks i ekspositsionnyi dizain," in *Problemy dizaina 5* (Moscow: Artproekt, 2009), 93–123.
109	Jack Masey, *Six Weeks in Sokolniki Park* (Moscow: US Embassy in Moscow; New York: Pepsi Cola Co, 2009).
110	For a more select audience, the Garage Museum of Contemporary Art in Moscow in 2015 organized an exhibit that recalled the 1959 show.
111	Konstantin I. Rozhdestvenskii, Letter to George Nelson, 13 April 1959; George Nelson, Letter to Konstantin Rozhdestvensii, 13 April 1959, Vitra Design Museum, Nelson Papers, MAR-10970.
112	The article was written by one of the designers of the exhibit: B. Rodionov, "Sovetskaia vystavka v New-Yorke," *Dekorativnoe iskusstvo SSSR*, no. 12 (1959): 3–5. See also Eisenbrand, *George Nelson*, 351–54 and Masey and Morgan, *Cold War Confrontations*, 246–47.

Soviet National Exhibition at the New York Coliseum, 1959. Catalogue.

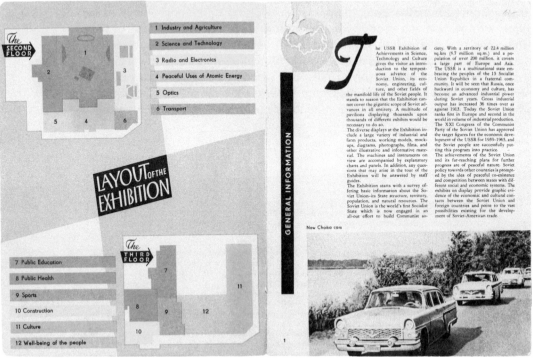

Layout of the exhibition

The Second Floor

1 Industry and Agriculture

2 Science and Technology

3 Radio and Electronics

4 Peaceful Uses of Atomic Energy

5 Optics

6 Transport

The Third Floor

7 Public Education

8 Public Health

9 Sports

10 Construction

11 Culture

12 Well-being of the people

GENERAL INFORMATION

The USSR Exhibition of Achievements in Science, Technology and Culture gives the visitor an introduction to the tempestuous advance of the Soviet Union, its economy, engineering, culture, and other fields of the manifold life of the Soviet people. It stands to reason that the Exhibition cannot cover the gigantic scope of Soviet advances in all entirety. A multitude of pavilions displaying thousands upon thousands of different exhibits would be necessary to do so.

The diverse displays at the Exhibition include a large variety of industrial and farm products, working models, mockups, diagrams, photographs, films, and other illustrative and informative material. The machines and instruments on view are accompanied by explanatory charts and panels. In addition, any questions that may arise in the tour of the Exhibition will be answered by staff guides.

The Exhibition starts with a survey offering basic information about the Soviet Union—its State structure, territory, population, and natural resources. The Soviet Union is the world's first Socialist State which is now engaged in an all-out effort to build Communist so-

ciety. With a territory of 22.4 million sq.km (8.7 million sq.m.) and a population of over 200 million, it covers a large part of Europe and Asia. The USSR is a multinational state embracing the peoples of the 15 Socialist Union Republics in a fraternal community. It will be seen that Russia, once backward in economy and culture, has become an advanced industrial power during Soviet years. Gross industrial output has increased 36 times over as against 1913. Today, the Soviet Union ranks first in Europe and second in the world in volume of industrial production. The XXI Congress of the Communist Party of the Soviet Union has approved the target figures for the economic development of the USSR for 1959–1965, and the Soviet people are successfully putting this program into practice.

The achievements of the Soviet Union and its far-reaching plans for further progress are of peaceful nature. Soviet policy towards other countries is prompted by the idea of peaceful co-existence and competition between states with different social and economic systems. The exhibits on display provide graphic evidence of the economic and cultural contacts between the Soviet Union and foreign countries and point to the vast possibilities existing for the development of Soviet-American trade.

New Chaika cars

Top: Cover with Sputnik 3;
Bottom: Double-page spread with the exhibition plan and a motorcade of GAZ-13 Chaika automobiles. Private collection.

The New York exhibit, like the Moscow event, addressed the issue of housing, insisting on heavy prefabrication using animated models and offering a three-bedroom apartment, arranged by the interior designer Olga Baiar—whose kitchen boasted a samovar—to the critical inspection of New Yorkers. In the automotive section, the Chaika manufactured by GAZ was proudly displayed. The exhibit's brochure even opened with a photograph of a fleet of limousines on a country road, as though these vehicles reserved to the nomenklatura were widely available, a fact which The New York Times did not fail to slyly point out[113]. Incidentally, the American public was not fooled by what they saw in the Coliseum and viewed the showcased interiors and everyday items as aspirational rather than as reflections of daily Soviet reality[114]. Of course, visitors could not but note the striking resemblance between the cars manufactured in the USSR and the Detroit automobiles that served as their inspiration[115].

The 1960s: A More Intimate Understanding

The 1959 American National Exhibition in the USSR was followed by a new cultural and scientific cooperation agreement signed in November of that same year, providing a framework for a long series of thematic travelling exhibits that disseminated the American message to specialized audiences throughout the country. Nelson was once again called upon by the USIA to curate Transportation USA, presented in Volgograd and Kharkov in 1961, and Industrial Design USA, presented in Moscow, Kiev, and Leningrad in 1967. This exhibit served as a rebuttal to the critiques articulated by the Moscow public, as it presented industrial equipment—which had been intentionally omitted in 1959—alongside mass-produced consumer goods[116]. In the first half of the 1960s, the new orientation advocated by Khrushchev, who was replaced by Leonid Brezhnev as the head of the party in 1964, materialized in Soviet architecture. The journalist Harrison E. Salisbury, who had been a Moscow correspondent for The New York Times from 1949 to 1954 remarked on this shift when he visited the exhibition of architectural designs in 1960: "There was nor

113   See the remarks of Max Frankel, who had seen the exhibit in Moscow: "Soviet Hopes on View: Coliseum Exhibition Depicts Nation Not as It is, but as It Wishes to Be," New York Times, 30 June 1959.
114   "U.S. Visitors to Soviet Exhibition in New York Express their Feelings," New York Times, 5 July 1959.
115   "In Sokolniki Park," 157.
116   Eisenbrand, George Nelson, 366–73.
117   Harrison E. Salisbury, To Moscow and Beyond: A Reporter's Narrative (New York: Harper & Bros., 1960), 113.
118   Alayne P. Reilly, America in Contemporary Soviet Literature (New York: New York University Press, 1971).
119   Kenneth Love, "Russian Curious about Beatniks: Soviet Writers Says Here He Would Like to Learn of Kerouac and Ginsberg," The New York Times, 6 August 1959.
120   "Otkrytie Ameriki: po tu storonu zanavesa," in Ottepel, ed. Marina Elzesser (Moscow: Gosudarstvennaia tretiakovskaia galereia, 2017), 370–75. On Kent's exhibit, see Pravda, 1 and 23 February 1958.
121   Nauchnaia organizatsiia triuda dvadtsatykh godov: sbornik dokumentov i materialov, intro. by Nikolai S. Ilenko and Kashaf Shamstudnikov (Kazan: Komb. im. Kamilia Iakuba, 1965). Another anthology was published at the very end of the Soviet era: U istokov NOT: zabytie diskussii i nerealizirovannye idei, Leningrad, Izd-vo Leningradskogo Universiteta, 1990. Gastev was among the founders of NOT whose biographies were collected in Edvard Koritskii, Yury Lavrikov, and Alim Omarov, Sovetskaia upravlencheskaia mysl 20-kh godov (Moscow: Ekonomika, 1990), 50–58.
122   Aksel I. Berg, "Lenin i nauchnaia organizatslia truda," Pravda, 24 October 1962.
123   Georgy Arbatov, The System: An Insider's Life in Soviet Politics (New York: Times Books, 1992). See S. Frederick Starr, "The Russian View of America," The Wilson Quarterly 1, no. 2 (Winter 1977): 106–17.
124   Nikolai P. Bylinkin, Istoria sovetskoi arkhitektury 1917–1958 (Moscow: Gos Izd-vo literatury po stroitelstve, arkhitekture i stroitelnym materialam, 1962), 31–32.
125   Viacheslav K. Oltarzhevskii, "Odnoobrazie po vertikali," Literaturnaia gazeta, 29 April 1965.
126   See the correspondence held in the MUAR's Oltarzhevskii archives.

a Kremlin tower in the lot, not an ornamental column, not a single hero-sized statue. Here were cool, clean, crisp, modern designs. Glass and metal and square planes. The architects had been studying the United Nations Secretariat Buildings, the new glass palaces of Park Avenue, the light and graceful concepts erected in Caracas and Rio de Janeiro."[117]

Despite successive events that offset the reconciliation initiated in 1956—the U-2 spy plane shot down above the Ural Region in 1960, the Berlin Crisis in 1961, and the Cuban Missile Crisis in 1962—, Amerikanizm prevailed in several fields. Seasoned writers like Valentin Kataev and, to a lesser degree, Viktor Nekrasov, as well as young poets such as Andrei Voznesenskii and Ievgenii Evtushenko, published their impressions and memories of America[118]. They were interested in the Beat Generation, as evidenced by the fact that Kataev, who had travelled to the Coliseum exhibit in 1959, wished to meet with Jack Kerouac and Allen Ginsberg, as reported by The New York Times[119]. Twenty-five years after Aleksandr Deineka, painters managed to be sent on artistic missions to sketch urban scenes in New York and Chicago. In 1959, Iakov Romas painted the UN headquarters, while Vadim Ryndin drew canyons surrounded by Manhattan skyscrapers. In 1960, in a more populist vein, Georgii Vereiskii depicted emaciated African-Americans loitering in the streets, while in 1958, Vitalii Goriaev's on-site caricatures garnered praise from Rockwell Kent, the first American painter to be exhibited in post-war USSR[120].

Among the rehabilitated victims of Stalin's purges—as part of a movement initiated in 1956—were some historical figures of Amerikanizm, such as Aleksei Gastev, poet of rationalized labour, whose work on the organization of labour had been unmentionable since the mid-1930s[121]. The discussion transcripts from his Central Institute of Labour and from Platon Kerzhentsev's League of Time, as well as political writings about the NOT, were reissued. In 1962, Axel Berg, the Soviet pioneer in the field of cybernetics, which was long considered a capitalist sham, wrote in the Pravda that "[m]odern cybernetics—the science of the rational, optimal control of complex processes and operations—may be looked upon in the USSR as the successor and heir of the scientific organization of labour."[122] In 1968, monitoring contemporary America was recognized as a legitimate scholarly activity, with the creation of the Institute of the USA and Canada of the Russian Academy of Sciences, headed by Georgii Arbatov, right-hand man of the Soviet leadership[123].

In the realm of architecture, the Russians' interest towards America shifted away from the 1950s focus on technology to encompass the discipline as a whole. Constructivists were also rediscovered and reinstated into the official discourse of the 1920s and 1930s. However, Albert Kahn's contribution to the development of the Soviet industrial system during the two earliest five-year plans remained entirely overlooked. A full page of Nikolai Bylinkin's 1962 official architectural history textbook was dedicated to the Cheliabinsk Tractor Plant in, but the project was credited to Anatolii Fisenko and V. Shevtsov instead of the American architect, whose "schematic" design Bylinkin criticized without naming him explicitly[124]. Kahn's name did not truly surface until the 1980s, when it was unearthed by the historian Boris Shpotov. The long rehabilitated Viacheslav Oltarzhevskii, however, became a particularly vocal figure. In a 1965 article in Literaturnaia gazeta, he criticized the "vertical monotony" of contemporary structures, while developing projects for vertical hotels and discarding not only Stalin-era "excesses" but also the ornamentations of his own 1920s projects[125]. Meanwhile, he repeatedly wrote to Khrushchev, invoking his "foreign experience" in the field of tourism complexes and department stores[126]. Another survivor was the constructivist Ivan Leonidov, who revisited the ideas he expressed in the 1934 Narkomtiazhprom in two theoretical projects: the "City of the Sun," inspired by the utopian work of Tommaso Campanella, and the United Nations Headquarters, which he envisioned as a skyscraper bouquet set on an island[127].

During this new cycle of relative thaw, which was interrupted by the Soviet invasion of Czechoslovakia in 1968, the Americans demonstrated the progress made in their relationship with the Soviet Union since the Stalin years—when the Moscow embassy was barricaded behind the pillars of a Palladian building by Ivan Zholtovskii—by opening new exhibitions in the wake of the Sokolniki show. In 1972, in addition to the two shows curated by Nelson, *Research and Development USA* was presented in Tbilisi, Moscow, Volgograd, Kazan, Donetsk, and Leningrad. Meanwhile, the USIA organized several other exhibits: *Plastics in America* (1961) in Kiev, Moscow, and Tbilisi, *Medicine USA* (1962) in Moscow, Kiev, and Leningrad, *Technical Books USA* (1963) in the same cities, and *Graphic Arts USA* (1963), in Alma-Ata, Moscow, Yerevan, and Leningrad, *Communication USA* (1965), in Leningrad, Kiev, and Moscow, *Hand Tools USA* (1966), in Kharkov, Rostov-on-Don, and Yerevan, *Education USA* (1979–1980) in Leningrad, Kiev, Moscow, Baku, Tashkent, and Novosibirsk, *Outdoor Recreation USA* (1973–1974), in Moscow, Ufa, Irkutsk, Yerevan, Kishinev, and Odessa, *Technology for the American Home* (1976) in Tashkent, Baku, Moscow, Zaporozhie, Leningrad, and Minsk, *USA 200 Years* (1976) in Moscow, *Photography USA* (1976), in Kiev, Alma-Ata, Tbilisi, Ufa, Novosibirsk, and Moscow, and *Agriculture USA* (1978–1979) in Kiev, Zelenograd, Dushanbe, Kishinev, Moscow, and Rostov-on-Don. In 1987–1989, after a hiatus that lasted a decade, the declining USSR still hosted *Information USA* in Moscow, Kiev, Rostov-on-Don, Tbilisi, Tashkent, Irkutsk, Magnitogorsk, Leningrad, and Minsk, and finally, in 1989–1991, *Design USA* was presented in Donetsk, Kishinev, Dushanbe, Alma-Ata, Novosibirsk, Volgograd, Baku, Vladivostok, and Khabarovsk[128].

Though tedious, this lengthy inventory is eloquent in showing that the spatial outreach of the American exhibitions extended to most major Soviet cities, with the exception of those whose secret factories made them inaccessible to foreigners. The USIA archives show that these events attracted a considerable total number of visitors, who collected *znachki* (buttons) as attendance trophies to boast about to their friends and colleagues[129]. There was thus a palpable sprawling presence of American civilization in the last decades of the USSR, with the impact of these exhibitions persisting well beyond their duration, namely through their catalogues, which quickly became collector's items.

In addition to these 15 exhibitions, *Architecture USA* had been developed at the Museum of Modern Art by Arthur Drexler with support from the Graham Foundation, and presented in Leningrad, Minsk, and Moscow in 1965. More diverse and inclusive than Blake's exhibition, Drexler's show was also denser and featured mostly architects patroned by the Museum, such as Mies van der Rohe, Richard Neutra, and Eero Saarinen, whose buildings were

127   Alessandro De Magistris and Irina Korobina, *Ivan Leonidov 1902–1959* (Milan: Electa, 2009), 246–61 and 265–67.
128   List compiled by Jochen Eisenbrand based on information in the USIA archives, in *George Nelson*, 465–83. See also Masey and Morgan, *Cold War Confrontations*, 284–307.
129   Ralph K. White described the significance of these souvenir buttons: Masey and Morgan, *Cold War Confrontations*, 249.

Ivan I. Leonidov. Project for the United Nations Headquarters, New York, 1947–1948. Perspective.
Graphite, gouache and watercolor on tracing paper. 17.7 × 20 cm. Tchoban Foundation, Museum for Architectural Drawing.

Viacheslav K. Oltarzhevskii. Left: Project of a hotel in Yalta, 1961. Perspective. Black and color pencil on paper, mounted on cardboard. 49.6 × 40 cm.
Right: Project for a hotel for 1,000 people, Type B, 1961. Perspective. Pencil and watercolour on paper, mounted on cardboard. 42.1 × 60.2 cm.
Shchusev State Museum of Architecture. RIa 7533/1. and RIa 7530/2.

Ivan I. Leonidov. Project for the United Nations Headquarters, New York, 1947-1948. Tempera, silver metallic ink, lacquer, bronze powder and ceruse on paper. 20 × 25 cm. Alex Lachmann Collection.

Ivan I. Leonidov. Project for the United Nations Headquarters, New York, 1947–1948.
Tempera and mixed media on paper. 19.8 × 26.5 cm. Alex Lachmann Collection, Drawing 402 - AG88:193.

illustrated with acclaimed photographs by Ezra Stoller and Julius Shulman[130]. As highlighted by Thomas Hines, with the original title, *Modern Architecture, USA*, the idea was to update a travelling exhibit that had been in circulation since the 1940s. The New York version, made up of large colour slides held in place by aluminum tubes, was presented from May to September in the MoMA galleries[131]. Drexler explained the selection criteria for the 71 chosen buildings as follows: "Some buildings are shown because they launched an idea; others because they carried an idea to its conclusion. All of them remind us that architectural excellence has many forms."[132] For *The New York Times* critic Ada Louise Huxtable, the exhibit showed "the twentieth century in the United States as a period of solid, stimulating, wide-ranging accomplishment in the building arts, with high points that have become international landmarks."[133]

The young Robert Venturi, with whom Drexler was then working on the publication of *Complexity and Contradiction in Architecture*, was invited to Moscow for the opening of the exhibit. Along with Paul Rudolph, he paid a memorable visit in an unofficial capacity to the Moscow Institute of Architecture[134].

130   A full-colour catalogue was published for the occasion: *Arkhitektura SShA* (Washington, DC; USIA, 1965).
131   Thomas S. Hines, *Architecture and Design at the Museum of Modern Art: The Arthur Drexler Years, 1951–1986* (Los Angeles: Getty Research Institute, 2018), 88–89.
132   Arthur Drexler, *Modern Architecture, USA* (New York: Museum of Modern Art, 1965), n.p.
133   Ada Louise Huxtable, "Modernism USA," *The New York Times*, 23 May 1965, quoted in Hines, *Architecture and Design*, 89.
134   Evgueni Asse, conversation with the author, Moscow: 17 March 2018.

United States Information Agency. Catalog for the exhibition *Industrial Aesthetics USA*, 1969.
Cover and interior spread. Graphic design by Ivan Chermayeff and Thomas H. Geismar. Private collection.

United States Information Agency. Catalogue for the exhibition *Architecture USA*, 1965. Cover.
Graphic design by Ivan Chermayeff and Thomas H. Geismar. Private collection.

Arthur Drexler, for the United States Information Agency. Catalogue of the exhibition *Architecture USA*, 1965:
Herb Greene, Prairie House, Norman, Oklahoma, 1961; Carl Koch, Techbuilt prefabricated house, 1956;
Richard J. Neutra, Kauffmann house, Palm Springs, California, 1946. Private collection.

Герберт Грин ↑
Загородный дом, Оклахома (1961)
Среди поклонников яркого индивидуализма
Франка Ллойда Райта немногие проявили
такую смелость архитектурного замысла,
как создатель этой деревянной несущей
конструкции, обшитой гонтом.
Пещерообразные комнаты — результат
свободного моделирования формы
и пространства.

Карл Кох →
Сборный дом фирмы «Техбуилт»
Дома проектируются с рассчетом
на популярность среди возможно бо́льшего
числа людей. Сборные панели для стен
и перекрытий из дерева или металла
могут быть установлены в несколько дней
по одному из нескольких предлагаемых
планов. Местный подрядчик-строитель
закладывает фундамент, подводит трубы
и электропроводку. Панели и другие детали
фирма поставляет на место строительства.

Рихард Нейтра
Загородный дом, Калифорния (1946)
Предназначающиеся для жизни в пустыне,
дома этого архитектора отличаются лёгкими,
тесно установленными стальными опорами,
плоскими крышами, переходящими
в нависающие консоли, и раздвижными
стеклянными стенами.

16

17

Louis I. Kahn travelled to Leningrad, not far from his native Estonia, and to Moscow, where, according to Mikhail Posokhin, he was struck by the prefabrication techniques, suggesting a stone cladding for the factory-made panels[135]. *Amerika*—another outlet for the USIA's Soviet activities with a distribution of 77,000 copies since the 1959 cooperation agreement, but still considered a political organ[136]—attached considerable importance to cities and architecture, with recurring reports on city neighbourhoods and profiles of major experts in the field. In 1964, its 90th issue was dedicated to architecture, with emphasis on urban renewal. In the feature item, the *Washington Post* critic Wolf von Eckhardt spoke of a "new stage" in American architecture, borrowing an expression from the Soviet rhetoric[137].

Drexler's exhibit contained no less than eight buildings by Frank Lloyd Wright, including the Guggenheim Museum, and earned him back his standing as the most celebrated American architect. Upon his death in 1959, four years after Aleksandr Vlasov's infamous visit to Taliesin, *Arkhitektura SSSR* dedicated a long obituary to Wright, making him the first Westerner to be featured in the publication since the 1930s[138]. The following year, his 1953 book *The Future of Architecture* was translated by Arkadii Goldshtein—who also penned the foreword together with Aleksandr Gegello, a prolific architect who had been active in 1920s Leningrad but had gone unnoticed ever since. They wrote that "Wright is interesting for us first of all as an innovator who understood, still at the end of the previous century, that the proper development of architecture had to shun the imitation of old forms and methods in order to invent solutions that responded to real conditions and expectations." However, they could not elude the official aesthetic principles and were forced to condemn his "formalism," declaring that while "the limitations of Wright tarnish his achievements, they do not cancel them. He was a superior master, in the same rank as the greatest architects in history."[139] The widespread acceptance of Wright's body of work was evidenced by his popularity at the Moscow Institute of Architecture, where the Guggenheim stood alongside the Parthenon and Palladio's Rotonda among the buildings used to teach students the basics of design. For instance, a drawing by Liudmila Smykovskai for a history class shows a sectional view of the building with a skyscraper used as a backdrop[140]. Despite this interest, the first monograph on Wright, by Arkadii Goldshtein, was not issued until 1973, over fifty years after Wasmuth's seminal publication[141]. Meanwhile, a more open-minded vision of Wright's oeuvre was gradually established in Soviet publications.

Amerikanizm was thus transformed when a more nuanced understanding of the work of individual architects became accessible. In its initial form, Amerikanizm was focused on programmes rather than on distinct approaches, which remained obscure or were simply impossible to reproduce, except perhaps that of Albert Kahn, which was based on a serial principle.

135   Mikhail V. Posokhin, *Dorogi zhizni: iz zapisok arkhitektora* (Moscow: Stroiizdat, 19950), 180.
136   "Report on the exchange of literature," 9 January 1961, TsKhSD, f. 5, 33, d. 189, quoted in Aucoin, "Deconstructing the American Way of Life," 168. On *Amerika* during this period, see Hixson, *Parting the Curtain*, 117–19.
137   Wolf von Eckhardt, "Amerikanskaia arkhitektura na novom etape," *Amerika*, no. 90 (1964): 16–31.
138   Arkadii F. Goldshtein, "Arkhitektor Frank Lloyd Wright," *Arkhitektura SSSR*, no. 6 (1959): 59–52.
139   Frank Lloyd Wright, *Budushchee arkhitektury*, trans. Arkadii F. Goldshtein, preface by Arkadii F. Goldshtein and Aleksandr I. Gegello (Moscow: Gos. Izd-vo literatury po stroitelstvu, arkhitekture i stroitelnym materialam, 1960[1953]).
140   The drawing is held at the Muzei MArkhI.
141   Arkadii F. Goldshtein, *Frank Lloyd Wright* (Moscow: Stroiizdat, 1973).

Ученый, изобретатель, инженер и философ — таков творческий облик Ричарда Бэкминстера Фуллера (см. «Обозрение», стр. 63). Но прежде всего Фуллер — строитель-новатор. Через несколько десятилетий, предсказывает он, человек, максимально используя поверхность земли, будет строить новые благоустроенные и экономичные городские центры. Это будут плавучие и воздушные поселения и покрытые прозрачным куполом города с искусственным климатом, проекты которых, по утверждению Фуллера, вполне осуществимы. Плавучий город (внизу) в форме пологого тетраэдра, будет вмещать от трех тысяч до миллиона жителей, деловые предприятия, общественные и культурные учреждения. Каждое жилище будет иметь веранду и сад. По мере разрастания города, площадь его можно увеличивать, не нарушая общей симметрии и плана. Город можно причалить в защищенной гавани или отбуксировать в море и поставить на якоря. Воздушный город с населением в несколько тысяч человек будет заключен в полиэтиленовый геодезический шар диаметром в полтора километра. Он может свободно плавать в атмосфере или пришвартовываться, скажем, к горной вершине. По словам Фуллера, воздушные поселения позволят большим массам людей «сосредотачиваться» в самых разных точках по всему земному шару, не сокращая производящих районов земли. Город под прозрачным геодезическим куполом будет защищен от холода, жары, снега и дождя, и жители в нем будут дышать свежим, очищенным от загрязнений воздухом.

Редки с плавучем городом самые высокие в мире здания покажутся как булавки.

По словам Фуллера, город под куполом (слева) окупит себя и десять лет одной лишь экономией средств, что повышения уборки снега. Воздушные города в геодезических шарах (внизу) смогут свободно передвигаться с места на место по всему земному шару.

"Charles Moore's House". Double page in *Amerika*, no. 168, October 1970. CCA, W.A4477.

507

Aleksandra M. Khristiani, *Recent Architecture in the United States (1945-1960)*, Moscow: Izd-vo literatury po stroitelstvu, arkhitekture i stroitelnym materialam, 1963. Cover with Walter Gropius's auditorium project for Tallahassee, Florida, and page with a view of the Seagram Building. Private collection.

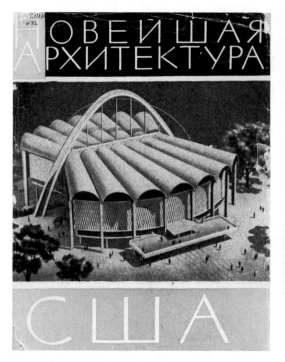

An idealized view devoid of practical effects was combined with a focus on a handful of venerated programmes, such as skyscrapers or factories, along with deficient knowledge of specific projects, which deepened only during the short-lived euphoria of the Allied victory. The 1963 publication of Aleksandra Khristiani's *The Latest Architecture in the United States (1945–1960)* was thus a significant milestone, as it was the first comprehensive Soviet study on American architecture. Strangely enough, its cover was illustrated by Walter Gropius's project for a concert hall in Tallahassee, whose arch was borrowed from Le Corbusier's Palace of the Soviets competition entry. Khristiani, the wife of the architect Viktor Asse, had worked under Lev Rudnev and for institutions related to the profession, translating British and American journals[142]. In this volume— whose breakdown by building type was in keeping with the conventions of Soviet literature on the topic—, the presence of industrial programmes was striking: factories of advanced technology giants such as General Electric were featured alongside well-known food industry brands like the Coca-Cola plant in Texas[143]. The fact that Khristiani included the 1959 project for Lincoln Center, entirely credited to Philip Johnson, is unsurprising, as Mikhail Posokhin had drawn inspiration from Max Abramovitz's disposition of Avery Fisher Hall to design the State Kremlin Palace, the last avatar of the Palace of Soviets project, permanently abandoned after the late 1950s competition. In his memoirs, Posokhin made no secret of his admiration for what he called "one of the best ensembles of New York[144]".

From a generational standpoint, though she paid a nearly ritual homage to Wright's Guggenheim Museum and Price Tower, Khristiani strongly emphasized Eero Saarinen's work—his buildings for MIT, the Ingalls Rink in New

Haven, and the Idlewild TWA Flight Center, whose traced perspective provided a logo for the book—and that of Mies van der Rohe, taken seriously for the first time in the USSR, with the Seagram Building, the Lake Shore Drive towers, Lafayette Park in Detroit, and the IIT campus. Louis I. Kahn was mentioned only in regards to his plan for downtown Philadelphia. Buckminster Fuller, present in many chapters of Khristiani's book, and well known among the Russian leaders since 1959, took part in the Dartmouth Conference that brought together American and Soviet scientists, whose first meeting took place in 1961. There, Fuller reflected upon the strategic balance between the two powers, namely during the July 1964 discussion in Leningrad, where his presence was widely acclaimed, including by the all-powerful president of the Academy of Sciences Mstislav Keldysh, who declared, according to Fuller himself: "From now on Buckminster Fuller will be ranked in the USSR side-by-side with Franklin and Edison."[145]

Victor Gruen: Los Angeles as a Model

Victor Gruen, another central figure of American architecture, was widely successful in the 1960s Soviet Union. His 1955 plan for Fort Worth was prominently showcased in the *Transportation USA* exhibit installed by George Nelson in Moscow's Gorky Park, in 1960[146]. The Los Angeles-based architect was mostly known for his main contribution to post-war architecture: the suburban mall, lost in a concrete sea of parking lots, whose prototype, Northland Centre, was featured in Khristiani's book[147]. In 1966, as Gruen's bestselling work, *Shopping Towns USA*—published with the economist Larry Smith in 1960—was translated into Russian, the mall came to occupy a dominant position at the crossroads between Soviet economics and architecture[148]. The relatively rapid translation bears witness to a sense of urgency and to the Soviet leaders' careful examination of commercial construction plans during their visits to America.

Gruen had already started to distance himself from the concept of the independent and autonomous mall to focus on urban centres, whose fabric had incidentally suffered as a result of his own schemes. In 1964, after developing several urban renovation projects such as the Midtown Plazza in Rochester, he articulated a theory on city centres in his book *The Heart of Our Cities*, where he called for an organic metropolitan model. From then on, he became dedicated to revitalizing city centres, while increasingly acting as a consultant in Europe until eventually moving back to his native Vienna in 1968[149]. The 1966 translation—introduced and edited by Avraam Urbakh, a market economist working for the Research Institute for Public Buildings—thus served to spread

142   Evgueni Asse, conversation with the author, 17 March 2018.
143   Aleksandra M. Khristiani, *Noveishaia arkhitektura SShA (1945–1960)* (Moscow: Izd-vo literatury po stroitelstvou, arkhitekture i stroitelnym materialam, 1963).
144   Possokhin, *Dorogi zhizni*, 190.
145   R. Buckminster Fuller, *Critical Path* (New York: St. Martin's Press, 1981), 190.
146   "Gradostroiteli Fort-Uorta planiruiut budushchii transport goroda," in *Transport USA*, Washington, DC, USIA, 1961, n.p. See Eisenbrand, *George Nelson*, 374.
147   Khristiani, *Noveishaia arkhitektura SShA*, 53.
148   Victor Gruen and Larry Smith, *Shopping Towns USA: The Planning of Shopping Centers* (New York: Reinhold, 1960).
149   Victor Gruen, *The Heart of Our Cities: The Urban Crisis, Diagnosis and Cure* (New York: Simon & Schuster, 1964).

a doctrine that had already been partly disavowed by its very author at the time. The translation was edited, as "a series of passages from the book do not resist to a sociological critique," specifically those where the authors "try to paint the American lifestyle in an idyllic light, by embellishing certain aspects of capitalism in the name of the 'prosperity' of American society. In those cases, they resort to pure glorification."[150] Urbakh spared his readers the "subjective thoughts of various individuals on the theme of malls" and their "'prospective' visions for customer growth and the possibility of building commercial constructions in urban centres while developing those located in the suburbs,"[151] in a straw-man portrayal of Gruen's views on city centres. As these paragraphs were removed, the translation was ideologically rectified, though it faithfully rendered the "scientific" and "technical" sections comprising the "healthy" core of the work. Its graphic austerity made it resemble a practical handbook. *Shopping Towns USA* was not translated into any other language, likely because English had become the lingua franca among post-war urban planners. In the Soviet Union, this book, akin to a project manual that could be put to immediate use, was a counterpart to the industrial project manuals of the 1930s. While Kahn's legacy was decisive for the development of productive infrastructure in the USSR, Gruen's contribution became vital for the shift towards a consumer economy undertaken under Khrushchev.

In 1963, Gruen received a visit from a Soviet delegation in his Los Angeles offices, and established fruitful relations during a night of eating and drinking where the urban planners of both countries united in solidarity against architects. Invited to the USSR the following fall, Gruen discovered Moscow, which he saw as a "a mixture of Paris and New York." To him, "the broad boulevards were Parisian, and the skyscrapers, where public institutions were housed, represented New York."[152] In the "Russian Report" he wrote upon his return, documenting the minutiae of his travels, Gruen noted that the new "purely utilitarian" architecture, with its "extremely poor quality," was "extremely dreary" and compared "very poorly with the Stalinistic [sic] period where at least the adornments of classisistic [sic] ornamentation [was] some relief. One of the problems of modern architecture, and we all have made our experiences in that respect, is if it isn't planned with good design and good feeling and if it isn't executed with good materials and good workmanship, the results are absolutely hopeless."[153] He lamented the poor quality of the newest dwellings, while the only redeemable structures in his view were the Kremlin Palace of Congresses and the new Pioneers Palace. In the city centre, Gruen was particularly interested in the GUM's "three parallel shopping malls," even noting a resemblance with the Topanga Plaza he had built in the San Fernando Valley. He described the scarcity he witnessed in the stores located in outlying districts, contrasting them with the more abundant ones on Gorky Street or on Nevsky Prospekt and commenting on the uneven distribution of goods.

150   Avraam I. Urbakh, preface to Victor Gruen and Larry Smith, *Torgovye tsentry SShA*, trans. V.M. Milonov (Moscow: Izd-vo literatury po stroitelstvu, 1966), 4–5.
151   Ibid., 8.
152   Annette Baldauf, ed., *Victor Gruen, Shopping Town: Memoiren eines Stadtplaners (1903–1980)* (Vienna: Böhlau Verlag, 2014), 253; in English: *Victor Gruen, Shopping Town: Designing the City in Suburban America* (Minneapolis, University of Minnesota Press, 201), 160.
153   Victor Gruen, "Russian Report," 1964, 7, Victor Gruen Papers, American Heritage Center, University of Wyoming, Laramie, box 4, file "Trips behind the Iron Curtain." Gruen's Soviet adventures are not covered in the principal monographs dedicated to his work: Alex Wall, *Victor Gruen: From Urban Shop to New City* (Barcelona: Actar, 2005); M. Jeffrey Hardwick, *Victor Gruen: Architect of an American Dream* (Philadelphia: University of Pennsylvania Press, 2004).

Рис. 29. Центр, расположенный вдоль прохода для пешеходов, с магнитом в середине

можно характеризовать как «развернутые наружу» типы. Их передние фасады повернуты в сторону шоссе и автомобильных стоянок. Их задние фасады, имеющие обычно непривлекательный вид, повернуты в сторону служебных дорог и непосредственно примыкающих к ним населенных участков.

Последующие исследуемые примеры В и Г можно назвать типом «Янус», или двухфасадным типом. Один из этих фасадов направлен в сторону автомобильной стоянки, а другой — в сторону прохода для пешеходов. Пример Д устанавливает связь между типом «Янус» и типом «Развернутый внутрь», который будет рассмотрен в примере Е.

если два мощных магнита, скажем, например, универсальный магазин и его филиал, располагались бы на концах 608-метровой полосы, то объем розничного движения, возникающего на участке между магазинами и проходящего через промежуточные магазины, также будет ограниченным и только немногие магазины будут иметь успех.

Торговые центры в этих двух примерах

Рис. 30 Центр Норсгет с магнитом в середине, г. Сиэтл, штат Вашингтон

56

Пример В.

Полоса земли длиной 608 м под магазины разделяется на две половины, образуя таким образом две полосы длиной каждая 304 м, расположенные друг против друга вдоль прохода

Рис. 31. Центр Норсленд области Детройта, планировка по типу пучка с главным магнитом в центре

для пешеходов. При этом автомобильные стоянки организуются с наружной стороны магазинов (рис. 25, а, б).

В этом примере рыночный поток пешеходов будет значительно больше по нескольким причинам:

1) место для пешеходов защищено от шума, запахов, беспорядка и опасностей, создаваемых автомобильным движением;

2) два главных магнита находятся на взаимном расстоянии, равном только 304 м, при условии их расположения на концах рассматриваемых полос. Поэтому вероятность взаимного обмена розничным потоком пешеходов между магазинами в этом случае будет значительно больше и магазины, расположенные между двумя магнитами, будут иметь за счет этого больший доход.

Если же имеется только один магнит, расположенный на одном конце прохода для пешеходов (рис. 26—28), то рыночный поток сократится вследствие недостатка взаимного обмена покупателями между магазинами. Наиболее удаленные от магнита магазины будут иметь доход от пешеходного движения, создаваемого этим магнитом, только в очень небольшой степени.

Пример Г.

В этом случае так же, как и в примере В, предусматривается благоустроенный проход для пешеходов. Однако магнит сдвигается к центру по одной стороне этого прохода (рис. 29, 30). Пешеходное движение в этом случае будет более интенсивным по сравнению с центром, имеющим магнит на конце прохода.

Рис. 32. Планировка по типу пучка

Рис. 33. План центра Норсленд

Пример Д.

Основной арендатор располагается в центре скомпонованных в пучок зданий (рис. 31—33). Таким образом, почти все магазины оказываются в непосредственной близости от наиболее мощного рыночного пешеходного потока. В противоположность ранее рассмотренным примерам, в которых все торговые точки развернуты в сторону движения автомобилей и пешеходов, данная планировка размещает основного арендатора только в направлении рыночного пешеходного движения. Ввиду большой притягательной силы основного универсального магазина такая планировка в результате не вредит его коммерческой деятельности.

57

ГЛАВА 2

График производства работ

Развитие торгового центра нельзя осуществлять быстрым темпом, и оно не должно идти по легкому пути.

Проектирование торгового центра — длительный процесс, в котором все стадии работы обычно логически следуют одна за другой. Поспешные и легкомысленные решения могут привести к плохим результатам. С момента зарождения идеи строительства в определенном месте торгового центра до момента открытия его дверей, как правило, проходит значительное время.

Рассмотрим более подробно стадии работы, которую должны выполнять отдельные члены бригады проектировщика. Сначала составляется в общих чертах предварительный график проектирования и строительства, который можно разделить на пять основных стадий: исследование, предварительная, заключительная стадия проектирования, стадия строительства, открытие торгового центра.

Для районных центров, вероятно, каждая из этих стадий должна определяться точно; при проектировании небольших центров строительство можно проводить при меньшем количестве стадий.

Стадия исследования

На этой стадии должен разрешаться вопрос — быть торговому центру или не стоит его создавать. В силу того, что ответ может быть отрицательным, застройщик часто не решается тратить достаточное количество времени и денежные средства в течение этого периода. Однако проведенные в этот момент бригадой проектировщиков поспешные и неполные исследования могут дать губительные результаты. В связи с этим в течение различных стадий работы в стадии исследования тщательно проверяются все благоприятные возможности и

условия, на основании чего создается принципиальное решение торгового центра.

1) Этап работы по установлению возможности проведения исследований. В зависимости от обстоятельств первый этап работы будет начинаться с исследования местности и выбора участка. Если участок уже установлен, то исследование будет начинаться с проверки пригодности участка с точки зрения экономики и планировки. Экономист и архитектор начинают работу с подбора всех подходящих сведений и анализа полученных данных. Эти экономист будет устанавливать коммерческий потенциал с надлежащим рассмотрением существующей конкуренции и возможного наличия основных арендаторов. Задача архитектора должна состоять в проверке пригодности участка с точки зрения физических характеристик участка и его доступности. Хорошо составленное заключение, основанное на опыте, позволит членам бригады существенно ограничить свои исследования и анализ на время этого этапа работы, избежав рассмотрения незначительных вопросов. При этом имеется в виду, что усилия экономиста и архитектора на этом этапе их работы сводятся только к доказательству возможности проведения исследования, а не к их окончанию.

2) Этап разработки принципиального решения планировки. Этот этап работы тесно связан по времени и действию с первым этапом. На принципиальное решение торгового центра, созданного в это время, будут оказывать влияние результаты экономического анализа. Однако только при изобретательном подходе можно создать выдающуюся планировку, тем самым в значительной мере увеличив притягательную силу центра, и изменить анализ коммерческого потенциала. Работа проводящего экономический анализ экономиста, и исследования, проводимые архитектором, на этом этапе должны проходить при

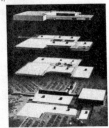

Рис. 21. Модели, сделанные во время оформления проектных материалов
а — торговый центр Бэй Фэйр, г. Сан Леандро, штат Калифорния; б — область Миннеаполиса. В связи с наличием несколько зданий этих планировочных моделях можно представить таким образом, что их можно было поднимать, раскрывая перекрытия

наиболее близком и возможном взаимном контакте между этими специалистами.

3) Этап оформления материалов. Поскольку члены бригады согласны условно с результатами, полученными на первых двух этапах, архитектор и экономист приступают к третьему этапу работы — они оформляют эти результаты в эффективной и наиболее понятной форме. Материалы, составляемые которых завершаются в течение этого этапа, будут состоять из планов использования земли, этажей, а также основного движения транспорта. Детальное представление проекта будет облегчаться при помощи многочисленных цветных и черно-белых перспективных изображений, включая вид центра с высоты птичьего полета, виды мест для пешеходов и виды центра с окружающих шоссейных дорог. Наиболее полезными являются модели (рис. 21, а, б), которые в случае сложных схем можно изготовлять без отдельных секций или междуэтажных перекрытий для того, чтобы дать арендаторам более ясное представление о пространственном решении центра. Кроме того, на этапе оформления материалов будет составляться брошюра, содержащая в ясной и краткой форме все данные по экономике и планировке. Вооруженная этим материалом бригада проектировщиков может продолжать работу дальше.

4) Этап развития подготовительных работ. В течение этого этапа на принципиальное решение проекта, выставленного для ознакомления, будут оказывать влияние различные агенты, организации и деловые круги, чья помощь должна быть обеспечена в будущем при условии строительства торгового центра. Надо будет добиться сотрудничества с местными властями, когда дело касается вопросов зонирования, разрешения строительства зданий, строительства дорог и контроля движения транспорта. Основные арендаторы, особенно универсальный магазин, филиал универсального магазина и магазин самообслуживания,

48   49

In terms of urban planning, Gruen compared Stalin's plan for Moscow to Haussmann's renovation of Paris but observed that circulation was becoming a pressing issue despite the city's wide roadways. During a visit to Moscow and Leningrad's urban planning institutes, whose members were "well acquainted with [his] work," he warned them against what they had to expect: "I gave them my opinion [about the private automobile] and told them that I thought what they had done with all the broad radial streets leading into the centre of Moscow would once prove to be a big problem. I promised them to send them my book and material of our various planning projects."[154] To the great relief of a portion of the audience, he criticized a new city project in Siberia for its excessive emphasis on automotive circulation, speaking out in favour of a plan for a Leningrad neighbourhood inspired by the new Finnish and Swedish cities. He noted that his hosts, among whom Mikhail Khauke, an expert on suburbs, were trying to surpass pre-existing solutions and were "striving for more differentiation, for more versatility, for a mixing of high buildings with low buildings, for a mixing of various building types, for the development of the *mikroraion* which we would call a village as an organic, more or less self-contained unit."[155]

In 1963, following a wintertime visit to Los Angeles in 1961 from a group headed by Mikhail Posokhin, a Soviet delegation travelled to Gruen's California offices. Appointed Moscow's chief architect the previous year, Posokhin was accompanied by his former associate Ashot Mndoiants, Dmitrii Chechulin, his former employer at the head of the capital's architectural services, and Vladimir Kucherenko, president of the State Committee for Construction. The trip was connected to the building of the Palace of Congresses and was in that sense a reiteration of Iofan's 1935 voyage. In New York, where the entrepreneur Robert W. Dowling organized a visit of several theatres, Posokhin was struck by Carnegie Hall and Radio City Music Hall[156]. He showed further interest for Edmund Bacon's urban planning endeavours in Philadelphia, whose model of the downtown area inspired him to create a similar tool for Moscow. In Los Angeles, the group discovered Clarence Stein's Baldwin Hills housing complex, William Pereira's Union Oil Center, and the 20th Century Fox studios, where they were shown a scale model of Century City, a set of offices being designed by Welton Becket for West Los Angeles[157]. Though Posokhin shed a wistful tear for Mary Pickford and Douglas Fairbanks upon seeing their stars on Hollywood Boulevard, he was mostly impressed by the road system surrounding the city. He also paid a visit to Mies van der Rohe in his Chicago offices, making him one of the rare—and likely the last—Soviet architects to have met him. The Chicago architect was beloved in the USSR, as evidenced by the fact that

154   Gruen, "Russian Report," 24.
155   Ibid., 25. Gruen wrote a more literary version of his recollections in Annette Baldauf, *Victor Gruen*, 189-190.
156   Posokhin, *Dorogi zhizni*, 165–67. On the Palace, see Mikhail V. Posokhin, Ashot A. Mndoiants, and Niss A. Pekareva, *Kremlevskii dvorets sezdov* (Moscow: Stroiizdat, 1965).
157   "Soviet Architects Here to Study City Planning," *Los Angeles Times*, 13 February 1960; "Russian Architects View LA Buildings," *Los Angeles Mirror News*, 13 February 1960.
158   Abram I. Damskii, "Iz putevogo dnevnika arkhitektora," *Dekorativnoe iskusstvo*, no. 6 (June 1960): 33–37.
159   Peter Self, *Goroda vykhodiat iz svoikh granits*, trans. Mikhail I. Khauke (Moscow: Gos Izd-vo Lit. po stroitelstvu, arkhitektury i stroitelnym materialam, 1962); originally: *Cities in Flood: The Problems of Urban Growth* (London: Faber and Faber, 1957).
160   Mikhail V. Posokhin, ed., *Gradostroitelstvo v SShA* (Moscow: Otdelenie nauchno-tekhnicheskoi informatsii pri NII teorii, istorii i perspektivnykh problem sovetskoi arkhitektury, 1968). The delegation comprised A.E. Biriukov, Aleksandr I. Naumov, E.A. Pylnik, and E.N. Sidorov.
161   Posokhin, *Gradostroitelstvo v SShA*, 33; Peter Blake, *God's Own Junkyard: The Planned Deterioration of America's Landscape* (New York: Holt Rinehart and Winston, 1964).
162   Posokhin, *Dorogi zhizni*, 184.

in a paper criticizing the "abstraction" of American interiors, Abram Damskii—an expert on lighting who was part of the delegation escorting the 1959 exhibition in New York—praised Mies, going as far as to credit him for the design of SOM's Lever House[158].

The Soviets' newfound interest in Los Angeles indicated a westward shift in the trend of Americanism. Though Sergei Eisenstein, Boris Pilniak, and Ilf and Petrov had travelled to the Californian metropolis, and despite Neutra's brief portrayal of the city in 1929, it had not yet taken shape in the minds of Soviet architects and urban planners. But Los Angeles soon became as appealing as New York or Chicago. The latter was at the centre of the Russians' focus, owing to its pioneering role in shaping modern commerce and consumer practices, and the prominent position allotted to the automobile. This last aspect was especially important considering that urban sprawl had become a concern among planners, as evidenced by the 1962 translation of Peter Self's book, *Cities in Flood*[159].

Investigative journeys thus became a cyclical endeavour, occurring roughly every decade since Iofan's 1934 expedition. After discovering New York in 1945 and following his eventful 1955 voyage, Posokhin crossed the Atlantic once again in 1965 as part of the preparations for Moscow's new general plan, heading a delegation of architects and builders escorted by a camera operator. The delegation was especially interested in urban planning and visited New York, Washington, Philadelphia, Los Angeles, San Francisco, Chicago, and Detroit. A detailed report was produced and its 1,500 copies were numbered to ensure their restricted dissemination to official organizations. It featured several buildings, including New York's Lever House, the Seagram Building, Lincoln Center, and Minoru Yamasaki's World Trade Center, which was of particular interest to Posokhin, as well as Bertrand Goldberg's Marina City in Chicago. A few malls were also included, confirming the trend revealed by the translation of Gruen's book[160]. Rather than emphasizing urban composition or the ordering of functions in keeping with the Athens Charter, the report stressed the intricacy of urban systems through the study of several major operations. The most in-depth analyses concerned Chicago and Philadelphia, whose systems were thoroughly examined, with a special focus on the placement of malls and their accessibility by motor vehicles. In the latter city, Posokhin also carefully studied Edmund Bacon's urban renovation project, Market East, and went on to befriend the urban planner. There were plenty of obligatory images of slums, but this time, they were printed next to a photograph of an advertisement-ridden street. The report noted that publicity "affects the expression of American cities," in a sentiment reminiscent of Peter Blake's newly published *God's Own Junkyard*[161].

In Los Angeles, Posokhin was struck by his visit to Disneyland, immediately imagining a Russian version of the amusement park for Moscow[162]. More importantly, he devoted no less than six entire pages of his report to blurry and airbrushed views of Los Angeles airports and projects like Century City or Bunker Hill, also in LA, while several others showed vertical parking lots. Based on a comprehensive analysis of the policies instated in the major cities he visited, Posokhin devised an action plan for his Soviet colleagues: "As shown by the American experience, it is reasonable to introduce trenches, tunnels, and installations to protect the population against noise, dust, and exhaust fumes, into the urban fabric. Not only do such insulation structures make for a healthier city, they also simplify the planning of large intersections, allow for a greater speed of traffic, and decrease the number of accidents. [...] To resolve circulation problems in major cities, research and project institutes

Mikhail V. Posokhin, *Urban Planning in the USA*, Moscow: Otd. nauchno-tekh. info. pri NII teorii, istorii i perspektivnykh problem sov. arkhitektury, 1965. Cover with the plan of Washington, DC, and aerial views of Los Angeles. Private collection.

Транспортная развязка в Лос-Анжелосе

Развязка скоростных магистралей в Чикаго является сложным инженерным сооружением, занимающим большую городскую территорию

must develop complex plans for the organization of transportation, and specifically efficient highway networks, while ensuring their organic connection with city structures. [...] American highway systems should be examined more closely and, after critical evaluation, introduced into the planning of Moscow, Leningrad, and other cities."[163] It was as though forty years after the fact, the Soviet urban planning technostructure set out to fulfill Valerian Obolenskii's prophecies, which became the foundation for Moscow's new general plan.

In his report, Posokhin mentioned Gruen's latest projects, professed his admiration for the man, and went on to consult with him some years later regarding his plan, approved in 1971[164]. He paid Gruen a visit in Vienna to show him his sketch, whose goals the urban planner found "laudable," as they "intended to stop further growth of the population [and] prevent the geographic spread of the urbanized area." He "congratulated [Posokhin] on his general concept, which would have prevented the sprawl that was occurring in Western cities." However, he was taken aback by his proud emphasis on the automobile, in conjunction with Brezhnev's industrial policy, and reminded Posokhin that Khrushchev had declared that an absurdity such as American traffic jams could exist only in capitalist countries. Gruen recalled: "I explained that this one aspect of his plan would erase all its other laudable intentions. The land requirements for the use of 1.5 million automobiles would be so great that limiting the urban area, increasing the green areas, and increasing the residential units would become impossible. He couldn't believe this, because many of the streets of Moscow were very broad." Gruen then showed him his calculations for the space necessary for traffic, parking, and all the ancillary services, remembering: "He checked my calculations and asked in consternation, 'Why didn't anyone tell me this? This is a disaster!' I suggested that he should revise his plan and leave out the proposed increase of the number of registered automobiles."[165] And thus, the creator of the horizontal American suburbs tried to talk the Soviets out of replicating his own model.

While still working on his plan for Moscow, Posokhin received a visit from the mayor of New York, John Lindsay, who convinced him that public transportation was the basis of urban planning[166]. In Brezhnev's USSR, Posokhin became a state architect, following in the footsteps of his teacher Aleksei Shchusev. He thus became a key figure in the monumental competition against the United States enacted in the various World's Fairs. In Montreal, the pavilion he designed with Ashot Mndoiants and Boris Tkhor echoed Buckminster Fuller's sphere from across the Le Moyne Channel[167]. In Osaka, a more distant dialogue was established between his pavilion and the one designed by Davis Brody and Chermayeff & Geismar, each located on opposite ends of the site. Posokhin's power can be observed in his monumental Soviet embassies, namely the one he built between 1969 and 1974 in Washington: a solid volume

163   Posokhin, *Gradostroitelstvo v SShA*, 193–94.
164   About the beginnings of shopping malls in the 1950s, see Timothy Mennel, "Victor Gruen and the Construction of Cold War Utopias," *Journal of Planning History* 3, no. 2 (2004): 116–50.
165   Victor Gruen, in Annette Baldauf, *Victor Gruen*, 293–94, in English in *Victor Gruen*, 190. Posokhin barely mentions this episode in his memoirs: *Dorogi zhizni*, 184.
166   Possokhine, *Dorogi*, 179.
167   Alexander Ortenberg, "The Soviet Pavilion at Expo 67 in Montreal: The Power and the Limits of a Symbol," in Aronova and Ortenberg, *A History of Russian Exposition and Festival Architecture*, 257–73.

clad in white stone[168], similar to the one he would build some years later for the Ministry of Defence in Moscow, nicknamed "the Pentagon." Not far from there, he erected the New Arbat, the main monumental construction created after Khrushchev to commemorate the 50th anniversary of the Revolution. Its construction involved the destruction of large portions of the neighbourhood, which were replaced by a road lined with tall buildings resting on low-rise volumes occupied by retail. Its New York City inspiration is apparent, most notably Edward Durell Stone's 1940 plan for Sixth Avenue.

There were multiple nods to American structures in Moscow's official stagnation-era architecture. The Intourist Hotel created between 1965 and 1969 at the bottom of Gorky Street by Vsevolod Voskresenskii, a student of Ivan Zholtovskii's, was offset from the street like the Seagram Building, but seemed to be inspired by the office buildings erected by Harrison & Abramovitz on Sixth Avenue[169]. Located north-west of Moscow, a new terminal was built for Sheremetyevo Airport by G. A. Elkin and G. V. Kriukov's team on a circular plan, crowned by a disk-shaped roof similar to that of Pan Am's Worldport, built in Idlewild in 1960 by Tippetts-Abbett-McCarthy-Stratton [ill. p. 518]. While the major figures of the profession observed their American counterparts, new approaches were emerging in opposition to the late International Style. In 1971, Iurii Platonov's project, which received a jury mention in the Centre Georges Pompidou competition, was a mannerist take on themes borrowed from Louis I. Kahn. During the same period, Robert Venturi's critical discourse became available to Russian readers, at least through excerpts of Complexity and Contradiction in Architecture[170]. His buildings were carefully examined by young Estonian architects such as Vilen Künappu. The latter received commissions from the wealthy milk farms of the Baltic republics that freed him from strict construction standards, allowing him to play with façades and rooftops with an irony reminiscent of his Philadelphia model[171].

Some fifteen years after Aleksandra Khristiani, Andrei Ikonnikov—probably the most knowledgeable Russian critic of Western built production—published a new book on the American architectural scene with the cautious subtitle, "An Architecture in the Bourgeois Culture System." Contrary to his previous publication, which was entirely based on journals, the book drew upon Ikonnikov's travels and featured his own photographs. After a long historical narrative informed by recent publications, the author focused on works of the 1960s and 1970s, with emphasis on Roche Dinkeloo's buildings, but without failing to include Kahn, Venturi, and Drop City's Zomes. In terms of urban planning, the new private cities of Columbia, Maryland, and Reston, Virginia were mentioned, as well as creations such as Disneyland, where Ikonnikov saw "the grotesquely magnified features" of America itself, in an updated version of his predecessors' condemnation of Coney Island.

168   On the embassy in Washington, see Fabien Bellat, Amériques–URSS Architectures du défi (Paris: Éditions Nicolas Chaudun, 2014), 262–65.

169   See what Feliks Novikov said after its demolition: Felix A. Novikov, "Razmyshlenia po povodu snosa gostinitsy Inturist," in Po susekam, arkhiva i pamiati (Ekaterinburg: Tatlin, 2017).

170   Robert Venturi, "Iz knigi 'Sloznost i protivorechia v arkhitekture'," in Mastera arkhitektury ob arkhitekture, texts collected by Andrei A. Ikonnikov (Moscow: Iskusstvo, 1972), 543–58.

171   Mart Kalm, "La tardive floraison des campagnes. L'architecture moderniste des kolkhozes dans l'Estonie soviétique," In Situ [online], no. 21 (2013). http://journals.openedition.org/insitu/10372 [accessed 2 September 2019].

172   Andrei A. Ikonnikov, Arkhitektura SShA: arkhitektura v sisteme burzhuaznoi kultury (Moscow: Iskusstvo, 1979), 190.

173   Posokhin, Dorogi zhizni, 196.

174   "Novoe pokolenie moskovkikh vysotok," Arkhitektura i stroitelstvo Moskvy, no. 11 (November 1988): 7–9.

To redeem himself after devoting a book to the great rival, Ikonnikov was careful to insist on the "crisis" of the production he portrayed, which he declared to be incoherent: "Nowadays, the global portrait of American architecture lacks a clear 'framework.' The reason for this is not the fact that the currently dominant generation has failed to produce prominent figures such as the now-extinct leaders that were Wright, Mies, or Neutra. The most notable reason is that no new ideas have emerged to make architecture a vital element of social life. The lack of a common social ideal and the shortage of ideas to believe in results in a contradiction between the wealth of resources and the narrowness of the ends to which they are allocated."[172] Perplexity regarding America's diverse production, which baffled even seasoned critics such as Ikonnikov—to his own admission—, soon made way for a new confidence instilled by the postmodern discourse that was reaching Russia. As of the late 1970s, Posokhin had perceived its early manifestations in projects by Philip Johnson's firm, such as the AT&T Building in New York[173]. A mere few years later, its effects could be noted on a generation of extravagantly shaped skyscrapers, which the political crisis of the late 1980s nipped in the bud[174].

Raymond Loewy's Industrial Designs

In the 1970s, the USSR was still reeling from the aftermath of the Sokolniki exhibition. Leonid Brezhnev's regime attempted to reinforce the production of consumer goods during the brief interlude preceding the revival of the arms race, rekindled in 1983 with Ronald Reagan's "Star Wars." Modernizing car designs became crucial, as automobiles were met with resounding success during the 1959 exhibition. The Soviet Union intended not only to feed a growing local market, but also to promote international exports. This goal was reached with Togliatti VAZ plant, which manufactured the first FIAT 124 models in 1970, while a project for a new Ford truck factory failed[175]. Shortly after the closing of the 1959 exhibit, the Soviet public demanded more original car designs, an initiative spearheaded by a collective from the Gorky Automobile Plant[176]. This citizen-driven movement was part of a more general awareness of the need for a deliberate industrial design policy, which would soon be devised.

The State Committee for New Technologies, in Moscow, turned to the most prominent American designer, Raymond Loewy, then considered to be the father of streamlining[177]. Invited by the Committee in 1961, he befriended Dzhermen Gvishiani, his head of protocol and the son-in-law of Prime Minister Aleksei Kosygin. In 1971, Loewy recalled having been greeted by the Minister of Industry along with Iurii Solovev, a trained graphic designer who had become a train wagon designer and who served as an interpreter: "The Minister explained that the USSR was in serious need of Industrial Design both for internal and export reasons. As the profession was inexistent in the

Soviet Union, he said, he invited me to come over to his country, with a team, in order to organize the profession throughout the USSR. [...] I dissuaded him and suggested instead that he places in charge Iurii Solovev, who had impressed me by his understanding of Industrial Design and his imaginative mind."[178] As for Solovev, he credited himself for inviting the American—along with the graphic designer Herbert Pinzke and designer Samuel Sherr—and stressed the importance of this first trip: "In Moscow, Leningrad, and Tbilisi Loewy lectured and talked about his work. These lectures created a strong impression and convincingly demonstrated to audiences, among whom were many intelligent leaders of industry and trade, how far behind we really were in the field of design. His lectures particularly impressed students. They provided a stimulus for initiating the training of industrial designers in educational institutions that had previously only turned out craftsmen."[179]

A few months later, in 1962, the Council of Ministers issued a decree aimed at "improving the quality of machines and everyday products by introducing methods of artistic construction."[180] Accordingly, the VNIITE (Union's Research Institute for Technical Aesthetics) was quickly created and established at the centre of the VDNKh, with Solovev at its helm. The term "technical aesthetics," chosen over *design* because of the latter's western undertones, was selected for denoting the official field of activity and gave its title to the journal published by the Institute starting in 1964. Solovev credited Loewy, who had created the Compagnie de l'esthétique industrielle in Paris in 1952—a name which seems to have inspired the Soviets, for providing the necessary impetus for this timely decision-making: "Without question Loewy's visit—the impression that he made and the materials that he placed at our disposal—contributed greatly to the development of industrial design in our country. Of course, such a resolution would have been adopted regardless of Loewy. But he accelerated its acceptance. Not only was Loewy a talented designer, but a brilliant propagandist of design, and in this capacity no borders existed or political differences existed for him. Moreover, he arrived at just the right time, at the height of the thaw. In my opinion, such a revolutionary government resolution would have been impossible two years later, in the period of stagnation under Leonid Brezhnev."[181]

After providing this initial impulse, Loewy retained close ties with Gvishiani and Solovev, whom he invited to New York in 1970 and in 1972, engaging in exploratory discussions that led him to be hired by Solovev as a consultant for a series of projects, ranging from the most experimental

175   David Lanier Lewis, *The Public Image of Henry Ford: An American Folk Hero and His Company* (Detroit: Wayne State University Press, 1976), 384. On the VAZ, see Siegelbaum, *Cars for Comrades*, 80–124.

176   "Sozdadim originalnuiu formu otechestvennogo avtomobila; obrashchenie khudozhnikov gorkovskogo avtozavoda," *Dekorativnoe iskusstvo SSSR*, no. 10 (October 1959): 13.

177   The Soviet general public discovered his production in the article by Leonard Reed, "Raymond Loewy, vedushchii amerikanskii khudozhnik-konstruktor," *Amerika*, no. 3 (1966): 43–45.

178   Raymond Loewy, "Visit to Moscow of Raymond and Viola Loewy, September 6 to 10, 1971," Raymond Loewy Archive, Hagley Museum and Library, Wilmington, DE, box 5, file 6, 4–5.

179   Yuri B. Soloviev, "Raymond Loewy in the USSR," in *Raymond Loewy: Pioneer of American Industrial Design,* ed. Angela Schönberger (Munich: Prestel, 1990), 196. See John Wall's comments in *Streamliner: Raymond Loewy and Image-Making in the Age of American Industrial Design* (Baltimore: Johns Hopkins University Press, 2018), 268–70.

180   "Ob uluchenii katchestva produktsii mashinostroenia i tovarov kulturno-bytovogo naznachenia putiom vnedrenia metodov khudozhestvennogo konstruirovania," USSR Council of Ministers Resolution no. 349, in *Reshenia partii i pravitelstva po khoziaistvennym voprosam: 1962–1965* (Moscow: Izd-vo polititcheskoi literatury, 1968), 65.

181   Soloviev, "Raymond Loewy in the USSR," 197.

Raymond Loewy, with the Compagnie de l'esthétique industrielle. Project for the Moskvich XRL automobile, 1975.
Top: Rendered perspective. Colour print on paper. Ever Endt collection.

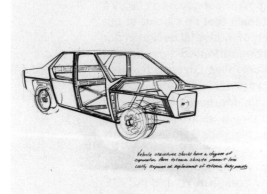

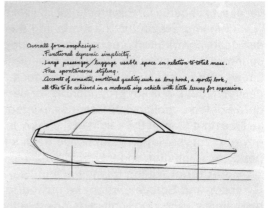

Center: Two study sketches. Gelatin silver print on paper and photostat, 27.9 × 21.6 cm. Raymond Loewy Archive, Hagley Museum and Library.
Bottom: Raymond Loewy, first row on the right, in Moscow, with Nikolai Smeliakov, Iurii Solovev, and other Soviet officials, 1973.
Gelatin silver print on paper, 27.9 × 21.6 cm. Raymond Loewy Archive, Hagley Museum and Library.

endeavours to simple household furnishings. The following years were punctuated by a dozen trips to Moscow, a series of framework agreements, and countless meetings. Loewy's Soviet experience turned out to be fun. He used his photos of Moscow's metro as an inspiration in his study for Montreal's metro. He was also amused and heartened to spot in the streets of the Soviet capital a vernacular copy of the Avanti, an innovative automobile he had designed for Studebaker, made of two motorcycles and a metal sheet shell[182].

During his 1972 trip, Loewy was commissioned by the Deputy Minister of Foreign Trade Nikolai Smeliakov to conduct a mission on the interior layout of the Tupolev Tu-144 supersonic transport aircraft[183]. The Soviets were aware that he had designed the exterior and the cabin for John F. Kennedy's Boeing 707, the original Air Force One. Loewy warned his collaborators that "the Tupolev 144 is as important to the Russian people's pride and to the top government team as the Concorde is to the French. Whoever is going to design the Tu-144 interiors will become somewhat of a Soviet Union's hero, a bit like an early astronaut."[184] The possibility of building a mock-up was considered, with Loewy insisting on including details that would show that his crew "understand[s] aircraft operation, where a sharp asperity may tear a dress, a hinge get loose, an ashtray get jammed, a moulding get warped, a switch has been located too far for comfort, a window screen does not slide easy, a toilet floor is hard to clean in the corners where airsick kids throw up. This is what the Russians call expertise; they know they don't have it, and this is why they come to see us."[185]

Loewy, whose every step in this process had to be approved by the Department of State, kindly offered to serve as a commercial broker for the American airline Braniff, which was about to acquire three Franco-British supersonics[186]. But the Goussainville catastrophe of 3 June 1973 tarnished the fate of the aircraft, when a prototype crashed to the ground during the Paris Air Show. After Tupolev's death in December 1972, a study of the Tu-154 three-engined airplane, a cousin of the Boeing 727, was abandoned. Furthermore, an operation intended for the Yakovlev Yak-40, meant to be distributed by Grumman in the United States, was also cancelled. But not all was lost, as Loewy was recruited by Air France to design the cabins of the Concorde. In 1974, a more sensitive matter arose, that of designing the Soviet space station. As Loewy had been working for NASA since 1967 and had designed the Skylab, enlisting him for the project was an obvious choice. He sent Solovev a great deal of material about this endeavour, but his efforts were thwarted by the American government and NASA, who reminded him that all interactions on the matter were restricted to official entities connected to the Soviet Academy of Sciences[187].

A framework agreement signed in 1973 with Lisensintorg, an organization in charge of technological transfers, contained an eclectic and ambitious list, including the following products: machine tools, forge hammers, equipment

182   Raymond Loewy Archive, Hagley Museum and Library, Wilmington, DL, box 1.
183   Iurii B. Solovev, Letter to Raymond Loewy, 18 December 1972. Raymond Loewy Archive, box 1.
184   Raymond Loewy, Note to Joseph Lovelace and David Butler, 8 June 1972, 2. Raymond Loewy Archive, box 1. Loewy uses the American term "astronaut" rather than the Russian "cosmonaut."
185   Ibid., 4.
186   Raymond Loewy, Letter to Robert White [State Department], 18 January 1972. Raymond Loewy, Telegram to Nikolai Smeliakov [USSR Minister of Foreign Trade], 20 March 1972. Raymond Loewy Archive, box 1.
187   Raymond Loewy, Letter to Iurii B. Solovev, 2 May 1974. Von R. Eshleman [Office of Space and Atmospheric Science Affairs], Letter to Joseph Lovelace, 31 January 1974. Raymond Loewy Archive, box 5.

for the food industry and medical equipment, motorcycles, bicycles, seagoing passenger ships, tractors, radio sets, watches, photo and film cameras, canned food packaging, vodka bottles, sports and hunting goods, and more importantly, cars[188]. This agreement came at a most opportune moment, as the first oil crisis affected the firm's business. The most complex and durable operation in which the New York firm Loewy & Snaith and the Compagnie de l'esthétique industrielle were involved as part of the 1975 agreement was in the design of a new sedan, the Moskvich XRL (Experimental Raymond Loewy), for the Moscow ZIL factory. This commission came about as Soviet automotive production was experiencing unprecedented growth. It went from 344,000 units in 1970 to 1,327,000 in 1980, and surpassed truck manufacturing by 100 per cent. While the fleet destined for the Russian population surged, exports quadrupled[189]. After three decades of relatively identical copies of Detroit models, American expertise was called upon to create models adapted to local production and usage conditions. Loewy examined not only the factory's entire production, but also that of western competitors, to offer a vehicle that would be "truly Russia—and highly saleable" as well as attractive, soliciting help from the American car expert Karl Eric Ludvigsen.

Paraphrasing the title of his 1951 bestseller *Never Leave Well Enough Alone*, Loewy wrote to his clients: "Pure function, a car with a purpose, soundly and correctly priced is not enough. Moskvich XRL needs romance, a sensuous overtone. It must be an automobile 'one falls in love with at first sight.'"[190] To reach "a high level of logic and sensibility," Loewy focused on redesigning the general shape of the vehicle, creating a double rather than a triple volume with five doors, ensuring its livability and attempting to combine contradictory qualities: "Looking fleet and racy, but also tough and stable, the Moskvich XRL will blend the grace of a ballet dancer with the mighty look of a tractor. Way ahead of any other car, it will reflect the power and prestige of the Nation."[191] [ill. p. 520] Created with numerous sketches and scale models, the designs were extremely elaborate and well regarded in the United States, a fact that Loewy boasted in his letters to Solovev, quoting remarks from the American population like "When can we buy one?" and "Detroit should have called you for help instead of Moscow."[192] But in April 1975, a telegram from Solovev closed the file in the following terms: "Further work for Moskvich not feasible stop perhaps Izhevsk [a Moskvich factory] will need your services in future stop then additional request will be sent regards."[193]

Concurrently to the XRL, Loewy designed a refrigerator for the American market, also meant to be manufactured by the ZIL. This is rather ironic considering that in 1951, the factory had produced the DKh-2, the first machine to be mass-produced in the USSR; its design, created by Sergei Kamishkirtsev, was reminiscent of the Coldspot, which Loewy himself had imagined in the 1930s for Sears, Roebuck & Co., in the spirit of automotive construction[194]. Loewy's team worked on interpreting Russian consumer habits to create a 400-litre refrigerator, while including certain elements of the Moscow production. On this theme, Loewy wrote to his friend Solovev: "We do feel that the ZIL three-chamber concept (with an all-purpose chamber) has good sales potential in the U.S. market, but not if it varies too much from U.S. customs of refrigerator use."[195]

1975 was a pivotal year in Loewy's Soviet adventures. Under the auspices of VNIITE, hoping to resume his work on the Moskvich, he presented an exhibition of his production in Moscow, building on materials from the exhibit held at the Renwick Gallery in Washington. More importantly, he signed a new framework agreement with Gvishiani, determining his working agenda for the five following years. This renewable agreement covered "a broad range of design activities, including product planning and design, packaging design, graphics, specialized architecture, interior planning and design (hotels, shopping centres, department stores, etc.), transportation design and product profile research."[196] More expansive than the 1973 deal, this arrangement turned Loewy into a marketing consultant, giving him free rein over product exports. Beyond the relatively vague list of products, Loewy was hired in order to conduct a global watch on "product demand in western markets, aesthetic tendencies, and emerging fields of innovation in terms of design, materials, and production techniques, as well as related aspects such as product utility, comfort, and security."[197] Always careful to cultivate his image as the saviour of humanity, Loewy gave an interview to *People* magazine, which proceeded to report: "The Kremlin wishes to entice not only increasingly sophisticated Soviet consumers but the spenders of Western hard currency who have previously shunned ineptly designed Soviet products. In asking Loewy to help sell their goods and improve their balance of payments, Soviet leaders are turning to an international designer with an unequalled record of commercial success."[198]

The last successful project developed in detail by Loewy's teams was the Kometa hydrofoil, ideated as of 1973 and completed in March 1976. The high-speed boat manufactured in the USSR since the early 1960s was among the rare Soviet vehicles widely distributed abroad, namely in Greece, among other countries. Loewy retained the technical principles of his previous projects, but updated the general shape, replacing the round contours of the body with an angular design, and making the inside more comfortable[199] [ill. p. 525]. He also designed a tractor for a factory in Minsk. All these projects came to a halt for two correlated reasons. Loewy seemed to be wary of losing his American business, as his major industrial clients were worried that the Soviets would obtain their trade secrets. Conversely, according to Solovev, the Soviet industry had no wish to renew its production, and interest for Loewy's projects remained limited to expert circles[200]. However, his relations with the Russians seemed to endure, as evidenced by an article published in *Design Magazine* in 1980, which reported that "though the recent furor over Afghanistan has made his work for the USSR harder to organize, the Kremlin has called to say how it wants to resume collaboration once the whole thing has blown over."[201]

188	"Approximate list of products on which collaboration is possible (items, produced by the USSR industry)," n.d. [March 1973], Raymond Loewy Archive, box 6.
189	Statistics reported in Siegelbaum, Cars for Comrades, 239.
190	Raymond Loewy, "Moskvich XRL," typoscript, 16 July 1973, 1. Raymond Loewy Archive, box 3. See Raymond Loewy, Never Leave Well Enough Alone: The Personal Record of an Industrial Designer (New York: Simon & Schuster, 1951).
191	Loewy, "Moskvich XRL," 2.
192	Raymond Loewy, Letter to Iurii Solovev, 6 February 1974, Raymond Loewy Archive, box 3.
193	Iurii Solovev, Telegram to Raymond Loewy, 15 April 1975, Raymond Loewy Archive, box 3.
194	Phil Patton, Made in USA: The Secret History of the Things That Made America (New York: Penguin Books, 1993), 245, 247, and 261.
195	Raymond Loewy, Letter to Iurii Solovev, 22 July 1974, Raymond Loewy Archive, box 5.
196	Press release, 16 June 1975, Raymond Loewy Archive, box 6.
197	Agreement between the State Committee for Science and Technology of the USSR Council of Ministers and Raymond Loewy International Inc., 14 June 1975, Raymond Loewy Archive, box 6.
198	"Still at the Drawing Board, Designer Raymond Loewy Shapes Up Russia's Exports," People, 10 March 1975.
199	Kometa hydrofoil deliverables, prepared by Raymond Loewy International, Inc., for Licensintorg, 29 March 1976, Raymond Loewy Archive, box 1.
200	Soloviev, "Raymond Loewy in the USSR," 201.
201	James Woudhuysen, "Raymond Loewy: A Message from a Grand Old Man," Design, 28 May 1980.

In 1986, *Tekhnicheskaia estetika* issued one last interview shortly after Loewy's death. In a rather vague discourse on "the future of design," he claimed to see one of the defining factors of "peaceful coexistence" in product design and urban planning, as though all that remained from his Soviet experience was the political jargon[202]. Despite the apparent neutrality of technical objects, Loewy's incomplete flirtation with Brezhnev's USSR is an eloquent expression of the Soviets' collective desire to acquire the functional and aesthetic qualities of American goods and to mimic them in their own production[203].

The success met by Welton Becket and Associates was in stark contrast with Loewy's failed attempts at dealing with the Soviets. The firm, whose Los Angeles offices were regularly visited by Soviet delegations, had designed one of the sections of the Sokolniki exhibition and was involved in a project meant to stabilize the technological exchanges initially endeavoured by Loewy. In 1976, the Moscow World Trade Centre project was borne from an agreement between Occidental Petroleum and Prommachimport, instigated by Armand Hammer, who had returned to Moscow in 1961, rekindling his relationship with his old acquaintance Anastas Mikoyan[204]. Its mixed financing by a group of American banks headed by the Chase Manhattan Bank and the Soviet government, unprecedented in the long history of economic relations between the two countries, was determined in 1974 and a four-hectare lot was chosen on the banks of the Moskva River, near the Hotel Ukraina, to erect the four buildings[205]. Overseen by the New York branch of the agency, the project was designed by MacDonald Becket with the Bechtel engineering firm, but co-signed by Posokhin, who supervised each step of the process[206]. Inaugurated in 1980, it was topped with two glass-clad towers, distant imitations of Minoru Yamasaki's New York structures. Posokhin had admired the towers during previous travels and had spent a whole day thoroughly visiting them in 1974, when Hammer loaned him his private jet to fly to relevant sites for the project[207]. The centre contained an apartment hotel, an unknown concept until then—though it could be viewed as a luxurious iteration of communal housing, stripped of its utopian dimension—, and a hotel whose lobby featured exterior elevators, according to a principle favored by John Portman, but invented by Ivan Leonidov [ill. p. 214].

202   Raymond Loewy, in Y.V. Shatin, "Reimond Loui", *Tekhnitcheskaia estetika*, no. 3 (1987): 26–30.
203   On the design of mass market goods, see Alexandra Sankova, *Designed in the USSR 1950-1989: From the Collection of the Moscow Design Museum* (London: Phaidon, 2018); Michael Idov, ed., *Made in Russia: Unsung Icons of Soviet Design* (New York: Rizzoli, 2011).
204   "Occidental Corp. To Help Soviets Build Moscow Trade Center," *Daily Commercial News*, 17 March 1976; Hammer and Lyndon, *Hammer*, 312–28.
205   "US, Soviets Sign Trade Center Pact," *Texas Morning News*, 20 April 1974; "Design Contract Signed for Moscow Trade Center," *Louisville Courier Journal*, 20 April 1974; "Soviet–US Contract Signed for International Trade Center," *Los Angeles Herald Examiner*, 21 April 1974.
206   MacDonald Becket, *Leadership in Architecture: My Passion in Life* (Bloomington, IN: AuthorHouse, 2014), 162–69.
207   Posokhin, *Dorogi zhizni*, 193–95.

Raymond Loewy and the Compagnie de l'esthétique industrielle. Project for a *Kometa* hydrofoil boat, 1976.
Model view. Gelatin silver print on paper, 21.4 × 27.9 cm. Raymond Loewy Archive, Hagley Museum and Library.

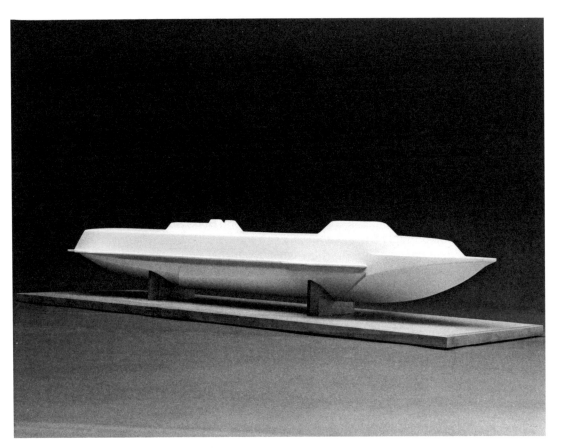

MacDonald Becket (second from left with pointer) shows to Mikhail Posokhin (third from left)
the model of the World Trade Center in Moscow, ca 1975.

Exhaustion and Oblivion

Though it was confined to rare joint ventures, the Soviet interest in the United States endured under Brezhnev and his successors. Distorted through multiple prisms, information nevertheless continued to circulate, namely in film production, which continued to peddle early Cold War-era stereotypes[208]. Jazz found new audiences, displaying the numerous ranks of its musicians and the fervour of its enthusiasts during the Tallinn festivals, the first of which was organized in 1967. The 50th anniversary of the official arrival of jazz in the USSR was celebrated in 1972, giving way to the publication of historical research such as that of Alexei Batashev, which was authorized by the censors in exchange for a few cuts to the initial text[209]. In the last years of the Soviet regime, when this musical genre, which was tolerated, but not encouraged, spread to numerous cities, the style that most inspired musicians was free jazz.[210]

New travel narratives followed the path opened by Ilf and Petrov, such as the one published by Vasili Peskov and Boris Strelnikov, which sold 100,000 copies in 1977[211]. *A California Encounter*, a 1975 bestseller by the former American correspondent of *Izvestiia*, Stanislav Kondrashov—who described the United States in half a dozen works—, was the first account of the emergence of an alternative culture on the West Coast[212]. Emigrant writings recorded their reactions to a real America—beyond the fantasy—as well as their previous fixations. In his 1987 novel *In Search of Melancholy Baby*, published in New York City, Vasilii Aksenov echoed some of his predecessors, revealing the presence of an intertextual network uniting previous figures of Americanism. This connection is apparent in his retelling of his experience with the "Maryland amazons," young girls whom he had met on the all-female campus of Goucher College. In *When Cathedrals Were White*, Le Corbusier had mentioned similar "amazons" who tore up his conference drawings to shreds at Vassar College in 1935[213]. To describe New York, a city which is "like a snazzy broad who fusses with her hair but forgets to wipe her ass," he stated in cruder

208   Andreï Kozovoï, "Présence des États-Unis en URSS, 1975–1985: Le grand public soviétique et les pratiques périaméricaines des pouvoirs," *Bulletin de l'Institut Pierre Renouvin* 25, n 1 (2007): 207–14; Id., "Les États-Unis réinventés sur les écrans soviétiques (1975–1985)," *Communisme*, no. 90 (2007): 119–39.

209   Alexei N. Batashev, *Sovetski djaz: istoricheskii ocherk* (Moscow: Muzyka, 1972); See also Aleksandr Medvedev and Olga Medvedeva, *Sovetskii djaz: problemy, sobytia, mastera* (Moscow: Sovetskii kompozitor, 1987).

210   Starr, *Red & Hot*, 316–34.

211   Vasilii M. Peskov and Boris G. Strelnikov, *Zemlia za okeanom: bolchoe puteshestvie po Amerike* (Moscow: Molodaia gvardia, 1977).

212   Stanislav N. Kondrashov, *Svidanie s Kaliforniei* (Moscow: Molodaia gvardia, 1975).

213   Le Corbusier, *When the Cathedrals Where White: A Journey to the Land of Timid People* [1937] (London: Routledge, 1947), 137.

214   Aksenov, *In Search of Melancholy Baby*, 23. See also D. B. Johnson, "Aksënov as Travel Writer," in *Vasiliy Pavlovich Aksënov: A Writer in Quest of Himself*, Edward Mozejko, Boris Briker and Per Dalgård, eds. (Columbus, OH: Slavica Publishers, 1986), 181–92.

215   Eduard Limonov, *His Butler's Story* [1980] (New York: Grove Press, 1986).

216   Vladimir Z. Paperny, *Mos-Angeles* (Moscow: Novoe literaturnoe obozrenie, 2004); *Mos-Angeles dva* (Moscow: Novoe literaturnoe obozrenie, 2009).

217   Yasha Klots, "The Ultimate City: New York In Russian Immigrant Narratives," *The Slavic and East European Journal* 55, no. 1 (Spring 2011): 38–57. See also Mikhail Iossel and Jeff Parker, eds., *Amerika: Russian Writers View the United States* (Normal, IL: Dalkey Archive Press, 2004); and Jean-Louis Cohen, "Retour d'Amérique: pages d'écriture russes," *Europe*, no. 1055 (March 2017), 43–54.

218   Maria Petrakova, "La perception de l'Amérique dans la société russe," *Quaderni*, no. 50–51 (Spring 2003): 249–64.

219   Jan Cermak, George J. Tamaro, "Foundations of High-Rise Structures in Moscow and New York City," in *Geotechnical Challenges in Megacities*, ed., V.P. Petrukhin (Saint Petersburg: GRF, 2010), 359–64.

220   Pavel Sudoplatov, *Special Tasks: The Memoirs of an Unwanted Witness: a Soviet Spymaster* (Boston; Toronto: Little - Brown, 1995).

terms what Ilya Ehrenburg and, to a certain extent, Konstantin Balmont had expressed before him: "Unfortunately, we émigrés inhabit her nether regions."[214] This was the New York inhabited by Eduard Limonov, whose writings, like Aksenov's, would only reach Russia after the fall of the Soviet Union[215]. Other cities, like Los Angeles, explored by Vladimir Paperny, were featured in books written by the last generations of travellers and émigrés[216]. The recent corpus of these writings is considerable and has become the subject of anthologies and studies, some of which have detected "Hudsonian tones" in a portion of the Russian literary production[217].

The United States remained a significant centre of interest for the post-Soviet public, which nevertheless maintained its phobic stance, following the official views[218]. But the many semantic borrowings demonstrate that despite the Russians' denials and repression, American hegemony persists, namely in the realm of urban culture. In Moscow's twenty-first century housing market, *developers* are kings, offering *penthouses*, *townhouses*, and *offices* for sale and to rent. These English terms have replaced the German or Dutch ones, such as *kontory*, previously used to characterize the workplace. In terms of urban planning projects, the set of office buildings called Moskva City over-shadows the now dwarflike towers of the World Trade Centre. Their invisible foundations were designed by Mueser Rutledge Consulting Engineers, the current avatar of Moran & Proctor, which had been involved in the Palace of the Soviets project and had preserved its surveys of Moscow's subsoil[219]. These distant echoes of unfinished Stalin-era projects extend to realizations that are dear to the Muscovites, such as high-rise buildings. The Triumph Palace, completed in 2007 by Andrei Trofimov, alludes to these structures, coupling their pyramidal arrangement with exceedingly vulgar ornamentation. As for the Oruzheinyi Building, located on the edge of the Garden Ring, it was directly inspired by New York, according to its creator Mikhail Posokhin, the son of Moscow's chief architect of the 1960s and 1970s.

The Soviet infrastructure built for its American policy has been dis-mantled. Amtorg was liquidated in 1998, and its innermost workings have since been revealed in spy memoirs such as those of Pavel Sudoplatov[220]. In the field of architecture, many of the Russian authors quoted in this book have admitted to the significance of West-to-East transfers that endured despite the chang-ing political discourse of the past decades, from the wartime alliance to the post-1945 Stalin era, all the way to Khrushchev's reforms and the subsequent stagnation. Though its leaders had strongly condemned "cosmopolitism" at various moments, Soviet material and visual culture has been shaped by a sometimes overt and often surreptitious Americanism. In many cases, this at-titude has had a tremendous impact on urban and architectural forms, making it a building block of contemporary Russian civilization. In Vladimir Putin's Russia, openly hostile to America to the point where it seems to be trying to undermine its political system, an unprecedented permeability has become the norm. Emigrants from the 1990s have maintained close connections to their homeland, and numerous forms of temporary mobility have emerged. The rising middle class now engages in a form of tourism taking its members to the re-motest areas of the United States.

This more privileged and sprawling relationship is also devoid of ide-alism, as evidenced by the song "Goodbye Amerika," interpreted by Viacheslav Butusov's rock band Nautilus Pompilius in 1985, the very year in which Mikhail Gorbachev came to power:

"Goodbye America, oh
Where I have never ever been
Farewell for ever!
Take your banjo
And play me for goodbye
la-la-la-la-la-la, la-la-la-la-la-la
Your worn-out blue jeans
Became too tight for me
We've been taught for too long
To be in love with your forbidden fruits."

As the USSR headed to its demise, America, finally better known among the Russians, lost most of its mystique. With it waned the desire to create a new and improved Russian America, a wish that had been fostered by many politicians, technicians, and artists ever since the nineteenth century. Meanwhile, the key moments of Amerikanizm—from Grigorii Aleksandrov's musicals to the Lend-Lease Act and the 1959 American National Exhibition in Moscow—remained ingrained in the post-Soviet collective memory, so much so that their long-term endurance could provide enough material for another book.

Index and credits

Verband Deutscher Elektrotechniker (Union of German Electrical Technicians) 115

Vkhutein: Vysshyi gosudarstvennyi khudozhestvenno-tekhnicheskii Institut (Higher State Artistic and Technical Institute), Moscow 153, *208*, 233, 254, 255

Vkhutemas: Vysshie gosudarstvennye khudozhestvenno-tekhnicheskie masterskie (Higher State Artistic and Technical Studios), Moscow *186*, 201, *206*, 207, *211*, *214*, 215, 233, 234, *235*, 244, 255, 290

VNIITE: Vsesoiuznyi institut tekhnicheskoi estetiki (Union's Institute for Technical Aesthetics), Moscow 519, 522

VOKS: Vsesoiuznoe obshchestvo kulturnoi sviazi s zagranitsei (Union Society for Cultural Relations with Foreign Countries), Moscow 110, 350, 353, 383, 385, 393, 418

VSNKh: Vekhovnyi soviet narodnogo khoziaistva (Supreme Council of the National Economy), Moscow 135, 147, 168, 201, 207, 314

VTSIK: Vserossiiskii tsentralnyi ispolnitelnyi komitet (Central Executive Committee of the Union), Moscow *214*, 215

W
World of Art society 256

Y
Yale University, New Haven 473
YMCA (Young Men's Christian Association) 225

Z
Zhivskulptarkh: Komissiia zhivopisno-skulpturno-arkhitekturnogo sinteza (Committee for the Synthesis of Painting, Sculpture and Architecture), Moscow 201
ZIL: Zavod imeni Likhacheva (Likhachev Factory), Moscow 354, 415, 466, 522
ZIS: Zavod imeni Stalina (Stalin Factory), Moscow 415

APRF: Arkhiv Prezidenta Rossiiskoi Federatsii (Archives of the President of the Russian Federation)

GARF: Gosudarstvennyi Arkhiv Rossiiskoi Federatsii (State Archives of the Russian Federation)

MUAR: Muzei arkhitektury im. Shchuseva (Shchusev Architecture Museum)

NARA (National Archive and Records Administration)

OKhD: Otdel Khranenia Dokumentov, Tsentralnyi Gosudarstvennyi Arkhiv Goroda Moskvy (Department for the Conservation of Records, Central State Archive of the City of Moscow)

RGAE: Rossiiskii Gosudarstvennyi Arkhiv Ekonomiki (State Russian Archives for the Economy)

RGASPI: Rossiiskii Gosudarstvennyi Arkhiv Sotsialno-Politicheskoi istorii (State Russian Archives for Social and Political History)

RGALI: Rossiiskii Gosudarstvennyi Arkhiv Literatury i Iskusstva (State Russian Archives for Literature and Art)

Chapter 1

p. 25
Moses King, *King's Views of New York: Four Hundred Illustrations*, New York: Moses King, ca. 1912. Drawing by Richard W. Rummell. CCA, ID:86-B1493.

p. 26-27
Samuel H. Gottscho. Night view of Luna Park at Coney Island, New York, 1904. Gelatin silver print. CCA, PH1979:0478:014.

p. 28-29
Moscow of the Future, advertising card published by the Einem candy factory in Moscow, 1912, CCA.

p. 30-31
Ernst Richard Nirnzee, High rise buiding, Bolshoi Gnezdikovskii pereulok, Moscow, 1912. Moskva kotoroi net.

p. 32
(top) Still image from *New York 1911*, produced by Svenska Biografteatern, 1911. Museum of Modern Art.
(bottom) Still image from *Moscow*, 1910.
Gaumont Pathé Archives.

Chapter 2

p. 89
Lillian M. and Frank B. Gilbreth. Motion study, image recorded with a chronocyclegraph, 1910. Purdue University Libraries, Frank and Lillian Gilbreth Papers.

p. 90-91
Tractor factory, Kharkov. Photograph by Iakov. N. Khalip, in *USSR in Construction*, June 1937. Private collection.

p. 92-93
Albert Kahn Associates. Tractor factory, Chelyabinsk, 1930-1932. Photograph by Leonid M. Surin, 1935. State Archive of the Sverdlovsk region.

p. 94-95
The oil industry in Baku, in *USSR in Construction*, May 1935. Private collection.

p. 96
Stalinets S-60 tractor produced in the Chelyabinsk factory. Fold-outs in *USSR in Construction*, 1933. Private collection.

Chapter 3

p. 177
Still image from *The Extraordinary Adventures of Mr. West in the Land of the Bolsheviks*, directed by Lev V. Kuleshov, produced by Goskino, 1924. Lobster films.

p. 178-179
Georgii and Vladimir Stenberg, Poster of the film *Chicago*, 1929. Merrill C. Berman Collection.

p. 180-181
Psychotechnical Laboratory of Vkhutemas. Ploglazometr, apparatus to measure areas. Illustrations in *Arkhitektura i Vkhutein* 1, no. 2, 1929. In Selim O. Khan-Magomedov, *Vhutemas*, 1991. CCA, N332.S65.M675 (ID:93-B1002).

p. 182
El Lissitzky. Wolkenbügel (cloud presser) project, 1925, view at the Nikitskie Vorota, Moscow. Getty Research Institute.

p. 183
Erich Mendelsohn, Street scene in Detroit, 1924, in *Amerika: Bilderbuch eines Architekten,* Berlin: Rudolf Mosse, 1926 CCA, NA44.M537.A35 1926.

p. 184
Fritz Lang, photograph of Times Square in New York, in Erich Mendelsohn's *Amerika: Bilderbuch eines Architekten,* 1926. CCA, NA44.M537.A35 1926.

Chapter 4

p. 265
Corbett, Harrison & MacMurray, Hood, Godley & Fouilhoux, and Reinhard & Hofmeister. Rockefeller Center, New York, 1930–1936. From the series of photographs of skyscrapers collected by Boris Iofan in New York. Alex Lachmann Collection.

p. 266
Viacheslav K. Oltarzhevskii. Plate in *Contemporary Babylon,* New York, 1933. Private Collection.

p. 267
Viacheslav K. Oltarzhevskii. Plate in *Contemporary Babylon,* New York, 1933. Private Collection.

p. 268–269
Ilya A. Ilf. Group of men on a street in the West, from the series of photographs taken in the United States, October 1935–January 1936. Russian State Archives for Literature and Art.

p. 270
Ivan I. Leonidov. Competition project of the People's Commissariat of Heavy Industry, Moscow, 1934. Shchusev State Museum of Architecture.

p. 271
Boris M. Iofan, with Vladimir G. Gelfreikh and Vladimir A. Shchuko. Project for the Palace of the Soviets, Moscow, 1934. Monumental statue of Vladimir I. Lenin. Private collection.

p. 272
Daniil F. Fridman and Gleb I. Glushchenko. House of Industry, Sverdlovsk, 1931–1935. CCA PH1993:0240.

Chapter 5

p. 361
Lev Rudnev shows to a group of students the model of the Moscow State University, in *USSR in Construction,* no. 11, 1949. Private collection.

p. 362–363
Lewis Hine. Riveters working on mooring mast of the Empire State Building, New York, 1931. CCA PH1984:0075.

p. 364–365
Panel of the Exhibition on American architecture sent to the Soviet Union by the National Council of American-Soviet Friendship, 1945. Douglas Putnam Haskell papers, Avery Architectural & Fine Arts Library, Columbia University.

p. 366
An American woman tastes the canned pork stew shipped by the thousands of tons to the USSR, New York, ca. 1944. National Archives and Records Administration.

p. 367
Alexander S. Zhitomirskii. *A Wolfish Appetite,* photomontage for *Literaturnaia gazeta,* 4 October 1947. Ne boltai! Collection.

p. 368
Nikolay M. Poliakov and Alexander B. Boretskii at the construction site of the Leningradskaia Hotel, in *USSR in Construction,* November 1949. Private collection.

Chapter 6

p. 449
Nikita S. Khrushchev and Richard Nixon at the American National Exposition, Moscow, 1959. National Archives and Records Administration.

p. 450
Cover of *Amerika* magazine, no. 36, 1963. CCA.

p. 451
Elliott Erwitt. The American National Exposition, Moscow, 1959. Harry Ransom Center, The University of Texas at Austin.

p. 452–453
Ivan Chermayeff and Thomas H. Geismar. *Industrial Design USA,* United States Information Agency, 1967, spread with tomatoes and knifes. Private collection.

p. 454
Aerial view of Los Angeles, in Mikhail V. Posokhin, *Urban Planning in the United States,* Moscow, 1965. Private collection.

p. 455
Ivan Chermayeff and Thomas H. Geismar. *Industrial Design USA,* United States Information Agency, 1967, cover. Private collection.

p. 456
Nikita S. Khrushchev and Roswell Garst at Garst's farm in Coon Rapids, Iowa, 1959. Alamy.

This book is the result of a lengthy process, stemming from publications issued in the late 1970s and from talks given on various occasions, including Hubert Damisch's weekly seminar at the École des hautes études en sciences sociales, then held on Rue de Tournon, in Paris. I articulated my first insights on this topic alongside Hubert, and later developed them as part of the "Américanisme et modernité" conference organized by the EHESS and the Institut français d'architecture in 1985. The conference proceedings were published in 1993, after a lengthy delay, with wholehearted support from Jean-François Barrielle, then the publishing director of Flammarion. In keeping with the spirit of these discussions, a fraction of the materials covered in this book was shown in the *Scenes of the World to Come* exhibit held at the Canadian Centre for Architecture in 1995. My warmest thoughts go to Hubert for being a constant inspiration and for our ongoing and challenging discussions.

I also wish to pay tribute to the late Anatole Kopp, who took part in the 1985 conference, but who—most importantly—ignited my passion for the Russian avant-garde. This interest initially led me to Moscow to explore the movement's remaining architectural traces and to meet with its survivors: the last of the 1920s architects. In 1987, I was able to observe him at work in Washington, where he was researching Albert Kahn's activities in the USSR, a topic that had previously scarcely been discussed. Incidentally, I must thank Henry Millon, who allowed me to spend that winter in the peculiar triangular offices of the Center for Advanced Study at the National Gallery of Art, which became my headquarters as I perused, exhilarated, the boundless stacks of the Library of Congress, then open to researchers day and night.

After the Washington collections allowed me to engage in more thorough scholarship, I pursued my investigations, making several research trips to the Getty Research Institute, first in Santa Monica, owing to the gracious hospitality of Kurt Forster, Herbert Hymans, and Thomas Reese, and later in Brentwood, where I was invited by Salvatore Settis and Tom Crow. In addition to support from the most obliging librarians, Alexander Weintraub and Jacob Stewart-Halevy helped me gather thousands of pages, in a pre-digital era. In Moscow, my explorations were made possible by the warm welcome extended to me by my friends Irina Kokkinaki and Andrei Gozak. David Sarkisian opened the doors to the Shchusev Museum of Architecture for me, in his unique and extravagant way, as did the friendly Irina Korobina, who took over the director position after his passing. In that same institution, I would like to thank the director Elizaveta Likhacheva and the efficient and thorough deputy director Pavel Kuznetsov for their tireless support, as well as the collection manager Maria Kostyuk and her assistant, Irina Finskaya. At the MArkhI Museum, I was graciously received by Larisa Ivanova-Veen and Tatiana Lysova. In the final phase of the project, Veronika Ushakova was instrumental in gathering documents and verifying obscure sources. In 2017, Nikita Sushkov was able to organize an expedition away from the Russian capital—to Ekaterinburg, Cheliabinsk, and Nizhnii Tagil—, enabling me to follow in Kahn's footsteps. The Ural architecture historians Larisa Piskunova and Igor Yankov gave me a clearer understanding of the context in which construction was undertaken in the region.

I would also like to extend my gratitude to Marc Dessauce, who gave me access to the papers of Knud Lonberg-Holm and Simon Breines, whom I was lucky enough to meet at the very beginning of the 3rd millennium, as well as to all those who provided me with documents and valuable advice. This includes my generous "Mos-Angeles" friends Marina Khrustaleva and Vladimir Paperny; Barbara Lamprecht, who provided me with information on the enigmatic Sergei Kozhin; Evgenii Asse, who shared memories of his mother Aleksandra Khristiani; Vladimir Shukhov, who presented me with documents on his grandfather; Sonia Melnikova-Raich, who told me about her investigations of Albert Kahn and Saul Bron; and Michał Dombrowski, who suggested a way of identifying the remarkable Moscow

perspective drawn by Henryk Dąbrowski. I retain fond memories of my frequent discussions about Albert Kahn with Claire Zimmerman, between Ann Arbor and Detroit. My utmost gratitude goes to Christina Crawford, Alla Vronskaya and Katherine Zubovich, who shared their outstanding doctoral dissertations with me prior to their publication. Seminars at the Princeton University School of Architecture (2013) and at the New York University Institute of Fine Arts (2015), as well as the lectures I gave at the Collège de France (2015) allowed me to further develop my ideas, fuelled by these lively exchanges. Masha Panteleyeva, Olena Chervonik, and English Cook helped me put these courses together. Da Hyung Jeong conducted complementary research in New York, while Sam Omans sifted through deeply buried archives and rare publications in Moscow and Los Angeles. Previously, my conversations with Richard Anderson during and after my 2005 seminar on World War II had been enlightening. Over the course of these four decades of intermittent research, I gave numerous talks and conference papers, during which my colleagues and their graduate students have asked me pointed questions that have compelled me to polish my analyses.

I am grateful to Valérie Pozner for her translation of Ilya Ehrenburg, as well as to Yvan Mignot for his elegant translations of several unpublished or poorly translated poems. The manuscript for this book was read in whole or in part by François Albera, Christina Crawford, Juliet Koss, and Danilo Udovički, whom I sincerely thank for their edits and notes. Natalia Solopova's review of the text, as well as her help in Paris and her welcome in Moscow, have been invaluable, as were our countless discussions and shared insights on "Uncle Sam in the Land of the Soviets," which, for a long time, was the secret code name for this project.

The exhibit that accompanied this book was made possible by the generosity of several collectors and numerous lenders, among whom I would like to give special credit to Alex Lachman, Merill Berman, Sergey Tchoban and his curator Nadja Bartels, Nancy Bartlett and Malgosia Myc at the University of Michigan Bentley Library, Janet Parks and Jennifer Gray at the Avery Library, as well as Sean Quimby and Jennifer B. Lee at Columbia University's Rare Book and Manuscript Library, Linda Skolarus at the Benson Ford Research Center, Andreas Nutz at the Vitra Design Museum, Lynn Catanese at the Hagley Museum, Gerd Zillner at the Frederick Kiesler Foundation in Vienna and Evert Endt, formerly from Raymond Loewy's Compagnie de l'esthétique industrielle in Paris.

At the Canadian Centre for Architecture, under Phyllis Lambert's gracious and watchful eye, the project was firmly supported by Mirko Zardini and Giovanna Borasi. The exhibit was overseen by Émilie Retailleau and Aude Renaud-Lorrain, with help from Helina Gebremedhen, and was made possible by technical assistance from Sébastien Larivière and Anh Truong, and administrative support from Christine Dalle-Vedove and Natasha Leeman. Martien de Vletter allowed the Centre's collection to acquire the books I gathered as part of my research. Within the gallery walls, the exhibit's discourse was ingeniously installed by Noëmi Mollet and Reto Geiser. Research and development of the models created to exemplify the main theses of this project was conducted by Mandana Bafghinia and Aurélien Catros, with guidance from Jean-Pierre Chupin, Canada Research Chair in Architecture, Competitions and Mediations for Excellence at the Université de Montréal.

Lastly, editorial production for this book was overseen by Albert Ferré and led by Geneviève Godbout and Nargisse Rafik for the French version, which was translated into English by Luba Markovskaia, while Stéphane Aleixandre collected its illustrations and Natasha Leeman delicately managed its implementation. This work, shaped into an attractive book thanks to Gregor Huber's design, has benefited from the editorial support of Katherine Boller at Yale University Press and Pierre Chabard at the Éditions de la Villette. My sincerest gratitude to all of those who were involved in this long-running project.

Colophon

Building a new New World: Amerikanizm in
Russian Architecture

This volume is published by the Canadian Centre for
Architecture and Yale University Press in conjunction with
the exhibition of the same title, organized by and presented
at the CCA from 12 November 2019 to 5 April 2020.

Curator and author
Jean-Louis Cohen

Publication
Editor-in-charge: Geneviève Godbout
Editorial assistance: Daria Der Kaloustian,
Helina Gebremedhen, Luba Markovskaia
Graphic design: Huber/Sterzinger, Sara Arzu
Translation: Luba Markovskaia
Rights and reproductions: Stéphane Aleixandre
Proof reading: Natasha Arora
Production management: Natasha Leeman
Printing and binding: DZA Druckerei zu Altenburg
Font: Basel by Chi-Long Trieu

Exhibition
Curatorial team: Aude Renaud-Lorrain,
Helina Gebremedhen, Émilie Retailleau
Design concept: MG&Co.
(Noëmi Mollet, Reto Geiser), Houston
Map concept: Studio Folder (Marco Ferrari,
Elisa Pasqual), Milan
Design development: Sébastien Larivière, Anh Truong
Research Assistants: Samuel Omans (New York and
Moscow), Veronika Ushakova (Moscow)

Lenders
Alex Lachmann Collection, London
Avery Architectural & Fine Arts Library, Columbia
    University, New York
Bentley Historical Library, University of Michigan,
    Ann Arbor, Albert Kahn Associates records and
    Albert Kahn Associates, Inc., Detroit
Butler Library, Rare Book & Manuscript Library,
    Columbia University, New York
Collection André-Raynaud, Direction des bibliothèques,
    Université de Montréal
Collection Merrill C. Berman, Rye, New York
Collection of The Henry Ford, Dearborn, Michigan
Getty Research Institute, Los Angeles
Hagley Museum and Library, Wilmington, Delaware
Österreichische Friedrich und Lillian Kiesler
    Privatstiftung, Vienna
Library of Congress, Washington, D.C.,
    Manuscript Division
Library of Congress, Washington, D.C.,
    General Collections
MOMus - Museum of Modern Art - Costakis Collection,
    Thessaloniki
Shchusev Museum of Architecture, Moscow
Private collection, Paris
Queen's University Library, Kingston, Ontario
Service des bibliothèques de l'UQAM, Montréal, Québec
Sprengel Museum Hannover
Tchoban Foundation, Museum for Architectural
    Drawing, Berlin

The Canadian Centre for Architecture is an international
research centre and museum founded by Phyllis Lambert
in 1979 on the conviction that architecture is a public
concern. Through its collection, exhibitions, public
programs, publications, and research opportunities the
CCA advances knowledge, promotes public understanding
and widens thought and debate on architecture, its
history, theory, practice, and its role in society today.

CCA Board of Trustees
Phyllis Lambert, Founding Director Emeritus
Bruce Kuwabara, Chair
Pierre-André Themens, Vice-Chair
Guido Beltramini; Giovanna Borasi; Stephen R. Bronfman;
Barry Campbell; Michael Conforti; Timur Galen;
Isabelle Jomphe; Sylvia Lavin; Greg Lynn;
Frederick Lowy; Gerald Sheff.
Honorary members: Serge Joyal, Warren Simpson

The CCA gratefully acknowledges the generous support
of the Ministère de la Culture et des Communications,
the Canada Council for the Arts, and the Conseil des arts
de Montréal.

© 2020 Canadian Centre for Architecture
All rights reserved under international copyright
conventions.

For more information on CCA publications,
please visit cca.qc.ca/publications.

978-1-927071-67-0
Canadian Centre for Architecture
1920 rue Baile
Montréal, Québec
Canada H3H 2S6
www.cca.qc.ca

978-0-300-24815-9
English edition distributed by Yale University Press,
New Haven and London
Yale University Press
302 Temple Street
P.O. Box 209040
New Haven, CT 06520-9040
www.yalebooks.com/art

Legal deposit: August 2020

Printed and bound in Germany

Bibliothèque et Archives nationales du Québec and
Library and Archives Canada cataloguing in publication

Title: Building a new New World: Amerikanizm in Russian
architecture / Jean-Louis Cohen ;
translated by Luba Markovskaia.
Other titles: Construire un nouveau Nouveau Monde.
Anglais
Names: Cohen, Jean-Louis, author. | Centre canadien
d'architecture, issuing body, host institution.
Description: Translation of: Construire un nouveau
Nouveau Monde. | Catalogue of an exhibition presented
at the Canadian Centre for Architecture. | Includes
bibliographical references and index.
Identifiers: Canadiana 20190040246 | ISBN
9781927071670
Subjects: LCSH: Architecture—Soviet Union—American
influences—Exhibitions. | LCSH: Architecture—Soviet
Union—History—Exhibitions.
Classification: LCC NA1188.C6414 2020 | DDC
720.94707471428—dc23